PENGUIN CLASSICS

DICKENS: SELECTED JOURNALISM 1850–1870

CHARLES DICKENS was born at Portsmouth on 7 February 1812, the second of eight children. Dickens's childhood experiences were similar to those depicted in *David Copperfield*. His father, who was a government clerk, was imprisoned for debt and Dickens was briefly sent to work in a blacking warehouse at the age of twelve. He received little formal education, but taught himself shorthand and became a reporter of parliamentary debates for the *Morning Chronicle*. He began to publish sketches in various periodicals, which were subsequently republished as *Sketches by Boz*. *The Pickwick Papers* was published in 1836–7 and after a slow start became a publishing phenomenon and Dickens's characters the centre of a popular cult. Part of the secret of his success was the method of cheap serial publication which Dickens used for all his novels. He began *Oliver Twist* in 1837, followed by *Nicholas Nickleby* (1838) and *The Old Curiosity Shop* (1840–41). After finishing *Barnaby Rudge* (1841) Dickens set off for America; he went full of enthusiasm for the young republic but, in spite of a triumphant reception, he returned disillusioned. His experiences are recorded in *American Notes* (1842). *Martin Chuzzlewit* (1843–4) did not repeat its predecessors' success but this was quickly redressed by the huge popularity of the *Christmas Books*, of which the first, *A Christmas Carol*, appeared in 1843. During 1844–6 Dickens travelled abroad and he began *Dombey and Son* while in Switzerland. This and *David Copperfield* (1849–50) were more serious in theme and more carefully planned than his early novels. In later works, such as *Bleak House* (1853) and *Little Dorrit* (1857), Dickens's social criticism became more radical and his comedy more savage. In 1850 Dickens started the weekly periodical *Household Words*, succeeded in 1859 by *All the Year Round*; in these he published *Hard Times* (1854), *A Tale of Two Cities* (1859) and *Great Expectations* (1860–61). Dickens's health was failing during the 1860s and the physical strain of the public readings which he began in 1858 hastened his decline, although *Our Mutual Friend* (1865) displays some of his strongest writing. His last novel, *The Mystery of Edwin Drood*, was never completed and he died on 9 June 1870. Public grief at his death was considerable and he was buried in the Poets' Corner of Westminster Abbey.

DAVID PASCOE was educated at King Edward School, Lytham, and Oriel College, Oxford, and is now Lecturer in English Literature at the University of Glasgow. He has published widely on Victorian and Modern writers, and is currently completing a book on the influence of Spiritualism on British and American literature. He has also edited Thackeray's *The Newcomes* for Penguin Classics.

CHARLES DICKENS

SELECTED JOURNALISM
1850–1870

Edited with an introduction and explanatory notes by
DAVID PASCOE

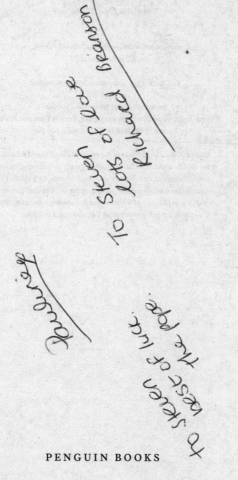

PENGUIN BOOKS

Published by the Penguin Group
Penguin Books Ltd, 27 Wrights Lane, London w8 5tz, England
Penguin Books USA Inc., 375 Hudson Street, New York, New York 10014, USA
Penguin Books Australia Ltd, Ringwood, Victoria, Australia
Penguin Books Canada Ltd, 10 Alcorn Avenue, Toronto, Ontario, Canada m4v 3b2
Penguin Books (NZ) Ltd, 182 – 190 Wairau Road, Auckland 10, New Zealand

Penguin Books Ltd, Registered Offices: Harmondsworth, Middlesex, England

This edition first published 1997
1 3 5 7 9 10 8 6 4 2

Set in 10/11.25 pt Monotype Fournier
Typeset by Rowland Phototypesetting Ltd, Bury St Edmunds, Suffolk
Printed in England by Clays Ltd, St Ives plc

CONTENTS

Introduction   ix

Select Bibliography   xxvii

A Note on the Texts   xxix

Dickens Chronology   xxxi

PERSONAL

A Christmas Tree (*Household Words*, 21 December 1850)   3
Our School (*Household Words*, 11 October 1851)   17
Lying Awake (*Household Words*, 30 October 1852)   24
Where We Stopped Growing (*Household Words*,
    1 January 1853)   30
Gone Astray (*Household Words*, 13 August 1853)   35
An Unsettled Neighbourhood (*Household Words*,
    11 November 1854)   45
Personal (*Household Words*, 12 June 1858)   51
New Year's Day (*Household Words*, 1 January 1859)   53
Dullborough Town (*All the Year Round*, 30 June 1860)   64
Night Walks (*All the Year Round*, 21 July 1860)   73
Chambers (*All the Year Round*, 18 August 1860)   81
Nurse's Stories (*All the Year Round*, 8 September 1860)   92
Some Recollections of Mortality (*All the Year Round*,
    16 May 1863)   102
Birthday Celebrations (*All the Year Round*,
    6 June 1863)   111

TRAVELLING ABROAD

A Narrative of Extraordinary Suffering (*Household Words*,
    12 July 1851)   123
Our Watering-Place (*Household Words*, 2 August 1851)   129
A Flight (*Household Words*, 30 August 1851)   137
Fire and Snow (*Household Words*, 21 January 1854)   146

Our French Watering-Place (*Household Words*, 4 November
   1854)   152
Out of Town (*Household Words*, 29 September 1855)   164
Railway Dreaming (*Household Words*, 10 May 1856)   170
Out of the Season (*Household Words*, 28 June 1856)   177
Refreshments for Travellers (*All the Year Round*, 24 March
   1860)   185
Travelling Abroad (*All the Year Round*, 7 April 1860)   193
Shy Neighbourhoods (*All the Year Round*, 26 May 1860)   204
Arcadian London (*All the Year Round*, 29 September 1860)   213
The Calais Night Mail (*All the Year Round*, 2 May 1863)   221
Chatham Dockyard (*All the Year Round*, 29 August 1863)   229

SLEEP TO STARTLE US

A Walk in a Workhouse (*Household Words*, 25 May 1850)   239
Detective Police (*Household Words*, 27 July and 10 August
   1850)   246
A Paper-Mill (*Household Words*, 31 August 1850)   263
Three 'Detective' Anecdotes (*Household Words*, 14 September
   1850)   269
Railway Strikes (*Household Words*, 11 January 1851)   277
Bill-Sticking (*Household Words*, 2 March 1851)   283
Spitalfields (*Household Words*, 5 April 1851)   294
On Duty With Inspector Field (*Household Words*, 14 June
   1851)   306
A Curious Dance Round a Curious Tree (*Household
   Words*, 17 January 1852)   318
A Sleep to Startle Us (*Household Words*, 13 March 1852)   327
A Plated Article (*Household Words*, 24 April 1852)   334
Down With the Tide (*Household Words*, 5 February 1853)   343
H. W. (*Household Words*, 16 April 1853)   352
A Nightly Scene in London (*Household Words*, 26 January
   1856)   361
Wapping Workhouse (*All the Year Round*, 3 February 1860)   366
A Small Star in the East (*All the Year Round*, 19 December
   1868)   376
On an Amateur Beat (*All the Year Round*, 27 February 1869)   386

INSULARITIES

Pet Prisoners (*Household Words*, 27 April 1850)   395
A Poor Man's Tale of a Patent (*Household Words*, 19 October
1850)   408
Lively Turtle (*Household Words*, 26 October 1850)   414
Red Tape (*Household Words*, 15 February 1851)   420
A Monument of French Folly (*Household Words*, 8 March
1851)   427
Trading in Death (*Household Words*, 27 November 1852)   438
Proposals for Amusing Posterity (*Household Words*,
12 February 1853)   447
On Strike (*Household Words*, 11 February 1854)   452
To Working Men (*Household Words*, 7 October 1854)   466
Insularities (*Household Words*, 19 January 1856)   470
The Demeanour of Murderers (*Household Words*, 14 June
1856)   476
Nobody, Somebody, and Everybody (*Household Words*,
30 August 1856)   481
The Murdered Person (*Household Words*, 11 October 1856)   485
The Best Authority (*Household Words*, 20 June 1857)   490

AMUSEMENTS OF THE PEOPLE

The Amusements of the People (*Household Words*, 30 March
and 13 April 1850)   499
Some Account of an Extraordinary Traveller (*Household
Words*, 20 April 1850)   511
Old Lamps for New Ones (*Household Words*, 15 June 1850)   521
The Ghost of Art (*Household Words*, 20 July 1850)   527
Epsom (*Household Words*, 7 June 1851)   534
Betting-Shops (*Household Words*, 26 June 1852)   546
The Spirit Business (*Household Words*, 7 May 1853)   553
The Noble Savage (*Household Words*, 11 June 1853)   560
Frauds on the Fairies (*Household Words*, 1 October 1853)   566
Gaslight Fairies (*Household Words*, 10 February 1855)   573
Well-Authenticated Rappings (*Household Words*,
20 February 1858)   579

Please to Leave Your Umbrella (*Household Words*,
1 May 1858)   586
In Memoriam W. M. Thackeray (*Cornhill Magazine*,
February 1864)   591

Explanatory Notes   595

Dickens's journalistic activities have rarely generated the high opinion he himself reserved for them when, late in his career, he told his American editors: 'To the wholesome training of severe newspaper-work, when I was a very young man, I constantly refer my first successes.'[1] In 1832, after leaving his job as a solicitor's clerk and acquiring a skill in shorthand, he became a correspondent for the *Mirror of Parliament*, and, two years later, was taken on as a reporter for the *Morning Chronicle*. Subsequently, some of the articles that he contributed to that paper between 1833 and 1836, and to other journals, the *Monthly Magazine* and the *Evening Chronicle*, were republished as his first full-length work, *Sketches by Boz*. After this, he concentrated his creative energies on novels. Nevertheless between 1837 and 1870, he continued to appear in newsprint; he was more than a reporter, but never other than one. On 20 May 1865, at the second annual dinner of the Newspaper Press Fund, after recalling some episodes in the life of a young journalist thirty years previously – recording important public speeches on the back of his hand, and wearing out his feet 'by standing to write in a preposterous pen in the old House of Lords' – Dickens confessed:

I never have forgotten the fascination of that old pursuit [cheers]. The pleasure that I used to feel in the rapidity and dexterity of its exercise has never faded out of my breast. Whatever little cunning of hand or head I took to it, or acquired in it, I have so retained that I fully believe I could resume it tomorrow, very little the worse for long disuse [cheers]. To this present year of my life, when I sit in this hall, or where not, hearing a dull speech (the phenomenon does occur), I sometimes beguile the tedium of the moment by mentally following the speaker in the old, old way; and sometimes, if you can believe me, I can find my hand going on the tablecloth, taking an imaginary note of it all [laughter]. Accept these little truths as a confirmation of what I know; as a confirmation of my undying interest in this old calling. Accept them as proof that my feeling for the vocation of my youth is not a sentiment taken up tonight to be thrown away tomorrow [hear, hear], but is a faithful sympathy which is a part of myself [cheers].[2]

In the first place, the discipline of reporting in shorthand amounted to a reflex manual action designed to cheat boredom by capturing the entirety of its manifestations in speech; but one might also suggest that, away from the dinner table and back at his writing desk, Dickens used this 'old, old way' to mould the 'rapidity and dexterity', and the native 'cunning' on which he so prided himself, and to strike the 'imaginary note' for which his mature journalism, that large body of miscellaneous work written between 1850 and 1870 with which this selection concerns itself, should be celebrated.

Of these writings, G. K. Chesterton observed: 'About these additional, miscellaneous, and even inferior works of Dickens, there is, moreover, another use and fascination which all Dickensians will understand; which after a manner, is not for the profane. All who love Dickens have a strange sense that he is really inexhaustible.'[3] That sense of plenty, however, owes more to manner than matter, as Dickens suggested to Forster: 'It does not seem to me to be enough to say of any description that it is the exact truth. The exact truth must be there; but the merit or art in the narrator, is the manner of stating the truth.'[4] Describing this manner, Chesterton claimed that Dickens 'always began with a fact';[5] however, in his famous essay, first published in 1938, George Orwell, clearly perplexed by such views, raised the matter of factuality. Rather than inexhaustibility, the unmistakable mark of Dickens's prose 'is the *unnecessary detail*', and he continued: 'Much that he wrote is extremely factual, and in the power of evoking visual images he has probably never been equalled,' but, on the *manner* of Dickens's presentation of facts, he added: 'wonderfully as he can describe an appearance, Dickens does not often describe a process.'[6] At the time he wrote these words, Orwell was receiving most of his income from freelance work for papers and magazines, and so it's perhaps odd that his account nowhere makes mention of Dickens's journalism. Yet if he had considered the articles in this selection, he would have found it impossible to maintain his line of argument, since these pieces habitually concern themselves with the inexhaustibility of process. In the journalism which follows, Dickens records goings-on about him, as he walks through London's slums alone ('A Walk in a Workhouse', 'A Sleep to Startle Us', 'Night Walks'), with trusted cohorts ('A Nightly Scene in London'), or with the detective police ('On Duty With Inspector Field'), and finds, as ever, poverty, desperation and criminality, and, just occasionally, the prospect of hope ('A Small Star in the East'). Alternatively, his columns record the occupations and amusements of the people ('Bill-Sticking', 'Epsom', 'Betting-Shops') or the means by which things are fabricated, either in manufacture ('A Plated Article', 'A Paper-Mill') and, more scandalously, in the political and legal process ('Red Tape', 'A Poor Man's Tale of a Patent', 'Proposals for Amusing Posterity', 'The Murdered Person'). Walter Bagehot once described Dickens as 'a special correspondent for posterity';[7] and certainly, the most memorable of these pieces are those in which he concentrates to set forth some sense of his own development, both as a writer and a man. In 'Gone Astray', he recalls how, as a youngster up from Kent, he lost his way in the City of London. After the initial terror, he soon becomes absorbed by the goings-on in the streets, and is then transported by the drama offered by a cheap theatre, before finally seeking out someone to take charge of him, and return him to his family. A later essay, 'New Year's Day', is a sequence of vivid recollections of various New Years in childhood and youth, leading to accounts of time spent in Genoa in 1845 and Paris in 1856; the editors of his correspondence are right to describe it as 'not an escape from the present to the happier past, but drawn from the timeless sources of the creative imagination'.[8] In all these cases, what emerges from Dickens's prose are images of worlds in flux, and evidence of an imagination at work; for though he felt acutely the responsibility of the journalist to give some account of the fact of this continuing process, he knew he could only achieve it through fancy.

In many respects, the best example of his approach is 'Lying Awake', the article Dickens wrote for *Household Words* in 1852. The piece begins with a quotation from Washington Irving, whom Dickens had met in 1842, and announces that Dickens will devote this paper to 'my train of thoughts as I lay awake', after which the argument pulls away into a quotation from Benjamin Franklin, and into a reminiscence of Niagara Falls. From there it loops back to London, into Clare Market, and to an inquiry into the equality of sleep, 'how many of its phenomena are common to all classes, to all degrees of wealth and poverty, to every grade of education and ignorance'. Now, the thread is broken, and Dickens finds himself revisiting the St Bernard Pass, which he saw in 1846; but once up there, he encounters a figure remembered from childhood chalked on a door in a country churchyard: a monstrous figure from which he ran. After this, his mind wanders to 'the balloon ascents of this last season', a craze in London in the early 1850s; but he cannot hang on to this new vehicle of thought and, in its place, hang the murderous Mannings, a married couple whose public execution had recently taken place, and so affected Dickens that he had written letters protesting against its brutality and tastelessness. He recalls a 'curious fantasy of the mind' involving the corpses of the murderers swinging from the gallows: 'strolling past the gloomy place one night, when the street was deserted and quiet, and actually seeing that the bodies were not there, my fancy was persuaded, as it were, to take them down and bury them within the precincts of the jail, where they have lain ever since'. Once more, his imagination returns to the ascending balloons, which are yet again deflated by a 'disagreeable intrusion': 'a man with his throat cut, dashing towards me as I lie awake'. This vision, however, is vicarious, 'a recollection of an old story' told by a kinsman of Dickens who once encountered a madman on the loose in Hampstead; and it eventually leads back to the balloons, and then to a consideration of the appeal of entertainments and amusements of the people. At this point, the morgue in Paris enters his mind, as it did so often; but on this occasion he is drawn to the water dripping on that 'swollen saturated something in the corner, like a heap of crushed over-ripe figs that I have seen in Italy'. He seeks to change the subject, and turns once more to crime, to 'the late brutal assaults' – a spate of street crime in the capital during 1851 – and his views on judicial punishments. Again, though, the dead begin 'to crowd into my thoughts' and he resolves to get up and go out for a night walk, 'which resolution was an acceptable relief to me, as I dare say it may prove now to a great many more'. The modesty of 'I dare say' coexists with the acceptance that what he excelled in (and what his public best enjoyed) were those works which emerged out of his nocturnal wanderings; which, in its own perverse way, is exactly what 'Lying Awake' amounts to. It is an extraordinary mélange of public and private, of news and recollection, of personality and impersonality; but, most crucially, the pun in its title gives some sense of the manner in which a powerful fancy may falsify the world around it.

Dickens had long harboured ambitions to be editor of his own journal. His first editorship, *Bentley's Miscellany* (1837), ended when he fell out with the proprietor, Richard Bentley, over editorial interference; after poor circulation figures, the second venture, *Master Humphrey's Clock* (1840), intended as an old-fashioned periodical, was quickly transformed into a vehicle for the publication of *The Old Curiosity Shop* and *Barnaby Rudge*; and the third attempt, the *Daily News*, ended in fiasco when, only a few days after the appearance of the launch issue, Dickens again resigned after clashing with Bradbury & Evans, his publishers. Anyway, none of these ventures offered him the freedom to blend fact with fancy which he had seen in the eighteenth-century periodicals he devoured in his youth: Addison and Steele's *Tatler* and *Spectator*; Johnson's *Idler* and Goldsmith's *Citizen of the World*. In late November 1846, when he was again formulating plans for his own periodical, he told Forster: 'I strongly incline to the notion of a kind of Spectator (Addison's) – very cheap and pretty frequent.' Eventually, in 1850, he came up with the idea of a weekly journal 'for the instruction and entertainment of all classes of readers'; but the title was a problem. Forster patiently records all of Dickens's suggestions:

'THE ROBIN. With this motto from Goldsmith. The redbreast, celebrated for its affection to mankind, continues with us the year round.' That however was rejected. Then came: 'MANKIND. This I think is very good.' It followed the other nevertheless. After it came: 'And here a strange idea, but with decided advantages. "CHARLES DICKENS. A weekly journal designed for the instruction and entertainment of all classes of readers. CONDUCTED BY HIMSELF"' Still something was wanting in that also. Next day there arrived: 'I really think if there be anything wanting in the other name, that this is very pretty, and just supplies it. THE HOUSEHOLD VOICE. I have thought of many others, as – THE HOUSEHOLD GUEST. THE HOUSEHOLD FACE. THE COMRADE. THE MICROSCOPE. THE HIGHWAY OF LIFE. THE LEVER. THE ROLLING YEARS. THE HOLLY TREE (with two lines from Southey for a motto). EVERYTHING. But I rather think the VOICE is it.' It was near indeed; but the following day came, 'HOUSEHOLD WORDS. This is a very pretty name': and the choice was made.[9]

And so on Saturday, 30 March 1850, the first number of *Household Words* was published, bearing the Shakespearean motto (taken from *Henry V*), 'Familiar in their mouths as Household Words'; and, as a vestige of the 'strange idea' of naming his journal after himself, the imprimatur 'Conducted by Charles Dickens' stood proudly at the top of every page. In the lead article, 'A Preliminary Word', the Conductor set out his thinking and intentions in founding the journal: 'We aspire to live in Household affections, and to be numbered among the Household thoughts of our readers,' who 'in this summer-dawn of time' will be introduced to 'the stirring world around us, the knowledge of many social wonders, good and evil', but will also be witness to 'no mere utilitarian spirits, no iron binding of the mind to grim realities'.[10]

Dickens always held that fancy was crucial for individual well-being, acting as a possible protective against the absurdities of the age.[11] Young David Copperfield comforts himself with the *Arabian Nights*, the *Tales of the Genii* and various eighteenth-century novels – 'They kept alive my fancy, and my hope of something beyond that place and time' (ch. 4); while in *Hard Times*, the novel serialized in the pages of *Household Words*, Sissy Jupe's father is lost in the East, 'forgetting all his troubles in wondering whether the sultan would let the lady go on with the story' (I ch. 9). An anonymous sonnet to Charles Dickens published in 1845 announced that he was unquestionably a 'potent wizard! painter of great skill! / Blending with life's realities the hues / Of a rich fancy'.[12] Certainly, he makes clear in the lead article that society needed to tenderly cherish that 'light of Fancy which is inherent in the human breast' or 'woe betide' the results. And just as Dickens had begun his literary career as a reporter – and through the powers of his own imagination, his fancy, had turned himself into a novelist – so *Household Words* would teach 'the hardest workers at this whirling wheel of toil, that their lot is not necessarily a moody brutal fact, excluded from the sympathies and graces of imagination'. His journalism would 'show to all, that in all familiar things, even in those which are repellant on the surface, there is Romance enough, if we will find it out'. Even such hideous manifestations of progress, 'towering chimneys spirting out fire and smoke upon the prospect', find a place in his vision, for these 'swart giants, Slaves of the Lamp of Knowledge, have their thousand and one tales, no less than the Genii of the East'.[13]

Hence, contributors were encouraged to observe his 'solemn and continual Conductorial Injunction': 'KEEP HOUSEHOLD WORDS IMAGIN-ATIVE.' He wrote to W. H. Wills, his most trusted editorial lieutenant, on 16 October 1851: 'I have been looking over the back Numbers. Wherever they fail, it is in wanting elegance of fancy. They lapse too much into a dreary, arithmetical, Cocker-cum-Walkingame [authors of mathematical texts] dustyness that is powerfully depressing.' In this harsh utilitarian age, fancy could not be allowed to be defeated by over-rationalization and mathematical precision; and if it were on the verge of extinction Dickens would have to take the necessary editorial steps to protect it. He soon became notorious for cutting and revising submissions to render them more fanciful and told E. de la Rue that 'I diffuse myself with infinite pains through Household Words, and leave very few papers indeed, untouched';[14] an admission which Percy Fitzgerald may also have heard when he observed how the journal 'displays his complete personality and is permeated with it, for the reason that he took such infinite unflagging pains to make himself present'.[15] The result of Dickens taking 'infinite pains' with his contributors' copy, was, for them, often just painful. Take, for instance, the experience of Henry Morley, a professional writer and man of letters, who had worked on *Household Words* since its inception; but who, by 1852, was exasperating its editor. Dickens wrote to him on 31 October of that year:

I am afraid you do not give sufficient consideration to some of your papers in Household Words. They are not to be done without trouble; and the main trouble necessary to them is, the devising of some pleasant means of telling what is to be told. The indispensible necessity of varying the manner of narration as much as possible, and investing it with some little grace or other, would be very evident to you if you knew as well as I do how severe the struggle is, to get the publication down into the masses of readers and to displace the prodigious heaps of nonsense and worse than nonsense which suffocate their better sense. I know of such 'perilous stuff' at present, produced at a cost about equal to the intrinsic worth of its literature and circulating six times the amount of Household Words.

My confidence in the ability of such people to receive and relish a good thing, is so far from being in the least shaken by this knowledge that I only feel the more strongly that the good thing must be done at its best. And what I particularly want to impress upon you is, that it is not enough to see a thing and go home and describe it, but that the necessity is, for ever upon us of patiently considering how to describe it so as to give some fanciful attraction or new air.

The disgruntlement may have begun late in the previous year when Dickens edited Morley's account of a visit to the Free Grammar School in Barnet, north of London, and came across this passage:

A sentence carries us a hundred miles and brings us to our journey's end. We pass through the little station house, and march on the high-road to Thistledown. That little country town is not far distant, as we see by the grey tower of its church, which peeps over the trees in yonder valley. It is a dull October afternoon; no blue whatever in the sky, no wind whatever in the trees.[16]

Dickens once wrote to his friend and biographer John Forster to tell him of 'the dreadful spectacle' he had made of someone's proofs – 'which look like an inky fishing-net'. Since Morley's account makes the dullness of the autumn day duller still, Dickens knew that a net needed to be cast over the copy. After Dickens's attentions, the passage in 'A Free and Easy School' read:

You put on the coat of Fortunatus, as a railway wrapper, and go with me as invisible companion. A sentence brings us to our journey's end. We pass through the little station house, and scorning the small fly at the door, which has blown itself into a railway omnibus, we march upon the high-road to Thistledown. That little country town is not far distant, as we see by the grey tower of its church, which peeps over the trees on yonder hill.

It is a dull October afternoon; no blue whatever in the sky, no wind whatever in the trees. On each side of the broad high-road, the fields are puffed up into notice by a series of undulations, as if it were determined that no effort should be spared to make the greatest possible display of melancholy oaks, and red and yellow copses, and every variety of autumn foliage which Nature has just now on hand. Dulled as we are by the dulness of the atmosphere, and little cheered by the dead leaves which make our path untidy, yet our London eyes are brightened at the first sight of a veritable five-barred gate, framed in blackberries. But blackberries, again, are melancholy things; they take our thoughts back to the days of trustful childhood, when we could crop those little joys by the wayside, and did not know that they are only safe while they are sour, and that the over-sweet have constantly a maggot coiled within. Alas for the experience of life. There goes the omnibus fly.[17]

This exhibits all those creative touches which show Dickens's imagination at work, even in the editor's chair. He adds an allusion to Fortunatus, always one of his favourite tales; but here the invisible cloak which concealed the hero is replaced by a travelling blanket.[18] The reduction of the length of the next sentence sensibly shortens the journey time. *Tempus fugit*; but, after all, Barnet was only twenty-five miles from the *Household Words* office. Look, too, at the way the carriage known as a fly, has first 'blown itself into a railway omnibus' – so implying that the (by now) flyblown interior of the coach might be a more suitable home for an insect than the station-house of the railway – and then returns to the scene at the close of the passage, immediately after Dickens has shown its origin (remembered from 'trustful childhood') as the maggot in a putrefying blackberry. The fields are 'puffed up into notice', putting on a show of decay, their action never far removed from the kind of distension that would characterize those bodies at the morgue in 'Lying Awake', 'swollen [and] saturated . . . like a heap of crushed over-ripe figs'; while the description of 'the red and yellow copses'[19] makes it sound like the tree trunks in the copses are turning into the trunks of corpses, carrying degeneration into unexpectedly familiar forms. In depicting the way no effort is spared by the processes of Nature, Dickens's prose is effortless; but then, even in an interpolated passage such as this, he is attempting nothing less than a darkly personal view of 'The Experience of Life'. His ambitions were inevitably so high for the journalism with which he was involved; for he was aiming for nothing less than an absolute engagement with the processes of the world around him: the way it was run, its goings-on, its falling into decay and final ends. He concluded his letter to Morley with the following observation:

. . . frequently it appears to me that you do not render justice to your many high powers, by thinking too slightingly of what you have in hand, instead of doing it, for the time being, as if there were nothing else to be done in the world – the only likely way I know of, of doing anything.

It was concentration on 'the time being' that Dickens missed in Morley's work, and yet so valued; that, and, with it, the ability to record everyday phenomena with a fanciful attraction, 'as if there were nothing else to be done in the world'.

Such concentration made for some wondrous and strange writing, especially when directed against satirical targets. For instance, in 'Lively Turtle', an attack on the City of London's opposition to much-needed sanitary reforms, a city alderman is mocked and transformed into a turtle; or in 'Red Tape', where Dickens imagines seeing a massive 'red tapeworm' which has been removed from the belly of a bureaucrat; or in 'The Murdered Person', an essay ostensibly dealing with the demise of a famous killer, where everything funnels down into the idea that the body of the United Kingdom itself has been abused and killed off by its corrupt and incompetent politicians. Such images, Dickens maintained, could provide the mass reading public with an alternative to the junk reading – 'Bastards of the Mountain, draggled fringe on the Red Cap, Panders to the basest passions of the lowest natures' – whose existence was a national disgrace, but also a threat to his own success. Moral crusading was never the intention; patronizing readers, Dickens maintained, was 'as great a mistake as can be made', so 'don't think that it is necessary to write down to any part of our audience' (12 October 1852). It did occasionally happen though. Rather than reporting on a serious industrial dispute, 'Railway Strikes' shows Dickens putting words into the mouths of the striking railwaymen in order to give comfort to his readers; while 'To Working Men' is hollowly patronizing, as Dickens knew as he wrote it that most of those to whom it was addressed would never be able to read it. Describing *Household Words*'s manner of handling material of social criticism, one contemporary reviewer wrote, 'isolated blemishes in the social system are magnified through the hazy medium of exaggerated phrases to the dimensions of the entire system, and casual exceptions are converted into a universal rule and practice'.[20] To a large extent, this exaggeration and twisting had its origins in Dickens's personality, and in his contributors' attempts to imitate his style – their following, as Fitzgerald said, its 'forms and "turns" and blemishes'.[21]

In this respect, consider the conclusion of *Household Words*'s manifesto:

The adventurer in the old fairy story, climbing towards the summit of the steep eminence on which the subject of his search was stationed, was surrounded by a roar of voices, crying to him, from the stones in the way, to turn back. All the voices *we* hear, cry Go on! The stones that call to us have sermons in them, as the trees have tongues, as there are books in the running brooks, as there is good in everything! They, and the Time, cry out to us Go on! With a fresh heart, a light step, and hopeful courage, we begin the journey.

This is Dickens at his most pompous and conceited. Unlike the hero in fairy tales of old, constrained by dissenting voices, he imagines the public sustaining him, urging him on in his quest. Yet for all this public support, he finds it hard to leave his old private self behind, since, amid the stones and trees, Dickens has buried allusions to *As You Like It*, in whose pastoral people find themselves after fleeing the horrors of the public world. Sweet, indeed, are the uses of adversity: Duke Senior now lives a newly private existence, and, 'exempt from public haunt, / Finds tongues in trees, books in the running brooks, / Sermons in stones, and good in every thing'. A noble ideal, to seek to discover good in everything, and one that Dickens, like Mr Mould in *Martin Chuzzlewit*,[22] sought to live by; nevertheless, what was more valuable to him than the final product – goodness – was the continuing process of discovery.

During the 1850s, that sheer act of continuation was a necessary thing not simply to Dickens's journalistic activities; it was also, paradoxically, a means of grounding himself. Worn out by work and worry, he was curiously rootless; a nomad convinced that somewhere – London, Dover, Folkestone, Calais, Boulogne, Paris – may be the ideal place. 'If I couldn't walk fast and far, I should just explode and perish,' he wrote to Forster in 1854; and Dickens's greatest journalism would not exist were it not for those trips he made not only between Britain and the Continent, but also between the past and the present; fiction and fact; the fancy and the reality. *Household Words* was, he told Leigh Hunt in January 1855, a 'great humming top . . . always going round with the weeks, and murmuring "Attend to me"'. And though he did attend to this toy, whipping his contributors, he was always on the move with a multitude of extra ventures: writing novels, speeches, plays; managing charities; organizing expeditions; giving readings; undertaking wanderings. As he oscillated between one activity and the next, it's not surprising that there is such a correspondence between his novels and his journalism at the time. Many of his most successful characters emerge, albeit fleetingly, in newsprint: Julia Mills, Dora's friend in *David Copperfield*, surfaces in 'Our Watering-Place'; Mrs Gamp, the chaotic umbrella-wielding nurse in *Martin Chuzzlewit*, turns up in 'Please to Leave Your Umbrella'; and Mrs Pipchin, the proprietress of the children's boarding-house in Brighton in *Dombey and Son*, makes an unwelcome reappearance in 'New Year's Day'. As Humphry House has suggested: 'The best commentaries on many parts of his novels are his own articles and short stories, and articles and stories he supervised as editor.'[23] Hence, 'Pet Prisoners', Dickens's polemical piece against the 'separate system' of prison discipline, is recalled in ch. 61 of *David Copperfield*, which shows Uriah Heep and Littimer as repentant inmates at Pentonville. Several commentators have shown how material gathered in Preston for 'On Strike' was used in *Hard Times*, which began in *Household Words* two months later in April 1854; and on 30 August 1856, by which time *Little Dorrit* was nine months old, Dickens published 'Nobody, Somebody and Everybody', an article written in the same ironic vein as the most topical chapters of the novel originally envisaged as 'Nobody's Fault'.[24]

On 13 December 1856, he described to an actor friend, W. C. Macready, how he was balancing 'Golden Marys [the special Christmas issue of *Household Words* for 1856], Little Dorrits, Household Wordses' while at the same time organizing a private performance.

Calm amidst the wrack, your aged friend glides away on the Dorrit stream, forgetting the uproar for a stretch of hours, refreshes himself with a ten or twelve miles' walk – pitches head-foremost into foaming rehearsals – placidly emerges for Editorial purposes – smokes over buckets of distemper with Mr Stanfield aforesaid – again calmly floats upon the Dorrit waters.

He was pushing himself to the limit, but it was a necessary labour in order to keep his head above the deluge. Without the pressure, he would have sunk into the oblivion he feared; he had seen his father go under and would not allow himself the same fate. Moreover, work took his mind away from home; his marriage had long been falling apart, and in May 1858 it was finally dissolved by a formal separation. The period prior to this had been especially difficult, with the need to choose sides between the couple's oldest friends, and the obligation – increasingly pressing – to scotch rumours of an affair with Ellen Ternan or a dalliance with his sister-in-law Georgina Hogarth; an obligation which eventually led to the extraordinary step of Dickens publishing a personal statement in *Household Words* (included in this selection). On 12 June 1858, the entire front page of the journal was given over to an announcement headed by the word 'Personal' and signed 'Charles Dickens', which, in oddly stilted phrases and vague allusions to 'some domestic trouble of mine, of long-standing', gave him an opportunity to acknowledge the separation, and quash the rumours:

By some means, arising out of wickedness, or out of folly, or out of inconceivable wild chance, or out of all three, this trouble has been made the occasion of misrepresentations, most grossly false, most monstrous, and most cruel – involving, not only me, but innocent persons dear to my heart, and innocent persons of whom I have no knowledge, if, indeed they have any existence – and so widely spread, that I doubt if one reader in a thousand will peruse these lines, by whom some touch of the breath of these slanders will not have passed, like an unwholesome air.

The 'unwholesome air' of the rumours was like a miasma surrounding the journal itself; and it was almost as if Dickens was seeking to move the whole affair into the sphere of sanitation and public health. He had assumed that his friends Bradbury and Evans, who published his novels, and who printed and partly owned *Household Words*, would also publish the notice in their comic magazine *Punch*. Not surprisingly, they elected not to do so, but for Dickens this betrayal was insupportable. After a reading tour in Ireland and the north of England, he broke off relations with his publishers, withdrew from the editorship of the magazine, blocked their attempts to continue with it, and, most crucially, started up another journal of his own.

The announcement of *All the Year Round* contained a promise to continue the policy of *Household Words* in offering 'that fusion of the graces of the imagination with the realities of life, which is vital to the welfare of any community'; and like its predecessor, it provided a medium for the publication of his novels, most notably *Great Expectations* (1860–61). But in other respects it was a departure from the informal tone of the previous magazine, which had moved far away from his ideal. When planning *Household Words* in October 1849, he wrote to Forster:

Now to bind all [the magazine] together, and to get a character established as it were which any of the writers may maintain without difficulty, I want to suppose a certain SHADOW... in which people will be perfectly willing to believe, and which is just as mysterious and quaint enough to have a sort of charm for their imagination, while it will represent common-sense and humanity.

Years later, his new journal would offer him the opportunity to modify the idea to his own personality, as in a series of articles written between 1860 and 1868, he set himself up as 'The Uncommercial Traveller'. The immediate inspiration for the persona was the work Dickens had undertaken in late 1859, preparing a speech for a benefit dinner for the Commercial Travellers' Schools. He told this gathering that he had considered whether anything could be done with the word Travellers; 'and I thought whether any fanciful analogy could be drawn between those travellers who diffuse the luxuries and necessities of existence', and other groups of travellers actual and metaphorical. In the first essay, the character introduces himself: 'Figuratively speaking, I travel for the great house of Human Interest Brothers, and have rather a large connexion in the fancy goods way.' Those fancy goods – 'the luxuries and necessities of existence' – are manufactured out of raw materials mined, in turn, from sources familiar to any reader of Dickens: prisons; theatres; dockyards; workhouses; slums; legal chambers; recollections of childhood in Kent and London, and of journeys to the Continent. 'Literally speaking, I am always wandering here and there from my rooms in Covent-garden, London – now about the city streets: now about the country by-roads – seeing many little things, and some great things, which because they interest me, I think may interest others.' Despite the humility, Dickens knew he was approaching the ideal of his journalistic ambitions; that the public interest was converging with his own private fancies.

As perhaps befits their origin in the Shadow, these late essays are darker, but show the obsession with death and mortality that he had added, seemingly incidentally, to Morley's copy, and which he had sought to expunge from 'Lying Awake'. In 'Travelling Abroad', memories of journeyings on the Continent, the narrator notes that whenever he is in Paris he is 'dragged by invisible force into the Morgue'. That verb has a peculiar force, since one of the corpses on view, as in the earlier piece, is that of a drowned man, this one, no doubt, dragged from the Seine. A few paragraphs later, the traveller takes a river bath, but while relaxing in the water is 'seized with an unreasonable idea that the large dark body was floating straight at me', and so flees in terror. 'Some Recollections of Mortality' features yet another visit to this 'obscene little Morgue, slinking on the brink of the river' to see a newly recovered body carried in an airy procession: 'Was it river, pistol, knife, love, gambling, robbery, hatred, how many stabs, how many bullets, fresh or decomposed, suicide or murder?' These are the staples of what a journalist might call human interest, that angle of inquiry which secures a continued readership. Unfortunately, the old man has died after being struck by falling masonry, and since this is 'not much' of a story, it requires embellishment:

He was calm of feature and undisfigured, as he lay on his back – having been struck upon the hinder part of his head, and thrown forward – and something like a tear or two had started from the closed eyes, and lay wet upon the face. The uncommercial interest, sated at a glance, directed itself upon the striving crowd on either side and behind.

That 'something like' announces the dissimulation, since he wished the tears to be river water dripping from his eyes; but in reporting the detail, the fancy is 'sated at a glance'. He finds it difficult to look any longer at the corpse; for now, the real interest is not in the body, but in others' reactions to it.

'Night Walks' is the most extraordinary of these essays, and again seems to recall 'Lying Awake'. The narrator, unable to sleep, undertakes a nightmare tour of London, now inhabited by the 'enormous hosts of dead [who] if they were raised while the living slept, there would not be the space of a pin's point in all the streets and ways for the living to come out into'. Imagining himself into a state of 'houselessness', the traveller returns once again to familiar haunts: Waterloo Bridge from whose parapets the suicides jump, as was reported in the *Household Words* piece 'Down With the Tide'; the theatres of Covent Garden, visited in 'Where We Stopped Growing'; Newgate Prison, an account of which appeared in *Sketches by Boz*; and Bethlehem Hospital for the Insane, where the heart of the essay emerges:

And the fancy was this: Are not the sane and the insane equal at night as the sane lie a dreaming? Are not all of us outside this hospital, who dream, more or less in the condition of those inside it, every night of our lives?

That 'more or less', however, announces the gap between liberty and limitation, fancy and fact; and it's a gap just wide enough for a writer like Dickens to step through. This is what the discipline of occasional journalism offered him in the last twenty years of his life: the private freedom to record the increasingly pressing shapes of his most fanciful visions, which coexisted with the compulsion to touch the realities which his novels could only reach out towards. This doubleness explains the extraordinary encounter with a beggar, which forms the climax of 'Night Walks':

The creature was like a beetle-browed hair-lipped youth of twenty, and it had a loose bundle of rags on, which it held together with one of its hands. It shivered from head to foot, and its teeth chattered, and as it stared at me – persecutor, devil, ghost, whatever it thought me – it made with its whining mouth as if it were snapping at me like a worried dog. Intending to give this ugly object money, I put out my hand to stay it – for it recoiled as it whined and snapped – and laid my hand upon its shoulder. Instantly, it twisted out of its garment, like the young man in the New Testament, and left me standing alone with its rags in my hands.

In the first place, the peculiarity of this lies in the impersonal objectivity of the pronouns; this creature is subhuman ('beetle-browed', 'a worried dog', an 'ugly object'), and unworthy of the simplest humane grammatical distinction.

However, after the attempt to offer money fails, the tone changes markedly, with the comparison with the young man in the New Testament. Dickens probably has in mind Mark 14: 51–2, where the young acolyte of Jesus, after the men attempt an arrest, drops his linen cloth and flees, naked. In alluding in this manner, who does Dickens think he is? Hardly the 'persecutor, devil, ghost' he offers himself as; but possibly a reporter offering sensational revelations about the urban underworld. Most obviously, however, he fancies himself (if only momentarily) as a kind of copper; someone whose hand – whose journalistic shorthand – could reach out to apprehend and move the world around him. But, standing in the early hours of the morning 'alone with its rags in my hands', Dickens must have realized that, at times, even *his* imagination was not potent enough to capture the human body breathing beneath the tattered fabric; at times even his inexhaustibility could be exhausted.

Dickens continued to run *All the Year Round* until a few months before his death in 1870; but after the second series of 'Uncommercial Traveller' articles appeared between May and October 1863, his journalistic contributions became more sporadic, and less distinctive, and culminated in the lifeless pieces published between December 1868 and February 1869 under the title 'New Uncommercial Samples'. The change in title is significant: the travels are over. As Philip Hobsbaum puts it: 'The Traveller . . . does not range quite far enough out of Dickens's now well-known territories,' and continues: 'one begins to feel [he] has done so much reporting of this nature, so consummately well for so many years, that by now we are entitled to ask for rather more enlightened approaches to criticism', before concluding: 'He is, as regards misfortunes of poverty and neglect, at last on the outside looking in'.[25] Part of this falling off may be attributable to the onset of circulatory problems in Dickens's feet which, of course, would have hampered the mobility on which he had come to rely for so much of his occasional writing; but he was also spending so much of his time travelling on lucrative but arduous reading tours that occasional writing may have proved increasingly difficult.

Nevertheless, in public he sought to maintain an air both of indefatigability and of self-effacement. He told Wills on 6 June 1867:

I shall never rest much while my faculties last, and (if I know myself) have a certain something in me that would still be active in rusting and corroding me, if I flattered myself that I was in repose. On the other hand, I think that my habit of easy self-abstraction and withdrawal into fancies has always refreshed and strengthened me in short intervals wonderfully. I always seem to myself to have rested far more than I have worked; and I do really believe that I have some exceptional faculty of accumulating young feelings in short pauses, which obliterates a quantity of wear and tear.[26]

Clearly, he was finding it difficult to know where the distinctions of his personality lay. In the processes of 'rusting and corroding', that internal decay caused inexorably by the reaction of life with art; or in the habits of self-preservation, manifested in the withdrawal into fancies so frequently seen in his journalism.

A couple of years before he wrote this letter, Dickens had suffered an experience which forced him to weigh up carefully the twin urges of action and repose; involvement and retreat. Exhausted, he had, as usual, taken his holidays abroad, in France, and, returning home on the tidal train from Folkestone on a hot Friday in early June 1865, he and his companions – his close friend Ellen Ternan and her mother – were involved in a railway accident. His train was approaching a small viaduct on which maintenance work (which involved the removal of several lengths of track) was taking place, but, having insufficient warning of the works, the driver approached the scene too quickly. The locomotive and six of the first-class carriages jumped the tracks and careered from the bridge, coming to rest in the mud of the River Beult fifteen feet below. Ten people were killed and scores were seriously injured. Luckily, Dickens's carriage lodged itself on the parapet of the bridge, and he and his companions emerged unscathed. In the minutes before help arrived, Dickens provided what little aid he could to the fatally injured passengers, offering them water from his top hat, or brandy from his flask.

The experience severely jolted his sensibility, as he found himself unable to report what had happened without shaking; and it is clear that his upset had its origins in the bloody aftermath of the accident rather than the derailment itself. On 12 June, the Monday following the disaster, he wrote to Macready: 'This is not all in my own hand, because I am too shaken to write many notes. Not by the beating and dragging of the carriage in which I was – it did not go over, but was caught on the turn, among the ruins of the bridge – but by the work afterwards to get out the dying and the dead, which was terrible.'[27] Dickens had seen corpses before in the Paris morgue; but here, the mangled bodies were still warm. The day after he dictated this note, the trauma was manifesting itself more directly in a long letter written to Thomas Mitton:

No imagination can conceive the ruin of the carriages, or the extraordinary weights under which the people were lying, or the complications into which they were twisted up among iron and wood, and mud and water . . . I don't want to write about it. I could do no good either way, and I could only seem to speak about myself, which, of course, I would rather not do. I am keeping very quiet here. I have a – I don't know what to call it – constitutional (I suppose) presence of mind, and was not in the least fluttered at the time. I instantly remembered that I had the MS of a number with me, and clambered back in the carriage for it. But in writing these scanty words of recollection I feel the shake and am obliged to stop.[28]

Dickens always sought to be in control of the situations in which he found himself; but here was something quite beyond the powers even of his imagination. So often in the previous fifteen years his journalistic writing presented the metaphorical weights under which the people suffered; the social complications which twisted them up. But he always remained the editor-in-chief who could decide the limits of the experience in question, and bring an article to a decent close. Here, the writer's instinct drives him back into the precariously balanced carriage to pick up the MS of the latest number of *Our Mutual Friend*; but, confronted with the carnage around him, he could no longer just stand idly by and observe. Although it meant that he would no longer be able to maintain what he had described a few weeks earlier to the gentlemen of the Newspaper Press Fund as his 'feeling for the vocation of my youth', Dickens abandoned the impulse to watch and relate, and, instead, held out a helping hand. It would be inaccurate to say that his journalistic career ended at this point; but, as he admitted to his estranged wife on 11 June 1865, the 'two or three hours' work afterwards among the dead and dying surrounded by terrific sights, render my hand unsteady':[29] too unsteady, in the years preceding his death on 9 June 1870 – the fifth anniversary of the accident – to take up again the old pursuit of shorthand reporting.

NOTES

1. John Forster, *The Life of Charles Dickens*, ed. A. J. Hoppé (London: Dent, 1966; revd 1969), I, p. 51.
2. *The Speeches of Charles Dickens*, ed. K. J. Fielding (Oxford: Clarendon Press, 1960), p. 348.
3. G. K. Chesterton, *Appreciations and Criticisms of the Works of Charles Dickens* (London: Dent, 1911), p. xx.
4. Forster II, p. 279.
5. Chesterton, p. xxvii.
6. George Orwell, 'Charles Dickens', in *The Collected Essays, Journalism and Letters*

of George Orwell, eds. Sonia Orwell and Ian Angus (Harmondsworth: Penguin, 1970), I, p. 493.

7. [Walter Bagehot] 'Charles Dickens', *National Review*, 7 (October 1858), reprinted in *Dickens: The Critical Heritage*, ed. Philip Collins (London: Routledge & Kegan Paul, 1971), p. 394.

8. *The Letters of Charles Dickens*, Pilgrim Edition, eds. Madeline House, Graham Storey, Kathleen Tillotson (Oxford: Clarendon Press, 1965–), VIII, p. xviii.

9. Forster II, pp. 65–6.

10. 'A Preliminary Word', *Household Words*, 30 March 1850.

11. On this topic, see Philip Collins's articles, 'Keep *Household Words* Imaginative!' *The Dickensian*, 52 (June 1956), pp. 117–23; and 'Queen Mab's Chariot Among the Steam Engines: Dickens and "Fancy"', *English Studies*, 42 (1961), pp. 78–90.

12. Quoted in Humphry House, *The Dickens World*, 2nd edn (Oxford: Clarendon Press, 1942), p. 41.

13. 'A Preliminary Word', op. cit.

14. Letter, 4 December 1853, Pilgrim edn.

15. Percy Fitzgerald, *Memories of Charles Dickens* (London: Simpkin, Marshall, 1913).

16. Henry Morley, *Gossip: Reprinted from Household Words* (London, 1857), p. 52. When he reprinted his piece, Morley, perhaps understandably, wanted to rid it of Dickens's additions. For further discussion of the textual issues raised, see Harry Stone ed., *The Uncollected Writings of Charles Dickens* (Harmondsworth: Allen Lane, 1968), I, p. 351.

17. 'A Free and Easy School', *Household Words*, 15 November 1851, pp. 169–73.

18. For further discussion of this allusion, see Kate Flint, *Dickens* (Brighton: Harvester, 1986), ch. 4.

19. In fact, 'copses' is misprinted as 'corpses' in Professor Stone's edition of *The Uncollected Writings*.

20. *The Press*, 22 October 1859.

21. Percy Fitzgerald, *Memoirs of an Author* (London: R. Bentley & Son, 1894), II, p. 56.

22. 'It only proves, sir, what was so forcibly observed by the lamented theatrical poet – buried at Stratford – that there is good in everything', *Martin Chuzzlewit*, ch. 19.

23. *The Dickens World*, p. 14.

24. On 'On Strike' and *Hard Times* see Sheila Smith, *The Other Nation: The Poor in English Novels of the 1840s and 1850s* (Oxford: Clarendon Press, 1980); on 'Nobody, Somebody, and Everybody' and *Little Dorrit*, see Kathleen Tillotson and John Butt, *Dickens at Work* (London: Methuen, 1957), pp. 229–30.

25. Philip Hobsbaum, *A Reader's Guide to Charles Dickens* (London: Thames & Hudson, 1972), pp. 138, 140.

26. Nonesuch Edition of *The Letters of Charles Dickens*, ed. Walter Dexter (London: Nonesuch Press, 1938), vol. III.

27. Ibid.

28. Ibid.

29. Ibid.

The standard biographies of Dickens are those by Edgar Johnson, *Charles Dickens: His Tragedy and Triumph*, 2 vols (New York: Simon and Schuster, 1952) and John Forster, *The Life of Charles Dickens*, 3 vols (1872–4); ed. A. J. Hoppé, 2 vols (London: Dent, 1966; revd 1969). More recently, Angus Wilson, *The World of Charles Dickens*, has some useful things to say on Dickens's involvement in journalism in the 1850s, and Peter Ackroyd's *Dickens* (London: Sinclair-Stevenson, 1990) has offered fine insights into the writer's mind. The most complete version of Dickens's letters is the three-volume edition, *The Letters of Charles Dickens*, edited by Walter Dexter (London: Nonesuch Press, 1938) as part of the limited Nonesuch Edition of Dickens's works. However, a much more comprehensive collection is being published: this is the Pilgrim Edition, edited by the late Madeline House, Graham Storey and Kathleen Tillotson, published by the Clarendon Press, Oxford. Volumes I (1965) to VIII (1995) dealing with the years 1820–58 have so far been published, and represent the pinnacle of Dickens scholarship. The following critical works touch on various aspects of Dickens's journalism:

John Butt and Kathleen Tillotson, *Dickens at Work* (London: Methuen, 1957). This is the seminal discussion of Dickens's methods of composition.
John Carey, *The Violent Effigy* (London: Faber, 1973). An imaginative and, at times, bizarre study of Dickens's imagination.
G. K. Chesterton, *Charles Dickens* (London: Methuen, 1906) is a quirky and readable account of the writings.
Philip A. W. Collins, '"Keep Household Words Imaginative!"', *The Dickensian*, 52 (1956), pp. 117–23.
—'Queen Mab's Chariot Among the Steam Engines: Dickens and "Fancy"', *English Studies*, 42 (1961), pp. 78–90.
—*Dickens and Education* (London: Macmillan, 1963).
—'"Inky Fishing Nets": Dickens as Editor', *The Dickensian*, 61 (1965), pp. 120–25.
—ed., *Dickens: The Critical Heritage* (London: Routledge & Kegan Paul, 1971).
—*Dickens and Crime*, 3rd edn (Basingstoke: Macmillan, 1995).

Percy Fitzgerald, *Memories of Charles Dickens with an Account of 'Household Words' and 'All the Year Round' and of the Contributors Thereto* (London: Simpkin, Marshall, Hamilton, Kent, 1913).

Robert Hamilton, 'The Creative Eye: Dickens as Essayist', *The Dickensian*, 64 (1968), pp. 36–42.

Humphry House, *The Dickens World* (Oxford: Clarendon Press, 2nd edn, 1942), was the first study to explore the social dimension of Dickens's writings, and makes use of much of the journalism.

George Orwell, 'Charles Dickens', *The Collected Essays, Journalism, and Letters of George Orwell*, eds. Sonia Orwell and Ian Angus, vol. I (Harmondsworth: Penguin, 1970), pp. 454–504. A characteristically brilliant, and, at times, wayward account of the distinctions of Dickens.

F. S. Schwarzbach, *Dickens and the City* (London: Athlone Press, 1979) includes some excellent discussion of *The Uncommercial Traveller*.

Harry Stone, 'Dickens and Interior Monologue', *Philological Quarterly*, 38 (1959), pp. 52–65.

—ed., *The Uncollected Writings of Charles Dickens: 'Household Words' 1850–1859*, 2 vols (Bloomington, Ind.: Indiana University Press and Harmondsworth: Allen Lane, both 1968). This is an important collection of Dickens's 'composite' writings as well as a valuable source of information about his editorial policies.

—'The Unknown Dickens: With a Sampling of Uncollected Writings', *Dickens Studies Annual*, ed. Robert B. Partlow, Jr, vol. I (Carbondale, Ill.: Southern Illinois University Press, 1970), pp. 1–22, 275–6.

Alexander Welsh, *The City of Dickens* (Oxford: Clarendon Press, 1971), makes good use of some of the *Household Words* pieces to further his arguments.

Where appropriate, the Explanatory Notes include more specific bibliographic references.

All the articles included in this selection were published between 1850 and 1870, but have their origins in a wide range of bibliographical sources. Some were collected and revised by Dickens in successive editions during his lifetime; other pieces were neglected, and have only recently been added to the canon of his writings.

At the time of his death, Dickens had published three selections of his journalistic writings. The earliest, *Sketches by Boz*, has been edited for Penguin by Dennis Walder; the others, *Reprinted Pieces* and *The Uncommercial Traveller*, provide the bulk of the material for this selection. *Reprinted Pieces*, the title given to volume 8 of the 1858 Library Edition of the works of Charles Dickens, consisted of over thirty essays, sketches and stories, which Dickens had first written for *Household Words*, and which he believed best represented his contribution to the journal. *The Uncommercial Traveller* was the collective title of a series of occasional papers Dickens produced in 1860 for his new magazine, *All the Year Round*, and which comprised of seventeen pieces when first published in book form in 1861. The series was continued in the journal during 1863 (so when *The Uncommercial Traveller* volume was included in the Dickens Edition of his works in 1868, eleven more papers were added); and resurrected again during 1868–9 (so that the Illustrated Library Edition (1875) added eight more items to *The Uncommercial Traveller*).

In 1908, B. W. Matz gathered together all the journalism supposed to have been written by Dickens and published it as volumes 35 and 36 of the National Edition. This was followed in 1937 by the sumptuous and rare Nonesuch Edition, edited by Walter Dexter, which also included two volumes of miscellaneous writings entitled *Collected Papers*. Since then, a number of other journalistic pieces have been identified as being wholly or partly by Dickens and these were included in Harry Stone's magisterial two-volume edition of *The Uncollected Writings of Charles Dickens* to which this selection is much indebted.

Head-notes identify the textual provenance of these pieces; and in each case the specified text has been closely followed, though the occasional obvious typographical error has been silently corrected. In general, I have based this selection on texts which appeared in those editions Dickens himself oversaw; but, where necessary, I have returned to the earliest published version of an essay for the copy-text. There is some inconsistency between the various texts in matters of italicization of titles and foreign words, and capitalization of names: these have been left in their original forms.

I would like to thank the staff of the Bodleian Library for their assistance and advice; and in particular, the Book Conservation Department, whose labours on early editions of *Household Words* have ensured the completion of this selection. I also wish to express my gratitude to Professor Philip Hobsbaum who read the introduction and kindly suggested several improvements; and to my patient copy-editor, Monica Schmoller, whose erudition and insight have made a particular impact on the Explanatory Notes. Of course, any errors which remain are mine alone.

1812   *7 February* Charles John Huffam Dickens born at Portsmouth, where
        his father is a clerk in the Navy Pay Office. The eldest son in a
        family of eight, two of whom die in childhood.

1817   Family move to Chatham.

1822   Family move to London.

1824   Dickens's father in Marshalsea Debtors' Prison for three months.
        Dickens employed in a blacking warehouse, labelling bottles. Attends
        Wellington House Academy, a private school, 1824–7.

1827   Becomes a solicitor's clerk.

1832   Becomes a parliamentary reporter after mastering shorthand. In love
        with Maria Beadnell, 1830–33.

1833   First published story, 'A Dinner at Poplar Walk', in the *Monthly
        Magazine*. Further stories and sketches in this and other periodicals,
        1834–5.

1834   Becomes reporter on the *Morning Chronicle*.

1835   Engaged to Catherine Hogarth, daughter of editor of the *Evening
        Chronicle*.

1836   *Sketches by Boz*, First and Second Series, published. Marries Catherine
        Hogarth. Meets John Forster, his literary adviser and future
        biographer.

1837   *The Pickwick Papers* published in one volume (issued in monthly
        parts, 1836–7). Birth of a son, the first of ten children. Death of
        Mary Hogarth, Dickens's sister-in-law. Edits *Bentley's Miscellany*,
        1837–9.

1838   *Oliver Twist* published in three volumes (serialized monthly in *Bent-
        ley's Miscellany*, 1837–9). Visits Yorkshire schools of the Dotheboys
        type.

1839   *Nicholas Nickleby* published in one volume (issued in monthly parts,
        1838–9).

1841   Declines invitation to stand for Parliament. *The Old Curiosity Shop*
        and *Barnaby Rudge* published in separate volumes after appearing in
        weekly numbers in *Master Humphrey's Clock*, 1840–41. Public dinner
        in his honour at Edinburgh.

1842 *January—June* First visit to North America, described in *American Notes*, two volumes.

1843 *A Christmas Carol* appears in December.

1844 *Martin Chuzzlewit* published in one volume (issued in monthly parts, 1843—4). Dickens and family leave for Italy, Switzerland and France. Dickens returns to London briefly to read *The Chimes* to friends before its publication in December.

1845 Dickens and family return from Italy. *The Cricket on the Hearth* published at Christmas. Writes autobiographical fragment, ?1845—6, not published until included in Forster's *Life* (three volumes, 1872—4).

1846 Becomes first editor of the *Daily News* but resigns after seventeen issues. *Pictures from Italy* published. Dickens and family in Switzerland and Paris. *The Battle of Life* published at Christmas.

1847 Returns to London. Helps Miss Burdett Coutts to set up, and later to run, a 'Home for Homeless Women'.

1848 *Dombey and Son* published in one volume (issued in monthly parts, 1846—8). Organizes and acts in charity performances of *The Merry Wives of Windsor* and *Every Man in His Humour* in London and elsewhere. *The Haunted Man* published at Christmas.

1850 *Household Words*, a weekly journal 'Conducted by Charles Dickens', begins in March and continues until 1859. Dickens makes speech at first meeting of Metropolitan Sanitary Association. *David Copperfield* published in one volume (issued in monthly parts, 1849—50).

1851 Death of Dickens's father. Further theatrical activities in aid of the Guild of Literature and Art, including a performance before Queen Victoria. *A Child's History of England* appears at intervals in *Household Words*, published in three volumes (1852, 1853, 1854).

1853 *Bleak House* published in one volume (issued in monthly parts, 1852—3). Dickens gives first public readings (from *A Christmas Carol*).

1854 Visits Preston, Lancashire, to observe industrial unrest. *Hard Times* appears weekly in *Household Words* and is published in book form.

1855 Speech in support of the Administrative Reform Association.

1856 Dickens buys Gad's Hill Place, near Rochester.

1857 *Little Dorrit* published in one volume (issued in monthly parts, 1855—7). Dickens acts in Wilkie Collins's melodrama *The Frozen Deep* and falls in love with the young actress Ellen Ternan. *The Lazy Tour of Two Idle Apprentices*, written jointly with Wilkie Collins about a holiday in Cumberland, appears in *Household Words*.

1858   Publishes *Reprinted Pieces* (articles from *Household Words*). Separation from his wife followed by statement in *Household Words*. Dickens household now largely run by his sister-in-law Georgina.

1859   *All the Year Round*, a weekly journal again 'Conducted by Charles Dickens', begins. *A Tale of Two Cities*, serialized both in *All the Year Round* and in monthly parts, appears in one volume.

1860   Dickens sells London house and moves family to Gad's Hill.

1861   *Great Expectations* published in three volumes after appearing weekly in *All the Year Round* (1860–61). *The Uncommercial Traveller* (papers from *All the Year Round*) appears: expanded edition, 1868. Further public readings, 1861–3.

1863   Death of Dickens's mother, and of his son Walter (in India). Reconciled with Thackeray, with whom he had quarrelled, shortly before the latter's death. Publishes 'Mrs Lirriper's Lodgings' in Christmas number of *All the Year Round*.

1865   *Our Mutual Friend* published in two volumes (issued in monthly parts, 1864–5). Dickens severely shocked after a train accident when returning from France with Ellen Ternan and her mother.

1866   Begins another series of readings. Takes a house for Ellen at Slough. 'Mugby Junction' appears in Christmas number of *All the Year Round*.

1867   Moves Ellen to Peckham. Second journey to America. Gives readings in Boston, New York, Washington and elsewhere, despite increasing ill-health. 'George Silverman's Explanation' appears in *Atlantic Monthly* (then in *All the Year Round*, 1868).

1868   Returns to England. Readings now include the sensational 'Sikes and Nancy' from *Oliver Twist*; Dickens's health further undermined.

1870   Farewell readings in London. *The Mystery of Edwin Drood* issued in six monthly parts, intended to be completed in twelve.

      9 June Dies, after collapse at Gad's Hill, aged fifty-eight. Buried in Westminster Abbey.

Stephen Wall, 1995

PERSONAL

A Christmas Tree

First published in the Christmas 1850 number of *Household Words*, 21 December 1850, and included in *Reprinted Pieces* (1858) in the Library Edition of Dickens's works, from which this text is reproduced.

I have been looking on, this evening, at a merry company of children assembled round that pretty German toy, a Christmas Tree. The tree was planted in the middle of a great round table, and towered high above their heads. It was brilliantly lighted by a multitude of little tapers; and everywhere sparkled and glittered with bright objects. There were rosy-cheeked dolls, hiding behind the green leaves; and there were real watches (with movable hands, at least, and an endless capacity of being wound up) dangling from innumerable twigs; there were French-polished tables, chairs, bedsteads, wardrobes, eight-day clocks, and various other articles of domestic furniture (wonderfully made, in tin, at Wolverhampton), perched among the boughs, as if in preparation for some fairy housekeeping; there were jolly, broad-faced little men, much more agreeable in appearance than many real men – and no wonder, for their heads took off, and showed them to be full of sugar-plums; there were fiddles and drums; there were tambourines, books, work-boxes, paint-boxes, sweet-meat boxes, peep-show boxes, and all kinds of boxes; there were trinkets for the elder girls, far brighter than any grown-up gold and jewels; there were baskets and pincushions in all devices; there were guns, swords, and banners; there were witches standing in enchanted rings of pasteboard, to tell fortunes; there were teetotums, humming-tops, needle-cases, pen-wipers, smelling-bottles, conversation-cards, bouquet-holders; real fruit, made artificially dazzling with gold leaf; imitation apples, pears, and walnuts, crammed with surprises; in short, as a pretty child, before me, delightedly whispered to another pretty child, her bosom friend, "There was everything, and more." This motley collection of odd objects, clustering on the tree like magic fruit, and flashing back the bright looks directed towards it from every side – some of the diamond-eyes admiring it were hardly on a level with the table, and a few were languishing in timid wonder on the bosoms of pretty mothers, aunts, and nurses – made a lively realisation of the fancies of childhood; and set me thinking how all the trees that grow and all the things that come into existence on the earth, have their wild adornments at that well-remembered time.

Being now at home again, and alone, the only person in the house awake, my thoughts are drawn back, by a fascination which I do not care to resist, to my own childhood. I begin to consider, what do we all remember best upon the branches of the Christmas Tree of our own young Christmas days, by which we climbed to real life.

Straight, in the middle of the room, cramped in the freedom of its growth by no encircling walls or soon-reached ceiling, a shadowy tree arises; and, looking up into the dreamy brightness of its top – for I observe in this tree the singular property that it appears to grow downward towards the earth – I look into my youngest Christmas recollections!

All toys at first, I find. Up yonder, among the green holly and red berries, is the Tumbler with his hands in his pockets, who wouldn't lie down, but whenever he was put upon the floor, persisted in rolling his fat body about, until he rolled himself still, and brought those lobster eyes of his to bear upon me – when I affected to laugh very much, but in my heart of hearts was extremely doubtful of him. Close beside him is that infernal snuff-box, out of which there sprang a demoniacal Counsellor in a black gown, with an obnoxious head of hair, and a red cloth mouth, wide open, who was not to be endured on any terms, but could not be put away either; for he used suddenly, in a highly magnified state, to fly out of Mammoth Snuff-boxes in dreams, when least expected. Nor is the frog with cobbler's wax on his tail, far off; for there was no knowing where he wouldn't jump; and when he flew over the candle, and came upon one's hand with that spotted back – red on a green ground – he was horrible. The cardboard lady in a blue-silk skirt, who was stood up against the candlestick to dance, and whom I see on the same branch, was milder, and was beautiful; but I can't say as much for the larger cardboard man, who used to be hung against the wall and pulled by a string; there was a sinister expression in that nose of his; and when he got his legs round his neck (which he very often did), he was ghastly, and not a creature to be alone with.

When did that dreadful Mask first look at me? Who put it on, and why was I so frightened that the sight of it is an era in my life? It is not a hideous visage in itself; it is even meant to be droll; why then were its stolid features so intolerable? Surely not because it hid the wearer's face. An apron would have done as much; and though I should have preferred even the apron away, it would not have been absolutely insupportable, like the mask. Was it the immovability of the mask? The doll's face was immovable, but I was not afraid of *her*. Perhaps that fixed and set change coming over a real face,

4

infused into my quickened heart some remote suggestion and dread of the universal change that is to come on every face, and make it still? Nothing reconciled me to it. No drummers, from whom proceeded a melancholy chirping on the turning of a handle; no regiment of soldiers, with a mute band, taken out of a box, and fitted, one by one, upon a stiff and lazy little set of lazy-tongs; no old woman, made of wires and a brown-paper composition, cutting up a pie for two small children; could give me a permanent comfort, for a long time. Nor was it any satisfaction to be shown the Mask, and see that it was made of paper, or to have it locked up and be assured that no one wore it. The mere recollection of that fixed face, the mere knowledge of its existence anywhere, was sufficient to awake me in the night all perspiration and horror, with, "O I know it's coming! O the mask!"

I never wondered what the dear old donkey with the panniers – there he is! was made of, then! His hide was real to the touch, I recollect. And the great black horse with the round red spots all over him – the horse that I could even get upon – I never wondered what had brought him to that strange condition, or thought that such a horse was not commonly seen at Newmarket. The four horses of no colour, next to him, that went into the waggon of cheeses, and could be taken out and stabled under the piano, appear to have bits of fur-tippet for their tails, and other bits for their manes, and to stand on pegs instead of legs, but it was not so when they were brought home for a Christmas present. They were all right, then; neither was their harness unceremoniously nailed into their chests, as appears to be the case now. The tinkling works of the music-cart, I *did* find out, to be made of quill toothpicks and wire; and I always thought that little tumbler in his shirt-sleeves, perpetually swarming up one side of a wooden frame, and coming down, head foremost, on the other, rather a weak-minded person – though good-natured; but the Jacob's Ladder, next him, made of little squares of red wood, that went flapping and clattering over one another, each developing a different picture, and the whole enlivened by small bells, was a mighty marvel and a great delight.

Ah! The Doll's house! – of which I was not proprietor, but where I visited. I don't admire the Houses of Parliament half so much as that stone-fronted mansion with real glass windows, and doorsteps, and a real balcony – greener than I ever see now, except at watering places; and even they afford but a poor imitation. And though it *did* open all at once, the entire house-front (which was a blow, I admit, as cancelling the fiction of a staircase), it was but to shut it up again, and I could believe. Even open, there were three distinct rooms in it: a sitting-room and bed-room, elegantly furnished, and best of all, a kitchen, with uncommonly soft fire-irons, a plentiful assortment of diminutive utensils – oh, the warming-pan! – and a tin man-cook in profile, who was always going to fry two fish. What Barmecide[1] justice have I done to the noble feasts wherein the set of wooden platters figured, each with its own peculiar delicacy, as a ham or turkey, glued tight on to it, and garnished with something green, which I recollect as moss! Could all the Temperance Societies of these later days, united, give me such a tea-drinking as I have had through the means of yonder little set of blue crockery, which really would hold liquid (it ran out of the small wooden cask, I recollect, and tasted of matches), and which made tea, nectar. And if the two legs of the ineffectual little sugar-tongs did tumble over one another, and want purpose, like Punch's hands,[2] what does it matter? And if I did once shriek out, as a poisoned child, and strike the fashionable company with consternation, by reason of having drunk a little teaspoon, inadvertently dissolved in too hot tea, I was never the worse for it, except by a powder!

Upon the next branches of the tree, lower down, hard by the green roller and miniature gardening-tools, how thick the books begin to hang. Thin books, in themselves, at first, but many of them, and with deliciously smooth covers of bright red or green. What fat black letters to begin with! "A was an archer, and shot at a frog." Of course he was. He was an apple-pie also, and there he is! He was a good many things in his time, was A, and so were most of his friends, except X, who had so little versatility, that I never knew him to get beyond Xerxes or Xantippe – like Y, who was always confined to a Yacht or a Yew Tree; and Z condemned for ever to be a Zebra or a Zany. But, now, the very tree itself changes, and becomes a bean-stalk – the marvellous bean-stalk up which Jack climbed to the Giant's house! And now, those deadfully interesting, double-headed giants, with their clubs over their shoulders, begin to stride along the boughs in a perfect throng, dragging knights and ladies home for dinner by the hair of their heads. And Jack – how noble, with his sword of sharpness, and his shoes of swiftness! Again those old meditations come upon me as I gaze up at him; and I debate within myself whether there was more than one Jack (which I am loth to believe possible), or only one genuine original admirable Jack, who achieved all the recorded exploits.[3]

Good for Christmas-time is the ruddy colour of the cloak, in which – the tree making a forest of itself for her to trip through, with her basket – Little Red Riding-Hood comes to me one Christmas Eve to give me information of the cruelty and treachery of that dissembling Wolf who ate her grandmother, without making any impression on his appetite, and then ate her, after making that ferocious joke about his teeth.[4] She was my first love. I felt that if I could have married Little Red Riding-Hood, I should have known perfect bliss. But, it was not to be; and there was nothing for it but to look out the Wolf in the Noah's Ark there, and put him late in the procession on the table, as a monster who was to be degraded. O the wonderful Noah's Ark! It was not found seaworthy when put in a washing-tub, and the animals were crammed in at the roof, and needed to have their legs well shaken down before they could be got in, even there – and then, ten to one but they began to tumble out at the door, which was but imperfectly fastened with a wire latch – but what was *that* against it! Consider the noble fly, a size or two smaller than the elephant: the lady-bird, the butterfly – all triumphs of art! Consider the goose, whose feet were so small, and whose balance was so indifferent, that he usually tumbled forward, and knocked down all the animal creation. Consider Noah and his family, like idiotic tobacco-stoppers; and how the leopard stuck to warm little fingers; and how the tails of the larger animals used gradually to resolve themselves into frayed bits of string!

Hush! Again a forest, and somebody up in a tree – not Robin Hood, not Valentine, not the Yellow Dwarf (I have passed him and all Mother Bunch's wonders,[5] without mention), but an Eastern King with a glittering scimitar and turban. By Allah! two Eastern Kings, for I see another, looking over his shoulder! Down upon the grass, at the tree's foot, lies the full length of a coal-black Giant, stretched asleep, with his head in a lady's lap; and near them is a glass box, fastened with four locks of shining steel, in which he keeps the lady prisoner when he is awake. I see the four keys at his girdle now. The lady makes signs to the two kings in the tree, who softly descend. It is the setting-in of the bright Arabian Nights.

Oh, now all common things become uncommon and enchanted to me. All lamps are wonderful; all rings are talismans. Common flower-pots are full of treasure, with a little earth scattered on the top; trees are for Ali Baba to hide in; beefsteaks are to throw down into the Valley of Diamonds, that the precious stones may stick to them, and be carried by the eagles to their nests, whence the traders, with loud cries, will scare them. Tarts are made, according to the recipe of the Vizier's son of Bussorah, who turned pastrycook after he was set down in his drawers at the gate of Damascus; cobblers are all Mustaphas, and in the habit of sewing up people cut into four pieces, to whom they are taken blind-fold.

Any iron ring let into stone is the entrance to a cave which only waits for the magician, and the little fire, and the necromancy, that will make the earth shake. All the dates imported come from the same tree as that unlucky date, with whose shell the merchant knocked out the eye of the genie's invisible son. All olives are of the stock of that fresh fruit, concerning which the Commander of the Faithful overheard the boy conduct the fictitious trial of the fraudulent olive merchant; all apples are akin to the apple purchased (with two others) from the Sultan's gardener for three sequins, and which the tall black slave stole from the child. All dogs are associated with the dog, really a transformed man, who jumped upon the baker's counter, and put his paw on the piece of bad money. All rice recalls the rice which the awful lady, who was a ghoule, could only peck by grains, because of her nightly feasts in the burial-place. My very rocking-horse, – there he is, with his nostrils turned completely inside-out, indicative of Blood! – should have a peg in his neck, by virtue thereof to fly away with me, as the wooden horse did with the Prince of Persia, in the sight of all his father's Court.

Yes, on every object that I recognise among those upper branches of my Christmas Tree, I see this fairy light! When I wake in bed, at daybreak, on the cold dark winter mornings, the white snow dimly beheld, outside, through the frost on the window-pane, I hear Dinarzade. "Sister, sister, if you are yet awake, I pray you finish the history of the Young King of the Black Islands." Scheherazade replies, "If my lord the Sultan will suffer me to live another day, sister, I will not only finish that, but tell you a more wonderful story yet." Then, the gracious Sultan goes out, giving no orders for the execution, and we all three breathe again.[6]

At this height of my tree I begin to see, cowering among the leaves – it may be born of turkey, or of pudding, or mince pie, or of these many fancies, jumbled with Robinson Crusoe on his desert island, Philip Quarll among the monkeys,[7] Sandford and Merton with Mr. Barlow,[8] Mother Bunch, and the Mask – or it may be the result of indigestion, assisted by imagination and over-doctoring – a prodigious nightmare. It is so exceedingly indistinct, that I don't know why it's frightful – but I know it is. I can only make out that it is an immense array of shapeless things, which appear to be planted on a vast exaggeration of the lazy-tongs that used to bear the toy soldiers, and to be slowly coming close to my eyes, and receding to an immeasurable distance. When it comes closest, it is worse. In connexion with it I descry remembrances of winter nights incredibly long; of being sent early to bed, as a punishment for some small offence, and waking in two hours, with a sensation of having been asleep two nights; of the laden hopelessness of morning ever dawning; and the oppression of a weight of remorse.

And now, I see a wonderful row of little lights rise smoothly out of the ground, before a vast green curtain. Now, a bell rings – a magic bell, which still sounds in my ears unlike all other bells – and music plays, amidst a buzz of voices, and a fragrant smell of orange-peel and oil. Anon, the magic bell commands the music to cease, and the great green curtain rolls itself up majestically, and The Play begins! The devoted dog of Montargis[9] avenges the death of his master, foully murdered in the Forest of Bondy; and a humorous Peasant with a red nose and a very little hat, whom I take from this hour forth to my bosom as a friend (I think he was a Waiter or an Hostler at a village Inn, but many years have passed since he and I have met), remarks that the sassigassity of that dog is indeed surprising; and evermore this jocular conceit will live in my remembrance fresh and unfading, overtopping all possible jokes, unto the end of time. Or now, I learn with bitter tears how poor Jane Shore,[10] dressed all in white, and with her brown hair hanging down, went starving through the streets; or how George Barnwell killed the worthiest uncle that ever man had,[11] and was afterwards so sorry for it that he ought to have been let off. Comes swift to comfort me, the Pantomime – stupendous Phenomenon! – when clowns are shot from loaded mortars into the great chandelier, bright constellation that it is; when Harlequins, covered all over with scales of pure gold, twist and sparkle, like amazing fish; when Pantaloon (whom I deem it no irreverence to compare in my own mind to my grandfather) puts red-hot pokers in his pocket, and cries "Here's somebody coming!" or taxes the Clown with petty larceny, by saying, "Now, I sawed you do it!" when Everything is capable, with the greatest ease, of being changed into Anything; and "Nothing is, but thinking makes it so."[12] Now, too, I perceive my first experience of the dreary sensation – often to return in after-life – of being unable, next day, to get back to the dull, settled world; of wanting to live for ever in the bright atmosphere I have quitted; of doting on the little Fairy, with the wand like a celestial Barber's Pole, and pining for a Fairy immortality along with her. Ah, she comes back, in many shapes, as my eyes wanders down the branches of my Christmas Tree, and goes as often, and has never yet stayed by me!

Out of this delight springs the toy-theatre,[13] – there it is, with its familiar proscenium, and ladies in feathers, in the boxes! – and all its attendant occupation with paste and glue, and gum, and water colours, in the getting-up of The Miller and his Men, and Elizabeth, or the Exile of Siberia. In spite of a few besetting accidents and failures (particularly an unreasonable disposition in the respectable Kelmar,[14] and some others, to become faint in the legs, and double up, at exciting points of the drama), a teeming world of fancies so suggestive and all-embracing, that, far below it on my Christmas

Tree, I see dark, dirty, real Theatres in the day-time, adorned with these associations as with the freshest garlands of the rarest flowers, and charming me yet.

But hark! The Waits are playing, and they break my childish sleep! What images do I associate with the Christmas music as I see them set forth on the Christmas Tree? Known before all the others, keeping far apart from all the others, they gather round my little bed. An angel, speaking to a group of shepherds in a field; some travellers, with eyes uplifted, following a star; a baby in a manger; a child in a spacious temple, talking with grave men; a solemn figure, with a mild and beautiful face, raising a dead girl by the hand; again, near a city gate, calling back the son of a widow, on his bier, to life; a crowd of people looking through the opened roof of a chamber where he sits, and letting down a sick person on a bed, with ropes; the same, in a tempest, walking on the water to a ship; again, on a sea-shore, teaching a great multitude; again, with a child upon his knee, and other children round; again, restoring sight to the blind, speech to the dumb, hearing to the deaf, health to the sick, strength to the lame, knowledge to the ignorant; again, dying upon a Cross, watched by armed soldiers, a thick darkness coming on, the earth beginning to shake, and only one voice heard, "Forgive them, for they know not what they do."[15]

Still, on the lower and maturer branches of the Tree, Christmas associations cluster thick. School-books shut up; Ovid and Virgil silenced; the Rule of Three,[16] with its cool impertinent inquiries, long disposed of; Terence and Plautus[17] acted no more, in an arena of huddled desks and forms, all chipped, and notched, and inked; cricket-bats, stumps, and balls, left higher up, with the smell of trodden grass and the softened noise of shouts in the evening air; the tree is still fresh, still gay. If I no more come home at Christmas-time, there will be boys and girls (thank Heaven!) while the World lasts; and they do! Yonder they dance and play upon the branches of my Tree, God bless them, merrily, and my heart dances and plays too!

And I *do* come home at Christmas. We all do, or we all should. We all come home, or ought to come home, for a short holiday – the longer, the better – from the great boarding-school, where we are for ever working at our arithmetical slates, to take, and give a rest. As to going a visiting, where can we not go, if we will; where have we not been, when we would; starting our fancy from our Christmas Tree!

Away into the winter prospect. There are many such upon the tree! On, by low-lying, misty grounds, through fens and fogs, up long hills, winding dark as caverns between thick plantations, almost shutting out the sparkling stars; so, out on broad heights, until we stop at last, with sudden silence, at an avenue. The gate-bell has a deep, half-awful sound in the frosty air; the gate swings open on its hinges; and, as we drive up to a great house, the glancing lights grow larger in the windows, and the opposing rows of trees seem to fall solemnly back on either side, to give us place. At intervals, all day, a frightened hare has shot across this whitened turf; or the distant clatter of a herd of deer trampling the hard frost, has, for the minute, crushed the silence too. Their watchful eyes beneath the fern may be shining now, if we could see them, like the icy dewdrops on the leaves; but they are still, and all is still. And so, the lights growing larger, and the trees falling back before us, and closing up again behind us, as if to forbid retreat, we come to the house.

There is probably a smell of roasted chestnuts and other good comfortable things all the time, for we are telling Winter Stories – Ghost Stories, or more shame for us – round the Christmas fire; and we have never stirred, except to draw a little nearer to it. But, no matter for that. We came to the house, and it is an old house, full of great chimneys where wood is burnt on ancient dogs upon the hearth, and grim portraits (some of them with grim legends, too) lower distrustfully from the oaken panels of the walls. We are a middle-aged nobleman, and we make a generous supper with our host and hostess and their guests – it being Christmas-time, and the old house full of company – and then we go to bed. Our room is a very old room. It is hung with tapestry. We don't like the portrait of a cavalier in green, over the fireplace. There are great black beams in the ceiling, and there is a great black bedstead, supported at the foot by two great black figures, who seem to have come off a couple of tombs in the old baronial church in the park, for our particular accommodation. But, we are not a superstitious nobleman, and we don't mind. Well! we dismiss our servant, lock the door, and sit before the fire in our dressing-gown, musing about a great many things. At length we go to bed. Well! we can't sleep. We toss and tumble, and can't sleep. The embers on the hearth burn fitfully and make the room look ghostly. We can't help peeping out over the counterpane, at the two black figures and the cavalier – that wicked-looking cavalier – in green. In the flickering light they seem to advance and retire: which, though we are not by any means a superstitious nobleman, is not agreeable. Well! we get nervous – more and more nervous. We say "This is very foolish, but we can't stand this; we'll pretend to be ill, and knock up somebody." Well! we are just going to do it, when the locked door opens, and there comes in a young woman, deadly pale, and with long fair hair, who glides to the fire, and sits down in the chair we have left there, wringing her hands. Then, we notice that her clothes are wet. Our tongue cleaves to the roof of our mouth, and we can't speak; but, we observe her accurately. Her clothes are wet; her long hair is dabbled with moist mud; she is dressed in the fashion of two hundred years ago; and she has at her girdle a bunch of rusty keys. Well! there she sits, and we can't even faint, we are in such a state about it. Presently she gets up, and tries all the locks in the room with the rusty keys, which won't fit one of them; then, she fixes her eyes on the portrait of the cavalier in green, and says, in a low, terrible voice, "The stags know it!" After that, she wrings her hands again, passes the bedside, and goes out at the door. We hurry on our dressing-gown, seize our pistols (we always travel with pistols), and are following, when we find the door locked. We turn the key, look out into the dark gallery; no one there. We wander away, and try to find our servant. Can't be done. We pace the gallery till daybreak; then return to our deserted room, fall asleep, and are awakened by our servant (nothing ever haunts *him*) and the shining sun. Well! we make a wretched breakfast, and all the company say we look queer. After breakfast, we go over the house with our host, and then we take him to the portrait of the cavalier in green, and then it all comes out. He was false to a young housekeeper once attached to that family, and famous for her beauty, who drowned herself in a pond, and whose body was discovered, after a long time, because the stags refused to drink of the water. Since which, it has been whispered that she traverses the house at midnight (but goes especially to that room where the cavalier in green was wont to sleep), trying the old locks with the rusty keys. Well! we tell our host of what we have seen, and a shade comes over his features, and he begs it may be hushed up; and so it is. But, it's all true; and we said so, before we died (we are dead now) to many responsible people.

There is no end to the old houses, with resounding galleries, and dismal state-bedchambers, and haunted wings shut up for many years, through which we may ramble, with an agreeable creeping up our back, and encounter any number of ghosts, but (it is worthy of remark perhaps) reducible to a very few general types and classes; for, ghosts have little originality, and "walk" in a beaten track. Thus, it comes to pass, that a certain room in a certain old hall, where a certain bad lord, baronet, knight, or gentleman, shot himself, has certain planks in the floor from which the blood *will not* be taken out. You may scrape and scrape, as the present owner has done, or plane and plane, as his father did, or scrub and scrub, as his grandfather did, or burn and burn with strong acids, as his great-grandfather did, but, there the blood will still be – no redder and no paler – no more and no less – always just the same. Thus, in such another house there is a haunted door, that never will keep open; or another door that never will keep shut; or a haunted sound of a spinning-wheel, or a hammer, or a footstep, or a cry, or a sigh, or a horse's tramp, or the rattling of a chain. Or else, there is a turret-clock, which, at the midnight hour, strikes thirteen when the head of the family is going to die; or a shadowy, immovable black carriage which at such a time is always seen by somebody, waiting near the great gates in the stable-yard. Or thus, it came to pass how Lady Mary went to pay a visit at a large wild house in the Scottish Highlands, and, being fatigued with her long journey, retired to bed early, and innocently said, next morning, at the breakfast-table, "How odd, to have so late a party last night, in this remote place, and not to tell me of it, before I went to bed!" Then, every one asked Lady Mary what she meant? Then, Lady Mary replied, "Why, all night long, the carriages were driving round and round the terrace, underneath my window!" Then, the owner of the house turned pale, and so did his Lady, and Charles Macdoodle of Macdoodle signed to Lady Mary to say no more, and every one was silent. After breakfast, Charles Macdoodle told Lady Mary that it was a tradition in the family that those rumbling carriages on the terrace betokened death. And so it proved, for, two months afterwards, the Lady of the mansion died. And Lady Mary, who was a Maid of Honour at Court, often told this story to the old Queen Charlotte; by this token that the old King[18] always said, "Eh, eh? What, what? Ghosts, ghosts? No such thing, no such thing!" And never left off saying so, until he went to bed.

Or, a friend of somebody's whom most of us know, when he was a young man at college, had a particular friend, with whom he made the compact that, if it were possible for the Spirit to return to this earth after its separation from the body, he of the twain who first died, should reappear to the other. In course of time, this compact was forgotten by our friend; the two young men having progressed in life, and taken diverging paths that were wide asunder. But, one night, many years afterwards, our friend being in the North of England, and staying for the night in an inn, on the Yorkshire Moors, happened to look out of bed; and there, in the moonlight, leaning on a bureau near the window, steadfastly regarding him, saw his old college friend! The appearance being solemnly addressed, replied, in a kind of whisper, but very audibly, "Do not come near me. I am dead. I am here to redeem my promise. I come from another world, but may not disclose its secrets!" Then, the whole form becoming paler, melted, as it were, into the moonlight, and faded away.

Or, there was the daughter of the first occupier of the picturesque Elizabethan house, so famous in our neighbourhood. You have heard about her? No! Why, *She* went out one summer evening at twilight, when she was a beautiful girl, just seventeen years of age, to gather flowers in the garden; and presently came running, terrified, into the hall to her father, saying, "Oh, dear father, I have met myself!" He took her in his arms, and told her it was fancy, but she said, "Oh no! I met myself in the broad walk, and I was pale and gathering withered flowers, and I turned my head, and held them up!" And, that night, she died; and a picture of her story was begun, though never finished, and they say it is somewhere in the house to this day, with its face to the wall.

Or, the uncle of my brother's wife was riding home on horseback, one mellow evening at sunset, when, in a green lane close to his own house, he saw a man standing before him, in the very centre of a narrow way. "Why does that man in the cloak stand there?" he thought. "Does he want me to ride over him?" But the figure never moved. He felt a strange sensation at seeing it so still, but slackened his trot and rode forward. When he was so close to it, as almost to touch it with his stirrup, his horse shied, and the figure glided up the bank, in a curious, unearthly manner – backward, and without seeming to use its feet – and was gone. The uncle of my brother's wife, exclaiming, "Good Heaven! It's my cousin Harry, from Bombay!" put spurs to his horse, which was suddenly in a profuse sweat, and, wondering at such strange behaviour, dashed round to the front of his house. There, he saw the same figure, just passing in at the long French window of the drawing-room, opening on the ground. He threw his bridle to a servant, and hastened in after it. His sister was sitting there, alone. "Alice, where's my cousin Harry?" "Your cousin Harry, John?" "Yes. From Bombay. I met him in the lane just now, and saw him enter here, this instant." Not a creature had been seen by any one; and in that hour and minute, as it afterwards appeared, this cousin died in India.

Or, it was a certain sensible old maiden lady, who died at ninety-nine, and retained her faculties to the last, who really did see the Orphan Boy; a story which has often been incorrectly told, but, of which the real truth is this – because it is, in fact, a story belonging to our family – and she was a connexion of our family. When she was about forty years of age, and still an uncommonly fine woman (her lover died young, which was the reason why she never married, though she had many offers), she went to stay at a place in Kent, which her brother, an Indian-Merchant, had newly bought. There was a story that this place had once been held in trust, by the guardian of a young boy; who was himself the next heir, and who killed the young boy by harsh and cruel treatment. She knew nothing of that. It has been said that there was a Cage in her bedroom in which the guardian used to put the boy. There was no such thing. There was only a closet. She went to bed, made no alarm whatever in the night, and in the morning said composedly to her maid when she came in, "Who is the pretty forlorn-looking child who has been peeping out of that closet all night?" The maid replied by giving a loud scream, and instantly decamping. She was surprised; but she was a woman of remarkable strength of mind, and she dressed herself and went downstairs, and closeted herself with her brother. "Now, Walter," she said, "I have been disturbed all night by a pretty, forlorn-looking boy, who has been constantly peeping out of that closet in my room, which I can't open. This is some trick." "I am afraid not, Charlotte," said he, "for it is the legend of the house. It is the Orphan Boy. What did he do?" "He opened the door softly," said she, "and peeped out. Sometimes, he came a step or two into the room. Then, I called to him, to encourage him, and he shrunk, and shuddered, and crept in again, and shut the door." "The closet has no communication, Charlotte," said her brother, "with any other part of the house, and it's nailed up." This was undeniably true, and it took two carpenters a whole forenoon to get it open, for examination. Then, she was satisfied that she had seen the Orphan Boy. But, the wild and terrible part of the story is, that he was also seen by three of her brother's sons, in succession, who all died young. On the occasion of each child being taken ill, he came home in a heat, twelve hours before, and said, Oh, mama, he had been playing under a particular oak-tree, in a certain meadow, with a strange boy – a pretty, forlorn-looking boy, who was very timid, and made signs! From fatal experience, the parents came to know that this was the Orphan Boy, and that the course of that child whom he chose for his little playmate was surely run.

Legion is the name[19] of the German castles, where we sit up alone to wait for the Spectre – where we are shown into a room, made comparatively cheerful for our reception – where we glance round at the shadows, thrown on the blank walls by the crackling fire – where we feel very lonely when the village innkeeper and his pretty daughter have retired, after laying down a fresh store of wood upon the hearth, and setting forth on the small table such supper-cheer as a cold roast capon, bread, grapes, and a flask of old Rhine wine – where the reverberating doors close on their retreat, one after another, like so many peals of sullen thunder – and where, about the small hours of the night, we come into the knowledge of divers supernatural mysteries. Legion is the name of the haunted German students, in whose society we draw yet nearer to the fire, while the schoolboy in the corner opens his eyes wide and round, and flies off the footstool he has chosen for his seat, when the door accidentally blows open. Vast is the crop of such fruit, shining on our Christmas Tree; in blossom, almost at the very top; ripening all down the boughs!

Among the later toys and fancies hanging there – as idle often and less pure – be the images once associated with the sweet old Waits, the softened music in the night, ever unalterable! Encircled by the social thoughts of Christmas-time, still let the benignant figure of my childhood stand unchanged! In every cheerful image and suggestion that the season brings, may the bright star that rested above the poor roof, be the star of all the Christian world! A moment's pause, O vanishing tree, of which the lower boughs are dark to me as yet, and let me look once more! I know there are blank spaces on thy branches, where eyes that I have loved, have shone and smiled; from which they are departed. But, far above, I see the raiser of the dead girl, and the widow's son; and God is good! If Age be hiding for me in the unseen portion of thy downward growth, O may I, with a grey head, turn a child's heart to that figure yet, and a child's trustfulness and confidence!

Now, the tree is decorated with bright merriment, and song, and dance, and cheerfulness. And they are welcome. Innocent and welcome be they ever held, beneath the branches of the Christmas Tree, which cast no gloomy shadow! But, as it sinks into the ground, I hear a whisper going through the leaves. "This, in commemoration of the law of love and kindness, mercy and compassion. This, in remembrance of Me!"[20]

Our School

First published in *Household Words*, 11 October 1851, and included in *Reprinted Pieces* from which this text is reproduced. Dickens wrote to Wills, 29 September 1851: 'The "sparkling" Muse has not been at all propitious . . . Today I have begun another [paper] called "Our School" – like that better but don't know when I may be able to finish it – doubt doing so tomorrow, for next No. – can't say – may be – may not.' The article, finished in time, begins with a recollection of the prep school Dickens attended with his sister Fanny in Rome Lane, Chatham, and then moves, for the remainder of the essay to a description of William Jones's Wellington House Classical and Commercial Academy, Hampstead Road, where Dickens was a pupil from the age of twelve to fourteen. This picture of the school is far less disagreeable than those offered in the Salem House chapters of *David Copperfield*, or in the speech made in 1857, where he claimed that the school was 'a pernicious and abominable humbug altogether', Forster, *Life* I, pp. 36–7, 42; and Philip Collins, *Dickens and Education*, pp. 10–12.

We went to look at it, only this last Midsummer, and found that the Railway had cut it up root and branch. A great trunk-line had swallowed the playground, sliced away the schoolroom, and pared off the corner of the house: which, thus curtailed of its proportions, presented itself, in a green stage of stucco, profilewise towards the road, like a forlorn flat-iron without a handle, standing on end.

It seems as if our schools were doomed to be the sport of change. We have faint recollections of a Preparatory Day-School, which we have sought in vain, and which must have been pulled down to make a new street, ages ago. We have dim impressions, scarcely amounting to a belief, that it was over a dyer's shop. We know that you went up steps to it; that you frequently grazed your knees in doing so; that you generally got your leg over the scraper, in trying to scrape the mud off a very unsteady little shoe. The mistress of the Establishment holds no place in our memory; but rampant on one eternal door-mat, in an eternal entry long and narrow, is a puffy pug-dog, with a personal animosity towards us, who triumphs over Time. The bark of that baleful Pug, a certain radiating way he had of snapping at our undefended legs, the ghastly grinning of his moist black muzzle and white teeth, and the insolence of his crisp tail curled like a pastoral crook, all live and flourish. From an otherwise unaccountable association of him with a fiddle, we conclude that he was of French extraction, and his name *Fidèle*. He belonged to some female, chiefly inhabiting a back-parlour, whose life appears to us to have been consumed in sniffing, and in wearing a brown beaver bonnet. For her, he would sit up and balance cake upon his nose, and not eat it until twenty had been counted. To the best of our belief we were once called in to witness this performance; when, unable, even in his milder moments, to endure our presence, he instantly made at us, cake and all.

Why a something in mourning, called "Miss Frost," should still connect itself with our preparatory school, we are unable to say. We retain no impression of the beauty of Miss Frost — if she were beautiful; or of the mental fascinations of Miss Frost — if she were accomplished; yet her name and her black dress hold an enduring place in our remembrance. An equally impersonal boy, whose name has long since shaped itself unalterably into "Master Mawls," is not to be dislodged from our brain. Retaining no vindictive feeling towards Mawls — no feeling whatever, indeed — we infer that neither he nor we can have loved Miss Frost. Our first impression of Death and Burial is associated with this formless pair. We all three nestled awfully in a corner one wintry day, when the wind was blowing shrill, with Miss Frost's pinafore over our heads; and Miss Frost told us in a whisper about somebody being "screwed down." It is the only distinct recollection we preserve of these impalpable creatures, except a suspicion that the manners of Master Mawls were susceptible of much improvement. Generally speaking, we may observe that whenever we see a child intently occupied with its nose, to the exclusion of all other subjects of interest, our mind reverts, in a flash, to Master Mawls.

But the School that was Our School before the Railroad came and overthrew it, was quite another sort of place. We were old enough to be put into Virgil when we went there, and to get Prizes for a variety of polishing on which the rust has long accumulated. It was a School of some celebrity in its neighbourhood — nobody could have said why — and we had the honour to attain and hold the eminent position of first boy. The master was supposed among us to know nothing, and one of the ushers was supposed to know everything. We are still inclined to think the first-named supposition perfectly correct.

We have a general idea that its subject had been in the leather trade, and had bought us — meaning Our School — of another proprietor who was immensely learned. Whether this belief had any real foundation, we are not likely ever to know now. The only branches of education with which he showed the least acquaintance, were, ruling and corporally punishing. He was always ruling ciphering-books with a bloated mahogany ruler, or smiting the palms of offenders with the same diabolical instrument, or viciously drawing a pair of pantaloons tight with one of his large hands, and caning the wearer with the other. We have no doubt whatever that this occupation was the principal solace of his existence.

A profound respect for money pervaded Our School, which was, of course, derived from its Chief. We remember an idiotic goggle-eyed boy, with a big head and half-crowns without end, who suddenly appeared as a parlour-boarder, and was rumoured to have come by sea from some mysterious part of the earth where his parents rolled in gold. He was usually called "Mr." by the Chief, and was said to feed in the parlour on steaks and gravy; likewise to drink currant wine. And he openly stated that if rolls and coffee were ever denied him at breakfast, he would write home to that unknown part of the globe from which he had come, and cause himself to be recalled to the regions of gold. He was put into no form or class, but learnt alone, as little as he liked – and he liked very little – and there was a belief among us that this was because he was too wealthy to be "taken down." His special treatment, and our vague association of him with the sea, and with storms, and sharks, and Coral Reefs occasioned the wildest legends to be circulated as his history. A tragedy in blank verse was written on the subject – if our memory does not deceive us, by the hand that now chronicles these recollections – in which his father figured as Pirate, and was shot for a voluminous catalogue of atrocities: first imparting to his wife the secret of the cave in which his wealth was stored, and from which his only son's half-crowns now issued. Dumbledon (the boy's name) was represented as "yet unborn" when his brave father met his fate; and the despair and grief of Mrs. Dumbledon at that calamity was movingly shadowed forth as having weakened the parlour-boarder's mind. This production was received with great favour, and was twice performed with closed doors in the dining-room. But it got wind, and was seized as libellous, and brought the unlucky poet into severe affliction. Some two years afterwards, all of a sudden one day, Dumbledon vanished. It was whispered that the Chief himself had taken him down to the Docks, and re-shipped him for the Spanish Main; but nothing certain was ever known about his disappearance. At this hour, we cannot thoroughly disconnect him from California.

Our School was rather famous for mysterious pupils. There was another – a heavy young man, with a large double-cased silver watch, and a fat knife the handle of which was a perfect tool-box – who unaccountably appeared one day at a special desk of his own, erected close to that of the Chief, with whom he held familiar converse. He lived in the parlour, and went out for his walks, and never took the least notice of us – even of us, the first boy – unless to give us a deprecatory kick, or grimly to take our hat off and throw it away, when he encountered us out of doors, which unpleasant ceremony he always performed as he passed – not even condescending to stop for the purpose. Some of us believed that the classical attainments of this phenomenon were terrific, but that his penmanship and arithmetic were defective, and he had come there to mend them; others, that he was going to set up a school, and had paid the Chief "twenty-five pound down," for leave to see Our School at work. The gloomier spirits even said that he was going to buy us; against which contingency, conspiracies were set on foot for a general defection and running away. However, he never did that. After staying for a quarter, during which period, though closely observed, he was never seen to do anything but make pens out of quills, write small hand in a secret portfolio, and punch the point of the sharpest blade in his knife into his desk all over it, he too disappeared, and his place knew him no more.

There was another boy, a fair, meek boy, with a delicate complexion and rich curling hair, who, we found out, or thought we found out (we have no idea now, and probably had none then, on what grounds, but it was confidentially revealed from mouth to mouth), was the son of a Viscount who had deserted his lovely mother. It was understood that if he had his rights, he would be worth twenty thousand a year. And that if his mother ever met his father, she would shoot him with a silver pistol, which she carried, always loaded to the muzzle, for that purpose. He was a very suggestive topic. So was a young Mulatto, who was always believed (though very amiable) to have a dagger about him somewhere. But we think they were both outshone, upon the whole, by another boy who claimed to have been born on the twenty-ninth of February, and to have only one birthday in five years. We suspect this to have been a fiction – but he lived upon it all the time he was at Our School.

The principal currency of Our School was slate pencil. It had some inexplicable value, that was never ascertained, never reduced to a standard. To have a great hoard of it was somehow to be rich. We used to bestow it in charity, and confer it as a precious boon upon our chosen friends. When the holidays were coming, contributions were solicited for certain boys whose relatives were in India, and who were appealed for under the generic name of "Holiday-stoppers," – appropriate marks of remembrance that should enliven and cheer them in their homeless state. Personally, we always contributed these tokens of sympathy in the form of slate pencil, and always felt that it would be a comfort and a treasure to them.

Our School was remarkable for white mice. Red-polls, linnets, and even canaries, were kept in desks, drawers, hat-boxes, and other strange refuges for birds; but white mice were the favourite stock. The boys trained the mice much better than the masters trained the boys. We recall one white mouse, who lived in the cover of a Latin dictionary, who ran up ladders, drew Roman chariots, shouldered muskets, turned wheels, and even made a very creditable appearance on the stage as the Dog of Montargis. He might have achieved greater things, but for having the misfortune to mistake his way in a triumphal procession to the Capitol, when he fell into a deep inkstand, and was dyed black and drowned. The mice were the occasion of some most ingenious engineering, in the construction of their houses and instruments of performance. The famous one belonged to a company of proprietors, some of whom have since made Railroads, Engines, and Telegraphs; the chairman has erected mills and bridges in New Zealand.

The usher at Our School, who was considered to know everything as opposed to the Chief, who was considered to know nothing, was a bony, gentle-faced, clerical-looking young man in rusty black. It was whispered that he was sweet upon one of Maxby's sisters (Maxby lived close by, and was a day pupil), and further that he "favoured Maxby." As we remember, he taught Italian to Maxby's sisters on half-holidays. He once went to the play with them, and wore a white waistcoat and a rose: which was considered among us equivalent to a declaration. We were of opinion on that occasion, that to the last moment he expected Maxby's father to ask him to dinner at five o'clock, and therefore neglected his own dinner at half-past one, and finally got none. We exaggerated in our imaginations the extent to which he punished Maxby's father's cold meat at supper; and we agreed to believe that he was elevated with wine and water when he came home. But we all liked him; for he had a good knowledge of boys, and would have made it a much better school if he had had more power. He was writing master, mathematical master, English master, made out the bills, mended the pens, and did all sorts of things. He divided the little boys with the Latin master (they were smuggled through their rudimentary books, at odd times when there was nothing else to do), and he always called at parents' houses to inquire after sick boys, because he had gentlemanly manners. He was rather musical, and on some remote quarter-day had bought an old trombone; but a bit of it was lost, and it made the most extraordinary sounds when he sometimes tried to play it of an evening. His holidays never began (on account of the bills) until long after ours; but in the summer vacations he used to take pedestrian excursions with a knapsack; and at Christmas time he went to see his father at Chipping Norton, who we all said (on no authority) was a dairy-fed pork-butcher. Poor fellow! He was very low all day on Maxby's sister's wedding-day, and afterwards was thought to favour Maxby more than ever, though he had been expected to spite him. He has been dead these twenty years. Poor fellow!

Our remembrance of Our School presents the Latin master as a colourless doubled-up near-sighted man with a crutch, who was always cold, and always putting onions into his ears for deafness, and always disclosing ends of flannel under all his garments, and almost always applying a ball of pocket-handkerchief to some part of his face with a screwing action round and round. He was a very good scholar, and took great pains where he saw intelligence and a desire to learn: otherwise, perhaps not. Our memory presents him (unless teased into a passion) with as little energy as colour – as having been worried and tormented into monotonous feebleness – as having had the best part of his life ground out of him in a Mill of boys. We remember with terror how he fell asleep one sultry afternoon with the little smuggled class before him, and awoke not when the footstep of the Chief fell heavy on the floor; how the Chief aroused him, in the midst of a dread silence, and said, "Mr. Blinkins, are you ill, sir?" how he blushingly replied, "Sir, rather so;" how the Chief retorted with severity, "Mr. Blinkins, this is no place to be ill in" (which was very, very true), and walked back solemn as the ghost in Hamlet, until, catching a wandering eye, he caned that boy for inattention, and happily expressed his feelings towards the Latin master through the medium of a substitute.

There was a fat little dancing-master who used to come in a gig, and taught the more advanced among us hornpipes (as an accomplishment in great social demand in after life); and there was a brisk little French master who used to come in the sunniest weather, with a handleless umbrella, and to whom the Chief was always polite, because (as we believed), if the Chief offended him, he would instantly address the Chief in French, and for ever confound him before the boys with his inability to understand or reply.

There was, besides, a serving man whose name was Phil. Our retrospective glance presents Phil as a shipwrecked carpenter, cast away upon the desert island of a school, and carrying into practice an ingenious inkling of many trades. He mended whatever was broken, and made whatever was wanted. He was general glazier, among other things, and mended all the broken windows – at the prime cost (as was darkly rumoured among us) of ninepence, for every square charged three-and-six to parents. We had a high opinion of his mechanical genius, and generally held that the Chief "knew something bad of him," and on pain of divulgence enforced Phil to be his bondsman. We particularly remember that Phil had a sovereign contempt for learning: which engenders in us a respect for his sagacity, as it implies his accurate observation of the relative positions of the Chief and the ushers. He was an impenetrable man, who waited at table between whiles, and throughout "the half" kept the boxes in severe custody. He was morose, even to the Chief, and never smiled, except at breaking-up, when, in acknowledgment of the toast, "Success to Phil! Hooray!" he would slowly carve a grin out of his wooden face, where it would remain until we were all gone. Nevertheless, one time when we had the scarlet fever in the school, Phil nursed all the sick boys of his own accord, and was like a mother to them.

There was another school not far off, and of course Our School could have nothing to say to that school. It is mostly the way with schools, whether of boys or men. Well! the railway has swallowed up ours, and the locomotives now run smoothly over its ashes.

> So fades and languishes, grows dim and dies,
> All that this world is proud of,[1]

– and is not proud of, too. It had little reason to be proud of Our School, and has done much better since in that way, and will do far better yet.

Lying Awake

First published in *Household Words*, 30 October 1852, and included in *Reprinted Pieces* from which this text is reproduced.

"My uncle lay with his eyes half closed, and his nightcap drawn almost down to his nose. His fancy was already wandering, and began to mingle up the present scene with the crater of Vesuvius, the French Opera, the Coliseum at Rome, Dolly's Chop-house in London, and all the farrago of noted places with which the brain of a traveller is crammed; in a word, he was just falling asleep."[1]

Thus, that delightful writer, WASHINGTON IRVING, in his Tales of a Traveller. But, it happened to me the other night to be lying: not with my eyes half closed, but with my eyes wide open; not with my nightcap drawn almost down to my nose, for on sanitary principles I never wear a nightcap: but with my hair pitchforked and touzled all over the pillow; not just falling asleep by any means, but glaringly, persistently, and obstinately, broad awake. Perhaps, with no scientific intention or invention, I was illustrating the theory of the Duality of the Brain; perhaps one part of my brain, being wakeful, sat up to watch the other part which was sleepy. Be that as it may, something in me was as desirous to go to sleep as it possibly could be, but something else in me *would not* go to sleep, and was as obstinate as George the Third.

Thinking of George the Third – for I devote this paper to my train of thoughts as I lay awake: most people lying awake sometimes, and having some interest in the subject – put me in mind of BENJAMIN FRANKLIN, and so Benjamin Franklin's paper on the art of procuring pleasant dreams, which would seem necessarily to include the art of going to sleep, came into my head. Now, as I often used to read that paper when I was a very small boy, and as I recollect everything I read then as perfectly as I forget everything I read now, I quoted "Get out of bed, beat up and turn your pillow, shake the bed-clothes well with at least twenty shakes, then throw the bed open and leave it to cool; in the meanwhile, continuing undrest, walk about your chamber. When you begin to feel the cold air unpleasant, then return to your bed, and you will soon fall asleep, and your sleep will be sweet and pleasant."[2] Not a bit of it! I performed the whole ceremony, and if it were possible for me to be more saucer-eyed than I was before, that was the only result that came of it.

Except Niagara. The two quotations from Washington Irving and Benjamin Franklin may have put it in my head by an American association of ideas; but there I was, and the Horse-shoe Fall was thundering and tumbling in my eyes and ears, and the very rainbows that I left upon the spray when I really did last look upon it, were beautiful to see.[3] The night-light being quite as plain, however, and sleep seeming to be many thousand miles further off than Niagara, I made up my mind to think a little about Sleep; which I no sooner did than I whirled off in spite of myself to Drury Lane Theatre, and there saw a great actor and dear friend of mine (whom I had been thinking of in the day) playing Macbeth, and heard him apostrophising "the death of each day's life,"[4] as I have heard him many a time, in the days that are gone.

But, Sleep. I *will* think about Sleep. I am determined to think (this is the way I went on) about Sleep. I must hold the word Sleep tight and fast, or I shall be off at a tangent in half a second. I feel myself unaccountably straying, already, into Clare Market. Sleep. It would be curious, as illustrating the equality of sleep, to inquire how many of its phenomena are common to all classes, to all degrees of wealth and poverty, to every grade of education and ignorance. Here, for example, is her Majesty Queen Victoria in her palace, this present blessed night, and here is Winking Charley, a sturdy vagrant, in one of her Majesty's jails. Her Majesty has fallen, many thousands of times, from that same Tower, which *I* claim a right to tumble off now and then. So has Winking Charley. Her Majesty in her sleep has opened or prorogued Parliament, or has held a Drawing Room, attired in some very scanty dress, the deficiencies and improprieties of which have caused her great uneasiness. I, in my degree, have suffered unspeakable agitation of mind from taking the chair at a public dinner at the London Tavern in my night-clothes, which not all the courtesy of my kind friend and host MR. BATHE[5] could persuade me were quite adapted to the occasion. Winking Charley has been repeatedly tried in a worse condition. Her Majesty is no stranger to a vault or firmament, of a sort of floorcloth,[6] with an indistinct pattern distantly resembling eyes, which occasionally obtrudes itself on her repose. Neither am I. Neither is Winking Charley. It is quite common to all three of us to skim along with airy strides a little above the ground; also to hold, with the deepest interest, dialogues with various people, all represented by ourselves; and to be at our wit's end to know what they are going to tell us; and to be indescribably astonished by the secrets they disclose. It is probable that we have all three committed murders and hidden bodies. It is pretty certain that we have all desperately wanted to cry out, and have had no voice; that we have all gone to the play and not been able to get in; that we have all dreamed much more of our youth than of our later lives; that – I have lost it! The thread's broken.

And up I go. I, lying here with the night-light before me, up I go, for no reason on earth that I can find out, and drawn by no links that are visible to me, up the Great Saint Bernard![7] I have lived in Switzerland, and rambled among the mountains; but why I should go there now, and why up the Great Saint Bernard in preference to any other mountain, I have no idea. As I lie here broad awake, and with every sense so sharpened that I can distinctly hear distant noises inaudible to me at another time, I make that journey, as I really did, on the same summer day, with the same happy party[8] – ah! two since dead, I grieve to think – and there is the same track, with the same black wooden arms to point the way, and there are the same storm-refuges here and there; and there is the same snow falling at the top, and there are the same frosty mists, and there is the same intensely cold convent with its ménagerie smell, and the same breed of dogs fast dying out, and the same breed of jolly young monks whom I mourn to know as humbugs, and the same convent parlour with its piano and the sitting round the fire, and the same supper, and the same lone night in a cell, and the same bright fresh morning when going out into the highly rarefied air was like a plunge into an icy bath. Now, see here what comes along; and why does this thing stalk into my mind on the top of a Swiss mountain!

It is a figure that I once saw, just after dark, chalked upon a door in a little back lane near a country church – my first church. How young a child I may have been at the time I don't know, but it horrified me so intensely – in connexion with the churchyard, I suppose, for it smokes a pipe, and has a big hat with each of its ears sticking out in a horizontal line under the brim, and is not in itself more oppressive than a mouth from ear to ear, a pair of goggle eyes, and hands like two bunches of carrots, five in each, can make it – that it is still vaguely alarming to me to recall (as I have often done before, lying awake) the running home, the looking behind, the horror, of its following me; though whether disconnected from the door, or door and all, I can't say, and perhaps never could. It lays a disagreeable train. I must resolve to think of something on the voluntary principle.

The balloon ascents of this last season. They will do to think about, while I lie awake, as well as anything else. I must hold them tight though, for I feel them sliding away, and in their stead are the Mannings, husband and wife, hanging on the top of Horsemonger Lane Jail.[9] In connexion with which dismal spectacle, I recall this curious fantasy of the mind. That, having beheld that execution, and having left those two forms dangling on the top of the entrance gateway – the man's, a limp, loose suit of clothes as if the man had gone out of them; the woman's, a fine shape, so elaborately corseted and artfully dressed, that it was quite unchanged in its trim appearance as it slowly swung from side to side – I never could, by my uttermost efforts, for some weeks, present the outside of that prison to myself (which the terrible impression I had received continually obliged me to do) without presenting it with the two figures still hanging in the morning air. Until, strolling past the gloomy place one night, when the street was deserted and quiet, and actually seeing that the bodies were not there, my fancy was persuaded, as it were, to take them down and bury them within the precincts of the jail, where they have lain ever since.

The balloon ascents of last season. Let me reckon them up. There were the horse, the bull, the parachute, and the tumbler hanging on – chiefly by his toes, I believe – below the car. Very wrong, indeed, and decidedly to be stopped. But, in connexion with these and similar dangerous exhibitions, it strikes me that that portion of the public whom they entertain, is unjustly reproached. Their pleasure is in the difficulty overcome. They are a public of great faith, and are quite confident that the gentleman will not fall off the horse, or the lady off the bull or out of the parachute, and that the tumbler has a firm hold with his toes. They do not go to see the adventurer vanquished, but triumphant. There is no parallel in public combats between men and beasts, because nobody can answer for the particular beast – unless it were always the same beast, in which case it would be a mere stage-show, which the same public would go in the same state of mind to see, entirely believing in the brute being beforehand safely subdued by the man. That they are not accustomed to calculate hazards and dangers with any nicety, we may know from their rash exposure of themselves in overcrowded steamboats, and unsafe conveyances and places of all kinds. And I cannot help thinking that instead of railing, and attributing savage motives to a people naturally well disposed and humane, it is better to teach them, and lead them argumentatively and reasonably – for they are very reasonable, if you will discuss a matter with them – to more considerate and wise conclusions.

This is a disagreeable intrusion! Here is a man with his throat cut, dashing towards me as I lie awake! A recollection of an old story of a kinsman of mine, who, going home one foggy winter night to Hampstead, when London was much smaller and the road lonesome, suddenly encountered such a figure rushing past him, and presently two keepers from a madhouse in pursuit. A very unpleasant creature indeed, to come into my mind unbidden, as I lie awake.

– The balloon ascents of last season. I must return to the balloons. Why did the bleeding man start out of them? Never mind; if I inquire, he will be back again. The balloons. This particular public have inherently a great pleasure in the contemplation of physical difficulties overcome; mainly, as I take it, because the lives of a large majority of them are exceedingly monotonous and real, and further, are a struggle against continual difficulties, and further still, because anything in the form of accidental injury, or any kind of illness or disability is so very serious in their own sphere. I will explain this seeming paradox of mine. Take the case of a Christmas Pantomime. Surely nobody supposes that the young mother in the pit who falls into fits of laughter when the baby is boiled or sat upon, would be at all diverted by such an occurrence off the stage. Nor is the decent workman in the gallery, who is transported beyond the ignorant present by the delight with which he sees a stout gentleman pushed out of a two pair of stairs window, to be slandered by the suspicion that he would be in the least entertained by such a spectacle in any street in London, Paris, or New York. It always appears to me that the secret of this enjoyment lies in the temporary superiority to the common hazards and mischances of life; in seeing casualties, attended when they really occur with bodily and mental suffering, tears, and poverty, happen through a very rough sort of poetry without the least harm being done to any one – the pretence of distress in a pantomime being so broadly humorous as to be no pretence at all. Much as in the comic fiction I can understand the mother with a very vulnerable baby at home, greatly relishing the invulnerable baby on the stage, so in the Cremorne reality[10] I can understand the mason who is always liable to fall off a scaffold in his working jacket and to be carried to the hospital, having an infinite admiration of the radiant personage in spangles who goes into the clouds upon a bull, or upside down, and who, he takes it for granted – not reflecting upon the thing – has, by uncommon skill and dexterity, conquered such mischances as those to which he and his acquaintance are continually exposed.

I wish the Morgue in Paris[11] would not come here as I lie awake, with its ghastly beds, and the swollen saturated clothes hanging up, and the water dripping, dripping all day long, upon that other swollen saturated something in the corner, like a heap of crushed over-ripe figs that I have seen in Italy! And this detestable Morgue comes back again at the head of a procession of forgotten ghost stories. This will never do. I must think of something else as I lie awake; or, like that sagacious animal in the United States who recognised the colonel who was such a dead shot, I am a gone 'Coon.[12] What shall I think of? The late brutal assaults. Very good subject. The late brutal assaults.

(Though whether, supposing I should see, here before me as I lie awake, the awful phantom described in one of those ghost stories, who, with a head-dress of shroud, was always seen looking in through a certain glass door at a certain dead hour – whether, in such a case it would be the least consolation to me to know on philosophical grounds that it was merely my imagination, is a question I can't help asking myself by the way.)

The late brutal assaults.[13] I strongly question the expediency of advocating the revival of whipping for those crimes. It is a natural and generous impulse to be indignant at the perpetration of inconceivable brutality, but I doubt the whipping panacea gravely. Not in the least regard or pity for the criminal, whom I hold in far lower estimation than a mad wolf, but in consideration for the general tone and feeling, which is very much improved since the whipping times. It is bad for a people to be familiarised with such punishments. When the whip went out of Bridewell, and ceased to be flourished at the cart's tail and at the whipping-post, it began to fade out of madhouses, and workhouses, and schools and families, and to give place to a better system everywhere, than cruel driving. It would be hasty, because a few brutes may be inadequately punished, to revive, in any aspect, what, in so many aspects, society is hardly yet happily rid of. The whip is a very contagious kind of thing, and difficult to confine within one set of bounds. Utterly abolish punishment by fine – a barbarous device, quite as much out of date as wager by battle, but particularly connected in the vulgar mind with this class of offence – at least quadruple the term of imprisonment for aggravated assaults – and above all let us, in such cases, have no Pet Prisoning,[14] vain glorifying, strong soup, and roasted meats, but hard work, and one unchanging and uncompromising dietary of bread and water, well or ill; and we shall do much better than by going down into the dark to grope for the whip among the rusty fragments of the rack, and the branding iron, and the chains and gibbet from the public roads, and the weights that pressed men to death in the cells of Newgate.

I had proceeded thus far, when I found I had been lying awake so long that the very dead began to wake too, and to crowd into my thoughts most sorrowfully. Therefore, I resolved to lie awake no more, but to get up and go out for a night walk – which resolution was an acceptable relief to me, as I dare say it may prove now to a great many more.

Where We Stopped Growing

First published in *Household Words*, 1 January 1853, from which this text is reproduced.

Few people who have been much in the society of children, are likely to be ignorant of the sorrowful feeling sometimes awakened in the mind by the idea of a favorite child's "growing up." This is intelligible enough. Childhood is usually so beautiful and engaging, that, setting aside the many subjects of profound interest which it offers to an ordinarily thoughtful observer; and even setting aside, too, the natural caprices of strong affection and prepossession; there is a mournful shadow of the common lot, in the notion of its changing and fading into anything else. The sentiment is unreasoning and vague, and does not shape itself into a wish. To consider what the dependent little creature would do without us, or in the course of how few years it would be in as bad a condition as those terrible immortals upon earth, engendered in the gloom of SWIFT's wise fancy,[1] is not within the range of so fleeting a thought. Neither does the imagination then enter into such details as the picturing of childhood come to old age, or of old age carried back to childhood, or of the pretty baby boy arrived at that perplexing state of immaturity when MR. CARLYLE, in mercy to society, would put him under a barrel for six years.[2] The regret is transitory, natural to a short-lived creature in a world of change, has no hold in the judgment, and so comes and passes away.

But we, the writer, having been conscious of the sensation the other night – for, at this present season most of us are much in childish company, and we among the rest – were led to consider whether there were any things as to which this individual We actually did stop growing when we were a child. We had a fear that the list would be very short; but, in writing it out as follows, were glad to find it longer than we had expected.

We have never grown the thousandth part of an inch out of Robinson Crusoe.[3] He fits us just as well, and in exactly the same way, as when we were among the smallest of the small. We have never grown out of his parrot, or his dog, or his fowling-piece, or the horrible old staring goat he came upon in the cave, or his rusty money, or his cap, or umbrella. There has been no change in the manufacture of telescopes, since that blessed ship's spy-glass was made, through which, lying on his breast at the top of his fortification, with the ladder drawn up after him and all made safe, he saw the black figures of those Cannibals moving round the fire on the sea-sand, as the monsters danced themselves into an appetite for dinner. We have never grown out of Friday, or the excellent old father he was so glad to see, or the grave and gentlemanly Spaniard, or the reprobate Will Atkins, or the knowing way in which he and those other mutineers were lured up into the Island when they came ashore there, and their boat was stove. We have got no nearer Heaven by the altitude of an atom, in respect of the tragi-comic bear whom Friday caused to dance upon a tree, or the awful array of howling wolves in the dismal weather, who were mad to make good entertainment of man and beast, and who were received with trains of gunpowder laid on fallen trees, and fired by the snapping of pistols; and who ran blazing into the forest darkness, or were blown up famously. Never sail we, idle, in a little boat, and hear the rippling water at the prow, and look upon the land, but we know that our boat-growth stopped for ever, when Robinson Crusoe sailed round the Island, and, having been nearly lost, was so affectionately awakened out of his sleep at home again by that immortal parrot, great progenitor of all the parrots we have ever known.

Our growth stopped, when the great Haroun Alraschid spelt his name so, and when nobody had ever heard of a Jin.[4] When the Sultan of the Indies was a mighty personage, to be approached respectfully even on the stage; and when all the dazzling wonders of those many nights held far too high a place in the imagination to be burlesqued and parodied. When Blue Beard,[5] condescending to come out of book at all, came over mountains, to the music of his own march, on an elephant, and knew no more of slang than of Sanscrit. Our growth stopped, when Don Quixote[6] might have been right after all in going about to succour the distressed, and when the priest and the barber were no more justified in burning his books than they would have been in making a bonfire of our own two bed-room shelves. When Gil Blas had a heart,[7] and was somehow or other, not at all worldly that we knew of: and when it was a wonderful accident that the end of that interesting story in the Sentimental Journey,[8] commencing with the windy night, and the notary, and the Pont Neuf, and the hat blown off, was not to be found in our Edition though we looked for it a thousand times.

We have never grown out of the real original roaring giants. We have seen modern giants, for various considerations ranging from a penny to half-a-crown; but, they have only had a head a-piece, and have been merely large men, and not always that. We have never outgrown the putting to ourselves of this supposititious case; Whether, if we, with a large company of brothers and sisters, had been put in his (by which we mean, of course, in Jack's) trying situation, we should have had at once the courage and the presence of mind to take the golden crowns (which it seems they always wore as night-caps) off the heads of the giant's children as they lay a-bed, and put them on our family; thus causing our treacherous host to batter his own offspring, and spare us. We have never outgrown a want of confidence in ourselves, in this particular.

There are real people and places that we have never outgrown, though they themselves may have passed away long since: which we always regard with the eye and mind of childhood. We miss a tea-tray shop, for many years at the corner of Bedford Street and King Street, Covent Garden, London, where there was a tea-tray in the window representing, with an exquisite Art[9] that we have not outgrown either, the departure from home for school, at breakfast time, of two boys – one boy used to it; the other, not. There was a charming mother in a bygone fashion, evidently much affected though trying to hide it; and a little sister, bearing, as we remember, a basket of fruit for the consolation of the unused brother; what time the used one, receiving advice we opine from his grandmother, drew on his glove in a manner we once considered unfeeling, but which we were afterwards inclined to hope might be only his brag. There were some corded boxes, and faithful servants; and there was a breakfast-table, with accessories (an urn and plate of toast particularly) our admiration of which, as perfect illusions, we never have outgrown and never shall outgrow.

We never have outgrown the whole region of Covent Garden. We preserve it as a fine, dissipated, insoluble mystery. We believe that the gentleman mentioned in Colman's Broad Grins[10] still lives in King Street. We have a general idea that the passages at the Old Hummums[11] lead to groves of gorgeous bed-rooms, eating out the whole of the adjacent houses: where Chamberlains who have never been in bed themselves for fifty years, show any country gentleman who rings at the bell, at any hour of the night, to luxurious repose in palatial apartments fitted up after the Eastern manner. (We have slept there in our time, but that makes no difference.) There is a fine secresy and mystery about the Piazza; – how you get up to those rooms above it, and what reckless deeds are done there. (We know some of those apartments very well, but that does not signify in the least.) We have not outgrown the two great Theatres.[12] Ghosts of great names are always getting up the most extraordinary pantomimes in them, with scenery and machinery on a tremendous scale. We have no doubt that the critics sit in the pit of both houses, every night. Even as we write in our common-place office, we behold from the window, four young ladies with peculiarly limp bonnets, and of a yellow or drab style of beauty, making for the stage-door of the Lyceum Theatre, in the dirty little fog-choked street over the way. Grown up wisdom whispers that these are beautiful fairies by night, and that they will find Fairy Land dirty even to their splashed skirts, and rather cold and dull (notwithstanding its mixed gas and daylight), this easterly morning. But, we don't believe it.

There was a poor demented woman who used to roam about the City, dressed all in black with cheeks staringly painted, and thence popularly known as *Rouge et Noire*; whom we have never outgrown by the height of a grain of mustard seed. The story went that her only brother, a Bank-clerk, was left for death for forgery; and that she, broken-hearted creature, lost her wits on the morning of his execution, and ever afterwards, while her confused dream of life lasted, flitted thus among the busy money-changers. A story, alas! all likely enough; but, likely or unlikely, true or untrue, never to take other shape in our mind. Evermore she wanders, as to our stopped growth, among the crowd, and takes her daily loaf out of the shop-window of the same charitable baker, and betweenwhiles sits in the old Bank office awaiting her brother. "Is he come yet?" Not yet, poor soul. "I will go walk for an hour and come back." It is then she passes our boyish figure in the street, with that strange air of vanity upon her, in which the comfortable self-sustainment of sane vanity (God help us all!) is wanting, and with her wildly-seeking, never resting, eyes. So she returns to his old Bank office, asking "Is he come yet?" Not yet, poor soul! So she goes home, leaving word that indeed she wonders he has been away from her so long, and that he must come to her however late at night he may arrive. He will come to thee, O stricken sister, with thy best friend – foe to the prosperous and happy – not to such as thou!

Another very different person who stopped our growth, we associate with Berners Street, Oxford Street; whether she was constantly on parade in that street only, or was ever to be seen elsewhere, we are unable to say. The White Woman is her name. She is dressed entirely in white, with a ghastly white plaiting round her head and face, inside her white bonnet. She even carries (we hope) a white umbrella. With white boots, we know she picks her way through the winter dirt. She is a conceited old creature, cold and formal in manner, and evidently went simpering mad on personal grounds alone – no doubt because a wealthy Quaker wouldn't marry her. This is her bridal dress. She is always walking up here, on her way to church to marry the false Quaker. We observe in her mincing step and fishy eye that she intends to lead him a sharp life. We stopped growing when we got at the conclusion that the Quaker had had a happy escape of the White Woman.

We have never outgrown the rugged walls of Newgate, or any other prison on the outside. All within, is still the same blank of remorse and misery. We have never outgrown Baron Trenck.[13] Among foreign fortifications, trenches, counterscarps, bastions, sentries, and what not, we always have him, filing at his chains down in some arched darkness far below, or taming the spiders to keep him company. We have never outgrown the wicked old Bastille. Here, in our mind at this present childish moment, is a distinct groundplan (wholly imaginative and resting on no sort of authority), of a maze of low vaulted passages with small black doors; and here, inside of this remote door on the left, where the black cobwebs hang like a veil from the arch, and the jailer's lamp will scarcely burn, was shut up, in black silence through so many years, that old man of the affecting anecdote, who was at last set free. But, who brought his white face, and his white hair, and his phantom figure, back again, to tell them what they had made him – how he had no wife, no child, no friend, no recognition of the light and air – and prayed to be shut up in his old dungeon till he died.

We received our earliest and most enduring impressions among barracks and soldiers, and ships and sailors. We have outgrown no story of voyage and travel, no love of adventure, no ardent interest in voyagers and travellers. We have outgrown no country inn – roadside, in the market-place, or on a solitary heath; no country landscape, no windy hill side, no old manor-house, no haunted place of any degree, not a drop in the sounding sea. Though we are equal (on strong provocation) to the Lancers, and may be heard of in the Polka, we have not outgrown Sir Roger de Coverley,[14] or any country dance in the music-book. We hope we have not outgrown the capacity of being easily pleased with what is meant to please us, or the simple folly of being gay upon occasion without the least regard to being grand.

Right thankful we are to have stopped in our growth at so many points – for each of these has a train of its own belonging to it – and particularly with the Old Year going out and the New Year coming in. Let none of us be ashamed to feel this gratitude. If we can only preserve ourselves from growing up, we shall never grow old, and the young may love us to the last. Not to be too wise, not to be too stately, not to be too rough with innocent fancies, or to treat them with too much lightness – which is as bad – are points to be remembered that may do us all good in our years to come. And the good they do us, may even stretch forth into the vast expanse beyond those years; for, this is the spirit inculcated by One on whose knees children sat confidingly, and from whom all our years dated.

Gone Astray

First published in *Household Words*, 13 August 1853, from which this text is reproduced.

When I was a very small boy indeed, both in years and stature, I got lost one day in the City of London. I was taken out by Somebody (shade of Somebody forgive me for remembering no more of thy identity!), as an immense treat, to be shown the outside of Saint Giles's Church.[1] I had romantic ideas in connexion with that religious edifice; firmly believing that all the beggars who pretended through the week to be blind, lame, one-armed, deaf and dumb, and otherwise physically afflicted, laid aside their pretences every Sunday, dressed themselves in holiday clothes, and attended divine service in the temple of their patron saint. I had a general idea that the reigning successor of Bamfylde Moore Carew[2] acted as a sort of church-warden on these occasions, and sat in a high pew with red curtains.

It was in the spring-time when these tender notions of mine, bursting forth into new shoots under the influence of the season, became sufficiently troublesome to my parents and guardians to occasion Somebody to volunteer to take me to see the outside of Saint Giles's Church, which was considered likely (I suppose) to quench my romantic fire, and bring me to a practical state. We set off after breakfast. I have an impression that Somebody was got up in a striking manner – in cord breeches of fine texture and milky hue, in long jean gaiters, in a green coat with bright buttons, in a blue neckerchief, and a monstrous shirt-collar. I think he must have newly come (as I had myself) out of the hop-grounds of Kent. I considered him the glass of fashion and the mould of form: a very Hamlet without the burden of his difficult family affairs.

We were conversational together, and saw the outside of Saint Giles's Church with sentiments of satisfaction, much enhanced by a flag flying from the steeple. I infer that we then went down to Northumberland House in the Strand to view the celebrated lion over the gateway.[3] At all events, I know that in the act of looking up with mingled awe and admiration at that famous animal I lost Somebody.

The child's unreasoning terror of being lost, comes as freshly on me now as it did then. I verily believe that if I had found myself astray at the North

Pole instead of in the narrow, crowded, inconvenient street over which the lion in those days presided, I could not have been more horrified. But, this first fright expended itself in a little crying and tearing up and down; and then I walked, with a feeling of dismal dignity upon me, into a court, and sat down on a step to consider how to get through life.

To the best of my belief, the idea of asking my way home never came into my head. It is possible that I may, for the time, have preferred the dismal dignity of being lost; but I have a serious conviction that in the wide scope of my arrangements for the future, I had no eyes for the nearest and most obvious course. I was but very juvenile; from eight to nine years old, I fancy.

I had one and fourpence in my pocket, and a pewter ring with a bit of red glass in it on my little finger. This jewel had been presented to me by the object of my affections, on my birthday, when we had sworn to marry, but had foreseen family obstacles to our union, in her being (she was six years old) of the Wesleyan persuasion, while I was devotedly attached to the Church of England. The one and fourpence were the remains of half-a-crown presented on the same anniversary by my godfather – a man who knew his duty and did it.

Armed with these amulets, I made up my little mind to seek my fortune. When I had found it, I thought I would drive home in a coach and six, and claim my bride. I cried a little more at the idea of such a triumph, but soon dried my eyes and came out of the court to pursue my plans. These were, first to go (as a species of investment) and see the Giants in Guildhall,[4] out of whom I felt it not improbable that some prosperous adventure would arise; failing that contingency, to try about the City for any opening of a Whittington nature; baffled in that too, to go into the army as a drummer.

So, I began to ask my way to Guildhall: which I thought meant, somehow, Gold or Golden Hall; I was too knowing to ask my way to the Giants, for I felt it would make people laugh. I remember how immensely broad the streets seemed now I was alone, how high the houses, how grand and mysterious everything. When I came to Temple Bar,[5] it took me half an hour to stare at it, and I left it unfinished even then. I had read about heads being exposed on the top of Temple Bar, and it seemed a wicked old place, albeit a noble monument of architecture and a paragon of utility. When at last I got away from it, behold I came, the next minute, on the figures at St. Dunstan's![6] Who could see those obliging monsters strike upon the bells and go? Between the quarters there was the toyshop to look at – still there, at this present writing, in a new form – and even when that enchanted spot was escaped from, after an hour and more, then Saint Paul's arose, and how was I to get beyond its dome, or to take my eyes from its cross of gold? I found it a long journey to the Giants, and a slow one.

I came into their presence at last, and gazed up at them with dread and veneration. They looked better-tempered, and were altogether more shiny-faced, than I had expected; but they were very big, and, as I judged their pedestals to be about forty feet high, I considered that they would be very big indeed if they were walking on the stone pavement. I was in a state of mind as to these and all such figures, which I suppose holds equally with most children. While I knew them to be images made of something that was not flesh and blood, I still invested them with attributes of life – with consciousness of my being there, for example, and the power of keeping a sly eye upon me. Being very tired I got into the corner under Magog, to be out of the way of his eye, and fell asleep.

When I started up after a long nap, I thought the giants were roaring, but it was only the City. The place was just the same as when I fell asleep: no beanstalk, no fairy, no princess, no dragon, no opening in life of any kind. So, being hungry, I thought I would buy something to eat, and bring it in there and eat it, before going forth to seek my fortune on the Whittington plan.[7]

I was not ashamed of buying a penny roll in a baker's shop, but I looked into a number of cooks' shops before I could muster courage to go into one. At last I saw a pile of cooked sausages in a window with the label, "Small Germans, A Penny." Emboldened by knowing what to ask for, I went in and said, "If you please will you sell me a small German?" which they did, and I took it, wrapped in paper in my pocket, to Guildhall.

The giants were still lying by, in their sly way, pretending to take no notice, so I sat down in another corner, when what should I see before me but a dog with his ears cocked. He was a black dog, with a bit of white over one eye, and bits of white and tan in his paws, and he wanted to play – frisking about me, rubbing his nose against me, dodging at me sideways, shaking his head and pretending to run away backwards, and making himself good-naturedly ridiculous, as if he had no consideration for himself, but wanted to raise my spirits. Now, when I saw this dog I thought of Whittington, and felt that things were coming right; I encouraged him by saying, "Hi, boy!" "Poor fellow!" "Good dog!" and was satisfied that he was to be my dog for ever afterwards, and that he would help me to seek my fortune.

Very much comforted by this (I had cried a little at odd times ever since I was lost), I took the small German out of my pocket, and began my dinner by biting off a bit and throwing it to the dog, who immediately swallowed it with a one-sided jerk, like a pill. While I took a bit myself, and he looked me in the face for a second piece, I considered by what name I should call him. I thought Merrychance would be an expressive name, under the circumstances; and I was elated, I recollect, by inventing such a good one, when Merrychance began to growl at me in a most ferocious manner.

I wondered he was not ashamed of himself, but he didn't care for that; on the contrary he growled a good deal more. With his mouth watering, and his eyes glistening, and his nose in a very damp state, and his head very much on one side, he sidled about on the pavement in a threatening manner and growled at me, until he suddenly made a snap at the small German, tore it out of my hand, and went off with it. He never came back to help me seek my fortune. From that hour to the present, when I am forty years of age, I have never seen my faithful Merrychance again.

I felt very lonely. Not so much for the loss of the small German, though it was delicious (I knew nothing about highly-peppered horse at that time), as on account of Merrychance's disappointing me so cruelly; for I had hoped he would do every friendly thing but speak, and perhaps even come to that. I cried a little more, and began to wish that the object of my affections had been lost with me, for company's sake. But, then I remembered that *she* could not go into the army as a drummer; and I dried my eyes and ate my loaf. Coming out, I met a milkwoman, of whom I bought a pennyworth of milk; quite set up again by my repast, I began to roam about the City, and to seek my fortune in the Whittington direction.

When I go into the City, now, it makes me sorrowful to think that I am quite an artful wretch. Strolling about it as a lost child, I thought of the British Merchant and the Lord Mayor, and was full of reverence. Strolling about it now, I laugh at the sacred liveries of state, and get indignant with the corporation as one of the strongest practical jokes of the present day. What did I know then, about the multitude who are always being disappointed in the City; who are always expecting to meet a party there, and to receive money there, and whose expectations are never fulfilled? What did I know then, about that wonderful person, the friend in the City, who is to do so many things for so many people; who is to get this one into a post at home, and that one into a post abroad; who is to settle with this man's creditors, provide for that man's son, and see that other man paid; who is to "throw himself" into this grand Joint-Stock certainty, and is to put his name down on that Life Assurance Directory, and never does anything predicted of him? What did I know, then, about him as the friend of gentlemen, Mosaic Arabs[8] and others, usually to be seen at races, and chiefly residing in the neighbourhood of Red Lion Square; and as being unable to discount the whole amount of that paper in money, but as happening to have by him a cask of remarkable fine sherry, a dressing-case, and a Venus by Titian, with which he would be willing to make up the balance? Had I ever heard of him, in those innocent days, as confiding information (which never by any chance turned out to be in the remotest degree correct) to solemn bald men, who mysteriously imparted it to breathless dinner tables? No. Had I ever learned to dread him as a shark, disregard him as a humbug, and know him for a myth? Not I. Had I ever heard of him as associated with tightness in the money market, gloom in consols, the exportation of gold, or that rock ahead in everybody's course, the bushel of wheat? Never. Had I the least idea what was meant by such terms as jobbery, rigging the market, cooking accounts, getting up a dividend, making things pleasant, and the like? Not the slightest. Should I have detected in Mr. Hudson[9] himself, a staring carcase of golden veal? By no manner of means. The City was to me a vast emporium of precious stones and metals, casks and bales, honour and generosity, foreign fruits and spices. Every merchant and banker was a compound of Mr. Fitz-Warren[10] and Sinbad the Sailor. Smith, Payne, and Smith, when the wind was fair for Barbary and the captain present, were in the habit of calling their servants together (the cross cook included) and asking them to produce their little shipments. Glyn and Halifax had personally undergone great hardships in the valley of diamonds. Baring Brothers had seen Rocs' eggs and travelled with caravans. Rothschild[11] had sat in the Bazaar at Bagdad with rich stuffs for sale; and a veiled lady from the Sultan's harem, riding on a donkey, had fallen in love with him.

Thus I wandered about the City, like a child in a dream, staring at the British merchants, and inspired by a mighty faith in the marvellousness of everything. Up courts and down courts – in and out of yards and little squares – peeping into counting-house passages and running away – poorly feeding the echoes in the court of the South Sea House with my timid steps – roaming down into Austin Friars,[12] and wondering how the Friars used to like it – ever staring at the British merchants, and never tired of the shops – I rambled on, all through the day. In such stories as I made, to account for the different places, I believed as devoutly as in the City itself. I particularly remember that when I found myself on 'Change,[13] and saw the shabby people sitting under the placards about ships, I settled that they were Misers, who had embarked all their wealth to go and buy gold-dust or something of that sort, and were waiting for their respective captains to come and tell them that they were ready to set sail. I observed that they all munched dry biscuits, and I thought it was to keep off sea-sickness.

This was very delightful; but it still produced no result according to the Whittington precedent. There was a dinner preparing at the Mansion House,[14] and when I peeped in at a grated kitchen window, and saw the men cooks at work in their white caps, my heart began to beat with hope that the Lord Mayor, or the Lady Mayoress, or one of the young Princesses their daughters, would look out of an upper apartment and direct me to be taken in. But, nothing of the kind occurred. It was not until I had been peeping in some time that one of the cooks called to me (the window was open) "Cut away, you sir!" which frightened me so, on account of his black whiskers, that I instantly obeyed.

After that, I came to the India House, and asked a boy what it was, who made faces and pulled my hair before he told me, and behaved altogether in an ungenteel and discourteous manner. Sir James Hogg himself might have been satisfied with the veneration in which I held the India House.[15] I had no doubt of its being the most wonderful, the most magnanimous, the most incorruptible, the most practically disinterested, the most in all respects astonishing, establishment on the face of the earth. I understood the nature of an oath, and would have sworn it to be one entire and perfect chrysolite.

Thinking much about boys who went to India, and who immediately, without being sick, smoked pipes like curled-up bell-ropes, terminating in a large cut-glass sugar basin upside down, I got among the outfitting shops. There, I read the lists of things that were necessary for an India-going boy, and when I came to "one brace of pistols," thought what happiness to be reserved for such a fate! Still no British merchant seemed at all disposed to take me into his house. The only exception was a chimney-sweep – he looked at me as if he thought me suitable to his business; but I ran away from him.

I suffered very much, all day, from boys; they chased me down turnings, brought me to bay in doorways, and treated me quite savagely, though I am sure I gave them no offence. One boy, who had a stump of black-lead pencil in his pocket, wrote his mother's name and address (as he said) on my white hat, outside the crown. MRS. BLORES, WOODEN LEG WALK, TOBACCO-STOPPER ROW, WAPPING. And I couldn't rub it out.

I recollect resting in a little churchyard after this persecution, disposed to think upon the whole, that if I and the object of my affections could be buried there together, at once, it would be comfortable. But, another nap, and a pump, and a bun, and above all a picture that I saw, brought me round again.

I must have strayed by that time, as I recall my course, into Goodman's Fields,[16] or somewhere thereabouts. The picture represented a scene in a play then performing at a theatre in that neighbourhood which is no longer in existence. It stimulated me to go to that theatre and see that play. I resolved, as there seemed to be nothing doing in the Whittington way, that on the conclusion of the entertainments I would ask my way to the barracks, knock at the gate, and tell them that I understood they were in want of drummers, and there I was. I think I must have been told, but I know I believed, that a soldier was always on duty, day and night, behind every barrack-gate, with a shilling; and that a boy who could by any means be prevailed on to accept it, instantly became a drummer, unless his father paid four hundred pounds.

I found out the theatre – of its external appearance I only remember the loyal initials G. R. untidily painted in yellow ochre on the front – and waited, with a pretty large crowd, for the opening of the gallery doors. The greater part of the sailors and others composing the crowd, were of the lowest description, and their conversation was not improving; but I understood little or nothing of what was bad in it then, and it had no depraving influence on me. I have wondered since, how long it would take, by means of such association, to corrupt a child nurtured as I had been, and innocent as I was.

Whenever I saw that my appearance attracted attention, either outside the doors or afterwards within the theatre, I pretended to look out for somebody who was taking care of me, and from whom I was separated, and to exchange nods and smiles with that creature of my imagination. This answered very well. I had my sixpence clutched in my hand ready to pay; and when the doors opened, with a clattering of bolts, and some screaming from women in the crowd, I went on with the current like a straw. My sixpence was rapidly swallowed up in the money-taker's pigeon-hole, which looked to me like a sort of mouth, and I got into the freer staircase above and ran on (as everybody else did) to get a good place. When I came to the back of the gallery, there were very few people in it, and the seats looked so horribly steep, and so like a diving arrangement to send me, headforemost, into the pit, that I held by one of them in a terrible fright. However, there was a good-natured baker with a young woman, who gave me his hand, and we all three scrambled over the seats together down into the corner of the first row. The baker was very fond of the young woman, and kissed her a good deal in the course of the evening.

I was no sooner comfortably settled, than a weight fell upon my mind, which tormented it most dreadfully, and which I must explain. It was a benefit night – the benefit of the comic actor – a little fat man with a very large face and, as I thought then, the smallest and most diverting hat that ever was seen. This comedian, for the gratification of his friends and patrons, had undertaken to sing a comic song on a donkey's back, and afterwards to give away the donkey so distinguished, by lottery. In this lottery, every person admitted to the pit and gallery had a chance. On paying my sixpence, I had received the number, forty-seven; and I now thought, in a perspiration of terror, what should I ever do if that number was to come up the prize, and I was to win the donkey!

It made me tremble all over to think of the possibility of my good fortune. I knew I never could conceal the fact of my holding forty-seven, in case that number came up, because, not to speak of my confusion, which would immediately condemn me, I had shewn my number to the baker. Then, I pictured to myself the being called upon to come down on the stage and receive the donkey. I thought how all the people would shriek when they saw it had fallen to a little fellow like me. How should I lead him out – for of course he wouldn't go? If he began to bray, what should I do? If he kicked, what would become of me? Suppose he backed into the stage-door, and stuck there, with me upon him? For I felt that if I won him, the comic actor would have me on his back, the moment he could touch me. Then if I got him out of the theatre, what was I to do with him? How was I to feed him? Where was I to stable him? It was bad enough to have gone astray by myself, but to go astray with a donkey, too, was a calamity more tremendous than I could bear to contemplate.

These apprehensions took away all my pleasure in the first piece. When the ship came on – a real man-of-war she was called in the bills – and rolled prodigiously in a very heavy sea, I couldn't, even in the terrors of the storm, forget the donkey. It was awful to see the sailors pitching about, with telescopes and speaking trumpets (they looked very tall indeed aboard the man-of-war), and it was awful to suspect the pilot of treachery, though impossible to avoid it, for when he cried – "We are lost! To the raft, to the raft! A thunderbolt has struck the main-mast!" – I myself saw him take the main-mast out of its socket and drop it overboard; but even these impressive circumstances paled before my dread of the donkey. Even, when the good sailor (and he was very good) came to good fortune, and the bad sailor (and he was very bad) threw himself into the ocean from the summit of a curious rock, presenting something of the appearance of a pair of steps, I saw the dreadful donkey through my tears.

At last the time came when the fiddlers struck up the comic song, and the dreaded animal, with new shoes on, as I inferred from the noise they made, came clattering in with the comic actor on his back. He was dressed out with ribbons (I mean the donkey was) and as he persisted in turning his tail to the audience, the comedian got off him, turned about, and sitting with his face that way, sang the song three times, amid thunders of applause. All this time, I was fearfully agitated; and when two pale people, a good deal splashed with the mud of the streets, were invited out of the pit to superintend the drawing of the lottery, and were received with a round of laughter from everybody else, I could have begged and prayed them to have mercy on me, and not draw number forty-seven.

But, I was soon put out of my pain now, for a gentleman behind me, in a flannel jacket and a yellow neck-kerchief, who had eaten two fried soles and all his pockets-full of nuts before the storm began to rage, answered to the winning number, and went down to take possession of the prize. This gentleman had appeared to know the donkey, rather, from the moment of his entrance, and had taken a great interest in his proceedings; driving him to himself, if I use an intelligible phrase, and saying, almost in my ear, when he made any mistake, "Kum up, you precious Moke. Kum up!" He was thrown by the donkey on first mounting him, to the great delight of the audience (including myself), but rode him off with great skill afterwards, and soon returned to his seat quite calm. Calmed myself by the immense relief I had sustained, I enjoyed the rest of the performance very much indeed. I remember there were a good many dances, some in fetters and some in roses, and one by a most divine little creature, who made the object of my affections look but common-place. In the concluding drama, she re-appeared as a boy (in arms, mostly), and was fought for, several times. I rather think a Baron wanted to drown her, and was on various occasions prevented by the comedian, a ghost, a Newfoundland dog, and a church bell. I only remember beyond this, that I wondered where the Baron expected to go to, and that he went there in a shower of sparks. The lights were turned out while the sparks died out, and it appeared to me as if the whole play – ship, donkey, men and women, divine little creature, and all – were a wonderful firework that had gone off, and left nothing but dust and darkness behind it.

It was late when I got out into the streets, and there was no moon, and there were no stars, and the rain fell heavily. When I emerged from the dispersing crowd, the ghost and the baron had an ugly look in my remembrance; I felt unspeakably forlorn; and now, for the first time, my little bed and the dear familiar faces came before me, and touched my heart. By daylight, I had never thought of the grief at home. I had never thought of my mother. I had never thought of anything but adapting myself to the circumstances in which I found myself, and going to seek my fortune.

For a boy who could do nothing but cry, and run about, saying, "O I am lost!" to think of going into the army was, I felt sensible, out of the question. I abandoned the idea of asking my way to the barracks – or rather the idea abandoned me – and ran about, until I found a watchman in his box. It is amazing to me, now, that he should have been sober; but I am inclined to think he was too feeble to get drunk.

This venerable man took me to the nearest watch-house; – I say he took me, but in fact I took him, for when I think of us in the rain, I recollect that we must have made a composition, like a vignette of Infancy leading Age. He had a dreadful cough, and was obliged to lean against a wall, whenever it came on. We got at last to the watch-house, a warm and drowsy sort of place embellished with great-coats and rattles hanging up. When a paralytic messenger had been sent to make inquiries about me, I fell asleep by the fire, and awoke no more until my eyes opened on my father's face. This is literally and exactly how I went astray. They used to say I was an odd child, and I suppose I was. I am an odd man perhaps.

Shade of Somebody, forgive me for the disquiet I must have caused thee! When I stand beneath the Lion, even now, I see thee rushing up and down, refusing to be comforted. I have gone astray since, many times, and farther afield. May I therein have given less disquiet to others, than herein I gave to thee!

An Unsettled Neighbourhood

First published in *Household Words*, 11 November 1854, from which this text is reproduced.

It is not my intention to treat of any of those new neighbourhoods which a wise legislature leaves to come into existence just as it may happen; overthrowing the trees, blotting out the face of the country, huddling together labyrinths of odious little streets of vilely constructed houses; heaping ugliness upon ugliness, inconvenience upon inconvenience, dirt upon dirt, and contagion upon contagion. Whenever a few hundreds of thousands of people of the classes most enormously increasing, shall happen to come to the conclusion that they have suffered enough from preventible disease (a moral phenomenon that may occur at any time), the said wise legislature will find itself called to a heavy reckoning. May it emerge from that extremity as agreeably as it slided in. Amen!

No. The unsettled neighbourhood on which I have my eye – in a literal sense, for I live in it, and am looking out of window – cannot be called a new neighbourhood.[1] It has been in existence, how long shall I say? Forty, fifty, years. It touched the outskirts of the fields, within a quarter of a century; at that period it was as shabby, dingy, damp, and mean a neighbourhood, as one would desire not to see. Its poverty was not of the demonstrative order. It shut the street-doors, pulled down the blinds, screened the parlour-windows with the wretchedest plants in pots, and made a desperate stand to keep up appearances. The genteeler part of the inhabitants, in answering knocks, got behind the door to keep out of sight, and endeavoured to diffuse the fiction that a servant of some sort was the ghostly warder. Lodgings were let, and many more were *to* let; but, with this exception, signboards and placards were discouraged. A few houses that became afflicted in their lower extremities with eruptions of mangling and clear-starching, were considered a disgrace to the neighbourhood. The working bookbinder with the large door-plate was looked down upon for keeping fowls, who were always going in and out. A corner house with "Ladies' School" on a board over the first floor windows, was barely tolerated for its educational facilities; and Miss Jamanne the dressmaker, who inhabited two parlours, and kept an obsolete work of art representing the Fashions, in the window of the front one, was held at a marked distance by the ladies of the neighbourhood – who patronised her, however, with far greater regularity than they paid her.

In those days, the neighbourhood was as quiet and dismal as any neighbourhood about London. Its crazily built houses – the largest, eight-roomed – were rarely shaken by any conveyance heavier than the spring van that came to carry off the goods of a "sold up" tenant. To be sold up was nothing particular. The whole neighbourhood felt itself liable, at any time, to that common casualty of life. A man used to come into the neighbourhood regularly, delivering the summonses for rates and taxes as if they were circulars. We never paid anything until the last extremity, and Heaven knows how we paid it then. The streets were positively hilly with the inequalities made in them by the man with the pickaxe who cut off the company's supply of water to defaulters. It seemed as if nobody had any money but old Miss Frowze, who lived with her mother at Number fourteen Little Twig Street, and who was rumoured to be immensely rich; though I don't know why, unless it was that she never went out of doors, and never wore a cap, and never brushed her hair, and was immensely dirty.

As to visitors, we really had no visitors at that time. Stabbers's Band used to come every Monday morning and play for three quarters of an hour on one particular spot by the Norwich Castle; but, how they first got into a habit of coming, or even how we knew them to be Stabbers's Band, I am unable to say. It was popular in the neighbourhood, and we used to contribute to it: dropping our halfpence into an exceedingly hard hat with a warm handkerchief in it, like a sort of bird's-nest (I am not aware whether it was Mr. Stabbers's hat or not), which came regularly round. They used to open with "Begone, dull Care!" and to end with a tune which the neighbourhood recognised as "I'd rather have a Guinea than a One-pound Note." I think any reference to money, that was not a summons or an execution, touched us melodiously. As to Punches, they knew better than to do anything but squeak and drum in the neighbourhood, unless a collection was made in advance – which never succeeded. Conjurors and strong men strayed among us, at long intervals; but, I never saw the donkey go up once. Even costermongers were shy of us, as a bad job: seeming to know instinctively that the neighbourhood ran scores with Mrs. Slaughter, Greengrocer, etc., of Great Twig Street, and consequently didn't dare to buy a ha'porth elsewhere: or very likely being told so by young Slaughter, who managed the business, and was always lurking in the Coal Department, practising Ramo Samee[2] with three potatoes.

As to shops, we had no shops either, worth mentioning. We had the

46

Norwich Castle, Truman Hanbury and Buxton, by J. Wigzell: a violent landlord, who was constantly eating in the bar, and constantly coming out with his mouth full and his hat on, to stop his amiable daughter from giving more credit; and we had Slaughter's; and we had a jobbing tailor's (in a kitchen), and a toy and hardbake[3] (in a parlour), and a Bottle Rag Bone Kitchen-stuff and Ladies' Wardrobe, and a tobacco and weekly paper. We used to run to the doors and windows to look at a cab, it was such a rare sight; the boys (we had no end of boys, but where *is* there any end of boys?) used to Fly the Garter[4] in the middle of the road; and if ever a man might have thought a neighbourhood was settled down until it dropped to pieces, a man might have thought ours was.

What made the fact quite the reverse, and totally changed the neighbourhood? I have known a neighbourhood changed, by many causes, for a time. I have known a miscellaneous vocal concert every evening, do it; I have known a mechanical waxwork with a drum and organ, do it; I have known a Zion Chapel do it; I have known a firework-maker's do it; or a murder, or a tallow-melter's. But, in such cases, the neighbourhood has mostly got round again, after a time, to its former character. I ask, what changed our neighbourhood altogether and for ever? I don't mean what knocked down rows of houses, took the whole of Little Twig Street into one immense hotel, substituted endless cab-ranks for Fly the garter, and shook us all day long to our foundations with waggons of heavy goods; but, what put the neighbourhood off its head, and wrought it to that feverish pitch that it has ever since been unable to settle down to any one thing, and will never settle down again? THE RAILROAD has done it all.

That the Railway Terminus springing up in the midst of the neighbourhood should make what I may call a physical change in it, was to be expected. That people who had not sufficient beds for themselves, should immediately begin offering to let beds to the travelling public, was to be expected. That coffee-pots, stale muffins, and egg-cups, should fly into parlour windows like tricks in a pantomime, and that everybody should write up Good Accommodation for Railway Travellers, was to be expected. Even that Miss Frowze should open a cigar-shop, with a what's-his-name that the Brahmins smoke,[5] in the middle of the window, and a thing outside like a Canoe stood on end, with a familiar invitation underneath it, to "Take a light," might have been expected. I don't wonder at house-fronts being broken out into shops, and particularly into Railway Dining Rooms, with powdered haunches of mutton, powdered cauliflowers, and great flat bunches of rhubarb, in the window. I don't complain of three eight-roomed houses out of every four taking upon themselves to set up as Private Hotels, and putting themselves, as such, into Bradshaw,[6] with a charge of so much a day for bed and breakfast, including boot-cleaning and attendance, and so much extra for a private sitting-room – though where the private sitting-rooms can be, in such an establishment, I leave you to judge. I don't make it any ground of objection to Mrs. Minderson (who is a most excellent widow woman with a young family) that, in exhibiting one empty soup-tureen with the cover on, she appears to have satisfied her mind that she is fully provisioned as "The Railway Larder." I don't point it out as a public evil that all the boys who are left in the neighbourhood, tout to carry carpet-bags. The Railway Ham, Beef, and German Sausage Warehouse, I was prepared for. The Railway Pie Shop, I have purchased pastry from. The Railway Hat and Travelling Cap Depot, I knew to be an establishment which in the nature of things must come. The Railway Hair-cutting Saloon, I have been operated upon in; the Railway Ironmongery, Nail and Tool Warehouse; the Railway Bakery; the Railway Oyster Rooms and General Shell Fish Shop; the Railway Medical Hall; and the Railway Hosiery and Travelling Outfitting Establishment; all these I don't complain of. In the same way, I know that the cabmen must and will have beer-shops, on the cellar-flaps of which they can smoke their pipes among the waterman's buckets, and dance the double shuffle. The railway porters must also have *their* houses of call; and at such places of refreshment I am prepared to find the Railway Double Stout at a gigantic threepence in your own jugs. I don't complain of this; neither do I complain of J. Wigzell having absorbed two houses on each side of him into The Railway Hotel (late Norwich Castle), and setting up an illuminated clock, and a vane at the top of a pole like a little golden Loco-motive. But what I do complain of, and what I am distressed at, is, the state of mind – the moral condition – into which the neighbourhood has got. It is unsettled, dissipated, wandering (I believe nomadic is the crack word for that sort of thing just at present), and don't know its own mind for an hour.

I have seen various causes of demoralisation learnedly pointed out in reports and speeches, and charges to grand juries; but, the most demoralising thing *I* know, is Luggage. I have come to the conclusion that the moment Luggage begins to be always shooting about a neighbourhood, that neigh-bourhood goes out of its mind. Everybody wants to be off somewhere. Everybody does everything in a hurry. Everybody has the strangest ideas of its being vaguely his or her business to go "down the line." If any Fast-train could take it, I believe the whole neighbourhood of which I write: bricks, stones, timber, ironwork, and everything else: would set off down the line.

Why, only look at it! What with houses being pulled down and houses being built up, is it possible to imagine a neighbourhood less collected in its intellects? There are not fifty houses of any sort in the whole place that know their own mind a month. Now, a shop says, "I'll be a toy-shop." To-morrow it says, "No I won't; I'll be a milliner's." Next week it says, "No I won't; I'll be a stationer's." Next week it says, "No I won't; I'll be a Berlin wool repository." Take the shop directly opposite my house. Within a year, it has gone through all these changes, and has likewise been a plumber's painter's and glazier's, a tailor's, a broker's, a school, a lecturing-hall, and a feeding-place, "established to supply the Railway public with a first-rate sandwich and a sparkling glass of Crowley's Alton Ale for threepence." I have seen the different people enter on these various lines of business, apparently in a sound and healthy state of mind. I have seen them, one after another, go off their heads with looking at the cabs rattling by, top-heavy with luggage, the driver obscured by boxes and portmanteaus crammed between his legs, and piled on the footboard – I say, I have seen them with my own eyes, fired out of their wits by luggage, put up the shutters, and set off down the line.

In the old state of the neighbourhood, if any young party was sent to the Norwich Castle to see what o'clock it was, the solid information would be brought back – say, for the sake of argument, twenty minutes to twelve. The smallest child in the neighbourhood who can tell the clock, is now convinced that it hasn't time to say twenty minutes to twelve, but comes back and jerks out, like a little Bradshaw, "Eleven forty." Eleven forty!

Mentioning the Norwich Castle, reminds me of J. Wigzell. That man is a type of the neighbourhood. He used to wear his shirt-sleeves and his stiff drab trowsers, like any other publican; and if he went out twice in a year, besides going to the Licensed Victuallers' Festival, it was as much as he did. What is the state of that man now? His pantaloons must be railway checks; his upper garment must be a cut-away coat, perfectly undermined by travelling pockets; he must keep a time-bill in his waistcoat – besides the two immense ones, UP and DOWN, that are framed in the bar – he must have a macintosh and a railway rug always lying ready on a chair; and he must habitually start off down the line, at five minutes' notice. Now, I *know* that J. Wigzell has no business down the line; he has no more occasion to go there than a Chinese. The fact is, he stops in the bar until he is rendered perfectly insane by the Luggage he sees flying up and down the street; then, catches up his macintosh and railway rug; goes down the line; gets out at a Common, two miles from a town; eats a dinner at the new little Railway Tavern there, in a choking hurry; comes back again by the next Up-train; and feels that he has done business!

We dream, in this said neighbourhood, of carpet-bags and packages. How can we help it? All night long, when passenger trains are flat, the Goods trains come in, banging and whanging over the turning-plates at the station like the siege of Sebastopol.[7] Then, the mails come in; then, the mail-carts come out; then, the cabs set in for the early parliamentary;[8] then, we are in for it through the rest of the day. Now, I don't complain of the whistle, I say nothing of the smoke and steam, I have got used to the red-hot burning smell from the Breaks[9] which I thought for the first twelve-month was my own house on fire, and going to burst out; but, my ground of offence is the moral inoculation of the neighbourhood. I am convinced that there is some mysterious sympathy between my hat on my head, and all the hats in hat-boxes that are always going down the line. My shirts and stockings put away in a chest of drawers, want to join the multitude of shirts and stockings that are always rushing everywhere, Express, at the rate of forty mile an hour. The trucks that clatter with such luggage, full trot, up and down the platform, tear into our spirits, and hurry us, and we can't be easy.

In a word, the Railway Terminus Works themselves are a picture of our moral state. They look confused and dissipated, with an air as if they were always up all night, and always giddy. Here, is a vast shed that was not here yesterday, and that may be pulled down to-morrow; there, a wall that is run up until some other building is ready; there, an open piece of ground, which is a quagmire in the middle, bounded on all four sides by a wilderness of houses, pulled down, shored up, broken-headed, crippled, on crutches, knocked about and mangled in all sorts of ways, and billed with fragments of all kinds of ideas. We are, mind and body, an unsettled neighbourhood. We are demoralised by the contemplation of luggage in perpetual motion. My conviction is, that you have only to circulate luggage enough − it is a mere question of quantity − through a Quakers' Meeting, and every broad-brimmed hat and slate-coloured bonnet there, will disperse to the four winds at the highest possible existing rate of locomotion.

Personal

First published in *Household Words*, 12 June 1858, from which this text is reproduced.

Three-and-twenty years have passed[1] since I entered on my present relations with the Public. They began when I was so young, that I find them to have existed for nearly a quarter of a century.

Through all that time I have tried to be as faithful to the Public, as they have been to me. It was my duty never to trifle with them, or deceive them, or presume upon their favor, or do any thing with it but work hard to justify it. I have always endeavoured to discharge that duty.

My conspicuous position has often made me the subject of fabulous stories and unaccountable statements. Occasionally, such things have chafed me, or even wounded me; but, I have always accepted them as the shadows inseparable from the light of my notoriety and success. I have never obtruded any such personal uneasiness of mine, upon the generous aggregate of my audience.

For the first time in my life, and I believe for the last, I now deviate from the principle I have so long observed, by presenting myself in my own Journal in my own private character, and entreating all my brethren (as they deem that they have reason to think well of me, and to know that I am a man who has ever been unaffectedly true to our common calling), to lend their aid to the dissemination of my present words.

Some domestic trouble of mine, of long-standing, on which I will make no further remark than that it claims to be respected, as being of a sacredly private nature, has lately been brought to an arrangement, which involves no anger or ill-will of any kind, and the whole origin, progress, and surrounding circumstances of which have been, throughout, within the knowledge of my children. It is amicably composed, and its details have now but to be forgotten by those concerned in it.

By some means, arising out of wickedness, or out of folly, or out of inconceivable wild chance, or out of all three, this trouble has been made the occasion of misrepresentations, most grossly false, most monstrous, and most cruel – involving, not only me, but innocent persons dear to my heart, and innocent persons of whom I have no knowledge, if, indeed, they have any existence – and so widely spread, that I doubt if one reader in a thousand will peruse these lines, by whom some touch of the breath of these slanders will not have passed, like an unwholesome air.

Those who know me and my nature, need no assurance under my hand that such calumnies are as irreconcileable with me, as they are, in their frantic incoherence, with one another. But, there is a great multitude who know me through my writings, and who do not know me otherwise; and I cannot bear that one of them should be left in doubt, or hazard of doubt, through my poorly shrinking from taking the unusual means to which I now resort, of circulating the Truth.

I most solemnly declare, then – and this I do, both in my own name and in my wife's name – that all the lately whispered rumours touching the trouble at which I have glanced, are abominably false. And that whosoever repeats one of them after this denial, will lie as wilfully and as foully as it is possible for any false witness to lie, before Heaven and earth.

CHARLES DICKENS.

New Year's Day

First published in *Household Words*, 1 January 1859, from which this text is reproduced.
Dickens is recalling festive periods spent in Genoa in 1845, Paris in 1856 and others.

When I was a little animal revolting to the sense of sight (for I date from the period when small boys had a dreadful high-shouldered sleeved strait-waistcoat put upon them by their keepers, over which their dreadful little trousers were buttoned tight, so that they roamed about disconsolate, with their hands in their pockets, like dreadful little pairs of tongs that were vainly looking for the rest of the fire-irons); when I was this object of just contempt and horror to all well-constituted minds, and when, according to the best of my remembrance and self-examination in the past, even my small shirt was an airy superstition which had no sleeves to it and stopped short at my chest; when I was this exceedingly uncomfortable and disreputable father of my present self, I remember to have been taken, upon a New Year's Day, to the Bazaar in Soho Square, London, to have a present bought for me. A distinct impression yet lingers in my soul that a grim and unsympathetic old personage of the female gender, flavoured with musty dry lavender, dressed in black crape, and wearing a pocket in which something clinked at my ear as we went along, conducted me on this occasion to the World of Toys. I remember to have been incidentally escorted a little way down some conveniently retired street diverging from Oxford Street, for the purpose of being shaken; and nothing has ever slaked the burning thirst for vengeance awakened in me by this female's manner of insisting upon wiping my nose herself (I had a cold and a pocket-handkerchief), on the screw principle. For many years I was unable to excogitate the reason why she should have undertaken to make me a present. In the exercise of a matured judgment, I have now no doubt that she had done something bad in her youth, and that she took me out in an act of expiation.

Nearly lifted off my legs by this adamantine woman's grasp of my glove (another fearful invention of those dark ages – a muffler, and fastened at the wrist like a hand-cuff), I was haled through the Bazaar. My tender imagination (or conscience) represented certain small apartments in corners, resembling wooden cages, wherein I have since seen reason to suppose that

53

ladies' collars and the like are tried on, as being, either dark places of confinement for refractory youth, or dens in which the lions were kept who fattened on boys who said they didn't care. Suffering tremendous terrors from the vicinity of these avenging mysteries, I was put before an expanse of toys, apparently about a hundred and twenty acres in extent, and was asked what I would have to the value of half-a-crown? Having first selected every object at half-a-guinea, and then staked all the aspirations of my nature on every object at five shillings, I hit, as a last resource, upon a Harlequin's Wand — painted particoloured, like Harlequin himself.

Although of a highly hopeful and imaginative temperament, I had no fond belief that the possession of this talisman would enable me to change Mrs. Pipchin[1] at my side into anything agreeable. When I tried the effect of the wand upon her, behind her bonnet, it was rather as a desperate experiment founded on the conviction that she could change into nothing worse, than with any latent hope that she would change into something better. Howbeit, I clung to the delusion that when I got home I should do something magical with this wand; and I did not resign all hope of it until I had, by many trials, proved the wand's total incapacity. It had no effect on the staring obstinacy of a rocking-horse; it produced no live Clown out of the hot beefsteak-pie at dinner; it could not even influence the minds of my honoured parents to the extent of suggesting the decency and propriety of their giving me an invitation to sit up to supper.

The failure of this wand is my first very memorable association with a New Year's Day. Other wands have failed me since, but the Day itself has become their substitute, and is always potent. It is the best Harlequin's Wand I have ever had. It has wrought strange transformations — no more of them — its power in reproducing the Past is admirable. Nothing ever goes wrong with that trick. I throw up and catch my little wand of New Year's Day, beat the dust of years from the ground at my feet with it, twinkle it a little, and Time reverses his hour-glass, and flies back, much faster than he ever flew forward.

New Year's Day. What Party can that have been, and what New Year's Day can that have been, which first rooted the phrase, "A New Year's Day Party," in my mind? So far back do my recollections of childhood extend, that I have a vivid remembrance of the sensation of being carried down-stairs in a woman's arms, and holding tight to her, in the terror of seeing the steep perspective below. Hence, I may have been carried into this Party, for anything I know; but, somehow or other, I most certainly got there, and was in a doorway looking on; and in that look a New Year's Party revealed itself to me, as a very long row of ladies and gentlemen sitting against a wall, all drinking at once out of little glass cups with handles, like custard-cups. What can this Party have been! I am afraid it must have been a dull one, but I *know* it came off. Where can this Party have been! I have not the faintest notion where, but I am absolutely certain it was somewhere. Why the company should all have been drinking at once, and especially why they should all have been drinking out of custard-cups, are points of fact over which the Waters of Oblivion have long rolled. I doubt if they can have been drinking the Old Year out and the New One in, because they were not at supper and had no table before them. There was no speech-making, no quick movement and change of action, no demonstration of any kind. They were all sitting in a long row against the wall – very like my first idea of the good people in Heaven, as I derived it from a wretched picture in a Prayer-book – and they had all got their heads a little thrown back, and were all drinking at once. It is possible enough that I, the baby, may have been caught up out of bed to have a peep at the company, and that the company may happen to have been thus occupied for the flash and space of a moment only. But, it has always seemed to me as if I looked at them for a long time – hours – during which they did nothing else; and to this present time, a casual mention in my hearing, of a Party on a New Year's Day, always revives that picture.

On what other early New Year's Day can I possibly have been an innocent accomplice in the secreting – in a coal cellar too – of a man with a wooden leg! There was no man with a wooden leg, in the circle of my acknowledged and lawful relations and friends. Yet, I clearly remember that we stealthily conducted the man with the wooden leg – whom we knew intimately – into the coal cellar, and that, in getting him over the coals to hide him behind some partition there was beyond, his wooden leg bored itself in among the small coals, and his hat flew off, and he fell backward and lay prone: a spectacle of helplessness. I clearly remember that his struggles to get up among the small coals, and to obtain any purchase on himself in those slippery and shifting circumstances, were a work of exceeding difficulty, involving delay and noise that occasioned us excessive terror. I have not the least idea who "we" were, except that I had a little sister for another innocent accomplice, and that there must have been a servant girl for principal: neither do I know whether the man with the wooden leg robbed the house, before or afterwards, or otherwise nefariously distin-guished himself. Nor, how a cat came to be connected with the occasion, and had a fit, and ran over the top of a door. But, I know that some awful reason compelled us to hush it all up, and that we "never told." For many years, I had this association with a New Year's Day entirely to myself, until at last, the anniversary being come round again, I said to the little sister, as she and I sat by chance among our children, "Do you remember the New Year's Day of the man with the wooden leg?" Whereupon, a thick black curtain which had overhung him from her infancy, went up, and she saw just this much of the man, and not a jot more. (A day or so before her death, that little sister told me that, in the night, the smell of the fallen leaves in the woods where we had habitually walked as very young children, had come upon her with such strength of reality that she had moved her weak head to look for strewn leaves on the floor at her bedside.)

New Year's Day. It was on a New Year's Day that I fought a duel. Furious with love and jealousy, I "went out" with another gentleman of honor, to assert my passion for the loveliest and falsest of her sex. I estimate the age of that young lady to have been about nine – my own age, about ten. I knew the Queen of my soul, as "the youngest Miss Clickitt but one." I had offered marriage, and my proposals had been very favorably received, though not definitively closed with. At which juncture, my enemy – Paynter, by name – arose out of some abyss or cavern, and came between us. The appearance of the Fiend Paynter, in the Clickitt Paradise, was altogether so mysterious and sudden, that I don't know where he came from; I only know that I found him, on the surface of this earth, one afternoon late in the month of December, playing at hot boiled beans and butter with the youngest Miss Clickitt but one. His conduct on that occasion was such, that I sent a friend to Paynter. After endeavouring with levity to evade the question, by pulling the friend's cap off and throwing it into a cabbage-garden, Paynter referred my messenger to his cousin – a goggle-eyed Being worthy of himself. Preliminaries were arranged, and by my own express stipulation the meeting was appointed for New Year's Day, in order that one of us might quit this state of existence on a day of mark. I passed a considerable portion of the last evening of the old year in arranging my affairs. I addressed a pathetic letter, and a goldfinch, to the youngest Miss Clickitt but one (to be delivered into her own hands by my friend, in case I should fall), and I wrote another letter for my mother, and made a disposition of my property: which consisted of books, some coloured engravings of Bamfylde Moore Carew, Mrs. Shipton,[2] and others, in a florid style of art, and a rather choice collection of marbles. While engaged in these last duties, I suffered the keenest anguish, and wept abundantly. The combat was to begin with fists, but was to end any how. Dark presentiments overshadowed my mind, because I had heard, on reliable authority, that Paynter (whose father was pay-master of some regiment stationed in the sea-port where the conflict impended), had a dirk and meant the worst. I had no other arms, myself, than a blank cartridge, of which ammunition we used to get driblets from the soldiers when they practised, by following them up with tobacco, and bribing them with pipes-full screwed in old copies, to pretend to load and not to do it. This cartridge my friend and second had specially recommended me, on the combat's assuming a mortal appearance, to explode on the fell Paynter: which I, with some indefinite view of blowing that gentleman up, had undertaken to do, though the engineering details of the operation were not at all adjusted. We met in a sequestered trench, among the fortifications. Paynter had access to some old military stores, and appeared on the ground in the regulation-cap of a full-grown Private of the Second Royal Veteran Battalion. – I see the boy now, coming from among the stinging-nettles in an angle of the trench, and making my blood run cold by his terrible appearance. Preliminaries were arranged, and we were to begin the struggle – this again was my express stipulation – on the word being given, "The youngest Miss Clickitt but one!" At this crisis, a difference of opinion arose between the seconds, touching the exact construction of that article in the code of honor which prohibits "hitting below the waistcoat;" and I rather think it arose from *my* second's having manœuvred the whole of *my* waistcoat into the neighbourhood of my chin. However it arose, expressions were used which Paynter, who I found had a very delicate sense of honor, could not permit to pass. He immediately dropped his guard, and appealed to me whether it was not our duty most reluctantly to forego our own gratification until the two gentlemen in attendance on us had established their honor? I warmly assented; I did more; I immediately took my friend aside, and lent him the cartridge. But, so unworthy of our confidence were those seconds that they declined, in spite alike of our encouragements and our indignant remonstrances, to engage. This made it plain both to Paynter and myself, that we had but one painful course to take; which was, to leave them ("with loathing," Paynter said, and I highly approved), and go away arm in arm. He gave me to understand as we went along that he too was a victim of the perfidy of the youngest Miss Clickitt but one, and I became exceedingly fond of him before we parted.

And here is another New Year's Day coming back, under the influence of the Wand which is better than Harlequin's! What New Year's Day is this? This is the New Year's Day of the annual gathering of later times at Boles's. Mr. Boles lives in a high, bleak, Down-country, where the wind never leaves off whistling all the year round, unless it takes to roaring. Mr. Boles has chimney-corners in his house, as big as other people's rooms; Mr. Boles's larder is as the larder of an amiable giant, and Mr. Boles's kitchen corresponds thereto. In Mr. Boles's boudoirs sits Miss Boles: a blessed creature: a Divinity. In Mr. Boles's bed-chambers, is a ghost. In Mr. Boles's house, in short, is everything desirable – and under Mr. Boles's house, is Mr. Boles's cellar. So many are the New Year's Days I have passed at Mr. Boles's, that I have won my way, like an enlisted Son of the vanished French Republic one and indivisible, through a regular series of promotions: beginning with the non-commissioned bed-rooms, passing through the subaltern bed-rooms, ascending in the scale until, on the New Year's Day now obedient to the Wand, I inhabit the Field-Marshal bed-room. But, where is Mr. Boles, now I have risen so high in the service? Alack! I go out, now-a-days, into the windy snow-drift, or the windy frost, or windy rain, or windy sunshine – of a certainty into the windy weather, let it be what else it may – to look at Mr. Boles's tomb in the little churchyard: where, while the avenue of elms is gustily tossed and troubled, like Life, the one dark yew-tree in the shadow of the bell-tower is solemnly at rest, like Death. And Miss Boles? She, too, is departed, though only into the world of matrons, not of shadows; and she is my hostess now; and she is a blessed creature (in the byegone sense of making the ground she walks on, worshipful), no more; and I have outlived my passion for her, and I perceive her appetite to be healthy, and her nose to be red. What of that? Are the seasons to stop for me? There are Boleses coming on, though under the different name into which the blessed creature gone for ever, (if she ever really came) sunk her own. In the old Boles boudoirs, there are still blessed creatures and divinities – to somebody, though not to me. If I suspect that the present non-commissioned officers and subalterns don't love as I did when I held those ranks, are not half as unselfishly faithful as I was, not half as tenderly devoted as I was, not half as passionately miserable as I was, what then? It may be so; it may not be so; but the world is, on the whole, round, and it is ever turning. If my old type has disappeared for the moment, it will come up again in its right place, when its right time brings it upward. Moreover, what am I, even as I know myself, that I should bemoan the disappearance, real or fancied, of the like of Me? Because I am *not* virtuous, shall there be no cakes but of my kneading, no ale but of my brewing? Far from me be the thought! When it comes near me, and stays by me, I may know of a surety that New Year's Days are finally closing in around me, and that, in a scheme where nothing created stops, I cannot too soon cease to be an insignificant anomaly. Therefore, O New Year's Days of the old Boles time, and of all my old time, may you be ever welcome! Therefore, non-commissioned officers, subalterns, lieutenants, all, of the Boles spare bed-rooms, I, from the Field-Marshal chamber stretch out my poor hand, entreating cordiality of union among all degrees, and cheerfully declaring my readiness to join as well as I can, in the last new figures of the Dance of Life, rather than growl and grumble, with no partner, down the Dance of Death.

And here is another New Year's Day responsive to the Wand of the season before I have dismissed the last. An Italian New Year's Day, this, and the bright Mediterranean, with a stretch of violet and purple shore, formed the first leaf in the book of the New Year that I turned at daybreak this morning. On the steep hill-sides between me and the sea, diversified by many a patch of cypress-trees and tangled vines, is a wild medley of roof upon roof, church upon church, terrace upon terrace, wall upon wall, tower upon tower. Questioning myself whether I am not descended, without having thought of it before, in a direct line from the good Haroun Alraschid, I tread the tesselated pavement of the garden-terrace, watch the gold-fish in the marble fountains, loiter in the pleasant grove of orange-trees, and become a moving pillar of fragrance by unromantically pocketing a green lemon, now and then, with an eye to Punch to-night in the English manner. It is not the New Year's Day of a dream, but of broad awake fact, that finds me housed in a palace, with a highly popular ghost and twenty-five spare bed-rooms: over the stone and marble floors of which deserted halls, the highly popular ghost (unquiet spirit of a Porter, one would think), drags all the heavy furniture at dead of night. Down in the town, in the street of Happy Charles, at the shop of the Swiss confectioner, there is at this moment, and is all day, an eager group examining the great Twelfth-cake – or, as my good friend and servant who speaks all languages and knows none, renders it to the natives, *pane dolce numero dodici* – sweet bread number twelve – which has come as a present all the way from Signor Gunter's, della Piazza Berkeley, Londra, Inghilterra[3] and which got cracked in coming, and is in the street of Happy Charles to be mended and the like of which has never been seen. It comes back at sunset (in order that the man who brings it on his head may get clear off before the ghost is due), and is set out as a show in the great hall. In the great hall, made as light as all our lights can make it – which is rather dark, it must be confessed – we assemble at night, to "keep it up," in the English manner; meaning by "we," the handful of English dwelling in that city, and the half handful of English who have married there into other nations, and the rare old Italian Cavaliere, who improvises, writes poetry, plays harps, composes music, paints pictures, and is always inaugurating somebody's bust in his little garden. Brown is the rare old Cavaliere's face, but green his young enthusiastic heart; and whatever we do upon this mad New Year's Night, the Cavaliere gaily bears his part in, and believes to be essentially an English custom, which all the English observe. When we enact grotesque charades, or disperse in the wildest exaggeration of an obsolete country-dance through the five-and-twenty empty rooms the Cavaliere, ever foremost, believes in his soul that all provincial respectability and metropolitan variety, all Canterbury Precinct, Whitfield Tabernacle, Saint James's Parish, Clapham, and Whitechapel, are religiously doing the same thing; and he cries "Dear England, merry England, the young and joyous, home of the Fancy, free as the air, playful as the child!" So enchanted is the dear Cavaliere (at about three in the morning, and after the lemons), that he folds my hand flat, inside his white waistcoat, folds his own two over it, and walks me up and down the Hall, meekly prisoner, while he improvises an enormous poem on the sports of England: which poem, I think, throughout, I am going to begin to understand presently, but of which I do not comprehend one lonely word. Nor, does even this severe intellectual exercise use up the Cavaliere, for after going home and playing the harp I don't know how many hours, he flies out of bed, seizes pen ink and paper − the mechanical appliances of the whole circle of the Arts are always at his bedside, ready against inspiration in the night − and writes quite a Work on the same subject: as the blotted piebald manuscript he sends to me before I am up next day, affectingly testifies. Said manuscript is inscribed to myself, most illustrious Signor, kissing my hands, and is munificently placed at the disposal of an English publisher whom it may please to undertake a translation.

And here is another New Year's Day invoked by the Wand of the time, and this New Year's Day is a French one, and a bitter, bitter cold one. All Paris is out of doors. Along the line of the Boulevards runs a double row of stalls, like the stalls at an English fair; and surely those are hard to please, in all small wares and all small gambling, who cannot be pleased here. Paris is out of doors in its newest and brightest clothes. Paris is making presents to the Universe − which is well known to be Paris. Paris will eat more bon-bons this day, than in the whole bon-bon eating year. Paris will dine out this day, more than ever. In homage to the day, the peculiar glory of the always-glorious plate-glass windows of the Restorers in the Palais Royal, where rare summer-vegetables from Algiers contend with wonderful great pears from the richest soils of France, and with little plump birds of exquisite plumage, direct from the skies. In homage to the day, the glittering brilliancy of the sweet-shops, teeming with beautiful arrangement of colours, and with beautiful tact and taste in trifles. In homage to the day, the new Review−Dramas at the Theatre of Varieties, and the Theatre of Vaudevilles, and the Theatre of the Palais Royal. In homage to the day, the new Drama in seven acts, and incalculable pictures, at the Ambiguously Comic Theatre, the Theatre of the Gate of Saint Martin, and the Theatre of Gaiety: at which last establishment particularly, a brooding Englishman can, by intensity of interest, get himself made wretched for a fortnight. In homage to the day, the extra-announcing of these Theatres, and fifty more, and the queues of blouses already, at three o'clock in the afternoon, penned up in the cold wind on the cold stone pavement outside them. Spite of wind and frost, the Elysian Fields and the Wood of Boulogne are filled with equipages, equestrians, and pedestrians: while the strange, rackety, rickety, up-all-night looking world of eating house, tombstone-maker, ball room, cemetery, and wine-shop outside the Barriers, is as thickly-peopled as the Paris streets themselves; with one universal tendency observable in both hemispheres, to sit down upon any public seat at a risk of being frozen to death, and to go round and round on a hobby-horse in any roundabout, to the music of a barrel organ, as a severe act of duty. And now, this New Year's Day tones down into night, and the brilliantly lighted city shines out like the gardens of the Wonderful Lamp, and the penned blouses flutter into the Theatres in orderly line, and the confidential men, not unaccustomed to lean on umbrellas as they survey mankind of an afternoon, who have tickets to sell cheap, are very busy among them, and the women money-takers shut up in strong iron-cages are busy too, and the three men all of a row behind a breast-work who take the checks are busy too, and the women box-openers with their footstools begin to be busy too, but as yet not very, and the curtain goes up for the curtain-rising piece, and the gloomy young gentleman with the tight black head and the new black moustache is as much in love as ever with the young lady whose eyebrows are very arched and whose voice is very thin, and the gloomy young gentleman's experienced friend (generally chewing something, by the bye, and I wonder what), who leans his back against the chimney-piece and reads him lessons of life, is just as cool as he always was, and an amazing circumstance to me is, that they are always doing this thing and no other thing, and that I don't find them to have any place in the great event of the evening, and that I want to know whether they go home when they have done it, or what becomes of them. Meanwhile, gushes of cookery rise with the night air from the Restorer's kitchens; and the guests at the Café of Paris, and the Café of the Three Provincial Brothers, and the Café Vefour, and the Café Verey, and the Gilded House, and others of first class, are reflected in wildernesses of looking glass, and sit on red velvet and order dinner out of red velvet books; while the citizens at the Café Champeaux near the Bourse, and others of second class, sit on rush-bottomed chairs, and have their dinner-library bound in plain leather, though they dine well too; while both kinds of company have plenty of children with them (which is pleasant to me, though I think they begin life biliously), and both unite in eating everything that is set before them. But, now it is eight o'clock upon this New Year's evening. The new Dramas being about to begin, bells ring violently in the Theatre lobbies and rooms, and cigars, coffee cups, and small glasses are hastily abandoned, and I find myself assisting at one of the Review-pieces: where I notice that the English gentleman's stomach isn't very like, because it doesn't fit him, and wherein I doubt the accurate nationality of the English lady's walking on her toes with an upward jerk behind. The Review is derived from various times and sources, and when I have seen David the Psalmist in his droll scene with Mahomet and Abd-el-Kader,[4] and have heard the best joke and best song that Eve (a charming young lady, but liable, I should fear, to take cold) has in her part (which occurs in her scene with the Sieur Framboisie[5]), I think I will step out to the Theatre of Gaiety, and see what they are about there. I am so fortunate as to arrive in the nick of time to find the very estimable man just eloped with the wife of the much less estimable man whom Destiny has made a bore, and to find her honest father just arriving from the country by one door, encountering the father of the very estimable man just arriving from the country by another door, and to hear them launch cross-curses – her father at him: his father at her – which so deeply affects a martial gentleman of tall stature and dark complexion, in the next stall to mine, that, taking his handkerchief from his hat to dry his eyes, he pulls out with it several very large lumps of sugar which he abstracted when he took his coffee, and showers them over my legs – exceedingly to my confusion, but not at all to his. The drop-curtain being, to appearance, down for a long time, I think I will step on a little further – say to the Theatre of the Scavengers – and see what they are doing there. At the Theatre of the Scavengers, I find Pierrot[6] on a voyage. I know he is aboard ship, because I can see nothing but sky; and I infer that the crew are aloft from the circumstance of two rope-ladders crossing the stage and meeting at top; about midway on each of which hangs, contemplating the public, an immovable young lady in male attire, with highly unseamanlike pink legs. This spectacle reminds me of another New Year's Day at home in England, where I saw the brave William, lover of Black Eyed Susan, tried by a Court Martial composed entirely of ladies, wearing perceptible combs in their heads: with the exception of the presiding Admiral, who was so far gone in liquor that I trembled to think what could possibly be done respecting the catastrophe, if he should take it in his head to record the verdict "Not guilty."[7] On this present New Year's Day, I find Pierrot suffering, in various ways, so very much from sea-sickness, that I soon leave the congregated Scavengers in possession of him; but not before I have gathered from the bill that in the case even of his drama, as of every other French piece, it takes at least two men to write it. So, I pass this New Year's evening, which is a French one, looking about me until midnight: when, going into a Boulevard café on my way home, I find the elderly men who are always playing dominos there, or always looking on at one another playing dominos there, hard at it still, not in the least moved by the stir and novelty of the day, not in the least minding the New Year.

Dullborough Town[1]

First published in *All the Year Round*, 30 June 1860. The text is that of the Charles Dickens Edition of *The Uncommercial Traveller* (1868).

It lately happened that I found myself rambling about the scenes among which my earliest days were passed; scenes from which I departed when I was a child, and which I did not revisit until I was a man. This is no uncommon chance, but one that befalls some of us any day; perhaps it may not be quite uninteresting to compare notes with the reader respecting an experience so familiar and a journey so uncommercial.

I call my boyhood's home (and I feel like a Tenor in an English Opera when I mention it) Dullborough. Most of us come from Dullborough who come from a country town.

As I left Dullborough in the days when there were no railroads in the land, I left it in a stage-coach. Through all the years that have since passed, have I ever lost the smell of the damp straw in which I was packed – like game – and forwarded, carriage paid, to the Cross Keys, Wood-street, Cheapside, London? There was no other inside passenger, and I consumed my sandwiches in solitude and dreariness, and it rained hard all the way, and I thought life sloppier than I had expected to find it.

With this tender remembrance upon me, I was cavalierly shunted back into Dullborough the other day, by train. My ticket had been previously collected, like my taxes, and my shining new portmanteau had had a great plaster stuck upon it, and I had been defied by Act of Parliament to offer an objection to anything that was done to it, or me, under a penalty of not less than forty shillings or more than five pounds, compoundable for a term of imprisonment. When I had sent my disfigured property on to the hotel, I began to look about me; and the first discovery I made, was, that the Station had swallowed up the playing-field.

It was gone. The two beautiful hawthorn-trees, the hedge, the turf, and all those buttercups and daisies, had given place to the stoniest of jolting roads: while, beyond the Station, an ugly dark monster of a tunnel kept its jaws open, as if it had swallowed them and were ravenous for more destruction. The coach that had carried me away, was melodiously called Timpson's Blue-Eyed Maid, and belonged to Timpson, at the coach-office

64

up-street; the locomotive engine that had brought me back, was called severely No. 97, and belonged to S.E.R.,[2] and was spitting ashes and hot water over the blighted ground.

When I had been let out at the platform-door, like a prisoner whom his turnkey grudgingly released, I looked in again over the low wall, at the scene of departed glories. Here, in the haymaking time, had I been delivered from the dungeons of Seringapatam,[3] an immense pile (of haycock), by my own countrymen, the victorious British (boy next door and his two cousins), and had been recognised with ecstasy by my affianced one (Miss Green), who had come all the way from England (second house in the terrace) to ransom me, and marry me. Here, had I first heard in confidence, from one whose father was greatly connected, being under Government, of the existence of a terrible banditti, called "The Radicals," whose principles were, that the Prince Regent wore stays, and that nobody had a right to any salary, and that the army and navy ought to be put down – horrors at which I trembled in my bed, after supplicating that the Radicals might be speedily taken and hanged. Here, too, had we, the small boys of Boles's, had that cricket match against the small boys of Coles's, when Boles and Coles had actually met upon the ground, and when, instead of instantly hitting out at one another with the utmost fury, as we had all hoped and expected, those sneaks had said respectively, "I hope Mrs. Boles is well," and "I hope Mrs. Coles and the baby are doing charmingly." Could it be that, after all this, and much more, the playing-field was a Station, and No. 97 expectorated boiling water and redhot cinders on it, and the whole belonged by Act of Parliament to S.E.R.?

As it could be, and was, I left the place with a heavy heart for a walk all over the town. And first of Timpson's up-street. When I departed from Dullborough in the strawy arms of Timpson's Blue-Eyed Maid, Timpson's was a moderate-sized coach-office (in fact, a little coach-office), with an oval transparency in the window, which looked beautiful by night, representing one of Timpson's coaches in the act of passing a milestone on the London road with great velocity, completely full inside and out, and all the passengers dressed in the first style of fashion, and enjoying themselves tremendously. I found no such place as Timpson's now – no such bricks and rafters, not to mention the name – no such edifice on the teeming earth. Pickford had come and knocked Timpson's down. Pickford had not only knocked Timpson's down, but had knocked two or three houses down on each side of Timpson's, and then had knocked the whole into one great establishment with a pair of big gates, in and out of which, his (Pickford's) waggons are, in these days, always rattling, with their drivers sitting up so high, that they look in at the second-floor windows of the old-fashioned houses in the High-street as they shake the town. I have not the honour of Pickford's acquaintance, but I felt that he had done me an injury, not to say committed an act of boyslaughter, in running over my childhood in this rough manner; and if ever I meet Pickford driving one of his own monsters, and smoking a pipe the while (which is the custom of his men), he shall know by the expression of my eye, if it catches his, that there is something wrong between us.

Moreover, I felt that Pickford had no right to come rushing into Dullborough and deprive the town of a public picture. He is not Napoleon Bonaparte. When he took down the transparent stage-coach, he ought to have given the town a transparent van. With a gloomy conviction that Pickford is wholly utilitarian and unimaginative, I proceeded on my way.

It is a mercy I have not a red and green lamp and a night-bell at my door, for in my very young days I was taken to so many lyings-in that I wonder I escaped becoming a professional martyr to them in after-life. I suppose I had a very sympathetic nurse, with a large circle of married acquaintance. However that was, as I continued my walk through Dullborough, I found many houses to be solely associated in my mind with this particular interest. At one little greengrocer's shop, down certain steps from the street, I remember to have waited on a lady who had had four children (I am afraid to write five, though I fully believe it was five) at a birth. This meritorious woman held quite a reception in her room on the morning when I was introduced there, and the sight of the house brought vividly to my mind how the four (five) deceased young people lay, side by side, on a clean cloth on a chest of drawers; reminding me by a homely association, which I suspect their complexion to have assisted, of pigs' feet as they are usually displayed at a neat tripe-shop. Hot caudle[4] was handed round on the occasion, and I further remembered as I stood contemplating the greengrocer's, that a subscription was entered into among the company, which became extremely alarming to my consciousness of having pocket-money on my person. This fact being known to my conductress, whoever she was, I was earnestly exhorted to contribute, but resolutely declined: therein disgusting the company, who gave me to understand that I must dismiss all expectations of going to Heaven.

How does it happen that when all else is change wherever one goes, there yet seem, in every place, to be some few people who never alter? As the sight of the greengrocer's house recalled these trivial incidents of long ago, the identical greengrocer appeared on the steps, with his hands in his pockets, and leaning his shoulder against the door-post, as my childish eyes had seen him many a time; indeed, there was his old mark on the door-post yet, as if his shadow had become a fixture there. It was he himself; he might formerly have been an old-looking young man, or he might now be a young-looking old man, but there he was. In walking along the street, I had as yet looked in vain for a familiar face, or even a transmitted face; here was the very greengrocer who had been weighing and handling baskets on the morning of the reception. As he brought with him a dawning remembrance that he had had no proprietary interest in those babies, I crossed the road, and accosted him on the subject. He was not in the least excited or gratified, or in any way roused, by the accuracy of my recollection, but said, Yes, summut out of the common – he didn't remember how many it was (as if half-a-dozen babes either way made no difference) – had happened to a Mrs. What's-her-name, as once lodged there – but he didn't call it to mind, particular. Nettled by this phlegmatic conduct, I informed him that I had left the town when I was a child. He slowly returned, quite unsoftened, and not without a sarcastic kind of complacency, *Had* I? Ah! And did I find it had got on tolerably well without me? Such is the difference (I thought, when I had left him a few hundred yards behind, and was by so much in a better temper) between going away from a place and remaining in it. I had no right, I reflected, to be angry with the greengrocer for his want of interest, I was nothing to him: whereas he was the town, the cathedral, the bridge, the river, my childhood, and a large slice of my life, to me.

Of course the town had shrunk fearfully, since I was a child there. I had entertained the impression that the High-street was at least as wide as Regent-street, London, or the Italian Boulevard at Paris. I found it little better than a lane. There was a public clock in it, which I had supposed to be the finest clock in the world: whereas it now turned out to be as inexpressive, moon-faced, and weak a clock as ever I saw. It belonged to a Town Hall, where I had seen an Indian (who I now suppose wasn't an Indian) swallow a sword (which I now suppose he didn't). The edifice had appeared to me in those days so glorious a structure, that I had set it up in my mind as the model on which the Genie of the Lamp built the palace for Aladdin.[5] A mean little brick heap, like a demented chapel, with a few yawning persons in leather gaiters, and in the last extremity for something to do, lounging at the door with their hands in their pockets, and calling themselves a Corn Exchange!

The Theatre was in existence, I found, on asking the fishmonger, who had a compact show of stock in his window, consisting of a sole and a quart of shrimps – and I resolved to comfort my mind by going to look at it.

Richard the Third, in a very uncomfortable cloak, had first appeared to me there, and had made my heart leap with terror by backing up against the stage-box in which I was posted, while struggling for life against the virtuous Richmond.[6] It was within those walls that I had learnt as from a page of English history, how that wicked King slept in war-time on a sofa much too short for him, and how fearfully his conscience troubled his boots. There, too, had I first seen the funny countryman, but countryman of noble principles, in a flowered waistcoat, crunch up his little hat and throw it on the ground, and pull off his coat, saying, "Dom thee, squire, coom on with thy fistes then!" At which the lovely young woman who kept company with him (and who went out gleaning, in a narrow white muslin apron with five beautiful bars of five different-coloured ribbons across it) was so frightened for his sake, that she fainted away. Many wondrous secrets of Nature had I come to the knowledge of in that sanctuary: of which not the least terrific were, that the witches in Macbeth bore an awful resemblance to the Thanes and other proper inhabitants of Scotland; and that the good King Duncan couldn't rest in his grave, but was constantly coming out of it and calling himself somebody else. To the Theatre, therefore, I repaired for consolation. But I found very little, for it was in a bad and declining way. A dealer in wine and bottled beer had already squeezed his trade into the box-office, and the theatrical money was taken – when it came – in a kind of meat-safe in the passage. The dealer in wine and bottled beer must have insinuated himself under the stage too; for he announced that he had various descriptions of alcoholic drinks "in the wood," and there was no possible stowage for the wood anywhere else. Evidently, he was by degrees eating the establishment away to the core, and would soon have sole possession of it. It was To Let, and hopelessly so, for its old purposes; and there had been no entertainment within its walls for a long time except a Panorama;[7] and even that had been announced as "pleasingly instructive," and I know too well the fatal meaning and the leaden import of those terrible expressions. No, there was no comfort in the Theatre. It was mysteriously gone, like my own youth. Unlike my own youth, it might be coming back some day; but there was little promise of it.

As the town was placarded with references to the Dullborough Mechanics' Institution, I thought I would go and look at that establishment next. There had been no such thing in the town, in my young day, and it occurred to me that its extreme prosperity might have brought adversity upon the Drama. I found the Institution with some difficulty, and should scarcely have known that I had found it if I had judged from its external appearance only; but this was attributable to its never having been finished, and having no front: consequently, it led a modest and retired existence up a stable-yard. It was (as I learnt, on inquiry) a most flourishing Institution, and of the highest benefit to the town: two triumphs which I was glad to understand were not at all impaired by the seeming drawbacks that no mechanics belonged to it, and that it was steeped in debt to the chimney-pots. It had a large room, which was approached by an infirm step-ladder: the builder having declined to construct the intended staircase, without a present payment in cash, which Dullborough (though profoundly appreciative of the Institution) seemed unaccountably bashful about subscribing. The large room had cost – or would, when paid for – five hundred pounds; and it had more mortar in it and more echoes than one might have expected to get for the money. It was fitted up with a platform, and the usual lecturing tools, including a large black board of a menacing appearance. On referring to lists of the courses of lectures that had been given in this thriving Hall, I fancied I detected a shyness in admitting that human nature when at leisure has any desire whatever to be relieved and diverted; and a furtive sliding in of any poor make-weight piece of amusement, shamefacedly and edgewise. Thus, I observed that it was necessary for the members to be knocked on the head with Gas, Air, Water, Food, the Solar System, the Geological periods, Criticism on Milton, the Steam-engine, John Bunyan, and Arrow-Headed Inscriptions, before they might be tickled by those unaccountable choristers, the negro singers in the court costume of the reign of George the Second. Likewise, that they must be stunned by a weighty inquiry whether there was internal evidence in Shakespeare's works, to prove that his uncle by the mother's side lived for some years at Stoke Newington, before they were brought-to by a Miscellaneous Concert. But, indeed, the masking of entertainment, and pretending it was something else – as people mask bedsteads when they are obliged to have them in sitting-rooms, and make believe that they are book-cases, sofas, chests of drawers, anything rather than bedsteads – was manifest even in the pretence of dreariness that the unfortunate entertainers themselves felt obliged in decency to put forth when they came here. One very agreeable professional singer, who travelled with two professional ladies, knew better than to introduce either of those ladies to sing the ballad "Comin' through the Rye"[8] without prefacing it himself, with some general remarks on wheat and clover; and even then, he dared not for his life call the song, a song, but disguised it in the bill as an "Illustration." In the library, also – fitted with shelves for three thousand books, and containing upwards of one hundred and seventy (presented copies mostly), seething their edges in damp plaster – there was such a painfully apologetic return of 62 offenders who had read Travels, Popular

Biography, and mere Fiction descriptive of the aspirations of the hearts and souls of mere human creatures like themselves; and such an elaborate parade of 2 bright examples who had had down Euclid after the day's occupation and confinement; and 3 who had had down Metaphysics after ditto; and 1 who had had down Theology after ditto; and 4 who had worried Grammar, Political Economy, Botany, and Logarithms all at once after ditto; that I suspected the boasted class to be one man, who had been hired to do it.

Emerging from the Mechanics' Institution and continuing my walk about the town, I still noticed everywhere the prevalence, to an extraordinary degree, of this custom of putting the natural demand for amusement out of sight, as some untidy housekeepers put dust, and pretending that it was swept away. And yet it was ministered to, in a dull and abortive manner, by all who made this feint. Looking in at what is called in Dullborough "the serious bookseller's," where, in my childhood, I had studied the faces of numbers of gentlemen depicted in rostrums with a gaslight on each side of them, and casting my eyes over the open pages of certain printed discourses there, I found a vast deal of aiming at jocosity and dramatic effect, even in them – yes, verily, even on the part of one very wrathful expounder who bitterly anathematised a poor little Circus. Similarly, in the reading provided for the young people enrolled in the Lasso of Love, and other excellent unions, I found the writers generally under a distressing sense that they must start (at all events) like story-tellers, and delude the young persons into the belief that they were going to be interesting. As I looked in at this window for twenty minutes by the clock, I am in a position to offer a friendly remonstrance – not bearing on this particular point – to the designers and engravers of the pictures in those publications. Have they considered the awful consequences likely to flow from their representations of Virtue? Have they asked themselves the question, whether the terrific prospect of acquiring that fearful chubbiness of head, unwieldiness of arm, feeble dislocation of leg, crispiness of hair, and enormity of shirt-collar, which they represent as inseparable from Goodness, may not tend to confirm sensitive waverers, in Evil? A most impressive example (if I had believed it) of what a Dustman and a Sailor may come to, when they mend their ways, was presented to me in this same shop-window. When they were leaning (they were intimate friends) against a post, drunk and reckless, with surpassingly bad hats on, and their hair over their foreheads, they were rather picturesque, and looked as if they might be agreeable men, if they would not be beasts. But, when they had got over their bad propensities, and when, as a consequence, their heads had swelled alarmingly, their hair had got so curly that it lifted their blown-out cheeks up, their coat-cuffs were so long that they never could do any work, and their eyes were so wide open that they never could do any sleep, they presented a spectacle calculated to plunge a timid nature into the depths of Infamy.

But, the clock that had so degenerated since I saw it last, admonished me that I had stayed here long enough; and I resumed my walk.

I had not gone fifty paces along the street when I was suddenly brought up by the sight of a man who got out of a little phaeton at the doctor's door, and went into the doctor's house. Immediately, the air was filled with the scent of trodden grass, and the perspective of years opened, and at the end of it was a little likeness of this man keeping a wicket, and I said, "God bless my soul! Joe Specks!"

Through many changes and much work, I had preserved a tenderness for the memory of Joe, forasmuch as we had made the acquaintance of Roderick Random[9] together, and had believed him to be no ruffian, but an ingenuous and engaging hero. Scorning to ask the boy left in the phaeton whether it was really Joe, and scorning even to read the brass plate on the door — so sure was I — I rang the bell and informed the servant maid that a stranger sought audience of Mr. Specks. Into a room, half surgery, half study, I was shown to await his coming, and I found it, by a series of elaborate accidents, bestrewn with testimonies to Joe. Portrait of Mr. Specks, bust of Mr. Specks, silver cup from grateful patient to Mr. Specks, presentation sermon from local clergyman, dedication poem from local poet, dinner-card from local nobleman, tract on balance of power from local refugee, inscribed *Hommage de l'auteur à Specks*.

When my old schoolfellow came in, and I informed him with a smile that I was not a patient, he seemed rather at a loss to perceive any reason for smiling in connexion with that fact, and inquired to what was he to attribute the honour? I asked him, with another smile, could he remember me at all? He had not (he said) that pleasure. I was beginning to have but a poor opinion of Mr. Specks, when he said reflectively, "And yet there's a something too." Upon that, I saw a boyish light in his eyes that looked well, and I asked him if he could inform me, as a stranger who desired to know and had not the means of reference at hand, what the name of the young lady was, who married Mr. Random? Upon that, he said "Narcissa," and, after staring for a moment, called me by my name, shook me by the hand, and melted into a roar of laughter. "Why, of course, you'll remember Lucy Green," he said, after we had talked a little. "Of course," said I. "Whom do you think she married?" said he. "You?" I hazarded. "Me," said Specks, "and you shall see her." So I saw her, and she was fat, and if all the hay in the world had been heaped upon her, it could scarcely have altered her face more than Time had altered it from my remembrance of the face that had once looked down upon me into the fragrant dungeons of Seringapatam. But when her youngest child came in after dinner (for I dined with them, and we had no other company than Specks, Junior, Barrister-at-law, who went away as soon as the cloth was removed, to look after the young lady to whom he was going to be married next week), I saw again, in that little daughter, the little face of the hayfield, unchanged, and it quite touched my foolish heart. We talked immensely, Specks and Mrs. Specks, and I, and we spoke of our old selves as though our old selves were dead and gone, and indeed indeed they were – dead and gone as the playing-field that had become a wilderness of rusty iron, and the property of S.E.R.

Specks, however, illuminated Dullborough with the rays of interest that I wanted and should otherwise have missed in it, and linked its present to its past, with a highly agreeable chain. And in Specks's society I had new occasion to observe what I had before noticed in similar communications among other men. All the schoolfellows and others of old, whom I inquired about, had either done superlatively well or superlatively ill – had either become uncertificated bankrupts, or been felonious and got themselves transported; or had made great hits in life, and done wonders. And this is so commonly the case, that I never can imagine what becomes of all the mediocre people of people's youth – especially considering that we find no lack of the species in our maturity. But, I did not propound this difficulty to Specks, for no pause in the conversation gave me an occasion. Nor, could I discover one single flaw in the good doctor – when he reads this, he will receive in a friendly spirit the pleasantly meant record – except that he had forgotten his Roderick Random, and that he confounded Strap with Lieutenant Hatchway;[10] who never knew Random, howsoever intimate with Pickle.

When I went alone to the Railway to catch my train at night (Specks had meant to go with me, but was inopportunely called out), I was in a more charitable mood with Dullborough than I had been all day; and yet in my heart I had loved it all day too. Ah! who was I that I should quarrel with the town for being changed to me, when I myself had come back, so changed, to it! All my early readings and early imaginations dated from this place, and I took them away so full of innocent construction and guileless belief, and I brought them back so worn and torn, so much the wiser and so much the worse!

Night Walks

First published in *All the Year Round*, 21 July 1860. The text here is taken from *The Uncommercial Traveller*.

Some years ago, a temporary inability to sleep, referable to a distressing impression, caused me to walk about the streets all night, for a series of several nights. The disorder might have taken a long time to conquer, if it had been faintly experimented on in bed; but, it was soon defeated by the brisk treatment of getting up directly after lying down, and going out, and coming home tired at sunrise.

In the course of those nights, I finished my education in a fair amateur experience of houselessness. My principal object being to get through the night, the pursuit of it brought me into sympathetic relations with people who have no other object every night in the year.

The month was March, and the weather damp, cloudy, and cold. The sun not rising before half-past five, the night perspective looked sufficiently long at half-past twelve: which was about my time for confronting it.

The restlessness of a great city, and the way in which it tumbles and tosses before it can get to sleep, formed one of the first entertainments offered to the contemplation of us houseless people. It lasted about two hours. We lost a great deal of companionship when the late public-houses turned their lamps out, and when the potmen thrust the last brawling drunkards into the street; but stray vehicles and stray people were left us, after that. If we were very lucky, a policeman's rattle sprang and a fray turned up; but, in general, surprisingly little of this diversion was provided. Except in the Haymarket,[1] which is the worst kept part of London, and about Kent-street in the Borough, and along a portion of the line of the Old Kent-road, the peace was seldom violently broken. But, it was always the case that London, as if in imitation of individual citizens belonging to it, had expiring fits and starts of restlessness. After all seemed quiet, if one cab rattled by, half-a-dozen would surely follow; and Houselessness even observed that intoxicated people appeared to be magnetically attracted towards each other: so that we knew when we saw one drunken object staggering against the shutters of a shop, that another drunken object would stagger up before five minutes were out, to fraternise or fight with it. When we made a divergence from the regular species of drunkard, the thin-armed, puff-faced, leaden-lipped gin-drinker, and encountered a rarer specimen of a more decent appearance, fifty to one but that specimen was dressed in soiled mourning. As the street experience in the night, so the street experience in the day; the common folk who come unexpectedly into a little property, come unexpectedly into a deal of liquor.

At length these flickering sparks would die away, worn out – the last veritable sparks of waking life trailed from some late pieman or hot-potato man – and London would sink to rest. And then the yearning of the houseless mind would be for any sign of company, any lighted place, any movement, anything suggestive of any one being up – nay, even so much as awake, for the houseless eye looked out for lights in windows.

Walking the streets under the pattering rain, Houselessness would walk and walk and walk, seeing nothing but the interminable tangle of streets, save at a corner, here and there, two policemen in conversation, or the sergeant or inspector looking after his men. Now and then in the night – but rarely – Houselessness would become aware of a furtive head peering out of a doorway a few yards before him, and, coming up with the head, would find a man standing bolt upright to keep within the doorway's shadow, and evidently intent upon no particular service to society. Under a kind of fascination, and in a ghostly silence suitable to the time, Houselessness and this gentleman would eye one another from head to foot, and so, without exchange of speech, part, mutually suspicious. Drip, drip, drip, from ledge and coping, splash from pipes and water-spouts, and by-and-by the houseless shadow would fall upon the stones that pave the way to Waterloo-bridge; it being in the houseless mind to have a halfpenny worth of excuse for saying "Good night" to the toll-keeper, and catching a glimpse of his fire. A good fire and a good great-coat and a good woollen neck-shawl, were comfortable things to see in conjunction with the toll-keeper; also his brisk wakefulness was excellent company when he rattled the change of halfpence down upon that metal table of his, like a man who defied the night, with all its sorrowful thoughts, and didn't care for the coming of dawn. There was need of encouragement on the threshold of the bridge, for the bridge was dreary. The chopped-up murdered man, had not been lowered with a rope over the parapet when those nights were; he was alive, and slept then quietly enough most likely, and undisturbed by any dream of where he was to come. But the river had an awful look, the buildings on the banks were muffled in black shrouds, and the reflected lights seemed to originate deep in the water, as if the spectres of suicides were holding them to show where they went down. The wild moon and clouds were as restless as an evil conscience in a tumbled bed, and the very shadow of the immensity of London seemed to lie oppressively upon the river.

Between the bridge and the two great theatres, there was but the distance of a few hundred paces, so the theatres came next. Grim and black within, at night, those great dry Wells, and lonesome to imagine, with the rows of faces faded out, the lights extinguished, and the seats all empty. One would think that nothing in them knew itself at such a time but Yorick's skull.[2] In one of my night walks, as the church steeples were shaking the March winds and rain with strokes of Four, I passed the outer boundary of one of these great deserts, and entered it. With a dim lantern in my hand, I groped my well-known way to the stage and looked over the orchestra – which was like a great grave dug for a time of pestilence – into the void beyond. A dismal cavern of an immense aspect, with the chandelier gone dead like everything else, and nothing visible through mist and fog and space, but tiers of winding-sheets. The ground at my feet where, when last there, I had seen the peasantry of Naples dancing among the vines, reckless of the burning mountain which threatened to overwhelm them, was now in possession of a strong serpent of engine-hose, watchfully lying in wait for the serpent Fire, and ready to fly at it if it showed its forked tongue. A ghost of a watchman, carrying a faint corpse candle, haunted the distant upper gallery and flitted away. Retiring within the proscenium, and holding my light above my head towards the rolled-up curtain – green no more, but black as ebony – my sight lost itself in a gloomy vault, showing faint indications in it of a shipwreck of canvas and cordage. Methought I felt much as a diver might, at the bottom of the sea.

In those small hours when there was no movement in the streets, it afforded matter for reflection to take Newgate[3] in the way, and, touching its rough stone, to think of the prisoners in their sleep, and then to glance in at the lodge over the spiked wicket, and see the fire and light of the watching turnkeys, on the white wall. Not an inappropriate time either, to linger by that wicked little Debtors' Door – shutting tighter than any other door one ever saw – which has been Death's Door to so many. In the days of the uttering of forged one-pound notes by people tempted up from the country, how many hundreds of wretched creatures of both sexes – many quite innocent – swung out of a pitiless and inconsistent world, with the tower of yonder Christian church of Saint Sepulchre[4] monstrously before their eyes! Is there any haunting of the Bank Parlour, by the remorseful souls of old directors, in the nights of these later days, I wonder, or is it as quiet as this degenerate Aceldama[5] of an Old Bailey?

To walk on to the Bank, lamenting the good old times and bemoaning the present evil period, would be an easy next step, so I would take it, and would make my houseless circuit of the Bank, and give a thought to the treasure within; likewise to the guard of soldiers passing the night there, and nodding over the fire. Next, I went to Billingsgate, in some hope of market-people, but it proving as yet too early, crossed London-bridge and got down by the waterside on the Surrey shore among the buildings of the great brewery. There was plenty going on at the brewery; and the reek, and the smell of grains, and the rattling of the plump dray horses at their mangers, were capital company. Quite refreshed by having mingled with this good society, I made a new start with a new heart, setting the old King's Bench prison[6] before me for my next object, and resolving, when I should come to the wall, to think of poor Horace Kinch, and the Dry Rot in men.

A very curious disease the Dry Rot in men, and difficult to detect the beginning of. It had carried Horace Kinch inside the wall of the old King's Bench prison, and it had carried him out with his feet foremost. He was a likely man to look at, in the prime of life, well to do, as clever as he needed to be, and popular among many friends. He was suitably married, and had healthy and pretty children. But, like some fair-looking houses or fair-looking ships, he took the Dry Rot. The first strong external revelation of the Dry Rot in men, is a tendency to lurk and lounge; to be at street-corners without intelligible reason; to be going anywhere when met; to be about many places rather than at any; to do nothing tangible, but to have an intention of performing a variety of intangible duties to-morrow or the day after. When this manifestation of the disease is observed, the observer will usually connect it with a vague impression once formed or received, that the patient was living a little too hard. He will scarcely have had leisure to turn it over in his mind and form the terrible suspicion "Dry Rot," when he will notice a change for the worse in the patient's appearance: a certain slovenliness and deterioration, which is not poverty, nor dirt, nor intoxication, nor ill-health, but simply Dry Rot. To this, succeeds a smell as of strong waters, in the morning; to that, a looseness respecting money; to that, a stronger smell as of strong waters, at all times; to that, a looseness respecting everything; to that, a trembling of the limbs, somnolency, misery, and crumbling to pieces. As it is in wood, so it is in men. Dry Rot advances at a compound usury quite incalculable. A plank is found infected with it, and the whole structure is devoted. Thus it had been with the unhappy Horace Kinch, lately buried by a small subscription. Those who knew him had not nigh done saying, "So well off, so comfortably established, with such hope before him – and yet, it is feared, with a slight touch of Dry Rot!" when lo! the man was all Dry Rot and dust.

From the dead wall associated on those houseless nights with this too common story, I chose next to wander by Bethlehem Hospital;[7] partly, because it lay on my road round to Westminster; partly, because I had a night fancy in my head which could be best pursued within sight of its walls and dome. And the fancy was this: Are not the sane and the insane equal at night as the sane lie a dreaming? Are not all of us outside this hospital, who dream, more or less in the condition of those inside it, every night of our lives? Are we not nightly persuaded, as they daily are, that we associate preposterously with kings and queens, emperors and empresses, and notabilities of all sorts? Do we not nightly jumble events and personages and times and places, as these do daily? Are we not sometimes troubled by our own sleeping inconsistencies, and do we not vexedly try to account for them or excuse them, just as these do sometimes in respect of their waking delusions? Said an afflicted man to me, when I was last in a hospital like this, "Sir, I can frequently fly." I was half ashamed to reflect that so could I – by night. Said a woman to me on the same occasion, "Queen Victoria frequently comes to dine with me, and her Majesty and I dine off peaches and maccaroni in our night-gowns, and his Royal Highness the Prince Consort does us the honour to make a third on horseback in a Field-Marshal's uniform." Could I refrain from reddening with consciousness when I remembered the amazing royal parties I myself had given (at night), the unaccountable viands I had put on table, and my extraordinary manner of conducting myself on those distinguished occasions? I wonder that the great master who knew everything, when he called Sleep the death of each day's life, did not call Dreams the insanity of each day's sanity.

By this time I had left the Hospital behind me, and was again setting towards the river; and in a short breathing space I was on Westminster-bridge, regaling my houseless eyes with the external walls of the British Parliament – the perfection of a stupendous institution, I know, and the admiration of all surrounding nations and succeeding ages, I do not doubt, but perhaps a little the better now and then for being pricked up to its work. Turning off into Old Palace-yard, the Courts of Law kept me company for a quarter of an hour; hinting in low whispers what numbers of people they were keeping awake, and how intensely wretched and horrible they were rendering the small hours to unfortunate suitors. Westminster Abbey was fine gloomy society for another quarter of an hour; suggesting a wonderful procession of its dead among the dark arches and pillars, each century more amazed by the century following it than by all the centuries going before.

And indeed in those houseless night walks – which even included cemeteries where watchmen went round among the graves at stated times, and moved the tell-tale handle of an index which recorded that they had touched it at such an hour – it was a solemn consideration what enormous hosts of dead belong to one old great city, and how, if they were raised while the living slept, there would not be the space of a pin's point in all the streets and ways for the living to come out into. Not only that, but the vast armies of dead would overflow the hills and valleys beyond the city, and would stretch away all round it, God knows how far.

When a church clock strikes, on houseless ears in the dead of the night, it may be at first mistaken for company and hailed as such. But, as the spreading circles of vibration, which you may perceive at such a time with great clearness, go opening out, for ever and ever afterwards widening perhaps (as the philosopher has suggested) in eternal space, the mistake is rectified and the sense of loneliness is profounder. Once – it was after leaving the Abbey and turning my face north – I came to the great steps of St. Martin's church[8] as the clock was striking Three. Suddenly, a thing that in a moment more I should have trodden upon without seeing, rose up at my feet with a cry of loneliness and houselessness, struck out of it by the bell, the like of which I never heard. We then stood face to face looking at one another, frightened by one another. The creature was like a beetle-browed hair-lipped youth of twenty, and it had a loose bundle of rags on, which it held together with one of its hands. It shivered from head to foot, and its teeth chattered, and as it stared at me – persecutor, devil, ghost, whatever it thought me – it made with its whining mouth as if it were snapping at me, like a worried dog. Intending to give this ugly object money, I put out my hand to stay it – for it recoiled as it whined and snapped – and laid my hand upon its shoulder. Instantly, it twisted out of its garment, like the young man in the New Testament,[9] and left me standing alone with its rags in my hands.

Covent-garden Market, when it was market morning, was wonderful company. The great waggons of cabbages, with growers' men and boys lying asleep under them, and with sharp dogs from market-garden neighbourhoods looking after the whole, were as good as a party. But one of the worst night sights I know in London, is to be found in the children who prowl about this place; who sleep in the baskets, fight for the offal, dart at any object they think they can lay their thieving hands on, dive under the carts and barrows, dodge the constables, and are perpetually making a blunt pattering on the pavement of the Piazza with the rain of their naked feet. A painful and unnatural result comes of the comparison one is forced to institute between the growth of corruption as displayed in the so much improved and cared for fruits of the earth, and the growth of corruption as displayed in these all uncared for (except inasmuch as ever-hunted) savages.

There was early coffee to be got about Covent-garden Market, and that was more company — warm company, too, which was better. Toast of a very substantial quality, was likewise procurable: though the towzled-headed man who made it, in an inner chamber within the coffee-room, hadn't got his coat on yet, and was so heavy with sleep that in every interval of toast and coffee he went off anew behind the partition into complicated cross-roads of choke and snore, and lost his way directly. Into one of these establishments (among the earliest) near Bow-street, there came one morning as I sat over my houseless cup, pondering where to go next, a man in a high and long snuff-coloured coat, and shoes, and, to the best of my belief, nothing else but a hat, who took out of his hat a large cold meat pudding; a meat pudding so large that it was a very tight fit, and brought the lining of the hat out with it. This mysterious man was known by his pudding, for on his entering, the man of sleep brought him a pint of hot tea, a small loaf, and a large knife and fork and plate. Left to himself in his box, he stood the pudding on the bare table, and, instead of cutting it, stabbed it, overhand, with the knife, like a mortal enemy; then took the knife out, wiped it on his sleeve, tore the pudding asunder with his fingers, and ate it all up. The remembrance of this man with the pudding remains with me as the remembrance of the most spectral person my houselessness encountered. Twice only was I in that establishment, and twice I saw him stalk in (as I should say, just out of bed, and presently going back to bed), take out his pudding, stab his pudding, wipe the dagger, and eat his pudding all up. He was a man whose figure promised cadaverousness, but who had an excessively red face, though shaped like a horse's. On the second occasion of my seeing him, he said huskily to the man of sleep, "Am I red to-night?" "You are," he uncompromisingly answered. "My mother," said the spectre, "was a red-faced woman that liked drink, and I looked at her hard when she laid in her coffin, and I took the complexion." Somehow, the pudding seemed an unwholesome pudding after that, and I put myself in its way no more.

When there was no market, or when I wanted variety, a railway terminus with the morning mails coming in, was remunerative company. But like most of the company to be had in this world, it lasted only a very short time. The station lamps would burst out ablaze, the porters would emerge from places of concealment, the cabs and trucks would rattle to their places (the post-office carts were already in theirs), and, finally, the bell would strike up, and the train would come banging in. But there were few passengers and little luggage, and everything scuttled away with the greatest expedition. The locomotive post-offices, with their great nets − as if they had been dragging the country for bodies − would fly open as to their doors, and would disgorge a smell of lamp, an exhausted clerk, a guard in a red coat, and their bags of letters; the engine would blow and heave and perspire, like an engine wiping its forehead and saying what a run it had had; and within ten minutes the lamps were out, and I was houseless and alone again.

But now, there were driven cattle on the high road near, wanting (as cattle always do) to turn into the midst of stone walls, and squeeze themselves through six inches' width of iron railing, and getting their heads down (also as cattle always do) for tossing-purchase at quite imaginary dogs, and giving themselves and every devoted creature associated with them a most extraordinary amount of unnecessary trouble. Now, too, the conscious gas began to grow pale with the knowledge that daylight was coming, and straggling work-people were already in the streets, and, as waking life had become extinguished with the last pieman's sparks, so it began to be rekindled with the fires of the first street-corner breakfast-sellers. And so by faster and faster degrees, until the last degrees were very fast, the day came, and I was tired and could sleep. And it is not, as I used to think, going home at such times, the least wonderful thing in London, that in the real desert region of the night, the houseless wanderer is alone there. I knew well enough where to find Vice and Misfortune of all kinds, if I had chosen; but they were put out of sight, and my houselessness had many miles upon miles of streets in which it could, and did, have its own solitary way.

Chambers

First published in *All the Year Round*, 18 August 1860. The text here is taken from *The Uncommercial Traveller*.

Having occasion to transact some business with a solicitor who occupies a highly suicidal set of chambers in Gray's Inn, I afterwards took a turn in the large square of that stronghold of Melancholy, reviewing, with congenial surroundings, my experiences of Chambers.

I began, as was natural, with the Chambers I had just left. They were an upper set on a rotten staircase, with a mysterious bunk or bulkhead on the landing outside them, of a rather nautical and Screw Collier-like appearance than otherwise, and painted an intense black. Many dusty years have passed since the appropriation of this Davy Jones's locker to any purpose, and during the whole period within the memory of living man, it has been hasped and padlocked. I cannot quite satisfy my mind whether it was originally meant for the reception of coals, or bodies, or as a place of temporary security for the plunder "looted" by laundresses; but I incline to the last opinion. It is about breast high, and usually serves as a bulk for defendants in reduced circumstances to lean against and ponder at, when they come on the hopeful errand of trying to make an arrangement without money – under which auspicious circumstances it mostly happens that the legal gentleman they want to see, is much engaged, and they pervade the staircase for a considerable period. Against this opposing bulk, in the absurdest manner, the tomb-like outer door of the solicitor's chambers (which is also of an intense black) stands in dark ambush, half open, and half shut, all day. The solicitor's apartments are three in number; consisting of a slice, a cell, and a wedge. The slice is assigned to the two clerks, the cell is occupied by the principal, and the wedge is devoted to stray papers, old game baskets from the country, a washing-stand, and a model of a patent Ship's Caboose[1] which was exhibited in Chancery at the commencement of the present century on an application for an injunction to restrain infringement. At about half-past nine on every week-day morning, the younger of the two clerks (who, I have reason to believe, leads the fashion at Pentonville in the articles of pipes and shirts) may be found knocking the dust out of his official door-key on the bunk or locker before mentioned; and so exceedingly subject to dust is his key, and so very retentive of that superfluity, that in exceptional summer weather when a ray of sunlight has fallen on the locker in my presence, I have noticed its inexpressive countenance to be deeply marked by a kind of Bramah erysipelas[2] or small-pox.

This set of chambers (as I have gradually discovered, when I have had restless occasion to make inquiries or leave messages, after office hours) is under the charge of a lady named Sweeney, in figure extremely like an old family-umbrella: whose dwelling confronts a dead wall in a court off Gray's Inn-lane, and who is usually fetched into the passage of that bower, when wanted, from some neighbouring home of industry, which has the curious property of imparting an inflammatory appearance to her visage. Mrs. Sweeney is one of the race of professed laundresses, and is the compiler of a remarkable manuscript volume entitled "Mrs. Sweeney's Book," from which much curious statistical information may be gathered respecting the high prices and small uses of soda, soap, sand, firewood, and other such articles. I have created a legend in my mind – and consequently I believe it with the utmost pertinacity – that the late Mr. Sweeney was a ticket-porter under the Honourable Society of Gray's Inn, and that, in consideration of his long and valuable services, Mrs. Sweeney was appointed to her present post. For, though devoid of personal charms, I have observed this lady to exercise a fascination over the elderly ticket-porter mind (particularly under the gateway, and in corners and entries), which I can only refer to her being one of the fraternity, yet not competing with it. All that need be said concerning this set of chambers, is said, when I have added that it is in a large double house in Gray's Inn-square, very much out of repair, and that the outer portal is ornamented in a hideous manner with certain stone remains, which have the appearance of the dismembered bust, torso, and limbs of a petrified bencher.

Indeed, I look upon Gray's Inn generally as one of the most depressing institutions in brick and mortar, known to the children of men. Can anything be more dreary than its arid Square, Sahara Desert of the law, with the ugly old tiled-topped tenements, the dirty windows, the bills To Let, To Let, the door-posts inscribed like gravestones, the crazy gateway giving upon the filthy Lane, the scowling iron-barred prison-like passage into Verulam-buildings,[3] the mouldy red-nosed ticket-porters with little coffin plates, and why with aprons, the dry hard atomy-like appearance of the whole dust-heap? When my uncommercial travels tend to this dismal spot, my comfort is its rickety state. Imagination gloats over the fulness of time when the staircases shall have quite tumbled down – they are daily wearing into an ill-savoured powder, but have not quite tumbled down yet – when the last old prolix bencher all of the olden time, shall have been got out of an upper window by means of a Fire Ladder, and carried off to the Holborn Union;[4] when the last clerk shall have engrossed the last parchment behind the last splash on the last of the mud-stained windows, which, all through the miry year, are pilloried out of recognition in Gray's Inn-lane. Then, shall a squalid little trench, with rank grass and a pump in it, lying between the coffee-house and South-square, be wholly given up to cats and rats, and not, as now, have its empire divided between those animals and a few briefless bipeds – surely called to the Bar by voices of deceiving spirits, seeing that they are wanted there by no mortal – who glance down, with eyes better glazed than their casements, from their dreary and lack-lustre rooms. Then shall the way Nor' Westward, now lying under a short grim colonnade where in summer-time pounce flies from law-stationering windows into the eyes of laymen, be choked with rubbish and happily become impassable. Then shall the gardens where turf, trees, and gravel wear a legal livery of black, run rank, and pilgrims go to Gorhambury to see Bacon's effigy as he sat, and not come here (which in truth they seldom do) to see where he walked. Then, in a word, shall the old-established vendor of periodicals sit alone in his little crib of a shop behind the Holborn Gate, like that lumbering Marius among the ruins of Carthage,[5] who has sat heavy on a thousand million of similes.

At one period of my uncommercial career I much frequented another set of chambers in Gray's Inn-square. They were what is familiarly called "a top set," and all the eatables and drinkables introduced into them acquired a flavour of Cockloft.[6] I have known an unopened Strasbourg pâté fresh from Fortnum and Mason's, to draw in this cockloft tone through its crockery dish, and become penetrated with cockloft to the core of its inmost truffle in three-quarters of an hour. This, however, was not the most curious feature of those chambers; that, consisted in the profound conviction entertained by my esteemed friend Parkle (their tenant) that they were clean. Whether it was an inborn hallucination, or whether it was imparted to him by Mrs. Miggot the laundress, I never could ascertain. But, I believe he would have gone to the stake upon the question. Now, they were so dirty that I could take off the distinctest impression of my figure on any article of furniture by merely lounging upon it for a few moments; and it used to be a private amusement of mine to print myself off – if I may use the expression – all over the rooms. It was the first large circulation I had. At other times I have accidentally shaken a window curtain while in animated conversation with Parkle, and struggling insects which were certainly red, and were certainly not ladybirds, have dropped on the back of my hand.

Yet Parkle lived in that top set years, bound body and soul to the superstition that they were clean. He used to say, when congratulated upon them, "Well, they are not like chambers in one respect, you know; they are clean." Concurrently, he had an idea which he could never explain, that Mrs. Miggot was in some way connected with the Church. When he was in particularly good spirits, he used to believe that a deceased uncle of hers had been a Dean; when he was poorly and low, he believed that her brother had been a Curate. I and Mrs. Miggot (she was a genteel woman) were on confidential terms, but I never knew her to commit herself to any distinct assertion on the subject; she merely claimed a proprietorship in the Church, by looking when it was mentioned, as if the reference awakened the slumbering Past, and were personal. It may have been his amiable confidence in Mrs. Miggot's better days that inspired my friend with his delusion respecting the chambers, but he never wavered in his fidelity to it for a moment, though he wallowed in dirt seven years.

Two of the windows of these chambers looked down into the garden; and we have sat up there together many a summer evening, saying how pleasant it was, and talking of many things. To my intimacy with that top set, I am indebted for three of my liveliest personal impressions of the loneliness of life in chambers. They shall follow here, in order; first, second, and third.

First. My Gray's Inn friend, on a time, hurt one of his legs, and it became seriously inflamed. Not knowing of his indisposition, I was on my way to visit him as usual, one summer evening, when I was much surprised by meeting a lively leech in Field-court, Gray's Inn, seemingly on his way to the West End of London. As the leech was alone, and was of course unable to explain his position, even if he had been inclined to do so (which he had not the appearance of being), I passed him and went on. Turning the corner of Gray's Inn-square, I was beyond expression amazed by meeting another leech − also entirely alone, and also proceeding in a westerly direction, though with less decision of purpose. Ruminating on this extraordinary circumstance, and endeavouring to remember whether I had ever read, in the Philosophical Transactions or any work on Natural History, of a migration of Leeches, I ascended to the top set, past the dreary series of closed outer doors of offices and an empty set or two, which intervened between that lofty region and the surface. Entering my friend's rooms, I found him stretched upon his back, like Prometheus Bound,[7] with a perfectly demented ticket-porter in attendance on him instead of the Vulture: which helpless individual, who was feeble and frightened, and had (my friend explained to me, in great choler) been endeavouring for some hours to apply leeches to his leg, and as yet had only got on two out of twenty. To this Unfortunate's distraction between a damp cloth on which he had placed the leeches to freshen them, and the wrathful adjurations of my friend to "Stick 'em on, sir!" I referred the phenomenon I had encountered: the rather as two fine specimens were at that moment going out at the door, while a general insurrection of the rest was in progress on the table. After a while our united efforts prevailed, and, when the leeches came off and had recovered their spirits, we carefully tied them up in a decanter. But I never heard more of them than that they were all gone next morning, and that the Out-of-door young man of Bickle Bush and Bodger, on the ground floor, had been bitten and blooded by some creature not identified. They never "took" on Mrs. Miggot, the laundress; but, I have always preserved fresh, the belief that she unconsciously carried several about her, until they gradually found openings in life.

Second. On the same staircase with my friend Parkle, and on the same floor, there lived a man of law who pursued his business elsewhere, and used those chambers as his place of residence. For three or four years, Parkle rather knew of him than knew him, but after that – for Englishmen – short pause of consideration, they began to speak. Parkle exchanged words with him in his private character only, and knew nothing of his business ways, or means. He was a man a good deal about town, but always alone. We used to remark to one another, that although we often encountered him in theatres, concert-rooms, and similar public places, he was always alone. Yet he was not a gloomy man, and was of a decidedly conversational turn; insomuch that he would sometimes of an evening lounge with a cigar in his mouth, half in and half out of Parkle's rooms, and discuss the topics of the day by the hour. He used to hint on these occasions that he had four faults to find with life; firstly, that it obliged a man to be always winding up his watch; secondly, that London was too small; thirdly, that it therefore wanted variety; fourthly, that there was too much dust in it. There was so much dust in his own faded chambers, certainly, that they reminded me of a sepulchre, furnished in prophetic anticipation of the present time, which had newly been brought to light, after having remained buried a few thousand years. One dry hot autumn evening at twilight, this man, being then five years turned of fifty, looked in upon Parkle in his usual lounging way, with his cigar in his mouth as usual, and said, "I am going out of town." As he never went out of town, Parkle said, "Oh indeed! At last?" "Yes," says he, "at last. For what is a man to do? London is so small! If you go West, you come to Hounslow. If you go East, you come to Bow. If you go South, there's Brixton or Norwood. If you go North, you can't get rid of Barnet. Then, the monotony of all the streets, streets, streets – and of all the roads, roads, roads – and the dust, dust, dust!" When he had said this, he wished Parkle a good evening, but came back again and said, with his watch in his hand, "Oh, I really cannot go on winding up this watch over and over again; I wish you would take care of it." So, Parkle laughed and consented, and the man went out of town. The man remained out of town so long, that his letter-box became choked, and no more letters could be got into it, and they began to be left at the lodge and to accumulate there. At last the head-porter decided, on conference with the steward, to use his master-key and look into the chambers, and give them the benefit of a whiff of air. Then, it was found that he had hanged himself to his bedstead, and had left this written memorandum: "I should prefer to be cut down by my neighbour and friend (if he will allow me to call him so), H. Parkle, Esq." This was an end of Parkle's occupancy of chambers. He went into lodgings immediately.

Third. While Parkle lived in Gray's Inn, and I myself was uncommercially preparing for the Bar – which is done, as everybody knows, by having a frayed old gown put on in a pantry by an old woman in a chronic state of Saint Anthony's fire[8] and dropsy, and, so decorated, bolting a bad dinner in a party of four, whereof each individual mistrusts the other three – I say, while these things were, there was a certain elderly gentleman who lived in a court of the Temple, and was a great judge and lover of port wine. Every day he dined at his club and drank his bottle or two of port wine, and every night came home to the Temple and went to bed in his lonely chambers. This had gone on many years without variation, when one night he had a fit on coming home, and fell and cut his head deep, but partly recovered and groped about in the dark to find the door. When he was afterwards discovered, dead, it was clearly established by the marks of his hands about the room that he must have done so. Now, this chanced on the night of Christmas Eve, and over him lived a young fellow who had sisters and young country friends, and who gave them a little party that night, in the course of which they played at Blindman's Buff. They played that game, for their greater sport, by the light of the fire only; and once, when they were all quietly rustling and stealing about, and the blindman was trying to pick out the prettiest sister (for which I am far from blaming him), somebody cried, Hark! The man below must be playing Blindman's Buff by himself to-night! They listened, and they heard sounds of some one falling about and stumbling against furniture, and they all laughed at the conceit, and went on with their play, more light-hearted and merry than ever. Thus, those two so different games of life and death were played out together, blindfolded, in the two sets of chambers.

Such are the occurrences, which, coming to my knowledge, imbued me long ago with a strong sense of the loneliness of chambers. There was a fantastic illustration to much the same purpose implicitly believed by a strange sort of man now dead, whom I knew when I had not quite arrived at legal years of discretion, though I was already in the uncommercial line.

This was a man who, though not more than thirty, had seen the world in divers irreconcilable capacities – had been an officer in a South American regiment among other odd things – but had not achieved much in any way of life, and was in debt, and in hiding. He occupied chambers of the dreariest nature in Lyons Inn;[9] his name, however, was not up on the door, or door-post, but in lieu of it stood the name of a friend who died in the chambers, and had given him the furniture. The story arose out of the furniture, and was to this effect: – Let the former holder of the chambers, whose name was still upon the door and door-post, be Mr. Testator.

Mr. Testator took a set of chambers in Lyons Inn when he had but very scanty furniture for his bedroom, and none for his sitting-room. He had lived some wintry months in this condition, and had found it very bare and cold. One night, past midnight, when he sat writing and still had writing to do that must be done before he went to bed, he found himself out of coals. He had coals down-stairs, but had never been to his cellar; however the cellar-key was on his mantelshelf, and if he went down and opened the cellar it fitted, he might fairly assume the coals in that cellar to be his. As to his laundress, she lived among the coal-waggons and Thames watermen – for there were Thames watermen at that time – in some unknown rat-hole by the river, down lanes and alleys on the other side of the Strand. As to any other person to meet him or obstruct him, Lyons Inn was dreaming, drunk, maudlin, moody, betting, brooding over bill-discounting or renewing – asleep or awake, minding its own affairs. Mr. Testator took his coal-scuttle in one hand, his candle and key in the other, and descended to the dismallest underground dens of Lyons Inn, where the late vehicles in the streets became thunderous, and all the water-pipes in the neighbourhood seemed to have Macbeth's Amen[10] sticking in their throats, and to be trying to get it out. After groping here and there among low doors to no purpose, Mr. Testator at length came to a door with a rusty padlock which his key fitted. Getting the door open with much trouble, and looking in, he found, no coals, but a confused pile of furniture. Alarmed by this intrusion on another man's property, he locked the door again, found his own cellar, filled his scuttle, and returned up-stairs.

But the furniture he had seen, ran on castors across and across Mr. Testator's mind incessantly, when, in the chill hour of five in the morning, he got to bed. He particularly wanted a table to write at, and a table expressly made to be written at, had been the piece of furniture in the foreground of the heap. When his laundress emerged from her burrow in the morning to make his kettle boil, he artfully led up to the subject of cellars and furniture; but the two ideas had evidently no connexion in her mind. When she left him, and he sat at his breakfast, thinking about the furniture, he recalled the rusty state of the padlock, and inferred that the furniture must have been stored in the cellars for a long time – was perhaps forgotten – owner dead, perhaps? After thinking it over, a few days, in the course of which he could pump nothing out of Lyons Inn about the furniture, he became desperate, and resolved to borrow that table. He did so, that night. He had not had the table long, when he determined to borrow an easy-chair; he had not had that long, when he made up his mind to borrow a bookcase; then, a couch; then, a carpet and rug. By that time, he felt he was "in furniture stepped in so far,"[11] as that it could be no worse to borrow it all. Consequently, he borrowed it all, and locked up the cellar for good. He had always locked it, after every visit. He had carried up every separate article in the dead of the night, and, at the best, had felt as wicked as a Resurrection Man. Every article was blue and furry when brought into his rooms, and he had had, in a murderous and guilty sort of way, to polish it up while London slept.

Mr. Testator lived in his furnished chambers two or three years, or more, and gradually lulled himself into the opinion that the furniture was his own. This was his convenient state of mind when, late one night, a step came up the stairs, and a hand passed over his door feeling for his knocker, and then one deep and solemn rap was rapped that might have been a spring in Mr. Testator's easy-chair to shoot him out of it; so promptly was it attended with that effect.

With a candle in his hand, Mr. Testator went to the door, and found there a very pale and very tall man; a man who stooped; a man with very high shoulders, a very narrow chest, and a very red nose; a shabby-genteel man. He was wrapped in a long threadbare black coat, fastened up the front with more pins than buttons, and under his arm he squeezed an umbrella without a handle, as if he were playing bagpipes. He said, "I ask your pardon, but can you tell me —" and stopped; his eyes resting on some object within the chambers.

"Can I tell you what?" asked Mr. Testator, noting his stoppage with quick alarm.

"I ask your pardon," said the stranger, "but — this is not the inquiry I was going to make — *do* I see in there, any small article of property belonging to *me*?"

Mr. Testator was beginning to stammer that he was not aware — when the visitor slipped past him into the chambers. There, in a goblin way which froze Mr. Testator to the marrow, he examined, first, the writing-table, and said, "Mine;" then, the easy-chair, and said, "Mine;" then, the bookcase, and said, "Mine;" then, turned up a corner of the carpet, and said, "Mine!" — in a word, inspected every item of furniture from the cellar, in succession, and said, "Mine!" Towards the end of this investigation, Mr. Testator perceived that he was sodden with liquor, and that the liquor was gin. He was not unsteady with gin, either in his speech or carriage; but he was stiff with gin in both particulars.

Mr. Testator was in a dreadful state, for (according to his making out of the story) the possible consequences of what he had done in recklessness and hardihood, flashed upon him in their fulness for the first time. When they had stood gazing at one another for a little while, he tremulously began:

"Sir, I am conscious that the fullest explanation, compensation, and restitution, are your due. They shall be yours. Allow me to entreat that, without temper, without even natural irritation on your part, we may have a little——"

"Drop of something to drink," interposed the stranger. "I am agreeable."

Mr. Testator had intended to say, "a little quiet conversation," but with great relief of mind adopted the amendment. He produced a decanter of gin, and was bustling about for hot water and sugar, when he found that his visitor had already drunk half of the decanter's contents. With hot water and sugar the visitor drank the remainder before he had been an hour in the chambers by the chimes of the church of St. Mary in the Strand; and during the process he frequently whispered to himself, "Mine!"

The gin gone, and Mr. Testator wondering what was to follow it, the visitor rose and said, with increased stiffness, "At what hour of the morning, sir, will it be convenient?" Mr. Testator hazarded, "At ten?" "Sir," said the visitor, "at ten, to the moment, I shall be here." He then contemplated Mr. Testator somewhat at leisure, and said, "God bless you! How is your wife?" Mr. Testator (who never had a wife) replied with much feeling, "Deeply anxious, poor soul, but otherwise well." The visitor thereupon turned and went away, and fell twice in going down-stairs. From that hour he was never heard of. Whether he was a ghost, or a spectral illusion of conscience, or a drunken man who had no business there, or the drunken rightful owner of the furniture, with a transitory gleam of memory; whether he got safe home, or had no home to get to; whether he died of liquor on the way, or lived in liquor ever afterwards; he never was heard of more. This was the story, received with the furniture and held to be as substantial, by its second possessor in an upper set of chambers in grim Lyons Inn.

It is to be remarked of chambers in general, that they must have been built for chambers, to have the right kind of loneliness. You may make a great dwelling-house very lonely, by isolating suites of rooms and calling them chambers, but you cannot make the true kind of loneliness. In dwelling-houses, there have been family festivals; children have grown in them, girls have bloomed into women in them, courtships and marriages have taken place in them. True chambers never were young, childish, maidenly; never had dolls in them, or rocking-horses, or christenings, or betrothals, or little coffins. Let Gray's Inn identify the child who first touched hands and hearts with Robinson Crusoe, in any one of its many "sets," and that child's little statue, in white marble with a golden inscription, shall be at its service, at my cost and charge, as a drinking fountain for the spirit, to freshen its thirsty square. Let Lincoln's produce from all its houses, a twentieth of the procession derivable from any dwelling-house one-twentieth of its age, of fair young brides who married for love and hope, not settlements, and all the Vice-Chancellors shall thence-forward be kept in nosegays for nothing, on application to the writer hereof. It is not denied that on the terrace of the Adelphi, or in any of the streets of that subterranean-stable-haunted spot, or about Bedford-row, or James-street of that ilk (a grewsome place), or anywhere among the neighbourhoods that have done flowering and have run to seed, you may find Chambers replete with the accommodations of Solitude, Closeness, and Darkness, where you may be as low-spirited as in the genuine article, and might be as easily murdered, with the placid reputation of having merely gone down to the sea-side. But, the many waters of life did run musical in those dry channels once; – among the Inns, never. The only popular legend known in relation to any one of the dull family of Inns, is a dark Old Bailey whisper concerning Clement's,[12] and importing how the black creature who holds the sun-dial there, was a negro who slew his master and built the dismal pile out of the contents of his strong box – for which architectural offence alone he ought to have been condemned to live in it. But, what populace would waste fancy upon such a place, or on New Inn, Staple Inn, Barnard's Inn,[13] or any of the shabby crew?

The genuine laundress, too, is an institution not to be had in its entirety out of and away from the genuine Chambers. Again, it is not denied that you may be robbed elsewhere. Elsewhere you may have – for money – dishonesty, drunkenness, dirt, laziness, and profound incapacity. But the veritable shining-red-faced shameless laundress; the true Mrs. Sweeney – in figure, colour, texture, and smell, like the old damp family umbrella; the tip-top complicated abomination of stockings, spirits, bonnet, limpness, looseness, and larceny; is only to be drawn at the fountain-head. Mrs. Sweeney is beyond the reach of individual art. It requires the united efforts of several men to ensure that great result, and it is only developed in perfection under an Honourable Society and in an Inn of Court.

Nurse's Stories

First published in *All the Year Round*, 8 September 1860. The text here is taken from *The Uncommercial Traveller*.

There are not many places that I find it more agreeable to revisit when I am in an idle mood, than some places to which I have never been. For, my acquaintance with those spots is of such long standing, and has ripened into an intimacy of so affectionate a nature, that I take a particular interest in assuring myself that they are unchanged.

I never was in Robinson Crusoe's Island, yet I frequently return there. The colony he established on it soon faded away, and it is uninhabited by any descendants of the grave and courteous Spaniards, or of Will Atkins and the other mutineers, and has relapsed into its original condition. Not a twig of its wicker houses remains, its goats have long run wild again, its screaming parrots would darken the sun with a cloud of many flaming colours if a gun were fired there, no face is ever reflected in the waters of the little creek which Friday swam across when pursued by his two brother cannibals with sharpened stomachs. After comparing notes with other travellers who have similarly revisited the Island and conscientiously inspected it, I have satisfied myself that it contains no vestige of Mr. Atkins's domesticity or theology, though his track on the memorable evening of his landing to set his captain ashore, when he was decoyed about and round about until it was dark, and his boat was stove, and his strength and spirits failed him, is yet plainly to be traced. So is the hill-top on which Robinson was struck dumb with joy when the reinstated captain pointed to the ship, riding within half a mile of the shore, that was to bear him away, in the nine-and-twentieth year of his seclusion in that lonely place. So is the sandy beach on which the memorable footstep was impressed, and where the savages hauled up their canoes when they came ashore for those dreadful public dinners, which led to a dancing worse than speech-making. So is the cave where the flaring eyes of the old goat made such a goblin appearance in the dark. So is the site of the hut where Robinson lived with the dog and the parrot and the cat, and where he endured those first agonies of solitude, which – strange to say – never involved any ghostly fancies; a circumstance so very remarkable, that perhaps he left out something in writing his record? Round hundreds of such objects, hidden in the dense tropical foliage, the tropical sea breaks evermore; and over them the tropical sky, saving in the short rainy season, shines bright and cloudless.

Neither was I ever belated among wolves, on the borders of France and Spain;[1] nor did I ever, when night was closing in and the ground was covered with snow, draw up my little company among some felled trees which served as a breastwork, and there fire a train of gunpowder so dexterously that suddenly we had three or four score blazing wolves illuminating the darkness around us. Nevertheless, I occasionally go back to that dismal region and perform the feat again; when indeed to smell the singeing and the frying of the wolves afire, and to see them setting one another alight as they rush and tumble, and to behold them rolling in the snow vainly attempting to put themselves out, and to hear their howlings taken up by all the echoes as well as by all the unseen wolves within the woods, makes me tremble.

I was never in the robbers' cave, where Gil Blas lived, but I often go back there and find the trap-door just as heavy to raise as it used to be, while that wicked old disabled Black lies everlastingly cursing in bed.[2] I was never in Don Quixote's study, where he read his books of chivalry until he rose and hacked at imaginary giants, and then refreshed himself with great draughts of water,[3] yet you couldn't move a book in it without my knowledge, or with my consent. I was never (thank Heaven) in company with the little old woman who hobbled out of the chest and told the merchant Abudah to go in search of the Talisman of Oromanes,[4] yet I make it my business to know that she is well preserved and as intolerable as ever. I was never at the school where the boy Horatio Nelson got out of bed to steal the pears: not because he wanted any, but because every other boy was afraid: yet I have several times been back to this Academy, to see him let down out of window with a sheet.[5] So with Damascus, and Bagdad, and Brobingnag[6] (which has the curious fate of being usually mis-spelt when written), and Lilliput, and Laputa, and the Nile, and Abyssinia, and the Ganges, and the North Pole, and many hundreds of places – I was never at them, yet it is an affair of my life to keep them intact, and I am always going back to them.

But, when I was at Dullborough one day, revisiting the associations of my childhood as recorded in previous pages of these notes, my experience in this wise was made quite inconsiderable and of no account, by the quantity of places and people – utterly impossible places and people, but none the less alarmingly real – that I found I had been introduced to by my nurse before I was six years old, and used to be forced to go back to at night

93

without at all wanting to go. If we all knew our own minds (in a more enlarged sense than the popular acceptation of that phrase), I suspect we should find our nurses responsible for most of the dark corners we are forced to go back to, against our wills.

The first diabolical character who intruded himself on my peaceful youth (as I called to mind that day at Dullborough), was a certain Captain Murderer. This wretch must have been an offshoot of the Blue Beard family, but I had no suspicion of the consanguinity in those times. His warning name would seem to have awakened no general prejudice against him, for he was admitted into the best society and possessed immense wealth. Captain Murderer's mission was matrimony, and the gratification of a cannibal appetite with tender brides. On his marriage morning, he always caused both sides of the way to church to be planted with curious flowers; and when his bride said, "Dear Captain Murderer, I never saw flowers like these before: what are they called?" he answered, "They are called Garnish for house-lamb," and laughed at his ferocious practical joke in a horrid manner, disquieting the minds of the noble bridal company, with a very sharp show of teeth, then displayed for the first time. He made love in a coach and six, and married in a coach and twelve, and all his horses were milk-white horses with one red spot on the back which he caused to be hidden by the harness. For, the spot *would* come there, though every horse was milk-white when Captain Murderer bought him. And the spot was young bride's blood. (To this terrific point I am indebted for my first personal experience of a shudder and cold beads on the forehead.) When Captain Murderer had made an end of feasting and revelry, and had dismissed the noble guests, and was alone with his wife on the day month after their marriage, it was his whimsical custom to produce a golden rolling-pin and a silver pie-board. Now, there was this special feature in the Captain's courtships, that he always asked if the young lady could make pie-crust; and if she couldn't by nature or education, she was taught. Well. When the bride saw Captain Murderer produce the golden rolling-pin and silver pie-board, she remembered this, and turned up her laced-silk sleeves to make a pie. The Captain brought out a silver pie-dish of immense capacity, and the Captain brought out flour and butter and eggs and all things needful, except the inside of the pie; of materials for the staple of the pie itself, the Captain brought out none. Then said the lovely bride, "Dear Captain Murderer, what pie is this to be?" He replied, "A meat pie." Then said the lovely bride, "Dear Captain Murderer, I see no meat." The Captain humorously retorted, "Look in the glass." She looked in the glass, but still she saw no meat, and then the Captain roared with laughter, and suddenly frowning and drawing his sword, bade her roll out the crust. So she rolled out the crust, dropping large tears upon it all the time because he was so cross, and when she had lined the dish with crust and had cut the crust all ready to fit the top, the Captain called out, "*I* see the meat in the glass!" And the bride looked up at the glass, just in time to see the Captain cutting her head off; and he chopped her in pieces, and peppered her, and salted her, and put her in the pie, and sent it to the baker's, and ate it all, and picked the bones.

Captain Murderer went on in this way, prospering exceedingly, until he came to choose a bride from two twin sisters, and at first didn't know which to choose. For, though one was fair and the other dark, they were both equally beautiful. But the fair twin loved him, and the dark twin hated him, so he chose the fair one. The dark twin would have prevented the marriage if she could, but she couldn't; however, on the night before it, much suspecting Captain Murderer, she stole out and climbed his garden wall, and looked in at his window through a chink in the shutter, and saw him having his teeth filed sharp. Next day she listened all day, and heard him make his joke about the house-lamb. And that day month, he had the paste rolled out, and cut the fair twin's head off, and chopped her in pieces, and peppered her, and salted her, and put her in the pie, and sent it to the baker's, and ate it all, and picked the bones.

Now, the dark twin had had her suspicions much increased by the filing of the Captain's teeth, and again by the house-lamb joke. Putting all things together when he gave out that her sister was dead, she divined the truth, and determined to be revenged. So, she went up to Captain Murderer's house, and knocked at the knocker and pulled at the bell, and when the Captain came to the door, said: "Dear Captain Murderer, marry me next, for I always loved you and was jealous of my sister." The Captain took it as a compliment, and made a polite answer, and the marriage was quickly arranged. On the night before it, the bride again climbed to his window, and again saw him having his teeth filed sharp. At this sight she laughed such a terrible laugh at the chink in the shutter, that the Captain's blood curdled, and he said: "I hope nothing has disagreed with me!" At that, she laughed again, a still more terrible laugh, and the shutter was opened and search made, but she was nimbly gone, and there was no one. Next day they went to church in a coach and twelve, and were married. And that day month, she rolled the pie-crust out, and Captain Murderer cut her head off, and chopped her in pieces, and peppered her, and salted her, and put her in the pie, and sent it to the baker's, and ate it all, and picked the bones.

But before she began to roll out the paste she had taken a deadly poison of a most awful character, distilled from toads' eyes and spiders' knees; and Captain Murderer had hardly picked her last bone, when he began to swell, and to turn blue, and to be all over spots, and to scream. And he went on swelling and turning bluer, and being more all over spots and screaming, until he reached from floor to ceiling and from wall to wall; and then, at one o'clock in the morning, he blew up with a loud explosion. At the sound of it, all the milk-white horses in the stables broke their halters and went mad, and then they galloped over everybody in Captain Murderer's house (beginning with the family blacksmith who had filed his teeth) until the whole were dead, and then they galloped away.

Hundreds of times did I hear this legend of Captain Murderer, in my early youth, and added hundreds of times was there a mental compulsion upon me in bed, to peep in at his window as the dark twin peeped, and to revisit his horrible house, and look at him in his blue and spotty and screaming stage, as he reached from floor to ceiling and from wall to wall. The young woman who brought me acquainted with Captain Murderer had a fiendish enjoyment of my terrors, and used to begin, I remember – as a sort of introductory overture – by clawing the air with both hands, and uttering a long low hollow groan. So acutely did I suffer from this ceremony in combination with this infernal Captain, that I sometimes used to plead I thought I was hardly strong enough and old enough to hear the story again just yet. But, she never spared me one word of it, and indeed commended the awful chalice to my lips as the only preservative known to science against "The Black Cat" – a weird and glaring-eyed supernatural Tom, who was reputed to prowl about the world by night, sucking the breath of infancy, and who was endowed with a special thirst (as I was given to understand) for mine.[7]

This female bard – may she have been repaid my debt of obligation to her in the matter of nightmares and perspirations! – reappears in my memory as the daughter of a shipwright. Her name was Mercy, though she had none on me. There was something of a shipbuilding flavour in the following story. As it always recurs to me in a vague association with calomel pills, I believe it to have been reserved for dull nights when I was low with medicine.

There was once a shipwright, and he wrought in a Government Yard, and his name was Chips. And his father's name before him was Chips, and *his* father's name before *him* was Chips, and they were all Chipses. And Chips the father had sold himself to the Devil for an iron pot and a bushel of tenpenny nails and half a ton of copper and a rat that could speak; and Chips the grandfather had sold himself to the Devil for an iron pot and a bushel of tenpenny nails and half a ton of copper and a rat that could speak; and Chips the great-grandfather had disposed of himself in the same direction on the same terms; and the bargain had run in the family for a long long time. So, one day, when young Chips was at work in the Dock Slip all alone, down in the dark hold of an old Seventy-four that was haled up for repairs, the Devil presented himself, and remarked:

> "A Lemon has pips,
> And a Yard has ships,
> And *I*'ll have Chips!"

(I don't know why, but this fact of the Devil's expressing himself in rhyme was peculiarly trying to me.) Chips looked up when he heard the words, and there he saw the Devil with saucer eyes that squinted on a terrible great scale, and that struck out sparks of blue fire continually. And whenever he winked his eyes, showers of blue sparks came out, and his eyelashes made a clattering like flints and steels striking lights. And hanging over one of his arms by the handle was an iron pot, and under that arm was a bushel of tenpenny nails, and under his other arm was half a ton of copper, and sitting on one of his shoulders was a rat that could speak. So, the Devil said again:

> "A Lemon has pips,
> And a Yard has ships,
> And *I*'ll have Chips!"

(The invariable effect of this alarming tautology on the part of the Evil Spirit was to deprive me of my senses for some moments.) So, Chips answered never a word, but went on with his work. "What are you doing, Chips?" said the rat that could speak. "I am putting in new planks where you and your gang have eaten old away," said Chips. "But we'll eat them too," said the rat that could speak; "and we'll let in the water and drown the crew, and we'll eat them too." Chips, being only a shipwright, and not a Man-of-war's man, said, "You are welcome to it." But he couldn't keep his eyes off the half a ton of copper or the bushel of tenpenny nails; for nails and copper are a shipwright's sweethearts, and shipwrights will run away with them whenever they can. So, the Devil said, "I see what you are looking at, Chips. You had better strike the bargain. You know the terms. Your father before you was well acquainted with them, and so were your grandfather and great-grandfather before him." Says Chips, "I like the copper, and I like the nails, and I don't mind the pot, but I don't like the rat." Says the Devil, fiercely, "You can't have the metal without him

– and *he's* a curiosity. I'm going." Chips, afraid of losing the half a ton of copper and the bushel of nails, then said, "Give us hold!" So, he got the copper and the nails and the pot and the rat that could speak, and the Devil vanished. Chips sold the copper, and he sold the nails, and he would have sold the pot; but whenever he offered it for sale, the rat was in it, and the dealers dropped it, and would have nothing to say to the bargain. So, Chips resolved to kill the rat, and, being at work in the Yard one day with a great kettle of hot pitch on one side of him and the iron pot with the rat in it on the other, he turned the scalding pitch into the pot, and filled it full. Then, he kept his eye upon it till it cooled and hardened, and then he let it stand for twenty days, and then he heated the pitch again and turned it back into the kettle, and then he sank the pot in water for twenty days more, and then he got the smelters to put it in the furnace for twenty days more, and then they gave it him out, red hot, and looking like red-hot glass instead of iron – yet there was the rat in it, just the same as ever! And the moment it caught his eye, it said with a jeer:

> "A Lemon has pips,
> And a Yard has ships,
> And *I*'ll have Chips!"

(For this Refrain I had waited since its last appearance, with inexpressible horror, which now culminated.) Chips now felt certain in his own mind that the rat would stick to him; the rat, answering his thought, said, "I will – like pitch!"

Now, as the rat leaped out of the pot when it had spoken, and made off, Chips began to hope that it wouldn't keep its word. But, a terrible thing happened next day. For, when dinner-time came, and the Dock-bell rang to strike work, he put his rule into the long pocket at the side of his trousers, and there he found a rat – not that rat, but another rat. And in his hat, he found another; and in his pocket-handkerchief, another; and in the sleeves of his coat, when he pulled it on to go to dinner, two more. And from that time he found himself so frightfully intimate with all the rats in the Yard, that they climbed up his legs when he was at work, and sat on his tools while he used them. And they could all speak to one another, and he understood what they said. And they got into his lodging, and into his bed, and into his teapot, and into his beer, and into his boots. And he was going to be married to a corn-chandler's daughter; and when he gave her a workbox he had himself made for her, a rat jumped out of it; and when he put his arm round her waist, a rat clung about her; so the marriage was broken off, though the banns were already twice put up – which the parish clerk well remembers, for, as he handed the book to the clergyman for the second time of asking, a large fat rat ran over the leaf. (By this time a special cascade of rats was rolling down my back, and the whole of my small listening person was overrun with them. At intervals ever since, I have been morbidly afraid of my own pocket, lest my exploring hand should find a specimen or two of those vermin in it.)

You may believe that all this was very terrible to Chips; but even all this was not the worst. He knew besides, what the rats were doing, wherever they were. So, sometimes he would cry aloud, when he was at his club at night, "Oh! Keep the rats out of the convicts' burying-ground! Don't let them do that!" Or, "There's one of them at the cheese down-stairs!" Or, "There's two of them smelling at the baby in the garret!" Or, other things of that sort. At last, he was voted mad, and lost his work in the Yard, and could get no other work. But King George wanted men, so before very long he got pressed for a sailor. And so he was taken off in a boat one evening to his ship, lying at Spithead, ready to sail. And so the first thing he made out in her as he got near her, was the figure-head of the old Seventy-four, where he had seen the Devil. She was called the Argonaut, and they rowed right under the bowsprit where the figure-head of the Argonaut, with a sheepskin in his hand and a blue gown on, was looking out to sea; and sitting staring on his forehead was the rat who could speak, and his exact words were these: "Chips ahoy! Old boy! We've pretty well eat them too, and we'll drown the crew, and will eat them too!" (Here I always became exceedingly faint, and would have asked for water, but that I was speechless.)

The ship was bound for the Indies; and if you don't know where that is, you ought to it, and angels will never love you. (Here I felt myself an outcast from a future state.) The ship set sail that very night, and she sailed, and sailed, and sailed. Chips's feelings were dreadful. Nothing ever equalled his terrors. No wonder. At last, one day he asked leave to speak to the Admiral. The Admiral giv' leave. Chips went down on his knees in the Great State Cabin. "Your Honour, unless your Honour, without a moment's loss of time, makes sail for the nearest shore, this is a doomed ship, and her name is the Coffin!" "Young man, your words are a madman's words." "Your Honour, no; they are nibbling us away." "They?" "Your Honour, them dreadful rats. Dust and hollowness where solid oak ought to be! Rats nibbling a grave for every man on board! Oh! Does your Honour love your Lady and your pretty children?" "Yes, my man, to be sure." "Then, for God's sake, make for the nearest shore, for at this present moment the rats are all stopping in their work, and are all looking straight towards you with bare teeth, and are all saying to one another that you shall never, never, never, never, see your Lady and your children more." "My poor fellow, you are a case for the doctor. Sentry, take care of this man!"

So, he was bled and he was blistered, and he was this and that, for six whole days and nights. So, then he again asked leave to speak to the Admiral. The Admiral giv' leave. He went down on his knees in the Great State Cabin. "Now, Admiral, you must die! You took no warning; you must die! The rats are never wrong in their calculations, and they make out that they'll be through, at twelve to-night. So, you must die! – With me and all the rest!" And so at twelve o'clock there was a great leak reported in the ship, and a torrent of water rushed in and nothing could stop it, and they all went down, every living soul. And what the rats – being water-rats – left of Chips, at last floated to shore, and sitting on him was an immense overgrown rat, laughing, that dived, when the corpse touched the beach and never came up. And there was a deal of seaweed on the remains. And if you get thirteen bits of seaweed, and dry them and burn them in the fire, they will go off like in these thirteen words as plain as plain can be:

> "A Lemon has pips,
> And a Yard has ships,
> And *I*'ve got Chips!"

The same female bard – descended, possibly, from those terrible old Scalds[8] who seem to have existed for the express purpose of addling the brains of mankind when they begin to investigate languages – made a standing pretence which greatly assisted in forcing me back to a number of hideous places that I would by all means have avoided. This pretence was, that all her ghost stories had occurred to her own relations. Politeness towards a meritorious family, therefore, forbade my doubting them, and they acquired an air of authentication that impaired my digestive powers for life. There was a narrative concerning an unearthly animal foreboding death, which appeared in the open street to a parlour-maid who "went to fetch the beer" for supper; first (as I now recall it) assuming the likeness of a black dog, and gradually rising on its hind-legs and swelling into the semblance of some quadruped greatly surpassing a hippopotamus: which apparition – not because I deemed it in the least improbable, but because I felt it to be really too large to bear – I feebly endeavoured to explain away. But, on Mercy's retorting with wounded dignity that the parlour-maid was her own sister-in-law, I perceived there was no hope, and resigned myself to this zoological phenomenon as one of my many pursuers. There was another narrative describing the apparition of a young woman who came out of a glass-case and haunted another young woman until the other young woman questioned it and elicited that its bones (Lord! To think of its being so particular about its bones!) were buried under the glass-case, whereas she required them to be interred, with every Undertaking solemnity up to twenty-four pound ten, in another particular place. This narrative I considered I had a personal interest in disproving, because we had glass-cases at home, and how, otherwise, was I to be guaranteed from the intrusion of young women requiring *me* to bury them up to twenty-four pound ten, when I had only twopence a week? But my remorseless nurse cut the ground from under my tender feet, by informing me that She was the other young woman; and I couldn't say "I don't believe you;" it was not possible.

Such are a few of the uncommercial journeys that I was forced to make, against my will, when I was very young and unreasoning. And really, as to the latter part of them, it is not so very long ago – now I come to think of it – that I was asked to undertake them once again, with a steady countenance.

Some Recollections of Mortality

First published in *All the Year Round*, 16 May 1863. The text here is taken from *The Uncommercial Traveller*.

I had parted from the small bird at somewhere about four o'clock in the morning, when he had got out at Arras, and had been received by two shovel-hats in waiting at the station, who presented an appropriately ornithological and crow-like appearance. My compatriot and I had gone on to Paris; my compatriot enlightening me occasionally with a long list of the enormous grievances of French railway travelling: every one of which, as I am a sinner, was perfectly new to me, though I have as much experience of French railways as most uncommercials. I had left him at the terminus (through his conviction, against all explanation and remonstrance, that his baggage-ticket was his passenger-ticket), insisting in a very high temper to the functionary on duty, that in his own personal identity he was four packages weighing so many kilogrammes – as if he had been Cassim Baba![1] I had bathed and breakfasted, and was strolling on the bright quays. The subject of my meditations was the question whether it is positively in the essence and nature of things, as a certain school of Britons would seem to think it, that a Capital must be ensnared and enslaved before it can be made beautiful: when I lifted up my eyes and found that my feet, straying like my mind, had brought me to Notre-Dame.

That is to say, Notre-Dame was before me, but there was a large open space between us. A very little while gone, I had left that space covered with buildings densely crowded; and now it was cleared for some new wonder in the way of public Street, Place, Garden, Fountain, or all four. Only the obscene little Morgue, slinking on the brink of the river and soon to come down, was left there, looking mortally ashamed of itself, and supremely wicked. I had but glanced at this old acquaintance, when I beheld an airy procession coming round in front of Notre-Dame, past the great hospital. It had something of a Masaniello look, with fluttering striped curtains in the midst of it, and it came dancing round the cathedral in the liveliest manner.

I was speculating on a marriage in Blouse-life,[2] or a Christening, or some other domestic festivity which I would see out, when I found, from the talk of a quick rush of Blouses past me, that it was a Body coming to the Morgue. Having never before chanced upon this initiation, I constituted myself a Blouse likewise, and ran into the Morgue with the rest. It was a very muddy day, and we took in a quantity of mire with us, and the procession coming in upon our heels brought a quantity more. The procession was in the highest spirits, and consisted of idlers who had come with the curtained litter from its starting-place, and of all the reinforcements it had picked up by the way. It set the litter down in the midst of the Morgue, and then two Custodians proclaimed aloud that we were all "invited" to go out. This invitation was rendered the more pressing, if not the more flattering, by our being shoved out, and the folding-gates being barred upon us.

Those who have never seen the Morgue, may see it perfectly, by presenting to themselves an indifferently paved coach-house accessible from the street by a pair of folding-gates; on the left of the coach-house, occupying its width, any large London tailor's or linendraper's plate-glass window reaching to the ground; within the window, on two rows of inclined plane, what the coach-house has to show; hanging above, like irregular stalactites from the roof of a cave, a quantity of clothes – the clothes of the dead and buried shows of the coach-house.

We had been excited in the highest degree by seeing the Custodians pull off their coats and tuck up their shirt-sleeves, as the procession came along. It looked so interestingly like business. Shut out in the muddy street, we now became quite ravenous to know all about it. Was it river, pistol, knife, love, gambling, robbery, hatred, how many stabs, how many bullets, fresh or decomposed, suicide or murder? All wedged together, and all staring at one another with our heads thrust forward, we propounded these inquiries and a hundred more such. Imperceptibly, it came to be known that Monsieur the tall and sallow mason yonder, was acquainted with the facts. Would Monsieur the tall and sallow mason, surged at by a new wave of us, have the goodness to impart? It was but a poor old man, passing along the street under one of the new buildings, on whom a stone had fallen, and who had tumbled dead. His age? Another wave surged up against the tall and sallow mason, and our wave swept on and broke, and he was any age from sixty-five to ninety.

An old man was not much: moreover, we could have wished he had been killed by human agency – his own, or somebody's else's: the latter, preferable – but our comfort was, that he had nothing about him to lend to his identification, and that his people must seek him here. Perhaps they were waiting dinner for him even now? We liked that. Such of us as had pocket-handkerchiefs took a slow intense protracted wipe at our noses, and then crammed our handkerchiefs into the breast of our blouses. Others of us who had no handkerchiefs administered a similar relief to our overwrought minds, by means of prolonged smears or wipes of our mouths on our sleeves. One man with a gloomy malformation of brow – a homicidal worker in white-lead, to judge from his blue tone of colour, and a certain flavour of paralysis pervading him – got his coat-collar between his teeth, and bit at it with an appetite. Several decent women arrived upon the outskirts of the crowd, and prepared to launch themselves into the dismal coach-house when opportunity should come, among them, a pretty young mother, pretending to bite the forefinger of her baby-boy, kept it between her rosy lips that it might be handy for guiding to point at the show. Meantime, all faces were turned towards the building, and we men waited with a fixed and stern resolution: – for the most part with folded arms. Surely, it was the only public French sight these uncommercial eyes had seen, at which the expectant people did not form *en queue*. But there was no such order of arrangement here; nothing but a general determination to make a rush for it, and a disposition to object to some boys who had mounted on the two stone posts by the hinges of the gates, with the design of swooping in when the hinges should turn.

Now, they turned, and we rushed! Great pressure, and a scream or two from the front. Then a laugh or two, some expressions of disappointment, and a slackening of the pressure and subsidence of the struggle. – Old man not there.

"But what would you have?" the Custodian reasonably argues, as he looks out at his little door. "Patience, patience! We make his toilette, gentlemen. He will be exposed presently. It is necessary to proceed according to rule. His toilette is not made all at a blow. He will be exposed in good time, gentlemen, in good time." And so retires, smoking, with a wave of his sleeveless arm towards the window, importing, "Entertain yourselves in the meanwhile with the other curiosities. Fortunately the Museum is not empty to-day."

Who would have thought of public fickleness even at the Morgue? But there it was, on that occasion. Three lately popular articles that had been attracting greatly when the litter was first descried coming dancing round the corner by the great cathedral, were so completely deposed now, that nobody save two little girls (one showing them to a doll) would look at them. Yet the chief of the three, the article in the front row, had received jagged injury of the left temple; and the other two in the back row, the drowned two lying side by side with their heads very slightly turned towards each other, seemed to be comparing notes about it. Indeed, those two of the back row were so furtive of appearance, and so (in their puffed way) assassinatingly knowing as to the one of the front, that it was hard to think the three had never come together in their lives, and were only chance companions after death. Whether or no this was the general, as it was the uncommercial, fancy, it is not to be disputed that the group had drawn exceedingly within ten minutes. Yet now, the inconstant public turned its back upon them, and even leaned its elbows carelessly against the bar outside the window and shook off the mud from its shoes, and also lent and borrowed fire for pipes.

Custodian re-enters from his door. "Again once, gentlemen, you are invited —" No further invitation necessary. Ready dash into the street. Toilette finished. Old man coming out.

This time, the interest was grown too hot to admit of toleration of the boys on the stone posts. The homicidal white-lead worker made a pounce upon one boy who was hoisting himself up, and brought him to earth amidst general commendation. Closely stowed as we were, we yet formed into groups – groups of conversation, without separation from the mass – to discuss the old man. Rivals of the tall and sallow mason sprang into being, and here again was popular inconstancy. These rivals attracted audiences, and were greedily listened to; and whereas they had derived their information solely from the tall and sallow one, officious members of the crowd now sought to enlighten *him* on their authority. Changed by this social experience into an iron-visaged and inveterate misanthrope, the mason glared at mankind, and evidently cherished in his breast the wish that the whole of the present company could change places with the deceased old man. And now listeners became inattentive, and people made a start forward at a slight sound, and an unholy fire kindled in the public eye, and those next the gates beat at them impatiently, as if they were of the cannibal species and hungry.

Again the hinges creaked, and we rushed. Disorderly pressure for some time ensued before the uncommercial unit got figured into the front row of the sum. It was strange to see so much heat and uproar seething about one poor spare white-haired old man, quiet for evermore. He was calm of feature and undisfigured, as he lay on his back – having been struck upon the hinder part of the head, and thrown forward – and something like a tear or two had started from the closed eyes, and lay wet upon the face. The uncommercial interest, sated at a glance, directed itself upon the striving crowd on either side and behind: wondering whether one might have guessed, from the expression of those faces merely, what kind of sight they were looking at. The differences of expression were not many. There was a little pity, but not much, and that mostly with a selfish touch in it – as who would say, "Shall I, poor I, look like that, when the time comes!" There was more of a secretly brooding contemplation and curiosity, as "That man I don't like, and have the grudge against; would such be his appearance, if some one – not to mention names – by any chance gave him an ugly knock?" There was a wolfish stare at the object, in which the homicidal white-lead worker shone conspicuous. And there was a much more general, purposeless, vacant staring at it – like looking at waxwork, without a catalogue, and not knowing what to make of it. But all these expressions concurred in possessing the one underlying expression of *looking at something that could not return a look*. The uncommercial notice had established this as very remarkable, when a new pressure all at once coming up from the street pinioned him ignominiously, and hurried him into the arms (now sleeved again) of the Custodian smoking at his door, and answering questions, between puffs, with a certain placid meritorious air of not being proud, though high in office. And mentioning pride, it may be observed, by the way, that one could not well help investing the original sole occupant of the front row with an air depreciatory of the legitimate attraction of the poor old man: while the two in the second row seemed to exult at this superseded popularity.

Pacing presently round the garden of the Tower of St. Jacques de la Boucherie,³ and presently again in front of the Hôtel de Ville, I called to mind a certain desolate open-air Morgue that I happened to light upon in London, one day in the hard winter of 1861, and which seemed as strange to me, at the time of seeing it, as if I had found it in China. Towards that hour of a winter's afternoon when the lamp-lighters are beginning to light the lamps in the streets a little before they are wanted, because the darkness thickens fast and soon, I was walking in from the country on the northern side of the Regent's Park – hard frozen and deserted – when I saw an empty Hansom cab drive up to the lodge at Gloucester-gate, and the driver with great agitation call to the man there: who quickly reached a long pole from a tree, and, deftly collared by the driver, jumped to the step of his little seat, and so the Hansom rattled out at the gate, galloping over the iron-bound road. I followed running, though not so fast but that when I came to the right-hand Canal Bridge, near the cross-path to Chalk Farm, the Hansom was stationary, the horse was smoking hot, the long pole was idle on the ground, and the driver and the park-keeper were looking over the bridge parapet. Looking over too, I saw, lying on the towing-path with her face turned up towards us, a woman, dead a day or two, and under thirty, as I guessed, poorly dressed in black. The feet were lightly crossed at the ankles, and the dark hair, all pushed back from the face, as though that had been the last action of her desperate hands, streamed over the ground. Dabbled all about her, was the water and the broken ice that had dropped from her dress, and had splashed as she was got out. The policeman who had just got her out, and the passing costermonger[4] who had helped him, were standing near the body; the latter with that stare at it which I have likened to being at a waxwork exhibition without a catalogue; the former, looking over his stock, with professional stiffness and coolness, in the direction in which the bearers he had sent for were expected. So dreadfully forlorn, so dreadfully sad, so dreadfully mysterious, this spectacle of our dear sister here departed! A barge came up, breaking the floating ice and the silence, and a woman steered it. The man with the horse that towed it, cared so little for the body, that the stumbling hoofs had been among the hair, and the tow-rope had caught and turned the head, before our cry of horror took him to the bridle. At which sound the steering woman looked up at us on the bridge, with contempt unutterable, and then looking down at the body with a similar expression – as if it were made in another likeness from herself, had been informed with other passions, had been lost by other chances, had had another nature dragged down to perdition – steered a spurning streak of mud at it, and passed on.

A better experience, but also of the Morgue kind, in which chance happily made me useful in a slight degree, arose to my remembrance as I took my way by the Boulevard de Sébastopol[5] to the brighter scenes of Paris.

The thing happened, say five-and-twenty years ago. I was a modest young uncommercial then, and timid and inexperienced. Many suns and winds have browned me in the line, but those were my pale days. Having newly taken the lease of a house in a certain distinguished metropolitan parish – a house which then appeared to me to be a frightfully first-class Family Mansion, involving awful responsibilities – I became the prey of a Beadle. I think the Beadle must have seen me going in or coming out, and must have observed that I tottered under the weight of my grandeur. Or he may have been in hiding under straw when I bought my first horse (in the desirable stable-yard attached to the first-class Family Mansion), and when the vendor remarked to me, in an original manner, on bringing him for approval, taking his cloth off and smacking him, "There, Sir! *There's* a Orse!" And when I said gallantly, "How much do you want for him?" and when the vendor said, "No more than sixty guineas, from you," and when I said smartly, "Why not more than sixty from *me*?" And when he said crushingly, "Because upon my soul and body he'd be considered cheap at seventy, by one who understood the subject – but you don't." – I say, the

Beadle may have been in hiding under straw, when this disgrace befell me, or he may have noted that I was too raw and young an Atlas to carry the first-class Family Mansion in a knowing manner. Be this as it may, the Beadle did what Melancholy did to the youth in Gray's Elegy[6] – he marked me for his own. And the way in which the Beadle did it, was this: he summoned me as a Juryman on his Coroner's Inquests.

In my first feverish alarm I repaired "for safety and for succour" – like those sagacious Northern shepherds who, having had no previous reason whatever to believe in young Norval,[7] very prudently did not originate the hazardous idea of believing in him – to a deep householder. This profound man informed me that the Beadle counted on my buying him off; on my bribing him not to summon me; and that if I would attend an Inquest with a cheerful countenance, and profess alacrity in that branch of my country's service, the Beadle would be disheartened, and would give up the game.

I roused my energies, and the next time the wily Beadle summoned me, I went. The Beadle was the blankest Beadle I have ever looked on when I answered to my name; and his discomfiture gave me courage to go through with it.

We were impanelled to inquire concerning the death of a very little mite of a child. It was the old miserable story. Whether the mother had committed the minor offence of concealing the birth, or whether she had committed the major offence of killing the child, was the question on which we were wanted. We must commit her on one of the two issues.

The Inquest came off in the parish workhouse, and I have yet a lively impression that I was unanimously received by my brother Jurymen as a brother of the utmost conceivable insignificance. Also, that before we began, a broker who had lately cheated me fearfully in the matter of a pair of card-tables, was for the utmost rigour of the law. I remember that we sat in a sort of board-room, on such very large square horse-hair chairs that I wondered what race of Patagonians[8] they were made for; and further, that an undertaker gave me his card when we were in the full moral freshness of having just been sworn, as "an inhabitant that was newly come into the parish, and was likely to have a young family." The case was then stated to us by the Coroner, and then we went down-stairs – led by the plotting Beadle – to view the body. From that day to this, the poor little figure, on which that sounding legal appellation was bestowed, has lain in the same place and with the same surroundings, to my thinking. In a kind of crypt devoted to the warehousing of the parochial coffins, and in the midst of a perfect Panorama of coffins of all sizes, it was stretched on a box; the mother had put it in her box – this box – almost as soon as it was born, and it had been presently found there. It had been opened, and neatly sewn up, and regarded from that point of view, it looked like a stuffed creature. It rested on a clean white cloth, with a surgical instrument or so at hand, and regarded from that point of view, it looked as if the cloth were "laid," and the Giant were coming to dinner. There was nothing repellant about the poor piece of innocence, and it demanded a mere form of looking at. So, we looked at an old pauper who was going about among the coffins with a foot rule, as if he were a case of Self-Measurement; and we looked at one another; and we said the place was well whitewashed anyhow; and then our conversational powers as a British Jury flagged, and the foreman said, "All right, gentleman? Back again, Mr. Beadle!"

The miserable young creature who had given birth to this child within a very few days, and who had cleaned the cold wet door-steps immediately afterwards, was brought before us when we resumed our horse-hair chairs, and was present during the proceedings. She had a horse-hair chair herself, being very weak and ill; and I remember how she turned to the unsympathetic nurse who attended her, and who might have been the figure-head of a pauper-ship, and how she hid her face and sobs and tears upon that wooden shoulder. I remember, too, how hard her mistress was upon her (she was a servant-of-all-work), and with what a cruel pertinacity that piece of Virtue spun her thread of evidence double, by intertwisting it with the sternest thread of construction. Smitten hard by the terrible low wail from the utterly friendless orphan girl, which never ceased during the whole inquiry, I took heart to ask this witness a question or two, which hopefully admitted of an answer that might give a favourable turn to the case. She made the turn as little favourable as it could be, but it did some good, and the Coroner, who was nobly patient and humane (he was the late Mr. Wakley), cast a look of strong encouragement in my direction. Then, we had the doctor who had made the examination, and the usual tests as to whether the child was born alive; but he was a timid muddle-headed doctor, and got confused and contradictory, and wouldn't say this, and couldn't answer for that, and the immaculate broker was too much for him, and our side slid back again. However, I tried again, and the Coroner backed me again, for which I ever afterwards felt grateful to him as I do now to his memory; and we got another favourable turn, out of some other witness, some member of the family with a strong prepossession against the sinner; and I think we had the doctor back again; and I know that the Coroner summed up for our side, and that I and my British brothers turned round to discuss our verdict, and get ourselves into great difficulties with our large chairs and the broker. At that stage of the case I tried hard again, being convinced that I had cause for it; and at last we found for the minor offence of only concealing the birth; and the poor desolate creature, who had been taken out during our deliberation, being brought in again to be told of the verdict, then dropped upon her knees before us, with protestations that we were right – protestations among the most affecting that I have ever heard in my life – and was carried away insensible.

(In private conversation after this was all over, the Coroner showed me his reasons as a trained surgeon, for perceiving it to be impossible that the child could, under the most favourable circumstances, have drawn many breaths, in the very doubtful case of its having ever breathed at all; this, owing to the discovery of some foreign matter in the wind-pipe, quite irreconcilable with many moments of life.)

When the agonised girl had made those final protestations, I had seen her face, and it was in unison with her distracted heartbroken voice, and it was very moving. It certainly did not impress me by any beauty that it had, and if I ever see it again in another world I shall only know it by the help of some new sense or intelligence. But it came to me in my sleep that night, and I selfishly dismissed it in the most efficient way I could think of. I caused some extra care to be taken of her in the prison, and counsel to be retained for her defence when she was tried at the Old Bailey; and her sentence was lenient, and her history and conduct proved that it was right. In doing the little I did for her, I remember to have had the kind help of some gentle-hearted functionary to whom I addressed myself – but what functionary I have long forgotten – who I suppose was officially present at the Inquest.

I regard this as a very notable uncommercial experience, because this good came of a Beadle. And to the best of my knowledge, information, and belief, it is the only good that ever did come of a Beadle since the first Beadle put on his cocked-hat.

Birthday Celebrations

First published in *All the Year Round*, 6 June 1863. The text is taken from *The Uncommercial Traveller*.

It came into my mind that I would recall in these notes a few of the many hostelries I have rested at in the course of my journeys; and, indeed, I had taken up my pen for the purpose, when I was baffled by an accidental circumstance. It was the having to leave off, to wish the owner of a certain bright face that looked in at my door, "many happy returns of the day." Thereupon a new thought came into my mind, driving its predecessor out, and I began to recall – instead of Inns – the birthdays that I have put up at, on my way to this present sheet of paper.

I can very well remember being taken out to visit some peach-faced creature in a blue sash, and shoes to correspond, whose life I supposed to consist entirely of birthdays. Upon seed-cake, sweet wine, and shining presents, that glorified young person seemed to me to be exclusively reared. At so early a stage of my travels did I assist at the anniversary of her nativity (and become enamoured of her), that I had not yet acquired the recondite knowledge that a birthday is the common property of all who are born, but supposed it to be a special gift bestowed by the favouring Heavens on that one distinguished infant. There was no other company, and we sat in a shady bower – under a table, as my better (or worse) knowledge leads me to believe – and were regaled with saccharine substances and liquids, until it was time to part. A bitter powder was administered to me next morning, and I was wretched. On the whole, a pretty accurate foreshadowing of my more mature experiences in such wise!

Then came the time when, inseparable from one's own birthday, was a certain sense of merit, a consciousness of well-earned distinction. When I regarded my birthday as a graceful achievement of my own, a monument of my perseverance, independence, and good sense, redounding greatly to my honour. This was at about the period when Olympia Squires became involved in the anniversary. Olympia was most beautiful (of course), and I loved her to that degree, that I used to be obliged to get out of my little bed in the night, expressly to exclaim to Solitude, "O, Olympia Squires!" Visions of Olympia, clothed entirely in sage-green, from which I infer a defectively educated taste on the part of her respected parents, who were necessarily unacquainted with the South Kensington Museum, still arise before me. Truth is sacred, and the visions are crowned by a shining white beaver bonnet, impossibly suggestive of a little feminine postboy. My memory presents a birthday when Olympia and I were taken by an unfeeling relative – some cruel uncle, or the like – to a slow torture called an Orrery.[1] The terrible instrument was set up at the local Theatre, and I had expressed a profane wish in the morning that it was a Play: for which a serious aunt had probed my conscience deep, and my pocket deeper, by reclaiming a bestowed half-crown. It was a venerable and a shabby Orrery, at least one thousand stars and twenty-five comets behind the age. Nevertheless, it was awful. When the low-spirited gentleman with a wand said, "Ladies and gentlemen" (meaning particularly Olympia and me), "the lights are about to be put out, but there is not the slightest cause for alarm," it was very alarming. Then the planets and stars began. Sometimes they wouldn't come on, sometimes they wouldn't go off, sometimes they had holes in them, and mostly they didn't seem to be good likenesses. All this time the gentleman with the wand was going on in the dark (tapping away at the heavenly bodies between whiles, like a wearisome woodpecker), about a sphere revolving on its own axis eight hundred and ninety-seven thousand millions of times – or miles – in two hundred and sixty-three thousand five hundred and twenty-four millions of something elses, until I thought if this was a birthday it were better never to have been born. Olympia, also, became much depressed, and we both slumbered and woke cross, and still the gentleman was going on in the dark – whether up in the stars, or down on the stage, it would have been hard to make out, if it had been worth trying – cyphering away about planes of orbits, to such an infamous extent that Olympia, stung to madness, actually kicked me. A pretty birthday spectacle, when the lights were turned up again, and all the schools in the town (including the National, who had come in for nothing, and serve them right, for they were always throwing stones) were discovered with exhausted countenances, screwing their knuckles into their eyes, or clutching their heads of hair. A pretty birthday speech when Dr. Sleek of the City-Free bobbed up his powdered head in the stage-box, and said that before this assembly dispersed he really must beg to express his entire approval of a lecture as improving, as informing, as devoid of anything that could call a blush into the cheek of youth, as any it had ever been his lot to hear delivered. A pretty birthday altogether, when Astronomy couldn't leave poor Small Olympia Squires and me alone, but must put an end to our loves! For, we never got over it; the threadbare Orrery outwore our mutual tenderness; the man with the wand was too much for the boy with the bow. •

When shall I disconnect the combined smells of oranges, brown paper, and straw, from those other birthdays at school, when the coming hamper casts its shadow before, and when a week of social harmony – shall I add of admiring and affectionate popularity – led up to that Institution? What noble sentiments were expressed to me in the days before the hamper, what vows of friendship were sworn to me, what exceedingly old knives were given me, what generous avowals of having been in the wrong emanated from else obstinate spirits once enrolled among my enemies! The birthday of the potted game and guava jelly, is still made special to me by the noble conduct of Bully Globson. Letters from home had mysteriously inquired whether I should be much surprised and disappointed if among the treasures in the coming hamper I discovered potted game, and guava jelly from the Western Indies. I had mentioned those hints in confidence to a few friends, and had promised to give away, as I now see reason to believe, a handsome covey of partridges potted, and about a hundredweight of guava jelly. It was now that Globson, Bully no more, sought me out in the playground. He was a big fat boy, with a big fat head and a big fat fist, and at the beginning of that Half had raised such a bump on my forehead that I couldn't get my hat of state on, to go to church. He said that after an interval of cool reflection (four months) he now felt this blow to have been an error of judgment, and that he wished to apologise for the same. Not only that, but holding down his big head between his two big hands in order that I might reach it conveniently, he requested me, as an act of justice which would appease his awakened conscience, to raise a retributive bump upon it, in the presence of witnesses. This handsome proposal I modestly declined, and he then embraced me, and we walked away conversing. We conversed respecting the West India Islands, and, in the pursuit of knowledge he asked me with much interest whether in the course of my reading I had met with any reliable description of the mode of manufacturing guava jelly; or whether I had ever happened to taste that conserve, which he had been given to understand was of rare excellence.

Seventeen, eighteen, nineteen, twenty; and then with the waning months came an ever augmenting sense of the dignity of twenty-one. Heaven knows I had nothing to "come into," save the bare birthday, and yet I esteemed it as a great possession. I now and then paved the way to my state of dignity, by beginning a proposition with the casual words, "say that a man of twenty-one," or by the incidental assumption of a fact that could not sanely be disputed, as, "for when a fellow comes to be a man of twenty-one." I gave a party on the occasion. She was there. It is unnecessary to name

Her more particularly; She was older than I, and had pervaded every chink and crevice of my mind for three or four years. I had held volumes of Imaginary Conversations with her mother on the subject of our union, and I had written letters more in number than Horace Walpole's,[2] to that discreet woman, soliciting her daughter's hand in marriage. I had never had the remotest intention of sending any of those letters; but to write them, and after a few days tear them up, had been a sublime occupation. Sometimes, I had begun "Honoured Madam. I think that a lady gifted with those powers of observation which I know you to possess, and endowed with those womanly sympathies with the young and ardent which it were more than heresy to doubt, can scarcely have failed to discover that I love your adorable daughter, deeply, devotedly." In less buoyant states of mind I had begun, "Bear with me, Dear Madam, bear with a daring wretch who is about to make a surprising confession to you, wholly unanticipated by yourself, and which he beseeches you to commit to the flames as soon as you have become aware to what a towering height his mad ambition soars." At other times – periods of profound mental depression, when She had gone out to balls where I was not – the draft took the affecting form of a paper to be left on my table after my departure to the confines of the globe. As thus: "For Mrs. Onowenever, these lines when the hand that traces them shall be far away. I could not bear the daily torture of hopelessly loving the dear one whom I will not name. Broiling on the coast of Africa, or congealing on the shores of Greenland, I am far far better there than here." (In this sentiment my cooler judgment perceives that the family of the beloved object would have most completely concurred.) "If I ever emerge from obscurity, and my name is ever heralded by Fame, it will be for her dear sake. If I ever amass Gold, it will be to pour it at her feet. Should I on the other hand become the prey of Ravens —" I doubt if I ever quite made up my mind what was to be done in that affecting case; I tried "then it is better so;" but not feeling convinced that it would be better so, I vacillated between leaving all else blank, which looked expressive and bleak, or winding up with "Farewell!"

This fictitious correspondence of mine is to blame for the foregoing digression. I was about to pursue the statement that on my twenty-first birthday I gave a party, and She was there. It was a beautiful party. There was not a single animate or inanimate object connected with it (except the company and myself) that I had ever seen before. Everything was hired, and the mercenaries in attendance were profound strangers to me. Behind a door, in the crumby part of the night when wine-glasses were to be found in unexpected spots, I spoke to Her – spoke out to Her. What passed, I cannot as a man of honour reveal. She was all angelical gentleness, but a word was mentioned – a short and dreadful word of three letters, beginning with a B – which, as I remarked at the moment, "scorched my brain." She went away soon afterwards, and when the hollow throng (though to be sure it was no fault of theirs) dispersed, I issued forth, with a dissipated scorner, and, as I mentioned expressly to him, "sought oblivion." It was found, with a dreadful headache in it, but it didn't last; for, in the shaming light of next day's noon, I raised my heavy head in bed, looking back to the birthdays behind me, and tracking the circle by which I had got round, after all, to the bitter powder and the wretchedness again.

This reactionary powder (taken so largely by the human race, I am inclined to regard it as the Universal Medicine once sought for in Laboratories) is capable of being made up in another form for birthday use. Anybody's long-lost brother will do ill to turn up on a birthday. If I had a long-lost brother I should know beforehand that he would prove a tremendous fraternal failure if he appointed to rush into my arms on my birthday. The first Magic Lantern I ever saw, was secretly and elaborately planned to be the great effect of a very juvenile birthday; but it wouldn't act, and its images were dim. My experience of adult birthday Magic Lanterns may possibly have been unfortunate, but has certainly been similar. I have an illustrative birthday in my eye: a birthday of my friend Flipfield, whose birthdays had long been remarkable as social successes. There had been nothing set or formal about them; Flipfield having been accustomed merely to say, two or three days before, "Don't forget to come and dine, old boy, according to custom;" – I don't know what he said to the ladies he invited, but I may safely assume it *not* to have been "old girl." Those were delightful gatherings, and were enjoyed by all participators. In an evil hour, a long-lost brother of Flipfield's came to light in foreign parts. Where he had been hidden, or what he had been doing, I don't know, for Flipfield vaguely informed me that he had turned up "on the banks of the Ganges" – speaking of him as if he had been washed ashore. The Long-lost was coming home, and Flipfield made an unfortunate calculation, based on the well-known regularity of the P. and O. Steamers,[3] that matters might be so contrived as that the Long-lost should appear in the nick of time on his (Flipfield's) birthday. Delicacy commanded that I should repress the gloomy anticipations with which my soul became fraught when I heard of this plan. The fatal day arrived, and we assembled in force. Mrs. Flipfield senior formed an interesting feature in the group, with a blue-veined miniature of the late Mr. Flipfield round her neck, in an oval, resembling a tart from the pastrycook's: his hair powdered, and the bright buttons on his coat, evidently very like. She was accompanied by Miss Flipfield, the eldest of her numerous family, who held her pocket-handkerchief to her bosom in a majestic manner, and spoke to all of us (none of us had ever seen her before), in pious and condoning tones, of all the quarrels that had taken place in the family, from her infancy – which must have been a long time ago – down to that hour. The Long-lost did not appear. Dinner, half an hour later than usual, was announced, and still no Long-lost. We sat down to table. The knife and fork of the Long-lost made a vacuum in Nature, and when the champagne came round for the first time, Flipfield gave him up for the day, and had them removed. It was then that the Long-lost gained the height of his popularity with the company; for my own part, I felt convinced that I loved him dearly. Flipfield's dinners are perfect, and he is the easiest and best of entertainers. Dinner went on brilliantly, and the more the Long-lost didn't come, the more comfortable we grew, and the more highly we thought of him. Flipfield's own man (who has a regard for me) was in the act of struggling with an ignorant stipendiary, to wrest from him the wooden leg of a Guinea-fowl which he was pressing on my acceptance, and to substitute a slice of the breast, when a ringing at the door-bell suspended the strife. I looked round me, and perceived the sudden pallor which I knew my own visage revealed, reflected in the faces of the company. Flipfield hurriedly excused himself, went out, was absent for about a minute or two, and then re-entered with the Long-lost.

I beg to say distinctly that if the stranger had brought Mont Blanc with him, or had come attended by a retinue of eternal snows, he could not have chilled the circle to the marrow in a more efficient manner. Embodied Failure sat enthroned upon the Long-lost's brow, and pervaded him to his Long-lost boots. In vain Mrs. Flipfield senior, opening her arms, exclaimed, "My Tom!" and pressed his nose against the counterfeit presentment of his other parent. In vain Miss Flipfield, in the first transports of this reunion, showed him a dint upon her maidenly cheek, and asked him if he remembered when he did that with the bellows? We, the bystanders, were overcome, but overcome by the palpable, undisguisable, utter, and total breakdown of the Long-lost. Nothing he could have done would have set him right with us but his instant return to the Ganges. In the very same moments it became established that the feeling was reciprocal, and that the Long-lost detested us. When a friend of the family (not myself, upon my honour), wishing to set things going again, asked him, while he partook of soup – asked him with an amiability of intention beyond all praise, but with a weakness of execution open to defeat – what kind of river he considered the Ganges, the Long-lost, scowling at the friend of the family over his spoon, as one of an abhorrent race, replied, "Why a river of water, I suppose," and spooned his soup into himself with a malignancy of hand and eye that blighted the amiable questioner. Not an opinion could be elicited from the Long-lost, in unison with the sentiments of any individual present. He contradicted Flipfield dead, before he had eaten his salmon. He had no idea – or affected to have no idea – that it was his brother's birthday, and on the communication of that interesting fact to him, merely wanted to make him out four years older than he was. He was an antipathetical being, with a peculiar power and gift of treading on everybody's tenderest place. They talk in America of a man's "Platform." I should describe the Platform of the Long-lost as a Platform composed of other people's corns, on which he had stumped his way, with all his might and main, to his present position. It is needless to add that Flipfield's great birthday went by the board, and that he was a wreck when I pretended at parting to wish him many happy returns of it.

There is another class of birthdays at which I have so frequently assisted, that I may assume such birthdays to be pretty well known to the human race. My friend Mayday's birthday is an example. The guests have no knowledge of one another except on that one day in the year, and are annually terrified for a week by the prospect of meeting one another again. There is a fiction among us that we have uncommon reasons for being particularly lively and spirited on the occasion, whereas deep despondency is no phrase for the expression of our feelings. But the wonderful feature of the case is, that we are in tacit accordance to avoid the subject – to keep it as far off as possible, as long as possible – and to talk about anything else, rather than the joyful event. I may even go so far as to assert that there is a dumb compact among us that we will pretend that it is NOT Mayday's birthday. A mysterious and gloomy Being, who is said to have gone to school with Mayday, and who is so lank and lean that he seriously impugns the Dietary of the establishment at which they were jointly educated, always leads us, as I may say, to the block, by laying his grisly hand on a decanter and begging us to fill our glasses. The devices and pretences that I have seen put in practice to defer the fatal moment, and to interpose between this man and his purpose, are innumerable. I have known desperate guests, when they saw the grisly hand approaching the decanter, wildly to begin, without any antecedent whatsoever, "That reminds me —" and to plunge into long stories. When at last the hand and the decanter come together, a shudder, a palpable perceptible shudder, goes round the table. We receive the reminder that it is Mayday's birthday, as if it were the anniversary of some profound disgrace he had undergone, and we sought to comfort him. And when we have drunk Mayday's health, and wished him many happy returns, we are seized for some moments with a ghastly blitheness, an unnatural levity, as if we were in the first flushed reaction of having undergone a surgical operation.

Birthdays of this species have a public as well as a private phase. My "boyhood's home," Dullborough,[4] presents a case in point. An Immortal Somebody was wanted in Dullborough, to dimple for a day the stagnant face of the waters; he was rather wanted by Dullborough generally, and much wanted by the principal hotel-keeper. The County history was looked up for a locally Immortal Somebody, but the registered Dullborough worthies were all Nobodies. In this state of things, it is hardly necessary to record that Dullborough did what every man does when he wants to write a book or deliver a lecture, and is provided with all the materials except a subject. It fell back upon Shakespeare.

No sooner was it resolved to celebrate Shakespeare's birthday in Dullborough, than the popularity of the immortal bard became surprising. You might have supposed the first edition of his works to have been published last week, and enthusiastic Dullborough to have got half through them. (I doubt, by the way, whether it had ever done half that, but this is a private opinion.) A young gentleman with a sonnet, the retention of which for two years had enfeebled his mind and undermined his knees, got the sonnet into the Dullborough Warden, and gained flesh. Portraits of Shakespeare broke out in the bookshop windows, and our principal artist painted a large original portrait in oils for the decoration of the dining-room. It was not in the least like any of the other portraits, and was exceedingly admired, the head being much swollen. At the Institution, the Debating Society discussed the new question, Was there sufficient ground for supposing that the Immortal Shakespeare ever stole deer?[5] This was indignantly decided by an overwhelming majority in the negative; indeed, there was but one vote on the Poaching side, and that was the vote of the orator who had undertaken to advocate it, and who became quite an obnoxious character – particularly to the Dullborough "roughs," who were about as well informed on the matter as most other people. Distinguished speakers were invited down, and very nearly came (but not quite). Subscriptions were opened, and committees sat, and it would have been far from a popular measure in the height of the excitement, to have told Dullborough that it wasn't Stratford-upon-Avon. Yet, after all these preparations, when the great festivity took place, and the portrait, elevated aloft, surveyed the company as if it were in danger of springing a mine of intellect and blowing itself up, it did undoubtedly happen, according to the inscrutable mysteries of things, that nobody could be induced, not to say to touch upon Shakespeare, but to come within a mile of him, until the crack speaker of Dullborough rose to propose the immortal memory. Which he did with the perplexing and astonishing result that before he had repeated the great name half-a-dozen times, or had been upon his legs as many minutes, he was assailed with a general shout of "Question."

TRAVELLING ABROAD

A Narrative of Extraordinary Suffering

First published in *Household Words*, 12 July 1851, from which this text is reproduced.

A gentleman of credit and of average ability, whose name we have permission to publish – Mr. Lost, of the Maze, Ware[1] – was recently desirous to make a certain journey in England. Previous to entering on this excursion, which we believe had a commercial object (though Mr. Lost has for some years retired from business as a Woolstapler, having been succeeded in 1831 by his son who now carries on the firm of Lost and Lost, in the old-established premises at Stratford on Avon, Warwickshire, where it may be interesting to our readers to know that he married, in 1834, a Miss Shakespeare, supposed to be a lineal descendant of the immortal bard), it was necessary that Mr. Lost should come to London, to adjust some unsettled accounts with a merchant in the Borough, arising out of a transaction in Hops. His Diary originating on the day previous to his leaving home is before us, and we shall present its rather voluminous information to our readers in a condensed form: endeavouring to extract its essence only.

It would appear that Mrs. Lost had a decided objection to her husband's undertaking the journey in question. She observed, "that he had much better stay at home, and not go and make a fool of himself" – which she seems to have had a strong presentiment that he would ultimately do. A young person in their employ as confidential domestic, also protested against his intention, remarking "that Master warn't the man as was fit for Railways, and Railways warn't the spearses as was fit for Master." Mr. Lost, however, adhering to his purpose, in spite of these dissuasions, Mrs. Lost made no effort (as she might easily have done with perfect success) to restrain him by force. But, she stipulated with Mr. Lost, that he should purchase an Assurance Ticket of the Railway Passengers' Assurance Company, entitling his representatives to three thousand pounds in case of the worst. It was also understood that in the event of his failing to write home by any single night's post, he would be advertised in the *Times*, at full length, next day.

These satisfactory preliminaries concluded, Mr. Lost sent out the confidential domestic (Mary Anne Mag by name, and born of poor but honest parents) to purchase a Railway Guide. This document was the first shock in connection with his extraordinary journey which Mr. Lost and family received. For, on referring to the Index, to ascertain how Ware stood in reference to the Railways of the United Kingdom and the Principality of Wales they encountered the following mysterious characters:—

WARE TU 6

No farther information could be obtained. They thought of page six, but there was no such page in the book, which had the sportive eccentricity of beginning at page eight. In desperate remembrance of the dark monosyllable TU, they turned to the "classification of Railways," but found nothing there under the letter T except "Taff Vale and Aberdare" – and who (as the confidential domestic said) could ever want *them*! Mr. Lost has placed it on record that his "brain reeled" when he glanced down the page, and found himself, in search of Ware, wandering among such names as Ravenglass, Bootle, and Sprouston.[2]

Reduced to the necessity of proceeding to London by turnpike-road, Mr. Lost made the best of his way to the metropolis in his own one-horse chaise, which he then dismissed in charge of his man, George Flay, who had accompanied him for that purpose. Proceeding to Southwark, he had the satisfaction of finding that the total of his loss upon the Hop transaction did not exceed three hundred and forty-seven pounds, four shillings, and twopence halfpenny. This, he justly regarded as, on the whole, a success for an amateur in that promising branch of speculation; in commemoration of his good fortune, he gave a plain but substantial dinner to the Hop Merchant and two friends at Tom's Coffee House on Ludgate Hill.

He did not sleep at that house of entertainment, but repaired in a hackney cab (No. 482) to the Euston Hotel, adjoining the terminus of the North-Western Railway. On the following morning his remarkable adventures may be considered to have commenced.

It appears that with a view to the farther prosecution of his contemplated journey, it was, in the first place, necessary for Mr. Lost to make for the ancient city of Worcester. Knowing that place to be attainable by way of Birmingham, he started by the train at eleven o'clock in the forenoon, and proceeded, pleasantly and at an even pace, to Leighton. Here he found, to his great amazement, a powerful black bar drawn across the road, hopelessly impeding his progress!

After some consideration, during which, as he informs us, his "brain reeled" again, Mr. Lost returned to London. Having partaken of some refreshment, and endeavoured to compose his mind with sleep (from which, however, he describes himself to have derived but little comfort, in consequence of being fitfully pursued by the mystic signs WARE TU 6), he awoke unrefreshed, and at five minutes past five in the afternoon once again set forth in quest of Birmingham. But now, he was even less fortunate than in the morning; for, on arriving at Tring, some ten miles short of his former place of stoppage, he suddenly found the dreaded black barrier across the road, and was thus warned by an insane voice, which seemed to have something supernatural in its awful sound. "RUGBY TO LEICESTER, NOTTINGHAM, AND DERBY!"

With the spirit of an Englishman, Mr. Lost absolutely refused to proceed to either of those towns. If such were the meaning of the voice, it fell powerless upon him. Why should he go to Leicester, Nottingham, and Derby; and what right had Rugby to interfere with him at Tring? He again returned to London, and, fearing that his mind was going, took the precaution of being bled.

When he arose on the following morning, it was with a haggard countenance, on which the most indifferent observer might have seen the traces of a corroding anxiety, and where the practised eye might have easily detected what was really wrong within. Even conscience does not sear like mystery. Where now were the glowing cheek, the double chin, the mellow nose, the dancing eye? Fled. And in their place —

In the silent watches of the night, he had formed the resolution of endeavouring to reach the object of his pursuit, by Gloucester, on the Great-Western Railway. Leaving London once more, this time at half an hour after twelve at noon, he proceeded to Swindon Junction. Not without difficulty. For, at Didcot, he again found the black barrier across the road, and was violently conducted to seven places, with none of which he had the least concern – in particular, to one dreadful spot with the savage appellation of Aynho.[3] But, escaping from these hostile towns after undergoing a variety of hardships, he arrived (as has been said) at Swindon Junction.

Here, all hope appeared to desert him. It was evident that the whole country was in a state of barricade, and that the insurgents (whoever they were) had taken their measures but too well. His imprisonment was of the severest kind. Tortures were applied, to induce him to go to Bath, to Bristol, Yatton, Clevedon Junction, Weston-super-Mare Junction, Exeter, Torquay, Plymouth, Falmouth, and the remotest fastnesses of West Cornwall. No chance of Gloucester was held out to him for a moment. Remaining firm, however, and watching his opportunity, he at length escaped – more by the aid of good fortune, he considers, than through his own exertions –

and sliding underneath the dreaded barrier, departed by way of Cheltenham for Gloucester.

And now indeed he might have thought that after combating with so many obstacles, and undergoing perils so extreme, his way at length lay clear before him, and a ray of sunshine fell upon his dismal path. The delusive hope, if any such were entertained by the forlorn man, was soon dispelled. It was his horrible fate to depart from Cirencester exactly an hour before he arrived there, and to leave Gloucester ten minutes before he got to it!

It were vain to endeavour to describe the condition to which Mr. Lost was reduced by this overwhelming culmination of his many hardships. It had been no light shock to find his native country in the hands of a nameless foe, cutting off the communication between one town and another, and carrying out a system of barricade, little if at all inferior, in strength and skill, to the fortification of Gibraltar. It had been no light shock to be addressed by maniac voices urging him to fly to various remote parts of the kingdom. But, this tremendous blow, the annihilation of time, the stupendous reversal of the natural sequence and order of things, was too much for his endurance – too much, perhaps for the endurance of humanity. He quailed beneath it, and became insensible.

When consciousness returned, he found himself again on the North-Western line of Railway, listlessly travelling anywhere. He remembers, he says, Four Ashes, Spread Eagle, and Penkridge.[4] They were black, he thinks, and coaly. He had no business there; he didn't care whether he was there or not. He knew where he wanted to go, and he knew he couldn't go where he wanted. He was taken to Manchester, Bangor, Liverpool, Windermere, Dundee and Montrose, Edinburgh and Glasgow. He repeatedly found himself in the Isle of Man; believes he was, several times, all over Wales; knows he was at Kingstown and Dublin, but has only a general idea how he got there. Once, when he thought he was going his own way at last, he was dropped at a North Staffordshire Station called (he thinks in mockery) Mow Cop. As a general rule he observed that whatsoever divergence he made, he came to Edinburgh. But, there were exceptions – as when he was set down on the extreme verge of land at Holyhead, or put aboard a Steamboat, and carried by way of Paris into the heart of France. He thinks the most remarkable journey he was made to take, was from Euston Square into Northamptonshire; so, by the fens of Lincolnshire round to Rugby; thence, through the whole of the North of England and a considerable part of Scotland, to Liverpool; thence, to Douglas in the Isle of Man; and back, by way of Ireland, Wales, Great Yarmouth, and Bishop

Stortford, to Windsor Castle. Throughout the whole of these travels, he observed the black-barrier system in active operation, and was always stopped when he least expected it. He invariably travelled against his will, and found a code of cabalistic signs in use all over the country.

Anxiety and disappointment had now produced their natural results. His face was wan, his voice much weakened, his hair scanty and grey, the whole man expressive of fatigue and endurance. It is an affecting instance of the influence of uneasiness and depression on the mind of Mr. Lost, that he now commenced wildly to seek the object of his journey in the strangest directions. Abandoning the Railroads on which he had undergone so much, he began to institute a feverish inquiry for it among a host of boarding-houses and hotels. "Bed, breakfast, boots, and attendance, two and sixpence per day." – "Bed and boots, seven shillings per week." – "Wines and spirits of the choicest quality." – "Night Porter in constant attendance." – "For night arrivals, ring the private door bell." – "Omnibuses to and from all parts of London, every minute." – "Do not confound this house with any other of the same name." Among such addresses to the public, did Mr. Lost now seek for a way to Worcester. As he might have anticipated – as he *did* anticipate in fact, for he was hopeless now – it was not to be found there. His intellect was greatly shaken.

Mr. Lost has left, in his Diary, a record so minute of the gradual deadening of his intelligence and benumbing of his faculties, that he can be followed downward, as it were step by step. Thus, we find that when he had exhausted the boarding-houses and hotels, family, commercial and otherwise (in which he found his intellect much enfeebled by the constant recurrence of the hieroglyphic "1–6–51–W. J. A."), he addressed himself, with the same dismal object, to Messrs. Moses and Son,[5] and to Mr. Medwin, bootmaker to His Royal Highness Prince Albert. After them, even to inanimate things, as the Patent Compendium Portmanteau, the improved Chaff Machines and Corn Crushers, the Norman Razor, the Bank of England Sealing Wax, Schweppe's Soda Water, the Extract of Sarsaparilla, the Registered Paletot, Rowlands' Kalydor, the Cycloidal Parasol, the Cough Lozenges, the universal night-light, the poncho, Allsopp's pale ale, and the patent knife-cleaner. Failing, naturally, in all these appeals, and in a final address to His Grace the Duke of Wellington in the gentlemanly summer garment, and to Mr. Burton of the General Furnishing Ironmongery Warehouse, he sank into a stupor, and abandoned hope.

Mr. Lost is now a ruin. He is at the Euston Square Hotel. When advised to return home he merely shakes his head and mutters "Ware Tu . . 6." No Cabman can be found who will take charge of him on those instructions.

He sits continually turning over the leaves of a small, dog's-eared quarto volume with a yellow cover, and babbling in a plaintive voice, "BRADSHAW, BRADSHAW."[6]

A few days since, Mrs. Lost, having been cautiously made acquainted with his condition, arrived at the hotel, accompanied by the confidential domestic. The first words of the heroic woman were:

"John Lost, don't make a spectacle of yourself, don't. Who am I?" He replied "BRADSHAW."

"John Lost," said Mrs. Lost, "I have no patience with you. Where have you been to?"

Fluttering the leaves of the book, he answered "To BRADSHAW."

"Stuff and nonsense you tiresome man," said Mrs. Lost. "You put me out of patience. What on earth has brought you to this stupid state?"

He feebly answered, "BRADSHAW."

No one knows what he means.

Our Watering-Place[1]

First published in *Household Words*, 2 August 1851, and then included in *Reprinted Pieces* from which this text is reproduced. Dickens wrote to Wills, 27 July 1851: 'I am glad you liked the Watering Place so much. It pleased me exceedingly.' The piece was widely quoted in the press, including *The Times*, 5 August 1851.

In the Autumn-time of the year, when the great metropolis is so much hotter, so much noisier, so much more dusty or so much more water-carted, so much more crowded, so much more disturbing and distracting in all respects, than it usually is, a quiet sea-beach becomes indeed a blessed spot. Half awake and half asleep, this idle morning in our sunny window on the edge of a chalk-cliff in the old-fashioned watering-place to which we are a faithful resorter, we feel a lazy inclination to sketch its picture.

The place seems to respond. Sky, sea, beach, and village, lie as still before us as if they were sitting for the picture. It is dead low-water. A ripple plays among the ripening corn upon the cliff, as if it were faintly trying from recollection to imitate the sea; and the world of butterflies hovering over the crop of radish-seed are as restless in their little way as the gulls are in their larger manner when the wind blows. But the ocean lies winking in the sunlight like a drowsy lion – its glassy waters scarcely curve upon the shore – the fishing-boats in the tiny harbour are all stranded in the mud – our two colliers (our watering-place has a maritime trade employing that amount of shipping) have not an inch of water within a quarter of a mile of them, and turn, exhausted, on their sides, like faint fish of an antediluvian species. Rusty cables and chains, ropes and rings, undermost parts of posts and piles and confused timber-defences against the waves, lie strewn about, in a brown litter of tangled sea-weed and fallen cliff which looks as if a family of giants had been making tea here for ages, and had observed an untidy custom of throwing their tea-leaves on the shore.

In truth, our watering-place itself has been left somewhat high and dry by the tide of years. Concerned as we are for its honour, we must reluctantly admit that the time when this pretty little semi-circular sweep of houses tapering off at the end of the wooden pier into a point in the sea, was a gay place, and when the lighthouse overlooking it shone at daybreak on company dispersing from public balls, is but dimly traditional now. There is a bleak chamber in our watering-place which is yet called the Assembly "Rooms," and understood to be available on hire for balls or concerts; and, some few seasons since, an ancient little gentleman came down and stayed at the hotel, who said that he had danced there, in bygone ages, with the Honourable Miss Peepy, well known to have been the Beauty of her day and the cruel occasion of innumerable duels. But he was so old and shrivelled, and so very rheumatic in the legs, that it demanded more imagination than our watering-place can usually muster, to believe him; therefore, except the Master of the "Rooms" (who to this hour wears knee-breeches, and who confirmed the statement with tears in his eyes), nobody did believe in the little lame old gentleman, or even in the Honourable Miss Peepy, long deceased.

As to subscription balls in the Assembly Rooms of our watering-place now red-hot cannon balls are less improbable. Sometimes, a misguided wanderer of a Ventriloquist, or an Infant Phenomenon, or a Juggler, or somebody with an Orrery that is several stars behind the time, takes the place for a night, and issues bills with the name of his last town lined out, and the name of ours ignominiously written in, but you may be sure this never happens twice to the same unfortunate person. On such occasions the discoloured old Billiard Table that is seldom played at (unless the ghost of the Honourable Miss Peepy plays at pool with other ghosts) is pushed into a corner, and benches are solemnly constituted into front seats, back seats, and reserved seats – which are much the same after you have paid – and a few dull candles are lighted – wind permitting – and the performer and the scanty audience play out a short match which shall make the other most low-spirited – which is usually a drawn game. After that the performer instantly departs with maledictory expressions, and is never heard of more.

But the most wonderful feature of our Assembly Rooms, is, that an annual sale of "Fancy and other China," is announced here with mysterious constancy and perseverance. Where the china comes from, where it goes to, why it is annually put up to auction when nobody ever thinks of bidding for it, how it comes to pass that it is always the same china, whether it would not have been cheaper, with the sea at hand, to have thrown it away, say in eighteen hundred and thirty, are standing enigmas. Every year the bills come out, every year the Master of the Rooms gets into a little pulpit on a table, and offers it for sale, every year nobody buys it, every year it is put away somewhere till next year, when it appears again as if the whole thing were a new idea. We have a faint remembrance of an unearthly collection of clocks, purporting to be the work of Parisian and Genovese artists – chiefly bilious-faced clocks, supported on sickly white crutches, with their pendulums dangling like lame legs – to which a similar course of events occurred for several years, until they seemed to lapse away, of mere imbecility.

Attached to our Assembly Rooms is a library. There is a wheel of fortune in it, but it is rusty and dusty, and never turns. A large doll, with moveable eyes, was put up to be raffled for, by five-and-twenty members at two shillings, seven years ago this autumn, and the list is not full yet. We are rather sanguine, now, that the raffle will come off next year. We think so, because we only want nine members, and should only want eight, but for number two having grown up since her name was entered, and withdrawn it when she was married. Down the street, there is a toy-ship of considerable burden, in the same condition. Two of the boys who were entered for that raffle have gone to India in real ships, since; and one was shot, and died in the arms of his sister's lover, by whom he sent his last words home.

This is the library for the Minerva Press.[2] If you want that kind of reading, come to our watering-place. The leaves of the romances, reduced to a condition very like curl-paper, are thickly studded with notes in pencil: sometimes complimentary, sometimes jocose. Some of these commentators, like commentators in a more extensive way, quarrel with one another. One young gentleman who sarcastically writes "Oh!!!" after every sentimental passage, is pursued through his literary career by another, who writes "Insulting Beast!" Miss Julia Mills has read the whole collection of these books.[3] She has left marginal notes on the pages, as "Is not this truly touching? J. M." "How thrilling! J. M." "Entranced here by the Magician's potent spell. J. M." She has also italicised her favourite traits in the description of the hero, as "his hair, which was *dark* and *wavy*, clustered in *rich profusion* around a *marble brow*, whose lofty paleness bespoke the intellect within." It reminds her of another hero. She adds, "How like B. L. Can this be mere coincidence? J. M."

You would hardly guess which is the main street of our watering-place, but you may know it by its being always stopped up with donkey-chaises. Whenever you come here, and see harnessed donkeys eating clover out of barrows drawn completely across a narrow thoroughfare, you may be quite sure you are in our High Street. Our Police you may know by his uniform, likewise by his never on any account interfering with anybody – especially the tramps and vagabonds. In our fancy shops we have a capital collection of damaged goods, among which the flies of countless summers "have been roaming."[4] We are great in obsolete seals, and in faded pin-cushions, and in rickety camp-stools, and in exploded cutlery, and in miniature vessels, and in stunted little telescopes, and in objects made of shells that pretend not to be shells. Diminutive spades, barrows, and baskets, are our principal articles of commerce; but even they don't look quite new somehow. They always seem to have been offered and refused somewhere else, before they came down to our watering-place.

Yet it must not be supposed that our watering-place is an empty place, deserted by all visitors except a few staunch persons of approved fidelity. On the contrary, the chances are that if you came down here in August or September, you wouldn't find a house to lay your head in. As to finding either house or lodging of which you could reduce the terms, you could scarcely engage in a more hopeless pursuit. For all this, you are to observe that every season is the worst season ever known, and that the householding population of our watering-place are ruined regularly every autumn. They are like the farmers, in regard that it is surprising how much ruin they will bear. We have an excellent hotel – capital baths, warm, cold, and shower – firstrate bathing-machines – and as good butchers, bakers, and grocers, as heart could desire. They all do business, it is to be presumed, from motives of philanthropy – but it is quite certain that they are all being ruined. Their interest in strangers, and their politeness under ruin, bespeak their amiable nature. You would say so, if you only saw the baker helping a new comer to find suitable apartments.

So far from being at a discount as to company, we are in fact what would be popularly called rather a nobby place. Some tip-top "Nobbs" come down occasionally – even Dukes and Duchesses. We have known such carriages to blaze among the donkey-chaises, as made beholders wink. Attendant on these equipages come resplendent creatures in plush and powder, who are sure to be stricken disgusted with the indifferent accommodation of our watering-place, and who, of an evening (particularly when it rains), may be seen very much out of drawing, in rooms far too small for their fine figures, looking discontentedly out of little back windows into bye-streets. The lords and ladies get on well enough and quite good-humouredly: but if you want to see the gorgeous phenomena who wait upon them at a perfect non-plus, you should come and look at the resplendent creatures with little back parlours for servants' halls, and turn-up bedsteads to sleep in, at our watering-place. You have no idea how they take it to heart.

We have a pier – a queer old wooden pier, fortunately without the slightest pretensions to architecture, and very picturesque in consequence. Boats are hauled up upon it, ropes are coiled all over it; lobster-pots, nets, masts, oars, spars, sails, ballast, and rickety capstans, make a perfect labyrinth of it. For ever hovering about this pier, with their hands in their pockets, or leaning over the rough bulwark it opposes to the sea, gazing through telescopes which they carry about in the same profound receptacles, are the Boatmen of our watering-place. Looking at them, you would say that surely these must be the laziest boatmen in the world. They lounge about, in obstinate and inflexible pantaloons that are apparently made of wood, the whole season through. Whether talking together about the shipping in the Channel, or gruffly unbending over mugs of beer at the public-house, you would consider them the slowest of men. The chances are a thousand to one that you might stay here for ten seasons, and never see a boatman in a hurry. A certain expression about his loose hands, when they are not in his pockets, as if he were carrying a considerable lump of iron in each, without any inconvenience, suggests strength, but he never seems to use it. He has the appearance of perpetually strolling – running is too inappropriate a word to be thought of – to seed. The only subject on which he seems to feel any approach to enthusiasm, is pitch. He pitches everything he can lay hold of, – the pier, the palings, his boat, his house, – when there is nothing else left he turns to and even pitches his hat, or his rough-weather clothing. Do not judge him by deceitful appearances. These are among the bravest and most skilful mariners that exist. Let a gale arise and swell into a storm, let a sea run that might appal the stoutest heart that ever beat, let the Light-boat on these dangerous sands throw up a rocket in the night, or let them hear through the angry roar the signal-guns of a ship in distress, and these men spring up into activity so dauntless, so valiant, and heroic, that the world cannot surpass it. Cavillers may object that they chiefly live upon the salvage of valuable cargoes. So they do, and God knows it is no great living that they get out of the deadly risks they run. But put that hope of gain aside. Let these rough fellows be asked, in any storm, who volunteers for the life-boat to save some perishing souls, as poor and empty-handed as themselves, whose lives the perfection of human reason does not rate at the value of a farthing each; and that boat will be manned, as surely and as cheerfully, as if a thousand pounds were told down on the weather-beaten pier. For this, and for the recollection of their comrades whom we have known, whom the raging sea has engulfed before their children's eyes in such brave efforts, whom the secret sand has buried, we hold the boatmen of our watering-place in our love and honour, and are tender of the fame they well deserve.

So many children are brought down to our watering-place that, when they are not out of doors, as they usually are in fine weather, it is wonderful where they are put: the whole village seeming much too small to hold them under cover. In the afternoons, you see no end of salt and sandy little boots drying on upper window-sills. At bathing-time in the morning, the little bay re-echoes with every shrill variety of shriek and splash – after which, if the weather be at all fresh, the sands teem with small blue mottled legs. The sands are the children's great resort. They cluster there, like ants: so busy burying their particular friends, and making castles with infinite labour which the next tide overthrows, that it is curious to consider how their play, to the music of the sea, foreshadows the realities of their after lives.

It is curious, too, to observe a natural ease of approach that there seems to be between the children and the boatmen. They mutually make acquaintance, and take individual likings, without any help. You will come upon one of those slow heavy fellows sitting down patiently mending a little ship for a mite of a boy, whom he could crush to death by throwing his lightest pair of trousers on him. You will be sensible of the oddest contrast between the smooth little creature, and the rough man who seems to be carved out of hard-grained wood – between the delicate hand expectantly held out, and the immense thumb and finger that can hardly feel the rigging of thread they mend – between the small voice and the gruff growl – and yet there is a natural propriety in the companionship: always to be noted in confidence between a child and a person who has any merit of reality and genuineness: which is admirably pleasant.

We have a preventive station at our watering-place, and much the same thing may be observed – in a lesser degree, because of their official character – of the coast blockade; a steady, trusty, well-conditioned, well-conducted set of men, with no misgiving about looking you full in the face, and with a quiet thorough-going way of passing along to their duty at night, carrying huge sou'-wester clothing in reserve, that is fraught with all good prepossession. They are handy fellows – neat about their houses – industrious at gardening – would get on with their wives, one thinks, in a desert island – and people it, too, soon.

As to the naval officer of the station, with his hearty fresh face, and his blue eye that has pierced all kinds of weather, it warms our hearts when he comes into church on a Sunday, with that bright mixture of blue coat, buff waistcoat, black neckerchief, and gold epaulette, that is associated in the minds of all Englishmen with brave, unpretending, cordial, national service. We like to look at him in his Sunday state; and if we were First Lord (really possessing the indispensable qualification for the office of knowing nothing whatever about the sea), we would give him a ship to-morrow.

We have a church, by-the-by, of course – a hideous temple of flint, like a great petrified haystack. Our chief clerical dignitary, who, to his honour, has done much for education both in time and money, and has established excellent schools, is a sound, shrewd, healthy gentleman, who has got into little occasional difficulties with the neighbouring farmers, but has had a pestilent trick of being right. Under a new regulation, he has yielded the church of our watering-place to another clergyman. Upon the whole we get on in church well. We are a little bilious sometimes, about these days of fraternisation, and about nations arriving at a new and more unprejudiced knowledge of each other (which our Christianity don't quite approve), but it soon goes off, and then we get on very well.

There are two dissenting chapels,[5] besides, in our small watering-place; being in about the proportion of a hundred and twenty guns to a yacht. But the dissension that has torn us lately, has not been a religious one. It has arisen on the novel question of Gas. Our watering-place has been convulsed by the agitation, Gas or No Gas. It was never reasoned why No Gas, but there was a great No Gas party. Broadsides were printed and stuck about – a startling circumstance in our watering-place. The No Gas party rested content with chalking "No Gas!" and "Down with Gas!" and other such angry war-whoops, on the few back gates and scraps of wall which the limits of our watering-place afford; but the Gas party printed and posted bills, wherein they took the high ground of proclaiming against the No Gas party, that it was said Let there be light and there was light; and that not to have light (that is gas-light) in our watering-place, was to contravene the great decree. Whether by these thunderbolts or not, the No Gas party were defeated; and in this present season we have had our handful of shops illuminated for the first time. Such of the No Gas party, however, as have got shops, remain in opposition and burn tallow – exhibiting in their windows the very picture of the sulkiness that punishes itself, and a new illustration of the old adage about cutting off your nose to be revenged on your face, in cutting off their gas to be revenged on their business.

Other population than we have indicated, our watering-place has none. There are a few old used-up boatmen who creep about in the sunlight with the help of sticks, and there is a poor imbecile shoemaker who wanders his lonely life away among the rocks, as if he were looking for his reason – which he will never find. Sojourners in neighbouring watering-places come occasionally in flys to stare at us, and drive away again as if they thought us very dull; Italian boys come, Punch comes, the Fantoccini come,[6] the Tumblers come, the Ethiopians come; Glee-singers come at night, and hum and vibrate (not always melodiously) under our windows. But they all go soon, and leave us to ourselves again. We once had a travelling Circus and Wombwell's Menagerie[7] at the same time. They both know better than ever to try it again; and the Menagerie had nearly razed us from the face of the earth in getting the elephant away – his caravan was so large, and the watering-place so small. We have a fine sea, wholesome for all people; profitable for the body, profitable for the mind. The poet's words[8] are sometimes on its awful lips:

> And the stately ships go on
> To their haven under the hill;
> But O for the touch of a vanish'd hand,
> And the sound of a voice that is still!

> Break, break, break,
> At the foot of thy crags, O sea!
> But the tender grace of a day that is dead
> Will never come back to me.

Yet it is not always so, for the speech of the sea is various, and wants not abundant resource of cheerfulness, hope, and lusty encouragement. And since I have been idling at the window here, the tide has risen. The boats are dancing on the bubbing water; the colliers are afloat again; the white-bordered waves rush in; the children

> Do chase the ebbing Neptune, and do fly him
> When he comes back;[9]

the radiant sails are gliding past the shore, and shining on the far horizon; all the sea is sparkling, heaving, swelling up with life and beauty, this bright morning.

A Flight

First published in *Household Words*, 30 August 1851, and included in *Reprinted Pieces* from which this text is reproduced. The paper is a fine account of what he once described as 'that queer sensation born of quick travelling'. On 13 August 1851 he informed Wills: 'I am now going to do the "Flight to France". I think I shall call it merely "A Flight" – which will be a good name for a fanciful paper.'

When Don Diego de – I forget his name – the inventor of the last new Flying Machines, price so many francs for ladies, so many more for gentlemen – when Don Diego, by permission of Deputy Chaff-wax[1] and his noble band, shall have taken out a Patent for the Queen's dominions, and shall have opened a commodious Warehouse in an airy situation; and when all persons of any gentility will keep at least a pair of wings, and be seen skimming about in every direction; I shall take a flight to Paris (as I soar round the world) in a cheap and independent manner. At present, my reliance is on the South-Eastern Railway Company, in whose Express Train here I sit, at eight of the clock on a very hot morning, under the very hot roof of the Terminus at London Bridge, in danger of being "forced" like a cucumber or a melon, or a pine-apple. And talking of pine-apples, I suppose there never were so many pine-apples in a Train as there appear to be in this Train.

Whew! The hot-house air is faint with pine-apples. Every French citizen or citizeness is carrying pine-apples home. The compact little Enchantress in the corner of my carriage (French actress, to whom I yielded up my heart under the auspices of that brave child, "MEAT-CHELL,"[2] at the St. James's Theatre the night before last) has a pine-apple in her lap. Compact Enchantress's friend, confidante, mother, mystery, Heaven knows what, has two pine-apples in her lap, and a bundle of them under the seat. Tobacco-smoky Frenchman in Algerine wrapper, with peaked hood behind, who might be Abd-el-Kader[3] dyed rifle-green, and who seems to be dressed entirely in dirt and braid, carries pine-apples in a covered basket. Tall, grave, melancholy Frenchman, with black Vandyke beard, and hair close-cropped, with expansive chest to waistcoat, and compressive waist to coat: saturnine as to his pantaloons, calm as to his feminine boots, precious as to his jewellery, smooth and white as to his linen: dark-eyed, high-foreheaded, hawk-nosed – got up, one thinks, like Lucifer or Mephistopheles, or Zamiel,[4] transformed into a highly genteel Parisian – has the green end of a pine-apple sticking out of his neat valise.

Whew! If I were to be kept here long, under this forcing-frame, I wonder what would become of me – whether I should be forced into a giant, or should sprout or blow into some other phenomenon! Compact Enchantress is not ruffled by the heat – she is always composed, always compact. O look at her little ribbons, frills, and edges, at her shawl, at her gloves, at her hair, at her bracelets, at her bonnet, at everything about her! How is it accomplished? What does she do to be so neat? How is it that every trifle she wears belongs to her, and cannot choose but be a part of her? And even Mystery, look at *her*! A model. Mystery is not young, not pretty, though still of an average candlelight passability; but she does such miracles in her own behalf, that, one of these days, when she dies, they'll be amazed to find an old woman in her bed, distantly like her. She was an actress once, I shouldn't wonder, and had a Mystery attendant on herself. Perhaps, Compact Enchantress will live to be a Mystery, and to wait with a shawl at the side-scenes, and to sit opposite to Mademoiselle in railway carriages, and smile and talk subserviently, as Mystery does now. That's hard to believe!

Two Englishmen, and now our carriage is full. First Englishman, in the monied interest – flushed, highly respectable – Stock Exchange, perhaps – City, certainly. Faculties of second Englishman entirely absorbed in hurry. Plunges into the carriage, blind. Calls out of window concerning his luggage, deaf. Suffocates himself under pillows of greatcoats, for no reason, and in a demented manner. Will receive no assurance from any porter whatsoever. Is stout and hot, and wipes his head, and makes himself hotter by breathing so hard. Is totally incredulous respecting assurance of Collected Guard, that "there's no hurry." No hurry! And a flight to Paris in eleven hours![5]

It is all one to me in this drowsy corner, hurry or no hurry. Until Don Diego shall send home my wings, my flight is with the South-Eastern Company. I can fly with the South-Eastern, more lazily, at all events, than in the upper air. I have but to sit here thinking as idly as I please, and be whisked away. I am not accountable to anybody for the idleness of my thoughts in such an idle summer flight; my flight is provided for by the South-Eastern and is no business of mine.

The bell! With all my heart. It does not require *me* to do so much as even to flap my wings. Something snorts for me, something shrieks for me, something proclaims to everything else that it had better keep out of my way, – and away I go.

Ah! The fresh air is pleasant after the forcing-frame, though it does blow over these interminable streets, and scatter the smoke of this vast wilderness of chimneys. Here we are – no, I mean there we were, for it has darted far into the rear – in Bermondsey where the tanners live. Flash! The distant shipping in the Thames is gone. Whirr! The little streets of new brick and red tile, with here and there a flagstaff growing like a tall weed out of the scarlet beans, and, everywhere, plenty of open sewer and ditch for the promotion of the public health, have been fired off in a volley. Whizz! Dust-heaps, market-gardens, and waste grounds. Rattle! New Cross Station. Shock! There we were at Croydon. Bur-r-r-r! The tunnel.

I wonder why it is that when I shut my eyes in a tunnel, I begin to feel as if I were going at an Express pace the other way. I am clearly going back to London now. Compact Enchantress must have forgotten something, and reversed the engine. No! After long darkness, pale fitful streaks of light appear. I am still flying on for Folkestone. The streaks grow stronger – become continuous – become the ghost of day – become the living day – became I mean – the tunnel is miles and miles away, and here I fly through sunlight, all among the harvest and the Kentish hops.

There is a dreamy pleasure in this flying. I wonder where it was, and when it was, that we exploded, blew into space somehow, a Parliamentary Train,[6] with a crowd of heads and faces looking at us out of cages, and some hats waving. Monied Interest says it was at Reigate Station. Expounds to Mystery how Reigate Station is so many miles from London, which Mystery again develops to Compact Enchantress. There might be neither a Reigate nor a London for me, as I fly away among the Kentish hops and harvest. What do *I* care?

Bang! We have let another Station off, and fly away regardless. Everything is flying. The hop-gardens turn gracefully towards me, presenting regular avenues of hops in rapid flight, then whirl away. So do the pools and rushes, haystacks, sheep, clover in full bloom delicious to the sight and smell, corn-sheaves, cherry-orchards, apple-orchards, reapers, gleaners, hedges, gates, fields that taper off into little angular corners, cottages, gardens, now and then a church. Bang, bang! A double-barrelled Station! Now a wood, now a bridge, now a landscape, now a cutting, now a — Bang! a single-barrelled Station – there was a cricket-match somewhere with two white tents, and then four flying cows, then turnips – now the wires of the electric telegraph are all alive, and spin, and blur their edges, and go up and down, and make the intervals between each other most irregular: contracting and expanding in the strangest manner. Now we slacken. With a screwing, and a grinding, and a smell of water thrown on ashes, now we stop!

Demented Traveller, who has been for two or three minutes watchful, clutches his great-coats, plunges at the door, rattles it, cries "Hi!" eager to embark on board of impossible packets, far inland. Collected Guard appears. "Are you for Tunbridge, sir?" "Tunbridge? No. Paris." "Plenty of time, sir. No hurry. Five minutes here, sir, for refreshment." I am so blest (anticipating Zamiel, by half a second) as to procure a glass of water for Compact Enchantress.

Who would suppose we had been flying at such a rate, and shall take wing again directly? Refreshment-room full, platform full, porter with watering-pot deliberately cooling a hot wheel, another porter with equal deliberation helping the rest of the wheels bountifully to ice cream. Monied Interest and I re-entering the carriage first, and being there alone, he intimates to me that the French are "no go" as a Nation. I ask why? He says, that Reign of Terror of theirs was quite enough. I ventured to inquire whether he remembers anything that preceded said Reign of Terror? He says not particularly. "Because," I remark, "the harvest that is reaped, has sometimes been sown." Monied Interest repeats, as quite enough for him, that the French are revolutionary, – "and always at it."

Bell. Compact Enchantress, helped in by Zamiel (whom the stars confound!), gives us her charming little side-box look, and smites me to the core. Mystery eating sponge-cake. Pine-apple atmosphere faintly tinged with suspicions of sherry. Demented Traveller flits past the carriage, looking for it. Is blind with agitation, and can't see it. Seems singled out by Destiny to be the only unhappy creature in the flight, who has any cause to hurry himself. Is nearly left behind. Is seized by Collected Guard after the Train is in motion, and bundled in. Still, has lingering suspicions that there must be a boat in the neighbourhood, and *will* look wildly out of window for it.

Flight resumed. Corn-sheaves, hop-gardens, reapers, gleaners, apple-orchards, cherry-orchards, Stations single and double-barrelled, Ashford. Compact Enchantress (constantly talking to Mystery, in an exquisite manner) gives a little scream; a sound that seems to come from high up in her precious little head; from behind her bright little eyebrows. "Great Heaven, my pine-apple! My Angel! It is lost!" Mystery is desolated. A search made. It is not lost. Zamiel finds it. I curse him (flying) in the Persian manner. May his face be turned upside down, and jackasses sit upon his uncle's grave!

Now fresher air, now glimpses of unenclosed Down-land with flapping crows flying over it whom we soon outfly, now the Sea, now Folkestone at a quarter after ten. "Tickets ready, gentlemen!" Demented dashes at the door. "For Paris, sir?" No hurry.

Not the least. We are dropped slowly down to the Port, and sidle to and fro (the whole Train) before the insensible Royal George Hotel, for some ten minutes. The Royal George takes no more heed of us than its namesake under water at Spithead, or under earth at Windsor, does. The Royal George's dog lies winking and blinking at us, without taking the trouble to sit up; and the Royal George's "wedding party" at the open window (who seem, I must say, rather tired of bliss) don't bestow a solitary glance upon us, flying thus to Paris in eleven hours. The first gentleman in Folkestone is evidently used up, on this subject.

Meanwhile, Demented chafes. Conceives that every man's hand is against him, and exerting itself to prevent his getting to Paris. Refuses consolation. Rattles door. Sees smoke on the horizon, and "knows" it's the boat gone without him. Monied Interest resentfully explains that *he* is going to Paris too. Demented signifies that if Monied Interest chooses to be left behind, *he* don't.

"Refreshments in the Waiting-Room, ladies and gentlemen. No hurry, ladies and gentlemen, for Paris. No hurry whatever!"

Twenty minutes' pause, by Folkestone clock, for looking at Enchantress while she eats a sandwich, and at Mystery while she eats of everything there that is eatable, from pork-pie, sausage, jam, and gooseberries, to lumps of sugar. All this time, there is a very waterfall of luggage, with a spray of dust, tumbling slantwise from the pier into the steamboat. All this time, Demented (who has no business with it) watches it with starting eyes, fiercely requiring to be shown *his* luggage. When it at last concludes the cataract, he rushes hotly to refresh — is shouted after, pursued, jostled, brought back, pitched into the departing steamer upside down, and caught by mariners disgracefully.

A lovely harvest-day, a cloudless sky, a tranquil sea. The piston-rods of the engines so regularly coming up from below, to look (as well they may) at the bright weather, and so regularly almost knocking their iron heads against the cross beam of the skylight, and never doing it! Another Parisian actress is on board, attended by another Mystery. Compact Enchantress greets her sister artist — Oh, the Compact One's pretty teeth! — and Mystery greets Mystery. *My* Mystery soon ceases to be conversational — is taken poorly, in a word, having lunched too miscellaneously — and goes below. The remaining Mystery then smiles upon the sister artists (who, I am afraid, wouldn't greatly mind stabbing each other), and is upon the whole ravished.

And now I find that all the French people on board begin to grow, and all the English people to shrink. The French are nearing home, and shaking off a disadvantage, whereas we are shaking it on. Zamiel is the same man, and Abd-el-Kader is the same man, but each seems to come into possession of an indescribable confidence that departs from us – from Monied Interest, for instance, and from me. Just what they gain, we lose. Certain British "Gents" about the steersman, intellectually nurtured at home on parody of everything and truth of nothing, become subdued, and in a manner forlorn; and when the steersman tells them (not exultingly) how he has "been upon this station now eight year, and never see the old town of Bullum yet," one of them, with an imbecile reliance on a reed, asks him what he considers to be the best hotel in Paris?

Now, I tread upon French ground, and am greeted by the three charming words, Liberty, Equality, Fraternity, painted up (in letters a little too thin for their height) on the Custom-house wall – also by the sight of large cocked hats, without which demonstrative head-gear nothing of a public nature can be done upon this soil. All the rabid Hotel population of Boulogne howl and shriek outside a distant barrier, frantic to get at us. Demented, by some unlucky means peculiar to himself, is delivered over to their fury, and is presently seen struggling in a whirlpool of Touters – is somehow understood to be going to Paris – is, with infinite noise, rescued by two cocked hats, and brought into Custom-house bondage with the rest of us.

Here, I resign the active duties of life to an eager being, of preternatural sharpness, with a shelving forehead and a shabby snuff-coloured coat, who (from the wharf) brought me down with his eye before the boat came into port. He darts upon my luggage, on the floor where all the luggage is strewn like a wreck at the bottom of the great deep; gets it proclaimed and weighed as the property of "Monsieur a traveller unknown;" pays certain francs for it, to a certain functionary behind a Pigeon Hole, like a pay-box at a Theatre (the arrangements in general are on a wholesale scale, half military and half theatrical); and I suppose I shall find it when I come to Paris – he says I shall. I know nothing about it, except that I pay him his small fee, and pocket the ticket he gives me, and sit upon a counter, involved in the general distraction.

Railway station. "Lunch or dinner, ladies and gentlemen. Plenty of time for Paris. Plenty of time!" Large hall, long counter, long strips of dining-table, bottles of wine, plates of meat, roast chickens, little loaves of bread, basins of soup, little caraffes of brandy, cakes, and fruit. Comfortably restored from these resources, I begin to fly again.

I saw Zamiel (before I took wing) presented to Compact Enchantress and Sister Artist, by an officer in uniform, with a waist like a wasp's, and pantaloons like two balloons. They all got into the next carriage together, accompanied by the two Mysteries. They laughed. I am alone in the carriage (for I don't consider Demented anybody) and alone in the world.

Fields, windmills, low grounds, pollard-trees, windmills, fields, fortifications, Abbeville, soldiering and drumming. I wonder where England is, and when I was there last – about two years ago, I should say. Flying in and out among these trenches and batteries, skimming the clattering drawbridges, looking down into the stagnant ditches, I become a prisoner of state, escaping. I am confined with a comrade in a fortress. Our room is in an upper story. We have tried to get up the chimney, but there's an iron grating across it, imbedded in the masonry. After months of labour, we have worked the grating loose with the poker, and can lift it up. We have also made a hook, and twisted our rugs and blankets into ropes. Our plan is, to go up the chimney, hook our ropes to the top, descend hand over hand upon the roof of the guard-house far below, shake the hook loose, watch the opportunity of the sentinel's pacing away, hook again, drop into the ditch, swim across it, creep into the shelter of the wood. The time is come – a wild and stormy night. We are up the chimney, we are on the guard-house roof, we are swimming in the murky ditch, when lo! "Qui v'là?" a bugle, the alarm, a crash! What is it? Death? No, Amiens.

More fortifications, more soldiering and drumming, more basins of soup, more little loaves of bread, more bottles of wine, more caraffes of brandy, more time for refreshment. Everything good, and everything ready. Bright, unsubstantial-looking, scenic sort of station. People waiting. Houses, uniforms, beards, moustaches, some sabots, plenty of neat women, and a few old-visaged children. Unless it be a delusion born of my giddy flight, the grown-up people and the children seem to change places in France. In general, the boys and girls are little old men and women, and the men and women lively boys and girls.

Bugle, shriek, flight resumed. Monied Interest has come into my carriage. Says the manner of refreshing is "not bad," but considers it French. Admits great dexterity and politeness in the attendants. Thinks a decimal currency may have something to do with their despatch in settling accounts, and don't know but what it's sensible and convenient. Adds, however, as a general protest, that they're a revolutionary people – and always at it.

Ramparts, canals, cathedral, river, soldiering and drumming, open country, river, earthenware manufactures, Creil.[7] Again ten minutes. Not even Demented in a hurry. Station, a drawing-room with a verandah: like a planter's house. Monied Interest considers it a band-box, and not made to last. Little round tables in it, at one of which the Sister Artists and attendant Mysteries are established with Wasp and Zamiel, as if they were going to stay a week.

Anon, with no more trouble than before, I am flying again, and lazily wondering as I fly. What has the South-Eastern done with all the horrible little villages we used to pass through, in the *Diligence*? What have they done with all the summer dust, with all the winter mud, with all the dreary avenues of little trees, with all the ramshackle post-yards, with all the beggars (who used to turn out at night with bits of lighted candle, to look in at the coach windows), with all the long-tailed horses who were always biting one another, with all the big postillions in jack-boots — with all the mouldy cafés that we used to stop at, where a long mildewed table-cloth, set forth with jovial bottles of vinegar and oil, and with a Siamese arrangement of pepper and salt, was never wanting? Where are the grass-grown little towns, the wonderful little market-places all unconscious of markets, the shops that nobody kept, the streets that nobody trod, the churches that nobody went to, the bells that nobody rang, the tumble-down old buildings plastered with many-coloured bills that nobody read? Where are the two-and-twenty weary hours of long long day and night journey, sure to be either insupportably hot or insupportably cold? Where are the pains in my bones, where are the fidgets in my legs, where is the Frenchman with the nightcap who never *would* have the little coupé-window down, and who always fell upon me when he went to sleep, and always slept all night snoring onions?

A voice breaks in with "Paris! Here we are!"

I have overflown myself, perhaps, but I can't believe it. I feel as if I were enchanted or bewitched. It is barely eight o'clock yet — it is nothing like half-past — when I have had my luggage examined at that briskest of Custom-houses attached to the station, and am rattling over the pavement in a hackney-cabriolet.

Surely, not the pavement of Paris? Yes, I think it is, too. I don't know any other place where there are all these high houses, all these haggard-looking wine shops, all these billiard tables, all these stocking-makers with flat red or yellow legs of wood for signboard, all these fuel shops with stacks of billets painted outside, and real billets sawing in the gutter, all these dirty corners of streets, all these cabinet pictures over dark doorways representing discreet matrons nursing babies. And yet this morning — I'll think of it in a warm-bath.

Very like a small room that I remember in the Chinese baths upon the Boulevard, certainly; and, though I see it through the steam, I think that I might swear to that peculiar hot-linen basket, like a large wicker hour-glass. When can it have been that I left home? When was it that I paid "through to Paris" at London Bridge, and discharged myself of all responsibility, except the preservation of a voucher ruled into three divisions, of which the first was snipped off at Folkestone, the second aboard the boat, and the third taken at my journey's end? It seems to have been ages ago. Calculation is useless. I will go out for a walk.

The crowds in the streets, the lights in the shops and balconies, the elegance, variety, and beauty of their decorations, the number of the theatres, the brilliant cafés with their windows thrown up high and their vivacious groups at little tables on the pavement, the light and glitter of the houses turned as it were inside out, soon convince me that it is no dream; that I am in Paris, howsoever I got here. I stroll down to the sparkling Palais Royal, up the Rue de Rivoli, to the Place Vendôme. As I glance into a print-shop window, Monied Interest, my late travelling companion, comes upon me, laughing with the highest relish of disdain. "Here's a people!" he says, pointing to Napoleon in the window and Napoleon on the column. "Only one idea all over Paris! A monomania!" Humph! I THINK I have seen Napoleon's match? There WAS a statue, when I came away, at Hyde Park Corner,[8] and another in the City, and a print or two in the shops.

I walk up to the Barrière de l'Etoile, sufficiently dazed by my flight to have a pleasant doubt of the reality of everything about me; of the lively crowd, the overhanging trees, the performing dogs, the hobby-horses, the beautiful perspectives of shining lamps: the hundred and one enclosures, where the singing is, in gleaming orchestras of azure and gold, and where a star-eyed Houri comes round with a box for voluntary offerings. So, I pass to my hotel, enchanted; sup, enchanted; go to bed, enchanted; pushing back this morning (if it really were this morning) into the remoteness of time, blessing the South-Eastern Company for realising the Arabian Nights in these prose days, murmuring, as I wing my idle flight into the land of dreams, "No hurry, ladies and gentlemen, going to Paris in eleven hours. It is so well done, that there really is no hurry!"

Fire and Snow

First published in *Household Words*, 21 January 1854, from which this text is reproduced. On 21 November 1853, Dickens wrote to Wills from Florence about the imminent trip he was to make to the Midlands: 'Can't a Saturday Night in a Truck District, or a Sunday Morning among the ironworkers (a fine subject) be knocked out in the course of the same visit?'

Can this be the region of cinders and coal-dust, which we have traversed before now, divers times, both by night and by day, when the dirty wind rattled as it came against us charged with fine particles of coal, and the natural colour of the earth and all its vegetation might have been black, for anything our eyes could see to the contrary in a waste of many miles? Indeed it is the same country, though so altered that on this present day when the old year is near its last, the North East wind blows white, and all the ground is white – pure white – insomuch that if our lives depended on our identifying a mound of ashes as we jar along this Birmingham and Wolverhampton Railway, we could not find a handful.

The sun shines brightly, though it is a cold cold sun, this piercing day; and when the Birmingham tunnel disgorges us into the frosty air, we find the pointsman housed in no mere box, but in a resplendent pavilion, all bejewelled with dazzling icicles, the least a yard long. A radiant pointsman he should be, we think, invested by fairies with a dress of rainbow hues, and going round and round in some gorgeously playful manner on a gold and silver pivot. But, he has changed neither his stout great coat, nor his stiff hat, nor his stiff attitude of watch; and as (like the ghostly dagger of Macbeth[1]) he marshals us the way that we were going, we observe him to be a mortal with a red face – red, in part from a seasonable joviality of spirit, and in part from frost and wind – with the encrusted snow dropping silently off his outstretched arm.

Redder than ever are the very red-brick little houses outside Birmingham – all staring at the railway in the snowy weather, like plethoric old men with white heads. Clean linen drying in yards seems ill-washed, against the intense white of the landscape. Far and near, the tall tall chimneys look out over one another's shoulders for the swart ashes familiar to them, and can discern nothing but snow. Is this the smoke of other chimneys setting in so heavily from the north-east, and overclouding the short brightness of the day? No. By the North Pole it is more snow!

Making directly at us, and flying almost horizontally before the wind, it rushes against the train, in a dark blast profusely speckled as it were with drifting white feathers. A sharp collision, though a harmless one! No wonder that the engine seems to have a fearful cold in his head. No wonder, with a deal of out-door work in such a winter, that he is very hoarse and very short of breath, very much blown when we come to the next station, and very much given to weeping, snorting and spitting, all the time he stops!

Which is short enough, for these little upstairs stations at the tops of high arches, whence we almost look down the chimneys of scattered workshops, and quite inhale their smoke as it comes puffing at us – these little upstairs stations rarely seem to do much business anywhere, and just now are like suicidal heights to dive from into depths of snow. So, away again over the moor, where the clanking serpents usually writhing above coal-pits, are dormant and whitened over – this being holiday time – but where those grave monsters, the blast-furnaces, which cannot stoop to recreation, are awake and roaring. Now, a smoky village; now, a chimney; now, a dormant serpent who seems to have been benumbed in the act of working his way for shelter into the lonely little engine-house by the pit's mouth; now, a pond with black specks sliding and skating; now, a drift with similar specks half sunken in it throwing snowballs; now, a cold white altar of snow with fire blazing on it; now, a dreary open space of mound and fell, snowed smoothly over, and closed in at last by sullen cities of chimneys. Not altogether agreeable to think of crossing such space without a guide, and being swallowed by a long-abandoned, long-forgotten shaft. Not even agreeable, in this undermined country, to think of half-a-dozen railway arches with the train upon them, suddenly vanishing through the snow into the excavated depths of a coal-forest.

Snow, wind, ice, and Wolverhampton – all together. No carriage at the station, everything snowed up. So much the better. The Swan will take us under its warm wing, walking or riding. Where is the Swan's nest? In the market-place. So much the better yet, for it is market-day, and there will be something to see from the Swan's nest.

Up the streets of Wolverhampton, where the doctor's bright door-plate is dimmed as if Old Winter's breath were on it, and the lawyer's office window is appropriately misty, to the market-place: where we find a cheerful bustle and plenty of people – for the most part pretending not to like the snow, but liking it very much, as people generally do. The Swan is a bird of a good substantial brood, worthy to be a country cousin of the hospitable

Hen and Chickens, whose company we have deserted for only a few hours and with whom we shall roost again at Birmingham to-night. The Swan has bountiful coal-country notions of firing, snug homely rooms, cheerful windows looking down upon the clusters of snowy umbrellas in the market-place, and on the chaffering and chattering which is pleasantly hushed by the thick white down lying so deep, and softly falling still. Neat bright-eyed waitresses do the honors of the Swan. The Swan is confident about its soup, is troubled with no distrust concerning cod-fish, speaks the word of promise in relation to an enormous chine of roast beef, one of the dishes at "the Ironmasters' dinner," which will be disengaged at four. The Ironmasters' dinner! It has an imposing sound. We think of the Ironmasters joking, drinking to their Ironmistresses, clinking their glasses with a metallic ring, and comporting themselves at the festive board with the might of men who have mastered Iron.

Now for a walk! Not in the direction of the furnaces, which we will see to-night when darkness shall set off the fires; but in the country, with our faces towards Wales. Say, ye hoary finger-posts whereon the name of picturesque old Shrewsbury is written in characters of frost; ye hedges lately bare, that have burst into snowy foliage; ye glittering trees from which the wind blows sparkling dust; ye high drifts by the roadside, which are blue a-top, where ye are seen opposed to the bright red and yellow of the horizon; say all of ye, is summer the only season for enjoyable walks! Answer, roguish crow, alighting on a sheep's back to pluck his wool off for an extra blanket, and skimming away, so black, over the white field; give us your opinion, swinging ale-house signs, and cosey little bars; speak out, farrier's shed with faces all a-glow, fountain of sparks, heaving bellows, and ringing music; tell us, cottage hearths and sprigs of holly in cottage windows; be eloquent in praise of wintry walks, you sudden blasts of wind that pass like shiverings of Nature, you deep roads, you solid fragments of old hayricks with your fragrance frozen in! Even you, drivers of toiling carts, coal-laden, keeping company together behind your charges, dog-attended and basket-bearing: even you, though it is no easy work to stop, every now and then, and chip the snow away from the clogged wheels with picks, will have a fair word to say for winter, will you not!

Down to the solitary factory in the dip of the road, deserted of holiday-makers, and where the water-mill is frozen up – then turn. As we draw nigh to our bright bird again, the early evening is closing in, the cold increases, the snow deadens and darkens, and lights spring up in the shops. A wet walk, ankle deep in snow the whole way. We must buy some stockings, and borrow the Swan's slippers before dinner.

It is a mercy that we step into the toy-shop to buy a pocket-comb too, or the pretty child-customer (as it seems to us, the only other customer the elderly lady of the toy-shop has lately had), might have stood divided between the two puzzles at one shilling each, until the putting up of the shutters. But, the incursion of our fiery faces and snowy dresses, coupled with our own individual recommendation of the puzzle on the right hand, happily turn the scale. The best of pocket-combs for a shilling, and now for the stockings. Dibbs "don't keep 'em," though he writes up that he does, and Jibbs is so beleaguered by country people making market-day and Christmas-week purchases, that his shop is choked to the pavement. Mibbs is the man for our money, and Mibbs keeps everything in the stocking line, though he may not exactly know where to find it. However, he finds what we want, in an inaccessible place, after going up ladders for it like a lamplighter; and a very good article it is, and a very civil worthy trader Mibbs is, and may Mibbs increase and multiply! Likewise young Mibbs, unacquainted with the price of anything in stock, and young Mibbs's aunt who attends to the ladies' department.

The Swan is rich in slippers – in those good old flip-flap inn slippers which nobody can keep on, which knock double knocks on every stair as their wearer comes down stairs, and fly away over the banisters before they have brought him to level ground. Rich also is the Swan in wholesome well-cooked dinner, and in tender chine of beef, so brave in size that the mining of all the powerful Ironmasters is but a sufficient outlet for its gravy. Rich in things wholesome and sound and unpretending is the Swan, except that we would recommend the good bird not to dip its beak into its sherry. Under the change from snow and wind to hot soup, drawn red curtains, fire and candle, we observe our demonstrations at first to be very like the engine's at the little station; but they subside, and we dine vigorously – another tribute to a winter walk! – and finding that the Swan's ideas of something hot to drink are just and laudable, we adopt the same, with emendations (in the matter of lemon chiefly) of which modesty and total abstinence principles forbid the record. Then, thinking drowsily and delightfully of all things that have occurred to us during the last four-and-twenty hours, and of most things that have occurred to us during the last four-and-twenty years, we sit in arm chairs, amiably basking before the fire – playthings for infancy – creatures to be asked a favour of – until aroused by the fragrance of hot tea and muffins. These we have ordered, principally as a perfume.

The bill of the Swan is to be commended as not out of proportion to its plumage; and now, our walking shoes being dried and baked, we must get them on somehow – for the rosy driver with his carriage and pair who is to take us among the fires on the blasted heath[2] by Bilston announces from under a few shawls, and the collars of three or four coats, that we must be going. Away we go, obedient to the summons, and, having taken leave of the lady in the Swan's bar opposite the door, who is almost rustled out of her glass case and blown upstairs whenever the door opens, we are presently in outer darkness grinding the snow.

Soon the fires begin to appear. In all this ashy country, there is still not a cinder visible; in all this land of smoke, not a stain upon the universal white. A very novel and curious sight is presented by the hundreds of great fires blazing in the midst of the cold dead snow. They illuminate it very little. Sometimes, the construction of a furnace, kiln, or chimney, admits of a tinge being thrown upon the pale ground near it; but, generally the fire burns in its own sullen ferocity, and the snow lies impassive and untouched. There is a glare in the sky, flickering now and then over the greater furnaces, but the earth lies stiff in its winding sheet, and the huge corpse candles burning above it affect it no more than colossal tapers of state move dead humanity.

Sacrificial altars, varying in size, but all gigantic, and all made of ice and snow, abound. Tongues of flame shoot up from them, and pillars of fire turn and twist upon them. Fortresses on fire, a whole town in a blaze, Moscow newly kindled, we see fifty times; rattling and crashing noises strike the ear, and the wind is loud. Thus, crushing the snow with our wheels, and sidling over hillocks of it, and sinking into drifts of it, we roll on softly through a forest of conflagration; the rosy-faced driver, concerned for the honor of his locality, much regretting that many fires are making holiday to-night, and that we see so few.

Come we at last to the precipitous wooden steps by which we are to be mast-headed at a railway station. Good night to rosy-face, the cheeriest man we know, and up. Station very gritty, as a general characteristic. Station very dark, the gas being frozen. Station very cold, as any timber cabin suspended in the air with such a wind making lunges at it, would be. Station very dreary, being a station. Man and boy behind money-taking partition, checking accounts, and not able to unravel a knot of seven and sixpence. Small boy, with a large package on his back, like Christian with his bundle of sins,[3] sent down into the snow an indefinite depth and distance, with instructions to "look sharp in delivering that, and then cut away back here for another." Second small boy in search of basket for Mr. Brown, unable to believe that it is not there, and that anybody can have dared to disappoint Brown. Six third-class passengers prowling about, and trying in the dim light of one oil lamp to read with interest the dismal time-bills[4] and notices about throwing stones at trains, upon the walls. Two more, scorching themselves at the rusty stove. Shivering porter going in and out, bell in hand, to look for the train, which is overdue, finally gives it up for the present, and puts down the bell – also the spirits of the passengers. In our own innocence we repeatedly mistake the roaring of the nearest furnace for the approach of the train, run out, and return covered with ignominy. Train in sight at last – but the other train – which don't stop here – and it seems to tear the trembling station limb from limb, as it rushes through. Finally, some half-an-hour behind its time through the tussle it has had with the snow, comes our expected engine, shrieking with indignation and grief. And as we pull the clean white coverlet over us in bed at Birmingham, we think of the whiteness lying on the broad landscape all around for many a frosty windy mile, and find that it makes bed very comfortable.

Our French Watering-Place[1]

First published in *Household Words*, 4 November 1854, and included in *Reprinted Pieces* from which this text is taken. Dickens originally intended to write the article in 1853, and he wrote to Wills on 25 September of that year: 'I have deferred our French Watering-Place, as an easy thing to write while I am away.' However, it wasn't until the following autumn that the piece appeared, and soon after he said to Wills: 'As I don't think that an Englishman wants to dissect a Frenchman's love at present, I would rather say nothing about France unless I had plenty to say about its gallantry and spirit.'

Having earned by many years of fidelity, the right to be sometimes inconstant to our English watering-place, we have dallied for two or three seasons with a French watering-place: once solely known to us as a town with a very long street, beginning with an abattoir and ending with a steam-boat, which it seemed our fate to behold only at daybreak on winter mornings, when (in the days before continental rail-roads), just sufficiently awake to know that we were most uncomfortably asleep, it was our destiny always to clatter through it, in the coupé of the diligence[2] from Paris, with a sea of mud behind us, and a sea of tumbling waves before. In relation to which latter monster, our mind's eye now recalls a worthy Frenchman in a seal-skin cap with a braided hood over it, once our travelling companion in the coupé aforesaid, who, waking up with a pale and crumpled visage, and looking ruefully out at the grim row of breakers enjoying themselves fanatically on an instrument of torture called "the Bar,"[3] inquired of us whether we were ever sick at sea? Both to prepare his mind for the abject creature we were presently to become, and also to afford him consolation, we replied, "Sir, your servant is always sick when it is possible to be so." He returned, altogether uncheered by the bright example, "Ah, Heaven, but I am always sick, even when it is *im*possible to be so."

The means of communication between the French capital and our French watering-place are wholly changed since those days; but the Channel remains unbridged as yet, and the old floundering and knocking about go on there. It must be confessed that saving in reasonable (and therefore rare) sea-weather, the act of arrival at our French watering-place from England is difficult to be achieved with dignity. Several little circumstances combine to render the visitor an object of humiliation. In the first place, the steamer no sooner touches the port, than all the passengers fall into captivity: being boarded by an overpowering force of Custom-house officers, and marched into a gloomy dungeon. In the second place, the road to this dungeon is fenced off with ropes breast-high, and outside those ropes all the English in the place who have lately been sea-sick and are now well, assemble in their best clothes to enjoy the degradation of their dilapidated fellow-creatures. "Oh, my gracious! how ill this one has been!" "Here's a damp one coming next!" "*Here's* a pale one!" "Oh! Ain't he green in the face, this next one!" Even we ourself (not deficient in natural dignity) have a lively remembrance of staggering up this detested lane one September day in a gale of wind, when we were received like an irresistible comic actor, with a burst of laughter and applause, occasioned by the extreme imbecility of our legs.

We were coming to the third place. In the third place, the captives, being shut up in the gloomy dungeon, are strained, two or three at a time, into an inner cell, to be examined as to passports; and across the doorway of communication, stands a military creature making a bar of his arm. Two ideas are generally present to the British mind during these ceremonies; first, that it is necessary to make for the cell with violent struggles, as if it were a life-boat and the dungeon a ship going down; secondly, that the military creature's arm is a national affront, which the government at home ought instantly to "take up." The British mind and body becoming heated by these fantasies, delirious answers are made to inquiries, and extravagant actions performed. Thus, Johnson persists in giving Johnson as his baptismal name, and substituting for his ancestral designation the national "Dam!" Neither can he by any means be brought to recognise the distinction between a portmanteau-key and a passport, but will obstinately persevere in tendering the one when asked for the other. This brings him to the fourth place, in a state of mere idiotcy; and when he is, in the fourth place, cast out at a little door into a howling wilderness of touters, he becomes a lunatic with wild eyes and floating hair until rescued and soothed. If friendless and unrescued, he is generally put into a railway omnibus and taken to Paris.

But our French watering-place, when it is once got into, is a very enjoyable place. It has a varied and beautiful country around it, and many characteristic and agreeable things within it. To be sure, it might have fewer bad smells and less decaying refuse, and it might be better drained, and much cleaner in many parts, and therefore infinitely more healthy. Still, it is a bright, airy, pleasant, cheerful town; and if you were to walk down either of its three well-paved main streets, towards five o'clock in the afternoon, when delicate odours of cookery fill the air, and its hotel windows (it is full of hotels) give glimpses of long tables set out for dinner, and made to look sumptuous by the aid of napkins folded fan-wise, you would rightly judge it to be an uncommonly good town to eat and drink in.

We have an old walled town, rich in cool public wells of water, on the top of a hill within and above the present business-town; and if it were some hundreds of miles further from England, instead of being, on a clear day, within sight of the grass growing in the crevices of the chalk-cliffs of Dover, you would long ago have been bored to death about that town. It is more picturesque and quaint than half the innocent places which tourists, following their leader like sheep, have made impostors of. To say nothing of its houses with grave courtyards, its queer by-corners, and its many-windowed streets white and quiet in the sunlight, there is an ancient belfry in it that would have been in all the Annuals and Albums, going and gone, these hundred years, if it had but been more expensive to get at. Happily it has escaped so well, being only in our French watering-place, that you may like it of your own accord in a natural manner, without being required to go into convulsions about it. We regard it as one of the later blessings of our life, that BILKINS,[4] the only authority on Taste, never took any notice that we can find out, of our French watering-place. Bilkins never wrote about it, never pointed out anything to be seen in it, never measured anything in it, always left it alone. For which relief, Heaven bless the town and the memory of the immortal Bilkins likewise!

There is a charming walk, arched and shaded by trees, on the old walls that form the four sides of this High Town, whence you get glimpses of the streets below, and changing views of the other town and of the river, and of the hills and of the sea. It is made more agreeable and peculiar by some of the solemn houses that are rooted in the deep streets below, bursting into a fresher existence a-top, and having doors and windows, and even gardens, on these ramparts. A child going in at the courtyard gate of one of these houses, climbing up the many stairs, and coming out at the fourth-floor window, might conceive himself another Jack, alighting on enchanted ground from another bean-stalk. It is a place wonderfully populous in children; English children, with governesses reading novels as they walk down the shady lanes of trees, or nursemaids interchanging gossip on the seats; French children with their smiling bonnes in snow-white caps, and themselves – if little boys – in straw head-gear like beehives, work-baskets and church hassocks. Three years ago, there were three weazen old men, one bearing a frayed red ribbon in his threadbare button-hole, always to be found walking together among these children, before dinner-time. If they walked for an appetite, they doubtless lived en pension – were contracted for – otherwise their poverty would have made it a rash action. They were stooping, blear-eyed, dull old men, slip-shod and shabby, in long-skirted short-waisted coats and meagre trousers, and yet with a ghost of gentility hovering in their company. They spoke little to each other, and looked as if they might have been politically discontented if they had had vitality enough. Once, we overheard red-ribbon feebly complain to the other two that somebody, or something, was "a Robber;" and then they all three set their mouths so that they would have ground their teeth if they had had any. The ensuing winter gathered red-ribbon unto the great company of faded ribbons, and next year the remaining two were there – getting themselves entangled with hoops and dolls – familiar mysteries to the children – probably in the eyes of most of them, harmless creatures who had never been like children, and whom children could never be like. Another winter came, and another old man went, and so, this present year, the last of the triumvirate left off walking – it was no good, now – and sat by himself on a little solitary bench, with the hoops and the dolls as lively as ever all about him.

In the Place d'Armes of this town, a little decayed market is held, which seems to slip through the old gateway, like water, and go rippling down the hill, to mingle with the murmuring market in the lower town, and get lost in its movement and bustle. It is very agreeable on an idle summer morning to pursue this market-stream from the hill-top. It begins, dozingly and dully, with a few sacks of corn; starts into a surprising collection of boots and shoes; goes brawling down the hill in a diversified channel of old cordage, old iron, old crockery, old clothes, civil and military, old rags, new cotton goods, flaming prints of saints, little looking-glasses, and incalculable lengths of tape; dives into a backway, keeping out of sight for a little while, as streams will, or only sparkling for a moment in the shape of a market drinking-shop; and suddenly reappears behind the great church, shooting itself into a bright confusion of white-capped women and blue-bloused men, poultry, vegetables, fruits, flowers, pots, pans, praying-chairs, soldiers, country butter, umbrellas and other sun-shades, girl-porters waiting to be hired with baskets at their backs, and one weazen little old man in a cocked hat, wearing a cuirass of drinking-glasses and carrying on his shoulder a crimson temple fluttering with flags, like a glorified pavior's rammer without the handle, who rings a little bell in all parts of the scene, and cries his cooling drink Hola, Hola, Ho-o-o! in a shrill cracked voice that somehow makes itself heard, above all the chaffering and vending hum. Early in the afternoon, the whole course of the stream is dry. The praying-chairs are put back in the church, the umbrellas are folded up, the unsold goods are carried away, the stalls and stands disappear, the square is swept, the hackney coaches lounge there to be hired, and on all the country roads (if you walk about, as much as we do) you will see the peasant women, always neatly and comfortably dressed, riding home, with the pleasantest saddle-furniture of clean milk-pails, bright butter-kegs, and the like, on the jolliest little donkeys in the world.

We have another market in our French watering-place – that is to say, a few wooden hutches in the open street, down by the Port – devoted to fish. Our fishing-boats are famous everywhere; and our fishing people, though they love lively colours and taste is neutral (see Bilkins), are among the most picturesque people we ever encountered. They have not only a quarter of their own in the town itself, but they occupy whole villages of their own on the neighbouring cliffs. Their churches and chapels are their own; they consort with one another, they intermarry among themselves, their customs are their own, and their costume is their own and never changes. As soon as one of their boys can walk, he is provided with a long bright red nightcap; and one of their men would as soon think of going afloat without his head, as without that indispensable appendage to it. Then, they wear the noblest boots, with the hugest tops – flapping and bulging over anyhow; above which, they encase themselves in such wonderful overalls and petticoat trousers, made to all appearance of tarry old sails, so additionally stiffened with pitch and salt, that the wearers have a walk of their own, and go straddling and swinging about among the boats and barrels and nets and rigging, a sight to see. Then, their younger women, by dint of going down to the sea barefoot, to fling their baskets into the boats as they come in with the tide, and bespeak the first fruits of the haul with propitiatory promises to love and marry that dear fisherman who shall fill that basket like an Angel, have the finest legs ever carved by Nature in the brightest mahogany, and they walk like Juno.[5] Their eyes, too, are so lustrous that their long gold ear-rings turn dull beside those brilliant neighbours; and when they are dressed, what with these beauties, and their fine fresh faces, and their many petticoats – striped petticoats, red petticoats, blue petticoats, always clean and smart, and never too long – and their home-made stockings, mulberry-coloured, blue, brown, purple, lilac – which the older women, taking care of the Dutch-looking children, sit in all sorts of places knitting, knitting, knitting from morning to night – and what with their little saucy bright blue jackets, knitted too, and fitting close to their handsome figures; and what with the natural grace with which they wear the commonest cap, or fold the commonest handkerchief round their luxuriant hair – we say, in a word and out of breath, that taking all those premises into our consideration, it has never been a matter of the least surprise to us that we have never once met, in the cornfields, on the dusty roads, by the breezy windmills, on the plots of short sweet grass overhanging the sea – anywhere – a young fisherman and fisherwoman of our French watering-place together, but the arm of that fisherman has invariably been, as a matter of course and without any absurd attempt to disguise so plain a necessity, round the neck or waist of that fisherwoman. And we have had no doubt whatever, standing looking at their uphill streets, house rising above house, and terrace above terrace, and bright garments here and there lying sunning on rough stone parapets, that the pleasant mist on all such objects, caused by their being seen through the brown nets hung across on poles to dry, is, in the eyes of every true young fisherman, a mist of love and beauty, setting off the goddess of his heart.

Moreover it is to be observed that these are an industrious people, and a domestic people, and an honest people. And though we are aware that at the bidding of Bilkins it is our duty to fall down and worship the Neapolitans, we make bold very much to prefer the fishing people of our French watering-place – especially since our last visit to Naples within these twelve months, when we found only four conditions of men remaining in the whole city: to wit, lazzaroni,[6] priests, spies, and soldiers, and all of them beggars; the paternal government having banished all its subjects except the rascals.

But we can never henceforth separate our French watering-place from our own landlord of two summers, M. Loyal Devasseur,[7] citizen and town-councillor. Permit us to have the pleasure of presenting M. Loyal Devasseur.

His own family name is simply Loyal; but as he is married, and as in that part of France a husband always adds to his own name the family name of his wife, he writes himself Loyal Devasseur. He owns a compact little estate of some twenty or thirty acres on a lofty hill-side, and on it he has built two country houses, which he lets furnished. They are by many degrees the best houses that are so let near our French watering-place; we have had the honour of living in both, and can testify. The entrance-hall of the first we inhabited was ornamented with a plan of the estate, representing it as about twice the size of Ireland; insomuch that when we were yet new to the property (M. Loyal always speaks of it as "La propriété") we went three miles straight on end in search of the bridge of Austerlitz – which we afterwards found to be immediately outside the window. The Château of the Old Guard, in another part of the grounds, and, according to the plan, about two leagues from the little dining-room, we sought in vain for a week, until, happening one evening to sit upon a bench in the forest (forest in the plan), a few yards from the house-door, we observed at our feet, in the ignominious circumstances of being upside down and greenly rotten, the Old Guard himself: that is to say, the painted effigy of a member of that distinguished corps, seven feet high, and in the act of carrying arms, who had had the misfortune to be blown down in the previous winter. It will be perceived that M. Loyal is a staunch admirer of the great Napoleon. He is an old soldier himself – captain of the National Guard, with a handsome gold vase on his chimney-piece, presented to him by his company – and his respect for the memory of the illustrious general is enthusiastic. Medallions of him, portraits of him, busts of him, pictures of him, are thickly sprinkled all over the property. During the first month of our occupation, it was our affliction to be constantly knocking down Napoleon: if we touched a shelf in a dark corner, he toppled over with a crash; and every door we opened, shook him to the soul. Yet M. Loyal is not a man of mere castles in the air, or, as he would say, in Spain.[8] He has a specially practical, contriving, clever, skilful eye and hand. His houses are delightful. He unites French elegance and English comfort, in a happy manner quite his own. He has an extraordinary genius for making tasteful little bedrooms in angles of his roofs, which an Englishman would as soon think of turning to any account as he would think of cultivating the Desert. We have ourself reposed deliciously in an elegant chamber of M. Loyal's construction, with our head as nearly in the kitchen chimney-pot as we can conceive it likely for the head of any gentleman, not by profession a Sweep, to be. And into whatsoever strange nook M. Loyal's genius penetrates, it, in that nook, infallibly constructs a cupboard and a row of pegs. In either of our houses, we could have put away the knap-sacks and hung up the hats of the whole regiment of Guides.

Aforetime, M. Loyal was a tradesman in the town. You can transact business with no present tradesman in the town, and give your card "chez M. Loyal," but a brighter face shines upon you directly. We doubt if there is, ever was, or ever will be, a man so universally pleasant in the minds of people as M. Loyal is in the minds of the citizens of our French watering-place. They rub their hands and laugh when they speak of him. Ah, but he is such a good child, such a brave boy, such a generous spirit, that Monsieur Loyal! It is the honest truth. M. Loyal's nature is the nature of a gentleman. He cultivates his ground with his own hands (assisted by one little labourer, who falls into a fit now and then); and he digs and delves from morn to eve in prodigious perspirations – "works always," as he says – but, cover him with dust, mud, weeds, water, any stains you will, you never can cover the gentleman in M. Loyal. A portly, upright, broad-shouldered, brown faced man, whose soldierly bearing gives him the appearance of being taller than he is, look into the bright eye of M. Loyal, standing before you in his working-blouse and cap, not particularly well shaved, and, it may be, very earthy, and you shall discern in M. Loyal a gentleman whose true politeness is in grain, and confirmation of whose word by his bond you would blush to think of. Not without reason is M. Loyal when he tells that story, in his own vivacious way, of his travelling to Fulham, near London, to buy all these hundreds and hundreds of trees you now see upon the Property, then a bare, bleak hill; and of his sojourning in Fulham three months; and of his jovial evenings with the market-gardeners; and of the crowning banquet before his departure, when the market-gardeners rose as one man, clinked their glasses all together (as the custom at Fulham is), and cried, "Vive Loyal!"

M. Loyal has an agreeable wife, but no family; and he loves to drill the children of his tenants, or run races with them, or do anything with them, or for them, that is good-natured. He is of a highly convivial temperament, and his hospitality is unbounded. Billet a soldier on him, and he is delighted. Five-and-thirty soldiers had M. Loyal billeted on him this present summer, and they all got fat and red-faced in two days. It became a legend among the troops that whosoever got billeted on M. Loyal rolled in clover; and so it fell out that the fortunate man who drew the billet "M. Loyal Devasseur" always leaped into the air, though in heavy marching order. M. Loyal cannot bear to admit anything that might seem by any implication to disparage the military profession. We hinted to him once, that we were conscious of a remote doubt arising in our mind, whether a sou a day for pocket-money, tobacco, stockings, drink, washing, and social pleasures in general, left a very large margin for a soldier's enjoyment. Pardon! said Monsieur Loyal, rather wincing. It was not a fortune, but – à la bonne heure – it was better than it used to be! What, we asked him on another occasion, were all those neighbouring peasants, each living with his family in one room, and each having a soldier (perhaps two) billeted on him every other night, required to provide for those soldiers? "Faith!" said M. Loyal, reluctantly; "a bed, monsieur, and fire to cook with, and a candle. And they share their supper with those soldiers. It is not possible that they could eat alone." – "And what allowance do they get for this?" said we. Monsieur Loyal drew himself up taller, took a step back, laid his hand upon his breast, and said, with majesty, as speaking for himself and all France, "Monsieur, it is a contribution to the State!"

It is never going to rain, according to M. Loyal. When it is impossible to deny that it is now raining in torrents, he says it will be fine – charming – magnificent – to-morrow. It is never hot on the Property, he contends. Likewise it is never cold. The flowers, he says, come out, delighting to grow there; it is like Paradise this morning; it is like the Garden of Eden. He is a little fanciful in his language: smilingly observing of Madame Loyal, when she is absent at vespers, that she is "gone to her salvation" – allée à son salut. He has a great enjoyment of tobacco, but nothing would induce him to continue smoking face to face with a lady. His short black pipe immediately goes into his breast pocket, scorches his blouse, and nearly sets him on fire. In the Town Council and on occasions of ceremony, he appears in a full suit of black, with a waistcoat of magnificent breadth across the chest, and a shirt-collar of fabulous proportions. Good M. Loyal! Under blouse or waistcoat, he carries one of the gentlest hearts that beat in a nation teeming with gentle people. He has had losses, and has been at his best under them. Not only the loss of his way by night in the Fulham times – when a bad subject of an Englishman, under pretence of seeing him home, took him into all the night public-houses, drank "arfanarf"[9] in every one at his expense, and finally fled, leaving him shipwrecked at Cleefeeway, which we apprehend to be Ratcliffe Highway[10] – but heavier losses than that. Long ago a family of children and a mother were left in one of his houses without money, a whole year. M. Loyal – anything but as rich as we wish he had been – had not the heart to say "you must go;" so they stayed on and stayed on, and paying-tenants who would have come in couldn't come in, and at last they managed to get helped home across the water; and M. Loyal kissed the whole group, and said, "Adieu, my poor infants!" and sat down in their deserted salon and smoked his pipe of peace. – "The rent, M. Loyal?" "Eh! well! The rent!" M. Loyal shakes his head. "Le bon Dieu," says M. Loyal presently, "will recompense me," and he laughs and smokes his pipe of peace. May he smoke it on the Property, and not be recompensed, these fifty years!

There are public amusements in our French watering-place, or it would not be French. They are very popular, and very cheap. The sea-bathing – which may rank as the most favoured daylight entertainment, inasmuch as the French visitors bathe all day long, and seldom appear to think of remaining less than an hour at a time in the water – is astoundingly cheap. Omnibuses convey you, if you please, from a convenient part of the town to the beach and back again; you have a clean and comfortable bathing-machine, dress, linen, and all appliances; and the charge for the whole is half-a-franc, or fivepence. On the pier, there is usually a guitar, which seems presumptuously enough to set its tinkling against the deep hoarseness of the sea, and there is always some boy or woman who sings, without any voice, little songs without any tune: the strain we have most frequently heard being an appeal to "the sportsman" not to bag that choicest of game, the swallow. For bathing purposes, we have also a subscription establishment with an esplanade, where people lounge about with telescopes, and seem to get a good deal of weariness for their money; and we have also an association of individual machine proprietors combined against this formidable rival. M. Féroce,[11] our own particular friend in the bathing line, is one of these. How he ever came by his name we cannot imagine. He is as gentle and polite a man as M. Loyal Devasseur himself; immensely stout withal, and of a beaming aspect. M. Féroce has saved so many people from drowning, and has been decorated with so many medals in consequence, that his stoutness seems a special dispensation of Providence to enable him to wear them; if his girth were the girth of an ordinary man, he could never hang them on, all at once. It is only on very great occasions that M. Féroce displays his shining honours. At other times they lie by, with rolls of manuscript testifying to the causes of their presentation, in a huge glass case in the red-sofa'd salon of his private residence on the beach, where M. Féroce also keeps his family pictures, his portraits of himself as he appears both in bathing life and in private life, his little boats that rock by clockwork, and his other ornamental possessions.

Then, we have a commodious and gay Theatre – or had, for it is burned down now – where the opera was always preceded by a vaudeville, in which (as usual) everybody, down to the little old man with the large hat and the little cane and tassel, who always played either my Uncle or my Papa, suddenly broke out of the dialogue into the mildest vocal snatches, to the great perplexity of unaccustomed strangers from Great Britain, who never could make out when they were singing and when they were talking – and indeed it was pretty much the same. But the caterers in the way of entertainment to whom we are most beholden are the Society of Welldoing, who are active all the summer, and give the proceeds of their good works to the poor. Some of the most agreeable fêtes they contrive are announced as "Dedicated to the children;" and the taste with which they turn a small public enclosure into an elegant garden beautifully illuminated, and the thorough-going heartiness and energy with which they personally direct the childish pleasures, are supremely delightful. For fivepence a head, we have on these occasions donkey races with English "Jokeis," and other rustic sports; lotteries for toys, roundabouts, dancing on the grass to the music of an admirable band, fire-balloons and fireworks. Further, almost every week all through the summer – never mind, now, on what day of the week – there is a fête in some adjoining village (called in that part of the country a Ducasse), where the people – really *the people* – dance on the green turf in the open air, round a little orchestra, that seems itself to dance, there is such an airy motion of flags and streamers all about it. And we do not suppose that between the Torrid Zone and the North Pole there are to be found male dancers with such astonishingly loose legs, furnished with so many joints in wrong places, utterly unknown to Professor Owen,[12] as those who here disport themselves. Sometimes the fête appertains to a particular trade; you will see among the cheerful young women at the joint Ducasse of the milliners and tailors, a wholesome knowledge of the art of making common and cheap things uncommon and pretty, by good sense and good taste, that is a practical lesson to any rank of society in a whole island we could mention. The oddest feature of those agreeable scenes is the everlasting Roundabout (we preserve an English word wherever we can, as we are writing the English language), on the wooden horses of which machine grown-up people of all ages are wound round and round with the utmost solemnity, while the proprietor's wife grinds an organ, capable of only one tune, in the centre.

As to the boarding-houses of our French watering-place, they are Legion, and would require a distinct treatise. It is not without a sentiment of national pride that we believe them to contain more bores from the shores of Albion than all the clubs in London. As you walk timidly in their neighbourhood, the very neckcloths and hats of your elderly compatriots cry to you from the stones of the streets, "We are Bores – avoid us!" We have never overheard at street corners such lunatic scraps of political and social discussion as among these dear countrymen of ours. They believe everything that is impossible and nothing that is true. They carry rumours, and ask questions, and make corrections and improvements on one another, staggering to the human intellect. And they are for ever rushing into the English library, propounding such incomprehensible paradoxes to the fair mistress of that establishment, that we beg to recommend her to her Majesty's gracious consideration as a fit object for a pension.

The English form a considerable part of the population of our French watering-place, and are deservedly addressed and respected in many ways. Some of the surface-addresses to them are odd enough, as when a laundress puts a placard outside her house announcing her possession of that curious British instrument, a "Mingle;" or when a tavern-keeper provides accommodation for the celebrated English game of "Nokemdon."[13] But, to us, it is not the least pleasant feature of our French watering-place that a long and constant fusion of the two great nations there has taught each to like the other, and to learn from the other, and to rise superior to the absurd prejudices that have lingered among the weak and ignorant in both countries equally.

Drumming and trumpeting of course go on for ever in our French watering-place. Flag-flying is at a premium, too; but we cheerfully avow that we consider a flag a very pretty object, and that we take such outward signs of innocent liveliness to our heart of hearts. The people, in the town and in the country, are a busy people who work hard; they are sober, temperate, good-humoured, light-hearted, and generally remarkable for their engaging manners. Few just men, not immoderately bilious, could see them in their recreations without very much respecting the character that is so easily, so harmlessly, and so simply, pleased.

Out of Town

First published in *Household Words*, 29 September 1855, and included in *Reprinted Pieces* from which this text is reproduced.

Sitting, on a bright September morning, among my books and papers at my open window on the cliff overhanging the sea-beach, I have the sky and ocean framed before me like a beautiful picture. A beautiful picture, but with such movement in it, such changes of light upon the sails of ships and wake of steamboats, such dazzling gleams of silver far out at sea, such fresh touches on the crisp wave-tops as they break and roll towards me – a picture with such music in the billowy rush upon the shingle, the blowing of morning wind through the corn-sheaves where the farmers' waggons are busy, the singing of the larks, and the distant voices of children at play – such charms of sight and sound as all the Galleries on earth can but poorly suggest.

So dreamy is the murmur of the sea below my window, that I may have been here, for anything I know, one hundred years. Not that I have grown old, for, daily on the neighbouring downs and grassy hill-sides, I find that I can still in reason walk any distance, jump over anything, and climb up anywhere; but that the sound of the ocean seems to have become so customary to my musings, and other realities seem so to have gone aboard ship and floated away over the horizon, that, for aught I will undertake to the contrary, I am the enchanted son of the King my father, shut up in a tower on the sea-shore, for protection against an old she-goblin who insisted on being my godmother, and who foresaw at the font – wonderful creature! – that I should get into a scrape before I was twenty-one. I remember to have been in a City (my Royal parent's dominions, I suppose), and apparently not long ago either, that was in the dreariest condition. The principal inhabitants had all been changed into old newspapers, and in that form were preserving their window-blinds from dust, and wrapping all their smaller household gods in curl-papers. I walked through gloomy streets where every house was shut up and newspapered, and where my solitary footsteps echoed on the deserted pavements. In the public rides there were no carriages, no horses, no animated existence, but a few sleepy policemen, and a few adventurous boys taking advantage of the devastation to swarm up the lamp-posts. In the Westward streets there was no traffic; in the Westward shops, no business. The water-patterns[1] which the 'Prentices had trickled out on the pavements early in the morning, remained uneffaced by human feet. At the corners of mews, Cochin-China fowls stalked gaunt and savage; nobody being left in the deserted city (as it appeared to me), to feed them. Public Houses, where splendid footmen swinging their legs over gorgeous hammer-cloths beside wigged coachmen were wont to regale, were silent, and the unused pewter pots shone, too bright for business, on the shelves. I beheld a Punch's Show leaning against a wall near Park Lane, as if it had fainted. It was deserted, and there were none to heed its desolation. In Belgrave Square I met the last man – an ostler – sitting on a post in a ragged red waistcoat, eating straw, and mildewing away.

If I recollect the name of the little town, on whose shore this sea is murmuring – but I am not just now, as I have premised, to be relied upon for anything – it is Pavilionstone.[2] Within a quarter of a century, it was a little fishing town, and they do say, that the time was, when it was a little smuggling town. I have heard that it was rather famous in the hollands[3] and brandy way, and that coevally with that reputation the lamplighter's was considered a bad life at the Assurance Offices. It was observed that if he were not particular about lighting up, he lived in peace; but that, if he made the best of the oil-lamps in the steep and narrow streets, he usually fell over the cliff at an early age. Now, gas and electricity run to the very water's edge, and the South-Eastern Railway Company screech at us in the dead of night.

But the old little fishing and smuggling town remains, and is so tempting a place for the latter purpose, that I think of going out some night next week, in a fur cap and a pair of petticoat trousers,[4] and running an empty tub, as a kind of archæological pursuit. Let nobody with corns come to Pavilionstone, for there are breakneck flights of ragged steps, connecting the principal streets by back-ways, which will cripple that visitor in half an hour. These are the ways by which, when I run that tub, I shall escape. I shall make a Thermopylæ[5] of the corner of one of them, defend it with my cutlass against the coast-guard until my brave companions have sheered off, then dive into the darkness, and regain my Susan's[6] arms. In connexion with these breakneck steps I observe some wooden cottages, with tumble-down out-houses, and back-yards three feet square, adorned with garlands of dried fish, in one of which (though the General Board of Health might object) my Susan dwells.

The South-Eastern Company have brought Pavilionstone into such vogue, with their tidal trains and splendid steam-packets, that a new

Pavilionstone is rising up. I am, myself, of New Pavilionstone. We are a little mortary and limey at present, but we are getting on capitally. Indeed, we were getting on so fast, at one time, that we rather overdid it, and built a street of shops, the business of which may be expected to arrive in about ten years. We are sensibly laid out in general; and with a little care and pains (by no means wanting, so far), shall become a very pretty place. We ought to be, for our situation is delightful, our air is delicious, and our breezy hills and downs, carpeted with wild thyme, and decorated with millions of wild flowers, are, on the faith of a pedestrian, perfect. In New Pavilionstone we are a little too much addicted to small windows with more bricks in them than glass, and we are not over-fanciful in the way of decorative architecture, and we get unexpected sea-views through cracks in the street doors; on the whole, however, we are very snug and comfortable, and well accommodated. But the Home Secretary (if there be such and officer) cannot too soon shut up the burial-ground of the old parish church. It is in the midst of us, and Pavilionstone will get no good of it, if it be too long left alone.

The lion of Pavilionstone is its Great Hotel.[7] A dozen years ago, going over to Paris by South-Eastern Tidal Steamer, you used to be dropped upon the platform of the main line Pavilionstone Station (not a junction then), at eleven o'clock on a dark winter's night, in a roaring wind; and in the howling wilderness outside the station, was a short omnibus which brought you up by the forehead the instant you got in at the door; and nobody cared about you, and you were alone in the world. You bumped over infinite chalk, until you were turned out at a strange building which had just left off being a barn without having quite begun to be a house, where nobody expected your coming, or knew what to do with you when you were come, and where you were usually blown about, until you happened to be blown against the cold beef, and finally into bed. At five in the morning you were blown out of bed, and after a dreary breakfast, with crumpled company, in the midst of confusion, were hustled on board a steamboat and lay wretched on deck until you saw France lunging and surging at you with great vehemence over the bowsprit.

Now, you come down to Pavilionstone in a free and easy manner, an irresponsible agent, made over in trust to the South-Eastern Company, until you get out of the railway-carriage at high-water mark. If you are crossing by the boat at once, you have nothing to do but walk on board and be happy there if you can – I can't. If you are going to our Great Pavilionstone Hotel, the sprightliest porters under the sun, whose cheerful looks are a pleasant welcome, shoulder your luggage, drive it off in vans, bowl it away in trucks, and enjoy themselves in playing athletic games with it. If you are for public life at our great Pavilionstone Hotel, you walk into that establishment as if it were your club; and find ready for you, your news-room, dining-room, smoking-room, billiard-room, music-room, public breakfast, public dinner twice a-day (one plain, one gorgeous), hot baths and cold baths. If you want to be bored, there are plenty of bores always ready for you, and from Saturday to Monday in particular, you can be bored (if you like it) through and through. Should you want to be private at our Great Pavilionstone Hotel, say but the word, look at the list of charges, choose your floor, name your figure – there you are, established in your castle, by the day, week, month, or year, innocent of all comers or goers, unless you have my fancy for walking early in the morning down the groves of boots and shoes, which so regularly flourish at all the chamber-doors before breakfast, that it seems to me as if nobody ever got up or took them in. Are you going across the Alps, and would you like to air your Italian at our Great Pavilionstone Hotel? Talk to the Manager – always conversational, accomplished, and polite. Do you want to be aided, abetted, comforted, or advised, at our Great Pavilionstone Hotel? Send for the good landlord,[8] and he is your friend. Should you, or any one belonging to you, ever be taken ill at our Great Pavilionstone Hotel, you will not soon forget him or his kind wife. And when you pay your bill at our Great Pavilionstone Hotel, you will not be put out of humour by anything you find in it.

A thoroughly good inn, in the days of coaching and posting, was a noble place. But no such inn would have been equal to the reception of four or five hundred people, all of them wet through, and half of them dead sick, every day in the year. This is where we shine, in our Pavilionstone Hotel. Again – who, coming and going, pitching and tossing, boating and training, hurrying in, and flying out, could ever have calculated the fees to be paid at an old-fashioned house? In our Pavilionstone Hotel vocabulary, there is no such word as fee. Everything is done for you; every service is provided at a fixed and reasonable charge; all the prices are hung up in all the rooms; and you can make out your own bill beforehand, as well as the book-keeper.

In the case of your being a pictorial artist, desirous of studying at small expense the physiognomies and beards of different nations, come, on receipt of this, to Pavilionstone. You shall find all the nations of the earth, and all the styles of shaving and not shaving, hair cutting and hair letting alone, for ever flowing through our hotel. Couriers you shall see by hundreds; fat leathern bags for five-franc pieces, closing with violent snaps, like discharges of fire-arms, by thousands; more luggage in a morning than, fifty years ago, all Europe saw in a week. Looking at trains, steamboats, sick travellers, and luggage, is our great Pavilionstone recreation. We are not strong in other public amusements. We have a Literary and Scientific Institution, and we have a Working Men's Institution — may it hold many gipsy holidays in summer fields, with the kettle boiling, the band of music playing, and the people dancing; and may I be on the hill-side, looking on with pleasure at a wholesome sight too rare in England! — and we have two or three churches, and more chapels than I have yet added up. But public amusements are scarce with us. If a poor theatrical manager comes with his company to give us, in a loft, Mary Bax, or the Murder on the Sand Hills,[9] we don't care much for him — starve him out, in fact. We take more kindly to wax-work, especially if it moves; in which case it keeps much clearer of the second commandment than when it is still. Cooke's Circus[10] (Mr. Cooke is my friend, and always leaves a good name behind him) gives us only a night in passing through. Nor does the travelling menagerie think us worth a longer visit. It gave us a look-in the other day, bringing with it the residentiary van with the stained glass windows, which Her Majesty kept ready-made at Windsor Castle, until she found a suitable opportunity of submitting it for the proprietor's acceptance. I brought away five wonderments from this exhibition. I have wondered ever since, Whether the beasts ever do get used to those small places of confinement; Whether the monkeys have that very horrible flavour in their free state; Whether wild animals have a natural ear for time and tune, and therefore every four-footed creature began to howl in despair when the band began to play; What the giraffe does with his neck when his cart is shut up; and, Whether the elephant feels ashamed of himself when he is brought out of his den to stand on his head in the presence of the whole Collection.

We are a tidal harbour at Pavilionstone, as indeed I have implied already in my mention of tidal trains. At low water, we are a heap of mud, with an empty channel in it where a couple of men in big boots always shovel and scoop: with what exact object, I am unable to say. At that time, all the stranded fishing-boats turn over on their sides, as if they were dead marine monsters; the colliers and other shipping stick disconsolate in the mud; the steamers look as if their white chimneys would never smoke more, and their red paddles never turn again; the green sea-slime and weed upon the rough stones at the entrance, seem records of obsolete high tides never more to flow; the flagstaff-halyards droop; the very little wooden lighthouse shrinks in the idle glare of the sun. And here I may observe of the very little wooden lighthouse, that when it is lighted at night, — red and green, — it looks so like a medical man's, that several distracted husbands have at various times been found, on occasions of premature domestic anxiety, going round and round it, trying to find the Night-bell.

But the moment the tide begins to make, the Pavilionstone Harbour begins to revive. It feels the breeze of the rising water before the water comes, and begins to flutter and stir. When the little shallow waves creep in, barely overlapping one another, the vanes at the mastheads wake, and become agitated. As the tide rises, the fishing-boats get into good spirits and dance, the flagstaff hoists a bright red flag, the steamboat smokes, cranes creak, horses and carriages dangle in the air, stray passengers and luggage appear. Now, the shipping is afloat, and comes up buoyantly, to look at the wharf. Now, the carts that have come down for coals, load away as hard as they can load. Now, the steamer smokes immensely, and occasionally blows at the paddle-boxes like a vaporous whale – greatly disturbing nervous loungers. Now, both the tide and the breeze have risen, and you are holding your hat on (if you want to see how the ladies hold *their* hats on, with a stay, passing over the broad brim and down the nose, come to Pavilionstone). Now, everything in the harbour splashes, dashes, and bobs. Now, the Down Tidal Train is telegraphed, and you know (without knowing how you know), that two hundred and eighty-seven people are coming. Now, the fishing-boats that have been out, sail in at the top of the tide. Now, the bell goes, and the locomotive hisses and shrieks, and the train comes gliding in, and the two hundred and eighty-seven come scuffling out. Now, there is not only a tide of water, but a tide of people, and a tide of luggage – all tumbling and flowing and bouncing about together. Now, after infinite bustle, the steamer steams out, and we (on the Pier) are all delighted when she rolls as if she would roll her funnel out, and are all disappointed when she don't. Now, the other steamer is coming in, and the Custom House prepares, and the wharf-labourers assemble, and the hawsers are made ready, and the Hotel Porters come rattling down with van and truck, eager to begin more Olympic games with more luggage. And this is the way in which we go on, down at Pavilionstone, every tide. And if you want to live a life of luggage, or to see it lived, or to breathe sweet air which will send you to sleep at a moment's notice at any period of the day or night, or to disport yourself upon or in the sea, or to scamper about Kent, or to come out of town for the enjoyment of all or any of these pleasures, come to Pavilionstone.

Railway Dreaming

First published in *Household Words*, 10 May 1856, from which this text is reproduced.

When was I last in France all the winter, deducting the many hours I passed upon the wet and windy way between France and England? In what autumn and spring was it that those Champs Elysées trees were yellow and scant of leaf when I first looked at them out of my balcony, and were a bright and tender green when I last looked at them on a beautiful May morning?

I can't make out. I am never sure of time or place upon a Railroad. I can't read, I can't think, I can't sleep – I can only dream. Rattling along in this railway carriage in a state of luxurious confusion, I take it for granted I am coming from somewhere, and going somewhere else. I seek to know no more. Why things come into my head and fly out again, whence they come and why they come, where they go and why they go, I am incapable of considering. It may be the guard's business, or the railway company's; I only know it is not mine. I know nothing about myself – for anything I know, I may be coming from the Moon.

If I am coming from the Moon, what an extraordinary people the Mooninians must be for sitting down in the open air! I have seen them wipe the hoar-frost off the seats in the public ways, on the faintest appearance of a gleam of sun, and sit down to enjoy themselves. I have seen them, two minutes after it has left off raining for the first time in eight-and-forty hours, take chairs in the midst of the mud and water, and begin to chat. I have seen them by the roadside, easily reclining on iron couches, when their beards have been all but blown off their chins by the east wind. I have seen them, with no protection from the black drizzle and dirt but a saturated canvas blind overhead, and a handful of sand underfoot, smoke and drink new beer, whole evenings. And the Mooninian babies. Heavens, what a surprising race are the Mooninian babies! Seventy-one of these innocents have I counted, with their nurses and chairs, spending the day outside the Café de la Lune,[1] in weather that would have satisfied Herod.[2] Thirty-nine have I beheld in that locality at once, with these eyes, partaking of their natural refreshment under umbrellas. Twenty-three have I seen engaged with skipping-ropes, in mire three inches thick. At three years old the Mooninian babies grow up. They are by that time familiar with coffee-houses, and used up as to truffles. They dine at six. Soup, fish, two entrées, a vegetable, a cold dish, or paté-de-foie-gras, a roast, a salad, a sweet, and a preserved peach or so, form (with occasional whets of sardines, radishes, and Lyons sausage) their frugal repast. They breakfast at eleven, on a light beefsteak with Madeira sauce, a kidney steeped in champagne, a trifle of sweetbread, a plate of fried potatoes, and a glass or two of wholesome Bordeaux wine. I have seen a marriageable young female aged five, in a mature bonnet and crinoline, finish off at a public establishment with her amiable parents, on coffee that would consign a child of any other nation to the family undertaker in one experiment. I have dined at a friendly party, sitting next to a Mooninian baby, who ate of nine dishes besides ice and fruit, and, wildly stimulated by sauces, in all leisure moments flourished its spoon about its head in the manner of a pictorial glory.

The Mooninian Exchange was a strange sight in my time. The Mooninians of all ranks and classes were gambling at that period (whenever it was), in the wildest manner – in a manner, which, in its extension to all possible subjects of gambling, and in the prevalence of the frenzy among all grades, has few parallels that I can recall. The steps of the Mooninian Bourse were thronged every day with a vast, hot, mad crowd, so expressive of the desperate game in which the whole City were players, that one stood aghast. In the Mooninian Journals I read, any day, without surprise, how such a Porter had rushed out of such a house and flung himself into the river, "because of losses on the Bourse;" or how such a man had robbed such another, with the intent of acquiring funds for speculation on the Bourse. In the great Mooninian Public Drive, every day, there were crowds of riders on blood-horses, and crowds of riders in dainty carriages red-velvet lined and white-leather harnessed, all of whom had the cards and counters in their pockets; who were all feeding the blood-horses on paper and stabling them on the board; who were leading a grand life at a great rate and with a mighty show; who were all profuse and prosperous while the cards could continue to be shuffled and the deals to go round.

In the same place, I saw, nearly every day, a curious spectacle. One pretty little child at a window, always waving his hand at, and cheering, an array of open carriages escorted by out-riders in green and gold; and no one echoing the child's acclamation. Occasional deference in carriages, occasional curiosity on foot, occasional adulation from foreigners, I noticed in that connexion, in that place; but, four great streams of determined indifference I always saw flowing up and down; and I never, in six months, knew a hand or heard a voice to come in real aid of the child.

I am not a lonely man, though I was once a lonely boy; but that was long ago. The Mooninian capital, however, is the place for lonely men to dwell in. I have tried it, and have condemned myself to solitary freedom expressly for the purpose. I sometimes like to pretend to be childless and companionless, and to wonder whether, if I were really so, I should be glad to find somebody to ask me out to dinner, instead of living under a constant terror of weakly making engagements that I don't want to make. Hence, I have been into many Mooninian restaurants as a lonely man. The company have regarded me as an unfortunate person of that description. The paternal character, occupying the next table with two little boys whose legs were difficult of administration in a narrow space, as never being the right legs in the right places, has regarded me, at first, with looks of envy. When the little boys have indecorously inflated themselves out of the seltzer-water bottle, I have seen discomfiture and social shame on that Mooninian's brow. Meanwhile I have sat majestically using my tooth-pick, in silent assertion of my counterfeit superiority. And yet it has been good to see how that family Mooninian has vanquished me in the long-run. I have never got so red in the face over my meat and wine, as he. I have never warmed up into such enjoyment of my meal as he has of his. I have never forgotten the legs of the little boys, whereas from that Mooninian's soul they have quickly walked into oblivion. And when, at last, under the ripening influence of dinner, those boys have both together pulled at that Mooninian's waistcoat (imploring him, as I conceived, to take them to the play-house, next door but one), I have shrunk under the glance he has given me; so emphatically has it said, with the virtuous farmer in the English domestic comedy,[3] "Dang it, Squoire, can'ee doa thic!" (I may explain in a parenthesis that "thic," which the virtuous farmer can do and the squire can't, is to lay his hand upon his heart − a result opposed to my experience in actual life, where the humbugs are always able to lay their hands upon their hearts, and do it far oftener and much better than the virtuous men.)

In my solitary character I have walked forth after eating my dinner and paying my bill − in the Mooninian capital we used to call the bill "the addition" − to take my coffee and cigar at some separate establishment devoted to such enjoyments. And in the customs belonging to these, as in many other easy and gracious customs, the Mooninians are highly deserving of imitation among ourselves. I have never had far to go, unless I have been particularly hard to please; a dozen houses at the utmost. A spring evening is in my mind when I sauntered from my dinner into one of these resorts, haphazard. The thoroughfare in which it stood, was not as wide as the Strand in London, by Somerset House; the houses were no larger and no better than are to be found in that place; the climate (we find ours a convenient scapegoat) had been, for months, quite as cold and wet, and very very often almost as dark, as the climate in the Strand. The place into which I turned, had been there all the winter just as it was then. It was like a Strand-shop, with the front altogether taken away. Within, it was sanded, prettily painted and papered, decorated with mirrors and glass chandeliers for gas; furnished with little round stone tables, crimson stools, and crimson benches. It was made much more tasteful (at the cost of three and fourpence a week) by two elegant baskets of flowers on pedestals. An inner raised-floor, answering to the back shop in the Strand, was partitioned off with glass, for those who might prefer to read the papers and play at dominoes, in an atmosphere free from tobacco-smoke. There, in her neat little tribune, sits the Lady of the Counter, surrounded at her needlework by lump-sugar and little punch-bowls. To whom I touch my hat; she graciously acknowledging the salute. Forth from her side comes a pleasant waiter, scrupulously clean, brisk, attentive, honest: a man to be very obliging to me, but expecting me to be obliging in return, and whom I cannot bully – which is no deprivation to me, as I don't at all want to do it. He brings me, at my request, my cup of coffee and cigar, and, of his own motion, a small decanter of brandy and a liqueur-glass. He gives me a light, and leaves me to my enjoyment. The place from which the shop-front has been taken makes a gay proscenium; as I sit and smoke, the street becomes a stage, with an endless procession of lively actors crossing and re-crossing. Women with children, carts and coaches, men on horseback, soldiers, water-carriers with their pails, family groups, more soldiers, lounging exquisites, more family groups (coming past, flushed, a little too late for the play), stone-masons leaving work on the new buildings and playing tricks with one another as they go along, two lovers, more soldiers, wonderfully neat young women from shops, carrying flat boxes to customers; a seller of cool drink, with the drink in a crimson velvet temple at his back, and a waistcoat of tumblers on; boys, dogs, more soldiers, horse-riders strolling to the Circus in amazing shirts of private life, and yellow kid gloves; family groups; pickers-up of refuse, with baskets at their backs and hooked rods in their hands to fill them with; more neat young women, more soldiers. The gas begins to spring up in the street; and my brisk waiter lighting our gas, enshrines me, like an idol, in a sparkling temple. A family group come in: father and mother and little child. Two short-throated old ladies come in, who will pocket their spare sugar, and out of whom I foresee that the establishment will get as little profit as possible. Workman in his common frock comes in; orders his small bottle of beer, and lights his pipe. We are all amused, sitting seeing the traffic in the street, and the traffic in the street is in its turn amused by seeing us. It is surely better for me, and for the family group, and for the two old ladies, and for the workman, to have thus much of community with the city life of all degrees, than to be getting bilious in hideous black-holes, and turning cross and suspicious in solitary places! I may never say a word to any of these people in my life, nor they to me; but, we are all interchanging enjoyment frankly and openly − not fencing ourselves off and boxing ourselves up. We are forming a habit of mutual consideration and allowance; and this institution of the café (for all my entertainment and pleasure in which, I pay tenpence), is a part of the civilised system that requires the giant to fall into his own place in a crowd, and will not allow him to take the dwarf's; and which renders the commonest person as certain of retaining his or her commonest seat in any public assembly, as the marquis is of holding his stall at the Opera through the evening.

There were many things among the Mooninians that might be changed for the better, and there were many things that they might learn from us. They could teach us, for all that, how to make and keep a Park − which we have been accustomed to think ourselves rather learned in − and how to trim up our ornamental streets, a dozen times a-day, with scrubbing-brushes, and sponges, and soap, and chloride of lime. As to the question of sweetness within doors, I would rather not have put my own residence, even under the perpetual influence of peat charcoal, in competition with the cheapest model lodging-house in England. And one strange sight, which I have contemplated many a time during the last dozen years, I think is not so well arranged in the Mooninian capital as in London, even though our coroners hold their dread courts at the little public-houses − a custom which I am of course prepared to hear is, and which I know beforehand must be, one of the Bulwarks of the British Constitution.

I am thinking of the Mooninian Morgue, where the bodies of all persons discovered dead, with no clue to their identity upon them, are placed to be seen by all who choose to go and look at them. All the world knows this custom, and perhaps all the world knows that the bodies lie on inclined planes within a great glass window, as though Holbein should represent Death, in his grim Dance, keeping a shop, and displaying his goods like a Regent Street or Boulevard linen-draper.[4] But, all the world may not have had the means of remarking perhaps, as I by chance have had from time to time, some of the accidental peculiarities of the place. The keeper seems to be fond of birds. In fair weather, there is always a cage outside his little window, and a something singing within it as such a something sang, thousands of ages ago, before ever a man died on this earth. The spot is sunny in the forenoon, and, there being a little open space there, and a market for fruit and vegetables close at hand, and a way to the Great Cathedral past the door, is a reasonably good spot for mountebanks. Accordingly, I have often found Paillasse[5] there, balancing a knife or a straw upon his nose, with such intentness that he has almost backed himself in at the doorway. The learned owls have elicited great mirth there, within my hearing, and once the performing dog who had a wait in his part, came and peeped in, with a red jacket on, while I was alone in the contemplation of five bodies, one with a bullet through the temple. It happened, on another occasion, that a handsome youth lay in front in the centre of the window, and that a press of people behind me rendered it a difficult and slow process to get out. As I gave place to the man at my right shoulder, he slipped into the position I had occupied, with his attention so concentrated on the dead figure that he seemed unaware of the change of place. I never saw a plainer expression than that upon his features, or one that struck more enduringly into my remembrance. He was an evil-looking fellow of two or three and twenty, and had his left hand at the draggled ends of his cravat, which he had put to his mouth, and his right hand feeling in his breast. His head was a little on one side; his eyes were intently fixed upon the figure. "Now, if I were to give that pretty young fellow, my rival, a stroke with a hatchet on the back of the head, or were to tumble him over into the river by night, he would look pretty much like that, I am thinking!" He could not have said it more plainly; – I have always an idea that he went away and did it.

It is wonderful to see the people at this place. Cheery married women, basket in hand, strolling in, on their way to or from the buying of the day's dinner; children in arms with little pointing fingers; young girls; prowling boys; comrades in working, soldiering, or what not. Ninety-nine times in a hundred, nobody about to cross the threshold, looking in the faces coming out, could form the least idea, from anything in their expression, of the nature of the sight. I have studied them attentively, and have reason for saying so.

But, I never derived so strange a sensation from this dismal establishment as on going in there once, and finding the keeper moving about among the bodies. I never saw any living creature in among them, before or since, and the wonder was that he looked so much more ghastly and intolerable than the dead, stark people. There is a strong light from above, and a general cold, clammy aspect; and I think that with the first start of seeing him must have come the impression that the bodies were all getting up! It was instantaneous; but he looked horribly incongruous there, even after it had departed. All about him was a library of mysterious books that I have often had my eyes on. From pegs and hooks and rods, hang, for a certain time, the clothes of the dead who have been buried without recognition. They mostly have been taken off people who were found in the water, and are swollen (as the people often are) out of shape and likeness. Such awful boots, with turned-up toes, and sand and gravel clinging to them, shall be seen in no other collection of dress; nor, such neckcloths, long and lank, still retaining the form of having been wrung out; nor, such slimy garments with puffed legs and arms; nor such hats and caps that have been battered against pile and bridge; nor, such dreadful rags. Whose work ornaments that decent blouse; who sewed that shirt? And the man who wore it. Did he ever stand at this window wondering, as I do, what sleepers shall be brought to these beds, and whether wonderers as to who should occupy them, have come to be laid down here themselves?

London! Please to get your tickets ready, gentlemen! I must have a coach. And that reminds me, how much better they manage coaches for the public in the capital of the Mooninians! But, it is done by Centralisation! somebody shrieks to me from some vestry's topmost height. Then, my good sir, let us have Centralisation. It is a long word, but I am not at all afraid of long words when they represent efficient things. Circumlocution[6] is a long word, but it represents inefficiency; inefficiency in everything; inefficiency from the state coach to my hackney cab.

Out of the Season

First published in *Household Words*, 28 June 1856, and included in *Reprinted Pieces* from which it is reproduced.

It fell to my lot, this last bleak Spring, to find myself in a watering-place out of the Season.[1] A vicious north-east squall blew me into it from foreign parts, and I tarried in it alone for three days, resolved to be exceedingly busy.

On the first day, I began business by looking for two hours at the sea, and staring the Foreign Militia out of countenance. Having disposed of these important engagements, I sat down at one of the two windows of my room, intent on doing something desperate in the way of literary composition, and writing a chapter of unheard-of excellence[2] – with which the present essay has no connexion.

It is a remarkable quality in a watering-place out of the season, that everything in it will and must be looked at. I had no previous suspicion of this fatal truth; but the moment I sat down to write, I began to perceive it. I had scarcely fallen into my most promising attitude, and dipped my pen in the ink, when I found the clock upon the pier – a red-faced clock with a white rim – importuning me in a highly vexatious manner to consult my watch, and see how I was off for Greenwich time. Having no intention of making a voyage or taking an observation, I had not the least need of Greenwich time, and could have put up with watering-place time as a sufficiently accurate article. The pier-clock, however, persisting, I felt it necessary to lay down my pen, compare my watch with him, and fall into a grave solicitude about half-seconds. I had taken up my pen again, and was about to commence that valuable chapter, when a Custom-house cutter under the window requested that I would hold a naval review of her, immediately.

It was impossible, under the circumstances, for any mental resolution, merely human, to dismiss the Custom-house cutter, because the shadow of her topmast fell upon my paper, and the vane played on the masterly blank chapter. I was therefore under the necessity of going to the other window; sitting astride of the chair there, like Napoleon bivouacking in the print; and inspecting the cutter as she lay, all, O! that day, in the way of my chapter. She was rigged to carry a quantity of canvas, but her hull was so very small that four giants aboard of her (three men and a boy) who were vigilantly scraping at her, all together, inspired me with a terror lest they should scrape her away. A fifth giant, who appeared to consider himself "below" – as indeed he was, from the waist downwards – meditated, in such close proximity with the little gusty chimney-pipe, that he seemed to be smoking it. Several boys looked on from the wharf, and, when the gigantic attention appeared to be fully occupied, one or other of these would furtively swing himself in mid-air over the Custom-house cutter, by means of a line pendant from her rigging, like a young spirit of the storm. Presently, a sixth hand brought down two little water-casks; presently afterwards a truck came and delivered a hamper. I was now under an obligation to consider that the cutter was going on a cruise, and to wonder where she was going, and when she was going, and why she was going, and at what date she might be expected back, and who commanded her? With these pressing questions I was fully occupied when the Packet, making ready to go across, and blowing off her spare steam, roared, "Look at me!"

It became a positive duty to look at the Packet preparing to go across; aboard of which, the people newly come down by the railroad were hurrying in a great fluster. The crew had got their tarry overalls on – and one knew what *that* meant – not to mention the white basins, ranged in neat little piles of a dozen each, behind the door of the after-cabin. One lady as I looked, one resigning and far-seeing woman, took her basin from the store of crockery, as she might have taken a refreshment-ticket, laid herself down on deck with that utensil at her ear, muffled her feet in one shawl, solemnly covered her countenance after the antique manner with another, and on the completion of these preparations appeared by the strength of her volition to become insensible. The mail-bags (O that I myself had the sea-legs of a mail-bag!) were tumbled aboard; the Packet left off roaring, warped out, and made at the white line upon the bar. One dip, one roll, one break of the sea over her bows, and Moore's Almanack or the sage Raphael[3] could not have told me more of the state of things aboard, than I knew.

The famous chapter was all but begun now, and would have been quite begun, but for the wind. It was blowing stiffly from the east, and it rumbled in the chimney and shook the house. That was not much; but, looking out into the wind's grey eye for inspiration, I laid down my pen again to make the remark to myself, how emphatically everything by the sea declares that it has a great concern in the state of the wind. The trees blown all one way; the defences of the harbour reared highest and strongest against the raging point; the shingle flung up on the beach from the same direction; the number of arrows pointed at the common enemy; the sea tumbling in and rushing towards them as if it were inflamed by the sight. This put it in my head that I really ought to go out and take a walk in the wind; so I gave up the magnificent chapter for that day, entirely persuading myself that I was under a moral obligation to have a blow.

I had a good one, and that on the high road – the very high road – on the top of the cliffs, where I met the stage-coach with all the outsides holding their hats on and themselves too, and overtook a flock of sheep with the wool about their necks blown into such great ruffs that they looked like fleecy owls. The wind played upon the lighthouse as if it were a great whistle, the spray was driven over the sea in a cloud of haze, the ships rolled and pitched heavily, and at intervals long slants and flaws of light made mountain-steeps of communication between the ocean and the sky. A walk of ten miles brought me to a seaside town without a cliff,⁴ which, like the town I had come from, was out of the season too. Half of the houses were shut up; half of the other half were to let; the town might have done as much business as it was doing then, if it had been at the bottom of the sea. Nobody seemed to flourish save the attorney; his clerk's pen was going in the bow-window of his wooden house; his brass door-plate alone was free from salt, and had been polished up that morning. On the beach, among the rough luggers and capstans, groups of storm-beaten boatmen, like a sort of marine monsters, watched under the lee of those objects, or stood leaning forward against the wind, looking out through battered spy-glasses. The parlour bell in the Admiral Benbow had grown so flat with being out of the season, that neither could I hear it ring when I pulled the handle for lunch, nor could the young woman in black stockings and strong shoes, who acted as waiter out of the season, until it had been tinkled three times.

Admiral Benbow's cheese was out of the season, but his home-made bread was good, and his beer was perfect. Deluded by some earlier spring day which had been warm and sunny, the Admiral had cleared the firing out of his parlour stove, and had put some flower-pots in – which was amiable and hopeful in the Admiral, but not judicious: the room being, at that present visiting, transcendantly cold. I therefore took the liberty of peeping out across a little stone passage into the Admiral's kitchen, and, seeing a high settle with its back towards me drawn out in front of the Admiral's kitchen fire, I strolled in, bread and cheese in hand, munching and looking about. One landsman and two boatmen were seated on the settle, smoking pipes and drinking beer out of thick pint crockery mugs – mugs peculiar to such places, with parti-coloured rings round them, and ornaments between the rings like frayed-out roots.[5] The landsman was relating his experiences, as yet only three nights old, of a fearful running-down case in the Channel, and therein presented to my imagination a sound of music that it will not soon forget.

"At that identical moment of time," said he (he was a prosy man by nature, who rose with his subject), "the night being light and calm, but with a grey mist upon the water that didn't seem to spread for more than two or three mile, I was walking up and down the wooden causeway next the pier, off where it happened, along with a friend of mine, which his name is Mr. Clocker. Mr. Clocker is a grocer over yonder." (From the direction in which he pointed the bowl of his pipe, I might have judged Mr. Clocker to be a merman, established in the grocery trade in five-and-twenty fathoms of water.) "We were smoking our pipes, and walking up and down the causeway, talking of one thing and talking of another. We were quite alone there, except that a few hovellers" (the Kentish name for 'long-shore boatmen like his companions) "were hanging about their lugs, waiting while the tide made, as hovellers will." (One of the two boatmen, thoughtfully regarding me, shut up one eye; this I understood to mean: first, that he took me into the conversation: secondly, that he confirmed the proposition: thirdly, that he announced himself as a hoveller.) "All of a sudden Mr. Clocker and me stood rooted to the spot, by hearing a sound come through the stillness, right over the sea, *like a great sorrowful flute or Æolian harp*. We didn't in the least know what it was, and judge of our surprise when we saw the hovellers, to a man, leap into the boats and tear about to hoist sail and get off, as if they had every one of 'em gone, in a moment, raving mad! But *they* knew it was the cry of distress from the sinking emigrant ship."

When I got back to my watering-place out of the season, and had done my twenty miles in good style, I found that the celebrated Black Mesmerist[6] intended favouring the public that evening in the Hall of the Muses, which he had engaged for the purpose. After a good dinner, seated by the fire in an easy chair, I began to waver in a design I had formed of waiting on the Black Mesmerist, and to incline towards the expediency of remaining where I was. Indeed a point of gallantry was involved in my doing so, inasmuch as I had not left France alone, but had come from the prisons of St. Pélagie with my distinguished and unfortunate friend Madame Roland[7] (in two volumes which I bought for two francs each, at the book-stall in the Place de la Concorde, Paris, at the corner of the Rue Royale). Deciding to pass the evening tête-à-tête with Madame Roland, I derived, as I always do, great pleasure from that spiritual woman's society, and the charms of her brave soul and engaging conversation. I must confess that if she had only some more faults, only a few more passionate failings of any kind, I might love her better; but I am content to believe that the deficiency is in me, and not in her. We spent some sadly interesting hours together on this occasion, and she told me again of her cruel discharge from the Abbaye, and of her being re-arrested before her free feet had sprung lightly up half-a-dozen steps of her own staircase, and carried off to the prison which she only left for the guillotine.

Madame Roland and I took leave of one another before midnight, and I went to bed full of vast intentions for next day, in connexion with the unparalleled chapter. To hear the foreign mail-steamers coming in at dawn of day, and to know that I was not aboard or obliged to get up, was very comfortable; so I rose for the chapter in great force.

I had advanced so far as to sit down at my window again on my second morning, and to write the first half-line of the chapter and strike it out, not liking it, when my conscience reproached me with not having surveyed the watering-place out of the season, after all, yesterday, but with having gone straight out of it at the rate of four miles and a half an hour. Obviously the best amends that I could make for this remissness was to go and look at it without another moment's delay. So — altogether as a matter of duty — I gave up the magnificent chapter for another day, and sauntered out with my hands in my pockets.

All the houses and lodgings ever let to visitors were to let that morning. It seemed to have snowed bills with To Let upon them. This put me upon thinking what the owners of all those apartments did, out of the season; how they employed their time, and occupied their minds. They could not be always going to the Methodist chapels, of which I passed one every other minute. They must have some other recreation. Whether they pretended to take one another's lodgings, and opened one another's tea-caddies in fun? Whether they cut slices off their own beef and mutton, and made believe that it belonged to somebody else? Whether they played little dramas of life, as children do, and said, "I ought to come and look at your apartments, and you ought to ask two guineas a week too much, and then I ought to say I must have the rest of the day to think of it, and then you ought to say that another lady and gentleman with no children in family had made an offer very close to your own terms, and you had passed your word to give them a positive answer in half an hour, and indeed were just going to take the bill down when you heard the knock, and then I ought to take them you know?" Twenty such speculations engaged my thoughts. Then, after passing, still clinging to the walls, defaced rags of the bills of last year's Circus, I came to a back field near a timber-yard where the Circus itself had been, and where there was yet a sort of monkish tonsure on the grass, indicating the spot where the young lady had gone round upon her pet steed Firefly in her daring flight. Turning into the town again, I came among the shops, and they were emphatically out of the season. The chemist had no boxes of ginger-beer powders, no beautifying sea-side soaps and washes, no attractive scents; nothing but his great goggle-eyed red bottles, looking as if the winds of winter and the drift of the salt sea had inflamed them. The grocers' hot pickles, Harvey's Sauce, Doctor Kitchener's Zest, Anchovy Paste, Dundee Marmalade, and the whole stock of luxurious helps to appetite, were hybernating somewhere underground. The china-shop had no trifles from anywhere. The Bazaar had given in altogether, and presented a notice on the shutters that this establishment would re-open at Whitsuntide, and that the proprietor in the meantime might be heard of at Wild Lodge, East Cliff. At the Sea-bathing Establishment, a row of neat little wooden houses seven or eight feet high, I *saw* the proprietor in bed in the shower-bath. As to the bathing-machines, they were (how they got there is not for me to say) at the top of a hill at least a mile and a half off. The library, which I had never seen otherwise than wide open, was tight shut; and two peevish bald old gentlemen seemed to be hermetically sealed up inside, eternally reading the paper. That wonderful mystery, the music-shop, carried it off as usual (except that it had more cabinet pianos in stock), as if season or no season were all one to it. It made the same prodigious display of bright brazen wind-instruments, horribly twisted, worth, as I should conceive, some thousands of pounds, and which it is utterly impossible that anybody in any season can ever play or want to play. It had five triangles in the window, six pairs of castanets, and three harps; likewise every polka with a coloured frontispiece that ever was published; from the original one where a smooth male and female Pole of high rank are coming at the observer with their arms a-kimbo, to the Ratcatcher's Daughter. Astonishing establishment, amazing enigma! Three other shops were pretty much out of the season, what they were used to be in it. First, the shop where they sell the sailors' watches, which had still the old collection of enormous timekeepers, apparently designed to break a fall from the masthead: with places to wind them up, like fire-plugs. Secondly, the shop where they sell the sailors' clothing, which displayed the old sou'-westers, and the old oily suits, and the old pea-jackets, and the old one sea-chest, with its handles like a pair of rope ear-rings. Thirdly, the unchangeable shop for the sale of literature that has been left behind. Here, Dr. Faustus was still going down to very red and yellow perdition, under the superintendence of three green personages of a scaly humour, with excrescential serpents growing out of their blade-bones.[8] Here, the Golden Dreamer and the Norwood Fortune Teller were still on sale at sixpence each, with instructions for making the dumb cake, and reading destinies in tea-cups, and with a picture of a young woman with a high waist lying on a sofa in an attitude so uncomfortable as almost to account for her dreaming at one and the same time of a conflagration, a shipwreck, an earthquake, a skeleton, a church-porch, lightning, funerals performed, and a young man in a bright blue coat and canary pantaloons. Here, were Little Warblers and Fairburn's Comic Songsters. Here, too, were ballads on the old ballad paper and in the old confusion of types; with an old man in a cocked hat, and an arm-chair, for the illustration to Will Watch the bold Smuggler; and the Friar of Orders Grey, represented by a little girl in a hoop, with a ship in the distance. All these as of yore, when they were infinite delights to me![9]

It took me so long fully to relish these many enjoyments, that I had not more than an hour before bedtime to devote to Madame Roland. We got on admirably together on the subject of her convent education, and I rose next morning with the full conviction that the day for the great chapter was at last arrived.

It had fallen calm, however, in the night, and as I sat at breakfast I blushed to remember that I had not yet been on the Downs.[10] I a walker, and not yet on the Downs! Really, on so quiet and bright a morning this must be set right. As an essential part of the Whole Duty of Man,[11] therefore, I left the chapter to itself – for the present – and went on the Downs. They were wonderfully green and beautiful, and gave me a good deal to do. When I had done with the free air and the view, I had to go down into the valley and look after the hops (which I know nothing about), and to be equally solicitous as to the cherry orchards. Then I took it on myself to cross-examine a tramping family in black (mother alleged, I have no doubt by herself in person, to have died last week), and to accompany eighteenpence, which produced a great effect, with moral admonitions which produced none at all. Finally, it was late in the afternoon before I got back to the unprecedented chapter, and then I determined that it was out of the season, as the place was, and put it away.

I went at night to the benefit of Mrs. B. Wedgington at the Theatre, who had placarded the town with the admonition, "DON'T FORGET IT!" I made the house, according to my calculation, four and ninepence to begin with, and it may have warmed up, in the course of the evening, to half a sovereign. There was nothing to offend any one, – the good Mr. Baines of

Leeds[12] excepted. Mrs. B. Wedgington sang to a grand piano. Mr. B. Wedgington did the like, and also took off his coat, tucked up his trousers, and danced in clogs. Master B. Wedgington, aged ten months, was nursed by a shivering young person in the boxes, and the eye of Mrs. B. Wedgington wandered that way more than once. Peace be with all the Wedgingtons from A. to Z. May they find themselves in the Season somewhere![13]

Refreshments for Travellers

First published in *All the Year Round*, 24 March 1860. The text here is taken from *The Uncommercial Traveller*.

In the late high winds I was blown to a great many places – and indeed, wind or no wind, I generally have extensive transactions on hand in the article of Air – but I have not been blown to any English place lately, and I very seldom have blown to any English place in my life, where I could get anything good to eat and drink in five minutes, or where, if I sought it, I was received with a welcome.

This is a curious thing to consider. But before (stimulated by my own experiences and the representations of many fellow-travellers of every uncommercial and commercial degree) I consider it further, I must utter a passing word of wonder concerning high winds.

I wonder why metropolitan gales always blow so hard at Walworth.[1] I cannot imagine what Walworth has done, to bring such windy punishment upon itself, as I never fail to find recorded in the newspapers when the wind has blown at all hard. Brixton seems to have something on its conscience; Peckham suffers more than a virtuous Peckham might be supposed to deserve; the howling neighbourhood of Deptford figures largely in the accounts of the ingenious gentlemen who are out in every wind that blows, and to whom it is an ill high wind that blows no good; but, there can hardly be any Walworth left by this time. It must surely be blown away. I have read of more chimney-stacks and house-copings coming down with terrific smashes at Walworth, and of more sacred edifices being nearly (not quite) blown out to sea from the same accursed locality, than I have read of practised thieves with the appearance and manners of gentlemen – a popular phenomenon which never existed on earth out of fiction and a police report. Again: I wonder why people are always blown into the Surrey Canal, and into no other piece of water! Why do people get up early and go out in groups, to be blown into the Surrey Canal? Do they say to one another, "Welcome death, so that we get into the newspapers?" Even that would be an insufficient explanation, because even then they might sometimes put themselves in the way of being blown into the Regent's Canal, instead of always saddling Surrey for the field. Some nameless policeman, too, is constantly, on the slightest provocation, getting himself blown into this same Surrey Canal. Will SIR RICHARD MAYNE[2] see to it, and restrain that weak-minded and feeble-bodied constable?

To resume the consideration of the curious question of Refreshment. I am a Briton, and, as such, I am aware that I never will be a slave – and yet I have latent suspicion that there must be some slavery of wrong custom in this matter.

I travel by railroad. I start from home at seven or eight in the morning, after breakfasting hurriedly. What with skimming over the open landscape, what with mining in the damp bowels of the earth, what with banging booming and shrieking the scores of miles away, I am hungry when I arrive at the "Refreshment" station where I am expected. Please to observe, expected. I have said, I am hungry; perhaps I might say, with greater point and force, that I am to some extent exhausted, and that I need – in the expressive French sense of the word – to be restored. What is provided for my restoration? The apartment that is to restore me is a wind-trap, cunningly set to inveigle all the draughts in that country-side, and to communicate a special intensity and velocity to them as they rotate in two hurricanes: one, about my wretched head: one, about my wretched legs. The training of the young ladies behind the counter who are to restore me, has been from their infancy directed to the assumption of a defiant dramatic show that I am *not* expected. It is in vain for me to represent to them by my humble and conciliatory manners, that I wish to be liberal. It is in vain for me to represent to myself, for the encouragement of my sinking soul, that the young ladies have a pecuniary interest in my arrival. Neither my reason nor my feelings can make head against the cold glazed glare of eye with which I am assured that I am not expected, and not wanted. The solitary man among the bottles would sometimes take pity on me, if he dared, but he is powerless against the rights and mights of Woman. (Of the page I make no account, for, he is a boy, and therefore the natural enemy of Creation.) Chilling fast, in the deadly tornadoes to which my upper and lower extremities are exposed, and subdued by the moral disadvantage at which I stand, I turn my disconsolate eyes on the refreshments that are to restore me. I find that I must either scald my throat by insanely ladling into it, against time and for no wager, brown hot water stiffened with flour; or I must make myself flaky and sick with Banbury cake; or, I must stuff into my delicate organisation, a currant pincushion which I know will swell into immeasurable dimensions when it has got there; or, I must extort from an iron-bound quarry, with a fork, as if I were farming an inhospitable soil, some glutinous lumps of gristle and grease, called pork-pie. While thus forlornly occupied, I find that the depressing banquet on the table is, in every phase of its profoundly unsatisfactory character, so like the banquet at the meanest and shabbiest of evening parties, that I begin to think I must have "brought down" to supper, the old lady unknown, blue with cold, who is setting her teeth on edge with a cool orange at my elbow – that the pastrycook who has compounded for the company on the lowest terms per head, is a fraudulent bankrupt, redeeming his contract with the stale stock from his window – that, for some unexplained reason, the family giving the party have become my mortal foes, and have given it on purpose to affront me. Or, I fancy that I am "breaking up" again, at the evening conversazione[3] at school, charged two-and-sixpence in the half-year's bill; or breaking down again at that celebrated evening party given at Mrs. Bogles's boarding-house when I was a boarder there, on which occasion Mrs. Bogles was taken in execution by a branch of the legal profession who got in as the harp, and was removed (with the keys and subscribed capital) to a place of durance, half an hour prior to the commencement of the festivities.

Take another case.

Mr. Grazinglands, of the Midland Counties, came to London by railroad one morning last week, accompanied by the amiable and fascinating Mrs. Grazinglands. Mr. G. is a gentleman of a comfortable property, and had a little business to transact at the Bank of England, which required the concurrence and signature of Mrs. G. Their business disposed of, Mr. and Mrs. Grazinglands viewed the Royal Exchange, and the exterior of St. Paul's Cathedral. The spirits of Mrs. Grazinglands then gradually beginning to flag, Mr. Grazinglands (who is the tenderest of husbands) remarked with sympathy, "Arabella, my dear, I fear you are faint." Mrs. Grazinglands replied, "Alexander, I am rather faint; but don't mind me, I shall be better presently." Touched by the feminine meekness of this answer, Mr. Grazinglands looked in at a pastry-cook's window, hesitating as to the expediency of lunching at that establishment. He beheld nothing to eat, but butter in various forms, slightly charged with jam, and languidly frizzling over tepid water. Two ancient turtle-shells, on which was inscribed the legend, "Soups," decorated a glass partition within, enclosing a stuffy alcove, from which a ghastly mockery of a marriage-breakfast spread on a rickety table, warned the terrified traveller. An oblong box of stale and broken pastry at reduced prices, mounted on a stool, ornamented the doorway; and two high chairs that looked as if they were performing on stilts, embellished the counter. Over the whole, a young lady presided, whose gloomy haughtiness as she surveyed the street, announced a deep-seated grievance against society, and an implacable determination to be avenged. From a beetle-haunted kitchen below this institution, fumes arose, suggestive of a class of soup which Mr. Grazinglands knew, from painful experience, enfeebles the mind, distends the stomach, forces itself into the complexion, and tries to ooze out at the eyes. As he decided against entering, and turned away, Mrs. Grazinglands becoming perceptibly weaker, repeated, "I am rather faint, Alexander, but don't mind me." Urged to new efforts by these words of resignation, Mr. Grazinglands looked in at a cold and floury baker's shop, where utilitarian buns unrelieved by a currant, consorted with hard biscuits, a stone filter of cold water, a hard pale clock, and a hard little old woman with flaxen hair, of an undeveloped-farinaceous aspect, as if she had been fed upon seeds. He might have entered even here, but for the timely remembrance coming upon him that Jairing's was but round the corner.

Now, Jairing's being an hotel for families and gentlemen, in high repute among the midland counties, Mr. Grazinglands plucked up a great spirit when he told Mrs. Grazinglands she should have a chop there. That lady likewise felt that she was going to see Life. Arriving on that gay and festive scene, they found the second waiter, in a flabby undress, cleaning the windows of the empty coffee-room; and the first waiter, denuded of his white tie, making up his cruets behind the Post-Office Directory. The latter (who took them in hand) was greatly put out by their patronage, and showed his mind to be troubled by a sense of the pressing necessity of instantly smuggling Mrs. Grazinglands into the obscurest corner of the building. This slighted lady (who is the pride of her division of the county) was immediately conveyed, by several dark passages, and up and down several steps, into a penitential apartment at the back of the house, where five invalided old plate-warmers leaned up against one another under a discarded old melancholy sideboard, and where the wintry leaves of all the dining-tables in the house lay thick. Also, a sofa, of incomprehensible form regarded from any sofane point of view, murmured "Bed;" while an air of mingled fluffiness and heeltaps, added, "Second Waiter's." Secreted in this dismal hold, objects of a mysterious distrust and suspicion, Mr. Grazinglands and his charming partner waited twenty minutes for the smoke (for it never came to a fire), twenty-five minutes for the sherry, half an hour for the tablecloth, forty minutes for the knives and forks, three-quarters of an hour for the chops, and an hour for the potatoes. On settling the little bill – which was not much more than the day's pay of a Lieutenant in the navy – Mr. Grazinglands took heart to remonstrate against the general quality and cost of his reception. To whom the waiter replied, substantially, that

Jairing's made it a merit to have accepted him on any terms: "for," added the waiter (unmistakably coughing at Mrs. Grazinglands, the pride of her division of the county), "when indiwiduals is not staying in the 'Ouse, their favours is not as a rule looked upon as making it worth Mr. Jairing's while; nor is it, indeed, a style of business Mr. Jairing wishes." Finally, Mr. and Mrs. Grazinglands passed out of Jairing's hotel for Families and Gentlemen, in a state of the greatest depression, scorned by the bar; and did not recover their self-respect for several days.

Or take another case. Take your own case.

You are going off by railway, from any Terminus. You have twenty minutes for dinner, before you go. You want your dinner, and like Dr. Johnson, Sir, you like to dine.[4] You present to your mind, a picture of the refreshment-table at that terminus. The conventional shabby evening-party supper – accepted as the model for all termini and all refreshment stations, because it is the last repast known to this state of existence of which any human creature would partake, but in the direst extremity – sickens your contemplation, and your words are these: "I cannot dine on stale sponge-cakes that turn to sand in the mouth. I cannot dine on shining brown patties, composed of unknown animals within, and offering to my view the device of an indigestible star-fish in leaden pie-crust without. I cannot dine on a sandwich that has long been pining under an exhausted receiver. I cannot dine on barley-sugar. I cannot dine on Toffee." You repair to the nearest hotel, and arrive, agitated, in the coffee-room.

It is a most astonishing fact that the waiter is very cold to you. Account for it how you may, smooth it over how you will, you cannot deny that he is cold to you. He is not glad to see you, he does not want you, he would much rather you hadn't come. He opposes to your flushed condition, an immovable composure. As if this were not enough, another waiter, born, as it would seem, expressly to look at you in this passage of your life, stands at a little distance, with his napkin under his arm and his hands folded, looking at you with all his might. You impress on your waiter that you have ten minutes for dinner, and he proposes that you shall begin with a bit of fish which will be ready in twenty. That proposal declined, he suggests – as a neat originality – "a weal or mutton cutlet." You close with either cutlet, any cutlet, anything. He goes, leisurely, behind a door and calls down some unseen shaft. A ventriloquial dialogue ensues, tending finally to the effect that weal only, is available on the spur of the moment. You anxiously call out, "Veal, then!" Your waiter having settled that point, returns to array your tablecloth, with a table napkin folded cocked-hat-wise (slowly, for something out of window engages his eye), a white wine-glass, a green wine-glass, a blue finger-glass, a tumbler, and a powerful field battery of fourteen casters with nothing in them; or at all events – which is enough for your purpose – with nothing in them that will come out. All this time, the other waiter looks at you – with an air of mental comparison and curiosity, now, as if it had occurred to him that you are rather like his brother. Half your time gone, and nothing come but the jug of ale and the bread, you implore your waiter to "see after that cutlet, waiter; pray do!" He cannot go at once, for he is carrying in seventeen pounds of American cheese for you to finish with, and a small Landed Estate of celery and water-cresses. The other waiter changes his leg, and takes a new view of you, doubtfully, now, as if he had rejected the resemblance to his brother, and had begun to think you more like his aunt or his grandmother. Again you beseech your waiter with pathetic indignation, to "see after that cutlet!" He steps out to see after it, and by-and-by, when you are going away without it, comes back with it. Even then, he will not take the sham silver cover off, without a pause for a flourish, and a look at the musty cutlet as if he were surprised to see it – which cannot possibly be the case, he must have seen it so often before. A sort of fur has been produced upon its surface by the cook's art, and in a sham silver vessel staggering on two feet instead of three, is a cutaneous kind of sauce, of brown pimples and pickled cucumber. You order the bill, but your waiter cannot bring your bill yet, because he is bringing, instead, three flinty-hearted potatoes and two grim head of broccoli, like the occasional ornaments on area railings, badly boiled. You know that you will never come to this pass, any more than to the cheese and celery, and you imperatively demand your bill; but, it takes time to get, even when gone for, because your waiter has to communicate with a lady who lives behind a sash-window in a corner, and who appears to have to refer to several Ledgers before she can make it out – as if you had been staying there a year. You become distracted to get away, and the other waiter, once more changing his leg, still looks at you – but suspiciously, now, as if you had begun to remind him of the party who took the great-coats last winter. Your bill at last brought and paid, at the rate of sixpence a mouthful, your waiter reproachfully reminds you that "attendance is not charged for a single meal," and you have to search in all your pockets for sixpence more. He has a worse opinion of you than ever, when you have given it to him, and lets you out into the street with the air of one saying to himself, as you cannot doubt he is, "I hope we shall never see *you* here again!"

Or, take any other of the numerous travelling instances in which, with more time at your disposal, you are, have been, or may be, equally ill served. Take the old-established Bull's Head with its old-established knife-boxes on its old-established sideboards, its old-established flue under its old-established four-post bedsteads in its old-established airless rooms, its old-established frouziness up-stairs and down-stairs, its old-established cookery, and its old-established principles of plunder. Count up your injuries, in its side-dishes of ailing sweetbreads in white poultices, of apothecaries' powders in rice for curry, of pale stewed bits of calf ineffectually relying for an adventitious interest on forcemeat balls. You have had experience of the old-established Bull's Head stringy fowls, with lower extremities like wooden legs, sticking up out of the dish; of its cannibalic boiled mutton, gushing horribly among its capers, when carved; of its little dishes of pastry – roofs of spermaceti ointment,[5] erected over half an apple or four gooseberries. Well for you if you have yet forgotten the old-established Bull's Head fruity port: whose reputation was gained solely by the old-established price the Bull's Head put upon it, and by the old-established air with which the Bull's Head set the glasses and D'Oyleys[6] on, and held that Liquid Gout to the three-and-sixpenny wax-candle, as if its old-established colour hadn't come from the dyer's.

Or lastly, take to finish with, two cases that we all know, every day.

We all know the new hotel near the station, where it is always gusty, going up the lane which is always muddy, where we are sure to arrive at night, and where we make the gas start awfully when we open the front door. We all know the flooring of the passages and staircases that is too new, and the walls that are too new, and the house that is haunted by the ghost of mortar. We all know the doors that have cracked, and the cracked shutters through which we get a glimpse of the disconsolate moon. We all know the new people, who have come to keep the new hotel, and who wish they had never come, and who (inevitable result) wish *we* had never come. We all know how much too scant and smooth and bright the new furniture is, and how it has never settled down, and cannot fit itself into right places, and will get into wrong places. We all know how the gas, being lighted, shows maps of Damp upon the walls. We all know how the ghost of mortar passes into our sandwich, stirs our negus, goes up to bed with us, ascends the pale bedroom chimney, and prevents the smoke from following. We all know how a leg of our chair comes off at breakfast in the morning, and how the dejected waiter attributes the accident to a general greenness pervading the establishment, and informs us, in reply to a local inquiry, that he is thankful to say he is an entire stranger in that part of the country, and is going back to his own connexion on Saturday.

We all know, on the other hand, the great station hotel belonging to the company of proprietors, which has suddenly sprung up in the back outskirts of any place we like to name, and where we look out of our palatial windows, at little back yards and gardens, old summer-houses, fowl-houses, pigeon-traps, and pigsties. We all know this hotel in which we can get anything we want, after its kind, for money; but where nobody is glad to see us, or sorry to see us, or minds (our bill paid) whether we come or go, or how, or when, or why, or cares about us. We all know this hotel, where we have no individuality, but put ourselves into the general post, as it were, and are sorted and disposed of according to our division. We all know that we can get on very well indeed at such a place, but still not perfectly well; and this may be, because the place is largely wholesale, and there is a lingering personal retail interest within us that asks to be satisfied.

To sum up. My uncommercial travelling has not yet brought me to the conclusion that we are close to perfection in these matters. And just as I do not believe that the end of the world will ever be near at hand, so long as any of the very tiresome and arrogant people who constantly predict that catastrophe are left in it, so, I shall have small faith in the Hotel Millennium, while any of the uncomfortable superstitions I have glanced at remain in existence.

Travelling Abroad

First published in *All the Year Round*, 7 April 1860. The text here is taken from *The Uncommercial Traveller*.

I got into the travelling chariot – it was of German make, roomy, heavy, and unvarnished – I got into the travelling chariot, pulled up the steps after me, shut myself in with a smart bang of the door, and gave the word, "Go on!"

Immediately, all that W. and S. W. division of London began to slide away at a pace so lively, that I was over the river, and past the Old Kent Road, and out on Blackheath, and even ascending Shooter's Hill,[1] before I had had time to look about me in the carriage, like a collected traveller.

I had two ample Imperials on the roof, other fitted storage for luggage in front, and other up behind; I had a net for books overhead, great pockets to all the windows, a leathern pouch or two hung up for odds and ends, and a reading lamp fixed in the back of the chariot, in case I should be benighted. I was amply provided in all respects, and had no idea where I was going (which was delightful), except that I was going abroad.

So smooth was the old high road, and so fresh were the horses, and so fast went I, that it was midway between Gravesend and Rochester, and the widening river was bearing the ships, white-sailed or black-smoked, out to sea, when I noticed by the wayside a very queer small boy.[2]

"Holloa!" said I, to the very queer small boy, "where do you live?"

"At Chatham," says he.

"What do you do there?" says I.

"I go to school," says he.

I took him up in a moment, and we went on. Presently, the very queer small boy says, "This is Gads-hill we are coming to, where Falstaff went out to rob those travellers, and ran away."[3]

"You know something about Falstaff, eh?" said I.

"All about him," said the very queer small boy. "I am old (I am nine), and I read all sorts of books. But *do* let us stop at the top of the hill, and look at the house there, if you please!"

"You admire that house?" said I.

"Bless you, sir," said the very queer small boy, "when I was not more than half as old as nine, it used to be a treat for me to be brought to look at it. And now, I am nine, I come by myself to look at it. And ever since I can recollect, my father, seeing me so fond of it, has often said to me, 'If you were to be very persevering and were to work hard, you might some day come to live in it.' Though that's impossible!" said the very queer small boy, drawing a low breath, and now staring at the house out of window with all his might.

I was rather amazed to be told this by the very queer small boy; for that house happens to be *my* house, and I have reason to believe that what he said was true.

Well! I made no halt there, and I soon dropped the very queer small boy and went on. Over the road where the old Romans used to march, over the road where the old Canterbury pilgrims used to go, over the road where the travelling trains of the old imperious priests and princes used to jingle on horseback between the continent and this Island through the mud and water, over the road where Shakespeare hummed to himself, "Blow, blow, thou winter wind,"[4] as he sat in the saddle at the gate of the inn yard noticing the carriers; all among the cherry orchards, apple orchards, corn-fields, and hop-gardens; so went I, by Canterbury to Dover. There, the sea was tumbling in, with deep sounds, after dark, and the revolving French light on Cape Grinez was seen regularly bursting out and becoming obscured, as if the head of a gigantic light-keeper in an anxious state of mind were interposed every half-minute, to look how it was burning.

Early in the morning I was on the deck of the steam-packet, and we were aiming at the bar in the usual intolerable manner, and the bar was aiming at us in the usual intolerable manner, and the bar got by far the best of it, and we got by far the worst – all in the usual intolerable manner.

But, when I was clear of the Custom House on the other side, and when I began to make the dust fly on the thirsty French roads, and when the twigsome trees by the wayside (which, I suppose, never will grow leafy, for they never did) guarded here and there a dusty soldier, or field labourer, baking on a heap of broken stones, sound asleep in a fiction of shade, I began to recover my travelling spirits. Coming upon the breaker of the broken stones, in a hard hot shining hat, on which the sun played at a distance as on a burning-glass, I felt that now, indeed, I was in the dear old France of my affections. I should have known it, without the well-remembered bottle of rough ordinary wine, the cold roast fowl, the loaf, and the pinch of salt, on which I lunched with unspeakable satisfaction, from one of the stuffed pockets of the chariot.

I must have fallen asleep after lunch, for when a bright face looked in at the window, I started, and said:

"Good God, Louis, I dreamed you were dead!"

My cheerful servant laughed, and answered:

"Me? Not at all, sir."

"How glad I am to wake! What are we doing, Louis?"

"We go to take relay of horses. Will you walk up the hill?"

"Certainly."

"Welcome the old French hill, with the old French lunatic (not in the most distant degree related to Sterne's Maria⁵) living in a thatched dog-kennel half-way up, and flying out with his crutch and his big head and extended nightcap, to be beforehand with the old men and women exhibiting crippled children, and with the children exhibiting old men and women, ugly and blind, who always seemed by resurrectionary process to be recalled out of the elements for the sudden peopling of the solitude!"

"It is well," said I, scattering among them what small coin I had; "here comes Louis, and I am quite roused from my nap."

We journeyed on again, and I welcomed every new assurance that France stood where I had left it. There were the posting-houses, with their archways, dirty stable-yards, and clean postmasters' wives, bright women of business, looking on at the putting-to of the horses; there were the postilions counting what money they got, into their hats, and never making enough of it; there were the standard population of grey horses of Flanders descent, invariably biting one another when they got a chance; there were the fleecy sheep-skins, looped on over their uniforms by the postilions, like bibbed aprons when it blew and rained; there were their jack-boots, and their cracking whips; there were the cathedrals that I got out to see, as under some cruel bondage, in no wise desiring to see them; there were the little towns that appeared to have no reason for being towns, since most of their houses were to let and nobody could be induced to look at them, except the people who couldn't let them and had nothing else to do but look at them all day. I lay a night upon the road and enjoyed delectable cookery of potatoes, and some other sensible things, adoption of which at home would inevitably be shown to be fraught with ruin, somehow or other, to that rickety national blessing, the British farmer; and at last I was rattled, like a single pill in a box, over leagues of stones, until – madly cracking, plunging, and flourishing two grey tails about – I made my triumphal entry into Paris.

At Paris, I took an upper apartment for a few days in one of the hotels of the Rue de Rivoli; my front windows looking into the garden of the

Tuileries (where the principal difference between the nursemaids and the flowers seemed to be that the former were locomotive and the latter not): my back windows looking at all the other back windows in the hotel, and deep down into a paved yard, where my German chariot had retired under a tight-fitting archway, to all appearance for life, and where bells rang all day without anybody's minding them but certain chamberlains with feather brooms and green baize caps, who here and there leaned out of some high window placidly looking down, and where neat waiters with trays on their left shoulders passed and repassed from morning to night.

Whenever I am at Paris, I am dragged by invisible force into the Morgue.[6] I never want to go there, but am always pulled there. One Christmas Day, when I would rather have been anywhere else, I was attracted in, to see an old grey man lying all alone on his cold bed, with a tap of water turned on over his grey hair, and running, drip, drip, drip, down his wretched face until it got to the corner of his mouth, where it took a turn, and made him look sly. One New Year's Morning (by the same token, the sun was shining outside, and there was a mountebank balancing a feather on his nose, within a yard of the gate), I was pulled in again to look at a flaxen-haired boy of eighteen, with a heart hanging on his breast – "from his mother," was engraven on it – who had come into the net across the river, with a bullet wound in his fair forehead and his hands cut with a knife, but whence or how was a blank mystery. This time, I was forced into the same dread place, to see a large dark man whose disfigurement by water was in a frightful manner comic, and whose expression was that of a prize-fighter who had closed his eyelids under a heavy blow, but was going immediately to open them, shake his head, and "come up smiling." Oh what this large dark man cost me in that bright city!

It was very hot weather, and he was none the better for that, and I was much the worse. Indeed, a very neat and pleasant little woman with the key of her lodging on her forefinger, who had been showing him to her little girl while she and the child ate sweetmeats, observed monsieur looking poorly as we came out together, and asked monsieur, with her wondering little eyebrows prettily raised, if there were anything the matter? Faintly replying in the negative, monsieur crossed the road to a wine-shop, got some brandy, and resolved to freshen himself with a dip in the great floating bath on the river.

The bath was crowded in the usual airy manner, by a male population in striped drawers of various gay colours, who walked up and down arm in arm, drank coffee, smoked cigars, sat at little tables, conversed politely with the damsels who dispensed the towels, and every now and then pitched themselves into the river head foremost, and came out again to repeat this social routine. I made haste to participate in the water part of the entertainments, and was in the full enjoyment of a delightful bath, when all in a moment I was seized with an unreasonable idea that the large dark body was floating straight at me.

I was out of the river, and dressing instantly. In the shock I had taken some water into my mouth, and it turned me sick, for I fancied that the contamination of the creature was in it. I had got back to my cool darkened room in the hotel, and was lying on a sofa there, before I began to reason with myself.

Of course, I knew perfectly well that the large dark creature was stone dead, and that I should no more come upon him out of the place where I had seen him dead, than I should come upon the cathedral of Notre-Dame in an entirely new situation. What troubled me was the picture of the creature; and that had so curiously and strongly painted itself upon my brain, that I could not get rid of it until it was worn out.

I noticed the peculiarities of this possession, while it was a real discomfort to me. That very day, at dinner, some morsel on my plate looked like a piece of him, and I was glad to get up and go out. Later in the evening, I was walking along the Rue St. Honoré, when I saw a bill at a public room there, announcing small-sword exercise, broad-sword exercise, wrestling, and other such feats. I went in, and some of the sword-play being very skilful, remained. A specimen of our own national sport, The British Boaxe,[7] was announced to be given at the close of the evening. In an evil hour, I determined to wait for this Boaxe, as became a Briton. It was a clumsy specimen (executed by two English grooms out of place), but one of the combatants, receiving a straight right-hander with the glove between his eyes, did exactly what the large dark creature in the Morgue had seemed going to do — and finished me for that night.

There was rather a sickly smell (not at all an unusual fragrance in Paris) in the little ante-room of my apartment at the hotel. The large dark creature in the Morgue was by no direct experience associated with my sense of smell, because, when I came to the knowledge of him, he lay behind a wall of thick plate-glass as good as a wall of steel or marble for that matter. Yet the whiff of the room never failed to reproduce him. What was more curious, was the capriciousness with which his portrait seemed to light itself up in my mind, elsewhere. I might be walking in the Palais Royal, lazily enjoying the shop windows, and might be regaling myself with one of the ready-made clothes shops that are set out there. My eyes, wandering over impossible-waisted dressing-gowns and luminous waistcoats, would fall upon the master, or the shopman, or even the very dummy at the door, and would suggest to me, "Something like him!" – and instantly I was sickened again.

This would happen at the theatre, in the same manner. Often it would happen in the street, when I certainly was not looking for the likeness, and when probably there was no likeness there. It was not because the creature was dead that I was so haunted, because I know that I might have been (and I know it because I have been) equally attended by the image of a living aversion. This lasted about a week. The picture did not fade by degrees, in the sense that it became a whit less forcible and distinct, but in the sense that it obtruded itself less and less frequently. The experience may be worth considering by some who have the care of children. It would be difficult to overstate the intensity and accuracy of an intelligent child's observation. At that impressible time of life, it must sometimes produce a fixed impression. If the fixed impression be of an object terrible to the child, it will be (for want of reasoning upon) inseparable from great fear. Force the child at such a time, be Spartan with it, send it into the dark against its will, leave it in a lonely bedroom against its will, and you had better murder it.

On a bright morning I rattled away from Paris, in the German chariot, and left the large dark creature behind me for good. I ought to confess, though, that I had been drawn back to the Morgue, after he was put underground, to look at his clothes, and that I found them frightfully like him – particularly his boots. However, I rattled away for Switzerland, looking forward and not backward, and so we parted company.

Welcome again, the long long spell of France, with the queer country inns, full of vases of flowers and clocks, in the dull little town, and with the little population not at all dull on the little Boulevard in the evening, under the little trees! Welcome Monsieur the Curé, walking alone in the early morning a short way out of the town, reading that eternal Breviary of yours, which surely might be almost read, without book, by this time! Welcome Monsieur the Curé, later in the day, jolting through the highway dust (as if you had already ascended to the cloudy region), in a very big-headed cabriolet, with the dried mud of a dozen winters on it. Welcome again Monsieur the Curé, as we exchange salutations; you, straightening your back to look at the German chariot, while picking in your little village garden a vegetable or two for the day's soup: I, looking out of the German chariot window in that delicious traveller's trance which knows no cares, no yesterdays, no to-morrows, nothing but the passing objects and the passing scents and sounds! And so I came, in due course of delight, to

Strasbourg, where I passed a wet Sunday evening at a window, while an idle trifle of a vaudeville was played for me at the opposite house.

How such a large house came to have only three people living in it, was its own affair. There were at least a score of windows in its high roof alone; how many in its grotesque front, I soon gave up counting. The owner was a shopkeeper, by name Straudenheim; by trade – I couldn't make out what by trade, for he had forborne to write that up, and his shop was shut.

At first, as I looked at Straudenheim's, through the steadily falling rain, I set him up in business in the goose-liver line. But, inspection of Straudenheim, who became visible at a window on the second floor, convinced me that there was something more precious than liver in the case. He wore a black velvet skull-cap, and looked usurious and rich. A large-lipped, pear-nosed old man, with white hair, and keen eyes, though near-sighted. He was writing at a desk, was Straudenheim, and ever and again left off writing, put his pen in his mouth, and went through actions with his right hand, like a man steadying piles of cash. Five-franc pieces, Straudenheim, or golden Napoleons? A jeweller, Straudenheim, a dealer in money, a diamond merchant, or what?

Below Straudenheim, at a window on the first floor, sat his housekeeper – far from young, but of a comely presence, suggestive of a well-matured foot and ankle. She was cheerily dressed, had a fan in her hand, and wore large gold earrings and a large gold cross. She would have been out holiday-making (as I settled it) but for the pestilent rain. Strasbourg had given up holiday-making for that once, as a bad job, because the rain was jerking in gushes out of the old roof-spouts, and running in a brook down the middle of the street. The housekeeper, her arms folded on her bosom and her fan tapping her chin, was bright and smiling at her open window, but otherwise Straudenheim's house front was very dreary. The house-keeper's was the only open window in it; Straudenheim kept himself close, though it was a sultry evening when air is pleasant, and though the rain had brought into the town that vague refreshing smell of grass which rain does bring in the summer-time.

The dim appearance of a man at Straudenheim's shoulder, inspired me with a misgiving that somebody had come to murder that flourishing merchant for the wealth with which I had handsomely endowed him: the rather, as it was an excited man, lean and long of figure, and evidently stealthy of foot. But, he conferred with Straudenheim instead of doing him a mortal injury, and then they both softly opened the other window of that room – which was immediately over the housekeeper's – and tried to see her by looking down. And my opinion of Straudenheim was much lowered when I saw that eminent citizen spit out of window, clearly with the hope of spitting on the housekeeper.

The unconscious housekeeper fanned herself, tossed her head, and laughed. Though unconscious of Straudenheim, she was conscious of some-body else – of me? – there was nobody else.

After leaning so far out of the window, that I confidently expected to see their heels tilt up, Straudenheim and the lean man drew their heads in and shut the window. Presently, the house door secretly opened, and they slowly and spitefully crept forth into the pouring rain. They were coming over to me (I thought) to demand satisfaction for my looking at the housekeeper, when they plunged into a recess in the architecture under my window and dragged out the puniest of little soldiers, begirt with the most innocent of little swords. The tall glazed head-dress of this warrior, Straudenheim instantly knocked off, and out of it fell two sugar-sticks, and three or four large lumps of sugar.

The warrior made no effort to recover his property or to pick up his shako,[8] but looked with an expression of attention at Straudenheim when he kicked him five times, and also at the lean man when *he* kicked him five times, and again at Straudenheim when he tore the breast of his (the warrior's) little coat open, and shook all his ten fingers in his face, as if they were ten thousand. When these outrages had been committed, Straudenheim and his man went into the house again and barred the door. A wonderful circumstance was, that the housekeeper who saw it all (and who could have taken six such warriors to her buxom bosom at once), only fanned herself and laughed as she had laughed before, and seemed to have no opinion about it, one way or other.

But, the chief effect of the drama was the remarkable vengeance taken by the little warrior. Left alone in the rain, he picked up his shako; put it on, all wet and dirty as it was; retired into a court, of which Straudenheim's house formed the corner; wheeled about; and bringing his two forefingers close to the top of his nose, rubbed them over one another, cross-wise, in derision, defiance, and contempt of Straudenheim. Although Straudenheim could not possibly be supposed to be conscious of this strange proceeding, it so inflated and comforted the little warrior's soul, that twice he went away, and twice came back into the court to repeat it, as though it must goad his enemy to madness. Not only that, but he afterwards came back with two other small warriors, and they all three did it together. Not only that – as I live to tell the tale! – but just as it was falling quite dark, the three came back, bringing with them a huge bearded Sapper, whom they moved, by recital of the original wrong, to go through the same performance, with the same complete absence of all possible knowledge of it on the part of Straudenheim. And then they all went away, arm in arm, singing.

I went away too, in the German chariot at sunrise, and rattled on, day after day, like one in a sweet dream; with so many clear little bells on the harness of the horses, that the nursery rhyme about Banbury Cross[9] and the venerable lady who rode in state there, was always in my ears. And now I came to the land of wooden houses, innocent cakes, thin butter soup, and spotless little inn bedrooms with a family likeness to Dairies. And now the Swiss marksmen were for ever rifle-shooting at marks across gorges, so exceedingly near my ear, that I felt like a new Gesler in a Canton of Tells,[10] and went in highly-deserved danger of my tyrannical life. The prizes at these shootings, were watches, smart handkerchiefs, hats, spoons, and (above all) tea-trays; and at these contests I came upon a more than usually accomplished and amiable countryman of my own, who had shot himself deaf in whole years of competition, and had won so many tea-trays that he went about the country with his carriage full of them, like a glorified Cheap-Jack.[11]

In the mountain-country into which I had now travelled, a yoke of oxen were sometimes hooked on before the post-horses, and I went lumbering up, up, up, through mist and rain, with the roar of falling water for change of music. Of a sudden, mist and rain would clear away, and I would come down into picturesque little towns with gleaming spires and odd towers; and would stroll afoot into market-places in steep winding streets, where a hundred women in bodices, sold eggs and honey, butter and fruit, and suckled their children as they sat by their clean baskets, and had such enormous goîtres (or glandular swellings in the throat) that it became a science to know where the nurse ended and the child began. About this time, I deserted my German chariot for the back of a mule (in colour and consistency so very like a dusty old hair trunk I once had at school, that I half expected to see my initials in brass-headed nails on his backbone), and went up a thousand rugged ways, and looked down at a thousand woods of fir and pine, and would on the whole have preferred my mule's keeping a little nearer to the inside, and not usually travelling with a hoof or two over the precipice – though much consoled by explanation that this was to be attributed to his great sagacity, by reason of his carrying broad loads of wood at other times, and not being clear but that I myself belonged to that station of life, and required as much room as they. He brought me safely, in his own wise way, among the passes of the Alps, and here I enjoyed a dozen climates a day; being now (like Don Quixote on the back of the wooden horse[12]) in the region of wind, now in the region of fire, now in the region of unmelting ice and snow. Here, I passed over trembling domes of ice, beneath which the cataract was roaring; and here was received under arches of icicles, of unspeakable beauty; and here the sweet air was so bracing and so light, that at halting-times I rolled in the snow when I saw my mule do it, thinking that he must know best. At this part of the journey we would come, at mid-day, into half an hour's thaw: when the rough mountain inn would be found on an island of deep mud in a sea of snow, while the baiting strings of mules, and the carts full of casks and bales, which had been in an Arctic condition a mile off, would steam again. By such ways and means, I would come to the cluster of châlets where I had to turn out of the track to see the waterfall; and then, uttering a howl like a young giant, on espying a traveller – in other words, something to eat – coming up the steep, the idiot lying on the wood-pile who sunned himself and nursed his goître, would rouse the woman-guide within the hut, who would stream out hastily, throwing her child over one of her shoulders and her goître over the other, as she came along. I slept at religious houses, and bleak refuges of many kinds, on this journey, and by the stove at night heard stories of travellers who had perished within call, in wreaths and drifts of snow. One night the stove within, and the cold outside, awakened childish associations long forgotten, and I dreamed I was in Russia – the identical serf out of a picture-book I had, before I could read it for myself – and that I was going to be knouted by a noble personage in a fur cap, boots, and earrings, who, I think, must have come out of some melodrama.

Commend me to the beautiful waters among these mountains! Though I was not of their mind: they, being inveterately bent on getting down into the level country, and I ardently desiring to linger where I was. What desperate leaps they took, what dark abysses they plunged into, what rocks they wore away, what echoes they invoked! In one part where I went, they were pressed into the service of carrying wood down, to be burnt next winter, as costly fuel, in Italy. But, their fierce savage nature was not to be easily constrained, and they fought with every limb of the wood; whirling it round and round, stripping its bark away, dashing it against pointed corners, driving it out of the course, and roaring and flying at the peasants who steered it back again from the bank with long stout poles. Alas! concurrent streams of time and water carried *me* down fast, and I came, on an exquisitely clear day, to the Lausanne shore of the Lake of Geneva, where I stood looking at the bright blue water, the flushed white mountains opposite, and the boats at my feet with their furled Mediterranean sails, showing like enormous magnifications of this goose-quill pen that is now in my hand.

– The sky became overcast without any notice; a wind very like the March east wind of England, blew across me; and a voice said, "How do you like it? Will it do?"

I had merely shut myself, for half a minute, in a German travelling chariot that stood for sale in the Carriage Department of the London Pantechnicon. I had a commission to buy it, for a friend who was going abroad; and the look and manner of the chariot, as I tried the cushions and the springs, brought all these hints of travelling remembrance before me.

"It will do very well," said I, rather sorrowfully, as I got out at the other door, and shut the carriage up.

Shy Neighbourhoods

First published in *All the Year Round*, 26 May 1860. The text is reproduced from *The Uncommercial Traveller*.

So much of my travelling is done on foot, that if I cherished betting propensities, I should probably be found registered in sporting newspapers under some such title as the Elastic Novice, challenging all eleven stone mankind to competition in walking. My last special feat was turning out of bed at two, after a hard day, pedestrian and otherwise, and walking thirty miles into the country to breakfast. The road was so lonely in the night, that I fell asleep to the monotonous sound of my own feet, doing their regular four miles an hour. Mile after mile I walked, without the slightest sense of exertion, dozing heavily and dreaming constantly. It was only when I made a stumble like a drunken man, or struck out into the road to avoid a horseman close upon me on the path – who had no existence – that I came to myself and looked about. The day broke mistily (it was autumn time), and I could not disembarrass myself of the idea that I had to climb those heights and banks of cloud, and that there was an Alpine Convent somewhere behind the sun, where I was going to breakfast. This sleepy notion was so much stronger than such substantial objects as villages and haystacks, that, after the sun was up and bright, and when I was sufficiently awake to have a sense of pleasure in the prospect, I still occasionally caught myself looking about for wooden arms to point the right track up the mountain, and wondering there was no snow yet. It is a curiosity of broken sleep that I made immense quantities of verses on that pedestrian occasion (of course I never make any when I am in my right senses), and that I spoke a certain language once pretty familiar to me, but which I have nearly forgotten from disuse, with fluency. Of both these phenomena I have such frequent experience in the state between sleeping and waking, that I sometimes argue with myself that I know I cannot be awake, for, if I were, I should not be half so ready. The readiness is not imaginary, because I often recall long strings of the verses, and many turns of the fluent speech, after I am broad awake.

My walking is of two kinds: one, straight on end to a definite goal at a round pace; one, objectless, loitering, and purely vagabond. In the latter state, no gipsy on earth is a greater vagabond than myself; it is so natural to me, and strong with me, that I think I must be the descendant, at no great distance, of some irreclaimable tramp.

One of the pleasantest things I have lately met with, in a vagabond course of shy metropolitan neighbourhoods and small shops, is the fancy of a humble artist, as exemplified in two portraits representing Mr. Thomas Sayers, of Great Britain, and Mr. John Heenan,[1] of the United States of America. These illustrious men are highly coloured in fighting trim, and fighting attitude. To suggest the pastoral and meditative nature of their peaceful calling, Mr. Heenan is represented on emerald sward, with primroses and other modest flowers springing up under the heels of his half-boots; while Mr. Sayers is impelled to the administration of his favourite blow, the Auctioneer, by the silent eloquence of a village church. The humble homes of England, with their domestic virtues and honeysuckle porches, urge both heroes to go in and win; and the lark and other singing birds are observable in the upper air, ecstatically carolling their thanks to Heaven for a fight. On the whole, the associations entwined with the pugilistic art by this artist are much in the manner of Izaak Walton.[2]

But, it is with the lower animals of back streets and by-ways that my present purpose rests. For human notes we may return to such neighbourhoods when leisure and opportunity serve.

Nothing in shy neighbourhoods perplexes my mind more, than the bad company birds keep. Foreign birds often get into good society, but British birds are inseparable from low associates. There is a whole street of them in St. Giles's;[3] and I always find them in poor and immoral neighbourhoods, convenient to the public-house and the pawnbroker's. They seem to lead people into drinking, and even the man who makes their cages usually gets into a chronic state of black eye. Why is this? Also, they will do things for people in short-skirted velveteen coats with bone buttons, or in sleeved waistcoats and fur caps, which they cannot be persuaded by the respectable orders of society to undertake. In a dirty court in Spitalfields,[4] once, I found a goldfinch drawing his own water, and drawing as much of it as if he were in a consuming fever. That goldfinch lived at a bird-shop, and offered, in writing, to barter himself against old clothes, empty bottles, or even kitchen stuff. Surely a low thing and a depraved taste in any finch! I bought that goldfinch for money. He was sent home, and hung upon a nail over against my table. He lived outside a counterfeit dwelling-house, supposed (as I argued) to be a dyer's; otherwise it would have been impossible to account for his perch sticking out of the garret window. From the time of his appearance in my room, either he left off being thirsty – which was not in the bond – or he could not make up his mind to hear his little bucket drop back into his well when he let it go: a shock which in the best of times had made him tremble. He drew no water but by stealth and under the cloak of night. After an interval of futile and at length hopeless expectation, the merchant who had educated him was appealed to. The merchant was a bow-legged character, with a flat and cushiony nose, like the last new strawberry. He wore a fur cap, and shorts, and was of the velveteen race, velveteeny. He sent word that he would "look round." He looked round, appeared in the doorway of the room, and slightly cocked up his evil eye at the goldfinch. Instantly a raging thirst beset that bird; when it was appeased, he still drew several unnecessary buckets of water; and finally, leaped about his perch and sharpened his bill, as if he had been to the nearest wine vaults and got drunk.

Donkeys again. I know shy neighbourhoods where the Donkey goes in at the street door, and appears to live up-stairs, for I have examined the back-yard from over the palings, and have been unable to make him out. Gentility, nobility, Royalty, would appeal to that donkey in vain to do what he does for a costermonger. Feed him with oats at the highest price, put an infant prince and princess in a pair of panniers on his back, adjust his delicate trappings to a nicety, take him to the softest slopes at Windsor, and try what pace you can get out of him. Then, starve him, harness him anyhow to a truck with a flat tray on it, and see him bowl from Whitechapel to Bayswater. There appears to be no particular private understanding between birds and donkeys, in a state of nature; but in the shy neighbourhood state, you shall see them always in the same hands and always developing their very best energies for the very worst company. I have known a donkey – by sight; we were not on speaking terms – who lived over on the Surrey side of London-bridge, among the fastnesses of Jacob's Island[5] and Dockhead. It was the habit of that animal, when his services were not in immediate requisition, to go out alone, idling. I have met him a mile from his place of residence, loitering about the streets; and the expression of his countenance at such times was most degraded. He was attached to the establishment of an elderly lady who sold periwinkles, and he used to stand on Saturday nights with a cartful of those delicacies outside a gin-shop, pricking up his ears when a customer came to the cart, and too evidently deriving satisfaction from the knowledge that they got bad measure. His mistress was sometimes overtaken by inebriety. The last time I ever saw him (about five years ago) he was in circumstances of difficulty, caused by this failing. Having been left alone with the cart of periwinkles, and forgotten, he went off idling. He prowled among his usual low haunts for some time, gratifying his depraved tastes, until, not taking the cart into his calculations, he endeavoured to turn up a narrow alley, and became greatly involved. He was taken into custody by the police, and, the Green Yard[6] of the district being near at hand, was backed into that place of durance. At that crisis, I encountered him; the stubborn sense he evinced of being – not to compromise the expression – a blackguard, I never saw exceeded in the human subject. A flaring candle in a paper shade, stuck in among his periwinkles, showed him, with his ragged harness broken and his cart extensively shattered, twitching his mouth and shaking his hanging head, a picture of disgrace and obduracy. I have seen boys being taken to station-houses, who were as like him as his own brother.

The dogs of shy neighbourhoods, I observe to avoid play, and to be conscious of poverty. They avoid work, too, if they can, of course; that is in the nature of all animals. I have the pleasure to know a dog in a back street in the neighbourhood of Walworth, who has greatly distinguished himself in the minor drama, and who takes his portrait with him when he makes an engagement, for the illustration of the play-bill. His portrait (which is not at all like him) represents him in the act of dragging to the earth a recreant Indian, who is supposed to have tomahawked, or essayed to tomahawk, a British officer. The design is pure poetry, for there is no such Indian in the piece, and no such incident. He is a dog of the Newfoundland breed, for whose honesty I would be bail to any amount; but whose intellectual qualities in association with dramatic fiction, I cannot rate high. Indeed, he is too honest for the profession he has entered. Being at a town in Yorkshire last summer, and seeing him posted in the bill of the night, I attended the performance. His first scene was eminently successful; but, as it occupied a second in its representation (and five lines in the bill), it scarcely afforded ground for a cool and deliberate judgment of his powers. He had merely to bark, run on, and jump through an inn window, after a comic fugitive. The next scene of importance to the fable was a little marred in its interest by his over-anxiety; forasmuch as while his master (a belated soldier in a den of robbers on a tempestuous night) was feelingly lamenting the absence of his faithful dog, and laying great stress on the fact that he was thirty leagues away, the faithful dog was barking furiously in the prompter's box, and clearly choking himself against his collar. But it was in his greatest scene of all, that his honesty got the better of him. He had to enter a dense and trackless forest, on the trail of the murderer, and there to fly at the murderer when he found him resting at the foot of a tree, with his victim bound ready for slaughter. It was a hot night, and he came into the forest from an altogether unexpected direction, in the sweetest temper, at a very deliberate trot, not in the least excited; trotted to the foot-lights with his tongue out; and there sat down, panting, and amiably surveying the audience, with his tail beating on the boards, like a Dutch clock. Meanwhile the murderer, impatient to receive his doom, was audibly calling to him "Co-o-ome here!" while the victim, struggling with his bonds, assailed him with the most injurious expressions. It happened through these means, that when he was in course of time persuaded to trot up and rend the murderer limb from limb, he made it (for dramatic purposes) a little too obvious that he worked out that awful retribution by licking butter off his blood-stained hands.

In a shy street, behind Long-acre, two honest dogs live, who perform in Punch's shows.[7] I may venture to say that I am on terms of intimacy with both, and that I never saw either guilty of the falsehood of failing to look down at the man inside the show, during the whole performance. The difficulty other dogs have in satisfying their minds about these dogs, appears to be never overcome by time. The same dogs must encounter them over and over again, as they trudge along in their off-minutes behind the legs of the show and beside the drum; but all dogs seem to suspect their frills and jackets, and to sniff at them as if they thought those articles of personal adornment, an eruption — a something in the nature of mange, perhaps. From this Covent-garden window of mine I noticed a country dog, only the other day, who had come up to Covent-garden Market under a cart, and had broken his cord, an end of which he still trailed along with him. He loitered about the corners of the four streets commanded by my window; and bad London dogs came up, and told him lies that he didn't believe; and worse London dogs came up, and made proposals to him to go and steal in the market, which his principles rejected; and the ways of the town confused him, and he crept aside and lay down in a doorway. He had scarcely got a wink of sleep, when up comes Punch with Toby. He was darting to Toby for consolation and advice, when he saw the frill, and stopped, in the middle of the street, appalled. The show was pitched, Toby retired behind the drapery, the audience formed, the drum and pipes struck up. My country dog remained immovable, intently staring at these strange appearances, until Toby opened the drama by appearing on his ledge, and to him entered Punch, who put a tobacco-pipe into Toby's mouth. At this spectacle, the country dog threw up his head, gave one terrible howl, and fled due west.

We talk of men keeping dogs, but we might often talk more expressively of dogs keeping men. I know a bull-dog in a shy corner of Hammersmith who keeps a man. He keeps him up a yard, and makes him go to public-houses and lay wagers on him, and obliges him to lean against posts and look at him, and forces him to neglect work for him, and keeps him under rigid coercion. I once knew a fancy terrier who kept a gentleman – a gentleman who had been brought up at Oxford, too. The dog kept the gentleman entirely for his glorification, and the gentleman never talked about anything but the terrier. This, however, was not in a shy neighbourhood, and is a digression consequently.

There are a great many dogs in shy neighbourhoods, who keep boys. I have my eye on a mongrel in Somerstown[8] who keeps three boys. He feigns that he can bring down sparrows, and unburrow rats (he can do neither), and he takes the boys out on sporting pretences into all sorts of suburban fields. He has likewise made them believe that he possesses some mysterious knowledge of the art of fishing, and they consider themselves incompletely equipped for the Hampstead ponds, with a pickle-jar and wide-mouthed bottle, unless he is with them and barking tremendously. There is a dog residing in the Borough of Southwark who keeps a blind man. He may be seen, most days, in Oxford-street, haling the blind man away on expeditions wholly uncontemplated by, and unintelligible to, the man: wholly of the dog's conception and execution. Contrariwise, when the man has projects, the dog will sit down in a crowded thoroughfare and meditate. I saw him yesterday, wearing the money-tray like an easy collar, instead of offering it to the public, taking the man against his will, on the invitation of a disreputable cur, apparently to visit a dog at Harrow – he was so intent on that direction. The north wall of Burlington House Gardens, between the Arcade and the Albany,[9] offers a shy spot for appointments among blind men at about two or three o'clock in the afternoon. They sit (very uncomfortably) on a sloping stone there, and compare notes. Their dogs may always be observed at the same time, openly disparaging the men they keep, to one another, and settling where they shall respectively take their men when they begin to move again. At a small butcher's, in a shy neighbourhood (there is no reason for suppressing the name; it is by Notting-hill,[10] and gives upon the district called the Potteries), I know a shaggy black and white dog who keeps a drover. He is a dog of an easy disposition, and too frequently allows this drover to get drunk. On these occasions, it is the dog's custom to sit outside the public-house, keeping his eye on a few sheep, and thinking. I have seen him with six sheep, plainly casting up in his mind how many he began with when he left the market, and at what places he has left the rest. I have seen him perplexed by not being able to account to himself for certain particular sheep. A light has gradually broken on him, he has remembered at what butcher's he left them, and in a burst of grave satisfaction has caught a fly off his nose, and shown himself much relieved. If I could at any time have doubted the fact that it was he who kept the drover, and not the drover who kept him, it would have been abundantly proved by his way of taking undivided charge of the six sheep, when the drover came out besmeared with red ochre and beer, and gave him wrong directions, which he calmly disregarded. He has taken the sheep entirely into his own hands, has merely remarked with respectful firmness, "That instruction would place them under an omnibus; you had better confine your attention to yourself − you will want it all;" and has driven his charge away, with an intelligence of ears and tail, and a knowledge of business, that has left his lout of a man very, very far behind.

As the dogs of shy neighbourhoods usually betray a slinking consciousness of being in poor circumstances − for the most part manifested in an aspect of anxiety, an awkwardness in their play, and a misgiving that somebody is going to harness them to something, to pick up a living − so the cats of shy neighbourhoods exhibit a strong tendency to relapse into barbarism. Not only are they made selfishly ferocious by ruminating on the surplus population[11] around them, and on the densely crowded state of all the avenues to cat's meat; not only is there a moral and politico-economical haggardness in them, traceable to these reflections; but they evince a physical deterioration. Their linen is not clean, and is wretchedly got up; their black turns rusty, like old mourning; they wear very indifferent fur; and take to the shabbiest cotton velvet, instead of silk velvet. I am on terms of recognition with several small streets of cats, about the Obelisk in Saint George's Fields,[12] and also in the vicinity of Clerkenwell-green, and also in the back settlements of Drury-lane. In appearance, they are very like the women among whom they live. They seem to turn out of their unwholesome beds into the street, without any preparation. They leave their young families to stagger about the gutters, unassisted, while they frouzily quarrel and swear and scratch and spit, at street corners. In particular, I remark that when they are about to increase their families (an event of frequent recurrence) the resemblance is strongly expressed in a certain dusty dowdiness, down-at-heel self-neglect, and general giving up of things. I cannot honestly report that I have ever seen a feline matron of this class washing her face when in an interesting condition.

Not to prolong these notes of uncommercial travel among the lower animals of shy neighbourhoods, by dwelling at length upon the exasperated moodiness of the tom-cats, and their resemblance in many respects to a man and a brother, I will come to a close with a word on the fowls of the same localities.

That anything born of an egg and invested with wings, should have got to the pass that it hops contentedly down a ladder into a cellar, and calls *that* going home, is a circumstance so amazing as to leave one nothing more in this connexion to wonder at. Otherwise I might wonder at the completeness with which these fowls have become separated from all the birds of the air – have taken to grovelling in bricks and mortar and mud – have forgotten all about live trees, and make roosting-places of shop-boards, barrows, oyster-tubs, bulk-heads, and door-scrapers. I wonder at nothing concerning them, and take them as they are. I accept as products of Nature and things of course, a reduced Bantam family of my acquaintance in the Hackney-road, who are incessantly at the pawnbroker's. I cannot say that they enjoy themselves, for they are of a melancholy temperament; but what enjoyment they are capable of, they derive from crowding together in the pawnbroker's side-entry. Here, they are always to be found in a feeble flutter, as if they were newly come down in the world, and were afraid of being identified. I know a low fellow, originally of a good family from Dorking, who takes his whole establishment of wives, in single file, in at the door of the Jug Department of a disorderly tavern near the Haymarket, manœuvres them among the company's legs, emerges with them at the Bottle Entrance, and so passes his life: seldom, in the season, going to bed before two in the morning. Over Waterloo-bridge, there is a shabby old speckled couple (they belong to the wooden French-bedstead, washing-stand, and towel-horse-making trade), who are always trying to get in at the door of a chapel. Whether the old lady, under a delusion reminding one of Mrs. Southcott,[13] has an idea of entrusting an egg to that particular denomination, or merely understands that she has no business in the building and is consequently frantic to enter it, I cannot determine; but she is constantly endeavouring to undermine the principal door: while her partner, who is infirm upon his legs, walks up and down, encouraging her and defying the Universe. But, the family I have been best acquainted with, since the removal from this trying sphere of a Chinese circle at Brentford, reside in the densest part of Bethnal-green.[14] Their abstraction from the objects among which they live, or rather their conviction that those objects have all come into existence in express subservience to fowls, has so enchanted me, that I have made them the subject of many journeys at divers hours. After careful observation of the two lords and the ten ladies of whom this family consists, I have come to the conclusion that their opinions are represented by the leading lord and leading lady: the latter, as I judge, an aged personage, afflicted with a paucity of feather and visibility of quill, that gives her the appearance of a bundle of office pens. When a railway goods van that would crush an elephant comes round the corner, tearing over these fowls, they emerge unharmed from under the horses, perfectly satisfied that the whole rush was a passing property in the air, which may have left something to eat behind it. They look upon old shoes, wrecks of kettles and saucepans, and fragments of bonnets, as a kind of meteoric discharge, for fowls to peck at. Peg-tops and hoops they account, I think, as a sort of hail; shuttlecocks, as rain, or dew. Gaslight comes quite as natural to them as any other light; and I have more than a suspicion that, in the minds of the two lords, the early public-house at the corner has superseded the sun. I have established it as a certain fact, that they always begin to crow when the public-house shutters begin to be taken down, and that they salute the potboy, the instant he appears to perform that duty, as if he were Phœbus[15] in person.

Arcadian London

First published in *All the Year Round*, 29 September 1860. The text here is taken from *The Uncommercial Traveller*. For an earlier account of the deserted city, see the letter to Mrs Richard Watson, 21 September 1853, Pilgrim *Letters*, vol. VII.

Being in a humour for complete solitude and uninterrupted meditation this autumn, I have taken a lodging for six weeks in the most unfrequented part of England – in a word, in London.

The retreat into which I have withdrawn myself, is Bond-street. From this lonely spot I make pilgrimages into the surrounding wilderness, and traverse extensive tracts of the Great Desert. The first solemn feeling of isolation overcome, the first oppressive consciousness of profound retirement conquered, I enjoy that sense of freedom, and feel reviving within me that latent wildness of the original savage, which has been (upon the whole somewhat frequently) noticed by Travellers.

My lodgings are at a hatter's – my own hatter's. After exhibiting no articles in his window for some weeks, but seaside wide-awakes, shooting-caps, and a choice of rough water-proof head-gear for the moors and mountains, he has put upon the heads of his family as much of this stock as they could carry, and has taken them off to the Isle of Thanet. His young man alone remains – and remains alone – in the shop. The young man has let out the fire at which the irons are heated, and, saving his strong sense of duty, I see no reason why he should take the shutters down.

Happily for himself and for his country, the young man is a Volunteer;[1] most happily for himself, or I think he would become the prey of a settled melancholy. For, to live surrounded by human hats, and alienated from human heads to fit them on, is surely a great endurance. But, the young man, sustained by practising his exercise, and by constantly furbishing up his regulation plume (it is unnecessary to observe that, as a hatter, he is in a cock's-feather corps), is resigned and uncomplaining. On a Saturday, when he closes early and gets his Knickerbockers[2] on, he is even cheerful. I am gratefully particular in this reference to him, because he is my companion through many peaceful hours. My hatter has a desk up certain steps behind his counter, enclosed like the clerk's desk at Church. I shut myself into this place of seclusion, after breakfast, and meditate. At such times, I observe the young man loading an imaginary rifle with the greatest precision, and maintaining a most galling and destructive fire upon the national enemy. I thank him publicly for his companionship and his patriotism.

The simple character of my life, and the calm nature of the scenes by which I am surrounded, occasion me to rise early. I go forth in my slippers, and promenade the pavement. It is pastoral to feel the freshness of the air in the uninhabited town, and to appreciate the shepherdess character of the few milkwomen who purvey so little milk that it would be worth nobody's while to adulterate it, if anybody were left to undertake the task. On the crowded sea-shore, the great demand for milk, combined with the strong local temptation of chalk, would betray itself in the lowered quality of the article. In Arcadian London I derive it from the cow.

The Arcadian simplicity of the metropolis altogether, and the primitive ways into which it has fallen in this autumnal Golden Age, make it entirely new to me. Within a few hundred yards of my retreat, is the house of a friend who maintains a most sumptuous butler. I never, until yesterday, saw that butler out of superfine black broadcloth. Until yesterday, I never saw him off duty, never saw him (he is the best of butlers) with the appearance of having any mind for anything but the glory of his master and his master's friends. Yesterday morning, walking in my slippers near the house of which he is the prop and ornament – a house now a waste of shutters – I encountered that butler, also in his slippers, and in a shooting suit of one colour, and in a low-crowned straw-hat, smoking an early cigar. He felt that we had formerly met in another state of existence, and that we were translated into a new sphere. Wisely and well, he passed me without recognition. Under his arm he carried the morning paper, and shortly afterwards I saw him sitting on a rail in the pleasant open landscape of Regent-street, perusing it at his ease under the ripening sun.

My landlord having taken his whole establishment to be salted down, I am waited on by an elderly woman labouring under a chronic sniff, who, at the shadowy hour of half-past nine o'clock of every evening, gives admittance at the street door to a meagre and mouldy old man whom I have never yet seen detached from a flat pint of beer in a pewter pot. The meagre and mouldy old man is her husband, and the pair have a dejected consciousness that they are not justified in appearing on the surface of the earth. They come out of some hole when London empties itself, and go in again when it fills. I saw them arrive on the evening when I myself took possession, and they arrived with the flat pint of beer, and their bed in a bundle. The old man is a weak old man, and appeared to me to get the bed down the kitchen stairs by tumbling down with and upon it. They make their bed in the lowest and remotest corner of the basement, and they smell of bed, and have no possession but bed: unless it be (which I rather infer from an under-current of flavour in them) cheese. I know their name, through the chance of having called the wife's attention, at half-past nine on the second evening of our acquaintance, to the circumstance of there being some one at the house door; when she apologetically explained, "It's only Mr. Klem." What becomes of Mr. Klem all day, or when he goes out, or why, is a mystery I cannot penetrate; but at half-past nine he never fails to turn up on the door-step with the flat pint of beer. And the pint of beer, flat as it is, is so much more important than himself, that it always seems to my fancy as if it had found him drivelling in the street and had humanely brought him home. In making his way below, Mr. Klem never goes down the middle of the passage, like another Christian, but shuffles against the wall as if entreating me to take notice that he is occupying as little space as possible in the house; and whenever I come upon him face to face, he backs from me in fascinated confusion. The most extraordinary circumstance I have traced in connexion with this aged couple, is, that there is a Miss Klem, their daughter, apparently ten years older than either of them, who has also a bed and smells of it, and carries it about the earth at dusk and hides it in deserted houses. I came into this piece of knowledge through Mrs. Klem's beseeching me to sanction the sheltering of Miss Klem under that roof for a single night, "between her takin' care of the upper part in Pall Mall which the family of his back, and a 'ouse in Serjameses-street, which the family of leaves towng ter-morrer." I gave my gracious consent (having nothing that I know of to do with it), and in the shadowy hours Miss Klem became perceptible on the doorstep, wrestling with a bed in a bundle. Where she made it up for the night I cannot positively state, but, I think, in a sink. I know that with the instinct of a reptile or an insect, she stowed it and herself away in deep obscurity. In the Klem family, I have noticed another remarkable gift of nature, and that is a power they possess of converting everything into flue. Such broken victuals as they take by stealth, appear (whatever the nature of the viands) invariably to generate flue; and even the nightly pint of beer, instead of assimilating naturally, strikes me as breaking out in that form, equally on the shabby gown of Mrs. Klem, and the threadbare coat of her husband.

Mrs. Klem has no idea of my name – as to Mr. Klem he has no idea of anything – and only knows me as her good gentleman. Thus, if doubtful whether I am in my room or no, Mrs. Klem taps at the door and says, "Is my good gentleman here?" Or, if a messenger desiring to see me were consistent with my solitude, she would show him in with "Here is my good gentleman." I find this to be a generic custom. For, I meant to have observed before now, that in its Arcadian time all my part of London is indistinctly pervaded by the Klem species. They creep about with beds, and go to bed in miles of deserted houses. They hold no companionship except that sometimes, after dark, two of them will emerge from opposite houses, and meet in the middle of the road as on neutral ground, or will peep from adjoining houses over an interposing barrier of area railings, and compare a few reserved mistrustful notes respecting their good ladies or good gentlemen. This I have discovered in the course of various solitary rambles I have taken Northward from my retirement, along the awful perspectives of Wimpole-street, Harley-street, and similar frowning regions. Their effect would be scarcely distinguishable from that of the primeval forests, but for the Klem stragglers; these may be dimly observed, when the heavy shadows fall, flitting to and fro, putting up the door-chain, taking in the pint of beer, lowering like phantoms at the dark parlour windows, or secretly consorting underground with the dust-bin and the water-cistern.

In the Burlington Arcade, I observe, with peculiar pleasure, a primitive state of manners to have superseded the baneful influences of ultra civilisation. Nothing can surpass the innocence of the ladies' shoe-shops, the artificial-flower repositories, and the head-dress depôts. They are in strange hands at this time of year – hands of unaccustomed persons, who are imperfectly acquainted with the prices of the goods, and contemplate them with unsophisticated delight and wonder. The children of these virtuous people exchange familiarities in the Arcade, and temper the asperity of the two tall beadles. Their youthful prattle blends in an unwonted manner with the harmonious shade of the scene, and the general effect is, as of the voices of birds in a grove. In this happy restoration of the golden time, it has been my privilege even to see the bigger beadle's wife. She brought him his dinner in a basin, and he ate it in his arm-chair, and afterwards fell asleep like a satiated child. At Mr. Truefitt's, the excellent hair-dresser's, they are learning French to beguile the time; and even the few solitaries left on guard at Mr. Atkinson's, the perfumer's round the corner (generally the most inexorable gentleman in London, and the most scornful of three-and-sixpence), condescend a little, as they drowsily bide or recall their turn for chasing the ebbing Neptune on the ribbed sea-sand.[3] From Messrs. Hunt and Roskell's, the jewellers, all things are absent but the precious stones, and the gold and silver, and the soldierly pensioner at the door with his decorated breast. I might stand night and day for a month to come, in Saville-row, with my tongue out, yet not find a doctor to look at it for love or money. The dentists' instruments are rusting in their drawers, and their horrible cool parlours, where people pretend to read the Every-Day Book[4] and not to be afraid, are doing penance for their grimness in white sheets. The light-weight of shrewd appearance, with one eye always shut up, as if he were eating a sharp gooseberry in all seasons, who usually stands at the gateway of the livery-stables on very little legs under a very large waistcoat, has gone to Doncaster. Of such undesigning aspect is his guileless yard now, with its gravel and scarlet beans, and the yellow Break housed under a glass roof in a corner, that I almost believe I could not be taken in there, if I tried. In the places of business of the great tailors, the cheval-glasses are dim and dusty for lack of being looked into. Ranges of brown paper coat and waistcoat bodies look as funereal as if they were the hatchments of the customers with whose names they are inscribed; the measuring tapes hang idle on the wall; the order-taker, left on the hopeless chance of some one looking in, yawns in the last extremity over the book of patterns, as if he were trying to read that entertaining library. The hotels in Brook-street have no one in them, and the staffs of servants stare disconsolately for next season out of all the windows. The very man who goes about like an erect Turtle, between two boards recommendatory of the Sixteen Shilling Trousers, is aware of himself as a hollow mockery, and eats filberts while he leans his hinder shell against a wall.

Among these tranquillising objects, it is my delight to walk and meditate. Soothed by the repose around me, I wander insensibly to considerable distances, and guide myself back by the stars. Thus, I enjoy the contrast of a few still partially inhabited and busy spots where all the lights are not fled, where all the garlands are not dead, whence all but I have not departed. Then, does it appear to me that in this age three things are clamorously required of Man in the miscellaneous thoroughfares of the metropolis. Firstly, that he have his boots cleaned. Secondly, that he eat a penny ice. Thirdly, that he get himself photographed. Then do I speculate, What have those seam-worn artists been who stand at the photograph doors in Greek caps, sample in hand, and mysteriously salute the public – the female public with a pressing tenderness – to come in and be "took"? What did they do with their greasy blandishments, before the era of cheap photography? Of what class were their previous victims, and how victimised? And how did they get, and how did they pay for, that large collection of likenesses, all purporting to have been taken inside, with the taking of none of which had that establishment any more to do than with the taking of Delhi?[5]

But, these are small oases, and I am soon back again in metropolitan Arcadia. It is my impression that much of its serene and peaceful character is attributable to the absence of customary Talk. How do I know but there may be subtle influences in Talk, to vex the souls of men who don't hear it? How do I know but that Talk, five, ten, twenty miles off, may get into the air and disagree with me? If I rise from my bed, vaguely troubled and wearied and sick of my life, in the session of Parliament, who shall say that my noble friend, my right reverend friend, my right honourable friend, my honourable friend, my honourable and learned friend, or my honourable and gallant friend, may not be responsible for that effect upon my nervous system? Too much Ozone in the air, I am informed and fully believe (though I have no idea what it is), would affect me in a marvellously disagreeable way; why may not too much Talk? I don't see or hear the Ozone; I don't see or hear the Talk. And there is so much Talk; so much too much; such loud cry, and such scant supply of wool; such a deal of fleecing, and so little fleece! Hence, in the Arcadian season, I find it a delicious triumph to walk down to deserted Westminster, and see the Courts shut up; to walk a little further and see the Two Houses shut up;[6] to stand in the Abbey Yard, like the New Zealander of the grand English History[7] (concerning which unfortunate man, a whole rookery of mares' nests is generally being discovered), and gloat upon the ruins of Talk. Returning to my primitive solitude and lying down to sleep, my grateful heart expands with the consciousness that there is no adjourned Debate, no ministerial explanation, nobody to give notice of intention to ask the noble Lord at the head of her Majesty's Government five-and-twenty bootless questions in one, no term time with legal argument, no Nisi Prius with eloquent appeal to British Jury; that the air will to-morrow, and to-morrow, and to-morrow,[8] remain untroubled by this superabundant generating of Talk. In a minor degree it is a delicious triumph to me to go into the club, and see the carpets up, and the Bores and the other dust dispersed to the four winds. Again New Zealander-like, I stand on the cold hearth, and say in the solitude, "Here I watched Bore A 1, with voice always mysteriously low and head always mysteriously dropped, whispering political secrets into the ears of Adam's confiding children. Accursed be his memory for ever and a day!"

But, I have all this time been coming to the point, that the happy nature of my retirement is most sweetly expressed in its being the abode of Love. It is, as it were, an inexpensive Agapemone:[9] nobody's speculation: everybody's profit. The one great result of the resumption of primitive habits, and (convertible terms) the not having much to do, is, the abounding of Love.

The Klem species are incapable of the softer emotions; probably, in that low nomadic race, the softer emotions have all degenerated into flue. But, with this exception, all the sharers of my retreat make love.

I have mentioned Saville-row. We all know the Doctor's servant. We all know what a respectable man he is, what a hard dry man, what a firm man, what a confidential man: how he lets us into the waiting-room, like a man who knows minutely what is the matter with us, but from whom the rack should not wring the secret. In the prosaic "season," he has distinctly the appearance of a man conscious of money in the savings bank, and taking his stand on his respectability with both feet. At that time it is as impossible to associate him with relaxation, or any human weakness, as it is to meet his eye without feeling guilty of indisposition. In the blest Arcadian time, how changed! I have seen him, in a pepper-and-salt jacket – jacket – and drab trousers, with his arm round the waist of a bootmaker's housemaid, smiling in open day. I have seen him at the pump by the Albany, unsolicitedly pumping for two fair young creatures, whose figures as they bent over their cans, were – if I may be allowed an original expression – a model for the sculptor. I have seen him trying the piano in the Doctor's drawing-room with his forefinger, and have heard him humming tunes in praise of lovely woman. I have seen him seated on a fire-engine, and going (obviously in search of excitement) to a fire. I saw him, one moonlight evening when the peace and purity of our Arcadian west were at their height, polk with the lovely daughter of a cleaner of gloves, from the door-steps of his own residence, across Saville-row, round by Clifford-street and Old Burlington-street, back to Burlington-gardens. Is this the Golden Age revived, or Iron London?

The Dentist's servant. Is that man no mystery to us, no type of invisible power? The tremendous individual knows (who else does?) what is done with the extracted teeth; he knows what goes on in the little room where something is always being washed or filed; he knows what warm spicy infusion is put into the comfortable tumbler from which we rinse our wounded mouth, with a gap in it that feels a foot wide; he knows whether the thing we spit into is a fixture communicating with the Thames, or could be cleared away for a dance; he sees the horrible parlour when there are no patients in it, and he could reveal, if he would, what becomes of the Every-Day Book then. The conviction of my coward conscience when I see that man in a professional light, is, that he knows all the statistics of my teeth and gums, my double teeth, my single teeth, my stopped teeth, and my sound. In this Arcadian rest, I am fearless of him as of a harmless, powerless creature in a Scotch cap, who adores a young lady in a voluminous crinoline, at a neighbouring billiard-room, and whose passion would be uninfluenced if every one of her teeth were false. They may be. He takes them all on trust.

In secluded corners of the place of my seclusion, there are little shops withdrawn from public curiosity, and never two together, where servants' perquisites are bought. The cook may dispose of grease at these modest and convenient marts; the butler, of bottles; the valet and lady's maid, of clothes; most servants, indeed, of most things they may happen to lay hold of. I have been told that in sterner times loving correspondence, otherwise interdicted, may be maintained by letter through the agency of some of these useful establishments. In the Arcadian autumn, no such device is necessary. Everybody loves, and openly and blamelessly loves. My landlord's young man loves the whole of one side of the way of Old Bond-street, and is beloved several doors up New Bond-street besides. I never look out of window but I see kissing of hands going on all around me. It is the morning custom to glide from shop to shop and exchange tender sentiments; it is the evening custom for couples to stand hand in hand at house doors, or roam, linked in that flowery manner, through the unpeopled streets. There is nothing else to do but love; and what there is to do, is done.

In unison with this pursuit, a chaste simplicity obtains in the domestic habits of Arcadia. Its few scattered people dine early, live moderately, sup socially, and sleep soundly. It is rumoured that the Beadles of the Arcade, from being the mortal enemies of boys, have signed with tears an address to Lord Shaftesbury, and subscribed to a ragged school.[10] No wonder! For, they might turn their heavy maces into crooks and tend sheep in the Arcade, to the purling of the water-carts as they give the thirsty streets much more to drink than they can carry.

A happy Golden Age, and a serene tranquillity. Charming picture, but it will fade. The iron age will return, London will come back to town, if I show my tongue then in Saville-row for half a minute I shall be prescribed for, the Doctor's man and the Dentist's man will then pretend that these days of unprofessional innocence never existed. Where Mr. and Mrs. Klem and their bed will be at that time, passes human knowledge; but my hatter hermitage will then know them no more, nor will it then know me. The desk at which I have written these meditations will retributively assist at the making out of my account, and the wheels of gorgeous carriages and the hoofs of high-stepping horses will crush the silence out of Bond-street – will grind Arcadia away, and give it to the elements in granite powder.

The Calais Night Mail

First published in *All the Year Round*, 2 May 1863. The text here is reproduced from *The Uncommercial Traveller*.

It is an unsettled question with me whether I shall leave Calais something handsome in my will, or whether I shall leave it my malediction. I hate it so much, and yet I am always so very glad to see it, that I am in a state of constant indecision on this subject. When I first made acquaintance with Calais, it was as a maundering young wretch in a clammy perspiration and dripping saline particles, who was conscious of no extremities but the one great extremity, sea-sickness – who was a mere bilious torso, with a mislaid headache somewhere in its stomach – who had been put into a horrible swing in Dover Harbour, and had tumbled giddily out of it on the French coast, or the Isle of Man, or anywhere. Times have changed, and now I enter Calais self-reliant and rational. I know where it is beforehand, I keep a look out for it, I recognise its landmarks when I see any of them, I am acquainted with its ways, and I know – and I can bear – its worst behaviour.

Malignant Calais! Low-lying alligator, evading the eyesight and discouraging hope! Dodging flat streak, now on this bow, now on that, now anywhere, now everywhere, now nowhere! In vain Cape Grinez, coming frankly forth into the sea, exhorts the failing to be stout of heart and stomach: sneaking Calais, prone behind its bar, invites emetically to despair. Even when it can no longer quite conceal itself in its muddy dock, it has an evil way of falling off, has Calais, which is more hopeless than its invisibility. The pier is all but on the bowsprit, and you think you are there – roll, roar, wash! – Calais has retired miles inland, and Dover has burst out to look for it. It has a last dip and slide in its character, has Calais, to be especially commended to the infernal gods. Thrice accursed be that garrison-town, when it dives under the boat's keel, and comes up a league or two to the right, with the packet shivering and spluttering and staring about for it!

Not but what I have my animosities towards Dover. I particularly detest Dover for the self-complacency with which it goes to bed. It always goes to bed (when I am going to Calais) with a more brilliant display of lamp and candle than any other town. Mr. and Mrs. Birmingham, host and hostess of the Lord Warden Hotel, are my much esteemed friends, but they are too conceited about the comforts of that establishment when the Night Mail is starting. I know it is a good house to stay at, and I don't want the fact insisted upon in all its warm bright windows at such an hour. I know the Warden is a stationary edifice that never rolls or pitches, and I object to its big outline seeming to insist upon that circumstance, and, as it were, to come over me with it, when I am reeling on the deck of the boat. Beshrew the Warden likewise for obstructing that corner, and making the wind so angry as it rushes round. Shall I not know that it blows quite soon enough, without the officious Warden's interference?

As I wait here on board the night packet, for the South-Eastern Train to come down with the Mail, Dover appears to me to be illuminated for some intensely aggravating festivity in my personal dishonour. All its noises smack of taunting praises of the land, and dispraises of the gloomy sea, and of me for going on it. The drums upon the heights have gone to bed, or I know they would rattle taunts against me for having my unsteady footing on this slippery deck. The many gas eyes of the Marine Parade twinkle in an offensive manner, as if with derision. The distant dogs of Dover bark at me in my mis-shapen wrappers, as if I were Richard the Third.[1]

A screech, a bell, and two red eyes come gliding down the Admiralty Pier with a smoothness of motion rendered more smooth by the heaving of the boat. The sea makes noises against the pier, as if several hippopotami were lapping at it, and were prevented by circumstances over which they had no control from drinking peaceably. We, the boat, become violently agitated – rumble, hum, scream, roar, and establish an immense family washing-day at each paddle-box. Bright patches break out in the train as the doors of the post-office vans are opened, and instantly stooping figures with sacks upon their backs begin to be beheld among the piles, descending as it would seem in ghostly procession to Davy Jones's Locker. The passengers come on board; a few shadowy Frenchmen, with hatboxes shaped like the stoppers of gigantic case-bottles; a few shadowy Germans in immense fur coats and boots; a few shadowy Englishmen prepared for the worst and pretending not to expect it. I cannot disguise from my uncommercial mind the miserable fact that we are a body of outcasts; that the attendants on us are as scant in number as may serve to get rid of us with the least possible delay; that there are no night-loungers interested in us; that the unwilling lamps shiver and shudder at us; that the sole object is to commit us to the deep and abandon us. Lo, the two red eyes glaring in increasing distance, and then the very train itself has gone to bed before we are off!

What is the moral support derived by some sea-going amateurs from an umbrella? Why do certain voyagers across the Channel always put up that article, and hold it up with a grim and fierce tenacity? A fellow-creature near me – whom I only know to *be* a fellow-creature, because of his umbrella: without which he might be a dark bit of cliff, pier, or bulkhead – clutches that instrument with a desperate grasp, that will not relax until he lands at Calais. Is there any analogy, in certain constitutions, between keeping an umbrella up, and keeping the spirits up? A hawser thrown on board with a flop replies "Stand by!" "Stand by, below!" "Half a turn a head!" "Half a turn a head!" "Half speed!" "Half speed!" "Port!" "Port!" "Steady!" "Steady!" "Go on!" "Go on!"

A stout wooden wedge driven in at my right temple and out at my left, a floating deposit of lukewarm oil in my throat, and a compression of the bridge of my nose in a blunt pair of pincers, – these are the personal sensations by which I know we are off, and by which I shall continue to know it until I am on the soil of France. My symptoms have scarcely established themselves comfortably, when two or three skating shadows that have been trying to walk or stand, get flung together, and other two or three shadows in tarpaulin slide with them into corners and cover them up. Then the South Foreland lights begin to hiccup at us in a way that bodes no good.

It is at about this period that my detestation of Calais knows no bounds. Inwardly I resolve afresh that I never will forgive that hated town. I have done so before, many times, but that is past. Let me register a vow. Implacable animosity to Calais everm — that was an awkward sea, and the funnel seems of my opinion, for it gives a complaining roar.

The wind blows stiffly from the Nor'-East, the sea runs high, we ship a deal of water, the night is dark and cold, and the shapeless passengers lie about in melancholy bundles, as if they were sorted out for the laundress; but for my own uncommercial part I cannot pretend that I am much inconvenienced by any of these things. A general howling whistling flopping gurgling and scooping, I am aware of, and a general knocking about of Nature; but the impressions I receive are very vague. In a sweet faint temper, something like the smell of damaged oranges, I think I should feel languidly benevolent if I had time. I have not time, because I am under a curious compulsion to occupy myself with the Irish melodies. "Rich and rare were the gems she wore,"[2] is the particular melody to which I find myself devoted. I sing it to myself in the most charming manner and with the greatest expression. Now and then, I raise my head (I am sitting on the hardest of wet seats, in the most uncomfortable of wet attitudes, but I don't mind it,) and notice that I am a whirling shuttlecock between a fiery battledore of a lighthouse on the French coast and a fiery battledore of a lighthouse on the English coast; but I don't notice it particularly, except to feel envenomed in my hatred of Calais. Then I go on again, "Rich and rare were the ge-ems she-e-e-e wore, And a bright gold ring on her wa-and she bo-ore, But O her beauty was fa-a-a-a-r beyond" – I am particularly proud of my execution here, when I become aware of another awkward shock from the sea, and another protest from the funnel, and a fellow-creature at the paddle-box more audibly indisposed than I think he need be – "Her sparkling gems, or snow-white wand, But O her beauty was fa-a-a-a-a-r beyond" – another awkward one here, and the fellow-creature with the umbrella down and picked up – "Her spa-a-rkling ge-ems, or her Port! port! steady! steady! snow-white fellow-creature at the paddle-box very selfishly audible, bump roar wash white wand."

As my execution of the Irish melodies partakes of my imperfect perceptions of what is going on around me, so what is going on around me becomes something else than what it is. The stokers open the furnace doors below, to feed the fires, and I am again on the box of the old Exeter Telegraph fast coach, and that is the light of the for ever extinguished coach-lamps, and the gleam on the hatches and paddle-boxes is *their* gleam on cottages and haystacks, and the monotonous noise of the engines is the steady jingle of the splendid team. Anon, the intermittent funnel roar of protest at every violent roll, becomes the regular blast of a high pressure engine, and I recognise the exceedingly explosive steamer in which I ascended the Mississippi[3] when the American civil war was not, and when only its causes were. A fragment of mast on which the light of a lantern falls, an end of rope, and a jerking block or so, become suggestive of Franconi's Circus[4] at Paris where I shall be this very night mayhap (for it must be morning now), and they dance to the self-same time and tune as the trained steed, Black Raven. What may be the speciality of these waves as they come rushing on, I cannot desert the pressing demands made upon me by the gems she wore, to inquire, but they are charged with something about Robinson Crusoe, and I think it was in Yarmouth Roads that he first went a seafaring and was near foundering (what a terrific sound that word had for me when I was a boy!) in his first gale of wind. Still, through all this, I must ask her (who *was* she, I wonder!) for the fiftieth time, and without ever stopping, Does she not fear to stray, So lone and lovely through this bleak way, And are Erin's sons so good or so cold, As not to be tempted by more fellow-creatures at the paddle-box or gold? Sir Knight I feel not the least alarm, No son of Erin will offer me harm, For though they love fellow-creature with umbrella down again and golden store, Sir Knight they what a tremendous one love honour and virtue more: For though they love Stewards with a bull's eye bright,[5] they'll trouble you for your ticket, sir – rough passage to-night!

I freely admit it to be a miserable piece of human weakness and inconsistency, but I no sooner become conscious of those last words from the steward than I begin to soften towards Calais. Whereas I have been vindictively wishing that those Calais burghers who came out of their town by a short cut into the History of England, with those fatal ropes round their necks[6] by which they have since been towed into so many cartoons, had all been hanged on the spot, I now begin to regard them as highly respectable and virtuous tradesmen. Looking about me, I see the light of Cape Grinez well astern of the boat on the davits to leeward, and the light of Calais Harbour undeniably at its old tricks, but still ahead and shining. Sentiments of forgiveness of Calais, not to say of attachment to Calais, begin to expand my bosom. I have weak notions that I will stay there a day or two on my way back. A faded and recumbent stranger pausing in a profound reverie over the rim of a basin, asked me what kind of place Calais is? I tell him (Heaven forgive me!) a very agreeable place indeed – rather hilly than otherwise.

So strangely goes the time, and on the whole so quickly – though still I seem to have been on board a week – that I am bumped rolled gurgled washed and pitched into Calais Harbour before her maiden smile has finally lighted her through the Green Isle, When blest for ever is she who relied, On entering Calais at the top of the tide. For we have not to land to-night down among those slimy timbers – covered with green hair as if it were the mermaids' favourite combing-place – where one crawls to the surface of the jetty, like a stranded shrimp, but we go steaming up the harbour to the Railway Station Quay. And as we go, the sea washes in and out among piles and planks, with dead heavy beats and in quite a furious manner (whereof we are proud), and the lamps shake in the wind, and the bells of Calais striking One seem to send their vibrations struggling against troubled air, as we have come struggling against troubled water. And now, in the sudden relief and wiping of faces, everybody on board seems to have had a prodigious double-tooth out, and to be this very instant free of the Dentist's hands. And now we all know for the first time how wet and cold we are, and how salt we are; and now I love Calais with my heart of hearts!

"Hôtel Dessin!" (but in this one case it is not a vocal cry; it is but a bright lustre in the eyes of the cheery representative of that best of inns). "Hôtel Meurice!" "Hôtel de France!" "Hôtel de Calais!" "The Royal Hôtel, Sir, Angaishe ouse!" "You going to Parry, Sir?" "Your baggage, registair froo, Sir?" Bless ye, my Touters, bless ye, my commissionaires, bless ye, my hungry-eyed mysteries in caps of a military form, who are always here, day or night, fair weather or foul, seeking inscrutable jobs which I never see you get! Bless ye, my Custom House officers in green and grey; permit me to grasp the welcome hands that descend into my travelling-bag, one on each side, and meet at the bottom to give my change of linen a peculiar shake up, as if it were a measure of chaff or grain! I have nothing to declare, Monsieur le Douanier, except that when I cease to breathe, Calais will be found written on my heart.[7] No article liable to local duty have I with me, Monsieur l'Officier de l'Octroi, unless the overflowing of a breast devoted to your charming town should be in that wise chargeable. Ah! see at the gangway by the twinkling lantern, my dearest brother and friend, he once of the Passport Office, he who collects the names! May he be for ever changeless in his buttoned black surtout, with his note-book in his hand, and his tall black hat surmounting his round smiling patient face! Let us embrace, my dearest brother. I am yours à tout jamais – for the whole of ever.

Calais up and doing at the railway station, and Calais down and dreaming in its bed; Calais with something of "an ancient and fish-like smell"[8] about it, and Calais blown and sea-washed pure; Calais represented at the Buffet by savoury roast fowls, hot coffee, cognac, and Bordeaux; and Calais represented everywhere by flitting persons with a monomania for changing money – though I never shall be able to understand in my present state of existence how they live by it, but I suppose I should, if I understood the currency question – Calais *en gros*, and Calais *en détail*, forgive one who has deeply wronged you. – I was not fully aware of it on the other side, but I meant Dover.

Ding, ding! To the carriages, gentlemen the travellers. Ascend then, gentlemen the travellers, for Hazebroucke, Lille, Douai, Bruxelles, Arras, Amiens, and Paris! I, humble representative of the uncommercial interest, ascend with the rest. The train is light to-night, and I share my compartment with but two fellow-travellers; one, a compatriot in an obsolete cravat, who thinks it a quite unaccountable thing that they don't keep "London time" on a French railway, and who is made angry by my modestly suggesting the possibility of Paris time being more in their way; the other, a young priest, with a very small bird in a very small cage, who feeds the small bird with a quill, and then puts him up in the network above his head, where he advances twittering, to his front wires, and seems to address me in an electioneering manner. The compatriot (who crossed in the boat, and whom I judge to be some person of distinction, as he was shut up, like a stately species of rabbit, in a private hutch on deck) and the young priest (who joined us at Calais) are soon asleep, and then the bird and I have it all to ourselves.

A stormy night still; a night that sweeps the wires of the electric telegraph with a wild and fitful hand; a night so very stormy, with the added storm of the train-progress through it, that when the Guard comes clambering round to mark the tickets while we are at full speed (a really horrible performance in an express train, though he holds on to the open window by his elbows in the most deliberate manner), he stands in such a whirlwind that I grip him fast by the collar, and feel it next to manslaughter to let him go. Still, when he is gone, the small small bird remains at his front wires feebly twittering to me – twittering and twittering, until, leaning back in my place and looking at him in drowsy fascination, I find that he seems to jog my memory as we rush along.

Uncommercial travels (thus the small small bird) have lain in their idle thriftless way through all this range of swamp and dyke, as through many other odd places; and about here, as you very well know, are the queer old stone farm-houses, approached by drawbridges, and the windmills that you get at by boats. Here, are the lands where the women hoe and dig, paddling canoe-wise from field to field, and here are the cabarets and other peasant-houses where the stone dove-cotes in the littered yards are as strong as warders' towers in old castles. Here, are the long monotonous miles of canal, with the great Dutch-built barges garishly painted, and the towing girls, sometimes harnessed by the forehead, sometimes by the girdle and the shoulders, not a pleasant sight to see. Scattered through this country are mighty works of VAUBAN,[9] whom you know about, and regiments of such corporals as you heard of once upon a time, and many a blue-eyed Bebelle.[10] Through these flat districts, in the shining summer days, walk those long grotesque files of young novices in enormous shovel-hats, whom you remember blackening the ground checkered by the avenues of leafy trees. And now that Hazebroucke slumbers certain kilometres ahead, recall the summer evening when your dusty feet strolling up from the station tended hap-hazard to a Fair there, where the oldest inhabitants were circling round and round a barrel-organ on hobby-horses, with the greatest gravity, and where the principal show in the Fair was a Religious Richardson's[11] – literally, on its own announcement in great letters, THEATRE RELIGIEUX. In which improving Temple, the dramatic representation was of "all the interesting events in the life of our Lord, from the Manger to the Tomb;" the principal female character without any reservation or exception, being at the moment of your arrival, engaged in trimming the external Moderators (as it was growing dusk), while the next principal female character took the money, and the Young Saint John disported himself upside down on the platform.

Looking up at this point to confirm the small small bird in every particular he has mentioned, I find he has ceased to twitter, and has put his head under his wing. Therefore, in my different way I follow the good example.

Chatham Dockyard

First published in *All the Year Round*, 29 August 1863. The text here is taken from *The Uncommercial Traveller*. Dickens had already written an article in collaboration with Wills on this topic, 'One Man in a Dockyard', *Household Words*, 6 September 1851.

There are some small out-of-the-way landing-places on the Thames and the Medway, where I do much of my summer idling. Running water is favourable to day-dreams, and a strong tidal river is the best of running water for mine. I like to watch the great ships standing out to sea or coming home richly laden, the active little steam-tugs confidently puffing with them to and from the sea-horizon, the fleet of barges that seem to have plucked their brown and russet sails from the ripe trees in the landscape, the heavy old colliers, light in ballast, floundering down before the tide, the light screw barks and schooners imperiously holding a straight course while the others patiently tack and go about, the yachts with their tiny hulls and great white sheets of canvas, the little sailing-boats bobbing to and fro on their errands of pleasure or business, and – as it is the nature of little people to do – making a prodigious fuss about their small affairs. Watching these objects, I still am under no obligation to think about them, or even so much as to see them, unless it perfectly suits my humour. As little am I obliged to hear the plash and flop of the tide, the ripple at my feet, the clinking windlass afar off, or the humming steam-ship paddles further away yet. These, with the creaking little jetty on which I sit, and the gaunt high-water marks and low-water marks in the mud, and the broken causeway, and the broken bank, and the broken stakes and piles leaning forward as if they were vain of their personal appearance and looking for their reflection in the water, will melt into any train of fancy. Equally adaptable to any purpose or to none, are the pasturing sheep and kine upon the marshes, the gulls that wheel and dip around me, the crows (well out of gunshot) going home from the rich harvest-fields, the heron that has been out a-fishing and looks as melancholy, up there in the sky, as if it hadn't agreed with him. Everything within the range of the senses will, by the aid of the running water, lend itself to everything beyond that range, and work into a drowsy whole, not unlike a kind of tune, but for which there is no exact definition.

One of these landing-places is near an old fort (I can see the Nore Light[1] from it with my pocket-glass), from which fort mysteriously emerges a boy, to whom I am much indebted for additions to my scanty stock of knowledge. He is a young boy, with an intelligent face burnt to a dust colour by the summer sun, and with crisp hair of the same hue. He is a boy in whom I have perceived nothing incompatible with habits of studious inquiry and meditation, unless an evanescent black eye (I was delicate of inquiring how occasioned) should be so considered. To him am I indebted for ability to identify a Custom-house boat at any distance, and for acquaint-ance with all the forms and ceremonies observed by a homeward-bound Indiaman coming up the river, when the Custom-house officers go aboard her. But for him, I might never have heard of "the dumb-ague,"[2] respecting which malady I am now learned. Had I never sat at his feet, I might have finished my mortal career and never known that when I see a white horse on a barge's sail, that barge is a lime barge. For precious secrets in reference to beer, am I likewise beholden to him, involving warning against the beer of a certain establishment, by reason of its having turned sour through failure in point of demand: though my young sage is not of opinion that similar deterioration has befallen the ale. He has also enlightened me touching the mushrooms of the marshes, and has gently reproved my ignorance in having supposed them to be impregnated with salt. His manner of imparting information, is thoughtful, and appropriate to the scene. As he reclines beside me, he pitches into the river, a little stone or piece of grit, and then delivers himself oracularly, as though he spoke out of the centre of the spreading circle that it makes in the water. He never improves my mind without observing this formula.

With the wise boy – whom I know by no other name than the Spirit of the Fort – I recently consorted on a breezy day when the river leaped about us and was full of life. I had seen the sheaved corn carrying in the golden fields as I came down to the river; and the rosy farmer, watching his labouring-men in the saddle on his cob, had told me how he had reaped his two hundred and sixty acres of long-strawed corn last week, and how a better week's work he had never done in all his days. Peace and abundance were on the country-side in beautiful forms and beautiful colours, and the harvest seemed even to be sailing out to grace the never-reaped sea in the yellow-laden barges that mellowed the distance.

It was on this occasion that the Spirit of the Fort, directing his remarks to a certain floating iron battery lately lying in that reach of the river, enriched my mind with his opinions on naval architecture, and informed me that he would like to be an engineer. I found him up to everything that is done in the contracting line by Messrs. Peto and Brassey – cunning in the article of concrete – mellow in the matter of iron – great on the subject of gunnery. When he spoke of pile-driving and sluice-making, he left me not a leg to stand on, and I can never sufficiently acknowledge his forbearance with me in my disabled state. While he thus discoursed, he several times directed his eyes to one distant quarter of the landscape, and spoke with vague mysterious awe of "the Yard." Pondering his lessons after we had parted, I bethought me that the Yard was one of our large public Dockyards, and that it lay hidden among the crops down in the dip behind the windmills, as if it modestly kept itself out of view in peaceful times, and sought to trouble no man. Taken with this modesty on the part of the Yard, I resolved to improve the Yard's acquaintance.

My good opinion of the Yard's retiring character was not dashed by nearer approach. It resounded with the noise of hammers beating upon iron; and the great sheds or slips under which the mighty men-of-war are built, loomed business-like when contemplated from the opposite side of the river. For all that, however, the Yard made no display, but kept itself snug under hill-sides of corn-fields, hop-gardens, and orchards; its great chimneys smoking with a quiet – almost a lazy – air, like giants smoking tobacco; and the great Shears moored off it, looking meekly and inoffensively out of proportion, like the Giraffe of the machinery creation. The store of cannon on the neighbouring gun-wharf, had an innocent toy-like appearance, and the one red-coated sentry on duty over them was a mere toy figure, with a clock-work movement. As the hot sunlight sparkled on him he might have passed for the identical little man who had the little gun, and whose bullets they were made of lead, lead, lead.

Crossing the river and landing at the Stairs, where a drift of chips and weed had been trying to land before me and had not succeeded, but had got into a corner instead, I found the very street posts to be cannon, and the architectural ornaments to be shells. And so I came to the Yard, which was shut up tight and strong with great folded gates, like an enormous patent safe. These gates devouring me, I became digested into the Yard; and it had, at first, a clean-swept holiday air, as if it had given over work until next war-time. Though indeed a quantity of hemp for rope was tumbling out of store-houses, even there, which would hardly be lying like so much hay on the white stones if the Yard were as placid as it pretended.

Ding, Clash, Dong, BANG, Boom, Rattle, Clash, BANG, Clink, BANG, Dong, BANG, Clatter, BANG BANG BANG! What on earth is this! This is, or soon will be, the Achilles,[3] iron armour-plated ship. Twelve hundred men are working at her now; twelve hundred men working on stages over her sides, over her bows, over her stern, under her keel, between her decks, down in her hold, within her and without, crawling and creeping into the finest curves of her lines wherever it is possible for men to twist. Twelve hundred hammerers, measurers, caulkers, armourers, forgers, smiths, ship-wrights; twelve hundred dingers, clashers, dongers, rattlers, clinkers, bangers bangers bangers! Yet all this stupendous uproar around the rising Achilles is as nothing to the reverberations with which the perfected Achilles shall resound upon the dreadful day when the full work is in hand for which this is but note of preparation – the day when the scuppers that are now fitting like great dry thirsty conduit-pipes, shall run red. All these busy figures between decks, dimly seen bending at their work in smoke and fire, are as nothing to the figures that shall do work here of another kind in smoke and fire, that day. These steam-worked engines alongside, helping the ship by travelling to and fro, and wafting tons of iron plates about, as though they were so many leaves of trees, would be rent limb from limb if they stood by her for a minute then. To think that this Achilles, monstrous compound of iron tank and oaken chest, can ever swim or roll! To think that any force of wind and wave could ever break her! To think that wherever I see a glowing red-hot iron point thrust out of her side from within – as I do now, there, and there, and there! – and two watching men on a stage without, with bared arms and sledge-hammers, strike at it fiercely, and repeat their blows until it is black and flat, I see a rivet being driven home, of which there are many in every iron plate, and thousands upon thousands in the ship! To think that the difficulty I experience in appreciating the ship's size when I am on board, arises from her being a series of iron tanks and oaken chests, so that internally she is ever finishing and ever beginning, and half of her might be smashed, and yet the remaining half suffice and be sound. Then, to go over the side again and down among the ooze and wet to the bottom of the dock, in the depths of the subterranean forest of dog-shores and stays that hold her up, and to see the immense mass bulging out against the upper light, and tapering down towards me, is, with great pains and much clambering, to arrive at an impossibility of realising that this is a ship at all, and to become possessed by the fancy that it is an enormous immovable edifice set up in an ancient amphitheatre (say, that at Verona),[4] and almost filling it! Yet what would even these things be, without the tributary workshops and the mechanical powers for piercing the iron plates – four inches and a half thick – for rivets, shaping them under hydraulic pressure to the finest tapering turns of the ship's lines, and paring them away, with knives shaped like the beaks of strong and cruel birds, to the nicest requirements of the design! These machines of tremendous force, so easily directed by one attentive face and presiding hand, seem to me to have in them something of the retiring character of the Yard. "Obedient monster, please to bite this mass of iron through and through, at equal distances, where these regular chalk-marks are, all round." Monster looks at its work, and lifting its ponderous head, replies, "I don't particularly want to do it; but if it must be done —!" The solid metal wriggles out, hot from the monster's crunching tooth, and it *is* done. "Dutiful monster, observe this other mass of iron. It is required to be pared away, according to this delicately lessening and arbitrary line, which please to look at." Monster (who has been in a reverie) brings down its blunt head, and, much in the manner of Doctor Johnson, closely looks along the line – very closely, being somewhat near-sighted.[5] "I don't particularly want to do it; but if it must be done—!" Monster takes another near-sighted look, takes aim, and the tortured piece writhes off, and falls, a hot tight-twisted snake, among the ashes. The making of the rivets is merely a pretty round game, played by a man and a boy, who put red-hot barley sugar in a Pope Joan board,[6] and immediately rivets fall out of window; but the tone of the great machines is the tone of the great Yard and the great country: "We don't particularly want to do it; but if it must be done —!"

How such a prodigious mass as the Achilles can ever be held by such comparatively little anchors as those intended for her and lying near her here, is a mystery of seamanship which I will refer to the wise boy. For my own part, I should as soon have thought of tethering an elephant to a tent-peg, or the larger hippopotamus in the Zoological Gardens to my shirt-pin. Yonder in the river, alongside a hulk, lie two of this ship's hollow iron masts. *They* are large enough for the eye, I find, and so are all her other appliances. I wonder why only her anchors look small.

I have no present time to think about it, for I am going to see the workshops where they make all the oars used in the British Navy. A pretty large pile of building, I opine, and a pretty long job! As to the building, I am soon disappointed, because the work is all done in one loft. And as to a long job – what is this? Two rather large mangles with a swarm of butterflies hovering over them? What can there be in the mangles that attracts butterflies?

Drawing nearer, I discern that these are not mangles, but intricate machines, set with knives and saws and planes, which cut smooth and straight here, and slantwise there, and now cut such a depth, and now miss cutting altogether, according to the predestined requirements of the pieces of wood that are pushed on below them: each of which pieces is to be an oar, and is roughly adapted to that purpose before it takes its final leave of far-off forests, and sails for England. Likewise I discern that the butterflies are not true butterflies, but wooden shavings, which, being spirted up from the wood by the violence of the machinery, and kept in rapid and not equal movement by the impulse of its rotation on the air, flutter and play, and rise and fall, and conduct themselves as like butterflies as heart could wish. Suddenly the noise and motion cease, and the butterflies drop dead. An oar has been made since I came in, wanting the shaped handle. As quickly as I can follow it with my eye and thought, the same oar is carried to a turning lathe. A whirl and a Nick! Handle made. Oar finished.

The exquisite beauty and efficiency of this machinery need no illustration, but happen to have a pointed illustration to-day. A pair of oars of unusual size chance to be wanted for a special purpose, and they have to be made by hand. Side by side with the subtle and facile machine, and side by side with the fast-growing pile of oars on the floor, a man shapes out these special oars with an axe. Attended by no butterflies, and chipping and dinting, by comparison as leisurely as if he were a labouring Pagan getting them ready against his decease at threescore and ten, to take with him as a present to Charon[7] for his boat, the man (aged about thirty) plies his task. The machine would make a regulation oar while the man wipes his forehead. The man might be buried in a mound made of the strips of thin broad wooden ribbon torn from the wood whirled into oars as the minutes fall from the clock, before he had done a forenoon's work with his axe.

Passing from this wonderful sight to the Ships again – for my heart, as to the Yard, is where the ships are – I notice certain unfinished wooden walls left seasoning on the stocks, pending the solution of the merits of the wood and iron question, and having an air of biding their time with surly confidence. The names of these worthies are set up beside them, together with their capacity in guns – a custom highly conducive to ease and satisfaction in social intercourse, if it could be adapted to mankind. By a plank more gracefully pendulous than substantial, I make bold to go aboard a transport ship (iron screw) just sent in from the contractor's yard to be inspected and passed. She is a very gratifying experience, in the simplicity and humanity of her arrangements for troops, in her provision for light and air and cleanliness, and in her care for women and children. It occurs to me, as I explore her, that I would require a handsome sum of money to go aboard her, at midnight by the Dockyard bell, and stay aboard alone till morning; for surely she must be haunted by a crowd of ghosts of obstinate old martinets, mournfully flapping their cherubic epaulettes over the changed times. Though still we may learn from the astounding ways and means in our Yards now, more highly than ever to respect the forefathers who got to sea, and fought the sea, and held the sea, without them. This remembrance putting me in the best of tempers with an old hulk, very green as to her copper, and generally dim and patched, I pull off my hat to her. Which salutation a callow and downy-faced young officer of Engineers, going by at the moment, perceiving, appropriates – and to which he is most heartily welcome, I am sure.

Having been torn to pieces (in imagination) by the steam circular saws, perpendicular saws, horizontal saws, and saws of eccentric action, I come to the sauntering part of my expedition, and consequently to the core of my Uncommercial pursuits.

Everywhere, as I saunter up and down the Yard, I meet with tokens of its quiet and retiring character. There is a gravity upon its red brick offices and houses, a staid pretence of having nothing worth mentioning to do, an avoidance of display, which I never saw out of England. The white stones of the pavement present no other trace of Achilles and his twelve hundred banging men (not one of whom strikes an attitude) than a few occasional echoes. But for a whisper in the air suggestive of sawdust and shavings, the oar-making and the saws of many movements might be miles away. Down below here, is the great reservoir of water where timber is steeped in various temperatures, as a part of its seasoning process. Above it, on a tramroad supported by pillars, is a Chinese Enchanter's Car, which fishes the logs up, when sufficiently steeped, and rolls smoothly away with them to stack them. When I was a child (the Yard being then familiar to me) I used to think that I should like to play at Chinese Enchanter, and to have that apparatus placed at my disposal for the purpose by a beneficent country. I still think that I should rather like to try the effect of writing a book in it. Its retirement is complete, and to go gliding to and fro among the stacks of timber would be a convenient kind of travelling in foreign countries – among the forests of North America, the sodden Honduras swamps, the dark pine woods, the Norwegian frosts, and the tropical heats, rainy seasons, and thunder-storms. The costly store of timber is stacked and stowed away in sequestered places, with the pervading avoidance of flourish or effect. It makes as little of itself as possible, and calls to no one "Come and look at me!" And yet it is picked out from the trees of the world; picked out for length, picked out for breadth, picked out for straightness, picked out for crookedness, chosen with an eye to every need of ship and boat. Strangely twisted pieces lie about, precious in the sight of shipwrights. Sauntering through these groves, I come upon an open glade where workmen are examining some timber recently delivered. Quite a pastoral scene, with a background of river and windmill! and no more like War than the American States are at present like an Union.

Sauntering among the ropemaking, I am spun into a state of blissful indolence, wherein my rope of life seems to be so untwisted by the process as that I can see back to very early days indeed, when my bad dreams – they were frightful, though my more mature understanding has never made out why – were of an interminable sort of ropemaking, with long minute filaments for strands, which, when they were spun home together close to my eyes, occasioned screaming. Next, I walk among the quiet lofts of stores – of sails, spars, rigging, ships' boats – determined to believe that somebody in authority wears a girdle and bends beneath the weight of a massive bunch of keys, and that, when such a thing is wanted, he comes telling his keys like Blue Beard, and opens such a door. Impassive as the long lofts look, let the electric battery send down the word, and the shutters and doors shall fly open, and such a fleet of armed ships, under steam and under sail, shall burst forth as will charge the old Medway – where the merry Stuart let the Dutch come, while his not so merry sailors starved in the streets[8] – with something worth looking at to carry to the sea. Thus I idle round to the Medway again, where it is now flood tide; and I find the river evincing a strong solicitude to force a way into the dry dock where Achilles is waited on by the twelve hundred bangers, with intent to bear the whole away before they are ready.

To the last, the Yard puts a quiet face upon it; for I make my way to the gates through a little quiet grove of trees, shading the quaintest of Dutch landing-places, where the leaf-speckled shadow of a shipwright just passing away at the further end might be the shadow of Russian Peter[9] himself. So, the doors of the great patent safe at last close upon me, and I take boat again: somehow, thinking as the oars dip, of braggart Pistol[10] and his brood, and of the quiet monsters of the Yard, with their "We don't particularly want to do it; but if it must be done —!" Scrunch.

SLEEP TO STARTLE US

A Walk in a Workhouse

First published in *Household Words*, 25 May 1850, and included in *Reprinted Pieces* from which this text is reproduced.

On a certain Sunday, I formed one of the congregation assembled in the chapel of a large metropolitan Workhouse.[1] With the exception of the clergyman and clerk, and a very few officials, there were none but paupers present. The children sat in the galleries; the women in the body of the chapel, and in one of the side aisles; the men in the remaining aisle. The service was decorously performed, though the sermon might have been much better adapted to the comprehension and to the circumstances of the hearers. The usual supplications were offered, with more than the usual significancy in such a place, for the fatherless children and widows, for all sick persons and young children, for all that were desolate and oppressed, for the comforting and helping of the weak-hearted, for the raising-up of them that had fallen; for all that were in danger, necessity, and tribulation. The prayers of the congregation were desired "for several persons in the various wards dangerously ill;" and others who were recovering returned their thanks to Heaven.

Among this congregation were some evil-looking young women, and beetle-browed young men; but not many – perhaps that kind of characters kept away. Generally, the faces (those of the children excepted) were depressed and subdued, and wanted colour. Aged people were there, in every variety. Mumbling, blear-eyed, spectacled, stupid, deaf, lame; vacantly winking in the gleams of sun that now and then crept in through the open doors, from the paved yard; shading their listening ears, or blinking eyes, with their withered hands; poring over their books, leering at nothing, going to sleep, crouching and drooping in corners. There were weird old women, all skeleton within, all bonnet and cloak without, continually wiping their eyes with dirty dusters of pocket-handkerchiefs; and there were ugly old crones, both male and female, with a ghastly kind of contentment upon them which was not at all comforting to see. Upon the whole, it was the dragon, Pauperism, in a very weak and impotent condition; toothless, fangless, drawing his breath heavily enough, and hardly worth chaining up.

When the service was over, I walked with the humane and conscientious gentleman whose duty it was to take that walk, that Sunday morning, through the little world of poverty enclosed within the workhouse walls. It was inhabited by a population of some fifteen hundred or two thousand paupers, ranging from the infant newly born or not yet come into the pauper world, to the old man dying on his bed.

In a room opening from a squalid yard, where a number of listless women were lounging to and fro, trying to get warm in the ineffectual sunshine of the tardy May morning – in the "Itch Ward," not to compromise the truth – a woman such as HOGARTH has often drawn,[2] was hurriedly getting on her gown before a dusty fire. She was the nurse, or wardswoman, of that insalubrious department – herself a pauper – flabby, raw-boned, untidy – unpromising and coarse of aspect as need be. But, on being spoken to about the patients whom she had in charge, she turned round, with her shabby gown half on, half off, and fell a crying with all her might. Not for show, not querulously, not in any mawkish sentiment, but in the deep grief and affliction of her heart; turning away her dishevelled head: sobbing most bitterly, wringing her hands, and letting fall abundance of great tears, that choked her utterance. What was the matter with the nurse of the itch-ward? Oh, "the dropped child" was dead! Oh, the child that was found in the street, and she had brought up ever since, had died an hour ago, and see where the little creature lay, beneath this cloth! The dear, the pretty dear!

The dropped child seemed too small and poor a thing for Death to be in earnest with, but Death had taken it; and already its diminutive form was neatly washed, composed, and stretched as if in sleep upon a box. I thought I heard a voice from Heaven saying, It shall be well for thee, O nurse of the itch-ward, when some less gentle pauper does those offices to thy cold form, that such as the dropped child are the angels who behold my Father's face!

In another room were several ugly old women crouching, witch-like, round a hearth, and chattering and nodding, after the manner of the monkeys. "All well here? And enough to eat?" A general chattering and chuckling; at last an answer from a volunteer. "Oh yes, gentleman! Bless you, gentleman! Lord bless the Parish of St. So-and-So! It feed the hungry, sir, and give drink to the thusty, and it warm them which is cold, so it do, and good luck to the parish of St. So-and-So, and thankee, gentleman!" Elsewhere, a party of pauper nurses were at dinner. "How do *you* get on?" "Oh pretty well, sir! We works hard, and we lives hard – like the sodgers!"[3]

In another room, a kind of purgatory or place of transition, six or eight noisy madwomen were gathered together, under the superintendence of one sane attendant. Among them was a girl of two or three and twenty, very prettily dressed, of most respectable appearance, and good manners, who had been brought in from the house where she had lived as domestic servant (having, I suppose, no friends), on account of being subject to epileptic fits, and requiring to be removed under the influence of a very bad one. She was by no means of the same stuff, or the same breeding, or the same experience, or in the same state of mind, as those by whom she was surrounded; and she pathetically complained that the daily association and the nightly noise made her worse, and was driving her mad – which was perfectly evident. The case was noted for inquiry and redress, but she said she had already been there for some weeks.

If this girl had stolen her mistress's watch, I do not hesitate to say she would have been infinitely better off. We have come to this absurd, this dangerous, this monstrous pass, that the dishonest felon is, in respect of cleanliness, order, diet, and accommodation, better provided for, and taken care of, than the honest pauper.

And this conveys no special imputation on the workhouse of the parish of St. So-and-So, where, on the contrary, I saw many things to commend. It was very agreeable, recollecting that most infamous and atrocious enormity committed at Tooting[4] – an enormity which, a hundred years hence, will still be vividly remembered in the bye-ways of English life, and which has done more to engender a gloomy discontent and suspicion among many thousands of the people than all the Chartist leaders could have done in all their lives – to find the pauper children in this workhouse looking robust and well, and apparently the objects of very great care. In the Infant School – a large, light, airy room at the top of the building – the little creatures, being at dinner, and eating their potatoes heartily, were not cowed by the presence of strange visitors, but stretched out their small hands to be shaken, with a very pleasant confidence. And it was comfortable to see two mangy pauper rocking-horses rampant in a corner. In the girls' school, where the dinner was also in progress, everything bore a cheerful and healthy aspect. The meal was over, in the boys' school, by the time of our arrival there, and the room was not yet quite re-arranged; but the boys were roaming unrestrained about a large and airy yard, as any other schoolboys might have done. Some of them had been drawing large ships upon the schoolroom wall; and if they had a mast with shrouds and stays set up for practice (as they have in the Middlesex House of Correction[5]), it would be so much the better. At present, if a boy should feel a strong impulse upon him to learn the art of going aloft, he could only gratify it, I presume, as the men and women paupers gratify their aspirations after better board and lodging, by smashing as many workhouse windows as possible, and being promoted to prison.

In one place, the Newgate of the Workhouse, a company of boys and youths were locked up in a yard alone; their day-room being a kind of kennel where the casual poor used formerly to be littered down at night. Divers of them had been there some long time. "Are they never going away?" was the natural inquiry. "Most of them are crippled, in some form or other," said the Wardsman, "and not fit for anything." They slunk about, like dispirited wolves or hyænas;[6] and made a pounce at their food when it was served out, much as those animals do. The big-headed idiot shuffling his feet along the pavement, in the sunlight outside, was a more agreeable object everyway.

Groves of babies in arms; groves of mothers and other sick women in bed; groves of lunatics; jungles of men in stone-paved down-stairs day-rooms, waiting for their dinners; longer and longer groves of old people, in up-stairs Infirmary wards, wearing out life, God knows how – this was the scenery through which the walk lay, for two hours. In some of these latter chambers, there were pictures stuck against the wall, and a neat display of crockery and pewter on a kind of side-board; now and then it was a treat to see a plant or two; in almost every ward there was a cat.

In all of these Long Walks of aged and infirm, some old people were bedridden, and had been for a long time; some were sitting on their beds half-naked; some dying in their beds; some out of bed, and sitting at a table near the fire. A sullen or lethargic indifference to what was asked, a blunted sensibility to everything but warmth and food, a moody absence of complaint as being of no use, a dogged silence and resentful desire to be left alone again, I thought were generally apparent. On our walking into the midst of one of these dreary perspectives of old men, nearly the following little dialogue took place, the nurse not being immediately at hand:

"All well here?"

No answer. An old man in a Scotch cap sitting among others on a form at the table, eating out of a tin porringer, pushes back his cap a little to look at us, claps it down on his forehead again with the palm of his hand, and goes on eating.

"All well here?" (repeated).

No answer. Another old man sitting on his bed, paralytically peeling a boiled potato, lifts his head and stares.

"Enough to eat?"

No answer. Another old man, in bed, turns himself and coughs.

"How are *you* to-day?" To the last old man.

That old man says nothing; but another old man, a tall old man of very good address, speaking with perfect correctness, comes forward from somewhere, and volunteers an answer. The reply almost always proceeds from a volunteer, and not from the person looked at or spoken to.

"We are very old, sir," in a mild, distinct voice. "We can't expect to be well, most of us."

"Are you comfortable?"

"I have no complaint to make, sir." With a half shake of his head, a half shrug of his shoulders, and a kind of apologetic smile.

"Enough to eat?"

"Why, sir, I have but a poor appetite," with the same air as before; "and yet I get through my allowance very easily."

"But," showing a porringer with a Sunday dinner in it; "here is a portion of mutton, and three potatoes. You can't starve on that?"

"Oh dear no, sir," with the same apologetic air. "Not starve."

"What do you want?"

"We have very little bread, sir. It's an exceedingly small quantity of bread."

The nurse, who is now rubbing her hands at the questioner's elbow, interferes with, "It ain't much raly, sir. You see they've only six ounces a day, and when they've took their breakfast, there *can* only be a little left for night, sir."

Another old man, hitherto invisible, rises out of his bed-clothes, as out of a grave, and looks on.

"You have tea at night?" The questioner is still addressing the well-spoken old man.

"Yes, sir, we have tea at night."

"And you save what bread you can from the morning, to eat with it?"

"Yes, sir – if we can save any."

"And you want more to eat with it?"

"Yes, sir." With a very anxious face.

The questioner, in the kindness of his heart, appears a little discomposed, and changes the subject.

"What has become of the old man who used to lie in that bed in the corner?"

The nurse don't remember what old man is referred to. There has been such a many old men. The well-spoken old man is doubtful. The spectral old man who has come to life in bed, says, "Billy Stevens." Another old man who has previously had his head in the fireplace, pipes out,

"Charley Walters."

Something like a feeble interest is awakened. I suppose Charley Walters had conversation in him.

"He's dead," says the piping old man.

Another old man, with one eye screwed up, hastily displaces the piping old man, and says:

"Yes! Charley Walters died in that bed, and – and —"

"Billy Stevens," persists the spectral old man.

"No, no! and Johnny Rogers died in that bed, and – and – they're both on 'em dead – and Sam'l Bowyer;" this seems very extraordinary to him; "he went out!"

With this he subsides, and all the old men (having had quite enough of it) subside, and the spectral old man goes into his grave again, and takes the shade of Billy Stevens with him.

As we turn to go out at the door, another previously invisible old man, a hoarse old man in a flannel gown, is standing there, as if he had just come up through the floor.

"I beg your pardon, sir, could I take the liberty of saying a word?"

"Yes; what is it?"

"I am greatly better in my health, sir; but what I want, to get me quite round," with his hand on his throat, "is a little fresh air, sir. It has always done my complaint so much good, sir. The regular leave for going out comes round so seldom, that if the gentlemen, next Friday, would give me leave to go out walking, now and then – for only an hour or so, sir! —"

Who could wonder, looking through those weary vistas of bed and infirmity, that it should do him good to meet with some other scenes, and assure himself that there was something else on earth? Who could help wondering why the old men lived on as they did; what grasp they had on life; what crumbs of interest or occupation they could pick up from its bare board; whether Charley Walters had ever described to them the days when he kept company with some old pauper woman in the bud, or Billy Stevens ever told them of the time when he was a dweller in the far-off foreign land called Home!

The morsel of burnt child, lying in another room, so patiently, in bed, wrapped in lint, and looking steadfastly at us with his bright quiet eyes when we spoke to him kindly, looked as if the knowledge of these things, and of all the tender things there are to think about, might have been in his mind – as if he thought, with us, that there was a fellow-feeling in the pauper nurses which appeared to make them more kind to their charges than the race of common nurses in the hospitals – as if he mused upon the Future of some older children lying around him in the same place, and thought it best, perhaps, all things considered, that he should die — as if he knew, without fear, of those many coffins, made and unmade, piled up in the store below — and of his unknown friend, "the dropped child," calm upon the box-lid covered with a cloth. But there was something wistful and appealing, too, in his tiny face, as if, in the midst of all the hard necessities and incongruities he pondered on, he pleaded, in behalf of the helpless and the aged poor, for a little more liberty — and a little more bread.

Detective Police

First published in two parts in *Household Words*, 27 July and 10 August 1850, and subsequently in one part, with some minor changes, in *Reprinted Pieces* from which this text is reproduced.

We are not by any means devout believers in the old Bow Street Police.[1] To say the truth, we think there was a vast amount of humbug about those worthies. Apart from many of them being men of very indifferent character, and far too much in the habit of consorting with thieves and the like, they never lost a public occasion of jobbing and trading in mystery and making the most of themselves. Continually puffed besides by incompetent magistrates anxious to conceal their own deficiencies, and hand-in-glove with the penny-a-liners[2] of that time, they became a sort of superstition. Although as a Preventive Police they were utterly ineffective, and as a Detective Police were very loose and uncertain in their operations, they remain with some people a superstition to the present day.

On the other hand, the Detective Force organised since the establishment of the existing Police, is so well chosen and trained, proceeds so systematically and quietly, does its business in such a workmanlike manner, and is always so calmly and steadily engaged in the service of the public, that the public really do not know enough of it, to know a tithe of its usefulness. Impressed with this conviction, and interested in the men themselves, we represented to the authorities at Scotland Yard, that we should be glad, if there were no official objection, to have some talk with the Detectives. A most obliging and ready permission being given, a certain evening was appointed with a certain Inspector for a social conference between ourselves and the Detectives, at The Household Words Office in Wellington Street, Strand, London. In consequence of which appointment the party "came off," which we are about to describe. And we beg to repeat that, avoiding such topics as it might for obvious reasons be injurious to the public, or disagreeable to respectable individuals, to touch upon in print, our description is as exact as we can make it.

The reader will have the goodness to imagine the Sanctum Sanctorum of Household Words. Anything that best suits the reader's fancy, will best represent that magnificent chamber. We merely stipulate for a round table in the middle, with some glasses and cigars arranged upon it; and the editorial sofa elegantly hemmed in between that stately piece of furniture and the wall.

It is a sultry evening at dusk. The stones of Wellington Street are hot and gritty, and the watermen and hackney-coachmen at the Theatre opposite,[3] are much flushed and aggravated. Carriages are constantly setting down the people who have come to Fairy-Land; and there is a mighty shouting and bellowing every now and then, deafening us for the moment, through the open windows.

Just at dusk, Inspectors Wield[4] and Stalker are announced; but we do not undertake to warrant the orthography of any of the names here mentioned. Inspector Wield presents Inspector Stalker. Inspector Wield is a middle-aged man of a portly presence, with a large, moist, knowing eye, a husky voice, and a habit of emphasising his conversation by the aid of a corpulent fore-finger, which is constantly in juxtaposition with his eyes or nose. Inspector Stalker is a shrewd, hard-headed Scotchman – in appearance not at all unlike a very acute, thoroughly-trained schoolmaster, from the Normal Establishment at Glasgow.[5] Inspector Wield one might have known, perhaps, for what he is – Inspector Stalker, never.

The ceremonies of reception over, Inspectors Wield and Stalker observe that they have brought some sergeants with them. The sergeants are presented[6] – five in number, Sergeant Dornton, Sergeant Witchem, Sergeant Mith, Sergeant Fendall, and Sergeant Straw. We have the whole Detective Force from Scotland Yard, with one exception. They sit down in a semi-circle (the two Inspectors at the two ends) at a little distance from the round table, facing the editorial sofa. Every man of them, in a glance, immediately takes an inventory of the furniture and an accurate sketch of the editorial presence. The Editor feels that any gentleman in company could take him up, if need should be, without the smallest hesitation, twenty years hence.

The whole party are in plain clothes. Sergeant Dornton about fifty years of age, with a ruddy face and a high sun-burnt forehead, has the air of one who has been a Sergeant in the army – he might have sat to Wilkie for the Soldier in the Reading of the Will.[7] He is famous for steadily pursuing the inductive process, and, from small beginnings, working on from clue to clue until he bags his man. Sergeant Witchem, shorter and thicker-set, and marked with the small-pox, has something of a reserved and thoughtful air; as if he were engaged in deep arithmetical calculations. He is renowned for his acquaintance with the swell mob.[8] Sergeant Mith, a smooth-faced man with a fresh bright complexion, and a strange air of simplicity, is a dab at housebreakers. Sergeant Fendall, a light-haired, well-spoken, polite person, is a prodigious hand at pursuing private inquiries of a delicate nature. Straw, a little wiry Sergeant of meek demeanour and strong sense, would knock at a door and ask a series of questions in any mild character you choose to prescribe to him, from a charity-boy upwards, and seem as innocent as an infant. They are, one and all, respectable-looking men; of perfectly good deportment and unusual intelligence; with nothing lounging or slinking in their manners; with an air of keen observation and quick perception when addressed; and generally presenting in their faces, traces more or less marked of habitually leading lives of strong mental excitement. They have all good eyes; and they all can, and they all do, look full at whomsoever they speak to.

We light the cigars, and hand round the glasses (which are very temperately used indeed), and the conversation begins by a modest amateur reference on the Editorial part to the swell mob. Inspector Wield immediately removes his cigar from his lips, waves his right hand, and says, "Regarding the swell mob, sir, I can't do better than call upon Sergeant Witchem. Because the reason why? I'll tell you. Sergeant Witchem is better acquainted with the swell mob than any officer in London."

Our heart leaping up when we beheld this rainbow in the sky, we turn to Sergeant Witchem, who very concisely, and in well-chosen language, goes into the subject forthwith. Meantime, the whole of his brother officers are closely interested in attending to what he says, and observing its effect. Presently they begin to strike in, one or two together, when an opportunity offers, and the conversation becomes general. But these brother officers only come in to the assistance of each other – not to the contradiction – and a more amicable brotherhood there could not be. From the swell mob, we diverge to the kindred topics of cracksmen, fences, public-house dancers, area-sneaks, designing young people who go out "gonophing,"[9] and other "schools." It is observable throughout these revelations, that Inspector Stalker, the Scotchman, is always exact and statistical, and that when any question of figures arises, everybody as by one consent pauses, and looks to him.

When we have exhausted the various schools of Art – during which discussion the whole body have remained profoundly attentive, except when some unusual noise at the Theatre over the way has induced some gentleman to glance inquiringly towards the window in that direction, behind his next neighbour's back – we burrow for information on such points as the following. Whether there really are any highway robberies in London, or whether some circumstances not convenient to be mentioned by the aggrieved party, usually precede the robberies complained of, under that head, which quite change their character? Certainly the latter, almost always.

Whether in the case of robberies in houses, where servants are necessarily exposed to doubt, innocence under suspicion ever becomes so like guilt in appearance, that a good officer need be cautious how he judges it? Undoubtedly. Nothing is so common or deceptive as such appearances at first. Whether in a place of public amusement, a thief knows an officer, and an officer knows a thief – supposing them, beforehand, strangers to each other – because each recognises in the other, under all disguise, an inattention to what is going on, and a purpose that is not the purpose of being entertained? Yes. That's the way exactly. Whether it is reasonable or ridiculous to trust to the alleged experiences of thieves as narrated by themselves, in prisons, or penitentiaries, or anywhere? In general, nothing more absurd. Lying is their habit and their trade; and they would rather lie – even if they hadn't an interest in it, and didn't want to make themselves agreeable – than tell the truth.

From these topics, we glide into a review of the most celebrated and horrible of the great crimes that have been committed within the last fifteen or twenty years. The men engaged in the discovery of almost all of them, and in the pursuit or apprehension of the murderers, are here, down to the very last instance. One of our guests gave chase to and boarded the emigrant ship, in which the murderess last hanged in London[10] was supposed to have embarked. We learn from him that his errand was not announced to the passengers, who may have no idea of it to this hour. That he went below, with the captain, lamp in hand – it being dark, and the whole steerage abed and sea-sick – and engaged the Mrs. Manning who *was* on board, in a conversation about her luggage, until she was, with no small pains, induced to raise her head, and turn her face towards the light. Satisfied that she was not the object of his search, he quietly re-embarked in the Government steamer alongside, and steamed home again with the intelligence.

When we have exhausted these subjects, too, which occupy a considerable time in the discussion, two or three leave their chairs, whisper Sergeant Witchem, and resume their seats. Sergeant Witchem leaning forward a little, and placing a hand on each of his legs, then modestly speaks as follows:

"My brother-officers wish me to relate a little account of my taking Tally-ho Thompson. A man oughtn't to tell what he has done himself; but still, as nobody was with me, and, consequently, as nobody but myself can tell it, I'll do it in the best way I can, if it should meet your approval."

We assure Sergeant Witchem that he will oblige us very much, and we all compose ourselves to listen with great interest and attention.

"Tally-ho Thompson," says Sergeant Witchem, after merely wetting his lips with his brandy-and-water, "Tally-ho Thompson was a famous horse-stealer, couper, and magsman. Thompson, in conjunction with a pal that occasionally worked with him, gammoned a countryman out of a good round sum of money, under pretence of getting him a situation – the regular old dodge – and was afterwards in the 'Hue and Cry' for a horse – a horse that he stole, down in Hertfordshire. I had to look after Thompson, and I applied myself, of course, in the first instance, to discovering where he was. Now, Thompson's wife lived, along with a little daughter, at Chelsea. Knowing that Thompson was somewhere in the country, I watched the house – especially at post-time in the morning – thinking Thompson was pretty likely to write to her. Sure enough, one morning the postman comes up, and delivers a letter at Mrs. Thompson's door. Little girl opens the door, and takes it in. We're not always sure of postmen, though the people at the post-offices are always very obliging. A postman may help us, or he may not, – just as it happens. However, I go across the road, and I say to the postman, after he has left the letter, 'Good morning! how are you?' 'How are *you*?' says he. 'You've just delivered a letter for Mrs. Thompson.' 'Yes, I have.' 'You didn't happen to remark what the post-mark was, perhaps?' 'No,' says he, 'I didn't.' 'Come,' says I, 'I'll be plain with you. I'm in a small way of business, and I have given Thompson credit, and I can't afford to lose what he owes me. I know he's got money, and I know he's in the country, and if you could tell me what the post-mark was, I should be very much obliged to you, and you'd do a service to a tradesman in a small way of business that can't afford a loss.' 'Well,' he said, 'I do assure you that I did not observe what the post-mark was; all I know is, that there was money in the letter – I should say a sovereign.' This was enough for me, because of course I knew that Thompson having sent his wife money, it was probable she'd write to Thompson, by return of post, to acknowledge the receipt. So I said 'Thankee' to the postman, and I kept on the watch. In the afternoon I saw the little girl come out. Of course I followed her. She went into a stationer's shop, and I needn't say to you that I looked in at the window. She bought some writing-paper and envelopes, and a pen. I think to myself, 'That'll do!' – watch her home again – and don't go away, you may be sure, knowing that Mrs. Thompson was writing her letter to Tally-ho, and that the letter would be posted presently. In about an hour or so, out came the little girl again, with the letter in her hand. I went up, and said something to the child, whatever it might have been; but I couldn't see the direction of the letter, because she held it with the seal upwards. However, I observed that on the back of the letter there was what we call a kiss – a drop of wax by the side of the seal

– and again, you understand, that was enough for me. I saw her post the letter, waited till she was gone, then went into the shop, and asked to see the Master. When he came out, I told him, 'Now, I'm an Officer in the Detective Force; there's a letter with a kiss been posted here just now, for a man that I'm in search of; and what I have to ask of you, is, that you will let me look at the direction of that letter.' He was very civil – took a lot of letters from the box in the window – shook 'em out on the counter with the faces downwards – and there among 'm was the identical letter with the kiss. It was directed, Mr. Thomas Pigeon, Post Office, B—, to be left 'till called for. Down I went to B — (a hundred and twenty miles or so) that night. Early next morning I went to the Post Office; saw the gentleman in charge of that department; told him who I was; and that my object was to see, and track, the party that should come for the letter for Mr. Thomas Pigeon. He was very polite, and said, 'You shall have every assistance we can give you; you can wait inside the office; and we'll take care to let you know when anybody comes for the letter.' Well, I waited there three days, and began to think that nobody ever *would* come. At last the clerk whispered to me, 'Here! Detective! Somebody's come for the letter!' 'Keep him a minute,' said I, and I ran round to the outside of the office. There I saw a young chap with the appearance of an Ostler, holding a horse by the bridle – stretching the bridle across the pavement, while he waited at the Post Office window for the letter. I began to pat the horse, and that; and I said to the boy, 'Why, this is Mr. Jones's Mare!' 'No. It an't.' 'No?' said I. 'She's very like Mr. Jones's Mare!' 'She an't Mr. Jones's Mare, anyhow,' says he. 'It's Mr. So and So's, of the Warwick Arms.' And up he jumped, and off he went – letter and all. I got a cab, followed on the box, and was so quick after him that I came into the stable-yard of the Warwick Arms, by one gate, just as he came in by another. I went into the bar, where there was a young woman serving, and called for a glass of brandy-and-water. He came in directly, and handed her the letter. She casually looked at it, without saying anything, and stuck it up behind the glass over the chimney-piece. What was to be done next?

"I turned it over in my mind while I drank my brandy-and-water (looking pretty sharp at the letter the while), but I couldn't see my way out of it at all. I tried to get lodgings in the house, but there had been a horse-fair, or something of that sort, and it was full. I was obliged to put up somewhere else, but I came backwards and forwards to the bar for a couple of days, and there was the letter always behind the glass. At last I thought I'd write a letter to Mr. Pigeon myself, and see what that would do. So I wrote one, and posted it, but I purposely addressed it, Mr. John Pigeon, instead of Mr.

Thomas Pigeon, to see what *that* would do. In the morning (a very wet morning it was) I watched the postman down the street, and cut into the bar, just before he reached the Warwick Arms. In he came presently with my letter. 'Is there a Mr. John Pigeon staying here?' 'No! – stop a bit though,' says the barmaid; and she took down the letter behind the glass. 'No,' says she, 'it's Thomas, and *he* is not staying here. Would you do me a favour, and post this for me, as it is so wet?' The postman said Yes; she folded it in another envelope, directed it, and gave it him. He put it in his hat, and away he went.

"I had no difficulty in finding out the direction of that letter. It was addressed Mr. Thomas Pigeon, Post Office, R——, Northamptonshire, to be left till called for. Off I started directly for R——; I said the same at the Post Office there, as I had said at B——; and again I waited three days before anybody came. At last another chap on horseback came. 'Any letters for Mr. Thomas Pigeon?' 'Where do you come from?' 'New Inn, near R——.' He got the letter, and away *he* went at a canter.

"I made my inquiries about the New Inn, near R——, and hearing it was a solitary sort of house, a little in the horse line, about a couple of miles from the station, I thought I'd go and have a look at it. I found it what it had been described, and sauntered in, to look about me. The landlady was in the bar, and I was trying to get into conversation with her; asked her how business was, and spoke about the wet weather, and so on; when I saw, through an open door, three men sitting by the fire in a sort of parlour, or kitchen; and one of those men, according to the description I had of him, was Tally-ho Thompson!

"I went and sat down among 'em, and tried to make things agreeable; but they were very shy – wouldn't talk at all – looked at me, and at one another, in a way quite the reverse of sociable. I reckoned 'em up, and finding that they were all three bigger men than me, and considering that their looks were ugly – that it was a lonely place – railroad station two miles off – and night coming on – thought I couldn't do better than have a drop of brandy-and-water to keep my courage up. So I called for my brandy-and-water; and as I was sitting drinking it by the fire, Thompson got up and went out.

"Now the difficulty of it was, that I wasn't sure it *was* Thompson, because I had never set eyes on him before; and what I had wanted was to be quite certain of him. However, there was nothing for it now, but to follow, and put a bold face upon it. I found him talking, outside in the yard, with the landlady. It turned out afterwards that he was wanted by a Northampton officer for something else, and that, knowing that officer to be pock-marked (as I am myself), he mistook me for him. As I have observed, I found him talking to the landlady, outside. I put my hand upon his shoulder – this way – and said, 'Tally-ho Thompson, it's no use. I know you. I'm an officer from London, and I take you into custody for felony!' 'That be d—d!' says Tally-ho Thompson.

"We went back into the house, and the two friends began to cut up rough, and their looks didn't please me at all, I assure you. 'Let the man go. What are you going to do with him?' 'I'll tell you what I'm going to do with him. I'm going to take him to London to-night, as sure as I'm alive. I'm not alone here, whatever you may think. You mind your own business, and keep yourselves to yourselves. It'll be better for you, for I know you both very well.' *I* 'd never seen or heard of 'em in all my life, but my bouncing cowed 'em a bit, and they kept off, while Thompson was making ready to go. I thought to myself, however, that they might be coming after me on the dark road, to rescue Thompson; so I said to the landlady, 'What men have you got in the house, Missis?' 'We haven't got no men here,' she says sulkily. 'You have got an ostler, I suppose?' 'Yes, we've got an ostler.' 'Let me see him.' Presently he came, and a shaggy-headed young fellow he was. 'Now attend to me, young man,' says I; 'I'm a Detective Officer from London. This man's name is Thompson. I have taken him into custody for felony. I am going to take him to the railroad station. I call upon you in the Queen's name to assist me; and mind you, my friend, you'll get yourself into more trouble than you know of, if you don't!' You never saw a person open his eyes so wide. 'Now, Thompson, come along!' says I. But when I took out the handcuffs, Thompson cries, 'No! None of that! I won't stand *them*! I'll go along with you quiet, but I won't bear none of that!' 'Tally-ho Thompson,' I said, 'I'm willing to behave as a man to you, if you are willing to behave as a man to me. Give me your word that you'll come peaceably along, and I don't want to handcuff you.' 'I will,' says Thompson, 'but I'll have a glass of brandy first.' 'I don't care if I've another,' said I. 'We'll have two more, Missis,' said the friends, 'and con-found you, Constable, you'll give your man a drop, won't you?' I was agreeable to that, so we had it all round, and then my man and I took Tally-ho Thompson safe to the railroad, and I carried him to London that night. He was afterwards acquitted, on account of a defect in the evidence; and I understand he always praises me up to the skies, and says I'm one of the best of men."

This story coming to a termination amidst general applause, Inspector Wield, after a little grave smoking, fixes his eye on his host, and thus delivers himself:

"It wasn't a bad plant that of mine, on Fikey,[11] the man accused of forging the Sou'-Western Railway debentures – it was only t'other day – because the reason why? I'll tell you.

"I had information that Fikey and his brother kept a factory over yonder there," – indicating any region on the Surrey side of the river – "where he bought second-hand carriages; so after I'd tried in vain to get hold of him by other means, I wrote him a letter in an assumed name, saying that I'd got a horse and shay to dispose of, and would drive down next day that he might view the lot, and make an offer – very reasonable it was, I said – a reg'lar bargain. Straw and me then went off to a friend of mine that's in the livery and job business, and hired a turn-out for the day, a precious smart turn-out it was – quite a slap-up thing! Down we drove, accordingly, with a friend (who's not in the Force himself); and leaving my friend in the shay near a public-house, to take care of the horse, we went to the factory, which was some little way off. In the factory, there was a number of strong fellows at work, and after reckoning 'em up, it was clear to me that it wouldn't do to try it on there. They were too many for us. We must get our man out of doors. 'Mr. Fikey at home?' 'No, he ain't.' 'Expected home soon?' 'Why, no, not soon.' 'Ah! Is his brother here?' '*I*'m his brother.' 'Oh! well, this is an ill-conwenience, this is. I wrote him a letter yesterday, saying I'd got a little turn-out to dispose of, and I've took the trouble to bring the turn-out down a' purpose, and now he ain't in the way.' 'No, he ain't in the way. You couldn't make it convenient to call again, could you?' 'Why, no, I couldn't. I want to sell; that's the fact; and I can't put it off. Could you find him anywheres?' At first he said No, he couldn't, and then he wasn't sure about it, and then he'd go and try. So at last he went up-stairs, where there was a sort of loft, and presently down comes my man himself in his shirt-sleeves.

" 'Well,' he says, 'this seems to be rayther a pressing matter of yours.' 'Yes,' I says, 'it *is* rayther a pressing matter, and you'll find it a bargain – dirt cheap.' 'I ain't in partickler want of a bargain just now,' he says, 'but where is it?' 'Why,' I says, 'the turn-out's just outside. Come and look at it.' He hasn't any suspicions, and away we go. And the first thing that happens is, that the horse runs away with my friend (who knows no more of driving than a child) when he takes a little trot along the road to show his paces. You never saw such a game in your life!

"When the bolt is over, and the turn-out has come to a standstill again, Fikey walks round and round it as grave as a judge – me too. 'There, sir!' I says. 'There's a neat thing!' 'It ain't a bad style of thing,' he says. 'I believe you,' says I. 'And there's a horse!' – for I saw him looking at it. 'Rising

254

eight!' I says, rubbing his fore-legs. (Bless you, there ain't a man in the world knows less of horses than I do, but I'd heard my friend at the Livery Stables say he was eight year old, so I says, as knowing as possible, 'Rising eight.') 'Rising eight, is he?' says he. 'Rising eight,' says I. 'Well,' he says, 'what do you want for it?' 'Why, the first and last figure for the whole concern is five-and-twenty pound!' 'That's very cheap!' he says, looking at me. 'Ain't it?' I says. 'I told you it was a bargain! Now, without any higgling and haggling about it, what I want is to sell, and that's my price. Further, I'll make it easy to you, and take half the money down, and you can do a bit of stiff* for the balance.' 'Well,' he says again, 'that's very cheap.' 'I believe you,' says I; 'get in and try it, and you'll buy it. Come! take a trial!'

"Ecod, he gets in, and we get in, and we drive along the road, to show him to one of the railway clerks that was hid in the public-house window to identify him. But the clerk was bothered, and didn't know whether it was him, or wasn't – because the reason why? I'll tell you, – on account of his having shaved his whiskers. 'It's a clever little horse,' he says, 'and trots well; and the shay runs light.' 'Not a doubt about it,' I says. 'And now, Mr. Fikey, I may as well make it all right, without wasting any more of your time. The fact is, I'm Inspector Wield, and you're my prisoner.' 'You don't mean that?' he says. 'I do, indeed.' 'Then burn my body,' says Fikey, 'if this ain't *too* bad!'

"Perhaps you never saw a man so knocked over with surprise. 'I hope you'll let me have my coat?' he says. 'By all means.' 'Well, then, let's drive to the factory.' 'Why, not exactly that, I think,' said I; 'I've been there, once before, to-day. Suppose we send for it.' He saw it was no go, so he sent for it, and put it on, and we drove him up to London, comfortable."

This reminiscence is in the height of its success, when a general proposal is made to the fresh-complexioned, smooth-faced officer, with the strange air of simplicity, to tell the "Butcher's Story."

[10 August 1850]

The fresh-complexioned, smooth-faced officer, with the strange air of simplicity, began with a rustic smile, and in a soft, wheedling tone of voice, to relate the Butcher's Story, thus:

"It's just about six years ago, now, since information was given at Scotland Yard of there being extensive robberies of lawns and silks going on, at some wholesale houses in the City. Directions were given for the business being looked into; and Straw, and Fendall, and me, we were all in it."

* Give a bill.

"When you received your instructions," said we, "you went away, and held a sort of Cabinet Council together!"

The smooth-faced officer coaxingly replied, "Ye-es. Just so. We turned it over among ourselves a good deal. It appeared, when we went into it, that the goods were sold by the receivers extraordinarily cheap – much cheaper than they could have been if they had been honestly come by. The receivers were in the trade, and kept capital shops – establishments of the first respectability – one of 'em at the West End, one down in Westminster. After a lot of watching and inquiry, and this and that among ourselves, we found that the job was managed, and the purchases of the stolen goods made, at a little public-house near Smithfield, down by Saint Bartholomew's; where the Warehouse Porters, who were the thieves, took 'em for that purpose, don't you see? and made appointments to meet the people that went between themselves and the receivers. This public-house was principally used by journeymen butchers from the country, out of place, and in want of situations; so, what did we do, but – ha, ha, ha! – we agreed that I should be dressed up like a butcher myself, and go and live there!"

Never, surely, was a faculty of observation better brought to bear upon a purpose, than that which picked out this officer for the part. Nothing in all creation could have suited him better. Even while he spoke, he became a greasy, sleepy, shy, good-natured, chuckle-headed, unsuspicious, and confiding young butcher. His very hair seemed to have suet in it, as he made it smooth upon his head, and his fresh complexion to be lubricated by large quantities of animal food.

" – So I – ha, ha, ha!" (always with the confiding snigger of the foolish young butcher) "so I dressed myself in the regular way, made up a little bundle of clothes, and went to the public-house, and asked if I could have a lodging there? They says, 'yes, you can have a lodging here,' and I got a bedroom, and settled myself down in the tap. There was a number of people about the place, and coming backwards and forwards to the house; and first one says, and then another says, 'Are you from the country, young man?' 'Yes,' I says, 'I am. I'm come out of Northamptonshire, and I'm quite lonely here, for I don't know London at all, and it's such a mighty big town.' 'It *is* a big town,' they says. 'Oh, it's a *very* big town!' I says. 'Really and truly I never was in such a town. It quite confuses of me!' – and all that, you know.

"When some of the Journeymen Butchers that used the house, found that I wanted a place, they says, 'Oh, we'll get you a place!' And they actually took me to a sight of places, in Newgate Market, Newport Market, Clare, Carnaby[12] – I don't know where all. But the wages was – ha, ha, ha! – was not sufficient, and I never could suit myself, don't you see? Some of the queer frequenters of the house were a little suspicious of me at first, and I was obliged to be very cautious indeed, how I communicated with Straw or Fendall. Sometimes, when I went out, pretending to stop and look into the shop windows, and just casting my eye round, I used to see some of 'em following me; but being perhaps better accustomed than they thought for, to that sort of thing, I used to lead 'em on as far as I thought necessary or convenient – sometimes a long way – and then turn sharp round, and meet 'em, and say, 'Oh, dear, how glad I am to come upon you so fortunate! This London's such a place, I'm blowed if I an't lost again!' And then we'd go back all together, to the public-house, and – ha, ha, ha! and smoke our pipes, don't you see?

"They were very attentive to me, I am sure. It was a common thing, while I was living there, for some of 'em to take me out, and show me London. They showed me the Prisons – showed me Newgate – and when they showed me Newgate, I stops at the place where the Porters pitch their loads, and says, 'Oh dear, is this where they hang the men? Oh Lor!' 'That!' they says, 'what a simple cove[13] he is! *That* ain't it!' And then, they pointed out which *was* it, and I says, 'Lor!' and they says, 'Now you'll know it agen, won't you?' And I said I thought I should if I tried hard – and I assure you I kept a sharp look out for the City Police when we were out in this way, for if any of 'em had happened to know me, and had spoke to me, it would have been all up in a minute. However, by good luck such a thing never happened, and all went on quiet: though the difficulties I had in communicating with my brother officers were quite extraordinary.

"The stolen goods that were brought to the public-house by the Warehouse Porters, were always disposed of in a back parlour. For a long time, I never could get into this parlour, or see what was done there. As I sat smoking my pipe, like an innocent young chap, by the tap-room fire, I'd hear some of the parties to the robbery, as they came in and out, say softly to the landlord, 'Who's that? What does *he* do here?' 'Bless your soul,' says the landlord, 'he's only a' – ha, ha, ha! – 'he's only a green young fellow from the country, as is looking for a butcher's situation. Don't mind *him*!' So, in course of time, they were so convinced of my being green, and got to be so accustomed to me, that I was as free of the parlour as any of 'em, and I have seen as much as Seventy Pounds' Worth of fine lawn sold there, in one night, that was stolen from a warehouse in Friday Street. After the sale the buyers always stood treat – hot supper, or dinner, or what not – and they'd say on those occasions, 'Come on, Butcher! Put your best leg foremost, young 'un, and walk into it!' Which I used to do – and hear, at table, all manner of particulars that it was very important for us Detectives to know.

"This went on for ten weeks. I lived in the public-house all the time, and never was out of the Butcher's dress – except in bed. At last, when I had followed seven of the thieves, and set 'em to rights – that's an expression of ours, don't you see, by which I mean to say that I traced 'em, and found out where the robberies were done, and all about 'em – Straw, and Fendall, and I, gave one another the office, and at a time agreed upon, a descent was made upon the public-house, and the apprehensions effected. One of the first things the officers did, was to collar me – for the parties to the robbery weren't to suppose yet, that I was anything but a Butcher – on which the landlord cries out, 'Don't take *him*,' he says, 'whatever you do! He's only a poor young chap from the country, and butter wouldn't melt in his mouth!' However, they – ha, ha, ha! – they took me, and pretended to search my bedroom, where nothing was found but an old fiddle belonging to the landlord, that had got there somehow or another. But it entirely changed the landlord's opinion, for when it was produced, he says, 'My fiddle! The Butcher's a pur-loiner! I give him into custody for the robbery of a musical instrument!'

"The man that had stolen the goods in Friday Street was not taken yet. He had told me, in confidence, that he had his suspicions there was something wrong (on account of the City Police having captured one of the party), and that he was going to make himself scarce. I asked him, 'Where do you mean to go, Mr. Shepherdson?' 'Why, Butcher,' says he, 'the Setting Moon, in the Commercial Road, is a snug house, and I shall hang out there for a time. I shall call myself Simpson, which appears to me to be a modest sort of a name. Perhaps you'll give us a look in, Butcher?' 'Well,' says I, 'I think I *will* give you a call' – which I fully intended, don't you see, because, of course, he was to be taken! I went over to the Setting Moon next day, with a brother officer, and asked at the bar for Simpson. They pointed out his room, up-stairs. As we were going up, he looks down over the banisters, and calls out, 'Halloa, Butcher! is that you?' 'Yes, it's me. How do you find yourself?' 'Bobbish,' he says; 'but who's that with you?' 'It's only a young man, that's a friend of mine,' I says. 'Come along, then,' says he; 'any friend of the Butcher's is as welcome as the Butcher!' So I made my friend acquainted with him, and we took him into custody.

"You have no idea, sir, what a sight it was, in Court, when they first knew that I wasn't a Butcher, after all! I wasn't produced at the first examination, when there was a remand; but I was at the second. And when I stepped into the box, in full police uniform, and the whole party saw how they had been done, actually a groan of horror and dismay proceeded from 'em in the dock!

"At the Old Bailey, when their trials came on, Mr. Clarkson was engaged for the defence, and he *couldn't* make out how it was, about the Butcher. He thought, all along, it was a real Butcher. When the counsel for the prosecution said, 'I will now call before you, gentlemen, the Police-officer,' meaning myself, Mr. Clarkson says, 'Why Police-officer? Why more Police-officers? I don't want Police. We have had a great deal too much of the Police. I want the Butcher!' However, sir, he had the Butcher and the Police-officer, both in one. Out of seven prisoners committed for trial, five were found guilty, and some of 'em were transported. The respectable firm at the West End got a term of imprisonment; and that's the Butcher's Story!"

The story done, the chuckle-headed Butcher again resolved himself into the smooth-faced Detective. But he was so extremely tickled by their having taken him about, when he was that Dragon in disguise, to show him London, that he could not help reverting to that point in his narrative; and gently repeating with the Butcher snigger, "'Oh, dear,' I says, 'is that where they hang the men? Oh, Lor!' '*That!*' says they. 'What a simple cove he is!'"

It being now late, and the party very modest in their fear of being too diffuse, there were some tokens of separation; when Sergeant Dornton, the soldierly-looking man, said, looking round him with a smile:

"Before we break up, sir, perhaps you might have some amusement in hearing of the Adventures of a Carpet Bag. They are very short; and, I think, curious."

We welcomed the Carpet Bag, as cordially as Mr. Shepherdson welcomed the false Butcher at the Setting Moon. Sergeant Dornton proceeded.

"In 1847, I was despatched to Chatham, in search of one Mesheck, a Jew. He had been carrying on, pretty heavily, in the bill-stealing way, getting acceptances from young men of good connexions (in the army chiefly), on pretence of discount, and bolting with the same.

"Mesheck was off, before I got to Chatham. All I could learn about him was, that he had gone, probably to London, and had with him – a Carpet Bag.

"I came back to town, by the last train from Blackwall, and made inquiries concerning a Jew passenger with – a Carpet Bag.

"The office was shut up, it being the last train. There were only two or three porters left. Looking after a Jew with a Carpet Bag, on the Blackwall Railway, which was then the high road to a great Military Depôt, was worse than looking after a needle in a hayrick. But it happened that one of these porters had carried, for a certain Jew, to a certain public-house, a certain – Carpet Bag.

"I went to the public-house, but the Jew had only left his luggage there for a few hours, and had called for it in a cab, and taken it away. I put such questions there, and to the porter, as I thought prudent, and got at this description of – the Carpet Bag.

"It was a bag which had, on one side of it, worked in worsted, a green parrot on a stand. A green parrot on a stand was the means by which to identify that – Carpet Bag.

"I traced Mesheck, by means of this green parrot on a stand, to Cheltenham, to Birmingham, to Liverpool, to the Atlantic Ocean. At Liverpool he was too many for me. He had gone to the United States, and I gave up all thoughts of Mesheck, and likewise of his – Carpet Bag.

"Many months afterwards – near a year afterwards – there was a bank in Ireland robbed of seven thousand pounds, by a person of the name of Doctor Dundey, who escaped to America; from which country some of the stolen notes came home. He was supposed to have bought a farm in New Jersey. Under proper management, that estate could be seized and sold, for the benefit of the parties he had defrauded. I was sent off to America for this purpose.

"I landed at Boston. I went on to New York. I found that he had lately changed New York paper-money for New Jersey paper-money, and had banked cash in New Brunswick. To take this Doctor Dundey, it was necessary to entrap him into the State of New York, which required a deal of artifice and trouble. At one time, he couldn't be drawn into an appointment. At another time, he appointed to come to meet me, and a New York officer, on a pretext I made; and then his children had the measles. At last he came, per steamboat, and I took him, and lodged him in a New York prison called the Tombs;[14] which I dare say you know, sir?"

Editorial acknowledgment to that effect.

"I went to the Tombs, on the morning after his capture, to attend the examination before the magistrate. I was passing through the magistrate's private room, when, happening to look round me to take notice of the place, as we generally have a habit of doing, I clapped my eyes, in one corner, on a – Carpet Bag.

"What did I see upon that Carpet Bag, if you'll believe me, but a green parrot on a stand, as large as life!

" 'That Carpet Bag, with the representation of a green parrot on a stand,' said I, 'belongs to an English Jew, name Aaron Mesheck, and to no other man, alive or dead!'

"I give you my word the New York Police Officers were doubled up with surprise.

"'How did you ever come to know that?' said they.

"'I think I ought to know that green parrot by this time,' said I; 'for I have had as pretty a dance after that bird, at home, as ever I had, in all my life!'"

"And was it Mesheck's?" we submissively inquired.

"Was it, sir? Of course it was! He was in custody for another offence, in that very identical Tombs, at that very identical time. And, more than that! Some memoranda, relating to the fraud for which I had vainly endeavoured to take him, were found to be, at that moment, lying in that very same individual – Carpet Bag!"

Such are the curious coincidences and such is the peculiar ability, always sharpening and being improved by practice, and always adapting itself to every variety of circumstances, and opposing itself to every new device that perverted ingenuity can invent, for which this important social branch of the public service is remarkable! For ever on the watch, with their wits stretched to the utmost, these officers have, from day to day and year to year, to set themselves against every novelty of trickery and dexterity that the combined imaginations of all the lawless rascals in England can devise, and to keep pace with every such invention that comes out. In the Courts of Justice, the materials of thousands of such stories as we have narrated – often elevated into the marvellous and romantic, by the circumstances of the case – are dryly compressed into the set phrase, "in consequence of information I received, I did so and so." Suspicion was to be directed, by careful inference and deduction, upon the right person; the right person was to be taken, wherever he had gone, or whatever he was doing to avoid detection: he is taken; there he is at the bar; that is enough. From information I, the officer, received, I did it; and, according to the custom in these cases, I say no more.

These games of chess, played with live pieces, are played before small audiences, and are chronicled nowhere. The interest of the game supports the player. Its results are enough for Justice. To compare great things with small, suppose LEVERRIER or ADAMS informing the public that from information he had received he had discovered a new planet;[15] or COLUMBUS informing the public of his day that from information he had received he had discovered a new continent; so the Detectives inform it that they have discovered a new fraud or an old offender, and the process is unknown.

Thus, at midnight, closed the proceedings of our curious and interesting party. But one other circumstance finally wound up the evening, after our Detective guests had left us. One of the sharpest among them, and the officer best acquainted with the Swell Mob, had his pocket picked, going home!

A Paper-Mill

First published in *Household Words*, 31 August 1850, this article was written in collaboration with Mark Lemon. The text reproduced here is that published in *The Uncollected Writings of Charles Dickens* (1968), edited by Harry Stone who suggests that Dickens was responsible for the portions from the opening up to 'I am rags' and from 'Of my being made' to the conclusion; and he certainly dictated the strategy of the essay.

Down at Dartford in Kent, on a fine bright day, I strolled through the pleasant green lanes, on my way to a Paper-Mill. Accustomed, mainly, to associate Dartford with Gunpowder Mills, and formidable tin canisters, illustrated in copperplate, with the outpourings of a generous cornucopia of dead game, I found it pleasant to think, on a summer morning when all living creatures were enjoying life, that it was only paper in my mind – not powder.

If sturdy Wat Tyler,[1] of this very town of Dartford in Kent (Deptford had the honour of him once, but that was a mistake) could only have anticipated and reversed the precept of the pious Orange-Lodges;[2] if he could only have put his trust in Providence, and kept his paper damp[3] – for printing – he need never have marched to London, the captain of a hundred thousand men, and summarily beheaded the archbishop of Canterbury as a bad adviser of the young king, Richard. Then, would William Walworth, Lord Mayor of London (and an obsequious courtier enough, may be) never have struck him from his charger, unawares. Then, might the "general enfranchisement of all bondmen" – the bold smith's demand – have come, a long time sooner than it did. Then, might working-men have maintained the decency and honour of their daughters, through many a hazy score of troubled and oppressive years, when they were yet as the clods of the valley, broken by the ploughshare, worried by the harrow. But, in those days, paper and printing for the people were not; so, Wat lay low in Smithfield, and Heaven knows what became of his daughter, and the old ferocious wheel went driving round, some centuries longer.

The wild flowers were blowing in these Dartford hedges, all those many summer-times; the larks were singing, high in air; the trees were rustling as they rustle to-day; the bees went humming by; the light clouds cast their shadows on the verdant fields. The pleasant little river Darent ran the same course; sparkled in the same sun; had, then as now, its tiny circles made by insects; and its plumps and plashes, made by fish. But, the river has changed, since Wat the Blacksmith, bending over with his bucket, saw his grimy face, impatient of unjust and grievous tribute, making remonstrance with him for his long endurance. Now, there are indeed books in the running brooks[4] – for they go to feed the Paper-Mill.

Time was, in the old Saxon days, when there stood a Mill here, "held in ferm by a Reve," but *that* was not a Paper-Mill. Then, came a Nunnery, with kings' fair daughters in it; then, a Palace; then, Queen Elizabeth, in her sixteenth year, to sojourn at the Palace two days; then, in that reign, a Paper-Mill. In the church yonder, hidden behind the trees, with many rooks discoursing in their lofty houses between me and it, is the tomb of Sir John Spielman,[5] jeweller to the Queen when she had grown to be a dame of a shrewd temper, aged fifty or so: who "built a Paper-Mill for the making of writing-paper," and to whom his Royal Mistress was pleased to grant a licence "for the sole gathering for ten years of all rags, &c., necessary for the making of such paper." There is a legend that the same Sir John, in coming here from Germany, to build his Mill, did bring with him two young lime-trees – then unknown in England – which he set before his Dartford dwelling-house, and which did flourish exceedingly; so, that they fanned him with their shadows, when he lay asleep in the upper story, an ancient gentleman. Now, God rest the soul of Sir John Spielman, for the love of all the sweet-smelling lime-trees that have ever greeted me in the land, and all the writing-paper I have ever blotted!

But, as I turn down by the hawthorn hedge into the valley, a sound comes in my ears – like the murmuring and throbbing of a mighty giant, labouring hard – that would have unbraced all the Saxon bows, and shaken all the heads off Temple Bar and London Bridge, ever lifted to those heights from the always butchering, always craving, never sufficiently-to-be-regretted, brave old English Block. It is the noise of the Steam Engine. And now, before me, white and clean without, and radiant in the sun, with the sweet clear river tumbling merrily down to kiss it, and help in the work it does, is the Paper-Mill I have come to see!

It is like the Mill of the child's story,[6] that ground old people young. Paper! White, pure, spick and span new paper, with that fresh smell which takes us back to school and school-books; can it ever come from rags like these? Is it from such bales of dusty rags, native and foreign, of every colour and of every kind, as now environ us, shutting out the summer air and putting cotton into our summer ears, that virgin paper, to be written on, and printed on, proceeds? We shall see presently. Enough to consider, at present, what a grave of dress this rag-store is; what a lesson of vanity it preaches. The coarse blouse of the Flemish labourer, and the fine cambric of the Parisian lady, the court dress of the Austrian jailer, and the miserable garb of the Italian peasant; the woollen petticoat of the Bavarian girl, the linen head-dress of the Neapolitan woman, the priest's vestment, the player's robe, the Cardinal's hat, and the ploughman's nightcap; all dwindle down to this, and bring their littleness or greatness in fractional portions here. As it is with the worn, it shall be with the wearers; but there shall be no dust in our eyes then, though there is plenty now. Not all the great ones of the earth will raise a grain of it, and nothing but the Truth will be.

My conductor leads the way into another room. I am to go, as the rags go, regularly and systematically through the Mill. I am to suppose myself a bale of rags. I *am* rags.

Here, in another room, are some three-score women at little tables, each with an awful scythe-shaped knife standing erect upon it, and looking like the veritable tooth of time. I am distributed among these women, and worried into smaller shreds – torn cross-wise at the knives. Already I begin to lose something of my grosser nature. The room is filled with my finest dust, and, as gratings of me drop from the knives, they fall through the perforated surface of the tables into receptacles beneath. When I am small enough, I am bundled up, carried away in baskets, and stowed in immense binns, until they want me in the Boiling-Room.

The Boiling-Room has enormous cauldrons in it, each with its own big lid, hanging to the beams of the roof, and put on by machinery when it is full. It is a very clean place, "coddled" by much boiling, like a washerwoman's fingers, and looks as if the kitchen of the Parish Union had gone into partnership with the Church Belfry. Here, I am pressed, and squeezed, and jammed, a dozen feet deep, I should think, into my own particular cauldron; where I simmer, boil, and stew, a long, long time. Then, I am a dense, tight mass, cut out in pieces like so much clay – very clean – faint as to my colour – greatly purified – and gradually becoming quite ethereal.

In this improved condition, I am taken to the Cutting-Room. I am very grateful to the clear fresh water, for the good it has done me; and I am glad to be put into some more of it, and subjected to the action of large rollers filled with transverse knives, revolving by steam power upon iron beds, which favour me with no fewer than two million cuts per minute, though, within the memory of man, the functions of this machine were performed by an ordinary pestle and mortar. Such a drumming and rattling, such a battering and clattering, such a delight in cutting and slashing, not even the

Austrian part of me ever witnessed before. This continues, to my great satisfaction, until I look like shaving lather; when I am run off into chambers underneath, to have my friend the water, from whom I am unwilling to be separated, drained out of me.

At this time, my colour is a light blue, if I have indigo in me, or a pale fawn, if I am rags from which the dyes have been expelled. As it is necessary to bleach the fawn-coloured pulp (the blue being used for paper of that tint), and as I *am* fawn-coloured pulp, I am placed in certain stone chambers, like catacombs, hermetically sealed, excepting the first compartment, which communicates with a gasometer containing manganese, vitriol, and salt. From these ingredients, a strong gas (not agreeable, I must say, to the sense of smell) is generated, and forced through all the chambers, each of which communicates with the other. These continue closed, if I remember right, some four-and-twenty hours, when a man opens them and takes to his heels immediately, to avoid the offensive gas that rushes out. After I have been aired a little, I am again conveyed (quite white now, and very spiritual indeed) to some more obliging rollers upstairs.

At it these grinders go, "Munch, munch, munch!" like the sailor's wife in MACBETH,[7] who had chestnuts in her lap. I look, at first, as if I were the most delicious curds and whey; presently, I find that I am changed to gruel − not thin oatmeal gruel, but rich, creamy, tempting, exalted gruel! As if I had been made from pearls, which some voluptuous Mr. Emden had converted into groats![8]

And now, I am ready to undergo my last astounding transformation, and be made into paper by the machine. Oh what can I say of the wonderful machine, which receives me, at one end of a long room, gruel, and dismisses me at the other, paper!

Where is the subtle mind of this Leviathan lodged? It must be somewhere − in a cylinder, a pipe, a wheel − or how could it ever do with me the miracles it does! How could it receive me on a sheet of wire-gauze, in my gruel-form, and slide me on, gradually assuming consistency − gently becoming a little paper-like, a little more, a little more still, very paper-like, indeed − clinging to wet blankets, holding tight by other surfaces, smoothly ascending Witney hills,[9] lightly coming down into a woolly open country, easily rolling over and under a planetary system of heated cylinders, large and small, and ever growing, as I proceed, stronger and more paper-like! How does the power that fights the wintry waves on the Atlantic, and cuts and drills adamantine slabs of metal like cheese, how does it draw me out, when I am frailest and most liable to tear, so tenderly and delicately, that a woman's hand − no, even though I were a man, very ill and helpless, and she my nurse who loved me – could never touch me with so light a touch, or with a movement so unerring! How can I believe, even on experience, that, being of itself insensible, and only informed with intellect at second hand, it changes me, in less time than I take to tell it, into any sort of paper that is wanted, dries me, cuts me into lengths, becomes charged, just before dismissing me, with electricity, and gathers up the hair of the attendant-watcher, as if with horror at the mischiefs and desertions from the right, in which I may be instrumental! Above all, how can I reconcile its being mere machinery, with its leaving off when it has cut me into sheets, and NOT conveying me to the Exciseman in the next room, whom it plainly thinks a most unnatural conclusion!

I am carried thither on trucks. I am examined, and my defective portions thrown out, for the Mill, again; I am made up into quires and reams; I am weighed and excised by the hundredweight; and I am ready for my work. Of my being made the subject of nonsensical defences of Excise duty, in the House of Commons, I need say nothing. All the world knows that when the Right Honourable the Chancellor of the Exchequer, for the time being, says I am only the worse by a duty of fifteen shillings per hundredweight, he is a Wrong Honourable, and either don't know, or don't care, anything about me. For, he leaves out of consideration all the vexatious, depressing, and preventing influences of Excise Duty on any trade, and all the extra cost and charge of packing and unpacking, carrying and re-carrying, imposed upon the manufacturer, and of course upon the public. But we must have it, in future, even with Right Honourables as with birds. The Chancellor of the Exchequer that can sing, and won't sing, must be made to sing – small.

My metempsychosis ends with the manufacture. I am rags no more, but a visitor to the Paper-Mill. I am a pleased visitor to see the Mill in such beautiful order, and the workpeople so thriving; and I think that my good friend the owner has reason for saying with an agreeable smile, as we come out upon the sparkling stream again, that he is never so contented, as when he is in rags.

Shining up in the blue sky, far above the Paper-Mill, a mere speck in the distance, is a Paper Kite. It is an appropriate thing at the moment – not to swear by (we have enough of that already) but to hope by, with a devout heart. May all the Paper that I sport with, soar as innocently upward as the paper kite, and be as harmless to the holder as the kite is to the boy! May it bring, to some few minds, such fresh associations; and to me no worse remembrances than the kite that once plucked at my own hand like an airy friend. May I always recollect that paper has a mighty Duty, set forth in no Schedule of Excise,[10] and that its names are love, forbearance, mercy, progress, scorn of the Hydra Cant with all its million heads!

So, back by the green lanes, and the old Priory – a farm now, and none the worse for that – and away among the lime-trees, thinking of Sir John.

Three 'Detective' Anecdotes

First published in *Household Words*, 14 September 1850, and subsequently included in *Reprinted Pieces* from which this text is reproduced.

I. THE PAIR OF GLOVES

"It's a singler story, sir," said Inspector Wield, of the Detective Police, who, in company with Sergeants Dornton and Mith, paid us another twilight visit, one July evening; "and I've been thinking you might like to know it.

"It's concerning the murder of the young woman, Eliza Grimwood,[1] some years ago, over in the Waterloo Road. She was commonly called The Countess, because of her handsome appearance and her proud way of carrying of herself; and when I saw the poor Countess (I had known her well to speak to), lying dead, with her throat cut, on the floor of her bedroom, you'll believe me that a variety of reflections calculated to make a man rather low in his spirits, came into my head.

"That's neither here nor there. I went to the house the morning after the murder, and examined the body, and made a general observation of the bedroom where it was. Turning down the pillow of the bed with my hand, I found, underneath it, a pair of gloves. A pair of gentleman's dress gloves, very dirty; and inside the lining, the letters T R, and a cross.

"Well, sir, I took them gloves away, and I showed 'em to the magistrate, over at Union Hall, before whom the case was. He says, 'Wield,' he says, 'there's no doubt this is a discovery that may lead to something very important; and what you have got to do, Wield, is to find out the owner of these gloves.'

"I was of the same opinion, of course, and I went at it immediately. I looked at the gloves pretty narrowly, and it was my opinion that they had been cleaned. There was a smell of sulphur and rosin about 'em, you know, which cleaned gloves usually have, more or less. I took 'em over to a friend of mine at Kennington, who was in that line, and I put it to him. 'What do you say now? Have these gloves been cleaned?' 'These gloves have been cleaned,' says he. 'Have you any idea who cleaned them?' says I. 'Not at all,' says he; 'I've a very distinct idea who *didn't* clean 'em, and that's myself. But I'll tell you what, Wield, there ain't above eight or nine reg'lar glove-cleaners in London,' – there were not, at that time, it seems – 'and I think I can give you their addresses, and you may find out, by that means, who did clean 'em.' Accordingly, he gave me the directions, and I went here, and I went there, and I looked up this man, and I looked up that man; but, though they all agreed that the gloves had been cleaned, I couldn't find the man, woman, or child, that had cleaned that aforesaid pair of gloves.

"What with this person not being at home, and that person being expected home in the afternoon, and so forth, the inquiry took me three days. On the evening of the third day, coming over Waterloo Bridge from the Surrey side of the river, quite beat, and very much vexed and disappointed, I thought I'd have a shilling's worth of entertainment at the Lyceum Theatre[2] to freshen myself up. So I went into the Pit, at half-price, and I sat myself down next to a very quiet, modest sort of young man. Seeing I was a stranger (which I thought it just as well to appear to be) he told me the names of the actors on the stage, and we got into conversation. When the play was over, we came out together, and I said, 'We've been very companionable and agreeable, and perhaps you wouldn't object to a drain?'[3] 'Well, you're very good,' says he; 'I *shouldn't* object to a drain.' Accordingly, we went to a public-house, near the Theatre, sat ourselves down in a quiet room up-stairs on the first floor, and called for a pint of half-and-half apiece, and a pipe.

"Well, sir, we put our pipes aboard, and we drank our half-and-half, and sat a-talking, very sociably, when the young man says, 'You must excuse me stopping very long,' he says, 'because I'm forced to go home in good time. I must be at work all night.' 'At work all night?' says I. 'You ain't a baker?' 'No,' he says, laughing, 'I ain't a baker.' 'I thought not,' says I, 'you haven't the looks of a baker.' 'No,' says he, 'I'm a glove-cleaner.'

"I never was more astonished in my life, than when I heard them words come out of his lips. 'You're a glove-cleaner, are you?' says I. 'Yes,' he says, 'I am.' 'Then, perhaps,' says I, taking the gloves out of my pocket, 'you can tell me who cleaned this pair of gloves? It's a rum story,' I says. 'I was dining over at Lambeth, the other day, at a free-and-easy[4] – quite promiscuous – with a public company – when some gentleman, he left these gloves behind him! Another gentleman and me, you see, we laid a wager of a sovereign, that I wouldn't find out who they belonged to. I've spent as much as seven shillings already, in trying to discover; but, if you could help me, I'd stand another seven and welcome. You see there's T R and a cross, inside.' '*I* see,' he says. 'Bless you, *I* know these gloves very well! I've seen dozens of pairs belonging to the same party.' 'No?' says I. 'Yes,' says he. 'Then you know who cleaned 'em?' says I. 'Rather so,' says he. 'My father cleaned 'em.'

" 'Where does your father live?' says I. 'Just round the corner,' says the young man, 'near Exeter Street, here. He'll tell you who they belong to, directly.' 'Would you come round with me now?' says I. 'Certainly,' says he, 'but you needn't tell my father that you found me at the play, you know, because he mightn't like it.' 'All right!' We went round to the place, and there we found an old man in a white apron, with two or three daughters, all rubbing and cleaning away at lots of gloves, in a front parlour. 'Oh, Father!' says the young man, 'here's a person been and made a bet about the ownership of a pair of gloves, and I've told him you can settle it.' 'Good evening, sir,' says I to the old gentleman. 'Here's the gloves your son speaks of. Letters T R, you see, and a cross.' 'Oh yes,' he says, 'I know these gloves very well; I've cleaned dozens of pairs of 'em. They belong to Mr. Trinkle, the great upholsterer in Cheapside.' 'Did you get 'em from Mr. Trinkle, direct,' says I, 'if you'll excuse my asking the question?' 'No,' says he; 'Mr. Trinkle always sends 'em to Mr. Phibbs's, the haberdasher's, opposite his shop, and the haberdasher sends 'em to me.' 'Perhaps *you* wouldn't object to a drain?' says I. 'Not in the least!' says he. So I took the old gentleman out, and had a little more talk with him and his son, over a glass, and we parted excellent friends.

"This was late on a Saturday night. First thing on the Monday morning, I went to the haberdasher's shop, opposite Mr. Trinkle's, the great upholsterer's in Cheapside. 'Mr. Phibbs in the way?' 'My name is Phibbs.' 'Oh! I believe you sent this pair of gloves to be cleaned?' 'Yes, I did, for young Mr. Trinkle over the way. There he is in the shop!' 'Oh! that's him in the shop, is it? Him in the green coat?' 'The same individual.' 'Well, Mr. Phibbs, this is an unpleasant affair; but the fact is, I am Inspector Wield of the Detective Police, and I found these gloves under the pillow of the young woman that was murdered the other day, over in the Waterloo Road.' 'Good Heaven!' says he. 'He's a most respectable young man, and if his father was to hear of it, it would be the ruin of him!' 'I'm very sorry for it,' says I, 'but I must take him into custody.' 'Good Heaven!' says Mr. Phibbs, again; 'can nothing be done!' 'Nothing,' says I. 'Will you allow me to call him over here,' says he, 'that his father may not see it done?' 'I don't object to that,' says I; 'but unfortunately, Mr. Phibbs, I can't allow of any communication between you. If any was attempted, I should have to interfere directly. Perhaps you'll beckon him over here?' Mr. Phibbs went to the door and beckoned, and the young fellow came across the street directly; a smart, brisk young fellow.

"'Good morning, sir,' says I. 'Good morning, sir,' says he. 'Would you allow me to inquire, sir,' says I, 'if you ever had any acquaintance with a party of the name of Grimwood?' 'Grimwood! Grimwood!' says he. 'No!' 'You know the Waterloo Road?' 'Oh! of course I know the Waterloo Road!' 'Happen to have heard of a young woman being murdered there?' 'Yes, I read it in the paper, and very sorry I was to read it.' 'Here's a pair of gloves belonging to you, that I found under her pillow the morning afterwards!'

"He was in a dreadful state, sir; a dreadful state! 'Mr. Wield,' he says, 'upon my solemn oath I never was there. I never so much as saw her, to my knowledge, in my life!' 'I am very sorry,' says I. 'To tell you the truth; I don't think you *are* the murderer, but I must take you to Union Hall in a cab. However, I think it's a case of that sort, that, at present, at all events, the magistrate will hear it in private.'

"A private examination took place, and then it came out that this young man was acquainted with a cousin of the unfortunate Eliza Grimwood, and that, calling to see this cousin a day or two before the murder, he left these gloves upon the table. Who should come in, shortly afterwards, but Eliza Grimwood! 'Whose gloves are these?' she says, taking 'em up. 'Those are Mr. Trinkle's gloves,' says her cousin. 'Oh!' says she, 'they are very dirty, and of no use to him, I am sure. I shall take 'em away for my girl to clean the stoves with.' And she put 'em in her pocket. The girl had used 'em to clean the stoves, and, I have no doubt, had left 'em lying on the bedroom mantelpiece, or on the drawers, or somewhere; and her mistress, looking round to see that the room was tidy, had caught 'em up and put 'em under the pillow where I found 'em.

"That's the story, sir."

II. THE ARTFUL TOUCH

"One of the most *beautiful* things that ever was done, perhaps," said Inspector Wield, emphasising the adjective, as preparing us to expect dexterity or ingenuity rather than strong interest, "was a move of Sergeant Witchem's. It was a lovely idea!

"Witchem and me were down at Epsom one Derby Day, waiting at the station for the Swell Mob. As I mentioned, when we were talking about these things before, we are ready at the station when there's races, or an

Agricultural Show, or a Chancellor sworn in for an university, or Jenny Lind,[5] or anything of that sort; and as the Swell Mob come down, we send 'em back again by the next train. But some of the Swell Mob, on the occasion of this Derby that I refer to, so far kidded us as to hire a horse and shay; start away from London by Whitechapel, and miles round; come into Epsom from the opposite direction; and go to work, right and left, on the course, while we were waiting for 'em at the Rail. That, however, ain't the point of what I'm going to tell you.

"While Witchem and me were waiting at the station, there comes up one Mr. Tatt; a gentleman formerly in the public line, quite an amateur Detective in his way, and very much respected. 'Halloa, Charley Wield,' he says. 'What are you doing here? On the look out for some of your old friends?' 'Yes, the old move, Mr. Tatt.' 'Come along,' he says, 'you and Witchem, and have a glass of sherry.' 'We can't stir from the place,' says I, 'till the next train comes in; but after that, we will with pleasure.' Mr. Tatt waits, and the train comes in, and then Witchem and me go off with him to the Hotel. Mr. Tatt he's got up quite regardless of expense, for the occasion; and in his shirt-front there's a beautiful diamond prop,[6] cost him fifteen or twenty pound – a very handsome pin indeed. We drink our sherry at the bar, and have had our three or four glasses, when Witchem cries suddenly, 'Look out, Mr. Wield! stand fast!' and a dash is made into the place by the Swell Mob – four of 'em – that have come down as I tell you, and in a moment Mr. Tatt's prop is gone! Witchem, he cuts 'em off at the door, I lay about me as hard as I can, Mr. Tatt shows fight like a good 'un, and there we are, all down together, heads and heels, knocking about on the floor of the bar – perhaps you never see such a scene of confusion! However, we stick to our men (Mr. Tatt being as good as any officer), and we take 'em all, and carry 'em off to the station. The station's full of people, who have been took on the course; and it's a precious piece of work to get 'em secured. However, we do it at last, and we search 'em; but nothing's found upon 'em, and they're locked up; and a pretty state of heat we are in by that time, I assure you!

"I was very blank over it, myself, to think that the prop had been passed away; and I said to Witchem, when we had set 'em to rights, and were cooling ourselves along with Mr. Tatt, 'we don't take much by *this* move, anyway, for nothing's found upon 'em, and it's only the braggadocia,[7] after all.' 'What do you mean, Mr. Wield?' says Witchem. 'Here's the diamond pin!' and in the palm of his hand there it was, safe and sound! 'Why, in the name of wonder,' says me and Mr. Tatt, in astonishment, 'how did you come by that?' 'I'll tell you how I come by it,' says he. 'I saw which of 'em took it; and when we were all down on the floor together, knocking about, I just gave him a little touch on the back of his hand, as I knew his pal would; and he thought it WAS his pal; and gave it me!' It was beautiful, beau-ti-ful!

"Even that was hardly the best of the case, for that chap was tried at the Quarter Sessions at Guildford. You know what Quarter Sessions are, sir. Well, if you'll believe me, while them slow justices[8] were looking over the Acts of Parliament, to see what they could do to him, I'm blowed if he didn't cut out of the dock before their faces! He cut out of the dock, sir, then and there; swam across a river; and got up into a tree to dry himself. In the tree he was took – an old woman having seen him climb up – and Witchem's artful touch transported him!"

III. THE SOFA

"What young men will do, sometimes, to ruin themselves and break their friends' hearts," said Sergeant Dornton, "it's surprising! I had a case at Saint Blank's Hospital which was of this sort. A bad case, indeed, with a bad end!"

"The Secretary, and the House-Surgeon, and the Treasurer, of Saint Blank's Hospital, came to Scotland Yard to give information of numerous robberies having been committed on the students. The students could leave nothing in the pockets of their great-coats, while the great-coats were hanging at the hospital, but it was almost certain to be stolen. Property of various descriptions was constantly being lost; and the gentlemen were naturally uneasy about it, and anxious, for the credit of the institution, that the thief or thieves should be discovered. The case was entrusted to me, and I went to the hospital.

" 'Now, gentlemen,' said I, after we had talked it over; 'I understand this property is usually lost from one room.'

"Yes, they said. It was.

" 'I should wish, if you please,' said I, 'to see the room.'

"It was a good-sized bare room down-stairs, with a few tables and forms in it, and a row of pegs, all round, for hats and coats.

" 'Next, gentlemen,' said I, 'do you suspect anybody?'

"Yes, they said. They did suspect somebody. They were sorry to say, they suspected one of the porters.

" 'I should like,' said I, 'to have that man pointed out to me, and to have a little time to look after him.'

"He was pointed out, and I looked after him, and then I went back to the hospital, and said, 'Now, gentlemen, it's not the porter. He's, unfortunately for himself, a little too fond of drink, but he's nothing worse. My suspicion is, that these robberies are committed by one of the students; and if you'll put me a sofa into that room where the pegs are – as there's no closet – I think I shall be able to detect the thief. I wish the sofa, if you please, to be covered with chintz, or something of that sort, so that I may lie on my chest, underneath it, without being seen.'

"The sofa was provided, and next day at eleven o'clock, before any of the students came, I went there, with those gentlemen, to get underneath it. It turned out to be one of those old-fashioned sofas with a great cross-beam at the bottom, that would have broken my back in no time if I could ever have got below it. We had quite a job to break all this away in the time; however, I fell to work, and they fell to work, and we broke it out, and made a clear place for me. I got under the sofa, lay down on my chest, took out my knife, and made a convenient hole in the chintz to look through. It was then settled between me and the gentlemen that when the students were all up in the wards, one of the gentlemen should come in, and hang up a great-coat on one of the pegs. And that that great-coat should have, in one of the pockets, a pocket-book containing marked money.

"After I had been there some time, the students began to drop into the room, by ones, and twos, and threes, and to talk about all sorts of things, little thinking there was any body under the sofa – and then to go up-stairs. At last there came in one who remained until he was alone in the room by himself. A tallish, good-looking young man of one or two and twenty, with a light whisker. He went to a particular hat-peg, took off a good hat that was hanging there, tried it on, hung his own hat in its place, and hung that hat on another peg, nearly opposite to me. I then felt quite certain that he was the thief, and would come back by-and-by.

"When they were all up-stairs, the gentleman came in with the great-coat. I showed him where to hang it, so that I might have a good view of it; and he went away; and I lay under the sofa on my chest, for a couple of hours or so, waiting.

"At last, the same young man came down. He walked across the room, whistling – stopped and listened – took another walk and whistled – stopped again, and listened – then began to go regularly round the pegs, feeling in the pockets of all the coats. When he came to THE great-coat, and felt the pocket-book, he was so eager and so hurried that he broke the strap in tearing it open. As he began to put the money in his pocket, I crawled out from under the sofa, and his eyes met mine.

"My face, as you may perceive, is brown now, but it was pale at that time, my health not being good; and looked as long as a horse's. Besides which, there was a great draught of air from the door, underneath the sofa, and I had tied a handkerchief round my head; so what I looked like, altogether, I don't know. He turned blue – literally blue – when he saw me crawling out, and I couldn't feel surprised at it.

"'I am an officer of the Detective Police,' said I, 'and have been lying here, since you first came in this morning. I regret, for the sake of yourself and your friends, that you should have done what you have; but this case is complete. You have the pocket-book in your hand and the money upon you; and I must take you into custody!'

"It was impossible to make out any case in his behalf, and on his trial he pleaded guilty. How or when he got the means I don't know; but while he was awaiting his sentence, he poisoned himself in Newgate."

We inquired of this officer, on the conclusion of the fore-going anecdote, whether the time appeared long, or short, when he lay in that constrained position under the sofa?

"Why, you see, sir," he replied, "if he hadn't come in, the first time, and I had not been quite sure he was the thief, and would return, the time would have seemed long. But, as it was, I being dead certain of my man, the time seemed pretty short."

Railway Strikes

First published in *Household Words*, 11 January 1851, from which this text is taken.

Everything that has a direct bearing on the prosperity, happiness, and reputation of the working-men of England should be a Household Word.

We offer a few remarks on a subject which has recently attracted their attention, and on which one particular and important branch of industry has made a demonstration, affecting, more or less, every other branch of industry, and the whole community; in the hope that there are few among the intelligent body of skilled mechanics who will suspect us of entertaining any other than friendly feelings towards them, or of regarding them with any sentiment but one of esteem and confidence.

The Engine Drivers and Firemen on the North Western line of Railway – the great iron high-road of the Kingdom, by which communication is maintained with Ireland, Scotland, Wales, the chief manufacturing towns of Great Britain, and the port which is the main artery of her commerce with the world[1] – have threatened, for the second time, a simultaneous abandonment of their work, and relinquishment of their engagements with the Company they have contracted to serve.

We dismiss from consideration, the merits of the case. It would be easy, we conceive, to show, that the complaints of the men, even assuming them to be beyond dispute, were not, from the beginning of the manifestation, of a grave character, or by any means hopeless of fair adjustment. But, we purposely dismiss that question. We purposely dismiss, also, the character of the Company, for careful, business-like, generous, and honourable management. We are content to assume that it stands no higher than the level of the very worst public servant bearing the name of railway, that the public possesses. We will suppose MR. GLYN'S[2] communications with the men, to have been characterised by overbearing evasion, and not (as they undoubtedly have been) by courtesy, good temper, self-command, and the perfect spirit of a gentleman. We will suppose the case of the Company to be the worst that such a case could be, in this country, and in these times. Even with such a reduction of it to its lowest possible point, and a corresponding elevation of the case of the skilled Railway servants to its highest, we must deny the moral right or justification of the latter to exert

277

the immense power they accidentally possess, to the public detriment and danger.

We say, accidentally possess, because this power has not been raised up by themselves. If there be ill-conditioned spirits among them who represent that it has been, they represent what is not true, and what a minute's rational consideration will show to be false. It is the result of a vast system of skilful combination, and a vast expenditure of wealth. The construction of the line, alone, against all the engineering difficulties it presented, involved an amount of outlay that was wonderful, even in England. To bring it to its present state of working efficiency, a thousand ingenious problems have been studied and solved, stupendous machines have been constructed, a variety of plans and schemes have been matured with incredible labour: a great whole has been pieced together by numerous capacities and appliances, and kept incessantly in motion. Even the character of the men, which stands deservedly high, has not been set up by themselves alone, but has been assisted by large contributions from these various sources. Without a good permanent way, and good engine power, they could not have established themselves in the public confidence as good drivers. Without good business management in the complicated arrangements of trains for goods and passengers, they could not possibly have avoided accidents. They have done their part manfully; but they could not have done it, without efficient aid in like manful sort, from every department of the great executive staff. And because it happens that the whole machine is dependent upon them in one important stage, and is delivered necessarily into their control – and because it happens that Railway accidents, when they do occur, are of a frightful nature, attended with horrible mutilation and loss of life[3] – and because such accidents, with the best precautions, probably *must* occur, in the event of their resignation in a body – is it, therefore, defensible to strike?

To that, the question comes. It is just so narrow, and no broader. We all know, perfectly well, that there would be no strike, but for the extent of the power possessed. Can such an exercise of it be defended, after due consideration, by any honest man?

We firmly believe that these are honest men – as honest men as the world can produce. But, we believe, also, that they have not well considered what it is that they do. They are laboriously and constantly employed; and it is the habit of many men, so engaged, to allow other men to think for them. These deputy-thinkers are not always the most judicious order of intellects. They are something quick at grievances. They drive Express Trains to that point, and Parliamentary to all other points. They are not always, perhaps, the best workmen, and are not so satisfied as the best workmen. They are, sometimes, not workmen at all, but designing persons, who have, for their own base purposes, immeshed the workmen in a system of tyranny and oppression. Through these, on the one hand, and through an imperfect or misguided view of the details of a case on the other, a strike (always supposing this great power in the strikers) may be easily set a going. Once begun, there is aroused a chivalrous spirit – much to be respected, however mistaken its manifestation – which forbids all reasoning. "I will stand by my order, and do as the rest do. I never flinch from my fellow-workman. I should not have thought of this myself; but I wish to be true to the backbone, and here I put my name among the others." Perhaps in no class of society, in any country, is this principle of honour so strong, as among most great bodies of English artisans.

But, there is a higher principle of honour yet; and it is that, we suggest to our friends the Engine Drivers and Firemen on the North Western Railway, which would lead to these greater considerations. First, what is my duty to the public, who are, after all, my chief employers? Secondly, what is my duty to my fellow workmen of all denominations: not only here, upon this Railway, but all over England?

We will suppose Engine Driver, John Safe, entering upon these considerations with his Fireman, Thomas Sparks. Sparks is one of the best of men, but he has a great belief in Caleb Coke, of Wolverhampton, and Coke says (because somebody else has said so, to him) "Strike!"

"But, Sparks," argues John Safe, sitting on the side of the tender, waiting for the Down Express, "to look at it in these two ways, before we take any measures. – Here we are, a body of men with a great public charge; hundreds and thousands of lives every day. Individuals among us may, of course, and of course do, every now and again give up their part of that charge, for one reason or another – and right too! But I'm not so sure that we can all turn our backs upon it at once, and do right."

Thomas Sparks inquires "Why not?"

"Why, it seems to me, Sparks," says John Safe, "rather a murdering mode of action."

Sparks, to whom the question has never presented itself in this light, turns pale.

"You see," John Safe pursues, "when I first came upon this line, I didn't know – how could I? – where there was a bridge and where a tunnel – where we took the turnpike road – where there was a cutting – where there was an embankment – where there was an incline – when full speed, when half, when slacken, when shut off, when your whistle going, when not. I got to know all such, by degrees; first, from them that was used to it; then, from my own use, Sparks."

"So you did, John," says Sparks.

"Well, Sparks! When we and all the rest that are used to it, Engine Drivers and Firemen, all down the line and up again, lay our heads together, and say to the public, 'if you don't back us up in what we want, we'll all go to the right-about, such a-day, so that Nobody shall know all such' — that's rather a murdering mode of action, it appears to me."

Thomas Sparks, still uncomfortably pale, wishes Coke of Wolverhampton were present, to reply.

"Because, it's saying to the public, 'if you *don't* back us up, we'll do our united best towards your being run away with, and run into, and smashed, and jammed, and dislocated, and having your heads took off, and your bodies gleaned for, in small pieces — and we hope you may!' Now, you know, that has a murdering appearance, Sparks, upon the whole!" says John Safe.

Sparks, much shocked, suggests that "it mightn't happen."

"True. But it might," returns John Safe, "and we know it might — no men better. We threaten that it might. Now, when we entered into this employment, Sparks, I doubt if it was any part of our fair bargain, that we should have a monopoly of this line, and a manslaughtering sort of a power over the public. What do *you* think?"

Thomas Sparks thinks certainly not. But, Coke of Wolverhampton said, last Wednesday (as somebody else had said to him), that every man worthy of the name of Briton must stick up for his rights.

"There again!" says John Safe. "To my mind, Sparks, it's not at all clear that any person's rights, *can be* another person's wrongs. And, that our strike must be a wrong to the persons we strike against, call 'em Company or Public, seems pretty plain."

"What do they go and unite against us for, then?" demands Thomas Sparks.

"I don't know that they do," replies John Safe. "We took service with this company, as Individuals, ourselves, and not as a body; and you know very well we no more ever thought, then, of turning them off, as one man, than they ever thought of turning us off as one man. If the Company is a body, now, it was a body all the same when we came into its employment with our eyes wide open, Sparks."

"Why do they make aggravating rules then, respecting the Locomotives?" demands Mr. Sparks, "which, Coke of Wolverhampton says, is Despotism!"

"Well, anyways they're made for the public safety, Sparks," returns John

Safe; "and what's for the public safety, is for yours and mine. The first things to go, in a smash, is, generally, the Engine and Tender."

"*I* don't want to be made more safe," growls Thomas Sparks. "*I* am safe enough, *I* am."

"But, it don't signify a cinder whether you want it or don't want it," returns his companion. "You must be made safe, Sparks, whether you like or not, – if not on your own account, on other people's."

"Coke of Wolverhampton says, Justice! That's what Coke says!" observes Mr. Sparks, after a little deliberation.

"And a very good thing it is to say," returns John Safe. "A better thing to do. But, let's be sure we do it. I can't see that we good workmen do it to ourselves and families, by letting in bad un's that are out of employment. That's as to ourselves. I am sure we don't do it to the Company or Public, by conspiring together, to turn an accidental advantage against 'em. Look at other people! Gentlemen don't strike. Union doctors are bad enough paid (which we are not), but *they* don't strike. Many dispensary and hospital-doctors are not over well treated, but *they* don't strike, and leave the sick a groaning in their beds. So much for use of power. Then for taste. The respectable young men and women that serve in the shops, *they* didn't strike, when they wanted early closing."

"All the world wasn't against *them*," Thomas Sparks puts in.

"No; if it had been, a man might have begun to doubt their being in the right," returns John Safe.

"Why, you don't doubt *our* being in the right, I hope?" says Sparks.

"If I do, I an't alone in it. You know there are scores and scores of us that, of their own accord, don't want no striking, nor anything of the kind."

"Suppose we all agreed that we was a prey to despotism, what then?" asks Sparks.

"Why, even then, I should recommend our doing our work, true to the public, and appealing to the public feeling against the same," replies John Safe. "It would very soon act on the Company. As to the Company and the Public siding together against us, I don't find the Public too apt to go along with the Company when it can help it."

"Don't we owe nothing to our order?" inquires Thomas Sparks.

"A good deal. And when we enter on a strike like this, we don't appear to me to pay it. We are rather of the upper sort of our order; and what we owe to other workmen, is, to set 'em a good example, and to represent them well. Now, there is, at present, a deal of general talk (here and there, with a good deal of truth in it) of combinations of capital, and one power and another, against workmen. I leave you to judge how it serves the workman's case, at such a time, to show a small body of his order, combined, in a misuse of power, against the whole community!"

It appears to us, not only that John Safe might reasonably urge these arguments and facts; but, that John Safe did actually present many of them, and not remotely suggest the rest, to the consideration of an aggregate meeting of the Engine Drivers and Firemen engaged on the Southern Division of the line, which was held at Camden Town on the day after Christmas Day. The sensible, moderate, and upright tone of some men who spoke at that meeting, as we find them reported in The Times, commands our admiration and respect, though it by no means surprises us. We would especially commend to the attention of our readers, the speech of an Engine Driver on the Great Western Railway, and the letter of the Enginemen and Firemen at the Bedford Station. Writing, in submission to the necessities of this publication, immediately after that meeting was held, we are, of course, in ignorance of the issue of the question, though it will probably have transpired before the present number appears. It can, however, in no wise affect the observations we have made, or those with which we will conclude.

To the men, we would submit, that if they fail in adjusting the difference to their complete satisfaction, the failure will be principally their own fault, as inseparable, in a great measure, from the injudicious and unjustifiable threat into which the more sensible portion of them have allowed themselves to be betrayed. What the Directors might have conceded to temperate remonstrance, it is easy to understand they may deem it culpable weakness to yield to so alarming a combination against the public service and safety.

To the Public, we would submit, that the steadiness and patriotism of English workmen may, in the long run, be safely trusted; and that this mistake, once remedied, may be calmly dismissed. It is natural, in the first hot reception of such a menace, to write letters to newspapers, urging strong-handed legislation, or the enforcement of pains and penalties, past, present, or to come, on such deserters from their posts. But, it is not agreeable, on calmer reflection, to contemplate the English artisan as working under a curb or yoke, or even as being supposed to require one. His spirit is of the highest; his nature is of the best. He comes of a great race, and his character is famous in the world. If a false step on the part of any man should be generously forgotten, it should be forgotten in him.

Bill-Sticking

First published in *Household Words*, 2 March 1851, and subsequently included in *Reprinted Pieces* from which this text is reproduced.

If I had an enemy whom I hated – which Heaven forbid! – and if I knew of something which sat heavy on his conscience, I think I would introduce that something into a Posting-Bill, and place a large impression in the hands of an active sticker. I can scarcely imagine a more terrible revenge. I should haunt him, by this means, night and day. I do not mean to say that I would publish his secret, in red letters two feet high, for all the town to read: I would darkly refer to it. It should be between him, and me, and the Posting-Bill. Say, for example, that, at a certain period of his life, my enemy had surreptitiously possessed himself of a key. I would then embark my capital in the lock business, and conduct that business on the advertising principle. In all my placards and advertisements, I would throw up the line SECRET KEYS. Thus, if my enemy passed an uninhabited house, he would see his conscience glaring down on him from the parapets, and peeping up at him from the cellars. If he took a dead wall in his walk, it would be alive with reproaches. If he sought refuge in an omnibus, the panels thereof would become Belshazzar's palace[1] to him. If he took boat, in a wild endeavour to escape, he would see the fatal words lurking under the arches of the bridges over the Thames. If he walked the streets with downcast eyes, he would recoil from the very stones of the pavement, made eloquent by lamp-black lithograph. If he drove or rode, his way would be blocked up by enormous vans, each proclaiming the same words over and over again from its whole extent of surface. Until, having gradually grown thinner and paler, and having at last totally rejected food, he would miserably perish, and I should be revenged. This conclusion I should, no doubt, celebrate by laughing a hoarse laugh in three syllables, and folding my arms tight upon my chest agreeably to most of the examples of glutted animosity that I have had an opportunity of observing in connexion with the Drama – which, by-the-by, as involving a good deal of noise, appears to me to be occasionally confounded with the Drummer.

The foregoing reflections presented themselves to my mind, the other day, as I contemplated (being newly come to London from the East Riding of Yorkshire, on a house-hunting expedition for next May) an old warehouse which rotting paste and rotting paper had brought down to the condition of an old cheese. It would have been impossible to say, on the most conscientious survey, how much of its front was brick and mortar, and how much decaying and decayed plaster. It was so thickly encrusted with fragments of bills, that no ship's keel after a long voyage could be half so foul. All traces of the broken windows were billed out, the doors were billed across, the water-spout was billed over. The building was shored up to prevent its tumbling into the street; and the very beams erected against it were less wood than paste and paper, they had been so continually posted and reposted. The forlorn dregs of old posters so encumbered this wreck, that there was no hold for new posters, and the stickers had abandoned the place in despair, except one enterprising man who had hoisted the last masquerade to a clear spot near the level of the stack of chimneys, where it waved and drooped like a shattered flag. Below the rusty cellar-grating, crumpled remnants of old bills torn down rotted away in wasting heaps of fallen leaves. Here and there, some of the thick rind of the house had peeled off in strips, and fluttered heavily down, littering the street; but still, below these rents and gashes, layers of decomposing posters showed themselves, as if they were interminable. I thought the building could never even be pulled down, but in one adhesive heap of rottenness and poster. As to getting in – I don't believe that if the Sleeping Beauty and her Court had been so billed up, the young Prince could have done it.

Knowing all the posters that were yet legible, intimately, and pondering on their ubiquitous nature, I was led into the reflections with which I began this paper, by considering what an awful thing it would be, ever to have wronged – say M. JULLIEN for example – and to have his avenging name in characters of fire incessantly before my eyes. Or to have injured MADAME TUSSAUD, and undergo a similar retribution. Has any man a self-reproachful thought associated with pills, or ointment? What an avenging spirit to that man is PROFESSOR HOLLOWAY! Have I sinned in oil? CABBURN pursues me. Have I a dark remembrance associated with any gentlemanly garments, bespoke or ready made? MOSES AND SON are on my track. Did I ever aim a blow at a defenceless fellow-creature's head? That head eternally being measured for a wig, or that worse head which was bald before it used the balsam, and hirsute afterwards – enforcing the benevolent moral, "Better to be bald as a Dutch cheese than come to this," – undoes me. Have I no sore places in my mind which MECHI touches – which NICOLL probes – which no registered article whatever lacerates? Does no discordant note within me thrill responsive to mysterious watchwords, as "Revalenta

Arabica," or "Number One St. Paul's Churchyard"? Then may I enjoy life, and be happy.[2]

Lifting up my eyes, as I was musing to this effect, I beheld advancing towards me (I was then on Cornhill, near to the Royal Exchange) a solemn procession of three advertising vans, of first-class dimensions, each drawn by a very little horse. As the cavalcade approached, I was at a loss to reconcile the careless deportment of the drivers of these vehicles with the terrific announcements they conducted through the city, which being a summary of the contents of a Sunday newspaper, were of the most thrilling kind. Robbery, fire, murder, and the ruin of the United Kingdom – each discharged in a line by itself, like a separate broadside of red-hot shot – were among the least of the warnings addressed to an unthinking people. Yet the Ministers of Fate, who drove the awful cars, leaned forward with their arms upon their knees in a state of extreme lassitude, for want of any subject of interest. The first man, whose hair I might naturally have expected to see standing on end, scratched his head – one of the smoothest I ever beheld – with profound indifference. The second whistled. The third yawned.

Pausing to dwell upon this apathy, it appeared to me, as the fatal cars came by me, that I descried in the second car, through the portal in which the charioteer was seated, a figure stretched upon the floor. At the same time, I thought I smelt tobacco. The latter impression passed quickly from me; the former remained. Curious to know whether this prostrate figure was the one impressible man of the whole capital who had been stricken insensible by the terrors revealed to him, and whose form had been placed in the car by the charioteer, from motives of humanity, I followed the procession. It turned into Leadenhall-market, and halted at a public-house.[3] Each driver dismounted. I then distinctly heard, proceeding from the second car, where I had dimly seen the prostrate form, the words:

"And a pipe!"

The driver entering the public-house with his fellows, apparently for purposes of refreshment, I could not refrain from mounting on the shaft of the second vehicle, and looking in at the portal. I then beheld, reclining on his back upon the floor, on a kind of mattress or divan, a little man in a shooting-coat. The exclamation "Dear me," which irresistibly escaped my lips, caused him to sit upright and survey me. I found him to be a good-looking little man of about fifty, with a shining face, a tight head, a bright eye, a moist wink, a quick speech, and a ready air. He had something of a sporting way with him.

He looked at me, and I looked at him, until the driver displaced me by handing in a pint of beer, a pipe, and what I understand is called "a screw" of tobacco – an object which has the appearance of a curl-paper taken off the bar-maid's head, with the curl in it.

"I beg your pardon," said I, when the removed person of the driver again admitted of my presenting my face at the portal. "But – excuse my curiosity, which I inherit from my mother – do you live here?"

"That's good, too!" returned the little man, composedly laying aside a pipe he had smoked out, and filling the pipe just brought to him.

"Oh, you *don't* live here then?" said I.

He shook his head, as he calmly lighted his pipe by means of a German tinder-box, and replied, "This is my carriage. When things are flat, I take a ride sometimes, and enjoy myself. I am the inventor of these wans."[4]

His pipe was now alight. He drank his beer all at once, and he smoked and he smiled at me.

"It was a great idea!" said I.

"Not so bad," returned the little man, with the modesty of merit.

"Might I be permitted to inscribe your name upon the tablets of my memory?" I asked.

"There's not much odds in the name," returned the little man, " – no name particular – I am the King of the Bill-Stickers."

"Good gracious!" said I.

The monarch informed me, with a smile, that he had never been crowned or installed with any public ceremonies, but that he was peaceably acknowledged as King of the Bill-Stickers in right of being the oldest and most respected member of "the old school of bill-sticking." He likewise gave me to understand that there was a Lord Mayor of the Bill-Stickers, whose genius was chiefly exercised within the limits of the city. He made some allusion, also, to an inferior potentate, called "Turkey-legs;" but I did not understand that this gentleman was invested with much power. I rather inferred that he derived his title from some peculiarity of gait, and that it was of an honorary character.

"My father," pursued the King of the Bill-Stickers, "was Engineer, Beadle, and Bill-Sticker to the parish of St. Andrew's, Holborn, in the year one thousand seven hundred and eighty. My father stuck bills at the time of the riots of London."

"You must be acquainted with the whole subject of bill-sticking, from that time to the present!" said I.

"Pretty well so," was the answer.

"Excuse me," said I; "but I am a sort of collector —"

"Not Income-tax?" cried His Majesty, hastily removing his pipe from his lips.

"No, no," said I.

"Water-rate?" said His Majesty.

"No, no," I returned.

"Gas? Assessed?[5] Sewers?" said His Majesty.

"You misunderstand me," I replied, soothingly. "Not that sort of collector at all: a collector of facts."

"Oh, if it's only facts," cried the King of the Bill-Stickers, recovering his good-humour, and banishing the great mistrust that had suddenly fallen upon him, "come in and welcome! If it had been income, or winders,[6] I think I should have pitched you out of the wan, upon my soul!"

Readily complying with the invitation, I squeezed myself in at the small aperture. His Majesty, graciously handing me a little three-legged stool on which I took my seat in a corner, inquired if I smoked.

"I do; – that is, I can," I answered.

"Pipe and a screw!" said His Majesty to the attendant charioteer. "Do you prefer a dry smoke, or do you moisten it?"

As unmitigated tobacco produces most disturbing effects upon my system (indeed, if I had perfect moral courage, I doubt if I should smoke at all, under any circumstances), I advocated moisture, and begged the Sovereign of the Bill-Stickers to name his usual liquor, and to concede to me the privilege of paying for it. After some delicate reluctance on his part, we were provided, through the instrumentality of the attendant charioteer, with a can of cold rum-and-water, flavoured with sugar and lemon. We were also furnished with a tumbler, and I was provided with a pipe. His Majesty, then observing that we might combine business with conversation, gave the word for the car to proceed; and, to my great delight, we jogged away at a foot pace.

I say to my great delight, because I am very fond of novelty, and it was a new sensation to be jolting through the tumult of the city in that secluded Temple, partly open to the sky, surrounded by the roar without, and seeing nothing but the clouds. Occasionally, blows from whips fell heavily on the Temple's walls, when by stopping up the road longer than usual, we irritated carters and coachmen to madness; but they fell harmless upon us within and disturbed not the serenity of our peaceful retreat. As I looked upward, I felt, I should imagine, like the Astronomer Royal. I was enchanted by the contrast between the freezing nature of our external mission on the blood of the populace, and the perfect composure reigning within those sacred precincts: where His Majesty, reclining easily on his left arm, smoked his pipe and drank his rum-and-water from his own side of the tumbler, which stood impartially between us. As I looked down from the clouds and caught his royal eye, he understood my reflections. "I have an idea," he observed, with an upward glance, "of training scarlet runners across in the season, – making a arbour of it, – and sometimes taking tea in the same, according to the song."[7]

I nodded approval.

"And here you repose and think?" said I.

"And think," said he, "of posters – walls – and hoardings."

We were both silent, contemplating the vastness of the subject. I remembered a surprising fancy of dear THOMAS HOOD's,[8] and wondered whether this monarch ever sighed to repair to the great wall of China, and stick bills all over it.

"And so," said he, rousing himself, "it's facts as you collect?"

"Facts," said I.

"The facts of bill-sticking," pursued His Majesty, in a benignant manner, "as known to myself, air as following. When my father was Engineer, Beadle, and Bill-Sticker to the parish of St. Andrew's, Holborn, he employed women to post bills for him. He employed women to post bills at the time of the riots of London. He died at the age of seventy-five year, and was buried by the murdered Eliza Grimwood,[9] over in the Waterloo Road."

As this was somewhat in the nature of a royal speech, I listened with deference and silently. His Majesty, taking a scroll from his pocket, proceeded, with great distinctness, to pour out the following flood of information:–

"'The bills being at that period mostly proclamations and declarations, and which were only a demy size, the manner of posting the bills (as they did not use brushes) was by means of a piece of wood which they called a "dabber." Thus things continued till such time as the State Lottery[10] was passed, and then the printers began to print larger bills, and men were employed instead of women, as the State Lottery Commissioners then began to send men all over England to post bills, and would keep them out for six or eight months at a time, and they were called by the London bill-stickers "*trampers*," their wages at the time being ten shillings per day, besides expenses. They used sometimes to be stationed in large towns for five or six months together, distributing the schemes to all the houses in the town. And then there were more caricature wood-block engravings for posting-bills than there are at the present time, the principal printers, at that time, of posting-bills being Messrs. Evans and Ruffy, of Budge Row; Thoroughgood and Whiting, of the present day; and Messrs. Gye and Balne, Gracechurch Street, City. The largest bills printed at that period were a two-sheet double crown; and when they commenced printing four-sheet bills, two bill-stickers would work together. They had no settled wages per week, but had a fixed price for their work, and the London bill-stickers, during a lottery week, have been known to earn, each, eight or nine pounds per week, till the day of drawing; likewise the men who carried boards in the street used to have one pound per week, and the bill-stickers at that time would not allow any one to wilfully cover or destroy their bills, as they had a society amongst themselves, and very frequently dined together at some public-house where they used to go of an evening to have their work delivered out untoo 'em.'"

All this His Majesty delivered in a gallant manner; posting it, as it were, before me, in a great proclamation. I took advantage of the pause he now made, to inquire what a "two-sheet double crown" might express?

"A two-sheet double crown," replied the King, "is a bill thirty-nine inches wide by thirty inches high."

"Is it possible," said I, my mind reverting to the gigantic admonitions we were then displaying to the multitude – which were as infants to some of the posting-bills on the rotten old warehouse – "that some few years ago the largest bill was no larger than that?"

"The fact," returned the King, "is undoubtedly so." Here he instantly rushed again into the scroll.

"'Since the abolishing of the State Lottery all that good feeling has gone, and nothing but jealousy exists, through the rivalry of each other. Several bill-sticking companies have started, but have failed. The first party that started a company was twelve year ago; but what was left of the old school and their dependants joined together and opposed them. And for some time we were quiet again, till a printer of Hatton Garden formed a company by hiring the sides of houses; but he was not supported by the public, and he left his wooden frames fixed up for rent. The last company that started, took advantage of the New Police Act,[11] and hired of Messrs. Grissell and Peto the hoarding of Trafalgar Square, and established a bill-sticking office in Cursitor Street, Chancery Lane, and engaged some of the new bill-stickers to do their work, and for a time got the half of all our work, and with such spirit did they carry on their opposition towards us, that they used to give us in charge before the magistrate, and get us fined; but they found it so expensive that they could not keep it up, for they were always employing a lot of ruffians from the Seven Dials[12] to come and fight us; and on one occasion the old bill-stickers went to Trafalgar Square to attempt to post bills, when they were given in custody by the watchman in their employ, and fined at Queen Square five pounds, as they would not allow any of us to speak in the office; but when they were gone, we had an interview with the magistrate, who mitigated the fine to fifteen shillings. During the time the men were waiting for the fine, this company started off to a public-house that we were in the habit of using, and waited for us coming back, where a fighting scene took place that beggars description. Shortly after this, the principal one day came and shook hands with us, and acknowledged that he had broken up the company, and that he himself had lost five hundred pound in trying to overthrow us. We then took possession of the hoarding in Trafalgar Square; but Messrs. Grissell and Peto would not allow us to post our bills on the said hoarding without paying them – and from first to last we paid upwards of two hundred pounds for that hoarding, and likewise the hoarding of the Reform Club-house, Pall Mall.'"

His Majesty, being now completely out of breath, laid down his scroll (which he appeared to have finished), puffed at his pipe, and took some rum-and-water. I embraced the opportunity of asking how many divisions the art and mystery of bill-sticking comprised? He replied, three – auctioneers' bill-sticking, theatrical bill-sticking, general bill-sticking.

"The auctioneers' porters," said the King, "who do their bill-sticking, are mostly respectable and intelligent, and generally well paid for their work, whether in town or country. The price paid by the principal auctioneers for country work is nine shillings per day; that is, seven shillings for day's work, one shilling for lodging, and one for paste. Town work is five shillings a day, including paste."

"Town work must be rather hot work," said I, "if there be many of those fighting scenes that beggar description, among the bill-stickers?"

"Well," replied the King, "I an't a stranger, I assure you, to black eyes; a bill-sticker ought to know how to handle his fists a bit. As to that row I have mentioned, that grew out of competition, conducted in an uncompromising spirit. Besides a man in a horse-and-shay continually following us about, the company had a watchman on duty, night and day, to prevent us sticking bills upon the hoarding in Trafalgar Square. We went there, early one morning, to stick bills and to black-wash their bills if we were interfered with. We *were* interfered with, and I gave the word for laying on the wash. It *was* laid on – pretty brisk – and we were all taken to Queen Square: but they couldn't fine *me*. *I* knew that," – with a bright smile – "I'd only give directions – I was only the General."

Charmed with this monarch's affability, I inquired if he had ever hired a hoarding himself.

"Hired a large one," he replied, "opposite the Lyceum Theatre, when the buildings was there. Paid thirty pound for it; let out places on it, and called it 'The External Paper-Hanging Station.' But it didn't answer. Ah!"

said His Majesty thoughtfully, as he filled the glass, "Bill-stickers have a deal to contend with. The bill-sticking clause was got into the Police Act by a member of Parliament that employed me at his election. The clause is pretty stiff respecting where bills go; but *he* didn't mind where *his* bills went. It was all right enough, so long as they was *his* bills!"

Fearful that I observed a shadow of misanthropy on the King's cheerful face, I asked whose ingenious invention that was, which I greatly admired, of sticking bills under the arches of the bridges.

"Mine!" said His Majesty. "I was the first that ever stuck a bill under a bridge! Imitators soon rose up, of course. – When don't they? But they stuck 'em at low-water, and the tide came and swept the bills clean away. *I* knew that!" The King laughed.

"What may be the name of that instrument, like an immense fishing-rod," I inquired, "with which bills are posted on high places?"

"The joints," returned His Majesty. "Now, we use the joints where formerly we used ladders – as they do still in country places. Once, when Madame" (Vestris, understood)[13] "was playing in Liverpool, another bill-sticker and me were at it together on the wall outside the Clarence Dock – me with the joints – him on a ladder. Lord! I had my bill up, right over his head, yards above him, ladder and all, while he was crawling to his work. The people going in and out of the docks stood and laughed! – It's about thirty years since the joints come in."

"Are there any bill-stickers who can't read?" I took the liberty of inquiring.

"Some," said the King. "But they know which is the right side up'ards of their work. They keep it as it's given out to 'em. I have seen a bill or so stuck wrong side up'ards. But it's very rare."

Our discourse sustained some interruption at this point, by the procession of cars occasioning a stoppage of about three-quarters of a mile in length, as nearly as I could judge. His Majesty, however, entreating me not to be discomposed by the contingent uproar, smoked with great placidity, and surveyed the firmament.

When we were again in motion, I begged to be informed what was the largest poster His Majesty had ever seen. The King replied, "A thirty-six sheet poster." I gathered, also, that there were about a hundred and fifty bill-stickers in London, and that his Majesty considered an average hand equal to the posting of one hundred bills (single sheets) in a day. The King was of opinion that, although posters had much increased in size, they had not increased in number; as the abolition of the State Lotteries had occasioned a great falling off, especially in the country. Over and above which change,

I bethought myself that the custom of advertising in newspapers had greatly increased. The completion of many London improvements, as Trafalgar Square (I particularly observed the singularity of His Majesty's calling *that* an improvement), the Royal Exchange, &c., had of late years reduced the number of advantageous posting-places. Bill-Stickers at present rather confine themselves to districts, than to particular descriptions of work. One man would strike over Whitechapel, another would take round Houndsditch, Shoreditch, and the City Road; one (the King said) would stick to the Surrey side; another would make a beat of the West-end.

His Majesty remarked, with some approach to severity, on the neglect of delicacy and taste, gradually introduced into the trade by the new school: a profligate and inferior race of impostors who took jobs at almost any price, to the detriment of the old school, and the confusion of their own misguided employers. He considered that the trade was overdone with competition, and observed, speaking of his subjects, "There are too many of 'em." He believed, still, that things were a little better than they had been; adducing, as a proof, the fact that particular posting-places were now reserved, by common consent, for particular posters; those places, however, must be regularly occupied by those posters, or, they lapsed and fell into other hands. It was of no use giving a man a Drury Lane bill this week and not next. Where was it to go? He was of opinion that going to the expense of putting up your own board on which your sticker could display your own bills, was the only complete way of posting yourself at the present time; but, even to effect this, on payment of a shilling a week to the keepers of steamboat piers and other such places, you must be able, besides, to give orders for theatres and public exhibitions, or you would be sure to be cut out by somebody. His Majesty regarded the passion for orders, as one of the most unappeasable appetites of human nature. If there were a building, or if there were repairs, going on anywhere, you could generally stand something and make it right with the foreman of the works; but orders would be expected from you, and the man who could give the most orders was the man who would come off best. There was this other objectionable point, in orders, that workmen sold them for drink, and often sold them to persons who were likewise troubled with the weakness of thirst: which led (His Majesty said) to the presentation of your orders at Theatre doors, by individuals who were "too shakery" to derive intellectual profit from the entertainments, and who brought a scandal on you. Finally, His Majesty said that you could hardly put too little in a poster; what you wanted was, two or three good catch-lines for the eye to rest on – then, leave it alone – and there you were!

These are the minutes of my conversation with His Majesty, as I noted them down shortly afterwards. I am not aware that I have been betrayed into any alteration or suppression. The manner of the King was frank in the extreme; and he seemed to me to avoid, at once, that slight tendency to repetition which may have been observed in the conversation of His Majesty King George the Third, and that slight under-current of egotism which the curious observer may perhaps detect in the conversation of Napoleon Bonaparte.

I must do the King the justice to say that it was I, and not he, who closed the dialogue. At this juncture, I became the subject of a remarkable optical delusion; the legs of my stool appeared to me to double up; the car to spin round and round with great violence; and a mist to arise between myself and His Majesty. In addition to these sensations, I felt extremely unwell. I refer these unpleasant effects, either to the paste with which the posters were affixed to the van: which may have contained some small portion of arsenic; or to the printer's ink, which may have contained some equally deleterious ingredient. Of this I cannot be sure. I am only sure that I was not affected, either by the smoke or the rum-and-water. I was assisted out of the vehicle in a state of mind which I have only experienced in two other places – I allude to the Pier at Dover, and to the corresponding portion of the town of Calais – and sat upon a door-step until I recovered. The procession had then disappeared. I have since looked anxiously for the King in several other cars, but I have not yet had the happiness of seeing His Majesty.

Spitalfields

First published in *Household Words*, 5 April 1851, this article was written in collaboration with W. H. Wills. The text reproduced here is that published in *The Uncollected Writings of Charles Dickens*. Harry Stone suggests that Dickens wrote the portion from 'And what strange streets' to 'in the streets'; and from 'We knock at the door' to the conclusion.

Have you any distinct idea of Spitalfields,[1] dear reader? A general one, no doubt you have – an impression that here are certain squalid streets, lying like narrow black trenches, far below the steeples, somewhere about London, – towards the East, perhaps, – where sallow, unshorn weavers, who have nothing to do, prowl languidly about, or lean against posts, or sit brooding on door-steps, and occasionally assemble together in a crowd to petition Parliament or the Queen; after which there is a Drawing-Room, or a Court Ball, where all the great ladies wear dresses of Spitalfields manufacture; and then the weavers dine for a day or two, and so relapse into prowling about the streets, leaning against the posts, and brooding on the door-steps. If your occupation in town or country ever oblige you to travel by the Eastern Counties Railway (you would never do so, of course, unless you were obliged) you may connect with this impression, a general idea that many pigeons are kept in Spitalfields, and you may remember to have thought, as you rattled along the dirty streets, observing the pigeon-hutches and pigeon-traps on the tops of the poor dwellings, that it was a natural aspiration in the inhabitants to connect themselves with any living creatures that could get out of that, and take a flight into the air. The smoky little bowers of scarlet-runners that you may have sometimes seen on the house-tops, among the pigeons, may have suggested to your fancy – I pay you the poor compliment of supposing it to be a vagrant fancy, like my own – abortions of the bean-stalk that led Jack to fortune: by the slender twigs of which, the Jacks of Spitalfields will never, never, climb to where the giant keeps his money.

Will you come to Spitalfields?

Turning eastward out of the most bustling part of Bishopsgate, we suddenly lose the noise that has been resounding in our ears, and fade into the quiet churchyard of the Priory of St. Mary, Spital, otherwise "Domus

Dei et Beatæ Mariæ, extra Bishopsgate, in the Parish of St. Botolph." Its modern name is Spital Square. Cells and cloisters were, at an early date, replaced by substantial burgher houses, which, since the Revocation of the Edict of Nantes, in 1685, have been chiefly the depositories of the silk manufacture introduced into London, by the French Huguenots, who flew from the perfidy of Louis the Fourteenth. But much of the old quiet cloistered air, still lingers in the place.

The house to which we are bound, stands at an angle with the spot where the Pulpit-cross was anciently planted; whence, on every Easter Monday and Tuesday, the Spital sermons were preached, in presence of the Lord Mayor and Corporation, and children of Christ's Hospital. We cross the many-cornered "square" and enter a sort of gateway.

Along a narrow passage, up a dark stair, through a crazy door, into a room not very light, not very large, not in the least splendid; with queer corners, and quaint carvings, and massive chimney-pieces; with tall cup-boards with prim doors, and squat counters with deep dumpy drawers; with desks behind thin rails, with aisles between thick towers of papered-up packages, out of whose ends flash all the colours of the rainbow – where all is as quiet as a playhouse at daybreak, or a church at midnight – where, in truth, there is nobody to make a noise, except one well-dressed man, one attendant porter (neither of whom seem to be doing anything particular), and one remarkably fine male cat, admiring, before the fire, the ends of his silky paws – where the door, as we enter, shuts with a deep, dull, muffled sound, that is more startling than a noise – where there is less bustle than at a Quakers' meeting, and less business going on than in a Government office – the well-dressed man threads the mazes of the piles, and desks, and cupboards, and counters, with a slow step, to greet us, and to assure us, in reply to our apology, that we have *not* made any mistake whatever, and that we are in the silk warehouse which we seek: a warehouse in which, we have previously been informed, by one whose word we never before doubted, that there is "turned over" an annual average of one hundred thousand pounds, of good and lawful money of Great Britain.

We may tell our informant, frankly, that, looking round upon the evidences of stagnation which present themselves, we utterly disbelieve his statement. Our faith, however, is soon strengthened. Somebody mounts the stairs, and enters the apartment with the deliberate air of a man who has nothing whatever to do, but to walk about in a beautifully brushed hat, a nicely-fitting coat admirably buttoned, symmetrical boots, and a stock of amazing satin; to crush his gloves tightly between his hands, and to call on his friends, to ask them – as this gentleman asks our friend – how he is getting on; and whether he has been down "yonder" lately (a jerk eastward of the glossy hat); and, if he hasn't, whether he intends going down next Sunday, because if he does, he (the visitor) means to go too, and will take him down in his "trap." He then, in a parenthetical, post-scriptum sort of way, alludes to certain "assorted Glacés," and indicates the pile of silks he means by the merest motion of his ring finger. "The figure is — " says he.

"Two and seven," replies the vendor; "How many pieces shall I put aside?"

"Well – fifty. By-the-bye, have you heard?" – Mr. Broadelle (our friend) has *not* heard, and the visitor proceeds to announce, from unimpeachable authority, that the match between Mr. Crumpley of Howell's, and Miss Lammy of Swan's, is to come off at last: in fact, next Thursday. Cordial "good bye;" graceful elevation of the polished hat to myself; and departure of, as Mr. Broadelle informs us, one of his best customers.

"Customer?"

"Yes? You heard? He has just bought fifty pieces of silk of various or 'assorted' colours."

"At two shillings and seven-pence per yard?"

"Just so. And there are eighty-four yards in a piece."

Our organs of calculation are instantly wound up, and set a-going. The result brought out when these phrenological works have run down, is, that this short, easy jaunty gossip began and ended a transaction involving the sum of five hundred and forty-two pounds ten shillings. No haggling about price; no puffing of quality, on one side, or depreciation of it on the other. The silks are not even looked at. How is this?

"Our trade," says our friend, in explanation, "has been reduced to a system that enables us to transact business with the fewest possible words, and in the easiest possible way. The gentleman who has just left, is Messrs. Treacy and McIntyre's silk-buyer. That department of their establishment is handed over to his management as unrestrictedly and unreservedly as if the whole concern were his own. In like manner, the different branches of large houses – such as cotton, woollen, hosiery, small wares, &c. – are placed under the controul of similar buyers. At the end of every half-year, an account is taken of the stewardship of each of these heads of department; and, if his particular branch has not flourished – should the stock on hand be large and unsaleable – the Buyer is called to account, and his situation jeopardised. The partners, of course, know the capabilities and peculiarities of their trade, and can tell, on investigation, how and why the Buyer has been at fault. If, on the contrary, the Buyer have narrowly watched the public taste, and fed it successfully, – if he have been vigilant in getting early possession of the most attractive patterns, or in pouncing on cheap markets, by taking advantage, for instance, of the embarrassments of a 'shaky' manufacturer or a French revolution (for he scours the country at home and abroad in all directions), and if his department come out at the six-monthly settlement with marked profit – his salary is possibly raised. Should this success be repeated, he is usually taken into the firm as a partner."

"But, *no* judgment was exercised in the bargain just made. The Buyer did not even look at your goods."

"That is the result of previous study and experience. It is the art that conceals art. He need not examine the goods. He has learned the characteristics of our dyes to a shade, and the qualities of our fabrics to a thread."

"Then, as to price. I suppose your friend is lounging about, in various other Spitalfields warehouses at this moment. Perhaps by this time he has run his firm into debt for a few thousand pounds more?"

"Very likely."

"Well; suppose a neighbour of yours were to offer him the same sort of silks as those he has just chosen here, for less money, could he not – as no writing has passed between you – be off his bargain with you?"

"Too late. The thing is done, and cannot be undone," answers Mr. Broadelle, made a little serious by the bare notion of such a breach of faith. "Our bargain is as tight as if it had been written on parchment and attested by a dozen witnesses. His very existence as a Buyer, and mine as a Manufacturer, depend upon the scrupulous performance of the contract. I shall send in the silks this afternoon. And I feel as certain of a check for the cash, at our periodical settlement, as I do of death and quarter-day."

It is difficult to reconcile the immense amount of capital which flows through such a house as this – the rich stores of satins, velvets, lutestrings, brocades, damasks, and other silk textures, which Mr. Broadelle brings to light from the quaint cupboards and drawers – with the poignant and often-repeated cry of poverty that proceeds from this quarter.

What says Mr. Broadelle to it? He says this:

"Although most masters make this locality their head-quarters, and employ the neighbouring weavers, yet they nearly all have factories in the provinces: chiefly in Lancashire. The Spitalfields weaver of plain silks and velvets, therefore, keeps up a hopeless contest against machinery and cheaper labour, and struggles against overwhelming odds. Will you step round and see a family engaged in this desperate encounter?"

"Is there no remedy?" we ask, as we go out together.

"A very simple one. In the country – say in Suffolk,[2] where we have a hand-weaving factory – food is cheaper and better; both food for the stomach, and food for the lungs."

"The air is better, so less money, you think, would be spent in drink?"

"Undoubtedly. Fancy yourself stewed up in a stifling room all day; imagine the lassitude into which your whole frame would collapse after fourteen hours' mere inhalation of a stale, bad, atmosphere – to say nothing of fourteen hours' hard work in addition; and consider what stern self-denial it would require to refrain from some stimulant – a glass of bad gin, perhaps – if you could get it. On the other hand, the fresh air which plays around country looms, exhilarates in itself, and is found to be a substitute for gin."

"I have also heard that the atmosphere of London is positively detrimental to the manufacture of silk. Is that so?"

"Why, sir," replies Mr. Broadelle, stopping short, and speaking like a deeply-injured man, "the two-days' fog we had in December last, was a dead loss to me of one hundred pounds. The blacks (London genuine particular) got into the white satins, despite the best precautions of the workpeople, and put them into an ugly, foxy, unsaleable half-mourning, sir. They would not even take a dye, decently. I had to send down, express, to our Suffolk branch to supply the deficiency; and the white satins, partly woven there on the same days, came up as white as driven snow."

Considering that both the worker and the work are deteriorated by an obstinate tenure of the present dense and unfit site, it seems wonderful that the weavers themselves are not as anxious to remove from a noxious and unprofitable neighbourhood, as their well-wishers can be to effect their removal. From fourteen to seventeen thousand looms are contained in from eleven to twelve thousand houses – although, at the time at which we write, not more than from nine to ten thousand of them are at work. The average number of houses per acre in the parish is seventeen; and the average per acre for all London being no more than five and a fifth, Spitalfields contains the densest population, perhaps, existing. Within its small boundaries, not less than eighty-five thousand human beings are huddled. "They are," says Mr. Broadelle, "so interlaced, and bound together, by debt, marriage, and prejudice, that, despite many inducements to remove to the country establishments of the masters they already serve, they prefer dragging on a miserable existence in their present abodes. Spitalfields was the Necropolis of Roman London; the Registrar-General's returns show that it is now the grave of modern Manufacturing London. The average mortality is higher in this Metropolitan district than in any other."

"And what strange streets they are, Mr. Broadelle! These high gaunt houses, all window on the upper story, and that window all small diamond panes, are like the houses in some foreign town, and have no trace of London in them – except its soot, which is indeed a large exception. It is as if the Huguenots had brought their streets along with them, and dropped them down here. And what a number of strange shops, that seem to be open for no earthly reason, having nothing to sell! A few halfpenny bundles of firewood, a few halfpenny kites, halfpenny battledores, and farthing shuttle-cocks, form quite an extensive stock in trade here. Eatables are so important in themselves, that there is no need to set them off. Be the loaves never so coarse in texture, and never so unattractively jumbled together in the baker's dirty window, they *are* loaves, and that is the main thing. Liver, lights, and sheep's-heads, freckled sausages, and strong black puddings, are sufficiently enticing without decoration. The mouths of Spitalfields will water for them, howsoever raw and ugly they be. Is its intellectual appetite sharp-set, I wonder, for that wolfish literature of highly-coloured show-bill and rampant wood-cut, filling the little shop-window over the way, and covering half the house? Do the poor weavers, by the dim light of their lamps, unravel those villanous fabrics, and nourish their care-worn hearts on the last strainings of the foulest filth of France?" "I can't say," replies Mr. Broadelle; "we have but little intercourse with them in their domestic lives. They are rather jealous and suspicious. We have tried Mechanics' Institutions, but they have not come to much."

"Is there any school here?"

"Yes. Here it is."

An old house, hastily adapted to the purpose, with too much darkness in it and too little air, but no want of scholars. An infant school on the ground floor, where the infants are, as usual, drowsily rubbing their noses, or poking their fore-fingers into the features of other infants on exploratory surveys. Intermediate schools above. At the top of all, in a large, long, light room – occupying the width of two dwelling-houses, as the room made for the weaving, in the old style of building, does – the "ragged school."[3]

"Heaven send that all these boys may not grow up to be weavers here, Mr. Broadelle, nor all these girls grow up to marry them!"

"We don't increase much, now," he says. "We go for soldiers, or we go to sea, or we take to something else, or we emigrate perhaps."

Now, for a sample of the parents of these children. Can you find us a man and wife who should be in Lancashire, or Suffolk, or anywhere rather than here? Nothing easier to find in Spitalfields. Enter by this doorway.

Up a dark narrow winding public stair, such as are numerous in Lyons or in the wynds and closes of the old town of Edinburgh, and into a room where there are four looms; one idle, three at work.

A wan thin eager-eyed man, weaving in his shirt and trousers, stops the jarring of his loom. He is the master of the place. Not an Irishman himself, but of Irish descent.

"Good day!"

"Good day!" Passing his hand over his rough chin, and feeling his lean throat.

"We are walking through Spitalfields, being interested in the place. Will you allow us to look at your work?"

"Oh! certainly."

"It is very beautiful. Black velvet?"

"Yes. Every time I throw the shuttle, I cut out this wire, as you see, and put it in again – so!" Jarring and clashing at the loom, and glancing at us with his eager eyes.

"It is slow work."

"Very slow." With a hard dry cough, and the glance.

"And hard work."

"Very hard." With the cough again.

After a while, he once more stops, perceiving that we really are interested, and says, laying his hand upon his hollow breast and speaking in an unusually loud voice, being used to speak through the clashing of the loom:

"It tries the chest, you see, leaning for'ard like this for fifteen or sixteen hours at a stretch."

"Do you work so long at a time?"

"Glad to do it when I can get it to do. A day's work like that, is worth a matter of three shillings."

"Eighteen shillings a week."

"Ah! But it ain't always eighteen shillings a week. I don't always get it, remember! One week with another, I hardly get more than ten, or ten-and-six."

"Is this Mr. Broadelle's loom?"

"Yes. This is. So is that one there;" the idle one.

"And that, where the man is working?"

"That's another party's. The young man working at it, pays me a shilling a week for leave to work here. That's a shilling, you know, off my rent of half-a-crown. It's rather a large room."

"Is that your wife at the other loom?"

"That's my wife. She's making a commoner sort of work, for bonnets and that."

Again his loom clashes and jars, and he leans forward over his toil. In the window by him, is a singing-bird in a little cage, which trolls its song, and seems to think the loom an instrument of music. The window, tightly closed, commands a maze of chimney-pots, and tiles, and gables. Among them, the ineffectual sun, faintly contending with the rain and mist, is going down. A yellow ray of light crossing the weaver's eager eyes and hollow white face, makes a shape something like a pike-head on the floor.

The room is unwholesome, close, and dirty. Through one part of it the staircase comes up in a bulk, and roughly partitions off a corner. In that corner are the bedstead and the fireplace, a table, a chair or two, a kettle, a tub of water, a little crockery. The looms claim all the superior space and have it. Like grim enchanters who provide the family with their scant food, they must be propitiated with the best accommodation. They bestride the room, and pitilessly squeeze the children – this heavy, watery-headed baby carried in the arms of its staggering little brother, for example – into corners. The children sleep at night between the legs of the monsters, who deafen their first cries with their whirr and rattle, and who roar the same tune to them when they die.

Come to the mother's loom.

"Have you any other children besides these?"

"I have had eight. I have six alive."

"Did we see any of them, just now, at the ——"

"Ragged School? O yes! You saw four of mine at the Ragged School!"

She looks up, quite bright about it – has a mother's pride in it – is not ashamed of the name: she, working for her bread, not begging it – not in the least.

She has stopped her loom for the moment. So has her husband. So has the young man.

"Weaver's children are born in the weaver's room," says the husband, with a nod at the bedstead. "Nursed there, brought up there – sick or well – and die there."

To which, the clash and jar of all three looms – the wife's, the husband's, and the young man's, as they go again – make a chorus.

"This man's work, now, Mr. Broadelle – he can't hear us apart here, in this noise? – "

"Oh, no!"

– "requires but little skill?"

"Very little skill. He is doing now, exactly what his grandfather did. Nothing would induce him to use a simple improvement (the 'fly shuttle') to prevent that contraction of the chest of which he complains. Nothing would turn him aside from his old ways. It is the old custom to work at home, in a crowded room, instead of in a factory. *I* couldn't change it, if I were to try."

Good Heaven, is the house falling! Is there an earthquake in Spitalfields! Has a volcano burst out in the heart of London! What is this appalling rush and tremble?

It is only the railroad.

The arches of the railroad span the house; the wires of the electric telegraph stretch over the confined scene of his daily life; the engines fly past him on their errands, and outstrip the birds; and what can the man of prejudice and usage hope for, but to be overthrown and flung into oblivion! Look to it, gentlemen of precedent and custom standing, daintily opposed to progress, in the bag-wigs and embroidered coats of another generation, you may learn from the weaver in his shirt and trousers!

There, we leave him in the dark, about to kindle at the poor fire the lamp that hangs upon his loom, to help him on his labouring way into the night. The sun has gone down, the reflection has vanished from the floor. There is nothing in the gloom but his eager eyes, made hungrier by the sight of our small present; the dark shapes of his fellow-workers mingling with their stopped looms; the mute bird in its little cage, duskily expressed against the window; and the watery-headed baby crooning in a corner God knows where.

We are again in the streets.

"The fluctuations in the silk trade, and, consequently, in the condition of the Spitalfields weaver," says our friend, "are sudden and unforeseen; for they depend upon a variety of uncontrollable causes. Let us take, for example, the past four or five years."

"But does that period afford a fair average of the condition of the trade? Were not the fluctuations extreme?"

"They were. In 1846 the price of raw silk was very low. The manufacturers bought all they could, and worked up all they bought. Not a hand was idle, not a loom at rest. Enormous stocks soon accumulated, silk became dearer; but in May, 1847, there came a sudden stop."

"Was it not, then, that the last loud cry of distress arose from Spitalfields, and that public meetings were held for finding means of 'redress'?"

"It was. The stagnation was prolonged by a dispute, in which the silk manufacturers and wholesale dealers were involved with the large retail houses. It got the name of the 'short measure question.' The retailers wanted us to give them thirty-seven inches to every yard. The autumn trade was completely crippled by this discussion; which did not end till the breaking out of the French Revolution in February 1848. West-end and wholesale buyers rushed over to Paris and Lyons, in regiments, and with unlimited capital. They bought for almost any price they chose to offer. This cut two ways; although wholesale and retail houses brought home great parcels of manufactured articles, we also bought raw silk, in France, from fifteen to twenty per cent. below the lowest price I ever knew it. What do you think, sir, of the finest French organzine for a guinea a pound?"

We answered by an exclamation of vague surprise.

"Such a price as this enabled us to set some of our looms at work for stock, and, during 1849, the French goods being exhausted, ours came into play. Indeed, during that year the British manufacturer was in a position to defy competition."

"The French had not recovered themselves?"

"Not only that – but we had bought nearly all their raw silk, and they were actually obliged to buy it back from us at advances of from twenty to fifty per cent.! From that time prices advanced here, and work kept on increasing, so that, during most of last year, Spitalfields was busy."

"A glut of stock has been again the consequence."

"Yes; and what with that and the advancing price of raw silk,* I have within the last fortnight been compelled to discharge one hundred hands."

Spitalfields, however, has its bright side. As yet machinery has not been taught to turn artist, or to guide the shuttle through the intricate niceties of the Jacquard loom, so as to execute designs. Figured and brocaded silks must still be done by hands, and those hands must be skilful.

"Our silks," Mr. Broadelle tells us, "have never been inferior, in quality, to those of our foreign rivals; but, we have always been beaten in taste. In the stolid assiduous pains-taking motion of the hand and treadle, the English weaver is unsurpassed; but, he has seldom exercised his fancy. Until lately, therefore, few designs originated in this country. We silk-manufacturers, like the Dramatic Authors' Society,[4] have been content to take our novelties from the French."

"You say, 'until lately.' Has the English manufacturer improved in that respect?"

"Decidedly. Schools of Design have done something: the encouragement given by masters to those who make available patterns, has done something

* The price of "organzine" during the month of March was: – French 32s; Piedmont 26s; China, 22s.

too; but, the great improver of the English silk trade was the last French revolution."

"How?"

"That political disaster brought the manufacturers of France to a dead-lock. During the whole of 1849, the English markets were stocked with the most splendid fashions that ever came into it. As *we* could not sell a yard of *our* manufacture, we had plenty of leisure to examine the different foreign goods minutely. So rich a variety had never fallen under our observation, and never before had such a flood of light been thrown on the manufactures of our greatest rivals. We profited by it. More important improvements have been effected in the fabric of fancy silk goods since 1848, than were made, down to that time, since the days of Jacquard."

"This shows the value of national intercourse, Mr. Broadelle. Will the Great Exhibition do much service in this way?"

"I have no doubt it will. But, we are now at the door of a figure-weaver; and you will compare this visit with our last."

We knock at the door of a cheerful little house, extremely clean. We are introduced into a little parlour, where a young artist sits at work with crayons and water-colours. He is a student of the School of Design.[5] He is at work on a new pattern for a table-cover. He has learnt to paint in oil. He has painted the portraits of his sisters – and of some one who I suspect is not a sister, but who may be

> A nearer one
> Yet and a dearer one,[6]

and they decorate the room. He has painted groups of flowers. He shows us one that was in last year's Exhibition of the Royal Academy. He shows us another that he means to finish in good time to send to the next Exhibition. He does these things over and above his regular work. He don't mind work – gets up early. There are cheap casts prettily arranged about the room, and it has a little collection of cheap books of a good sort in it. The intrinsic worth of every simple article of furniture or embellishment is enhanced a hundred-fold (as it always may be) by neatness and order. Is father at home? Yes, and will be glad to see the visitors. Pray walk up!

The young artist shows us the way to the top of the house, apologising cheerfully for the ladder-staircase by which we mount at last. In a bright clean room, as pure as soap and water, scrubbing, and fresh air, can make it, we find a sister whose portrait is downstairs – we are able to claim her instantly for the original, to the general satisfaction. We find also, father, who is working at his Jacquard loom, making a pretty pattern of cravat, in blue upon a black ground. He is as cordial, sensible, intelligent a man, as any one would wish to know. He has a reason for everything he says, and everything he does. He is learned in sanitary matters among other necessary knowledge, and says the first thing you have to do, is, to make your place wholesome, or you can't expect to work heartily. Wholesome it is, as his own pleasant face, and the pleasant faces of his children well brought up. He has made various improvements in his own loom; he has made an improvement in his daughter's, who works near him, which prevents her having to contract her chest, although she is doing very ordinary work. Industry, contentment, sense, and self-respect, are the hopeful characteristics of everything animate and inanimate in this little house. If the veritable summer light were shining, and the veritable summer air were rustling, in it, which the young artist has tried to get into the sketches of green glades from Epping Forest that hang near father's loom, and can be seen by father while he is at work, it could not be more cheering to our hearts, oppressed with what we have left.

I meant to have had a talk with our good friend Mr. Broadelle, respecting a cruel persistence in one inflexible principle which gave the New Poor Law a particular severity in its application to Spitalfields, a few years back, but which I hope may have been amended. Work in the stone-yard was the test of all able-bodied applicants for relief. Now, the weaver's hands are soft and delicate, and *must be so* for his work. No matter. The weaver wanting relief, must work in the stone-yard with the rest. So, the Union blistered his hands before it relieved him, and incapacitated him from doing his work when he could get it.

But, let us leave Spitalfields with an agreeable impression, and be thankful that we can.

On Duty With Inspector Field

First published in *Household Words*, 14 June 1851, and subsequently published in *Reprinted Pieces* from which this text is taken.

How goes the night? Saint Giles's clock[1] is striking nine. The weather is dull and wet, and the long lines of street lamps are blurred, as if we saw them through tears. A damp wind blows and rakes the pieman's fire out, when he opens the door of his little furnace, carrying away an eddy of sparks.

Saint Giles's clock strikes nine. We are punctual. Where is Inspector Field? Assistant Commissioner of Police is already here, enwrapped in oil-skin cloak, and standing in the shadow of Saint Giles's steeple. Detective Sergeant, weary of speaking French all day to foreigners unpacking at the Great Exhibition, is already here. Where is Inspector Field?

Inspector Field is, to-night, the guardian genius of the British Museum. He is bringing his shrewd eye to bear on every corner of its solitary galleries, before he reports "all right." Suspicious of the Elgin marbles, and not to be done by cat-faced Egyptian giants with their hands upon their knees, Inspector Field, sagacious, vigilant, lamp in hand, throwing monstrous shadows on the walls and ceilings, passes through the spacious rooms. If a mummy trembled in an atom of its dusty covering, Inspector Field would say, "Come out of that, Tom Green. I know you!" If the smallest "Gonoph"[2] about town were crouching at the bottom of a classic bath, Inspector Field would nose him with a finer scent than the ogre's, when adventurous Jack lay trembling in his kitchen copper. But all is quiet, and Inspector Field goes warily on, making little outward show of attending to anything in particular, just recognising the Ichthyosaurus as a familiar acquaintance, and wondering, perhaps, how the detectives did it in the days before the Flood.

Will Inspector Field be long about this work? He may be half-an-hour longer. He sends his compliments by Police Constable, and proposes that we meet at St. Giles's Station House, across the road. Good. It were as well to stand by the fire, there, as in the shadow of Saint Giles's steeple.

Anything doing here to-night? Not much. We are very quiet. A lost boy, extremely calm and small, sitting by the fire, whom we now confide

306

to a constable to take home, for the child says that if you show him Newgate Street, he can show you where he lives – a raving drunken woman in the cells, who has screeched her voice away, and has hardly power enough left to declare, even with the passionate help of her feet and arms, that she is the daughter of a British officer, and, strike her blind and dead, but she'll write a letter to the Queen! but who is soothed with a drink of water – in another cell, a quiet woman, with a child at her breast, for begging – in another, her husband in a smock-frock, with a basket of watercresses – in another, a pickpocket – in another, a meek tremulous old pauper man who has been out for a holiday "and has took but a little drop, but it has overcome him after so many months in the house" – and that's all as yet. Presently, a sensation at the Station House door. Mr. Field, gentlemen!

Inspector Field comes in, wiping his forehead, for he is of a burly figure, and has come fast from the ores and metals of the deep mines of the earth, and from the Parrot Gods of the South Sea Islands, and from the birds and beetles of the tropics, and from the Arts of Greece and Rome, and from the Sculptures of Nineveh, and from the traces of an elder world, when these were not. Is Rogers ready? Rogers is ready, strapped and great-coated, with a flaming eye in the middle of his waist,[3] like a deformed Cyclops. Lead on, Rogers, to Rats' Castle!

How many people may there be in London, who, if we had brought them deviously and blindfold, to this street, fifty paces from the Station House, and within call of Saint Giles's church, would know it for a not remote part of the city in which their lives are passed? How many, who amidst this compound of sickening smells, these heaps of filth, these tumbling houses, with all their vile contents, animate and inanimate, slimily over-flowing into the black road, would believe that they breathe *this* air? How much Red Tape may there be, that could look round on the faces which now hem us in – for our appearance here has caused a rush from all points to a common centre – the lowering foreheads, the sallow cheeks, the brutal eyes, the matted hair, the infected, vermin-haunted heaps of rags – and say, "I have thought of this. I have not dismissed the thing. I have neither blustered it away, nor frozen it away, nor tied it up and put it away, nor smoothly said pooh, pooh! to it when it has been shown to me?"

This is not what Rogers wants to know, however. What Rogers wants to know is, whether you *will* clear the way here, some of you, or whether you won't; because if you don't do it right on end, he'll lock you up! "What! *You* are there, are you, Bob Miles? You haven't had enough of it yet, haven't you? You want three months more, do you? Come away from that gentleman! What are you creeping round there for?"

"What am I a doing, thinn, Mr. Rogers?" says Bob Miles, appearing, villainous, at the end of a lane of light, made by the lantern.

"I'll let you know pretty quick, if you don't hook it. WILL you hook it?"

A sycophantic murmur rises from the crowd. "Hook it, Bob, when Mr. Rogers and Mr. Field tells you! Why don't you hook it, when you are told to?"

The most importunate of the voices strikes familiarly on Mr. Rogers's ear. He suddenly turns his lantern on the owner.

"What! *You* are there, are you, Mister Click? You hook it too — come!"

"What for?" says Mr. Click, discomfited.

"You hook it, will you!" says Mr. Rogers with stern emphasis.

Both Click and Miles *do* "hook it," without another word, or, in plainer English, sneak away.

"Close up there, my men!" says Inspector Field to two constables on duty who have followed. "Keep together, gentlemen; we are going down here. Heads!"

Saint Giles's church strikes half-past ten. We stoop low, and creep down a precipitous flight of steps into a dark close cellar. There is a fire. There is a long deal table. There are benches. The cellar is full of company, chiefly very young men in various conditions of dirt and raggedness. Some are eating supper. There are no girls or women present. Welcome to Rats' Castle, gentlemen, and to this company of noted thieves!

"Well, my lads! How are you, my lads? What have you been doing to-day? Here's some company come to see you, my lads! *There's* a plate of beefsteak, sir, for the supper of a fine young man! And there's a mouth for a steak, sir! Why, I should be too proud of such a mouth as that, if I had it myself! Stand up and show it, sir! Take off your cap. There's a fine young man for a nice little party, sir! An't he?"

Inspector Field is the bustling speaker. Inspector Field's eye is the roving eye that searches every corner of the cellar as he talks. Inspector Field's hand is the well-known hand that has collared half the people here, and motioned their brothers, sisters, fathers, mothers, male and female friends, inexorably to New South Wales. Yet Inspector Field stands in this den, the Sultan of the place. Every thief here cowers before him, like a schoolboy before his schoolmaster. All watch him, all answer when addressed, all laugh at his jokes, all seek to propitiate him. This cellar company alone — to say nothing of the crowd surrounding the entrance from the street above, and making the steps shine with eyes — is strong enough to murder us all, and willing enough to do it; but let Inspector Field have a mind to pick out one thief here, and take him; let him produce that ghostly truncheon from his pocket, and say, with his business-air, "My lad, I want you!" and all Rats' Castle shall be stricken with paralysis, and not a finger move against him, as he fits the handcuffs on!

Where's the Earl of Warwick? — Here he is, Mr. Field! Here's the Earl of Warwick, Mr. Field! — O, there you are, my Lord. Come for'ard. There's a chest, sir, not to have a clean shirt on. An't it? Take your hat off, my Lord. Why, I should be ashamed if I was you — and an Earl, too — to show myself to a gentleman with my hat on! — The Earl of Warwick laughs and uncovers. All the company laugh. One pickpocket, especially, laughs with great enthusiasm. O what a jolly game it is, when Mr. Field comes down — and don't want nobody!

"So, *you* are here, too, are you, you tall, grey, soldierly-looking, grave man, standing by the fire? — Yes, sir. Good evening, Mr. Field! — Let us see. You lived servant to a nobleman once? — Yes, Mr. Field. — And what is it you do now; I forget? — Well, Mr. Field, I job about as well as I can. I left my employment on account of delicate health. The family is still kind to me. Mr. Wix of Piccadilly is also very kind to me when I am hard up. Likewise Mr. Nix of Oxford Street. I get a trifle from them occasionally, and rub on as well as I can, Mr. Field. Mr. Field's eye rolls enjoyingly, for this man is a notorious begging-letter writer. — Good night, my lads! — Good night, Mr. Field, and thank'ee, sir!

Clear the street here, half a thousand of you! Cut it, Mrs. Stalker — none of that — we don't want you! Rogers of the flaming eye, lead on to the tramps' lodging-house!

A dream of baleful faces attends to the door. Now, stand back all of you! In the rear Detective Sergeant plants himself, composedly whistling, with his strong right arm across the narrow passage. Mrs. Stalker, I am something'd that need not be written here, if you won't get yourself into trouble, in about half a minute, if I see that face of yours again!

Saint Giles's church clock, striking eleven, hums through our hand from the dilapidated door of a dark outhouse as we open it, and are stricken back by the pestilent breath that issues from within. Rogers to the front with the light, and let us look!

Ten, twenty, thirty — who can count them! Men, women, children, for the most part naked, heaped upon the floor like maggots in a cheese! Ho! In that dark corner yonder! Does anybody lie there? Me sir, Irish me, a widder, with six children. And yonder? Me sir, Irish me, with me wife and eight poor babes. And to the left there? Me sir, Irish me, along with two more Irish boys as is me friends. And to the right there? Me sir and the Murphy fam'ly, numbering five blessed souls. And what's this, coiling, now, about my foot? Another Irish me, pitifully in want of shaving, whom I have awakened from sleep – and across my other foot lies his wife – and by the shoes of Inspector Field lie their three eldest – and their three youngest are at present squeezed between the open door and the wall. And why is there no one on that little mat before the sullen fire? Because O'Donovan, with his wife and daughter, is not come in from selling Lucifers! Nor on the bit of sacking in the nearest corner? Bad luck! Because that Irish family is late to-night, a-cadging in the streets!

They are all awake now, the children excepted, and most of them sit up, to stare. Wheresoever Mr. Rogers turns the flaming eye, there is a spectral figure rising, unshrouded, from a grave of rags. Who is the landlord here? – I am, Mr. Field! says a bundle of ribs and parchment against the wall, scratching itself. – Will you spend this money fairly, in the morning, to buy coffee for 'em all? – Yes, sir, I will! – O he'll do it, sir, he'll do it fair. He's honest! cry the spectres. And with thanks and Good Night sink into their graves again.

Thus, we make our New Oxford Streets,[4] and our other new streets, never heeding, never asking, where the wretches whom we clear out, crowd. With such scenes at our doors, with all the plagues of Egypt tied up with bits of cobweb in kennels so near our homes, we timorously make our Nuisance Bills and Boards of Health, nonentities, and think to keep away the Wolves of Crime and Filth, by our electioneering ducking to little vestrymen[5] and our gentlemanly handling of Red Tape!

Intelligence of the coffee-money has got abroad. The yard is full, and Rogers of the flaming eye is beleaguered with entreaties to show other Lodging Houses. Mine next! Mine! Mine! Rogers, military, obdurate, stiff-necked, immovable, replies not, but leads away; all falling back before him. Inspector Field follows. Detective Sergeant, with his barrier of arm across the little passage, deliberately waits to close the procession. He sees behind him, without any effort, and exceedingly disturbs one individual far in the rear by coolly calling out, "It won't do, Mr. Michael! Don't try it!"

After council holden in the street, we enter other lodging-houses, public-houses, many lairs and holes; all noisome and offensive; none so filthy and so crowded as where Irish are. In one, The Ethiopian party are expected home presently – were in Oxford Street when last heard of – shall be fetched, for our delight, within ten minutes. In another, one of the two or three Professors who draw Napoleon Buonaparte and a couple of mackerel, on the pavement, and then let the work of art out to a speculator, is refreshing after his labours. In another, the vested interest of the profitable nuisance has been in one family for a hundred years, and the landlord drives in comfortably from the country to his snug little stew in town. In all, Inspector Field is received with warmth. Coiners and smashers droop before him; pickpockets defer to him; the gentle sex (not very gentle here) smile upon him. Half-drunken hags check themselves in the midst of pots of beer, or pints of gin, to drink to Mr. Field, and pressingly to ask the honour of his finishing the draught. One beldame in rusty black has such admiration for him, that she runs a whole street's length to shake him by the hand; tumbling into a heap of mud by the way, and still pressing her attentions when her very form has ceased to be distinguishable through it. Before the power of the law, the power of superior sense – for common thieves are fools beside these men – and the power of a perfect mastery of their character, the garrison of Rats' Castle and the adjacent Fortresses make but a skulking show indeed when reviewed by Inspector Field.

Saint Giles's clock says it will be midnight in half-an-hour, and Inspector Field says we must hurry to the Old Mint in the Borough.[6] The cab-driver is low-spirited, and has a solemn sense of his responsibility. Now, what's your fare, my lad? – O *you* know, Inspector Field, what's the good of asking *me*!

Say, Parker, strapped and great-coated, and waiting in dim Borough doorway by appointment, to replace the trusty Rogers whom we left deep in Saint Giles's, are you ready? Ready, Inspector Field, and at a motion of my wrist behold my flaming eye.

This narrow street, sir, is the chief part of the Old Mint, full of low lodging-houses, as you see by the transparent canvas-lamps and blinds, announcing beds for travellers! But it is greatly changed, friend Field, from my former knowledge of it; it is infinitely quieter and more subdued than when I was here last, some seven years ago? O yes! Inspector Haynes, a first-rate man, is on this station now and plays the Devil with them!

Well, my lads! How are you to-night, my lads? Playing cards here, eh? Who wins? – Why, Mr. Field, I, the sulky gentleman with the damp flat side-curls, rubbing my bleared eye with the end of my neckerchief which is like a dirty eel-skin, am losing just at present, but I suppose I must take my pipe out of my mouth, and be submissive to *you* – I hope I see you well, Mr. Field? – Aye, all right, my lad. Deputy, who have you got up-stairs? Be pleased to show the rooms!

Why Deputy, Inspector Field can't say. He only knows that the man who takes care of the beds and lodgers is always called so. Steady, O Deputy, with the flaring candle in the blacking-bottle, for this is a slushy back-yard, and the wooden staircase outside the house creaks and has holes in it.

Again, in these confined intolerable rooms, burrowed out like the holes of rats or the nests of insect-vermin, but fuller of intolerable smells, are crowds of sleepers, each on his foul truckle-bed coiled up beneath a rug. Halloa here! Come! Let us see you! Show your face! Pilot Parker goes from bed to bed and turns their slumbering heads towards us, as a salesman might turn sheep. Some wake up with an execration and a threat. – What! who spoke? O! If it's the accursed glaring eye that fixes me, go where I will, I am helpless. Here! I sit up to be looked at. Is it me you want? Not you, lie down again! and I lie down, with a woful growl.

Wherever the turning lane of light becomes stationary for a moment, some sleeper appears at the end of it, submits himself to be scrutinised, and fades away into the darkness.

There should be strange dreams here, Deputy. They sleep sound enough, says Deputy, taking the candle out of the blacking-bottle, snuffing it with his fingers, throwing the snuff into the bottle, and corking it up with the candle; that's all *I* know. What is the inscription, Deputy, on all the discoloured sheets? A precaution against loss of linen. Deputy turns down the rug of an unoccupied bed and discloses it. STOP THIEF!

To lie at night, wrapped in the legend of my slinking life; to take the cry that pursues me, waking, to my breast in sleep; to have it staring at me, and clamouring for me, as soon as consciousness returns; to have it for my first-foot on New-Year's day, my Valentine, my Birthday salute, my Christmas greeting, my parting with the old year. STOP THIEF!

And to know that I *must* be stopped, come what will. To know that I am no match for this individual energy and keenness, or this organised and steady system! Come across the street, here, and, entering by a little shop, and yard, examine these intricate passages and doors, contrived for escape, flapping and counter-flapping, like the lids of the conjurer's boxes. But what avail they? Who gets in by a nod, and shows their secret working to us? Inspector Field.

Don't forget the old Farm House, Parker! Parker is not the man to forget it. We are going there, now. It is the old Manor-House of these parts, and stood in the country once. Then, perhaps, there was something, which was not the beastly street, to see from the shattered low fronts of the overhanging wooden houses we are passing under – shut up now, pasted over with bills about the literature and drama of the Mint, and mouldering away. This long paved yard was a paddock or a garden once, or a court in front of the Farm House. Perchance, with a dovecot in the centre, and fowls pecking about – with fair elm trees, then, where discoloured chimney-stacks and gables are now – noisy, then, with rooks which have yielded to a different sort of rookery. It's likelier than not, Inspector Field thinks, as we turn into the common kitchen, which is in the yard, and many paces from the house.

Well, my lads and lasses, how are you all? Where's Blackey, who has stood near London Bridge these five-and-twenty years, with a painted skin to represent disease? – Here he is, Mr. Field! – How are you, Blackey? – Jolly, sa! Not playing the fiddle to-night, Blackey! – Not a night, sa! A sharp, smiling youth, the wit of the kitchen, interposes. He an't musical to-night, sir. I've been giving him a moral lecture; I've been a talking to him about his latter end, you see. A good many of these are my pupils, sir. This here young man (smoothing down the hair of one near him, reading a Sunday paper) is a pupil of mine. I'm a teaching of him to read, sir. He's a promising cove, sir. He's a smith, he is, and gets his living by the sweat of the brow, sir. So do I, myself, sir. This young woman is my sister, Mr. Field. *She's* getting on very well too. I've a deal of trouble with 'em, sir, but I'm richly rewarded, now I see 'em all a doing so well, and growing up so creditable. That's a great comfort, that is, an't it, sir? – In the midst of the kitchen (the whole kitchen is in ecstasies with this impromptu "chaff") sits a young, modest, gentle-looking creature, with a beautiful child in her lap. She seems to belong to the company, but is so strangely unlike it. She has such a pretty, quiet face and voice, and is so proud to hear the child admired – thinks you would hardly believe that he is only nine months old! Is she as bad as the rest, I wonder? Inspectorial experience does not engender a belief contrariwise, but prompts the answer, Not a ha'porth of difference!

There is a piano going in the old Farm House as we approach. It stops. Landlady appears. Has no objections, Mr. Field, to gentlemen being brought, but wishes it were at earlier hours, the lodgers complaining of ill-conwenience. Inspector Field is polite and soothing – knows his woman and the sex. Deputy (a girl in this case) shows the way up a heavy broad old staircase, kept very clean, into clean rooms where many sleepers are, and where painted panels of an older time look strangely on the truckle-beds. The sight of whitewash and the smell of soap – two things we seem by this time to have parted from in infancy – make the old Farm House a phenomenon, and connect themselves with the so curiously misplaced picture of the pretty mother and child long after we have left it, – long after we have left, besides, the neighbouring nook with something of a rustic flavour in it yet, where once, beneath a low wooden colonnade still standing as of yore, the eminent Jack Sheppard[7] condescended to regale himself, and where, now, two old bachelor brothers in broad hats (who are whispered in the Mint to have made a compact long ago that if either should ever marry, he must forfeit his share of the joint property) still keep a sequestered tavern, and sit o' nights smoking pipes in the bar, among ancient bottles and glasses, as our eyes behold them.

How goes the night now? Saint George of Southwark[8] answers with twelve blows upon his bell. Parker, good night, for Williams is already waiting over in the region of Ratcliffe Highway, to show the houses where the sailors dance.

I should like to know where Inspector Field was born. In Ratcliffe Highway, I would have answered with confidence, but for his being equally at home wherever we go. *He* does not trouble his head as I do, about the river at night. *He* does not care for its creeping, black and silent, on our right there, rushing through sluice-gates, lapping at piles and posts and iron rings, hiding strange things in its mud, running away with suicides and accidentally drowned bodies faster than midnight funeral should, and acquiring such various experience between its cradle and its grave. It has no mystery for *him*. Is there not the Thames Police?

Accordingly, Williams leads the way. We are a little late, for some of the houses are already closing. No matter. You show us plenty. All the landlords know Inspector Field. All pass him, freely and good-humouredly, wheresoever he wants to go. So thoroughly are all these houses open to him and our local guide, that, granting that sailors must be entertained in their own way – as I suppose they must, and have a right to be – I hardly know how such places could be better regulated. Not that I call the company very select, or the dancing very graceful – even so graceful as that of the German Sugar Bakers, whose assembly, by the Minories,[9] we stopped to visit – but there is watchful maintenance of order in every house, and swift expulsion where need is. Even in the midst of drunkenness, both of the lethargic kind and the lively, there is sharp landlord supervision, and pockets are in less peril than out of doors. These houses show, singularly, how much of the picturesque and romantic there truly is in the sailor, requiring to be especially addressed. All the songs (sung in a hailstorm of halfpence, which are pitched at the singer without the least tenderness for the time or tune – mostly from great rolls of copper carried for the purpose – and which he occasionally dodges like shot as they fly near his head) are of the sentimental sea sort. All the rooms are decorated with nautical subjects. Wrecks, engagements, ships on fire, ships passing lighthouses on iron-bound coasts, ships blowing up, ships going down, ships running ashore, men lying out upon the main-yard in a gale of wind, sailors and ships in every variety of peril, constitute the illustrations of fact. Nothing can be done in the fanciful way, without a thumping boy upon a scaly dolphin.

How goes the night now? Past one. Black and Green are waiting in Whitechapel to unveil the mysteries of Wentworth Street.[10] Williams, the best of friends must part. Adieu!

Are not Black and Green ready at the appointed place? O yes! They glide out of shadow as we stop. Imperturbable Black opens the cab-door; Imperturbable Green takes a mental note of the driver. Both Green and Black then open, each his flaming eye, and marshal us the way that we are going.

The lodging-house we want is hidden in a maze of streets and courts. It is fast shut. We knock at the door, and stand hushed looking up for a light at one or other of the begrimed old lattice windows in its ugly front, when another constable comes up — supposes that we want "to see the school." Detective Sergeant meanwhile has got over a rail, opened a gate, dropped down an area, overcome some other little obstacles, and tapped at a window. Now returns. The landlord will send a deputy immediately.

Deputy is heard to stumble out of bed. Deputy lights a candle, draws back a bolt or two, and appears at the door. Deputy is a shivering shirt and trousers by no means clean, a yawning face, a shock head much confused externally and internally. We want to look for some one. You may go up with the light, and take 'em all, if you like, says Deputy, resigning it, and sitting down upon a bench in the kitchen with his ten fingers sleepily twisting in his hair.

Holloa here! Now then! Show yourselves. That'll do. It's not you. Don't disturb yourself any more! So on, through a labyrinth of airless rooms, each man responding, like a wild beast, to the keeper who has tamed him, and who goes into his cage. What, you haven't found him, then? says Deputy, when we came down. A woman mysteriously sitting up all night in the dark by the smouldering ashes of the kitchen fire, says it's only tramps and cadgers here; it's gonophs over the way. A man mysteriously walking about the kitchen all night in the dark, bids her hold her tongue. We come out. Deputy fastens the door and goes to bed again.

Black and Green, you know Bark, lodging-house keeper and receiver of stolen goods? — O yes, Inspector Field. — Go to Bark's next.

Bark sleeps in an inner wooden hutch, near his street door. As we parley on the step with Bark's Deputy, Bark growls in his bed. We enter, and Bark flies out of bed. Bark is a red villain and a wrathful, with a sanguine throat that looks very much as if it were expressly made for hanging, as he stretches it out, in pale defiance, over the half-door of his hutch. Bark's parts of speech are of an awful sort – principally adjectives. I won't, says Bark, have no adjective police and adjective strangers in my adjective premises! I won't, by adjective and substantive! Give me my trousers, and I'll send the whole adjective police to adjective and substantive! Give me, says Bark, my adjective trousers! I'll put an adjective knife in the whole bileing of 'em. I'll punch their adjective heads. I'll rip up their adjective substantives. Give me my adjective trousers! says Bark, and I'll spile the bileing of 'em!

Now, Bark, what's the use of this? Here's Black and Green, Detective Sergeant, and Inspector Field. You know we will come in. – I know you won't! says Bark. Somebody give me my adjective trousers! Bark's trousers seem difficult to find. He calls for them as Hercules might for his club. Give me my adjective trousers! says Bark, and I'll spile the bileing of 'em.

Inspector Field holds that it's all one whether Bark likes the visit or don't like it. He, Inspector Field, is an Inspector of the Detective Police, Detective Sergeant *is* Detective Sergeant, Black and Green are constables in uniform. Don't you be a fool, Bark, or you know it will be the worse for you. – I don't care, says Bark. Give me my adjective trousers!

At two o'clock in the morning, we descend into Bark's low kitchen, leaving Bark to foam at the mouth above, and Imperturbable Black and Green to look at him. Bark's kitchen is crammed full of thieves, holding a *conversazione* there by lamp-light. It is by far the most dangerous assembly we have seen yet. Stimulated by the ravings of Bark, above, their looks are sullen, but not a man speaks. We ascend again. Bark has got his trousers, and is in a state of madness in the passage with his back against a door that shuts off the upper staircase. We observe, in other respects, a ferocious individuality in Bark. Instead of "STOP THIEF!" on his linen, he prints "STOLEN FROM BARK'S!"

Now, Bark, we are going up-stairs! – No, you ain't! – You refuse admission to the Police, do you, Bark? – Yes, I do! I refuse it to all the adjective police, and to all the adjective substantives. If the adjective coves in the kitchen was men, they'd come up now, and do for you! Shut me that there door! says Bark, and suddenly we are enclosed in the passage. They'd come up and do for you! cries Bark, and waits. Not a sound in the kitchen! They'd come up and do for you! cries Bark again, and waits. Not a sound in the kitchen! We are shut up, half-a-dozen of us, in Bark's house in the innermost recesses of the worst part of London, in the dead of the night – the house is crammed with notorious robbers and ruffians – and not a man stirs. No, Bark. They know the weight of the law, and they know Inspector Field and Co. too well.

We leave bully Bark to subside at leisure out of his passion and his trousers, and I dare say, to be inconveniently reminded of this little brush before long. Black and Green do ordinary duty here, and look serious.

As to White, who waits on Holborn Hill to show the courts that are eaten out of Rotten Gray's Inn Lane, where other lodging-houses are, and where (in one blind alley) the Thieves' Kitchen and Seminary for the teaching of the art to children, is, the night has so worn away, being now

almost at odds with morning, which is which,[11]

that they are quiet, and no light shines through the chinks in the shutters. As undistinctive Death will come here, one day, sleep comes now. The wicked cease from troubling sometimes, even in this life.

A Curious Dance Round a Curious Tree

First published in *Household Words*, 17 January 1852, this article was written in collaboration with W. H. Wills. The text reproduced here is that published in *The Uncollected Writings of Charles Dickens*. Harry Stone suggests that Dickens wrote the portion from 'How came I' to 'followed my leader'; and from 'It was playing' to the conclusion.

On the 13th day of January, 1750 – when the corn that grew near Moorfields was ground on the top of Windmill Hill, "Fensbury;"[1] when Bethlehem Hospital was "a dry walk for loiterers," and a show; when lunatics were chained, naked, in rows of cages that flanked a promenade, and were wondered and jeered at through iron bars by London loungers – Sir Thomas Ladbroke the banker, Bonnel Thornton[2] the wit, and half-a-dozen other gentlemen, met together to found a new asylum for the insane. Towards this object they put down, before separating, one guinea each. In a year from that time the windmill had been given to the winds, and on its ancient site, there stood a hospital for the gratuitous treatment of the insane poor.

With the benevolence which thus originated an additional madhouse, was mixed, as was usual in that age, a curious degree of unconscious cruelty. Coercion for the outward man, and rabid physicking for the inward man, were then the specifics for lunacy. Chains, straw, filthy solitude, darkness, and starvation; jalap, syrup of buckthorn, tartarised antimony, and ipecacuanha administered every spring and fall in fabulous doses to every patient, whether well or ill; spinning in whirligigs, corporal punishment, gagging, "continued intoxication;" nothing was too wildly extravagant, nothing too monstrously cruel to be prescribed by mad-doctors. It was their monomania;[3] and, under their influence, the directors of Lunatic Asylums acted. In other respects these physicians were grave men, of mild dispositions, and – in their ample-flapped, ample-cuffed coats, with a certain gravity and air of state in the skirts; with their large buttons and gold-headed canes, their hair-powder and ruffles – were men of benevolent aspects. Imagine one of them turning back his lace and tightening his wig to supply a maniac who *would* keep his mouth shut, with food or physic. He employed a flat oval ring, with a handle to it. "The head being placed between the knees of the operator, the patient, blinded and properly secured, an opportunity is watched. When

318

he opens his mouth to speak, the instrument is thrust in and allows the food or medicine to be introduced without difficulty. A sternutatory of any kind" (say a pepper-castor of cayenne, or half an ounce of rappee) "always forces the mouth open, in spite of the patient's determination to keep it shut." "In cases of great fury and violence," says the amiable practitioner from whom I quote, "the patient should be kept in a dark room, confined by one leg, with metallic manacles on the wrist; the skin being less liable to be injured," – here the Good Doctor becomes especially considerate and mild, – "the skin being less liable to be injured by the friction of polished metal than by that of linen or cotton."[4]

These practitioners of old, would seem to have been, without knowing it, early homœopathists; their motto must have been, *Similia similibus curantur*; they believed that the most violent and certain means of driving a man mad, were the only hopeful means of restoring him to reason. The inside of the new hospital, therefore, even when, in 1782, it was removed, under the name of "Saint Luke's,"[5] from Windmill Hill to its present site in the Old Street Road, must have appeared, to the least irrational new patient, like a collection of chambers of horrors. What sane person indeed, seeing, on his entrance into any place, gyves and manacles (however highly polished) yawning for his ankles and wrists; swings dangling in the air, to spin him round like an impaled cockchafer; gags and strait-waistcoats ready at a moment's notice to muzzle and bind him; would be likely to retain the perfect command of his senses? Even now, an outside view of Saint Luke's Hospital is gloomy enough; and, when on that cold, misty, cheerless afternoon which followed Christmas Day, I looked up at the high walls, and saw, grimly peering over them, its upper stories and dismal little iron-bound windows, I did not ring the porter's bell (albeit I was only a visitor, and free to go, if I would, without ringing it at all) in the most cheerful frame of mind.

How came I, it may be asked, on the day after Christmas Day, of all days in the year, to be hovering outside Saint Luke's, after dark, when I might have betaken myself to that jocund world of Pantomime, where there is no affliction or calamity that leaves the least impression; where a man may tumble into the broken ice, or dive into the kitchen fire, and only be the droller for the accident; where babies may be knocked about and sat upon, or choked with gravy spoons, in the process of feeding, and yet no Coroner be wanted, nor anybody made uncomfortable; where workmen may fall from the top of a house to the bottom, or even from the bottom of a house to the top, and sustain no injury to the brain, need no hospital, leave no young children; where every one, in short, is so superior to all the accidents of life, though encountering them at every turn, that I suspect this to be the secret (though many persons may not present it to themselves) of the general enjoyment which an audience of vulnerable spectators, liable to pain and sorrow, find in this class of entertainment.

Not long before the Christmas Night in question, I had been told of a patient in Saint Luke's, a woman of great strength and energy, who had been driven mad by an infuriated ox in the streets – an inconvenience not in itself worth mentioning, for which the inhabitants of London are frequently indebted to their inestimable Corporation.[6] She seized the creature literally by the horns, and so, as long as limb and life were in peril, vigorously held him; but, the danger over, she lost her senses, and became one of the most ungovernable of the inmates of the asylum. Why was I there to see this poor creature, when I might have seen a Pantomimic woman gored to any extent by a Pantomimic ox, at any height of ferocity, and have gone home to bed with the comforting assurance that she had rather enjoyed it than otherwise?

The reason of my choice was this. I had received a notification that on that night there would be, in Saint Luke's, "a Christmas Tree for the Patients." And further, that the "usual fortnightly dancing" would take place before the distribution of the gifts upon the tree. So there I was, in the street, looking about for a knocker and finding none.

There was a line of hackney cabriolets by the dead wall; some of the drivers, asleep; some, vigilant; some, with their legs not inexpressive of "Boxing," sticking out of the open doors of their vehicles, while their bodies were reposing on the straw within.[7] There were flaming gas-lights, oranges, oysters, paper lanterns, butchers and grocers, bakers and public-houses, over the way; there were omnibuses rattling by; there were ballad-singers, street cries, street passengers, street beggars, and street music; there were cheap theatres within call, which you would do better to be at some pains to improve, my worthy friends, than to shut up – for, if you will not have them with your own consent at their best, you may be sure that you *must* have them, without it, at their worst; there were wretched little chapels too, where the officiating prophets certainly were not inspired with grammar; there were homes, great and small, by the hundred thousand, east, west, north, and south; all the busy ripple of sane life (or of life, as sane as it ever is) came murmuring on from far away, and broke against the blank walls of the Madhouse, like a sea upon a desert shore.

Abandoning further search for the non-existent knocker, I discovered and rang the bell, and gained admission into Saint Luke's – through a stone courtyard and a hall, adorned with wreaths of holly and like seasonable garniture. I felt disposed to wonder how it looked to patients when they were first received, and whether they distorted it to their own wild fancies, or left it a matter of fact. But, as there was time for a walk through the building before the festivities began, I discarded idle speculation and followed my leader.

Into a long, long gallery: on one side, a few windows; on the other, a great many doors leading to sleeping cells. Dead silence – not utter solitude; for, outside the iron cage enclosing the fire-place between two of the windows, stood a motionless woman. The fire cast a red glare upon the walls, upon the ceiling, and upon the floor, polished by the daily friction of many feet. At the end of the gallery, the common sitting-room. Seated on benches around another caged fire-place, several women: all silent, except one. She, sewing a mad sort of seam, and scolding some imaginary person. (Taciturnity is a symptom of nearly every kind of mania, unless under pressure of excitement. Although the whole lives of some patients are passed together in the same apartment, they are passed in solitude; there is no solitude more complete.) Forms and tables, the only furniture. Nothing in the rooms to remind their inmates of the world outside. No domestic articles to occupy, to interest, or to entice the mind away from its malady. Utter vacuity. Except the scolding woman sewing a purposeless seam, every patient in the room either silently looking at the fire, or silently looking on the ground – or rather through the ground, and at Heaven knows what, beyond.

It was a relief to come to a work-room; with coloured prints over the mantel-shelf, and china shepherdesses upon it; furnished also with tables, a carpet, stuffed chairs, and an open fire. I observed a great difference between the demeanour of the occupants of this apartment and that of the immates of the other room. They were neither so listless nor so sad. Although they did not, while I was present, speak much, they worked with earnestness and diligence. A few noticed my going away, and returned my parting salutation. In a niche – not in a room – but at one end of a cheerless gallery – stood a pianoforte, with a few ragged music-leaves upon the desk. Of course, the music was turned upside down.

Several such galleries on the "female side;" all exactly alike. One, set apart for "boarders" who are incurable; and, towards whose maintenance their friends are required to pay a small weekly sum. The experience of this asylum did not differ, I found, from that of similar establishments, in proving that insanity is more prevalent among women than among men. Of the eighteen thousand seven hundred and fifty-nine inmates, Saint Luke's Hospital has received in the century of its existence, eleven thousand one hundred and sixty-two have been women, and seven thousand five hundred and eighty-seven, men. Female servants are, as is well known, more frequently afflicted with lunacy than any other class of persons. The table, published in the Directors' Report, of the condition in life of the one hundred and seven female inmates admitted in 1850, sets forth that while, under the vague description of "wife of labourer" there were only nine admissions, and under the equally indefinite term "housekeeper," no more than six; there were of women servants, twenty-four.

I passed into one of the galleries on the male side. Three men, engaged at a game of bagatelle; another patient kneeling against the wall apparently in deep prayer; two, walking rapidly up and down the long gallery arm-in-arm, but, as usual, without speaking together; a handsome young man deriving intense gratification from the motion of his fingers as he played with them in the air; two men standing like pillars before the fire-cage; one man, with a newspaper under his arm, walking with great rapidity from one end of the corridor to the other, as if engaged in some important mission which admitted of not a moment's delay. The only furniture in the common sitting-room not peculiar to a prison or a lunatic asylum of the old school, was a newspaper, which was being read by a demented publican. The same oppressive silence – except when the publican complained, in tones of the bitterest satire, against one of the keepers, or (said the publican) "attendant, as I suppose I must call him." The same listless vacuity here, as in the room occupied by the female patients. Despite the large amount of cures effected in the hospital, (upwards of sixty-nine per cent. during the past year,) testifying to the general efficacy of the treatment pursued in it, I think that, if the system of finding the inmates employment, so successful in other hospitals, were introduced into Saint Luke's, the proportion of cures would be much greater. Appended to the latest report of the charity is a table of the weights of the new-comers, compared with the weights of the same individuals when discharged. From this, it appears that their inactivity occasions a rapid accumulation of flesh. Of thirty patients, whose average residence in the hospital extended over eleven weeks, twenty-nine had gained at the average rate of more than one pound per week, each. This can hardly be a gain of health.

On the walls of some of the sleeping cells were the marks of what looked like small alcoves, that had been removed. These indicated the places to which the chairs, which patients were made to sit in for indefinite periods, were, in the good old times, nailed. A couple of these chairs have been preserved in a lumber-room, and are hideous curiosities indeed. As high as the seat, are boxes to enclose the legs, which used to be shut in with spring bolts. The thighs were locked down by a strong cross-board, which also served as a table. The back of this cramping prison is so constructed that the victim could only use his arms and hands in a forward direction; not backward or sideways.

Each sleeping cell has two articles of furniture – a bed and a stool; the latter serving instead of a wardrobe. Many of the patients sleep in single-bedded rooms; but the larger cells are occupied by four inmates. The bedding is comfortable, and the clothing ample. On one bed-place the clothes were folded up, and the bedding had been removed. In its stead, was a small bundle, made up of a pair of boots, a waistcoat, and some stockings. "*That* poor fellow," said my conductor, "died last night – in a fit."

As I was looking at the marks in the walls of the galleries, of the posts to which the patients were formerly chained, sounds of music were heard from a distance. The ball had begun, and we hurried off in the direction of the music.

It was playing in another gallery – a brown sombre place, not brilliantly illuminated by a light at either end, adorned with holly. The staircase by which this gallery was approached, was curtained off at the top, and near the curtain the musicians were cheerfully engaged in getting all the vivacity that could be got, out of their two instruments. At one end were a number of mad men, at the other, a number of mad women, seated on forms. Two or three sets of quadrille dancers were arranged down the centre, and the ball was proceeding with great spirit, but with great decorum.

There were the patients usually to be found in all such asylums, among the dancers. There was the brisk, vain, pippin-faced little old lady, in a fantastic cap – proud of her foot and ankle; there was the old-young woman, with the dishevelled long light hair, spare figure, and weird gentility; there was the vacantly-laughing girl, requiring now and then a warning finger to admonish her; there was the quiet young woman, almost well, and soon going out. For partners, there were the sturdy bull-necked thick-set little fellow who had tried to get away last week; the wry-faced tailor, formerly suicidal, but much improved; the suspicious patient with a countenance of gloom, wandering round and round strangers, furtively eyeing them behind from head to foot, and not indisposed to resent their intrusion. There was the man of happy silliness, pleased with everything. But the only chain that made any clatter was Ladies' Chain;[8] and there was no straiter waistcoat in company than the polka-garment of the old-young woman with the weird gentility, which was of a faded black satin, and languished through the dance with a love-lorn affability and condescension to the force of circumstances, in itself a faint reflection of all Bedlam.

Among those seated on the forms, the usual loss of social habits and the usual solitude in society, were again to be observed. It was very remarkable to see how they huddled together without communicating; how some watched the dancing with lack-lustre eyes, scarcely seeming to know what they watched; how others rested weary heads on hands, and moped; how others had the air of eternally expecting some miraculous visitor who never came, and looking out for some deliverances that never happened. The last figure of the set danced out, the women-dancers instantly returned to their station at one end of the gallery, the men-dancers repaired to *their* station at the other; and all were shut up within themselves in a moment.

The dancers were not all patients. Among them, and dancing with right good will, were attendants, male and female − pleasant-looking men, not at all realising the conventional idea of "keepers" − and pretty women, gracefully though not at all inappropriately dressed, and with looks and smiles as sparkling as one might hope to see in any dance in any place. Also, there were sundry bright young ladies who had helped to make the Christmas tree; and a few members of the resident-officer's family; and, shining above them all, and shining everywhere, his wife;[9] whose clear head and strong heart Heaven inspired to have no Christmas wish beyond this place, but to look upon it as her home, and on its inmates as her afflicted children. And may I see as seasonable a sight as that gentle Christian lady every Christmas that I live, and leave its counterpart in as fair a form in many a nook and corner of the world, to shine, like a star in a dark spot, through all the Christmases to come!

The tree was in a bye room by itself, not lighted yet, but presently to be displayed in all its glory. The porter of the Institution, a brisk young fellow with no end of dancing in him, now proclaimed a song. The announcement being received with loud applause, one of the dancing sisterhood of attendants sang the song, which the musicians accompanied. It was very pretty, and we all applauded to the echo, and seemed (the mad part of us I mean) to like our share in the applause prodigiously, and to take it as a capital point, that we were led by the popular porter. It was so great a success that we very soon called for another song, and then we danced a country-dance, (Porter perpetually going down the middle and up again with Weird-gentility) until the quaint pictures of the Founders, hanging in the adjacent committee-chamber, might have trembled in their frames.

The moment the dance was over, away the porter ran, not in the least out of breath, to help light up the tree. Presently it stood in the centre of its room, growing out of the floor, a blaze of light and glitter; blossoming in that place (as the story goes of the American aloe[10]) for the first time in a hundred years. O shades of Mad Doctors with laced ruffles and powdered wigs, O shades of patients who went mad in the only good old times to be mad or sane in, and who were therefore physicked, whirligigged, chained, handcuffed, beaten, cramped, and tortured, look from

> Wherever in your sightless substances,
> You wait —[11]

on this outlandish weed in the degenerate garden of Saint Luke's!

To one coming freshly from outer life, unused to such scenes, it was a very sad and touching spectacle, when the patients were admitted in a line, to pass round the lighted tree, and admire. I could not but remember with what happy, hopefully-flushed faces, the brilliant toy was associated in my usual knowledge of it, and compare them with the worn cheek, the listless stare, the dull eye raised for a moment and then confusedly dropped, the restless eagerness, the moody surprise, so different from the sweet expectancy and astonishment of children, that came in melancholy array before me. And when the sorrowful procession was closed by "Tommy," the favourite of the house, the harmless old man, with a giggle and a chuckle and a nod for every one, I think I would have rather that Tommy had charged at the tree like a Bull, than that Tommy had been, at once so childish and so dreadfully un-childlike.

We all went out into the gallery again after this survey, and the dazzling fruits of the tree were taken from their boughs, and distributed. The porter, an undeveloped genius in stage-management and mastership of ceremonies, was very active in the distribution, blew all the whistles, played all the trumpets, and nursed all the dolls. That done, we had a wonderful concluding dance, compounded of a country dance and galopade, during which all the popular couples were honored with a general clapping of hands, as they galoped down the middle; and the porter in particular was overwhelmed with plaudits. Finally, we had God Save the Queen, with the whole force of the company; solo parts by the female attendant with the pretty voice who had sung before; chorus led, with loyal animation, by the porter. When I came away, the porter, surrounded by bearers of trays, and busy in the midst of the forms, was delivering out mugs and cake, like a banker dealing at a colossal round game. I daresay he was asleep before I got home; but I left him in that stage of social briskness which is usually described among people who are at large, as "beginning to spend the evening."

Now, there is doubtless a great deal that is mournfully affecting in such a sight. I close this little record of my visit with the statement that the fact is so, because I am not sure but that many people expect far too much. I have known some, after visiting the noblest of our Institutions for this terrible calamity, express their disappointment at the many deplorable cases they had observed with pain, and hint that, after all, the better system could do little. Something of what it can do, and daily does, has been faintly shadowed forth, even in this paper. Wonderful things have been done for the Blind, and for the Deaf and Dumb; but, the utmost is necessarily far inferior to the restoration of the senses of which they are deprived. To lighten the affliction of insanity by all human means, is not to restore the greatest of the Divine gifts; and those who devote themselves to the task do not pretend that it is. They find their sustainment and reward in the substitution of humanity for brutality, kindness for maltreatment, peace for raging fury; in the acquisition of love instead of hatred; and in the knowledge that, from such treatment, improvement, and hope of final restoration will come, if such hope be possible. It may be little to have abolished from mad-houses all that is abolished, and to have substituted all that is substituted. Nevertheless, reader, if you can do a little in any good direction – do it. It will be much, some day.

A Sleep to Startle Us

First published in *Household Words*, 13 March 1852, from which this text is reproduced. Dickens wrote to Miss Burdett Coutts on 19 February 1852 to inform her that on Monday evening he would call on the 'Ragged School Dormitory', and this article is the result of that visit.

At the top of Farringdon Street in the City of London, once adorned by the Fleet Prison and by a diabolical jumble of nuisances in the middle of the road called Fleet Market, is a broad new thoroughfare in a state of transition.[1] A few years hence, and we of the present generation will find it not an easy task to recall, in the thriving street which will arise upon this spot, the wooden barriers and hoardings – the passages that lead to nothing – the glimpses of obscene Field Lane and Saffron Hill – the mounds of earth, old bricks, and oyster-shells – the arched foundations of unbuilt houses – the backs of miserable tenements with patched windows – the odds and ends of fever-stricken courts and alleys – which are the present features of the place. Not less perplexing do I find it now, to reckon how many years have passed since I traversed these byeways one night before they were laid bare, to find out the first Ragged School.[2]

If I say it is ten years ago, I leave a handsome margin. The discovery was then newly made, that to talk soundingly in Parliament, and cheer for Church and State, or to consecrate and confirm without end, or to perorate to any extent in a thousand market-places about all the ordinary topics of patriotic songs and sentiments, was merely to embellish England on a great scale with whited sepulchres, while there was, in every corner of the land where its people were closely accumulated, profound ignorance and perfect barbarism. It was also newly discovered, that out of these noxious sinks where they were born to perish, and where the general ruin was hatching day and night, the people *would not come* to be improved. The gulf between them and all wholesome humanity had swollen to such a depth and breadth, that they were separated from it as by impassable seas or deserts; and so they lived, and so they died: an always-increasing band of outlaws in body and soul, against whom it were to suppose the reversal of all laws, human and divine, to believe that Society could at last prevail.

In this condition of things, a few unaccredited messengers of Christianity, whom no Bishop had ever heard of, and no Government-office Porter had ever seen, resolved to go to the miserable wretches who had lost the way to them; and to set up places of instruction in their own degraded haunts. I found my first Ragged School, in an obscure place called West Street, Saffron Hill, pitifully struggling for life, under every disadvantage. It had no means, it had no suitable rooms, it derived no power or protection from being recognised by any authority, it attracted within its wretched walls a fluctuating swarm of faces − young in years but youthful in nothing else − that scowled Hope out of countenance. It was held in a low-roofed den, in a sickening atmosphere, in the midst of taint and dirt and pestilence: with all the deadly sins let loose, howling and shrieking at the doors. Zeal did not supply the place of method and training; the teachers knew little of their office; the pupils, with an evil sharpness, found them out, got the better of them, derided them, made blasphemous answers to scriptural questions, sang, fought, danced, robbed each other; seemed possessed by legions of devils. The place was stormed and carried, over and over again; the lights were blown out, the books strewn in the gutters, and the female scholars carried off triumphantly to their old wickedness. With no strength in it but its purpose, the school stood it all out and made its way. Some two years since, I found it, one of many such, in a large convenient loft in this transition part of Farringdon Street − quiet and orderly, full, lighted with gas, well whitewashed, numerously attended, and thoroughly established.

The number of houseless creatures who resorted to it, and who were necessarily turned out when it closed, to hide where they could in heaps of moral and physical pollution, filled the managers with pity. To relieve some of the more constant and deserving scholars, they rented a wretched house, where a few common beds − a dozen or a dozen-and-a-half perhaps − were made upon the floors. This was the Ragged School Dormitory; and when I found the School in Farringdon Street, I found the Dormitory in a court hard by, which in the time of the Cholera had acquired a dismal fame. The Dormitory was, in all respects, save as a small beginning, a very discouraging Institution. The air was bad; the dark and ruinous building, with its small close rooms, was quite unsuited to the purpose; and a general supervision of the scattered sleepers was impossible. I had great doubts at the time whether, excepting that they found a crazy shelter for their heads, they were better there than in the streets.

Having heard, in the course of last month, that this Dormitory (there are others elsewhere) had grown as the School had grown, I went the other night to make another visit to it. I found the School in the same place, still advancing. It was now an Industrial School too; and besides the men and boys who were learning – some, aptly enough; some, with painful difficulty; some, sluggishly and wearily; some, not at all – to read and write and cipher; there were two groups, one of shoemakers, and one (in a gallery) of tailors, working with great industry and satisfaction. Each was taught and superintended by a regular workman engaged for the purpose, who delivered out the necessary means and implements. All were employed in mending, either their own dilapidated clothes or shoes, or the dilapidated clothes or shoes of some of the other pupils. They were of all ages, from young boys to old men. They were quiet, and intent upon their work. Some of them were almost as unused to it as I should have shown myself to be if I had tried my hand, but all were deeply interested and profoundly anxious to do it somehow or other. They presented a very remarkable instance of the general desire there is, after all, even in the vagabond breast, to know something useful. One shock-headed man when he had mended his own scrap of a coat, drew it on with such an air of satisfaction, and put himself to so much inconvenience to look at the elbow he had darned, that I thought a new coat (and the mind could not imagine a period when that coat of his was new!) would not have pleased him better. In the other part of the School, where each class was partitioned off by screens adjusted like the boxes in a coffee-room, was some very good writing, and some singing of the multiplication table – the latter, on a principle much too juvenile and innocent for some of the singers. There was also a ciphering-class, where a young pupil teacher[3] out of the streets, who refreshed himself by spitting every half-minute, had written a legible sum in compound addition, on a broken slate, and was walking backward and forward before it, as he worked it, for the instruction of his class, in this way:

Now then! Look here, all on you! Seven and five, how many?

SHARP BOY (in no particular clothes). Twelve!

PUPIL TEACHER. Twelve – and eight?

DULL YOUNG MAN (with water on the brain). Forty-five!

SHARP BOY. Twenty!

PUPIL TEACHER. Twenty. You're right. And nine?

DULL YOUNG MAN (after great consideration). Twenty-nine!

PUPIL TEACHER. Twenty-nine it is. And nine?

RECKLESS GUESSER. Seventy-four!

PUPIL TEACHER. (drawing nine strokes). How can that be! Here's nine on 'em! Look! Twenty-nine, and one's thirty, and one's thirty-one, and one's thirty-two, and one's thirty-three, and one's thirty-four, and one's thirty-five, and one's thirty-six, and one's thirty-seven, and one's what?

RECKLESS GUESSER. Four-and-two-pence farden!

DULL YOUNG MAN (who has been absorbed in the demonstration). Thirty-eight!

PUPIL TEACHER. (restraining sharp boy's ardor). Of course it is! Thirty-eight pence. There they are! (writing 38 in slate-corner). Now what do you make of thirty-eight pence? Thirty-eight pence, how much? (Dull young man slowly considers and gives it up, under a week). How much, you? (to sleepy boy, who stares and says nothing). How much, *you?*

SHARP BOY. Three-and-twopence!

PUPIL TEACHER. Three-and-twopence. How do I put down three-and-twopence?

SHARP BOY. You puts down the two, and you carries the three.

PUPIL TEACHER. Very good. Where do I carry the three?

RECKLESS GUESSER. T' other side the slate!

SHARP BOY. You carries him to the next column on the left hand, and adds him on!

PUPIL TEACHER. And adds him on! and eight and three's eleven, and eight's nineteen, and seven's what?

— And so on.

The best and most spirited teacher was a young man, himself reclaimed through the agency of this School from the lowest depths of misery and debasement, whom the Committee were about to send out to Australia. He appeared quite to deserve the interest they took in him, and his appearance and manner were a strong testimony to the merits of the establishment.

All this was not the Dormitory, but it was the preparation for it. No man or boy is admitted to the Dormitory, unless he is a regular attendant at the school, and unless he has been in the school two hours before the time of opening the Dormitory. If there be reason to suppose that he can get any work to do and will not do it, he is admitted no more, and his place is assigned to some other candidate for the nightly refuge: of whom there are always plenty. There is very little to tempt the idle and profligate. A scanty supper and a scanty breakfast, each of six ounces of bread and nothing else (this quantity is less than the present penny-loaf), would scarcely be regarded by MR. CHADWICK[4] himself as a festive or uproarious entertainment.

I found the Dormitory below the School: with its bare walls and rafters, and bare floor, the building looked rather like an extensive coach-house, well lighted with gas. A wooden gallery had been recently erected on three sides of it; and, abutting from the centre of the wall on the fourth side, was a kind of glazed meat-safe, accessible by a ladder; in which the presiding officer is posted every night, and all night. In the centre of the room, which was very cool, and perfectly sweet, stood a small fixed stove; on two sides, there were windows; on all sides, simple means of admitting fresh air, and releasing foul air. The ventilation of the place, devised by DOCTOR ARNOTT,[5] and particularly the expedient for relieving the sleepers in the galleries from receiving the breath of the sleepers below, is a wonder of simplicity, cheapness, efficiency, and practical good sense. If it had cost five or ten thousand pounds, it would have been famous.

The whole floor of the building, with the exception of a few narrow pathways, was partitioned off into wooden troughs, or shallow boxes without lids – not unlike the fittings in the shop of a dealer in corn and flour, and seeds. The galleries were parcelled out in the same way. Some of these berths were very short – for boys; some, longer – for men. The largest were of very contracted limits; all were composed of the bare boards; each was furnished only with one coarse rug, rolled up. In the brick pathways were iron gratings communicating with trapped drains, enabling the entire surface of these sleeping-places to be soused and flooded with water every morning. The floor of the galleries was cased with zinc, and fitted with gutters and escape-pipes, for the same reason. A supply of water, both for drinking and for washing, and some tin vessels for either purpose, were at hand. A little shed, used by one of the industrial classes, for the chopping up of firewood, did not occupy the whole of the spare space in that corner; and the remainder was devoted to some excellent baths, available also as washing troughs, in order that those who have any rags of linen may clean them once a-week. In aid of this object, a drying-closet, charged with hot-air, was about to be erected in the wood-chopping shed. All these appliances were constructed in the simplest manner, with the commonest means, in the narrowest space, at the lowest cost; but were perfectly adapted to their respective purposes.

I had scarcely made the round of the Dormitory, and looked at all these things, when a moving of feet overhead announced that the School was breaking up for the night. It was succeeded by profound silence, and then by a hymn, sung in a subdued tone, and in very good time and tune, by the learners we had lately seen. Separated from their miserable bodies, the effect of their voices, united in this strain, was infinitely solemn. It was as if their souls were singing – as if the outward differences that parted us had fallen away, and the time was come when all the perverted good that was in them, or that ever might have been in them, arose imploringly to Heaven.

The baker who had brought the bread, and who leaned against a pillar while the singing was in progress, meditating in his way, whatever his way was, now shouldered his basket and retired. The two half-starved attendants (rewarded with a double portion for their pains) heaped the six-ounce loaves into other baskets, and made ready to distribute them. The night-officer arrived, mounted to his meat-safe, unlocked it, hung up his hat, and prepared to spend the evening. I found him to be a very respectable-looking person in black, with a wife and family; engaged in an office all day, and passing his spare time here, from half-past nine every night to six every morning, for a pound a-week. He had carried the post against two hundred competitors.

The door was now opened, and the men and boys who were to pass that night in the Dormitory, in number one hundred and sixty-seven (including a man for whom there was no trough, but who was allowed to rest in the seat by the stove, once occupied by the night-officer before the meat-safe was), came in. They passed to their different sleeping-places, quietly and in good order. Every one sat down in his own crib, where he became presented in a curiously foreshortened manner; and those who had shoes took them off, and placed them in the adjoining path. There were, in the assembly, thieves, cadgers, trampers, vagrants, common outcasts of all sorts. In casual wards and many other Refuges, they would have been very difficult to deal with; but they were restrained here by the law of kindness, and had long since arrived at the knowledge that those who gave them that shelter could have no possible inducement save to do them good. Neighbours spoke little together – they were almost as uncompanionable as mad people – but everybody took his small loaf when the baskets went round, with a thankfulness more or less cheerful, and immediately ate it up.

There was some excitement in consequence of one man being missing; "the lame old man." Everybody had seen the lame old man up-stairs asleep, but he had unaccountably disappeared. What he had been doing with himself was a mystery, but, when the inquiry was at its height, he came shuffling and tumbling in, with his palsied head hanging on his breast – an emaciated drunkard, once a compositor, dying of starvation and decay. He was so near death, that he could not be kept there, lest he should die in the night; and, while it was under deliberation what to do with him, and while his dull lips tried to shape out answers to what was said to him, he was held up by two men. Beside this wreck, but all unconnected with it and with the whole world, was an orphan boy with burning cheeks and great gaunt eager eyes, who was in pressing peril of death too, and who had no possession under the broad sky but a bottle of physic and a scrap of writing. He brought both from the house-surgeon of a Hospital that was too full to admit him, and stood, giddily staggering in one of the little pathways, while the Chief Samaritan read, in hasty characters underlined, how momentous his necessities were. He held the bottle of physic in his claw of a hand, and stood, apparently unconscious of it, staggering, and staring with his bright glazed eyes; a creature, surely, as forlorn and desolate as Mother Earth can have supported on her breast that night. He was gently taken away, along with the dying man, to the workhouse; and he passed into the darkness with his physic-bottle as if he were going into his grave.[6]

The bread eaten to the last crumb; and some drinking of water and washing in water having taken place, with very little stir or noise indeed; preparations were made for passing the night. Some, took off their rags of smock frocks; some, their rags of coats or jackets, and spread them out within their narrow bounds for beds: designing to lie upon them, and use their rugs as a covering. Some, sat up, pondering, on the edges of their troughs; others, who were very tired, rested their unkempt heads upon their hands and their elbows on their knees, and dozed. When there were no more who desired to drink or wash, and all were in their places, the night officer, standing below the meat-safe, read a short evening service, including perhaps as inappropriate a prayer as could possibly be read (as though the Lord's Prayer stood in need of it by way of Rider), and a portion of a chapter from the New Testament. Then, they all sang the Evening Hymn, and then they all lay down to sleep.

It was an awful thing, looking round upon those one hundred and sixty-seven representatives of many thousands, to reflect that a Government, unable, with the least regard to truth, to plead ignorance of the existence of such a place, should proceed as if the sleepers never were to wake again. I do not hesitate to say – why should I, for I know it to be true! – that an annual sum of money, contemptible in amount as compared with any charges upon any list, freely granted in behalf of these Schools, and shackled with no preposterous Red Tape conditions, would relieve the prisons, diminish county rates, clear loads of shame and guilt out of the streets, recruit the army and navy, waft to new countries, Fleets full of useful labor, for which their inhabitants would be thankful and beholden to us. It is no depreciation of the devoted people whom I found presiding here, to add, that with such assistance as a trained knowledge of the business of instruction, and a sound system adjusted to the peculiar difficulties and conditions of this sphere of action, their usefulness could be increased fifty-fold in a few months.

My Lords and Gentlemen, can you, at the present time, consider this at last, and agree to do some little easy thing! Dearly beloved brethren elsewhere, do you know that between Gorham controversies, and Pusey controversies, and Newman controversies, and twenty other edifying controversies, a certain large class of minds in the community is gradually being driven out of all religion? Would it be well, do you think, to come out of the controversies for a little while, and be simply Apostolic thus low down![7]

A Plated Article

First published in *Household Words*, 24 April 1852. This article was written in collaboration with W. H. Wills, and included in the latter's own collection *Old Leaves: Gathered from Household Words* (1860). Nevertheless, Dickens had already selected it for inclusion in *Reprinted Pieces* from which this text is reproduced. Professor Stone suggests that Dickens was responsible for 'writing the long nontechnical opening and the concluding paragraph, and perhaps rewriting portions of the remainder'; and adds: 'why it was included in *Reprinted Pieces*, whether by design or oversight, is a mystery, though the opening of the piece is very fine'.

Putting up for the night in one of the chiefest towns of Staffordshire,[1] I find it to be by no means a lively town. In fact it is as dull and dead a town as any one could desire not to see. It seems as if its whole population might be imprisoned in its Railway Station. The Refreshment Room at that Station is a vortex of dissipation compared with the extinct town-inn, the Dodo, in the dull High Street.[2]

Why High Street? Why not rather Low Street, Flat Street, Low-Spirited Street, Used-up Street? Where are the people who belong to the High Street? Can they all be dispersed over the face of the country, seeking the unfortunate Strolling Manager who decamped from the mouldy little Theatre last week, in the beginning of his season (as his play-bills testify), repentantly resolved to bring him back, and feed him, and be entertained? Or, can they all be gathered to their fathers in the two old churchyards near to the High Street – retirement into which churchyards appears to be a mere ceremony, there is so very little life outside their confines, and such small discernible difference between being buried alive in the town, and buried dead in the town tombs? Over the way, opposite to the staring blank bow windows of the Dodo, are a little ironmonger's shop, a little tailor's shop (with a picture of the Fashions in the small window and a bandy-legged baby on the pavement staring at it) – a watchmaker's shop, where all the clocks and watches must be stopped, I am sure, for they could never have the courage to go, with the town in general, and the Dodo in particular, looking at them. Shade of Miss Linwood, erst of Leicester Square,[3] London, thou art welcome here, and thy retreat is fitly chosen! I myself was one of the last visitors to that awful storehouse of thy life's work, where an anchorite old

334

man and woman took my shilling with a solemn wonder, and conducting me to a gloomy sepulchre of needlework dropping to pieces with dust and age and shrouded in twilight at high noon, left me there, chilled, frightened, and alone. And now, in ghostly letters on all the dead walls of this dead town, I read thy honoured name, and find that thy Last Supper, worked in Berlin Wool, invites inspection as a powerful excitement!

Where are the people who are bidden with so much cry to this feast of little wool? Where are they? Who are they? They are not the bandy-legged baby studying the fashions in the tailor's window. They are not the two earthy ploughmen lounging outside the saddler's shop, in the stiff square where the Town Hall stands, like a brick and mortar private on parade. They are not the landlady of the Dodo in the empty bar, whose eye had trouble in it and no welcome, when I asked for dinner. They are not the turnkeys of the Town Jail, looking out of the gateway in their uniforms, as if they had locked up all the balance (as my American friends would say) of the inhabitants, and could now rest a little. They are not the two dusty millers in the white mill down by the river, where the great water-wheel goes heavily round and round, like the monotonous days and nights in this forgotten place. Then who are they, for there is no one else? No; this deponent maketh oath and saith that there is no one else, save and except the waiter at the Dodo, now laying the cloth. I have paced the streets, and stared at the houses, and am come back to the blank bow window of the Dodo; and the town clocks strike seven, and the reluctant echoes seem to cry, "Don't wake us!" and the bandy-legged baby has gone home to bed.

If the Dodo were only a gregarious bird – if he had only some confused idea of making a comfortable nest – I could hope to get through the hours between this and bed-time, without being consumed by devouring melancholy. But, the Dodo's habits are all wrong. It provides me with a trackless desert of sitting-room, with a chair for every day in the year, a table for every month, and a waste of side-board where a lonely China vase pines in a corner for its mate long departed, and will never make a match with the candlestick in the opposite corner if it live till Doomsday. The Dodo has nothing in the larder. Even now, I behold the Boots returning with my sole in a piece of paper; and with that portion of my dinner, the Boots, perceiving me at the blank bow window, slaps his leg as he comes across the road, pretending it is something else. The Dodo excludes the outer air. When I mount up to my bedroom, a smell of closeness and flue gets lazily up my nose like sleepy snuff. The loose little bits of carpet writhe under my tread, and take wormy shapes. I don't know the ridiculous man in the looking-glass, beyond having met him once or twice in a dish-cover

— and I can never shave *him* to-morrow morning! The Dodo is narrow-minded as to towels; expects me to wash on a freemason's apron without the trimming: when I asked for soap, gives me a stony-hearted something white, with no more lather in it than the Elgin marbles. The Dodo has seen better days, and possesses interminable stables at the back — silent, grass-grown, broken-windowed, horseless.

This mournful bird can fry a sole, however, which is much. Can cook a steak, too, which is more. I wonder where it gets its Sherry? If I were to send my pint of wine to some famous chemist to be analysed, what would it turn out to be made of? It tastes of pepper, sugar, bitter-almonds, vinegar, warm knives, any flat drinks, and a little brandy. Would it unman a Spanish exile by reminding him of his native land at all? I think not. If there really be any townspeople out of the churchyards, and if a caravan of them ever do dine, with a bottle of wine per man, in this desert of the Dodo, it must make good for the doctor next day!

Where was the waiter born? How did he come here? Has he any hope of getting away from here? Does he ever receive a letter, or take a ride upon the railway, or see anything but the Dodo? Perhaps he has seen the Berlin Wool. He appears to have a silent sorrow on him, and it may be that. He clears the table; draws the dingy curtains of the great bow window, which so unwillingly consent to meet, that they must be pinned together; leaves me by the fire with my pint decanter, and a little thin funnel-shaped wine-glass, and a plate of pale biscuits — in themselves engendering desperation.

No book, no newspaper! I left the Arabian Nights in the railway carriage, and have nothing to read but Bradshaw, and "that way madness lies."[4] Remembering what prisoners and shipwrecked mariners have done to exercise their minds in solitude, I repeat the multiplication table, the pence table, and the shilling table: which are all the tables I happen to know. What if I write something? The Dodo keeps no pens but steel pens; and those I always stick through the paper, and can turn to no other account.

What am I to do? Even if I could have the bandy-legged baby knocked up and brought here, I could offer him nothing but sherry, and that would be the death of him. He would never hold up his head again if he touched it. I can't go to bed, because I have conceived a mortal hatred for my bedroom; and I can't go away, because there is no train for my place of destination until morning. To burn the biscuits will be but a fleeting joy; still it is a temporary relief, and here they go on the fire! Shall I break the plate? First let me look at the back, and see who made it. COPELAND.[5]

Copeland! Stop a moment. Was it yesterday I visited Copeland's works, and saw them making plates? In the confusion of travelling about, it might be yesterday or it might be yesterday month; but I think it was yesterday. I appeal to the plate. The plate says, decidedly, yesterday. I find the plate, as I look at it, growing into a companion.

Don't you remember (says the plate) how you steamed away, yesterday morning, in the bright sun and the east wind, along the valley of the sparkling Trent? Don't you recollect how many kilns you flew past, looking like the bowls of gigantic tobacco-pipes, cut short off from the stem and turned upside down? And the fires – and the smoke – and the roads made with bits of crockery, as if all the plates and dishes in the civilised world had been Macadamised[6] expressly for the laming of all the horses? Of course I do!

And don't you remember (says the plate) how you alighted at Stoke – a picturesque heap of houses, kilns, smoke, wharfs, canals, and river, lying (as was most appropriate) in a basin – and how, after climbing up the sides of the basin to look at the prospect, you trundled down again at a walking-match pace, and straight proceeded to my father's, Copeland's, where the whole of my family, high and low, rich and poor, are turned out upon the world from our nursery and seminary, covering some fourteen acres of ground? And don't you remember what we spring from: – heaps of lumps of clay, partially prepared and cleaned in Devonshire and Dorsetshire, whence said clay principally comes – and hills of flint, without which we should want our ringing sound, and should never be musical? And as to the flint, don't you recollect that it is first burnt in kilns, and is then laid under the four iron feet of a demon slave, subject to violent stamping fits, who, when they come on, stamps away insanely with his four iron legs, and would crush all the flint in the Isle of Thanet to powder, without leaving off? And as to the clay, don't you recollect how it is put into mills or teazers, and is sliced, and dug, and cut at, by endless knives, clogged and sticky, but persistent – and is pressed out of that machine through a square trough, whose form it takes – and is cut off in square lumps and thrown into a vat, and there mixed with water, and beaten to a pulp by paddle-wheels – and is then run into a rough house, all rugged beams and ladders splashed with white, – superintended by Grindoff the Miller in his working clothes, all splashed with white, – where it passes through no end of machinery-moved sieves all splashed with white, arranged in an ascending scale of fineness (some so fine, that three hundred silk threads cross each other in a single square inch of their surface), and all in a violent state of ague with their teeth for ever chattering, and their bodies for ever shivering! And as to the flint again, isn't it mashed and mollified and troubled and soothed, exactly

337

as rags are in a paper-mill, until it is reduced to a pap so fine that it contains no atom of "grit" perceptible to the nicest taste? And as to the flint and the clay together, are they not, after all this, mixed in the proportion of five of clay to one of flint, and isn't the compound – known as "slip" – run into oblong troughs, where its superfluous moisture may evaporate; and finally, isn't it slapped and banged and beaten and patted and kneaded and wedged and knocked about like butter, until it becomes a beautiful grey dough, ready for the potter's use?

In regard of the potter, popularly so called (says the plate), you don't mean to say you have forgotten that a workman called a Thrower is the man under whose hand this grey dough takes the shapes of the simpler household vessels as quickly as the eye can follow? You don't mean to say you cannot call him up before you, sitting, with his attendant woman, at his potter's wheel – a disc about the size of a dinner-plate, revolving on two drums slowly or quickly as he wills – who made you a complete breakfast-set for a bachelor, as a good-humoured little off-hand joke. You remember how he took up as much dough as he wanted, and, throwing it on his wheel, in a moment fashioned it into a teacup – caught up more clay and made a saucer – a larger dab and whirled it into a teapot – winked at a smaller dab and converted it into the lid of the teapot, accurately fitting by the measurement of his eye alone – coaxed a middle-sized dab for two seconds, broke it, turned it over at the rim, and made a milkpot – laughed, and turned out a slop-basin – coughed, and provided for the sugar? Neither, I think, are you oblivious of the newer mode of making various articles, but especially basins, according to which improvement a mould revolves instead of a disc? For you *must* remember (says the plate) how you saw the mould of a little basin spinning round and round, and how the workman smoothed and pressed a handful of dough upon it, and how with an instrument called a profile (a piece of wood, representing the profile of a basin's foot) he cleverly scraped and carved the ring which makes the base of any such basin, and then took the basin off the lathe like a doughy skull-cap to be dried, and afterwards (in what is called a green state) to be put into a second lathe, there to be finished and burnished with a steel burnisher? And as to moulding in general (says the plate), it can't be necessary for me to remind you that all ornamental articles, and indeed all articles not quite circular, are made in moulds. For you must remember how you saw the vegetable dishes, for example, being made in moulds; and how the handles of teacups, and the spouts of teapots, and the feet of tureens, and so forth, are all made in little separate moulds, and are each stuck on to the body corporate, of which it is destined to form a part, with a stuff called "slag," as quickly as you can recollect it. Further, you learnt – you know you did – in the same visit, how the beautiful sculptures in the delicate new material called Parian,[7] are all constructed in moulds; how, into that material, animal bones are ground up, because the phosphate of lime contained in bones makes it translucent; how everything is moulded, before going into the fire, one-fourth larger than it is intended to come out of the fire, because it shrinks in that proportion in the intense heat; how, when a figure shrinks unequally, it is spoiled – emerging from the furnace a misshapen birth; a big head and a little body, or a little head and a big body, or a Quasimodo with long arms and short legs, or a Miss Biffin[8] with neither legs nor arms worth mentioning.

And as to the kilns, in which the firing takes place, and in which some of the more precious articles are burnt repeatedly, in various stages of their process towards completion, – as to the kilns (says the plate, warming with the recollection), if you don't remember THEM with a horrible interest, what did you ever go to Copeland's for? When you stood inside of one of those inverted bowls of a pre-Adamite[9] tobacco-pipe, looking up at the blue sky through the open top far off, as you might have looked up from a well, sunk under the centre of the pavement of the Pantheon at Rome, had you the least idea where you were? And when you found yourself surrounded, in that dome-shaped cavern, by innumerable columns of an unearthly order of architecture, supporting nothing, and squeezed close together as if a pre-Adamite Samson had taken a vast Hall in his arms and crushed it into the smallest possible space, had you the least idea what they were? No (says the plate), of course not! And when you found that each of those pillars was a pile of ingeniously made vessels of coarse clay – called Saggers – looking, when separate, like raised-pies for the table of the mighty Giant Blunderbore,[10] and now all full of various articles of pottery ranged in them in baking order, the bottom of each vessel serving for the cover of the one below, and the whole kiln rapidly filling with these, tier upon tier, until the last workman should have barely room to crawl out, before the closing of the jagged aperture in the wall and the kindling of the gradual fire; did you not stand amazed to think that all the year round these dread chambers are heating, white hot – and cooling – and filling – and emptying – and being bricked up – and broken open – humanly speaking, for ever and ever? To be sure you did! And standing in one of those kilns nearly full, and seeing a free crow shoot across the aperture a-top, and learning how the fire would wax hotter and hotter by slow degrees, and would cool similarly through a space of from forty to sixty hours, did no remembrance of the days when human clay was burnt oppress you? Yes. I think so! I suspect that some fancy of a fiery haze and a shortening breath, and a growing heat, and a gasping prayer; and a figure in black interposing between you and the sky (as figures in black are very apt to do), and looking down, before it grew too hot to look and live, upon the Heretic in his edifying agony – I say I suspect (says the plate) that some such fancy was pretty strong upon you when you went out into the air, and blessed God for the bright spring day and the degenerate times!

After that, I needn't remind you what a relief it was to see the simplest process of ornamenting this "biscuit" (as it is called when baked) with brown circles and blue trees – converting it into the common crockery-ware that is exported to Africa, and used in cottages at home. For (says the plate) I am well persuaded that you bear in mind how those particular jugs and mugs were once more set upon a lathe and put in motion; and how a man blew the brown colour (having a strong natural affinity with the material in that condition) on them from a blowpipe as they twirled; and how his daughter, with a common brush, dropped blotches of blue upon them in the right places; and how, tilting the blotches upside down, she made them run into rude images of trees, and there an end.

And didn't you see (says the plate) planted upon my own brother that astounding blue willow, with knobbed and gnarled trunk, and foliage of blue ostrich feathers, which gives our family the title of "willow pattern"? And didn't you observe, transferred upon him at the same time, that blue bridge which spans nothing, growing out from the roots of the willow; and the three blue Chinese going over it into a blue temple, which has a fine crop of blue bushes sprouting out of the roof; and a blue boat sailing above them, the mast of which is burglariously sticking itself into the foundations of a blue villa, suspended sky-high, surmounted by a lump of blue rock, sky-higher, and a couple of billing blue birds, sky-highest – together with the rest of that amusing blue landscape, which has, in deference to our revered ancestors of the Cerulean Empire,[11] and in defiance of every known law of perspective, adorned millions of our family ever since the days of platters? Didn't you inspect the copper-plate on which my pattern was deeply engraved? Didn't you perceive an impression of it taken in cobalt colour at a cylindrical press, upon a leaf of thin paper, streaming from a plunge-bath of soap and water? Wasn't the paper impression daintily spread, by a light-fingered damsel (you *know* you admired her!), over the surface of the plate, and the back of the paper rubbed prodigiously hard – with a long tight roll of flannel, tied up like a round of hung beef – without so much as ruffling the paper, wet as it was? Then (says the plate), was not the paper washed away with a sponge, and didn't there appear, set off upon the plate, *this* identical piece of pre-Raphaelite blue distemper which you now behold? Not to be denied! I had seen all this – and more. I had been shown, at Copeland's, patterns of beautiful design, in faultless perspective, which are causing the ugly old willow to wither out of public favour; and which, being quite as cheap, insinuate good wholesome natural art into the humblest households. When Mr. and Mrs. Sprat[12] have satisfied their material tastes by that equal division of fat and lean which has made their *ménage* immortal; and have, after the elegant tradition, "licked the platter clean," they can – thanks to modern artists in clay – feast their intellectual tastes upon excellent delineations of natural objects.

This reflection prompts me to transfer my attention from the blue plate to the forlorn but cheerfully painted vase on the sideboard. And surely (says the plate) you have not forgotten how the outlines of such groups of flowers as you see there, are printed, just as I was printed, and are afterwards shaded and filled in with metallic colours by women and girls? As to the aristocracy of our order, made of the finer clay – porcelain peers and peeresses; – the slabs, and panels, and table-tops, and tazze; the endless nobility and gentry of dessert, breakfast, and tea services; the gemmed perfume bottles, and scarlet and gold salvers; you saw that they were painted by artists, with metallic colours laid on with camel-hair pencils, and afterwards burnt in.

And talking of burning in (says the plate), didn't you find that every subject, from the willow pattern to the landscape after Turner[13] – having been framed upon clay or porcelain biscuit – has to be glazed? Of course, you saw the glaze – composed of various vitreous materials – laid over every article; and of course you witnessed the close imprisonment of each piece in saggers upon the separate system rigidly enforced by means of fine-pointed earthenware stilts placed between the articles to prevent the slightest communication or contact. We had in my time – and I suppose it is the same now – fourteen hours' firing to fix the glaze and to make it "run" all over us equally, so as to put a good shiny and unscratchable surface upon us. Doubtless, you observed that one sort of glaze – called printing-body – is burnt into the better sort of ware *before* it is printed. Upon this you saw some of the finest steel engravings transferred, to be fixed by an after glazing – didn't you? Why, of course you did!

Of course I did. I had seen and enjoyed everything that the plate recalled to me, and had beheld with admiration how the rotatory motion which keeps this ball of ours in its place in the great scheme, with all its busy mites upon it, was necessary throughout the process, and could only be dispensed with in the fire. So, listening to the plate's reminders, and musing upon them, I got through the evening after all, and went to bed. I made but one sleep of it – for which I have no doubt I am also indebted to the plate – and left the lonely Dodo in the morning, quite at peace with it, before the bandy-legged baby was up.

Down With the Tide

First published in *Household Words*, 5 February 1853, and subsequently published in *Reprinted Pieces* from which this text is taken. Dickens wrote to Wills on 7 October 1852 with an idea: 'If the Waterloo Bridge people would give us a little information about the change in their affair since the railroad – and would let us lay hold of one of their Night Toll-takers, a very fine thing might be perhaps made of it.' A few days later he suggested that they contacted the Thames Police. 'I have a misty notion of some capital papers coming out of it.'

A very dark night it was, and bitter cold; the east wind blowing bleak, and bringing with it stinging particles from marsh, and moor, and fen – from the Great Desert and Old Egypt, may be. Some of the component parts of the sharp-edged vapour that came flying up the Thames at London might be mummy-dust, dry atoms from the Temple at Jerusalem, camels' foot-prints, crocodiles' hatching-places, loosened grains of expression from the visages of blunt-nosed sphynxes, waifs and strays from caravans of turbaned merchants, vegetation from jungles, frozen snow from the Himalayas. O! It was very very dark upon the Thames, and it was bitter bitter cold.

"And yet," said the voice within the great pea-coat[1] at my side, "you'll have seen a good many rivers too, I dare say?"

"Truly," said I, "when I come to think of it, not a few. From the Niagara, downward to the mountain rivers of Italy, which are like the national spirit – very tame, or chafing suddenly and bursting bounds, only to dwindle away again. The Moselle, and the Rhine, and the Rhone; and the Seine, and the Saone; and the St. Lawrence, Mississippi, and Ohio; and the Tiber, the Po, and the Arno; and the —"

Peacoat coughing as if he had had enough of that, I said no more. I could have carried the catalogue on to a teasing length, though, if I had been in the cruel mind.

"And after all," said he, "this looks so dismal?"

"So awful," I returned, "at night. The Seine at Paris is very gloomy too, at such a time, and is probably the scene of far more crime and greater wickedness; but this river looks so broad and vast, so murky and silent, seems such an image of death in the midst of the great city's life, that —"

That Peacoat coughed again. He *could not* stand my holding forth.

We were in a four-oared Thames Police Galley, lying on our oars in the deep shadow of Southwark Bridge – under the corner arch on the Surrey side – having come down with the tide from Vauxhall. We were fain to hold on pretty tight, though close in shore, for the river was swollen and the tide running down very strong. We were watching certain water-rats of human growth, and lay in the deep shade as quiet as mice; our light hidden and our scraps of conversation carried on in whispers. Above us, the massive iron girders of the arch were faintly visible, and below us its ponderous shadow seemed to sink down to the bottom of the stream.

We had been lying here some half an hour. With our backs to the wind, it is true; but the wind being in a determined temper blew straight through us, and would not take the trouble to go round. I would have boarded a fireship to get into action, and mildly suggested as much to my friend Pea.

"No doubt," says he as patiently as possible; "but shore-going tactics wouldn't do with us. River-thieves can always get rid of stolen property in a moment by dropping it overboard. We want to take them *with* the property, so we lurk about and come out upon 'em sharp. If they see us or hear us, over it goes."

Pea's wisdom being indisputable, there was nothing for it but to sit there and be blown through, for another half-hour. The water-rats thinking it wise to abscond at the end of that time without commission of felony, we shot out, disappointed, with the tide.

"Grim they look, don't they?" said Pea, seeing me glance over my shoulder at the lights upon the bridge, and downward at their long crooked reflections in the river.

"Very," said I, "and make one think with a shudder of Suicides. What a night for a dreadful leap from that parapet!"

"Aye, but Waterloo's the favourite bridge for making holes in the water from," returned Pea. "By the bye – avast pulling, lads! – would you like to speak to Waterloo on the subject?"

My face confessing a surprised desire to have some friendly conversation with Waterloo Bridge, and my friend Pea being the most obliging of men, we put about, pulled out of the force of the stream, and in place of going at great speed with the tide, began to strive against it, close in shore again. Every colour but black seemed to have departed from the world. The air was black, the water was black, the barges and hulks were black, the piles were black, the buildings were black, the shadows were only a deeper shade of black upon a black ground. Here and there, a coal fire in an iron cresset blazed upon a wharf; but one knew that it too had been black a little while ago, and would be black again soon. Uncomfortable rushes of water suggestive of gurgling and drowning, ghostly rattlings of iron chains, dismal clankings of discordant engines, formed the music that accompanied the dip of our oars and their rattling in the rullocks. Even the noises had a black sound to me – as the trumpet sounded red to the blind man.

Our dexterous boat's crew made nothing of the tide, and pulled us gallantly up to Waterloo Bridge. Here Pea and I disembarked, passed under the black stone archway, and climbed the steep stone steps. Within a few feet of their summit, Pea presented me to Waterloo (or an eminent toll-taker representing that structure), muffled up to the eyes in a thick shawl, and amply great-coated and fur-capped.

Waterloo received us with cordiality, and observed of the night that it was "a Searcher." He had been originally called the Strand Bridge, he informed us, but had received his present name at the suggestion of the proprietors, when Parliament had resolved to vote three hundred thousand pound for the erection of a monument in honour of the victory. Parliament took the hint (said Waterloo, with the least flavour of misanthropy) and saved the money. Of course the late Duke of Wellington was the first passenger, and of course he paid his penny, and of course a noble lord preserved it evermore. The treadle and index at the toll-house (a most ingenious contrivance for rendering fraud impossible), were invented by Mr. Lethbridge, then property-man at Drury Lane Theatre.

Was it suicide, we wanted to know about? said Waterloo. Ha! Well, he had seen a good deal of that work, he did assure us. He had prevented some. Why, one day a woman, poorish looking, came in between the hatch, slapped down a penny, and wanted to go on without the change! Waterloo suspected this, and says to his mate, "give an eye to the gate," and bolted after her. She had got to the third seat between the piers, and was on the parapet just a going over, when he caught her and gave her in charge. At the police office next morning, she said it was along of trouble and a bad husband.

"Likely enough," observed Waterloo to Pea and myself, as he adjusted his chin in his shawl. "There's a deal of trouble about, you see – and bad husbands too!"

Another time, a young woman at twelve o'clock in the open day, got through, darted along; and, before Waterloo could come near her, jumped upon the parapet, and shot herself over sideways. Alarm given, watermen put off, lucky escape. – Clothes buoyed her up.

"This is where it is," said Waterloo. "If people jump off straight forwards from the middle of the parapet of the bays of the bridge, they are seldom killed by drowning, but are smashed, poor things; that's what *they* are; they dash themselves upon the buttress of the bridge. But you jump off," said Waterloo to me, putting his forefinger in a button-hole of my great-coat; "you jump off from the side of the bay, and you'll tumble, true, into the stream under the arch. What you have got to do, is to mind how you jump in! There was poor Tom Steele from Dublin. Didn't dive! Bless you, didn't dive at all! Fell down so flat into the water, that he broke his breast-bone, and lived two days!"

I asked Waterloo if there were a favourite side of his bridge for this dreadful purpose? He reflected, and thought yes, there was. He should say the Surrey side.

Three decent-looking men went through one day, soberly and quietly, and went on abreast for about a dozen yards: when the middle one, he sung out, all of a sudden, "Here goes, Jack!" and was over in a minute.

Body found? Well. Waterloo didn't rightly recollect about that. They were compositors, *they* were.

He considered it astonishing how quick people were! Why, there was a cab came up one Boxing-night, with a young woman in it, who looked, according to Waterloo's opinion of her, a little the worse for liquor; very handsome she was too – very handsome. She stopped the cab at the gate, and said she'd pay the cabman then, which she did, though there was a little hankering about the fare, because at first she didn't seem quite to know where she wanted to be drove to. However, she paid the man, and the toll too, and looking Waterloo in the face (he thought she knew him, don't you see!) said, "I'll finish it somehow!" Well, the cab went off, leaving Waterloo a little doubtful in his mind, and while it was going on at full speed the young woman jumped out, never fell, hardly staggered, ran along the bridge pavement a little way, passing several people, and jumped over from the second opening. At the inquest it was giv' in evidence that she had been quarrelling at the Hero of Waterloo, and it was brought in jealousy. (One of the results of Waterloo's experience was, that there was a deal of jealousy about.)

"Do we ever get madmen?" said Waterloo, in answer to an inquiry of mine. "Well, we *do* get madmen. Yes, we have had one or two; escaped from 'Sylums, I suppose. One hadn't a halfpenny; and because I wouldn't let him through, he went back a little way, stooped down, took a run, and butted at the hatch like a ram. He smashed his hat rarely, but his head didn't seem no worse – in my opinion on account of his being wrong in it afore. Sometimes people haven't got a halfpenny. If they are really tired and poor we give 'em one and let 'em through. Other people will leave things – pocket-handkerchiefs mostly. I *have* taken cravats and gloves, pocket-knives, tooth-picks, studs, shirt-pins, rings (generally from young gents, early in the morning), but handkerchiefs is the general thing."

"Regular customers?" said Waterloo. "Lord, yes! We have regular customers. One, such a worn-out used-up old file as you can scarcely picter, comes from the Surrey side as regular as ten o'clock at night comes; and goes over, *I* think, to some flash house on the Middlesex side. He comes back, he does, as reg'lar as the clock strikes three in the morning, and then can hardly drag one of his old legs after the other. He always turns down the water-stairs, comes up again, and then goes on down the Waterloo Road. He always does the same thing, and never varies a minute. Does it every night – even Sundays."

I asked Waterloo if he had given his mind to the possibility of this particular customer going down the water-stairs at three o'clock some morning, and never coming up again? He didn't think *that* of him, he replied. In fact, it was Waterloo's opinion, founded on his observation of that file, that he know'd a trick worth two of it.

"There's another queer old customer," said Waterloo, "comes over, as punctual as the almanack, at eleven o'clock on the sixth of January, at eleven o'clock on the fifth of April, at eleven o'clock on the sixth of July, at eleven o'clock on the tenth of October. Drives a shaggy little, rough pony, in a sort of a rattle-trap arm-chair sort of a thing. White hair he has, and white whiskers, and muffles himself up with all manner of shawls. He comes back again the same afternoon, and we never see more of him for three months. He is a captain in the navy – retired – wery old – wery odd – and served with Lord Nelson. He is particular about drawing his pension at Somerset House² afore the clock strikes twelve every quarter. I *have* heerd say that he thinks it wouldn't be according to the Act of Parliament, if he didn't draw it afore twelve."

Having related these anecdotes in a natural manner, which was the best warranty in the world for their genuine nature, our friend Waterloo was sinking deep into his shawl again, as having exhausted his communicative powers and taken in enough east wind, when my other friend Pea in a moment brought him to the surface by asking whether he had not been occasionally the subject of assault and battery in the execution of his duty? Waterloo recovering his spirits, instantly dashed into a new branch of his subject. We learnt how "both these teeth" – here he pointed to the places where two front teeth were not – were knocked out by an ugly customer who one night made a dash at him (Waterloo) while his (the ugly customer's) pal and coadjutor made a dash at the toll-taking apron where the money-pockets were; how Waterloo, letting the teeth go (to Blazes, he observed indefinitely), grappled with the apron-seizer, permitting the ugly one to run away; and how he saved the bank, and captured his man, and consigned him to fine and imprisonment. Also how, on another night, "a Cove" laid hold of Waterloo, then presiding at the horse-gate of his bridge, and threw him unceremoniously over his knee, having first cut his head open with his whip. How Waterloo "got right," and started after the Cove all down the Waterloo Road, through Stamford Street, and round to the foot of Blackfriars Bridge, where the Cove "cut into" a public-house. How Waterloo cut in too; but how an aider and abettor of the Cove's, who happened to be taking a promiscuous drain at the bar, stopped Waterloo; and the Cove cut out again, ran across the road down Holland Street, and where not, and into a beer-shop. How Waterloo breaking away from his detainer was close upon the Cove's heels, attended by no end of people, who, seeing him running with the blood streaming down his face, thought something worse was "up," and roared Fire! and Murder! on the hopeful chance of the matter in hand being one or both. How the Cove was ignominiously taken, in a shed where he had run to hide, and how at the Police Court they at first wanted to make a sessions job of it; but eventually Waterloo was allowed to be "spoke to," and the Cove made it square with Waterloo by paying his doctor's bill (W. was laid up for a week) and giving him "Three, ten." Likewise we learnt what we had faintly suspected before, that your sporting amateur on the Derby day, albeit a captain, can be – "if he be," as Captain Bobadil observes, "so generously minded"[3] – anything but a man of honour and a gentleman; not sufficiently gratifying his nice sense of humour by the witty scattering of flour and rotten eggs on obtuse civilians, but requiring the further excitement of "bilking the toll," and "pitching into" Waterloo, and "cutting him about the head with his whip;" finally being, when called upon to answer for the assault, what Waterloo described as "Minus," or, as I humbly conceived it, not to be found. Likewise did Waterloo inform us, in reply to my inquiries, admiringly and deferentially preferred through my friend Pea, that the takings at the Bridge had more than doubled in amount, since the reduction of the toll one half. And being asked if the aforesaid takings included much bad money, Waterloo responded, with a look far deeper than the deepest part of the river, *he* should think not! – and so retired into his shawl for the rest of the night.

Then did Pea and I once more embark in our four-oared galley, and glide swiftly down the river with the tide. And while the shrewd East rasped and notched us, as with jagged razors, did my friend Pea impart to me confidences of interest relating to the Thames Police; we between whiles

finding "duty boats" hanging in dark corners under banks, like weeds –
our own was a "supervision boat" – and they, as they reported "all right!"
flashing their hidden light on us, and we flashing ours on them. These duty
boats had one sitter in each: an Inspector: and were rowed "Ran-dan,"
which – for the information of those who never graduated, as I was once
proud to do, under a fireman-waterman and winner of Kean's Prize Wherry:[4]
who, in the course of his tuition, took hundreds of gallons of rum and egg
(at my expense) at the various houses of note above and below bridge; not
by any means because he liked it, but to cure a weakness in his liver, for
which the faculty had particularly recommended it – may be explained as
rowed by three men, two pulling an oar each, and one a pair of sculls.

Thus, floating down our black highway, sullenly frowned upon by the
knitted brows of Blackfriars, Southwark, and London, each in his lowering
turn, I was shown by my friend Pea that there are, in the Thames Police
Force, whose district extends from Battersea to Barking Creek, ninety-eight
men, eight duty boats, and two supervision boats; and that these go about
so silently, and lie in wait in such dark places, and so seem to be nowhere,
and so may be anywhere, that they have gradually become a police of
prevention, keeping the river almost clear of any great crimes, even while
the increased vigilance on shore has made it much harder than of yore to
live by "thieving" in the streets. And as to the various kinds of water-thieves,
said my friend Pea, there were the Tier-rangers, who silently dropped
alongside the tiers of shipping in the Pool,[5] by night, and who, going to
the companion-head, listened for two snores – snore number one, the
skipper's; snore number two, the mate's – mates and skippers always snoring
great guns, and being dead sure to be hard at it if they had turned in and
were asleep. Hearing the double fire, down went the Rangers into the
skippers' cabins; groped for the skippers' inexpressibles, which it was the
custom of those gentleman to shake off, watch, money, braces, boots, and
all together, on the floor; and therewith made off as silently as might be.
Then there were the Lumpers, or labourers employed to unload vessels.
They wore loose canvas jackets with a broad hem in the bottom, turned
inside, so as to form a large circular pocket in which they could conceal,
like clowns in pantomimes, packages of surprising sizes. A great deal of
property was stolen in this manner (Pea confided to me) from steamers;
first, because steamers carry a larger number of small packages than other
ships; next, because of the extreme rapidity with which they are obliged to
be unladen for their return voyages. The Lumpers dispose of their booty
easily to marine store dealers, and the only remedy to be suggested is that
marine store shops should be licensed, and thus brought under the eye of

the police as rigidly as public-houses. Lumpers also smuggle goods ashore for the crews of vessels. The smuggling of tobacco is so considerable, that it is well worth the while of the sellers of smuggled tobacco to use hydraulic presses, to squeeze a single pound into a package small enough to be contained in an ordinary pocket. Next, said my friend Pea, there were the Truckers – less thieves than smugglers, whose business it was to land more considerable parcels of goods than the Lumpers could manage. They sometimes sold articles of grocery and so forth, to the crews, in order to cloak their real calling, and get aboard without suspicion. Many of them had boats of their own, and made money. Besides these, there were the Dredgermen, who, under pretence of dredging up coals and such like from the bottom of the river, hung about barges and other undecked craft, and when they saw an opportunity, threw any property they could lay their hands on overboard: in order slyly to dredge it up when the vessel was gone. Sometimes, they dexterously used their dredges to whip away anything that might lie within reach. Some of them were mighty neat at this, and the accomplishment was called dry dredging. Then, there was a vast deal of property, such as copper nails, sheathing, hardwood, &c., habitually brought away by shipwrights and other workmen from their employers' yards, and disposed of to marine store dealers, many of whom escaped detection through hard swearing, and their extraordinary artful ways of accounting for the possession of stolen property. Likewise, there were special-pleading practitioners, for whom barges "drifted away of their own selves" – they having no hand in it, except first cutting them loose, and afterwards plundering them – innocents, meaning no harm, who had the misfortune to observe those foundlings wandering about the Thames.

We were now going in and out, with little noise and great nicety, among the tiers of shipping, whose many hulls, lying close together, rose out of the water like black streets. Here and there, a Scotch, an Irish, or a foreign steamer, getting up her steam as the tide made, looked, with her great chimney and high sides, like a quiet factory among the common buildings. Now, the streets opened into clearer spaces, now contracted into alleys; but the tiers were so like houses, in the dark, that I could almost have believed myself in the narrower bye-ways of Venice. Everything was wonderfully still; for it wanted full three hours of flood, and nothing seemed awake but a dog here and there.

So we took no Tier-rangers captive, nor any Lumpers, nor Truckers, not Dredgermen, nor other evil-disposed person or persons; but went ashore at Wapping, where the old Thames Police-office is now a station-house, and where the old Court, with its cabin windows looking on the river, is a quaint charge-room: with nothing worse in it usually than a stuffed cat in a glass case, and a portrait, pleasant to behold, of a rare old Thames Police officer, Mr. Superintendent Evans, now succeeded by his son. We looked over the charge books, admirably kept, and found the prevention so good that there were not five hundred entries (including drunken and disorderly) in a whole year. Then, we looked into the store-room; where there was an oakum smell, and a nautical seasoning of dreadnought clothing, rope yarn, boat-hooks, sculls and oars, spare stretchers, rudders, pistols, cutlasses, and the like. Then, into the cell, aired high up in the wooden wall through an opening like a kitchen plate-rack: wherein there was a drunken man, not at all warm, and very wishful to know if it were morning yet. Then, into a better sort of watch and ward room, where there was a squadron of stone bottles drawn up, ready to be filled with hot water and applied to any unfortunate creature who might be brought in apparently drowned. Finally, we shook hands with our worthy friend Pea, and ran all the way to Tower Hill, under strong Police suspicion occasionally, before we got warm.

H. W.

First published in *Household Words*, 16 April 1853, this article was written in collaboration with Henry Morley. The text reproduced here is that published in *The Uncollected Writings of Charles Dickens*. Harry Stone suggests that Dickens wrote the portion from the opening to 'undergone or seen', and from 'The copies' to the conclusion.

The subject of this paper is not – as from its title might at first seem probable – the individual who never will go home on affectionate persuasion, to save the life of his nearest and dearest relative. Nor is it that other individual who leaves mysterious trunks, horses, ponies, greyhounds, gigs, watches, wheelbarrows, down long-suffering yards or in patient lodgings, where they run into debt and must at last be sold, unless fetched away within fourteen days. Nor is it that Somebody who appears to have an unaccountable objection to come forward and hear of something to his advantage; nor that impalpable creature who from year's end to year's end is in a convulsive state of advertisement about a lever, or an anchor, or a dove, or a scorpion, or a trumpeter, or a turbot, or some other cabalistic sign tending to the general confusion and madness. H. W. is the shorter name for Household Words by which this Journal is familiarly known among the persons employed in its production; and we purpose to describe the processes by which this Journal is produced.

We have already described the manufacture of paper.[1] But before we can possibly go to the printer's we have to dispose (as we know to our cost) of our Voluntary Correspondent. We will give our readers some account of him in his most irrational aspect.

His name is Legion.[2] He writes everything – on every description of paper, and with every conceivable and inconceivable quality of illegible ink. Like the players in Hamlet, nothing comes amiss to him; "tragedy, comedy, history, pastoral, pastoral-comical, historical-pastoral, tragical-historical, tragical-comical, historical-pastoral, scene individable, or poem unlimited."[3] But if he particularly excel in any one species of composition, it is perhaps, as to our experience, in the poem unlimited.

He has a general idea that literature is the easiest amusement in the world. He figures a successful author as a radiant personage whose whole time is

352

devoted to idleness and pastime – who keeps a prolific mind in a sort of corn-sieve, and lightly shakes a bushel of it out sometimes, in an odd half hour after breakfast. It would amaze his incredulity beyond all measure, to be told that such elements as patience, study, punctuality, determination, self-denial, training of mind and body, hours of application and seclusion to produce what he reads in seconds, enter into such a career. He has no more conception of the necessity of entire devotion to it, than he has of an eternity from the beginning. Correction and re-correction in the blotted manuscript, consideration, new observation, the patient massing of many reflections, experiences and imaginings for one minute purpose, and the patient separation from the heap of all the fragments that will unite to serve it – these would be Unicorns or Griffins to him – fables altogether. Hence, he can often afford to dispense with the low rudiments of orthography; and of the principles of composition it is obvious that he need know nothing.

He is fond of applying himself to literature in a leisure hour, or "a few leisure moments." He "throws his thoughts" upon paper. He rarely sends what he considers his best production. His best production is not copied – somehow, it seldom is. He is aware that there are many remarkable defects in the manuscript he encloses, but if we will insert that, "on the usual terms," he has another at home that will astonish us. He is not at all vain, but he "knows he has it in him." It is possible that it may be in him; but it is certain that under these circumstances it very, very, seldom comes out.

Sometimes he will write, without sending anything, to know "if we are open to voluntary contributors?" He will be informed "Yes, decidedly. If their contributions be adapted to these pages." He will then write again, to know what style of contribution would be preferred? He will be informed in answer that he had better try his own style. He writes back, to the effect that he has no style, no subject, no knowledge, and nothing to tell; and will therefore feel obliged to us for a few suggestions.

He calls sometimes. When he calls, he has often been a captain or a major. He comes with a foregone conclusion that we are always sitting in a padded chair (after a little early corn-sieve practice) open, like some competition of a sporting nature, to All England. He takes it very ill that we don't see him. Considers it ungentlemanly. Had supposed we were a public character, and doesn't understand it. He comes on behalf of a gifted friend, with a tragedy in five acts, a poem in twelve books, or a story that would occupy a volume or two of this publication. He brings it out of a cab, and leaves it in the office, rolled up in paper like a whitey-brown bolster. It bears evident traces of having been in every other office in the wide world, whence any composition in the English language is disseminated through the agency of print and paper. He is written to, and politely informed that the excessive bulk of this treasure renders it (without reference to its intrinsic merits or demerits) quite unsuitable as a blessing to the unhappy H. W. He reappears with all speed, red-faced and ireful, reproduces card, demands explanatory interview, and terrifies publisher. Nothing coming of it, he, on the spot, indites a letter, wherein he communicates to us that as we decline to accept the contribution of his gifted friend, he requires to be informed in writing, for the information of his gifted friend, what our critical opinion is, in detail, of the bolster, and what publisher we recommend for it; for which critical opinion he will call to-morrow afternoon at four precisely. He is again politely written to and informed that we cannot undertake to form and deliver such opinion, having our little hallucinations and labouring under the delusion that we have something else to do. Then he reappears with the cab, and takes the bolster away in extraordinary dudgeon; protesting to the last that he had supposed we were a public character, and that he don't understand it.

She (God bless her! − Mrs. or Miss Legion) is not so angry, but she is an unreasonable Angel, too. She brings little beneficent schemes in bags of Berlin wool, and, though they won't suit us, thinks they will suit our friends: among whom she begs us to distribute two hundred and fifty copies. She is the most amiable woman in the world − but she is impracticable; she is, indeed, though we love her! She brings the flattest and thinnest of little crimson or blue books, published by subscription, and wants to read them to us aloud. When she writes, it is on scented paper, highly glazed, over which all the letters seem to skate, and all the looped letters to tumble down. Her favorite title for poetry is "To a Child," or "To —." We don't know who — is, but we wish he would lead her to the altar. In prose, she addresses the Gentle Reader constantly, and sprinkles with French words. She is invariably persuaded that blanks heighten the interest, and convey an air of reality. She generally begins, "It was on a summer evening in the year eighteen hundred and (blank), near the pretty little town of (blank), where the (blank) river murmurs its rippling way among the rushes, that a youth of handsome mien and fine figure, who might have numbered two-and-twenty summers, and whose expressive countenance was cast in the pure Greek mould." Occasionally, she presents herself in the serious aspect of having some relative to support, and is particularly deserving of the gentlest consideration and respect. Then it is our misery to endeavour to explain to her that what is written for publication can be read for its own merits only; and that it would be as hopeful a resource to play a church organ without any knowledge of, or aptitude for, the instrument, as to play the muse's lyre. In any case and every case, she always forms a profound conviction (and will die in it) that we have never read her manuscript.

What inventors write and come, and what people with grievances of immense duration, and often real grievances too, we will not endeavour to set forth. What numbers of people suppose that to smuggle manuscripts in at our private door is a means of beguiling us into despatching them by express to the printer, instead of an infallible means of delaying their consideration, we will not record. Through how many of these various rocks and shoals every devoted number of H. W. steers its course, our readers may infer from the following facts. In the last year, we read nine hundred manuscripts, of which eleven were available for this journal, after being entirely re-written. In the same period, we received and answered two thousand letters, and made appointments with an odd two or three hundred more of our fellow creatures than there were pounds to pay for the celebrated nails in the horse's shoes, which will go down to posterity rusty with the tears of school-boys.[4] On the other hand, it is delightful to state that five of our very best regular fellow labourers first became known to us, as volunteers, at various periods within the three years and upwards of our existence;[5] and that some remarkable descriptions in this Journal have come to us from wholly unaccustomed writers, who have faithfully and in thorough earnest put down what they have undergone or seen.

Let us suppose a Number of H. W. "made up." In other words, let us suppose the articles it is to contain, their length, their nature, their order of succession, all duly calculated, considered, and decided on. We then go to the printer's.

Since the whole mind of our own nation finds its way into type, a London printing-office is a sort of compound brain, in which the busy working of the thoughts of the community are represented by the rapid flowing of the fount of lead between the fingers of compositors. Permutations and combinations of the letters of the alphabet are carried on incessantly upon the premises of Messrs. Bradbury and Evans, the printers of H. W., and the work of the printer goes on there, as elsewhere, with a rapidity that would have made the blood flush to the head of Guttenberg, or Faust, or Peter Schæffer.[6] Really the world is not greatly to be blamed for idleness, when we consider that it is, after all, only about four hundred years since the art of printing was invented. The legend of the men of Strasburg, who will have it that their townsman Johann Mentelin cut the first types of wood and strung them like beads, side by side, and that Guttenberg was prompted by a runaway from Strasburg – Mentelin's servant, Gänsfleisch (by interpretation Goose meat) – is but among the tales of yesterday. When the art of printing was invented, more than half the knowledge of the best educated portion of the world was nothing beyond what had been taught two thousand years before.

As for the acres of white paper and the ponds of writing ink, the mileage of finger movement that precede the issue of each week's allowance of print to the world, it is enough for us to have indicated how much of that comes under our notice in connexion with the printing of H. W., which is dispersed every week over the country. It is indeed not easy to forget the past when out attention is directed to the mass of printer's labour that is set in action by the pence of our subscribers. When the first printers used their types on the first printed Bible, they were in despair because it had cost them four thousand florins by the time they had printed to the end of the twelfth sheet; and the works issued by them, though some ten times cheaper than written copies, were still what we should now think enormously expensive.

The most familiar portion of the printer's work, as it is done at this day, it is not necessary to describe. Few do not know how the scrap of written paper, placed conveniently before him, is regarded by the compositor in the most literal sense as the production of a man of letters; and how all the author's a's and b's, translated into lead, are reproduced with an impartial fidelity that never troubles itself to consider whether it is reproducing sense or nonsense. From the types arranged, line under line, in lines of a fit length, forming a long column, a rough impression is taken of each article upon three or four long slips of paper, as a proof of the accuracy of the printer's handiwork. A reader in the printing-office then corrects all errors of the kind for which that office is responsible. The printer's work being made so far accurate, and fresh proofs having been printed, those are sent to the office; to which the responsibility attaches of the truth and fitness of the literary workmanship. Alterations are then often made in the matter or the manner of the article. In that case the compositors undo much that they have done; and, with the expedition of good generals, break up their lines to form them again into solid columns. The work of two-fold correction has then of course to be repeated.

The long irregular columns broken into detachments of an equal size, are paired into pages again. Two pages are wedded and bound together, and then, bondage within bondage, four of these couples are wedged within an iron frame or chase, into a square. A set is thus made of eight pages, cunningly arranged with a view to the subsequent folding of the half sheet of paper upon which they will be printed at a single stroke. H. W. is in this form – and in this form only, we would hope – a desperately heavy journal. The mass of type prepared thus for eight pages of a number contains more than forty thousand separate fragments of type, and weighs eighty-seven pounds and a half.

Three such iron-bound tablets of lead contain the matter of one number; and, from these, several proofs are again struck for final correction and revision. When the last amendments have been made, and all is so far accounted satisfactory, the frames containing the compositors' work are carried down into the domains of Vulcan: – for H. W. never appears until it has gone through fire and water.

The two hundred and sixty-two pounds and a half weight of unpublished H. W. are taken down into a vault, which may be regarded as a workshop of Vulcan by reason of the strong fire-heat that is in it. We observe, too, by the light of its three furnaces, a pan of Vulcan's broth – boiling-hot lead soup – in a corner. In other respects we might take the workers in this hot cave for the miller and his men;[7] for they are all covered with a white dust, and white is the prevailing colour of all the splash and soil that is to be seen about the walls and floors and benches. There is a bin filled with white powder in the middle of the room; and, from one corner, there proceeds the sound of water flowing from a tap. In another corner is a gas-jet; for the gloom natural to this work-shop on the basement story is dispelled by gas.

Each stereotype plate is the casting of two pages. The workman takes therefore one pair of leaden pages bound in its frame, lays it before him and beats upon its surface with a broad, flat wooden mallet. The blows of the mallet are intended to abase all stuck-up leads, and to produce a perfect evenness upon the surface of the type from which it is designed to make a casting. After they have had their beating the two pages are carried to another part of the long work-bench, or dresser, that runs along the wall; and, being set down by another workman near the water tap and sink, are covered with a thin cream. "Plaster of Paris mixed with water," the stereotyper tells us. "That's for the quads."

"O yes, certainly. The quads of course. By the bye, what are the quads?"

"Quadrats, sir. We call 'em quads."

"Exactly. Yes. And so you take a casting?"

"Bless you, no, sir, you don't seem to understand. Quads are the spaces left between the paragraphs that come white on the paper. If you look here, at this page that is set-up, you will see that they are deeper than the spaces left between the words and letters – regular little trenches. We don't want any of them. We must have all the spaces of an equal depth."

"And so you cover the whole mass with a thin mud of plaster; which that mischievous young monkey there is washing off again."

"Yes, he's bound to do that, and then I, with a soft brush, go and rub at it; but, look you, my brush sweeps the plaster from about the letters and between them, but it passes over the top of the deep quads and smooths it into *them*. I made the heights all even with a mallet, now I'm evening the depths with plaster and a hair-brush."

Cunning workman, you are understood. You need not explain why you in the next place with a delicate touch wipe fine oil over the types you have prepared; you are about to take a casting of those pages of the work whose title you and your brethren so irreverently shorten.

A collar is placed about the lump of H. W. which fits it, and sticks up around it, sloping outwards. The type and its new collar together make a pudding-pan; and, into the pan plaster pudding – mixed by hand in a large bowl – is, in the next place, carefully poured. Carefully, because at first it must be rubbed and smoothed, and perfectly insinuated between every crevice; the sharp outline of no letter must be rounded by a bubble. When the pan is full, the pudding stands to set, the top of it being in the meantime scraped smooth and flat. In less than a quarter of an hour, it is firm enough to be lifted by its frame, upon the bevelled sides of which it is supported, and the heavy types, forming the false bottom to the pan, are left behind. A plaster cast, shaped like a little Yorkshire pudding, has upon one side of it an accurate impression of those two pages of H. W. The characters inscribed thus upon pudding remind one very much of Nineveh and Babylon, but not at all of sixteen, Wellington Street North, Strand, London.[8] Since this cast is the mould or sop which will be dipped presently into the pan of Vulcan's gravy, "you see, sir," says the cunning workman, "if I hadn't made the back of it quite even, the hot lead would lie more on one part than another, and the plaster then would crack. Next-a-ways all the damp must be got out, and so we put the casts into these ovens to be dried. They want care. I don't understand what they want in thermometer degrees, but I know the exact heat by practice – this way: with my bare arm thrust into the oven."

The mould being quite dry, the demonstrator takes a piece of metal that resembles it in shape and size. "This," he says, "is a float. You see there's a rim round the cast side of the mould. The plaster was allowed to run down for the purpose of a making of it. I just smooth that with a knife, and nick it in a place or two, and lay the plaster cast side downwards, on the float. Now when that goes into the metal, metal can flow in between the nicks. Nextly here is the great pan without a lid, full of metal whereof stereotype plates are made; six parts lead, hardened with one part antimony. The metal's now at melting heat. Here's a crane over it, with a fixed plate hanging to it. Under the plate we put the plaster mould, with the float or swimming jacket under that, and down they all go for a warm bath. Now you see the float won't sink willingly, and the plate fastened to the crane can't rise: the plaster is between the two, and the float at the bottom. What's the results? The float pushes the plaster up, and keeps it fastened tight with its flat back against the plate above it. The metal forces in between the notches, but the float won't be shoved down by the metal, and forces that up consequently into every cranny of the plaster mould. What's the results again? We take it out and cool it with a little water, and there you have two pages of H. W. stereotyped on one plate – beautiful to look at! Just like a married couple."

From this plate the two pages will be printed, if it be not found faulty in another room, to which we follow it. It is there subjected to the criticism of another censor; who looks through it letter by letter, picks it over with a graver, and rejects it if it contain any flaw that cannot be removed in his department. If accepted by him it is subjected to further treatment. The pair of pages, now existing as a solid plate, will be again united under the printing press with the pairs from which it had parted; they will all meet again in their new form, and when they do meet, it will be as necessary that the separate stereotype plates should lie evenly side by side under the paper, as that the letters in each plate should present a level surface. Their edges are therefore cut by a machine. Their backs are first smoothed by a turning lathe. They are then placed on a flat table, and passed under a blade, so adjusted as to produce among all plates submitted to its cutting scrutiny, an almost perfect uniformity of thickness. Out of this room the plate of H. W., containing as we have said two pages, is sent to be used in its place for the actual printing of a weekly number.

Under the press, however, it is again subjected to criticism. The plates that belong together are slipped into nests prepared for their reception; of which the outer rims print off as borders to the pages. An impression is then taken, upon paper, of the entire set of pages, and the printed sheet is carefully examined; faults corrected, and then the great steam-press begins its labour. Under its two revolving cylinders are grouped the plates which represent the two halves of the forthcoming number of H. W. The two halves correspond to the two sides of our weekly sheet. Upon a peak covered with snowy paper that commands the upper surface of one cylinder there is a youth. He dexterously fits the paper, sheet by sheet, upon the lips of the devouring engine. As it heaves and works, the paper is drawn rapidly into a black abyss. It is rolled over the mass of metal characters, which is perpetually fertilised with printer's ink by mystic rollers. One cylinder passes the sheet printed upon one side, to another. Over that it leaps, and from under that it is delivered perfect, and placed quietly upon a table, ready to the fingers of a little boy, who helps it in its easy birth. The press works, one among many that appear to be engaged in voluntary labour side by side. Men and boys are reaping the advantage of their industry. Our youth upon the peak administers white sheets of paper to the busy monster labouring on our behalf. As fast as they are put into its mouth, like great square lozenges, they are all sucked away at the rate of nine hundred an hour. At the same rate, completely printed copies of H. W. are laid upon the table of the second boy and piled by him into a cube. The dimensions of the cube are constantly kept under by other boys who carry parts of it away. But our H. W. is not even yet ready to appear before the public.

Who does not entertain a proper horror of damp sheets? The sheets of H. W. are sent out of the great hall of steam-presses into a drying room. There they are hung up and aired. The sheets of H. W. are in the next place mangled. They endure a whole day under a powerful hydraulic press. The sheets of H. W. are neatly folded by the tidy hands of women.

The copies of each number which has in this way run the gauntlet down so long a lane of labour, are, at last, brought by boys upon their heads, upon their shoulders, upon their backs, upon their breasts, over their arms, and under them, to sixteen, Wellington Street North, in the Strand. From that place, on a given day, and punctually after a given hour, they are issued to a race of individuals who carry them away in bags, in pouches, in pockets; in hands, on heads, shoulders, backs; in cabs, in carts, and in trucks to the warehouses and shops of the metropolis to be sold to the public. From the warehouses they travel in detachments to the railway stations, and from railway stations many travel to the ships. So each number at last finds its owner out, who by some article he sees in it is perhaps prompted to become a sensible Voluntary Correspondent, and send up to H. W. a little bag – or a large sack – of grist. So the mill goes.

A Nightly Scene in London

First published in *Household Words*, 26 January 1856, from which this text is reproduced. On 9 January 1856 Dickens sent the proof to Wills and said of his account: 'It is perfectly accurate, except that the case is under-stated.'

On the fifth of last November, I, the Conductor of this journal,[1] accompanied by a friend well-known to the public,[2] accidentally strayed into Whitechapel. It was a miserable evening; very dark, very muddy, and raining hard.

There are many woful sights in that part of London, and it has been well-known to me in most of its aspects for many years. We had forgotten the mud and rain in slowly walking along and looking about us, when we found ourselves, at eight o'clock, before the Workhouse.

Crouched against the wall of the Workhouse, in the dark street, on the muddy pavement-stones, with the rain raining upon them, were five bundles of rags. They were motionless, and had no resemblance to the human form. Five great beehives, covered with rags – five dead bodies taken out of graves, tied neck and heels, and covered with rags – would have looked like those five bundles upon which the rain rained down in the public street.

"What is this!" said my companion. "What *is* this!"

"Some miserable people shut out of the Casual Ward,[3] I think," said I.

We had stopped before the five ragged mounds, and were quite rooted to the spot by their horrible appearance. Five awful Sphinxes by the wayside, crying to every passer-by, "Stop and guess! What is to be the end of a state of society that leaves us here!"

As we stood looking at them, a decent working-man, having the appearance of a stone-mason, touched me on the shoulder.

"This is an awful sight, sir," said he, "in a Christian country!"

"God knows it is, my friend," said I.

"I have often seen it much worse than this, as I have been going home from my work. I have counted fifteen, twenty, five-and-twenty, many a time. It's a shocking thing to see."

"A shocking thing, indeed," said I and my companion together. The man lingered near us a little while, wished us good-night, and went on.

We should have felt it brutal in us who had a better chance of being heard than the working-man, to leave the thing as it was, so we knocked at the Workhouse Gate. I undertook to be spokesman. The moment the gate was opened by an old pauper, I went in, followed close by my companion. I lost no time in passing the old porter, for I saw in his watery eye a disposition to shut us out.

"Be so good as to give that card to the master of the Workhouse, and say I shall be glad to speak to him for a moment."

We were in a kind of covered gateway, and the old porter went across it with the card. Before he had got to a door on our left, a man in a cloak and hat bounced out of it very sharply, as if he were in the nightly habit of being bullied and of returning the compliment.

"Now, gentlemen," said he in a loud voice, "what do you want here?"

"First," said I, "will you do me the favour to look at that card in your hand. Perhaps you may know my name."

"Yes," says he, looking at it. "I know this name."

"Good. I only want to ask you a plain question in a civil manner, and there is not the least occasion for either of us to be angry. It would be very foolish in me to blame you, and I don't blame you. I may find fault with the system you administer, but pray understand that I know you are here to do a duty pointed out to you, and that I have no doubt you do it. Now, I hope you won't object to tell me what I want to know."

"No," said he, quite mollified, and very reasonable, "not at all. What is it?"

"Do you know that there are five wretched creatures outside?"

"I haven't seen them, but I dare say there are."

"Do you doubt that there are?"

"No, not at all. There might be many more."

"Are they men? Or women?"

"Women, I suppose. Very likely one or two of them were there last night, and the night before last."

"There all night, do you mean?"

"Very likely."

My companion and I looked at one another, and the master of the Workhouse added quickly, "Why, Lord bless my soul, what am I to do? What can I do? The place is full. The place is always full – every night. I must give the preference to women with children, mustn't I? You wouldn't have me not do that?"

"Surely not," said I. "It is a very humane principle, and quite right; and I am glad to hear of it. Don't forget that I don't blame *you*."

"Well!" said he. And subdued himself again.

"What I want to ask you," I went on, "is whether you know anything against those five miserable beings outside?"

"Don't know anything about them," said he, with a wave of his arm.

"I ask, for this reason: that we mean to give them a trifle to get a lodging – if they are not shelterless because they are thieves for instance. – You don't know them to be thieves?"

"I don't know anything about them," he repeated emphatically.

"That is to say, they are shut out, solely because the Ward is full?"

"Because the Ward is full."

"And if they got in, they would only have a roof for the night and a bit of bread in the morning, I suppose?"

"That's all. You'll use your own discretion about what you give them. Only understand that I don't know anything about them beyond what I have told you."

"Just so. I wanted to know no more. You have answered my question civilly and readily, and I am much obliged to you. I have nothing to say against you, but quite the contrary. Good-night!"

"Good-night, gentlemen!" And out we came again.

We went to the ragged bundle nearest to the Workhouse-door, and I touched it. No movement replying, I gently shook it. The rags began to be slowly stirred within, and by little and little a head was unshrouded. The head of a young woman of three or four and twenty, as I should judge; gaunt with want, and foul with dirt; but not naturally ugly.

"Tell us," said I, stooping down. "Why are you lying here?"

"Because I can't get into the Workhouse."

She spoke in a faint dull way, and had no curiosity or interest left. She looked dreamily at the black sky and the falling rain, but never looked at me or my companion.

"Were you here last night?"

"Yes. All last night. And the night afore too."

"Do you know any of these others?"

"I know her next but one. She was here last night, and she told me she come out of Essex. I don't know no more of her."

"You were here all last night, but you have not been here all day?"

"No. Not all day."

"Where have you been all day?"

"About the streets."

"What have you had to eat?"

"Nothing."

"Come!" said I. "Think a little. You are tired and have been asleep, and

363

don't quite consider what you are saying to us. You have had something to eat to-day. Come! Think of it!"

"No I haven't. Nothing but such bits as I could pick up about the market. *Why, look at me!*"

She bared her neck, and I covered it up again.

"If you had a shilling to get some supper and a lodging, should you know where to get it?"

"Yes. I could do that."

"FOR GOD's sake get it then!"

I put the money into her hand, and she feebly rose up and went away. She never thanked me, never looked at me – melted away into the miserable night, in the strangest manner I ever saw. I have seen many strange things, but not one that has left a deeper impression on my memory than the dull impassive way in which that worn-out heap of misery took that piece of money, and was lost.

One by one I spoke to all the five. In every one, interest and curiosity were as extinct as in the first. They were all dull and languid. No one made any sort of profession or complaint; no one cared to look at me; no one thanked me. When I came to the third, I suppose she saw that my companion and I glanced, with a new horror upon us, at the last two, who had dropped against each other in their sleep, and were lying like broken images. She said, she believed they were young sisters. These were the only words that were originated among the five.

And now let me close this terrible account with a redeeming and beautiful trait of the poorest of the poor. When we came out of the Workhouse, we had gone across the road to a public house, finding ourselves without silver, to get change for a sovereign. I held the money in my hand while I was speaking to the five apparitions. Our being so engaged, attracted the attention of many people of the very poor sort usual to that place; as we leaned over the mounds of rags, they eagerly leaned over us to see and hear; what I had in my hand, and what I said, and what I did, must have been plain to nearly all the concourse. When the last of the five had got up and faded away, the spectators opened to let us pass; and not one of them, by word, or look, or gesture, begged of us. Many of the observant faces were quick enough to know that it would have been a relief to us to have got rid of the rest of the money with any hope of doing good with it. But, there was a feeling among them all, that their necessities were not to be placed by the side of such a spectacle; and they opened a way for us in profound silence, and let us go.

My companion wrote to me, next day, that the five ragged bundles had been upon his bed all night. I debated how to add our testimony to that of many other persons who from time to time are impelled to write to the newspapers, by having come upon some shameful and shocking sight of this description. I resolved to write in these pages an exact account of what we had seen, but to wait until after Christmas, in order that there might be no heat or haste. I know that the unreasonable disciples of a reasonable school, demented disciples who push arithmetic and political economy beyond all bounds of sense (not to speak of such a weakness as humanity), and hold them to be all-sufficient for every case, can easily prove that such things ought to be, and that no man has any business to mind them. Without disparaging those indispensable sciences in their sanity, I utterly renounce and abominate them in their insanity; and I address people with a respect for the spirit of the New Testament, who do mind such things, and who think them infamous in our streets.

Wapping Workhouse

First published in *All the Year Round*, 3 February 1860, and subsequently in *The Uncommercial Traveller* from which this text is taken.

My day's no-business beckoning me to the East-end of London, I had turned my face to that point of the metropolitan compass on leaving Covent-garden, and had got past the India House, thinking in my idle manner of Tippoo-Sahib and Charles Lamb,[1] and had got past my little wooden mid-shipman,[2] after affectionately patting him on one leg of his knee-shorts for old acquaintance' sake, and had got past Aldgate Pump,[3] and had got past the Saracen's Head[4] (with an ignominious rash of posting bills disfiguring his swarthy countenance), and had strolled up the empty yard of his ancient neighbour the Black or Blue Boar, or Bull,[5] who departed this life I don't know when, and whose coaches are all gone I don't know where; and I had come out again into the age of railways, and I had got past Whitechapel Church, and was – rather inappropriately for an Uncommercial Traveller – in the Commercial Road. Pleasantly wallowing in the abundant mud of that thoroughfare, and greatly enjoying the huge piles of building belonging to the sugar refiners, the little masts and vanes in small back gardens in back streets, the neighbouring canals and docks, the India vans lumbering along their stone tramway, and the pawnbrokers' shops where hard-up Mates had pawned so many sextants and quadrants, that I should have bought a few cheap if I had the least notion how to use them, I at last began to file off to the right, towards Wapping.

Not that I intended to take boat at Wapping Old Stairs, or that I was going to look at the locality, because I believe (for I don't) in the constancy of the young woman who told her sea-going lover, to such a beautiful old tune, that she had ever continued the same, since she gave him the 'baccer-box marked with his name; I am afraid he usually got the worst of those transactions, and was frightfully taken in.[6] No, I was going to Wapping, because an Eastern police magistrate had said, through the morning papers, that there was no classification at the Wapping workhouse for women, and that it was a disgrace and a shame, and divers other hard names, and because I wished to see how the fact really stood. For, that Eastern police magistrates are not always the wisest men of the East, may be inferred from their course of procedure respecting the fancy-dressing and pantomime-posturing at St. George's[7] in that quarter: which is usually, to discuss the matter at issue, in a state of mind betokening the weakest perplexity, with all parties concerned and unconcerned, and, for a final expedient, to consult the complainant as to what he thinks ought to be done with the defendant, and take the defendant's opinion as to what he would recommend to be done with himself.

Long before I reached Wapping, I gave myself up as having lost my way, and, abandoning myself to the narrow streets in a Turkish frame of mind, relied on predestination to bring me somehow or other to the place I wanted if I were ever to get there. When I had ceased for an hour or so to take any trouble about the matter, I found myself on a swing-bridge looking down at some dark locks in some dirty water. Over against me, stood a creature remotely in the likeness of a young man, with a puffed sallow face, and a figure all dirty and shiny and slimy, who may have been the youngest son of his filthy old father, Thames, or the drowned man about whom there was a placard on the granite post like a large thimble, that stood between us.

I asked this apparition what it called the place? Unto which, it replied, with a ghastly grin and a sound like gurgling water in its throat:

"Mr. Baker's trap."

As it is a point of great sensitiveness with me on such occasions to be equal to the intellectual pressure of the conversation, I deeply considered the meaning of this speech, while I eyed the apparition – then engaged in hugging and sucking a horizontal iron bar at the top of the locks. Inspiration suggested to me that Mr. Baker was the acting coroner of that neighbourhood.

"A common place for suicide," said I, looking down at the locks.

"Sue?" returned the ghost, with a stare. "Yes! And Poll. Likewise Emily. And Nancy. And Jane;" he sucked the iron between each name; "and all the bileing. Ketches off their bonnets or shorls, takes a run, and headers down here, they doos. Always a headerin' down here, they is. Like one o'clock."

"And at about that hour of the morning, I suppose?"

"Ah!" said the apparition. "*They* an't partickler. Two 'ull do for *them*. Three. All times o' night. On'y mind you!" Here the apparition rested his profile on the bar, and gurgled in a sarcastic manner. "There must be somebody comin'. They don't go a headerin' down here, wen there an't no Bobby nor gen'ral Cove, fur to hear the splash."

According to my interpretation of these words, I was myself a General Cove, or member of the miscellaneous public. In which modest character I remarked:

"They are often taken out, are they, and restored?"

"I dunno about restored," said the apparition, who, for some occult reason, very much objected to that word; "they're carried into the werkiss and put into a 'ot bath, and brought round. But I dunno about restored," said the apparition; "blow *that!*" – and vanished.

As it had shown a desire to become offensive, I was not sorry to find myself alone, especially as the "werkiss" it had indicated with a twist of its matted head, was close at hand. So I left Mr. Baker's terrible trap (baited with a scum that was like the soapy rinsing of sooty chimneys), and made bold to ring at the workhouse gate, where I was wholly unexpected and quite unknown.

A very bright and nimble little matron, with a bunch of keys in her hand, responded to my request to see the House. I began to doubt whether the police magistrate was quite right in his facts, when I noticed her quick active little figure and her intelligent eyes.

The Traveller (the matron intimated) should see the worst first. He was welcome to see everything. Such as it was, there it all was.

This was the only preparation for our entering "the Foul wards." They were in an old building squeezed away in a corner of a paved yard, quite detached from the more modern and spacious main body of the workhouse. They were in a building most monstrously behind the time – a mere series of garrets or lofts, with every inconvenient and objectionable circumstance in their construction, and only accessible by steep and narrow staircases, infamously ill-adapted for the passage up-stairs of the sick or down-stairs of the dead.

A-bed in these miserable rooms, here on bedsteads, there (for a change, as I understood it) on the floor, were women in every stage of distress and disease. None but those who have attentively observed such scenes, can conceive the extraordinary variety of expression still latent under the general monotony and uniformity of colour, attitude, and condition. The form a little coiled up and turned away, as though it had turned its back on this world for ever; the uninterested face at once lead-coloured and yellow, looking passively upward from the pillow; the haggard mouth a little dropped, the hand outside the coverlet, so dull and indifferent, so light, and yet so heavy; these were on every pallet; but when I stopped beside a bed, and said ever so slight a word to the figure lying there, the ghost of the old character came into the face, and made the Foul ward as various as the fair world. No one appeared to care to live, but no one complained; all who could speak, said that as much was done for them as could be done there, that the attendance was kind and patient, that their suffering was very heavy, but they had nothing to ask for. The wretched rooms were as clean and sweet as it is possible for such rooms to be; they would become a pest-house in a single week, if they were ill-kept.

I accompanied the brisk matron up another barbarous staircase, into a better kind of loft devoted to the idiotic and imbecile. There was at least Light in it, whereas the windows in the former wards had been like sides of school-boys' bird-cages. There was a strong grating over the fire here, and, holding a kind of state on either side of the hearth, separated by the breadth of this grating, were two old ladies in a condition of feeble dignity, which was surely the very last and lowest reduction of self-complacency, to be found in this wonderful humanity of ours. They were evidently jealous of each other, and passed their whole time (as some people do, whose fires are not grated) in mentally disparaging each other, and contemptuously watching their neighbours. One of these parodies on provincial gentlewomen was extremely talkative, and expressed a strong desire to attend the service on Sundays, from which she represented herself to have derived the greatest interest and consolation when allowed that privilege. She gossiped so well, and looked altogether so cheery and harmless, that I began to think this a case for the Eastern magistrate, until I found that on the last occasion of her attending chapel she had secreted a small stick, and had caused some confusion in the responses by suddenly producing it and belabouring the congregation.

So, these two old ladies, separated by the breadth of the grating – otherwise they would fly at one another's caps – sat all day long, suspecting one another, and contemplating a world of fits. For, everybody else in the room had fits, except the wards-woman; an elderly, able-bodied pauperess, with a large upper lip, and an air of repressing and saving her strength, as she stood with her hands folded before her, and her eyes slowly rolling, biding her time for catching or holding somebody. This civil personage (in whom I regretted to identify a reduced member of my honourable friend Mrs. Gamp's[8] family) said, "They has 'em continiwal, sir. They drops without no more notice than if they was coach-horses dropped from the moon, sir. And when one drops, another drops, and sometimes there'll be as many as four or five on 'em at once, dear me, a rolling and a tearin', bless you! – this young woman, now, has 'em dreadful bad."

She turned up this young woman's face with her hand as she said it. This young woman was seated on the floor, pondering in the foreground of the afflicted. There was nothing repellant either in her face or head. Many, apparently worse, varieties of epilepsy and hysteria were about her, but she was said to be the worst here. When I had spoken to her a little, she still sat with her face turned up, pondering, and a gleam of the mid-day sun shone in upon her.

— Whether this young woman, and the rest of these so sorely troubled, as they sit or lie pondering in their confused dull way, ever get mental glimpses among the motes in the sunlight, of healthy people and healthy things? Whether this young woman, brooding like this in the summer season, ever thinks that somewhere there are trees and flowers, even mountains and the great sea? Whether, not to go so far, this young woman ever has any dim revelation of that young woman — that young woman who is not here and never will come here; who is courted, and caressed, and loved, and has a husband, and bears children, and lives in a home, and who never knows what it is to have this lashing and tearing coming upon her? And whether this young woman, God help her, gives herself up then and drops like a coach-horse from the moon?

I hardly knew whether the voices of infant children, penetrating into so hopeless a place, made a sound that was pleasant or painful to me. It was something to be reminded that the weary world was not all aweary, and was ever renewing itself; but, this young woman was a child not long ago, and a child not long hence might be such as she. Howbeit, the active step and eye of the vigilant matron conducted me past the two provincial gentlewomen (whose dignity was ruffled by the children), and into the adjacent nursery.

There were many babies here, and more than one handsome young mother. There were ugly young mothers also, and sullen young mothers, and callous young mothers. But, the babies had not appropriated to themselves any bad expression yet, and might have been, for anything that appeared to the contrary in their soft faces, Princes Imperial, and Princesses Royal. I had the pleasure of giving a poetical commission to the baker's man to make a cake with all despatch and toss it into the oven for one red-headed young pauper and myself, and felt much the better for it. Without that refreshment, I doubt if I should have been in a condition for "the Refractories," towards whom my quick little matron — for whose adaptation to her office I had by this time conceived a genuine respect — drew me next, and marshalled me the way that I was going.

The Refractories were picking oakum,[9] in a small room giving on a yard. They sat in line on a form, with their backs to a window; before them, a table, and their work. The oldest Refractory was, say twenty; youngest

Refractory, say sixteen. I have never yet ascertained in the course of my uncommercial travels, why a Refractory habit should affect the tonsils and uvula; but, I have always observed that Refractories of both sexes and every grade, between a Ragged School and the Old Bailey, have one voice, in which the tonsils and uvula gain a diseased ascendency.

"Five pound indeed! I hain't a going fur to pick five pound," said the Chief of the Refractories, keeping time to herself with her head and chin. "More than enough to pick what we picks now, in sich a place as this, and on wot we gets here!"

(This was in acknowledgment of a delicate intimation that the amount of work was likely to be increased. It certainly was not heavy then, for one Refractory had already done her day's task – it was barely two o'clock – and was sitting behind it, with a head exactly matching it.)

"A pretty Ouse this is, matron, ain't it?" said Refractory Two, "where a pleeseman's called in, if a gal says a word!"

"And wen you're sent to prison for nothink or less!" said the Chief, tugging at her oakum as if it were the matron's hair. "But any place is better than this; that's one thing, and be thankful!"

A laugh of Refractories led by Oakum Head with folded arms – who originated nothing, but who was in command of the skirmishers outside the conversation.

"If any place is better than this," said my brisk guide, in the calmest manner, "it is a pity you left a good place when you had one."

"Ho, no, I didn't, matron," returned the Chief, with another pull at her oakum, and a very expressive look at the enemy's forehead. "Don't say that, matron, cos it's lies!"

Oakum Head brought up the skirmishers again, skirmished, and retired.

"And *I* warn't a going," exclaimed Refractory Two, "though I was in one place for as long as four year – *I* warn't a going fur to stop in a place that warn't fit for me – there! And where the family warn't 'spectable characters – there! And where I fort'nately or hunfort'nately, found that the people warn't what they pretended to make theirselves out to be – there! And where it wasn't their faults, by chalks, if I warn't made bad and ruinated – Hah!"

During this speech, Oakum Head had again made a diversion with the skirmishers, and had again withdrawn.

The Uncommercial Traveller ventured to remark that he supposed Chief Refractory and Number One, to be the two young women who had been taken before the magistrate?

"Yes!" said the Chief, "we har! and the wonder is, that a pleeseman an't 'ad in now, and we took off agen. You can't open your lips here, without a pleeseman.''

Number Two laughed (very uvularly), and the skirmishers followed suit.

"I'm sure I'd be thankful," protested the Chief, looking sideways at the Uncommercial, "if I could be got into a place, or got abroad. I'm sick and tired of this precious Ouse, I am, with reason.''

So would be, and so was, Number Two. So would be, and so was, Oakum Head. So would be, and so were, Skirmishers.

The Uncommercial took the liberty of hinting that he hardly thought it probable that any lady or gentleman in want of a likely young domestic of retiring manners, would be tempted into the engagement of either of the two leading Refractories, on her own presentation of herself as per sample.

"It ain't no good being nothink else here," said the Chief.

The Uncommercial thought it might be worth trying.

"Oh no, it ain't," said the Chief.

"Not a bit of good," said Number Two.

"And I'm sure I'd be very thankful to be got into a place, or got abroad," said the Chief.

"And so should I," said Number Two. "Truly thankful, I should."

Oakum Head then rose, and announced as an entirely new idea, the mention of which profound novelty might be naturally expected to startle her unprepared hearers, that she would be very thankful to be got into a place, or got abroad. And, as if she had then said, "Chorus, ladies!" all the Skirmishers struck up to the same purpose. We left them, thereupon, and began a long walk among the women who were simply old and infirm; but whenever, in the course of this same walk, I looked out of any high window that commanded the yard, I saw Oakum Head and all the other Refractories looking out at their low window for me, and never failing to catch me, the moment I showed my head.

In ten minutes I had ceased to believe in such fables of a golden time as youth, the prime of life, or a hale old age. In ten minutes, all the lights of womankind seemed to have been blown out, and nothing in that way to be left this vault to brag of, but the flickering and expiring snuffs.

And what was very curious, was, that these dim old women had one company notion which was the fashion of the place. Every old woman who became aware of a visitor and was not in bed hobbled over a form into her accustomed seat, and became one of a line of dim old women confronting another line of dim old women across a narrow table. There was no obligation whatever upon them to range themselves in this way; it was their manner of "receiving." As a rule, they made no attempt to talk to one another, or to look at the visitor, or to look at anything, but sat silently working their mouths, like a sort of poor old Cows. In some of these wards, it was good to see a few green plants; in others, an isolated Refractory acting as nurse, who did well enough in that capacity, when separated from her compeers; every one of these wards, day room, night room, or both combined, was scrupulously clean and fresh. I have seen as many such places as most travellers in my line, and I never saw one such, better kept.

Among the bedridden there was great patience, great reliance on the books under the pillow, great faith in G O D. All cared for sympathy, but none much cared to be encouraged with hope of recovery; on the whole, I should say, it was considered rather a distinction to have a complication of disorders, and to be in a worse way than the rest. From some of the windows, the river could be seen with all its life and movement; the day was bright, but I came upon no one who was looking out.

In one large ward, sitting by the fire in arm-chairs of distinction, like the President and Vice of the good company, were two old women, upwards of ninety years of age. The younger of the two, just turned ninety, was deaf, but not very, and could easily be made to hear. In her early time she had nursed a child, who was now another old woman, more infirm than herself, inhabiting the very same chamber. She perfectly understood this when the matron told it, and, with sundry nods and motions of her forefinger, pointed out the woman in question. The elder of this pair, ninety-three, seated before an illustrated newspaper (but not reading it), was a bright-eyed old soul, really not deaf, wonderfully preserved, and amazingly conversational. She had not long lost her husband, and had been in that place little more than a year. At Boston, in the State of Massachusetts,[10] this poor creature would have been individually addressed, would have been tended in her own room, and would have had her life gently assimilated to a comfortable life out of doors. Would that be much to do in England for a woman who has kept herself out of a workhouse more than ninety rough long years? When Britain first, at Heaven's command, arose, with a great deal of allegorical confusion, from out the azure main, did her guardian angels positively forbid it in the Charter which has been so much besung?[11]

The object of my journey was accomplished when the nimble matron had no more to show me. As I shook hands with her at the gate, I told her that I thought Justice had not used her very well, and that the wise men of the East were not infallible.

Now, I reasoned with myself, as I made my journey home again, concerning those Foul wards. They ought not to exist; no person of common decency and humanity can see them and doubt it. But what is this Union to do? The necessary alteration would cost several thousands of pounds; it has already to support three workhouses; its inhabitants work hard for their bare lives, and are already rated for the relief of the Poor to the utmost extent of reasonable endurance. One poor parish in this very Union is rated to the amount of FIVE AND SIXPENCE in the pound, at the very same time when the rich parish of Saint George's, Hanover-square, is rated at about SEVENPENCE in the pound, Paddington at about FOURPENCE, Saint James's, Westminster, at about TENPENCE! It is only through the equalisation of Poor Rates[12] that what is left undone in this wise, can be done. Much more is left undone, or is ill-done, than I have space to suggest in these notes of a single uncommercial journey; but, the wise men of the East, before they can reasonably hold forth about it, must look to the North and South and West; let them also, any morning before taking the seat of Solomon, look into the shops and dwellings all around the Temple, and first ask themselves "how much more can these poor people – many of whom keep themselves with difficulty enough out of the workhouse – bear?"

I had yet other matter for reflection as I journeyed home, inasmuch as, before I altogether departed from the neighbourhood of Mr. Baker's trap, I had knocked at the gate of the workhouse of St. George's-in-the-East, and had found it to be an establishment highly creditable to those parts, and thoroughly well administered by a most intelligent master. I remarked in it, an instance of the collateral harm that obstinate vanity and folly can do. "This was the Hall where those old paupers, male and female, whom I had just seen, met for the Church service, was it?" – "Yes." – "Did they sing the Psalms to any instrument?" – "They would like to, very much; they would have an extraordinary interest in doing so." – "And could none be got?" – "Well, a piano could even have been got for nothing, but these unfortunate dissensions—" Ah! better, far better, my Christian friend in the beautiful garment, to have let the singing boys alone, and left the multitude to sing for themselves! You should know better than I, but I think I have read that they did so, once upon a time, and that "when they had sung an hymn," Some one (not in a beautiful garment) went up unto the Mount of Olives.

It made my heart ache to think of this miserable trifling, in the streets of a city where every stone seemed to call to me, as I walked along, "Turn this way, man, and see what waits to be done!" So I decoyed myself into another train of thought to ease my heart. But, I don't know that I did it, for I was so full of paupers, that it was, after all, only a change to a single pauper, who took possession of my remembrance instead of a thousand.

"I beg your pardon, sir," he had said, in a confidential manner, on another occasion, taking me aside; "but I have seen better days."

"I am very sorry to hear it."

"Sir, I have a complaint to make against the master."

"I have no power here, I assure you. And if I had —"

"But, allow me, sir, to mention it, as between yourself and a man who has seen better days, sir. The master and myself are both masons, sir, and I make him the sign continually; but, because I am in this unfortunate position, sir, he won't give me the countersign!"[13]

A Small Star in the East

First published in *All the Year Round*, 19 December 1868, from which this text is taken.

I had been looking, yesternight, through the famous "Dance of Death,"[1] and to-day the grim old woodcuts arose in my mind with the new significance of a ghastly monotony not to be found in the original. The weird skeleton rattled along the streets before me, and struck fiercely; but it was never at the pains of assuming a disguise. It played on no dulcimer here, was crowned with no flowers, waved no plume, minced in no flowing robe or train, lifted no winecup, sat at no feast, cast no dice, counted no gold. It was simply a bare, gaunt, famished skeleton, slaying his way along.

The borders of Ratcliff[2] and Stepney, eastward of London, and giving on the impure river, were the scene of this uncompromising dance of death, upon a drizzling November day. A squalid maze of streets, courts, and alleys of miserable houses let out in single rooms. A wilderness of dirt, rags, and hunger. A mud-desert, chiefly inhabited by a tribe from whom employment has departed, or to whom it comes but fitfully and rarely. They are not skilled mechanics in any wise. They are but labourers, — dock-labourers, water-side labourers, coal-porters, ballast-heavers, such-like hewers of wood and drawers of water. But they have come into existence, and they propagate their wretched race.

One grisly joke alone, methought, the skeleton seemed to play off here. It had stuck election-bills on the walls, which the wind and rain had deteriorated into suitable rags. It had even summed up the state of the poll, in chalk, on the shutters of one ruined house. It adjured the free and independent starvers to vote for Thisman and vote for Thatman; not to plump, as they valued the state of parties and the national prosperity (both of great importance to them, I think); but, by returning Thisman and Thatman, each naught without the other, to compound a glorious and immortal whole. Surely the skeleton is nowhere more cruelly ironical in the original monkish idea!

Pondering in my mind the far-seeing schemes of Thisman and Thatman, and of the public blessing called Party, for staying the degeneracy, physical and moral, of many thousands (who shall say how many?) of the English race; for devising employment useful to the community for those who want but to work and live; for equalising rates, cultivating waste lands, facilitating emigration, and, above all things, saving and utilising the oncoming generations, and thereby changing ever-growing national weakness into strength: pondering in my mind, I say, these hopeful exertions, I turned down a narrow street to look into a house or two.

It was a dark street with a dead wall on one side. Nearly all the outer doors of the houses stood open. I took the first entry, and knocked at a parlour-door. Might I come in? I might, if I plased, sur.

The woman of the room (Irish) had picked up some long strips of wood, about some wharf or barge; and they had just now been thrust into the otherwise empty grate to make two iron pots boil. There was some fish in one, and there were some potatoes in the other. The flare of the burning wood enabled me to see a table, and a broken chair or so, and some old cheap crockery ornaments about the chimney-piece. It was not until I had spoken with the woman a few minutes, that I saw a horrible brown heap on the floor in the corner, which, but for previous experience in this dismal wise, I might not have suspected to be "the bed." There was something thrown upon it; and I asked what that was.

"'Tis the poor craythur that stays here, sur; and 'tis very bad she is, and 'tis very bad she's been this long time, and 'tis better she'll never be, and 'tis slape she does all day, and 'tis wake she does all night, and 'tis the lead, sur."

"The what?"

"The lead, sur. Sure 'tis the lead-mills, where the women gets took on at eighteen-pence a day, sur, when they makes application early enough, and is lucky and wanted; and 'tis lead-pisoned she is, sur, and some of them gets lead-pisoned soon, and some of them gets lead-pisoned later, and some, but not many, niver; and 'tis all according to the constitooshun, sur, and some constitooshuns is strong, and some is weak, and her constitooshun is lead-pisoned, bad as can be, sur; and her brain is coming out at her ear, and it hurts her dreadful; and that's what it is, and niver no more, and niver no less, sur."

The sick young woman moaning here, the speaker bent over her, took a bandage from her head, and threw open a back door to let in the daylight upon it, from the smallest and most miserable back-yard I ever saw.

"That's what cooms from her, sur, being lead-pisoned; and it cooms from her night and day, the poor, sick craythur; and the pain of it is dreadful; and God he knows that my husband has walked the streets these four days, being a labourer, and is walking them now, and is ready to work, and no work for him, and no fire and no food but the bit in the pot, and no more than ten shillings in a fortnight; God be good to us! and it is poor we are, and dark it is and could it is indeed."

Knowing that I could compensate myself thereafter for my self-denial, if I saw fit, I had resolved that I would give nothing in the course of these visits. I did this to try the people. I may state at once that my closest observation could not detect any indication whatever of an expectation that I would give money: they were grateful to be talked to about their miserable affairs, and sympathy was plainly a comfort to them; but they neither asked for money in any case, nor showed the least trace of surprise or disappointment or resentment at my giving none.

The woman's married daughter had by this time come down from her room on the floor above, to join in the conversation. She herself had been to the lead-mills[3] very early that morning to be "took on," but had not succeeded. She had four children; and her husband, also a water-side labourer, and then out seeking work, seemed in no better case as to finding it than her father. She was English, and by nature of a buxom figure and cheerful. Both in her poor dress and in her mother's there was an effort to keep up some appearance of neatness. She knew all about the sufferings of the unfortunate invalid, and all about the lead-poisoning, and how the symptoms came on, and how they grew, — having often seen them. The very smell when you stood inside the door of the works was enough to knock you down, she said: yet she was going back again to get "took on:" What could she do? Better be ulcerated and paralyzed for eighteen-pence a day, while it lasted, than see the children starve.

A dark and squalid cupboard in this room, touching the back door and all manner of offence, had been for some time the sleeping-place of the sick young woman. But the nights being now wintry, and the blankets and coverlets "gone to the leaving shop," she lay all night where she lay all day, and was lying then. The woman of the room, her husband, this most miserable patient, and two others, lay on the one brown heap together for warmth.

"God bless you, sir, and thank you!" were the parting words from these people, — gratefully spoken too, — with which I left this place.

Some streets away, I tapped at another parlour-door on another ground-floor. Looking in, I found a man, his wife, and four children, sitting at a washing-stool by way of table, at their dinner of bread and infused tea-leaves. There was a very scanty cinderous fire in the grate by which they sat; and there was a tent bedstead in the room with a bed upon it and a coverlet. The man did not rise when I went in, nor during my stay, but civilly inclined his head on my pulling off my hat, and, in answer to my inquiry whether I might ask him a question or two, said, "Certainly." There being a window at each end of this room, back and front, it might have been ventilated; but it was shut up tight, to keep the cold out, and was very sickening.

The wife, an intelligent, quick woman, rose and stood at her husband's elbow; and he glanced up at her as if for help. It soon appeared that he was rather deaf. He was a slow, simple fellow of about thirty.

"What was he by trade?"

"Gentleman asks what are you by trade, John?"

"I am a boilermaker;" looking about him with an exceedingly perplexed air, as if for a boiler that had unaccountably vanished.

"He ain't a mechanic, you understand, sir," the wife put in: "he's only a labourer."

"Are you in work?"

He looked up at his wife again. "Gentleman says are you in work, John?"

"In work!" cried this forlorn boilermaker, staring aghast at his wife, and then working his vision's way very slowly round to me: "Lord no!"

"Ah, he ain't indeed!" said the poor woman, shaking her head, as she looked at the four children in succession, and then at him.

"Work!" said the boilermaker, still seeking that evaporated boiler, first in my countenance, then in the air, and then in the features of his second son at his knee: "I wish I *was* in work! I haven't had more than a day's work to do this three weeks."

"How have you lived?"

A faint gleam of admiration lighted up the face of the would-be boiler-maker, as he stretched out the short sleeve of his threadbare canvas jacket, and replied, pointing her out, "On the work of the wife."

I forget where boilermaking had gone to, or where he supposed it had gone to; but he added some resigned information on that head, coupled with an expression of his belief that it was never coming back.

The cheery helpfulness of the wife was very remarkable. She did slop-work;[4] made pea-jackets. She produced the pea-jacket then in hand, and spread it out upon the bed, – the only piece of furniture in the room on which to spread it. She showed how much of it she made, and how much was afterwards finished off by the machine. According to her calculation at the moment, deducting what her trimming cost her, she got for making a pea-jacket tenpence half-penny, and she could make one in something less than two days.

But, you see, it come to her through two hands, and of course it didn't come through the second hand for nothing. Why did it come through the second hand at all? Why, this way. The second hand took the risk of the given-out work, you see. If she had money enough to pay the security deposit, − call it two pound, − she could get the work from the first hand, and so the second would not have to be deducted for. But, having no money at all, the second hand come in and took its profit, and so the whole worked down to tenpence half-penny. Having explained all this with great intelligence, even with some little pride, and without a whine or murmur, she folded her work again, sat down by her husband's side at the washing-stool, and resumed her dinner of dry bread. Mean as the meal was, on the bare board, with its old gallipots for cups, and what not other sordid makeshifts: shabby as the woman was in dress, and toning down towards the Bosjesman[5] colour, with want of nutriment and washing, − there was positively a dignity in her, as the family anchor just holding the poor shipwrecked boilermaker's bark. When I left the room, the boilermaker's eyes were slowly turned towards her, as if his last hope of ever again seeing that vanished boiler lay in her direction.

These people had never applied for parish relief but once; and that was when the husband met with a disabling accident at his work.

Not many doors from here, I went into a room on the first floor. The woman apologised for its being in "an untidy mess." The day was Saturday, and she was boiling the children's clothes in a saucepan on the hearth. There was nothing else into which she could have put them. There was no crockery, or tinware, or tub, or bucket. There was an old gallipot or two, and there was a broken bottle or so, and there were some broken boxes for seats. The last small scraping of coals left was raked together in a corner of the floor. There were some rags in an open cupboard, also on the floor. In a corner of the room was a crazy old French bedstead, with a man lying on his back upon it in a ragged pilot jacket, and rough oil-skin fantail hat. The room was perfectly black. It was difficult to believe, at first, that it was not purposely coloured black, the walls were so begrimed.

As I stood opposite the woman boiling the children's clothes, − she had not even a piece of soap to wash them with, − and apologising for her occupation, I could take in all these things without appearing to notice them, and could even correct my inventory. I had missed, at the first glance, some half a pound of bread in the otherwise empty safe, an old red ragged crinoline hanging on the handle of the door by which I had entered, and certain fragments of rusty iron scattered on the floor, which looked like broken tools and a piece of stove-pipe. A child stood looking on. On the box nearest to the fire sat two younger children; one a delicate and pretty little creature, whom the other sometimes kissed.

This woman, like the last, was wofully shabby, and was degenerating to the Bosjesman complexion. But her figure, and the ghost of a certain vivacity about her, and the spectre of a dimple in her cheek, carried my memory strangely back to the old days of the Adelphi Theatre, London, when Mrs. Fitzwilliam was the friend of Victorine.[6]

"May I ask you what your husband is?"

"He's a coal-porter, sir," – with a glance and a sigh towards the bed.

"Is he out of work?"

"Oh, yes, sir! and work's at all times very, very scanty with him; and now he's laid up."

"It's my legs," said the man upon the bed. "I'll unroll 'em." And immediately began.

"Have you any older children?"

"I have a daughter that does the needle-work, and I have a son that does what he can. She's at her work now, and he's trying for work."

"Do they live here?"

"They sleep here. They can't afford to pay more rent, and so they come here at night. The rent is very hard upon us. It's rose upon us too, now, – sixpence a week, – on account of these new changes in the law, about the rates. We are a week behind; the landlord's been shaking and rattling at that door frightfully; he says he'll turn us out. I don't know what's to come of it."

The man upon the bed ruefully interposed, "Here's my legs. The skin's broke, besides the swelling. I have had a many kicks, working, one way and another."

He looked at his legs (which were much discoloured and misshapen) for a while, and then appearing to remember that they were not popular with his family, rolled them up again, as if they were something in the nature of maps or plans that were not wanted to be referred to, lay hopelessly down on his back once more with his fantail hat over his face, and stirred not.

"Do your eldest son and daughter sleep in that cupboard?"

"Yes," replied the woman.

"With the children?"

"Yes. We have to get together for warmth. We have little to cover us."

"Have you nothing by you to eat but the piece of bread I see there?"

"Nothing. And we had the rest of the loaf for our breakfast, with water. I don't know what's to come of it."

"Have you no prospect of improvement?"

"If my eldest son earns anything to-day, he'll bring it home. Then we shall have something to eat to-night, and may be able to do something towards the rent. If not, I don't know what's to come of it."

"This is a sad state of things."

"Yes, sir; it's a hard, hard life. Take care of the stairs as you go, sir – they're broken, – and good day, sir!"

These people had a mortal dread of entering the workhouse, and received no out-of-door relief.

In another room, in still another tenement, I found a very decent woman with five children, – the last a baby, and she herself a patient of the parish doctor, – to whom, her husband being in the hospital, the Union allowed for the support of herself and family, four shillings a week and five loaves. I suppose when Thisman, M.P., and Thatman, M.P., and the Public-blessing Party, lay their heads together in course of time, and come to an equalisation of rating, she may go down to the dance of death to the tune of sixpence more.

I could enter no other houses for that one while, for I could not bear the contemplation of the children. Such heart as I had summoned to sustain me against the miseries of the adults failed me when I looked at the children. I saw how young they were, how hungry, how serious and still. I thought of them, sick and dying in those lairs. I think of them dead without anguish; but to think of them so suffering and so dying quite unmanned me.

Down by the river's bank in Ratcliff, I was turning upward by a side street, therefore, to regain the railway, when my eyes rested on the inscription across the road, "East London Children's Hospital." I could scarcely have seen an inscription better suited to my frame of mind; and I went across and went straight in.

I found the children's hospital established in an old sail-loft or storehouse, of the roughest nature, and on the simplest means. There were trap-doors in the floors, where goods had been hoisted up and down; heavy feet and heavy weights had started every knot in the well-trodden planking: inconvenient bulks and beams and awkward staircases perplexed my passage through the wards. But I found it airy, sweet, and clean. In its seven and thirty beds I saw but little beauty; for starvation in the second or third generation takes a pinched look: but I saw the sufferings both of infancy and childhood tenderly assuaged; I heard the little patients answering to pet playful names, the light touch of a delicate lady laid bare the wasted sticks of arms for me to pity; and the claw-like little hands, as she did so, twined themselves lovingly around her wedding-ring.

One baby mite there was as pretty as any of Raphael's angels. The tiny head was bandaged for water on the brain; and it was suffering with acute bronchitis too, and made from time to time a plaintive, though not impatient or complaining, little sound. The smooth curve of the cheeks and of the chin was faultless in its condensation of infantine beauty, and the large bright eyes were most lovely. It happened as I stopped at the foot of the bed, that these eyes rested upon mine with that wistful expression of wondering thoughtfulness which we all know sometimes in very little children. They remained fixed on mine, and never turned from me while I stood there. When the utterance of that plaintive sound shook the little form, the gaze still remained unchanged. I felt as though the child implored me to tell the story of the little hospital in which it was sheltered to any gentle heart I could address. Laying my world-worn hand upon the little unmarked clasped hand at the chin, I gave it a silent promise that I would do so.

A gentleman and lady,[7] a young husband and wife, have bought and fitted up this building for its present noble use, and have quietly settled themselves in it as its medical officers and directors. Both have had considerable practical experience of medicine and surgery; he as house-surgeon of a great London hospital; she as a very earnest student, tested by severe examination, and also as a nurse of the sick poor during the prevalence of cholera.

With every qualification to lure them away, with youth and accomplishments and tastes and habits that can have no response in any breast near them, close begirt by every repulsive circumstance inseparable from such a neighbourhood, there they dwell. They live in the hospital itself, and their rooms are on its first floor. Sitting at their dinner-table, they could hear the cry of one of the children in pain. The lady's piano, drawing-materials, books, and other such evidences of refinement are as much a part of the rough place as the iron bedsteads of the little patients. They are put to shifts for room, like passengers on board ship. The dispenser of medicines (attracted to them not by self-interest, but by their own magnetism and that of their cause) sleeps in a recess in the dining-room, and has his washing apparatus in the sideboard.

Their contented manner of making the best of the things around them, I found so pleasantly inseparable from their usefulness! Their pride in this partition that we put up ourselves, or in that partition that we took down, or in that other partition that we moved, or in the stove that was given us for the waiting-room, or in our nightly conversion of the little consulting-room into a smoking-room! Their admiration of the situation, if we could only get rid of its one objectionable incident, the coal-yard at the back! "Our hospital carriage, presented by a friend, and very useful." That was my presentation to a perambulator, for which a coach-house had been discovered in a corner down-stairs, just large enough to hold it. Coloured prints, in all stages of preparation for being added to those already decorating the wards, were plentiful; a charming wooden phenomenon of a bird, with an impossible top-knot, who ducked his head when you set a counter weight going, had been inaugurated as a public statue that very morning; and trotting about among the beds, on familiar terms with all the patients, was a comical mongrel dog, called Poodles. This comical dog (quite a tonic in himself) was found characteristically starving at the door of the institution, and was taken in and fed, and has lived here ever since. An admirer of his mental endowments has presented him with a collar bearing the legend, "Judge not Poodles by external appearances." He was merrily wagging his tail on a boy's pillow when he made this modest appeal to me.

When this hospital was first opened, in January of the present year, the people could not possibly conceive but that somebody paid for the services rendered there; and were disposed to claim them as a right, and to find fault if out of temper. They soon came to understand the case better, and have much increased in gratitude. The mothers of the patients avail themselves very freely of the visiting rules; the fathers often on Sundays. There is an unreasonable (but still, I think, touching and intelligible) tendency in the parents to take a child away to its wretched home, if on the point of death. One boy who had been thus carried off on a rainy night, when in a violent state of inflammation, and who had been afterwards brought back, had been recovered with exceeding difficulty; but he was a jolly boy, with a specially strong interest in his dinner, when I saw him.

Insufficient food and unwholesome living are the main causes of disease among these small patients. So nourishment, cleanliness, and ventilation are the main remedies. Discharged patients are looked after, and invited to come and dine now and then; so are certain famishing creatures who were never patients. Both the lady and the gentleman are well acquainted, not only with the histories of the patients and their families, but with the characters and circumstances of great numbers of their neighbours: of these they keep a register. It is their common experience, that people, sinking down by inches into deeper and deeper poverty, will conceal it, even from them, if possible, unto the very last extremity.

The nurses of this hospital are all young, – ranging, say, from nineteen to four and twenty. They have even within these narrow limits, what many well-endowed hospitals would not give them, a comfortable room of their own in which to take their meals. It is a beautiful truth, that interest in the children and sympathy with their sorrows bind these young women to their places far more strongly than any other consideration could. The best skilled of the nurses came originally from a kindred neighbourhood, almost as poor; and she knew how much the work was needed. She is a fair dressmaker. The hospital cannot pay her as many pounds in the year as there are months in it; and one day the lady regarded it as a duty to speak to her about her improving her prospects and following her trade. "No," she said: she could never be so useful or so happy elsewhere any more; she must stay among the children. And she stays. One of the nurses, as I passed her, was washing a baby-boy. Liking her pleasant face, I stopped to speak to her charge, – a common, bullet-headed, frowning charge enough, laying hold of his own nose with a slippery grasp, and staring very solemnly out of a blanket. The melting of the pleasant face into delighted smiles, as this young gentleman gave an unexpected kick, and laughed at me, was almost worth my previous pain.

An affecting play was acted in Paris years ago, called "The Children's Doctor."[8] As I parted from my children's doctor, now in question, I saw in his easy black necktie, in his loose buttoned black frock-coat, in his pensive face, in the flow of his dark hair, in his eyelashes, in the very turn of his moustache, the exact realisation of the Paris artist's ideal as it was presented on the stage. But no romancer that I know of has had the boldness to prefigure the life and home of this young husband and young wife in the Children's Hospital in the east of London.

I came away from Ratcliff by the Stepney railway station to the terminus at Fenchurch Street. Any one who will reverse that route may retrace my steps.

On an Amateur Beat

First published in *All the Year Round*, 27 February 1869, from which this text is reproduced.

It is one of my fancies, that even my idlest walk must always have its appointed destination. I set myself a task before I leave my lodging in Covent-garden on a street expedition, and should no more think of altering my route by the way, or turning back and leaving a part of it unachieved, than I should think of fraudulently violating an agreement entered into with somebody else. The other day, finding myself under this kind of obligation to proceed to Limehouse, I started punctually at noon, in compliance with the terms of the contract with myself to which my good faith was pledged.

On such an occasion, it is my habit to regard my walk as my beat, and myself as a higher sort of police-constable doing duty on the same. There is many a ruffian in the streets whom I mentally collar and clear out of them, who would see mighty little of London, I can tell him, if I could deal with him physically.

Issuing forth upon this very beat, and following with my eyes three hulking garrotters on their way home, – which home I could confidently swear to be within so many yards of Drury-lane, in such a narrow and restricted direction (though they live in their lodging quite as undisturbed as I in mine), – I went on duty with a consideration which I respectfully offer to the new Chief Commissioner,[1] – in whom I thoroughly confide as a tried and efficient public servant. How often (thought I) have I been forced to swallow, in police-reports, the intolerable stereotyped pill of nonsense, how that the police-constable informed the worthy magistrate how that the associates of the prisoner did, at that present speaking, dwell in a street or court which no man dared go down, and how that the worthy magistrate had heard of the dark reputation of such street or court, and how that our readers would doubtless remember that it was always the same street or court which was thus edifyingly discoursed about, say once a fortnight.

Now, suppose that a Chief Commissioner sent round a circular to every division of police employed in London, requiring instantly the names in all districts of all such much-puffed streets or courts which no man durst go down; and suppose that in such circular he gave plain warning, "If those places really exist, they are a proof of police inefficiency which I mean to punish; and if they do not exist, but are a conventional fiction, then they are a proof of lazy tacit police connivance with professional crime, which I also mean to punish" – what then? Fictions or realities, could they survive the touchstone of this atom of common sense? To tell us in open court, until it has become as trite a feature of news as the great gooseberry, that a costly police-system such as was never before heard of, has left in London, in the days of steam and gas and photographs of thieves and electric telegraphs, the sanctuaries and stews of the Stuarts! Why, a parity of practice, in all departments, would bring back the Plague in two summers, and the Druids in a century!

Walking faster under my share of this public injury, I overturned a wretched little creature, who, clutching at the rags of a pair of trousers with one of its claws, and at its ragged hair with the other, pattered with bare feet over the muddy stones. I stopped to raise and succour this poor weeping wretch, and fifty like it, but of both sexes, were about me in a moment, begging, tumbling, fighting, clamouring, yelling, shivering in their nakedness and hunger. The piece of money I had put into the claw of the child I had overturned was clawed out of it, and was again clawed out of that wolfish gripe, and again out of that, and soon I had no notion in what part of the obscene scuffle in the mud, of rags and legs and arms and dirt, the money might be. In raising the child, I had drawn it aside out of the main thoroughfare, and this took place among some wooden hoardings and barriers and ruins of demolished buildings, hard by Temple Bar.

Unexpectedly, from among them emerged a genuine police constable, before whom the dreadful brood dispersed in various directions, he making feints and darts in this direction and in that, and catching nothing. When all were frightened away, he took off his hat, pulled out a handkerchief from it, wiped his heated brow, and restored the handkerchief and hat to their places, with the air of a man who had discharged a great moral duty, – as indeed he had, in doing what was set down for him. I looked at him, and I looked about at the disorderly traces in the mud, and I thought of the drops of rain and the footprints of an extinct creature, hoary ages upon ages old, that geologists have identified on the face of a clift; and this speculation came over me: If this mud could petrify at this moment, and could lie concealed here for ten thousand years, I wonder whether the race of men then to be our successors on the earth could, from these or any marks, by the utmost force of the human intellect, unassisted by tradition, deduce such an astounding inference as the existence of a polished state of society that bore with the public savagery of neglected children in the streets of its capital city, and was proud of its power by sea and land, and never used its power to seize and save them!

After this, when I came to the Old Bailey and glanced up it towards Newgate, I found that the prison had an inconsistent look. There seemed to be some unlucky inconsistency in the atmosphere that day; for though the proportions of St. Paul's Cathedral are very beautiful, it had an air of being somewhat out of drawing, in my eyes. I felt as though the cross were too high up, and perched upon the intervening golden ball too far away.

Facing eastward, I left behind me Smithfield and Old Bailey, – fire and faggot, condemned hold, public hanging, whipping through the city at the cart-tail, pillory, branding-iron, and other beautiful ancestral landmarks, which rude hands have rooted up, without bringing the stars quite down upon us as yet, – and went my way upon my beat, noting how oddly characteristic neighbourhoods are divided from one another, hereabout, as though by an invisible line across the way. Here shall cease the bankers and the money-changers; here shall begin the shipping interest and the nautical-instrument shops; here shall follow a scarcely perceptible flavouring of groceries and drugs; here shall come a strong infusion of butchers; now, small hosiers shall be in the ascendant; henceforth, everything exposed for sale shall have its ticketed price attached. All this as if specially ordered and appointed.

A single stride at Houndsditch Church,[2] no wider than sufficed to cross the kennel at the bottom of the Canon-gate, which the debtors in Holyrood sanctuary were wont to relieve their minds by skipping over, as Scott relates, and standing in delightful daring of catchpoles on the free side,[3] – a single stride, and everything is entirely changed in grain and character. West of the stride, a table, or a chest of drawers on sale, shall be of mahogany and French-polished; east of the stride, it shall be of deal, smeared with a cheap counterfeit resembling lip-salve. West of the stride, a penny loaf or bun shall be compact and self-contained; east of the stride, it shall be of a sprawling and splay-footed character, as seeking to make more of itself for the money. My beat lying round by Whitechapel Church, and the adjacent sugar-refineries, – great buildings, tier upon tier, that have the appearance of being nearly related to the dock-warehouses at Liverpool, – I turned off to my right, and, passing round the awkward corner on my left, came suddenly on an apparition familiar to London streets afar off.

What London peripatetic of these times has not seen the woman who has fallen forward, double, through some affection of the spine, and whose head has of late taken a turn to one side, so that it now droops over the back of one of her arms at about the wrist? Who does not know her staff, and her shawl, and her basket, as she gropes her way along, capable of seeing nothing but the pavement, never begging, never stopping, for ever going somewhere on no business? How does she live, whence does she come, whither does she go, and why? I mind the time when her yellow arms were naught but bone and parchment. Slight changes steal over her; for there is a shadowy suggestion of human skin on them now. The Strand may be taken as the central point about which she revolves in a half-mile orbit. How comes she so far east as this? And coming back too! Having been how much farther? She is a rare spectacle in this neighbourhood. I receive intelligent information to this effect from a dog – a lop-sided mongrel with a foolish tail, plodding along with his tail up, and his ears pricked, and displaying an amiable interest in the ways of his fellow-men, – if I may be allowed the expression. After pausing at a pork-shop, he is jogging eastward like myself, with a benevolent countenance and a watery mouth, as though musing on the many excellences of pork, when he beholds this doubled-up bundle approaching. He is not so much astonished at the bundle (though amazed by that), as the circumstance that it has within itself the means of locomotion. He stops, pricks his ears higher, makes a slight point, stares, utters a short, low growl, and glistens at the nose, – as I conceive with terror. The bundle continuing to approach, he barks, turns tail, and is about to fly, when, arguing with himself that flight is not becoming in a dog, he turns, and once more faces the advancing heap of clothes. After much hesitation, it occurs to him that there may be a face in it somewhere. Desperately resolving to undertake the adventure, and pursue the inquiry, he goes slowly up to the bundle, goes slowly round it, and coming at length upon the human countenance down there where never human countenance should be, gives a yelp of horror, and flies for the East India Docks.

Being now in the Commercial Road district of my beat, and bethinking myself that Stepney Station is near, I quicken my pace that I may turn out of the road at that point, and see how my small eastern star is shining.

The Children's Hospital, to which I gave that name, is in full force. All its beds are occupied. There is a new face on the bed where my pretty baby lay, and that sweet little child is now at rest for ever.[4] Much kind sympathy has been here since my former visit, and it is good to see the walls profusely garnished with dolls. I wonder what Poodles may think of them, as they stretch out their arms above the beds, and stare, and display their splendid dresses. Poodles has a greater interest in the patients. I find him making the round of the beds, like a house-surgeon, attended by another dog, – a friend, – who appears to trot about with him in the character of his pupil dresser. Poodles is anxious to make me known to a pretty little girl looking wonderfully healthy, who had had a leg taken off for cancer of the knee. A difficult operation, Poodles intimates, wagging his tail on the counterpane, but perfectly successful, as you see, dear sir! The patient, patting Poodles, adds with a smile, "The leg was so much trouble to me, that I am glad it's gone." I never saw anything in doggery finer than the deportment of Poodles, when another little girl opens her mouth to show a peculiar enlargement of the tongue. Poodles (at that time on a table, to be on a level with the occasion) looks at the tongue (with his own sympathetically out) so very gravely and knowingly, that I feel inclined to put my hand in my waistcoat-pocket, and give him a guinea, wrapped in paper.

On my beat again, and close to Limehouse Church, its termination, I found myself near to certain "Lead-Mills." Struck by the name, which was fresh in my memory, and finding, on inquiry, that these same lead-mills were identified with those same lead-mills of which I made mention when I first visited the East London Children's Hospital and its neighbourhood as Uncommercial Traveller, I resolved to have a look at them.

Received by two very intelligent gentlemen, brothers, and partners with their father in the concern, and who testified every desire to show their works to me freely, I went over the lead-mills. The purport of such works is the conversion of pig-lead into white-lead. This conversion is brought about by the slow and gradual effecting of certain successive chemical changes in the lead itself. The processes are picturesque and interesting, – the most so, being the burying of the lead, at a certain stage of preparation, in pots, each pot containing a certain quantity of acid besides, and all the pots being buried in vast numbers, in layers, under tan, for some ten weeks.

Hopping up ladders, and across planks, and on elevated perches, until I was uncertain whether to liken myself to a bird or a bricklayer, I became conscious of standing on nothing particular, looking down into one of a series of large cocklofts, with the outer day peeping in through the chinks in the tiled roof above. A number of women were ascending to, and descending from, this cockloft, each carrying on the upward journey a pot of prepared lead and acid, for deposition under the smoking tan. When one layer of pots was completely filled, it was carefully covered in with planks, and those were carefully covered with tan again, and then another layer of pots was begun above; sufficient means of ventilation being preserved through wooden tubes. Going down into the cockloft then filling, I found the heat of the tan to be surprisingly great, and also the odour of the lead and acid to be not absolutely exquisite, though I believe not noxious at that stage. In other cocklofts, where the pots were being exhumed, the heat of the steaming tan was much greater, and the smell was penetrating and peculiar. There were cocklofts in all stages; full and empty, half filled and half emptied; strong, active women were clambering about them busily; and the whole thing had rather the air of the upper part of the house of some immensely rich old Turk, whose faithful seraglio were hiding his money because the sultan or the pasha was coming.

As is the case with most pulps or pigments, so in the instance of this white-lead, processes of stirring, separating, washing, grinding, rolling, and pressing succeed. Some of these are unquestionably inimical to health, the danger arising from inhalation of particles of lead, or from contact between the lead and the touch, or both. Against these dangers, I found good respirators provided (simply made of flannel and muslin, so as to be inexpensively renewed, and in some instances washed with scented soap), and gauntlet gloves, and loose gowns. Everywhere, there was as much fresh air as windows, well placed and opened, could possibly admit. And it was explained that the precaution of frequently changing the women employed in the worst parts of the work (a precaution originating in their own experience or apprehension of its ill effects) was found salutary. They had a mysterious and singular appearance, with the mouth and nose covered, and the loose gown on, and yet bore out the simile of the old Turk and the seraglio all the better for the disguise.

At last this vexed white-lead, having been buried and resuscitated, and heated and cooled and stirred, and separated and washed and ground, and rolled and pressed, is subjected to the action of intense fiery heat. A row of women, dressed as above described, stood, let us say, in a large stone bake-house, passing on the baking-dishes as they were given out by the cooks, from hand to hand, into the ovens. The oven, or stove, cold as yet, looked as high as an ordinary house, and was full of men and women on temporary footholds, briskly passing up and stowing away the dishes. The door of another oven, or stove, about to be cooled and emptied, was opened from above, for the uncommercial countenance to peer down into. The uncommercial countenance withdrew itself, with expedition and a sense of suffocation, from the dull-glowing heat and the overpowering smell. On the whole, perhaps the going into these stoves to work, when they are freshly opened, may be the worst part of the occupation.

But I made it out to be indubitable that the owners of these lead-mills honestly and sedulously try to reduce the dangers of the occupation to the lowest point.

A washing-place is provided for the women (I thought there might have been more towels), and a room in which they hang their clothes, and take their meals, and where they have a good fire-range and fire, and a female attendant to help them, and to watch that they do not neglect the cleansing of their hands before touching their food. An experienced medical attendant is provided for them, and any premonitory symptoms of lead-poisoning are carefully treated. Their teapots and such things were set out on tables ready for their afternoon meal, when I saw their room; and it had a homely look. It is found that they bear the work much better than men: some few of them have been at it for years, and the great majority of those I observed were strong and active. On the other hand, it should be remembered that most of them are very capricious and irregular in their attendance.

American inventiveness would seem to indicate that before very long white-lead may be made entirely by machinery. The sooner, the better. In the meantime, I parted from my two frank conductors over the mills, by telling them that they had nothing there to be concealed, and nothing to be blamed for. As to the rest, the philosophy of the matter of lead-poisoning and workpeople seems to me to have been pretty fairly summed up by the Irish-woman whom I quoted in my former paper: "Some of them gets lead-pisoned soon, and some of them gets lead-pisoned later, and some, but not many, niver; and 'tis all according to the constitooshun, sur; and some constitooshuns is strong and some is weak."

Retracing my footsteps over my beat, I went off duty.

INSULARITIES

Pet Prisoners

First published in *Household Words*, 27 April 1850, from which this text is reproduced.

The system of separate confinement[1] first experimented on in England at the model prison, Pentonville, London, and now spreading through the country, appears to us to require a little calm consideration and reflection on the part of the public. We purpose, in this paper, to suggest what we consider some grave objections to this system.

We shall do this temperately, and without considering it necessary to regard every one from whom we differ, as a scoundrel, actuated by base motives, to whom the most unprincipled conduct may be recklessly attributed. Our faith in most questions where the good men are represented to be all *pro*, and the bad men to be all *con*, is very small. There is a hot class of riders of hobby-horses in the field, in this century, who think they do nothing unless they make a steeple-chase of their object, throw a vast quantity of mud about, and spurn every sort of decent restraint and reasonable consideration under their horses' heels. This question has not escaped such championship. It has its steeple-chase riders, who hold the dangerous principle that the end justifies any means, and to whom no means, truth and fair-dealing usually excepted, come amiss.

Considering the separate system of imprisonment, here, solely in reference to England, we discard, for the purpose of this discussion, the objection founded on its extreme severity, which would immediately arise if we were considering it with any reference to the State of Pennsylvania in America. For whereas in that State it may be inflicted for a dozen years, the idea is quite abandoned at home of extending it usually, beyond a dozen months, or in any case beyond eighteen months. Besides which, the school and the chapel afford periods of comparative relief here, which are not afforded in America.

Though it has been represented by the steeple-chase riders as a most enormous heresy to contemplate the possibility of any prisoner going mad or idiotic, under the prolonged effects of separate confinement; and although any one who should have the temerity to maintain such a doubt in Pennsylvania would have a chance of becoming a profane St. Stephen;[2] Lord Grey,[3] in his very last speech in the House of Lords on this subject, made in the present session of Parliament, in praise of this separate system, said of it:

395

"Wherever it has been fairly tried, one of its great defects has been discovered to be this, – that it cannot be continued for a sufficient length of time without danger to the individual, and that human nature cannot bear it beyond a limited period. The evidence of medical authorities proves beyond dispute that, if it is protracted beyond twelve months, the health of the convict, mental and physical, would require the most close and vigilant superintendence. Eighteen months is stated to be the *maximum* time for the continuance of its infliction, and, as a general rule, it is advised that it never be continued for more than twelve months." This being conceded, and it being clear that the prisoner's mind, and all the apprehensions weighing upon it, must be influenced from the first hour of his imprisonment by the greater or less extent of its duration in perspective before him, we are content to regard the system as dissociated in England from the American objection of too great severity.

We shall consider it, first in the relation of the extraordinary contrast it presents, in a country circumstanced as England is, between the physical condition of the convict in prison, and that of the hard-working man outside, or the pauper outside. We shall then inquire, and endeavour to lay before our readers some means of judging, whether its proved or probable efficiency in producing a real, trustworthy, practically repentant state of mind, is such as to justify the presentation of that extraordinary contrast. If, in the end, we indicate the conclusion that the associated silent system is less objectionable, it is not because we consider it in the abstract a good secondary punishment, but because it is a severe one, capable of judicious administration, much less expensive, not presenting the objectionable contrast so strongly, and not calculated to pet and pamper the mind of the prisoner and swell his sense of his own importance. We are not acquainted with any system of secondary punishment that we think reformatory, except the mark system of Captain Macconnochie,[4] formerly governor of Norfolk Island, which proceeds upon the principle of obliging the convict to some exercise of self-denial and resolution in every act of his prison life, and which would condemn him to a sentence of so much labour and good conduct instead of so much time. There are details in Captain Macconnochie's scheme on which we have our doubts (rigid silence we consider indispensable); but, in the main, we regard it as embodying sound and wise principles. We infer from the writings of Archbishop Whateley,[5] that those principles have presented themselves to his profound and acute mind in a similar light.

We will first contrast the dietary of The Model Prison at Pentonville, with the dietary of what we take to be the nearest workhouse, namely, that of Saint Pancras. In the prison, every man receives twenty-eight ounces of meat weekly. In the workhouse, every able-bodied adult receives eighteen. In the prison, every man receives one hundred and forty ounces of bread weekly. In the workhouse, every able-bodied adult receives ninety-six. In the prison, every man receives one hundred and twelve ounces of potatoes weekly. In the workhouse, every able-bodied adult receives thirty-six. In the prison, every man receives five pints and a quarter of liquid cocoa weekly, (made of flaked cocoa or cocoa-nibs,) with fourteen ounces of milk and forty-two drams of molasses; also seven pints of gruel weekly, sweetened with forty-two drams of molasses. In the workhouse, every able-bodied adult receives fourteen pints and a half of milk-porridge weekly, and no cocoa, and no gruel. In the prison, every man receives three pints and a half of soup weekly. In the workhouse, every able-bodied adult male receives four pints and a half, and a pint of Irish stew. This, with seven pints of table-beer weekly, and six ounces of cheese, is all the man in the workhouse has to set off against the immensely superior advantages of the prisoner in all the other respects we have stated. His lodging is very inferior to the prisoner's, the costly nature of whose accommodation we shall presently show.

Let us reflect upon this contrast in another aspect. We beg the reader to glance once more at The Model Prison dietary, and consider its frightful disproportion to the dietary of the free labourer in any of the rural parts of England. What shall we take his wages at? Will twelve shillings a week do? It cannot be called a low average, at all events. Twelve shillings a week make thirty-one pounds four a year. The cost, in 1848, for the victualling and management of every prisoner in the Model Prison was within a little of thirty-six pounds. Consequently, that free labourer, with young children to support, with cottage-rent to pay, and clothes to buy, and no advantage of purchasing his food in large amounts by contracts, has, for the whole subsistence of himself and family, between four and five pounds a year *less* than the cost of feeding and overlooking one man in the Model Prison. Surely to his enlightened mind, and sometimes low morality, this must be an extraordinary good reason for keeping out of it!

But we will not confine ourselves to the contrast between the labourer's scanty fare and the prisoner's "flaked cocoa or cocoa-nibs," and daily dinner of soup, meat, and potatoes. We will rise a little higher in the scale. Let us see what advertisers in the *Times* newspaper can board the middle classes at, and get a profit out of, too.

A LADY, residing in a cottage, with a large garden, in a pleasant and healthful locality, would be happy to receive one or two LADIES to BOARD with her.

Two ladies occupying the same apartment may be accommodated for 12s. a week each. The cottage is within a quarter of an hour's walk of a good market town, 10 minutes' of a South-Western Railway Station, and an hour's distance from town.

These two ladies could not be so cheaply boarded in the Model Prison.

BOARD and RESIDENCE, at £70 per annum, for a married couple, or in proportion for a single gentleman or lady, with a respectable family. Rooms large and airy, in an eligible dwelling, at Islington, about 20 minutes' walk from the Bank. Dinner hour six o'clock. There are one or two vacancies to complete a small, cheerful, and agreeable circle.

Still cheaper than the Model Prison!

BOARD and RESIDENCE. – A lady, keeping a select school, in a town, about 30 miles from London, would be happy to meet with a LADY to BOARD and RESIDE with her. She would have her own bedroom and a sitting-room. Any lady wishing for accomplishments would find this desirable. Terms £30 per annum. References will be expected and given.

Again, some six pounds a year less than the Model Prison! And if we were to pursue the contrast through the newspaper file for a month, or through the advertising pages of two or three numbers of Bradshaw's Railway Guide, we might probably fill the present number of this publication with similar examples, many of them including a decent education into the bargain.

This Model Prison had cost at the close of 1847, under the heads of "building" and "repairs" alone, the insignificant sum of ninety-three thousand pounds – within seven thousand pounds of the amount of the last Government grant for the Education of the whole people, and enough to pay for the emigration to Australia of four thousand, six hundred and fifty poor persons at twenty pounds per head. Upon the work done by five hundred prisoners in the Model Prison, in the year 1848, (we collate these figures from the Reports, and from Mr. Hepworth Dixon's useful work on the London Prisons,) there was no profit, but an actual loss of upwards of eight hundred pounds. The cost of instruction, and the time occupied in instruction, when the labour is necessarily unskilled and unproductive, may be pleaded in explanation of this astonishing fact. We are ready to allow all due weight to such considerations, but we put it to our readers whether the whole system is right or wrong; whether the money ought or ought not rather to be spent in instructing the unskilled and neglected outside the prison walls. It will be urged that it is expended in preparing the convict for the exile to which he is doomed. We submit to our readers, who are the jury in the case, that all this should be done outside the prison, first; that the first persons to be prepared for emigration are the miserable children who are consigned to the tender mercies of a DROUET,[6] or who disgrace our streets; and that in this beginning at the wrong end, a spectacle of monstrous inconsistency is presented, shocking to the mind. Where is our Model House of Youthful Industry, where is our Model Ragged School, costing, for building and repairs, from ninety to a hundred thousand pounds, and for its annual maintenance upwards of twenty thousand pounds a year? Would it be a Christian act to build that, first? To breed our skilful labour there? To take the hewers of wood and drawers of water in a strange country from the convict ranks, until those men by earnest working, zeal, and perseverance, proved themselves, and raised themselves? Here are two sets of people in a densely populated land, always in the balance before the general eye. Is Crime for ever to carry it against Poverty, and to have a manifest advantage? There are the scales before all men. Whirlwinds of dust scattered in men's eyes – and there is plenty flying about – cannot blind them to the real state of the balance.

We now come to inquire into the condition of mind produced by the seclusion (limited in duration as Lord Grey limits it) which is purchased at this great cost in money, and this greater cost in stupendous injustice. That it is a consummation much to be desired, that a respectable man, lapsing into crime, should expiate his offence without incurring the liability of being afterwards recognised by hardened offenders who were his fellow-prisoners, we most readily admit. But, that this object, howsoever desirable and benevolent, is in itself sufficient to outweigh such objections as we have set forth, we cannot for a moment concede. Nor have we any sufficient guarantee that even this solitary point is gained. Under how many apparently insuperable difficulties, men immured in solitary cells, will by some means obtain a knowledge of other men immured in other solitary cells, most of us know from all the accounts and anecdotes we have read of secret prisons and secret prisoners from our school-time upwards. That there is a fascination in the desire to know something of the hidden presence beyond the blank wall of the cell; that the listening ear is often laid against the wall; that there is an overpowering temptation to respond to the muffled knock, or any other signal which sharpened ingenuity pondering day after day on one idea can devise: is in that constitution of human nature which impels mankind to communication with one another, and makes solitude a false condition against which nature strives. That such communication within the Model Prison, is not only probable, but indisputably proved to be possible by its actual discovery, we have no hesitation in stating as a fact. Some pains have been taken to hush the matter, but the truth is, that when the Prisoners at Pentonville ceased to be selected Prisoners, especially picked out and chosen for the purposes of that experiment, an extensive conspiracy was found out among them, involving, it is needless to say, extensive communication. Small pieces of paper with writing upon them, had been crushed into balls, and shot into the apertures of cell doors, by prisoners passing along the passages; false responses had been made during Divine Service in the chapel, in which responses they addressed one another; and armed men were secretly dispersed by the Governor in various parts of the building, to prevent the general rising, which was anticipated as the consequence of this plot. Undiscovered communication, under this system, we assume to be frequent.

The state of mind into which a man is brought who is the lonely inhabitant of his own small world, and who is only visited by certain regular visitors, all addressing themselves to him individually and personally, as the object of their particular solicitude – we believe in most cases to have very little promise in it, and very little of solid foundation. A strange absorbing selfishness – a spiritual egotism and vanity, real or assumed – is the first result. It is most remarkable to observe, in the cases of murderers who become this kind of object of interest, when they are at last consigned to the condemned cell, how the rule is (of course there are exceptions,) that the murdered person disappears from the stage of their thoughts, except as a part of their own important story; and how they occupy the whole scene. *I* did this, *I* feel that, *I* confide in the mercy of Heaven being extended to *me*; this is the autograph of *me*, the unfortunate and unhappy; in my childhood I was so and so; in my youth I did such a thing, to which I attribute my downfall – not this thing of basely and barbarously defacing the image of my Creator, and sending an immortal soul into eternity without a moment's warning, but something else of a venial kind that many unpunished people do. I don't want the forgiveness of this foully murdered person's bereaved wife, husband, brother, sister, child, friend; I don't ask for it, I don't care for it. I make no inquiry of the clergyman concerning the salvation of that murdered person's soul; *mine* is the matter; and I am almost happy that I came here, as to the gate of Paradise. "I never liked him," said the repentant Mr. Manning, false of heart to the last, calling a crowbar by a milder name, to lessen the cowardly horror of it, "and I beat in his skull with the ripping chisel."[7] I am going to bliss, exclaims the same authority, in effect. Where my victim went to, is not my business at all. Now, G o d forbid that we, unworthily believing in the Redeemer, should shut out hope, or even humble trustfulness, from any criminal at that dread pass; but, it is not in us to call this state of mind repentance.

The present question is with a state of mind analogous to this (as we conceive) but with a far stronger tendency to hypocrisy; the dread of death not being present, and there being every possible inducement, either to feign contrition, or to set up an unreliable semblance of it. If I, John Styles, the prisoner, don't do my work, and outwardly conform to the rules of the prison, I am a mere fool. There is nothing here to tempt me to do anything else, and everything to tempt me to do that. The capital dietary (and every meal is a great event in this lonely life) depends upon it; the alternative is a pound of bread a day. I should be weary of myself without occupation. I should be much more dull if I didn't hold these dialogues with the gentlemen who are so anxious about me. I shouldn't be half the object of interest I am, if I didn't make the professions I do. Therefore, I John Styles go in for what is popular here, and I may mean it, or I may not.

There will always, under any decent system, be certain prisoners betrayed into crime by a variety of circumstances, who will do well in exile, and offend against the laws no more. Upon this class, we think the Associated Silent System[8] would have quite as good an influence as this expensive and anomalous one; and we cannot accept them as evidence of the efficiency of separate confinement. Assuming John Styles to mean what he professes, for the time being, we desire to track the workings of his mind, and to try to test the value of his professions. Where shall we find an account of John Styles, proceeding from no objector to this system, but from a staunch supporter of it? We will take it from a work called "Prison Discipline, and the advantages of the separate system of imprisonment," written by the Reverend Mr. Field, chaplain of the new County Gaol at Reading; pointing out to Mr. Field, in passing, that the question is not justly, as he would sometimes make it, a question between this system and the profligate abuses and customs of the old unreformed gaols, but between it and the improved gaols of this time, which are not constructed on his favourite principles.*[9]

* As Mr. Field condescends to quote some vapouring about the account given by Mr. Charles Dickens in his "American Notes," of the Solitary Prison at Philadelphia, he may perhaps really wish for some few words of information on the subject. For this purpose, Mr. Charles Dickens has referred to the entry in his Diary, made at the close of that day.

He left his hotel for the Prison at twelve o'clock, being waited on, by appointment, by the gentlemen who showed it to him; and he returned between seven and eight at night; dining in the Prison in the course of that time; which, according to his calculation, in despite of the Philadelphia Newspaper, rather exceeds two hours. He found the Prison admirably conducted, extremely clean, and the system administered in a most intelligent, kind, orderly, tender, and careful manner. He did not consider (nor should he, if he were to visit Pentonville to-morrow)

Now, here is John Styles, twenty years of age, in prison for a felony. He has been there five months, and he writes to his sister, "Don't fret, my dear sister, about my being here. I cannot help fretting when I think about my usage to my father and mother: when I think about it, it makes me quite ill. I hope God will forgive me; I pray for it night and day from my heart. Instead of fretting about imprisonment, I ought to thank God for it, for before I came here, I was living quite a careless life; neither was God in all my thoughts; all I thought about was ways that led me towards destruction. Give my respects to my wretched companions, and I hope they will alter their wicked course, for they don't know for a day nor an hour but what they may be cut off. I have seen my folly, and I hope they may see their folly; but I shouldn't if I had not been in trouble. It is good for me that I have been in trouble. Go to church, my sister, every Sunday, and don't give your mind to going to playhouses and theatres, for that is no good to you. There are a great many temptations."

---

that the book in which visitors were expected to record their observation of the place, was intended for the insertion of criticisms on the system, but for honest testimony to the manner of its administration; and to that, he bore, as an impartial visitor, the highest testimony in his power. In returning thanks for his health being drunk, at the dinner within the walls, he said that what he had seen that day was running in his mind; that he could not help reflecting on it; and that it was an awful punishment. If the American officer who rode back with him afterwards should ever see these words, he will perhaps recall his conversation with Mr. Dickens on the road, as to Mr. Dickens having said so very plainly and strongly. In reference to the ridiculous assertion that Mr. Dickens in his book termed a woman "quite beautiful" who was a Negress, he positively believes that he was shown no Negress in the Prison, but one who was nursing a woman much diseased, and to whom no reference whatever is made in his published account. In describing three young women, "all convicted at the same time of a conspiracy," he may, *possibly*, among many cases, have substituted in his memory for one of them whom he did not see, some other prisoner, confined for some other crime, whom he did see; but he has not the least doubt of having been guilty of the (American) enormity of detecting beauty in a pensive quadroon or mulatto girl, or of having seen exactly what he describes; and he remembers the girl more particularly described in this connexion, perfectly. Can Mr. Field really suppose that Mr. Dickens had any interest or purpose in misrepresenting the system, or that if he could be guilty of such unworthy conduct, or desire to do it anything but justice, he would have volunteered the narrative of a man's having, of his own choice, undergone it for two years?

We will not notice the objection of Mr. Field (who strengthens the truth of Burns to nature, by the testimony of Mr. Pitt!) to the discussion of such a topic as the present in a work of "mere amusement;" though, we had thought we remembered in that book a word or two about slavery, which, although very amusing, can scarcely be considered an unmitigatedly comic theme. We are quite content to believe, without seeking to make a convert of the Reverend Mr. Field, that no work need be one of "mere amusement"; and that some works to which he would apply that designation have done a little good in advancing principles to which, we hope, and will believe, for the credit of his Christian office, he is not indifferent.

Observe! John Styles, who has committed the felony, has been "living quite a careless life." That is his worst opinion of it, whereas his companions, who did not commit the felony, are "wretched companions." John saw *his* "folly," and sees *their* "wicked course." It is playhouses and theatres which many unfelonious people go to, that prey upon John's mind – not felony. John is shut up in that pulpit to lecture his companions and his sister about the wickedness of the unfelonious world. Always supposing him to be sincere, is there no exaggeration of himself in this? Go to church where I can go, and don't go to theatres where I can't! Is there any tinge of the fox and the grapes in it? Is this the kind of penitence that will wear outside! Put the case that he had written, of his own mind, "My dear sister, I feel that I have disgraced you and all who should be dear to me, and if it please God that I live to be free, I will try hard to repair that, and to be a credit to you. My dear sister, when I committed this felony, I stole something – and these pining five months have not put it back – and I will work my fingers to the bone to make restitution, and oh! my dear sister, seek out my late companions, and tell Tom Jones, that poor boy, who was younger and littler than me, that I am grieved I ever led him so wrong, and I am suffering for it now!" Would that be better? Would it be more like solid truth?

But no. This is not the pattern penitence. There would seem to be a pattern penitence, of a particular form, shape, limits, and dimensions, like the cells. While Mr. Field is correcting his proof-sheets for the press, another letter is brought to him, and in that letter too, that man, also a felon, speaks of his "past folly," and lectures his mother about labouring under "strong delusions of the devil." Does this overweening readiness to lecture other people, suggest the suspicion of any parrot-like imitation of Mr. Field, who lectures him, and any presumptuous confounding of their relative positions?

We venture altogether to protest against the citation, in support of this system, of assumed repentance which has stood no test or trial in the working world. We consider that it proves nothing, and is worth nothing, except as a discouraging sign of that spiritual egotism and presumption of which we have already spoken. It is not peculiar to the separate system at Reading; Miss Martineau,[10] who was on the whole decidedly favourable to the separate prison at Philadelphia, observed it there. "The cases I became acquainted with," says she, "were not all hopeful. Some of the convicts were so stupid as not to be relied upon, more or less. Others canted so detestably, and were (always in connexion with their cant) so certain that they should never sin more, that I have every expectation that they will find themselves in prison again some day. One fellow, a sailor, notorious for having taken more lives than probably any man in the United States, was quite confident that he should be perfectly virtuous henceforth. He should never touch anything stronger than tea, or lift his hand against money or life. I told him I thought he could not be sure of all this till he was within sight of money and the smell of strong liquors; and that he was more confident than I should like to be. He shook his shock of red hair at me, and glared with his one ferocious eye, as he said he knew all about it. He had been the worst of men, and Christ had had mercy on his poor soul." (Observe again, as in the general case we have put, that he is not at all troubled about the souls of the people whom he had killed.)

Let us submit to our readers another instance from Mr. Field, of the wholesome state of mind produced by the separate system. "The 25th of March, in the last year, was the day appointed for a general fast, on account of the threatened famine. The following note is in my journal of that day. 'During the evening I visited many prisoners, and found with much satisfaction that a large proportion of them had observed the day in a manner becoming their own situation, and the purpose for which it had been set apart. I think it right to record the following remarkable proof of the effect of discipline. ✱ ✱ ✱ ✱ ✱ They were all supplied with their usual rations. I went first this evening to the cells of the prisoners recently committed for trial (Ward A. 1.), and amongst these (upwards of twenty) I found that but three had abstained from any portion of their food. I then visited twenty-one convicted prisoners who had spent some considerable time in the gaol (Ward C. 1.), and amongst them I found that some had altogether abstained from food, and of the whole number two-thirds had partially abstained.' " We will take it for granted that this was not because they had more than they could eat, though we know that with such a dietary even that sometimes happens, especially in the case of persons long confined. "The remark of one prisoner whom I questioned concerning his abstinence was, I believe, sincere, and was very pleasing. 'Sir, I have not felt able to eat to-day, whilst I have thought of those poor starving people; but I hope that I have prayed a good deal that God will give *them* something to eat.' "

If this were not pattern penitence, and the thought of those poor starving people had honestly originated with that man, and were really on his mind, we want to know why he was not uneasy, every day, in the contemplation of his soup, meat, bread, potatoes, cocoa-nibs, milk, molasses, and gruel, and its contrast to the fare of "those poor starving people" who, in some form or other, were taxed to pay for it?

We do not deem it necessary to comment on the authorities quoted by Mr. Field to show what a fine thing the separate system is, for the health of the body; how it never affects the mind except for good; how it is the true preventive of pulmonary disease; and so on. The deduction we must draw from such things is, that Providence was quite mistaken in making us gregarious, and that we had better all shut ourselves up directly. Neither will we refer to that "talented criminal," Dr. Dodd,[11] whose exceedingly indifferent verses applied to a system now extinct, in reference to our penitentiaries for convicted prisoners. Neither, after what we have quoted from Lord Grey, need we refer to the likewise quoted report of the American authorities, who are perfectly sure that no extent of confinement in the Philadelphia prison has ever affected the intellectual powers of any prisoner. Mr. Croker cogently observes, in the Good-Natured Man, that either his hat must be on his head or it must be off.[12] By a parity of reasoning, we conclude that both Lord Grey and the American authorities, cannot possibly be right – unless indeed the notoriously settled habits of the American people, and the absence of any approach to restlessness in the national character, render them unusually good subjects for protracted seclusion, and an exception from the rest of mankind.

In using the term "pattern penitence" we beg it to be understood that we do not apply it to Mr. Field, or to any other chaplain, but to the system; which appears to us to make these doubtful converts all alike. Although Mr. Field has not shown any remarkable courtesy in the instance we have set forth in a note, it is our wish to show all courtesy to him, and to his office, and to his sincerity in the discharge of its duties. In our desire to represent him with fairness and impartiality, we will not take leave of him without the following quotation from his book:

"Scarcely sufficient time has yet expired, since the present system was introduced, for me to report much concerning discharged criminals. Out of a class so degraded – the very dregs of the community – it can be no wonder that some, of whose improvement I cherished the hope, should have relapsed. Disappointed in a few cases I have been, yet by no means discouraged, since I can with pleasure refer to many whose conduct is affording proof of reformation. Gratifying indeed have been some accounts received from liberated offenders themselves, as well as from clergymen of parishes to which they have returned. I have also myself visited the homes of some of our former prisoners, and have been cheered by the testimony given, and the evident signs of improved character which I have there observed. Although I do not venture at present to describe the particular cases of prisoners, concerning whose reformation I feel much confidence, because, as I have stated, the time of trial has hitherto been short; yet I can with pleasure refer to some public documents which prove the happy effects of similar discipline in other establishments."

It should also be stated that the Reverend Mr. Kingsmill, the chaplain of the Model Prison at Pentonville, in his calm and intelligent report made to the Commissioners on the first of February 1849, expresses his belief "that the effects produced here upon the character of prisoners, have been encouraging in a high degree."

But, we entreat our readers once again to look at that Model Prison dietary (which is essential to the system, though the system is so very healthy of itself); to remember the other enormous expenses of the establishment; to consider the circumstances of this old country, with the inevitable anomalies and contrasts it must present; and to decide, on temperate reflection, whether there are any sufficient reasons for adding this monstrous contrast to the rest. Let us impress upon our readers that the existing question is, not between this system and the old abuses of the old profligate gaols (with which, thank Heaven, we have nothing to do), but between this system, and the associated silent system, where the dietary is much lower, where the annual cost of provision, management, repairs, clothing, etc., does not exceed, on a liberal average, £25 for each prisoner; where many prisoners are, and every prisoner would be (if due accommodation were provided in some overcrowded prisons), locked up alone, for twelve hours out of every twenty-four, and where, while preserved from contamination, he is still one of a society of men, and not an isolated being, filling his whole sphere of view with a diseased dilation of himself. We hear that the associated silent system is objectionable, because of the number of punishments it involves for breaches of the prison discipline; but how can we, in the same breath, be told that the resolutions of prisoners for the misty future are to be trusted, and that, on the least temptation, they are so little to be relied on, as to the solid present? How can I set the pattern penitence against the career that preceded it, when I am told that if I put that man with other men, and lay a solemn charge upon him not to address them by word or sign, there are such and such great chances that he will want the resolution to obey?

Remember that this separate system, though commended in the English Parliament and spreading in England, has not spread in America, despite of all the steeple-chase riders in the United States. Remember that it has never reached the State most distinguished for its learning, for its moderation, for its remarkable men of European reputation, for the excellence of its public Institutions. Let it be tried here, on a limited scale, if you will, with fair representatives of all classes of prisoners: let Captain Macconnochie's system be tried: let anything with a ray of hope in it be tried: but, only as a part of some general system for raising up the prostrate portion of the people of this country, and not as an exhibition of such astonishing consideration for crime, in comparison with want and work. Any prison built, at a great expenditure, for this system, is comparatively useless for any other; and the ratepayers will do well to think of this, before they take it for granted that it is a proved boon to the country which will be enduring.

Under the separate system, the prisoners work at trades. Under the associated silent system, the Magistrates of Middlesex have almost abolished the treadmill. Is it no part of the legitimate consideration of this important point of work, to discover what kind of work the people always filtering through the gaols of large towns – the pickpocket, the sturdy vagrant, the habitual drunkard, and the begging-letter impostor – like least, and to give them that work to do in preference to any other? It is out of fashion with the steeple-chase riders we know; but we would have, for all such characters, a kind of work in gaols, badged and degraded as belonging to gaols only, and never done elsewhere. And we must avow that, in a country circumstanced as England is, with respect to labour and labourers, we have strong doubts of the propriety of bringing the results of prison labour into the over-stocked market. On this subject some public remonstrances have recently been made by tradesmen; and we cannot shut our eyes to the fact that they are well-founded.

A Poor Man's Tale of a Patent

First published in *Household Words*, 19 October 1850, from which this text is reproduced. On 25 September 1850, Dickens wrote to Henry Cole (1808–82), whose account of the absurdities of the current patent laws, 'The Rights of Inventors', he had seen in proof, and told him that he was at work on a paper for *Household Words*, 'which I hope may help the question in a taking manner'. The article is heavily based on Cole's account of the numerous stages an inventor had to undergo to acquire a patent; and it's possible that this account provides the basis for the bureaucratic terrors visited upon the inventor Daniel Doyce in *Little Dorrit*.

I am not used to writing for print. What working-man, that never labours less (some Mondays, and Christmas Time and Easter Time excepted) than twelve or fourteen hours a day, is? But I have been asked to put down, plain, what I have got to say; and so I take pen-and-ink, and do it to the best of my power, hoping defects will find excuse.

I was born nigh London, but have worked in a shop at Birmingham (what you would call Manufactories, we call Shops) almost ever since I was out of my time. I served my apprenticeship at Deptford, nigh where I was born, and I am a smith by trade. My name is John. I have been called "Old John" ever since I was nineteen year of age, on account of not having much hair. I am fifty-six year of age at the present time, and I don't find myself with more hair, nor yet with less, to signify, than at nineteen year of age aforesaid.

I have been married five and thirty year, come next April. I was married on All Fools' Day. Let them laugh that win. I won a good wife that day, and it was as sensible a day to me as ever I had.

We have had a matter of ten children, six whereof are living. My eldest son is engineer in the Italian steam-packet "Mezzo Giorno, plying between Marseilles and Naples, and calling at Genoa, Leghorn, and Civita Vecchia." He was a good workman. He invented a many useful little things that brought him in – nothing. I have two sons doing well at Sydney, New South Wales – single, when last heard from. One of my sons (James) went wild and for a soldier, where he was shot in India, living six weeks in hospital with a musket-ball lodged in his shoulder-blade, which he wrote with his own hand. He was the best looking. One of my two daughters

(Mary) is comfortable in her circumstances, but water on the chest. The other (Charlotte), her husband run away from her in the basest manner, and she and her three children live with us. The youngest, six year old, has a turn for mechanics.

I am not a Chartist,[1] and I never was. I don't mean to say but what I see a good many public points to complain of, still I don't think that's the way to set them right. If I did think so, I should be a Chartist. But I don't think so, and I am not a Chartist. I read the paper, and hear discussion, at what we call "a parlour," in Birmingham, and I know many good men and workmen who are Chartists. Note. Not Physical force.

It won't be took as boastful in me, if I make the remark (for I can't put down what I have got to say, without putting that down before going any further), that I have always been of an ingenious turn. I once got twenty pound by a screw, and it's in use now. I have been twenty year, off and on, completing an Invention and perfecting it. I perfected of it, last Christmas Eve at ten o'clock at night. Me and my wife stood and let some tears fall over the Model, when it was done and I brought her in to take a look at it.

A friend of mine, by the name of William Butcher, is a Chartist. Moderate. He is a good speaker. He is very animated. I have often heard him deliver that what is, at every turn, in the way of us working-men, is, that too many places have been made, in the course of time, to provide for people that never ought to have been provided for; and that we have to obey forms and to pay fees to support those places when we shouldn't ought. "True," (delivers William Butcher), "all the public has to do this, but it falls heaviest on the working-man, because he has least to spare; and likewise because impediments shouldn't be put in his way, when he wants redress of wrong or furtherance of right." Note. I have wrote down those words from William Butcher's own mouth. W. B. delivering them fresh for the aforesaid purpose.

Now, to my Model again. There it was, perfected of, on Christmas Eve, gone nigh a year, at ten o'clock at night. All the money I could spare I had laid out upon the Model; and when times was bad, or my daughter Charlotte's children sickly, or both, it had stood still, months at a spell. I had pulled it to pieces, and made it over again with improvements, I don't know how often. There it stood, at last, a perfected Model as aforesaid.

William Butcher and me had a long talk, Christmas Day, respecting of the Model. William is very sensible. But sometimes cranky. William said, "What will you do with it, John?" I said, "Patent it." William said, "How patent it, John?" I said, "By taking out a Patent." William then delivered that the law of Patent was a cruel wrong. William said, "John, if you make

409

your invention public, before you get a Patent, any one may rob you of the fruits of your hard work. You are put in a cleft stick, John. Either you must drive a bargain very much against yourself, by getting a party to come forward beforehand with the great expenses of the Patent; or, you must be put about, from post to pillar, among so many parties, trying to make a better bargain for yourself, and showing your invention, that your invention will be took from you over your head." I said, "William Butcher, are you cranky? You are sometimes cranky." William said, "No, John, I tell you the truth;" which he then delivered more at length. I said to W. B. I would Patent the invention myself.

My wife's brother, George Bury of West Bromwich (his wife unfortunately took to drinking, made away with everything, and seventeen times committed to Birmingham Jail before happy release in every point of view), left my wife, his sister, when he died, a legacy of one hundred and twenty-eight pound ten, Bank of England Stocks. Me and my wife never broke into that money yet. Note. We might come to be old and past our work. We now agreed to Patent the invention. We said we would make a hole in it – I mean in the aforesaid money – and Patent the invention. William Butcher wrote me a letter to Thomas Joy, in London. T. J. is a carpenter, six foot four in height, and plays quoits well. He lives in Chelsea, London, by the church. I got leave from the shop, to be took on again when I come back. I am a good workman. Not a Teetotaller; but never drunk. When the Christmas holidays were over, I went up to London by the Parliamentary Train, and hired a lodging for a week with Thomas Joy. He is married. He has one son gone to sea.

Thomas Joy delivered (from a book he had) that the first step to be took, in Patenting the invention, was to prepare a petition unto Queen Victoria. William Butcher had delivered similar, and drawn it up. Note. William is a ready writer. A declaration before a Master in Chancery was to be added to it. That, we likewise drew up. After a deal of trouble I found out a Master, in Southampton Buildings, Chancery Lane, nigh Temple Bar, where I made the declaration, and paid eighteen-pence. I was told to take the declaration and petition to the Home Office, in Whitehall, where I left it to be signed by the Home Secretary (after I had found the office out), and where I paid two pound, two, and sixpence. In six days he signed it, and I was told to take it to the Attorney-General's chambers, and leave it there for a report. I did so, and paid four pound, four. Note. Nobody all through, ever thankful for their money, but all uncivil.

My lodging at Thomas Joy's was now hired for another week, whereof five days were gone. The Attorney-General made what they called a

Report-of-course (my invention being, as William Butcher had delivered before starting, unopposed), and I was sent back with it to the Home Office. They made a Copy of it, which was called a Warrant. For this warrant, I paid seven pound, thirteen, and six. It was sent to the Queen, to sign. The Queen sent it back, signed. The Home Secretary signed it again. The gentleman throwed it at me when I called, and said, "Now take it to the Patent Office in Lincoln's Inn." I was then in my third week at Thomas Joy's, living very sparing, on account of fees. I found myself losing heart.

At the Patent Office in Lincoln's Inn, they made "a draft of the Queen's bill," of my invention, and a "docket of the bill." I paid five pound, ten, and six, for this. They "engrossed two copies of the bill; one for the Signet Office, and one for the Privy-Seal Office." I paid one pound, seven, and six, for this. Stamp duty over and above, three pound. The Engrossing Clerk of the same office engrossed the Queen's bill for signature. I paid him one pound, one. Stamp duty, again, one pound, ten. I was next to take the Queen's bill to the Attorney-General again, and get it signed again. I took it, and paid five pound more. I fetched it away, and took it to the Home Secretary again. He sent it to the Queen again. She signed it again. I paid seven pound, thirteen, and six, more, for this. I had been over a month at Thomas Joy's. I was quite wore out, patience and pocket.

Thomas Joy delivered all this, as it went on, to William Butcher. William Butcher delivered it again to three Birmingham Parlours, from which it got to all the other Parlours, and was took, as I have been told since, right through all the shops in the North of England. Note. William Butcher delivered, at his Parlour, in a speech, that it was a Patent way of making Chartists.

But I hadn't nigh done yet. The Queen's bill was to be took to the Signet Office in Somerset House, Strand – where the stamp shop is. The Clerk of the Signet made "a Signet bill for the Lord Keeper of the Privy Seal." I paid him four pound, seven. The Clerk of the Lord Keeper of the Privy Seal made "a Privy-Seal bill for the Lord Chancellor." I paid him four pound, two. The Privy-Seal bill was handed over to the Clerk of the Patents, who engrossed the aforesaid. I paid him five pound, seventeen, and eight; at the same time, I paid Stamp-duty for the Patent, in one lump, thirty pound. I next paid for "boxes for the Patent," nine and sixpence. Note. Thomas Joy would have made the same at a profit for eighteen-pence. I next paid "fees to the Deputy, the Lord Chancellor's Purse-bearer," two pound, two. I next paid "fees to the Clerk of the Hanaper,"[2] seven pound, thirteen. I next paid "fees to the Deputy Clerk of the Hanaper," ten shillings. I next paid, to the Lord Chancellor again, one pound, eleven, and six. Last of all, I paid "fees to the Deputy Sealer, and Deputy Chaff-wax,"[3] ten shillings and sixpence. I had lodged at Thomas Joy's over six weeks, and the unopposed Patent for my invention, for England only, had cost me ninety-six pound, seven, and eightpence. If I had taken it out for the United Kingdom, it would have cost me more than three hundred pound.

Now, teaching had not come up but very limited when I was young. So much the worse for me, you'll say. I say the same. William Butcher is twenty year younger than me. He knows a hundred year more. If William Butcher had wanted to Patent an invention, he might have been sharper than myself when hustled backwards and forwards among all those offices, though I doubt if so patient. Note. William being sometimes cranky, and consider porters, messengers, and clerks.

Thereby I say nothing of my being tired of my life, while I was Patenting my invention. But I put this: Is it reasonable to make a man feel as if, in inventing an ingenious improvement meant to do good, he had done something wrong? How else can a man feel, when he is met by such difficulties at every turn? All inventors taking out a Patent MUST feel so. And look at the expense. How hard on me, and how hard on the country if there's any merit in me (and my invention is took up now, I am thankful to say, and doing well), to put me to all that expense before I can move a finger! Make the addition yourself, and it'll come to ninety-six pound, seven, and eightpence. No more, and no less.

What can I say against William Butcher, about places? Look at the Home Secretary, the Attorney-General, the Patent Office, the Engrossing Clerk, the Lord Chancellor, the Privy Seal, the Clerk of the Patents, the Lord Chancellor's Purse-bearer, the Clerk of the Hanaper, the Deputy Clerk of the Hanaper, the Deputy Sealer, and the Deputy Chaff-wax. No man in England could get a Patent for an Indian-rubber band, or an iron-hoop, without feeing all of them. Some of them, over and over again. I went through thirty-five stages. I began with the Queen upon the Throne. I ended with the Deputy Chaff-wax. Note. I should like to see the Deputy Chaff-wax. Is it a man, or what is it?

What I had to tell, I have told. I have wrote it down. I hope it's plain. Not so much in the handwriting (though nothing to boast of there), as in the sense of it. I will now conclude with Thomas Joy. Thomas said to me, when we parted, "John, if the laws of this country were as honest as they ought to be, you would have come to London – registered an exact description and drawing of your invention – paid half-a-crown or so for doing of it – and therein and thereby have got your Patent."

My opinion is the same as Thomas Joy. Further. In William Butcher's delivering "that the whole gang of Hanapers and Chaff-waxes must be done away with, and that England has been chaffed and waxed sufficient," I agree.

Lively Turtle

First published in *Household Words*, 26 October 1850, from which this text is reproduced.

I have a comfortable property. What I spend, I spend upon myself; and what I don't spend I save. Those are my principles. I am warmly attached to my principles, and stick to them on all occasions.

I am not, as some people have represented, a mean man. I never denied myself anything that I thought I should like to have. I may have said to myself "SNOADY" – that is my name – "you will get those peaches cheaper if you wait till next week;" or, I may have said to myself, "Snoady, you will get that wine for nothing, if you wait till you are asked out to dine;" but I never deny myself anything. If I can't get what I want without buying it, and paying its price for it, I *do* buy it and pay its price for it. I have an appetite bestowed upon me; and, if I baulked it, I should consider that I was flying in the face of Providence.

I have no near relation but a brother. If he wants anything of me, he don't get it. All men are my brothers; and I see no reason why I should make his, an exceptional case.

I live at a cathedral town where there is an old corporation. I am not in the Church, but it may be that I hold a little place of some sort. Never mind. It may be profitable. Perhaps yes, perhaps no. It may, or it may not, be a sinecure. I don't choose to say. I never enlightened my brother on these subjects, and I consider all men my brothers. The Negro is a man and a brother – should I hold myself accountable for my position in life, *to him*? Certainly not.

I often run up to London. I like London. The way I look at it, is this. London is not a cheap place, but, on the whole, you can get more of the real thing for your money there – I mean the best thing, whatever it is – than you can get in most places. Therefore, I say to the man who has got the money, and wants the thing, "Go to London for it, and treat yourself."

When *I* go, I do it in this manner. I go to Mrs. Skim's Private Hotel and Commercial Lodging House, near Aldersgate Street, City, (it is advertised in "Bradshaw's Railway Guide," where I first found it), and there I pay, "for bed and breakfast, with meat, two and ninepence per day, including servants." Now, I have made a calculation, and I am satisfied that Mrs. Skim cannot possibly make much profit out of *me*. In fact, if all her patrons were like me, my opinion is, the woman would be in the Gazette next month.

Why do I go to Mrs. Skim's when I could go to the Clarendon,[1] you may ask? Let us argue that point. If I went to the Clarendon I could get nothing in bed but sleep; could I? No. Now, sleep at the Clarendon is an expensive article; whereas sleep, at Mrs. Skim's, is decidedly cheap. I have made a calculation, and I don't hesitate to say, all things considered, that it's cheap. Is it an inferior article, as compared with the Clarendon sleep, or is it of the same quality? I am a heavy sleeper, and it is of the same quality. Then why should I go to the Clarendon?

But as to breakfast? you may say. – Very well. As to breakfast. I could get a variety of delicacies for breakfast at the Clarendon, that are out of the question at Mrs. Skim's. Granted. But I don't want to have them! My opinion is, that we are not entirely animal and sensual. Man has an intellect bestowed upon him. If he clogs that intellect by too good a breakfast, how can he properly exert that intellect in meditation, during the day, upon his dinner? That's the point. We are not to enchain the soul. We are to let it soar. It is expected of us.

At Mrs. Skim's, I get enough for breakfast (there is no limitation to the bread and butter, though there is to the meat) and not too much. I have all my faculties about me, to concentrate upon the object I have mentioned, and I can say to myself besides, "Snoady, you have saved six, eight, ten, fifteen, shillings, already to-day. If there is anything you fancy for your dinner, have it. Snoady, you have earned your reward."

My objection to London, is, that it is the head-quarters of the worst radical sentiments that are broached in England. I consider that it has a great many dangerous people in it. I consider the present publication (if it's "Household Words") very dangerous, and I write this with the view of neutralising some of its bad effects. My political creed is, let us be comfortable. We are all very comfortable as we are – *I* am very comfortable as I am – leave us alone!

All mankind are my brothers, and I don't think it Christian – if you come to that – to tell my brother that he is ignorant, or degraded, or dirty, or anything of the kind. I think it's abusive, and low. You meet me with the observation that I am required to love my brother. I reply, "I do." I am sure I am always willing to say to my brother, "My good fellow, I love you very much; go along with you; keep to your own road; leave me to mine; whatever is, is right; whatever isn't, is wrong; don't make a disturbance!" It seems to me, that this is at once the whole duty of man, and the only temper to go to dinner in.

Going to dinner in this temper in the City of London, one day not long ago, after a bed at Mrs. Skim's, with meat-breakfast and servants included, I was reminded of the observation which, if my memory does not deceive me, was formerly made by somebody on some occasion, that man may learn wisdom from the lower animals. It is a beautiful fact, in my opinion, that great wisdom is to be learnt from that noble animal the Turtle.

I had made up my mind, in the course of the day I speak of, to have a Turtle dinner. I mean a dinner mainly composed of Turtle. Just a comfortable tureen of soup, with a pint of punch; and nothing solid to follow, but a tender juicy steak. I like a tender juicy steak. I generally say to myself when I order one, "Snoady, you have done right."

When I make up my mind to have a delicacy, expense is no consideration. The question resolves itself, then, into a question of the very best. I went to a friend of mine who is a Member of the Common Council,[2] and with that friend I held the following conversation.

Said I to him, "Mr. Groggles,[3] the best Turtle is where?"

Says he, "If you want a basin for lunch, my opinion is, you can't do better than drop into Birch's."[4]

Said I, "Mr. Groggles, I thought you had known me better, than to suppose me capable of a basin. My intention is to dine. A tureen."

Says Mr. Groggles, without a moment's consideration, and in a determined voice. "Right opposite the India House, Leadenhall Street."

We parted. My mind was not inactive during the day, and at six in the afternoon I repaired to the house of Mr. Groggles's recommendation.[5] At the end of the passage, leading from the street into the coffee-room, I observed a vast and solid chest, in which I then supposed that a Turtle of unusual size might be deposited. But, the correspondence between its bulk and that of the charge made for my dinner, afterwards satisfied me that it must be the till of the establishment.

I stated to the waiter what had brought me there, and I mentioned Mr. Groggles's name. He feelingly repeated after me, "A tureen of Turtle, and a tender juicy steak." His manner, added to the manner of Mr. Groggles in the morning, satisfied me that all was well. The atmosphere of the coffee-room was odoriferous with Turtle, and the steams of thousands of gallons, consumed within its walls, hung, in savoury grease, upon their surface. I could have inscribed my name with a pen-knife, if I had been so disposed, in the essence of innumerable Turtles. I preferred to fall into a hungry reverie, brought on by the warm breath of the place, and to think of the West Indies and the Island of Ascension.

My dinner came – and went. I will draw a veil over the meal, I will put the cover on the empty tureen, and merely say that it was wonderful – and that I paid for it.

I sat meditating, when all was over, on the imperfect nature of our present existence, in which we can eat only for a limited time, when the waiter roused me with these words.

Said he to me, as he brushed the crumbs off the table, "Would you like to see the Turtle, Sir?"

"To see what Turtle, waiter?" said I (calmly) to him.

"The tanks of Turtle below, Sir," said he to me.

Tanks of Turtle! Good Gracious! "Yes!"

The waiter lighted a candle, and conducted me down stairs to a range of vaulted apartments, cleanly whitewashed and illuminated with gas, where I saw a sight of the most astonishing and gratifying description, illustrative of the greatness of my native country. "Snoady," was my first observation to myself, "Rule Britannia, Britannia rules the waves!"

There were two or three hundred Turtle in the vaulted apartments – all alive. Some in tanks, and some taking the air in long dry walks littered down with straw. They were of all sizes; many of them enormous. Some of the enormous ones had entangled themselves with the smaller ones, and pushed and squeezed themselves into corners, with their fins over water-pipes, and their heads downwards, where they were apoplectically struggling and splashing, apparently in the last extremity. Others were calm at the bottom of the tanks; others languidly rising to the surface. The Turtle in the walks littered down with straw, were calm and motionless. It was a thrilling sight. I admire such a sight. It rouses my imagination. If you wish to try its effect on yours, make a call right opposite the India House any day you please – dine – pay – and ask to be taken below.

Two athletic young men, without coats, and with the sleeves of their shirts tucked up to the shoulders, were in attendance on these noble animals. One of them, wrestling with the most enormous Turtle in company, and dragging him up to the edge of the tank, for me to look at, presented an idea to me which I never had before. I ought to observe that I like an idea. I say, when I get a new one, "Snoady, book that!"

My idea, on the present occasion, was, – Mr. Groggles! It was not a Turtle that I saw, but Mr. Groggles. It was the dead image of Mr. Groggles. He was dragged up to confront me, with his waistcoat – if I may be allowed the expression – towards me; and it was identically the waistcoat of Mr.

Groggles. It was the same shape, very nearly the same colour, only wanted a gold watch-chain and a bunch of seals, to BE the waistcoat of Mr. Groggles. There was what I should call a bursting expression about him in general, which was accurately the expression of Mr. Groggles. I had never closely observed a Turtle's throat before. The folds of his loose cravat, I found to be precisely those of Mr. Groggles's cravat. Even the intelligent eye – I mean to say, intelligent enough for a person of correct principles, and not dangerously so – was the eye of Mr. Groggles. When the athletic young man let him go, and, with a roll of his head, he flopped heavily down into the tank, it was exactly the manner of Mr. Groggles as I have seen him ooze away into his seat, after opposing a sanitary motion in the Court of Common Council!

"Snoady," I couldn't help saying to myself, "you have done it. You have got an idea, Snoady, in which a great principle is involved. I congratulate you!" I followed the young man, who dragged up several Turtle to the brinks of the various tanks. I found them all the same – all varieties of Mr. Groggles – all extraordinarily like the gentlemen who usually eat them. "Now, Snoady," was my next remark, "what do you deduce from this?"

"Sir," said I, "what I deduce from this, is, confusion to those Radicals and other Revolutionists who talk about improvement. Sir," said I, "what I deduce from this, is, that there isn't this resemblance between the Turtles and the Groggleses for nothing. It's meant to show mankind that the proper model for a Groggles, is a Turtle; and that the liveliness we want in a Groggles, is the liveliness of a Turtle, and no more." "Snoady," was my reply to this, "You have hit it. You are right!"

I admired the idea very much, because, if I hate anything in the world, it's change. Change has evidently no business in the world, has nothing to do with it, and isn't intended. What we want is (as I think I have mentioned) to be comfortable. I look at it that way. Let us be comfortable, and leave us alone. Now, when the young man dragged a Groggles – I mean a Turtle – out of his tank, this was exactly what the noble animal expressed as he floundered back again.

I have several friends besides Mr. Groggles in the Common Council, and it might be a week after this, when I said, "Snoady, if I was you, I would go to that court, and hear the debate to-day." I went. A good deal of it was what I call a sound, old English discussion. One eloquent speaker objected to the French as wearing wooden shoes; and a friend of his reminded him of another objection to that foreign people, namely, that they eat frogs. I had feared, for many years, I am sorry to say, that these wholesome principles were gone out. How delightful to find them still remaining among the great men of the City of London, in the year one thousand eight hundred and fifty! It made me think of the Lively Turtle.

But, I soon thought more of the Lively Turtle. Some Radicals and Revolutionists have penetrated even to the Common Council — which otherwise I regard as one of the last strongholds of our afflicted constitution; and speeches were made, about removing Smithfield Market — which I consider to be a part of that Constitution — and about appointing a Medical Officer for the City, and about preserving the public health; and other treasonable practices, opposed to Church and State. These proposals Mr. Groggles, as might have been expected of such a man, resisted; so warmly, that, as I afterwards understood from Mrs. Groggles, he had rather a sharp attack of blood to the head that night. All the Groggles party resisted them too, and it was a fine constitutional sight to see waistcoat after waistcoat rise up in resistance of them and subside. But what struck me in the sight was this, "Snoady," said I, "here is your idea carried out, Sir! These Radicals and Revolutionists are the athletic young men in shirt sleeves, dragging the Lively Turtle to the edges of the tank. The Groggleses are the Turtle, looking out for a moment, and flopping down again. Honour to the Groggleses! Honour to the Court of Lively Turtle! The wisdom of the Turtle is the hope of England!"

There are three heads in the moral of what I had to say. First, Turtle and Groggles are identical; wonderfully alike externally, wonderfully alike mentally. Secondly, Turtle is a good thing every way, and the liveliness of the Turtle is intended as an example for the liveliness of man; you are not to go beyond that. Thirdly, we are all quite comfortable. Leave us alone!

Red Tape

First published in *Household Words*, 15 February 1851, from which this text is reproduced. In late January 1851, Dickens wrote to his brother-in-law, Henry Austin, and asked if he had 'any printed particulars in any Reports, concerning the more obvious absurdities & evils of the Window Tax?'.

Your public functionary who delights in Red Tape – the purpose of whose existence is to tie up public questions, great and small, in an abundance of this official article – to make the neatest possible parcels of them, ticket them, and carefully put them away on a top shelf out of human reach – is the peculiar curse and nuisance of England. Iron, steel, adamant, can make no such drag-chain as Red Tape. An invasion of Red Ants in innumerable millions, would not be half so prejudicial to Great Britain, as its intolerable Red Tape.

Your Red Tapist is everywhere. He is always at hand, with a coil of Red Tape, prepared to make a small official parcel of the largest subject. In the reception-room of a Government Office, he will wind Red Tape round and round the sternest deputation that the country can send to him. In either House of Parliament, he will pull more Red Tape out of his mouth, at a moment's notice, than a conjuror at a Fair. In letters, memoranda, and dispatches, he will spin himself into Red Tape, by the thousand yards. He will bind you up vast colonies, in Red Tape, like cold roast chickens at a rout-supper;[1] and when the most valuable of them break it (a mere question of time), he will be amazed to find that they were too expansive for his favourite commodity. He will put a girdle of Red Tape round the earth, in quicker time than Ariel.[2] He will measure, from Downing Street to the North Pole, or the heart of New Zealand, or the highest summit of the Himalaya Mountains, by inches of Red Tape. He will rig all the ships in the British Navy with it, weave all the colours in the British Army from it, completely equip and fit out the officers and men of both services in it. He bound Nelson and Wellington hand and foot with it – ornamented them, all over, with bunches of it – and sent them forth to do impossibilities. He will stand over the side of the steamship of the state, sounding with Red Tape, for imaginary obstacles; and when the office-seal at the end of his pet line touches a floating weed, will cry majestically, "Back her! Stop her!"

He hangs great social efforts, in Red Tape, about the public offices, to terrify like evil-minded reformers, as great highwaymen used to be hanged in chains on Hounslow Heath. He has but one answer to every demonstration of right, or exposition of wrong; and it is, "My good Sir, this is a question of Tape."

He is the most gentlemanly of men. He is mysterious; but not more so than a man who is cognisant of so much Tape ought to be. Butterflies and gadflies who disport themselves, unconscious of the amount of Red Tape required to keep Creation together, may wear their hearts upon their sleeves; but he is another sort of person. Not that he is wanting in conversation. By no means. Every question mooted, he has to tie up according to form, and put away. Church, state, territory native and foreign, ignorance, poverty, crime, punishment, popes, cardinals, jesuits, taxes, agriculture and commerce, land and sea – all Tape. "Nothing but Tape, Sir, I assure you. Will you allow me to tie this subject up, with a few years, according to the official form? Thank you. Thus, you see. A knot here; the end cut off there; a twist in this place; a loop in that. Nothing can be more complete. Quite compact, you observe. I ticket it, you perceive, and put it on the shelf. It is now disposed of. What is the next article?"

The quantity of Red Tape officially employed in the defence of such an imposition (in more senses than one) as the Window Tax;[3] the array of Red Tapists and the amount of Red Taping employed in its behalf, within the last six or seven years, is something so astounding in itself, and so illustrative of the enormous quantities of Tape devoted to the public confusion, that we take the liberty, at this appropriate time, of disentangling an odd thousand fathoms or so, as a sample of the commodity.

The Window Tax is a tax of that just and equitable description, that it charges a house with twenty windows at the rate of six shillings and twopence farthing a window; and houses with nine times as many windows, to wit a hundred and eighty, at the rate of eightpence a window, *less*. It is a beautiful feature in this tax (and a mighty convenient one for large country-houses) that, after progressing in a gradually ascending scale or charge, from eight windows to seventy-nine, it then begins to descend again, and charges a house with five hundred windows, just a farthing a window more than a house with nine. This has been, for so many years, proved – by Red Tape – to be the perfection of human reason, that we merely remark upon the circumstance, and there leave it, for another ornamental branch of the subject.

Light and air are the first essentials of our being. Among the facts demonstrated by Physical Science, there is not one more indisputable, than that a large amount of Solar Light is necessary to the development of the nervous system. Lettuces, and some other vegetables, may be grown in the dark, at no greater disadvantage than a change in their natural colour; but, the nervous system of Animals must be developed by Light. The higher the Animal, the more stringent and absolute the necessity of a free admission to it of the Sun's bright rays. All human creatures bred in darkness, droop, and become degenerate. Among the diseases distinctly known to be engendered and propagated by the want of Light, and by its necessary concomitant, the want of free Air, those dreadful maladies, Scrofula and Consumption, occupy the foremost place.

At this time of day, and when the labours of Sanitary Reformers and Boards of Health have educated the general mind in the knowledge of such truths, we almost hesitate to recapitulate these simple facts: which are as palpable and certain as the growth of a tree, or the curling of a wave. But, within a few years, it was a main fault of practical Philosophy, to hold too much herself apart from the daily business and concerns of life. Consequently, within a few years, even these truths were imperfectly and narrowly known. Red Tape, as a great institution quite superior to Nature, positively refused to receive them – strangled them, out of hand – labelled them Impositions, and shelved them with great resentment.

This is so incredible, that our readers will naturally inquire, when, where, and how? Thus. In the Spring of 1844, there sat enthroned, in the office of the Chancellor of the Exchequer,[4] Downing Street, London, the Incarnation of Red Tape. There waited upon this enshrinement of Red Tape in the body and flesh of man, a Deputation from the Master Carpenters' Society, and another from the Metropolitan Improvement Society: which latter, comprising among its members some distinguished students of Natural Philosophy, took the liberty of representing the before-mentioned fact in connexion with Light, as a small result of Infinite Wisdom, eternally established before Tape was. And, forasmuch as the Window Tax excluded light from the dwellings of the poor in large towns, where the poor lived, crowded together in large old houses; by tempting the landlords of those houses to block up windows and save themselves the payment of duty, which they notoriously did – and, forasmuch, as in every room and corner thus made dark and airless, the poor, for want of space, were fain to huddle beds – and, forasmuch, as a large and a most unnatural percentage of them, were, in consequence, scrofulous, and consumptive, and always sliding downwards into Pauperism – the Deputation prayed the Right Honourable Red Tape, M.P., at least so to modify this tax, as to modify that inhuman and expensive wrong. To which, the Right Honourable Red Tape, M.P., made reply, that he didn't believe that the Tax had anything to do with scrofula; "for," said he, "the window-duties don't affect the cottager; and I have seen numerous instances of scrofula in my own neighbourhood, among the families of the agricultural peasantry." Now, this was the perfection of what may be called Red Tapeosophy. For, not to mention the fact, well known to every traveller about England, that the cottages of agricultural labourers, in general, are a perfect model of sanitary arrangement, and are, in particular remarkable for the capacious dimensions of their windows (which are usually of the bay or oriel form: never less than six feet high, commonly fitted with plate glass, and always capable of being opened freely), it is to be carefully noticed that such cottages always contain a superabundance of room, and especially of sleeping-room: also, that nothing can be farther from the custom of a cottager than to let a sleeping-room to a single man, to diminish his rent and to crowd himself and family into one small chamber, where by reason of the dearness of fuel he stops up crevices, and shuts out air. These being things which no English landlord, dead or alive, ever heard of, it is clear – as clear as the agricultural labourer's cottage is light and airy – that the exclusion of light and air can have nothing to do with Scrofula. So, the Right Honourable Red Tape, M.P., gave the lie (politely) to the Deputation, and proved his case against Nature, to the great admiration of the office Messengers!

Well! But, on the same occasion, there was more Red Tape yet, in the background, ready, in nautical phrase, to be paid out. The Deputation, rather pertinaciously dwelling on the murderous effects of a prohibition of ventilation in the thickly-peopled habitations of the poor, the same authority returned, "You *can* ventilate them if you choose. Here is Deputy Red Tape, from the Stamp Office, at my elbow: and he tells you, that perforated plates of zinc, may be placed in the external walls of houses, without becoming liable to duty." Now, the Deputation were very glad to hear this, because they knew it to be a part of the perfect wisdom of the Acts of Parliament establishing the Window Tax, that they required all stopped-up windows to be stopped up with precisely the same substance as that of which the external walls of a house were made; and that, in a variety of cases, where such walls were of stone, for example, and such windows were stopped up with wood, they were held to be chargeable with duty: though they admitted no ray of light through that usually opaque material. Besides which, the Deputation knew, from the Government Returns, that, under the same Acts of Parliament, a little unglazed hole in a wall, made for a cat to creep through, and a little trap in a cellar to shoot coals down, had been solemnly decided to be windows. Therefore, they were so much relieved by this perforated-zinc discovery, that the good and indefatigable Doctor Southwood Smith[5] (who was one of the deputation) was seen, by Private John Towler, of the Second Grenadier Guards, sentry on duty at the Treasury, to fall upon the neck of Mr. Toynbee (who was another of the deputation) and shed tears of joy in Parliament Street.

But, the President of the Carpenters' Society, a man of rule and compasses, whose organ of veneration appears (in respect of Red Tape) to have been imperfectly developed, doubted. And he, writing to the Stamp Office on the point, caused more Red Tape to be spun into this piece of information, "that perforated plates of zinc would be chargeable if so perforated as to afford light, but not if so as to serve the purpose of ventilation only!" It not being within the knowledge of the Carpenters' Society (which was a merely practical body) how to construct perforations of such a peculiar double-barrelled action as at once to let in air and shut out light, the Right Honourable Red Tape, M.P., himself, was referred to for an explanation. This, he gave in the following skein, which has justly been considered the highest specimen of the manufacture. "There has been no mistake, as the parties suppose, in stating that openings for ventilation might be made which would not be chargeable as windows, and I cannot think it at all inconsistent with such a statement to decline expressing, beforehand, a general opinion as to whether certain openings when made would or would not be considered as windows, and as such liable to charge."

To crown all, with a wreath of blushing Tape of the first official quality, it may be briefly mentioned, that no existing Act of Parliament made any such exception, and that it had no existence out of Tape. For, a local act, for Liverpool only, was *afterwards passed*, exempting from the Window Tax circular ventilating apertures, not exceeding seven inches in diameter; provided, that if they were made in a direct line, they should be protected by a grating of cast-iron, the interstices thereof not exceeding one quarter of an inch in width.

One other choice sample of the best Red Tape presents itself in the nefarious history of the Window Tax. In July of the same year, Lord Althorp[6] − whose name is ever to be respected, as having, perhaps, less association with Red Tape than that of any Minister whomsoever − made a short speech in the House of Commons, descriptive of an enactment he then introduced, for allaying something of the indignation which this tax had raised. It was, he said, "a clause, enabling persons to open fresh windows in houses at present existing, without any additional charge. Its only effect is, to prevent an increase of the revenue, in the case of houses already existing." On the faith of this statement, numbers of house-occupiers opened new windows. The instant the clause got into the Government offices, it was immeshed in a very net of Red Tape. The Stamp Office, in its construction of it, substituted existing occupiers, for existing houses; into the clause itself were introduced, before it became law, words, confining this privilege to persons "duly assessed for the year ending 5th April 1835." What followed? Red Tape made the discovery that no one who took advantage of that clause, and opened new windows, WAS duly assessed in 1835 – the whole Government Assessment: made, be it remembered, by Government Assessors: having been loosely and carelessly made – and all those openers of new windows, upon the faith of that plain speech of a plain gentleman, were surcharged; to the increase of the revenue, the dishonour of the public character of the country, and the very canonisation of Red Tape.

For the collection and clear statement of these facts, we are indebted to an excellent pamphlet reprinted, at the time, from the Westminster Review.[7] The facts and the subject are worthy of one another.

O give your public functionary, who delights in Red Tape, a good social improvement to deal with! Let him come back to his Tape-wits, after being frightened out of them, for a little while, by the ravages of a Plague; and count, if you can, the miles of Red Tape he will pile into barriers, against – a General Interment Bill, say, or a Law for the suppression of infectious and disgusting nuisances! O the cables of Red Tape he will coil away in dispatch boxes, the handcuffs he will make of Red Tape to fetter useful hands; the interminable perspectives of Exchequers, Woods and Forests, and what not, all hung with Red Tape, up and down which he will languidly wander, to the weariness of all whose hard fate it is, to have to pursue him!

But, give him something to play with – give him a park to slice away – a hideous scarecrow to set up in a public place, where it may become the ludicrous horror of the civilised earth – a marble arch to move – and who so brisk as he! He will rig you up a scaffolding with Red Tape, and fall to, joyfully. These are the things in which he finds relief from unlucky Acts of Parliament that are more troublesome improvements than they were meant to be. Across and across them, he can spin his little webs of Red Tape, and catch summer flies; or, near them, litter down official dozing-places, and roll himself over and over in Red Tape, like the Hippopotamus wallowing in his bath.

Once upon a time, there was a dusty dry old shop in Long Acre, London, where, displayed in the windows, in tall slim bottles, were numerous preparations, looking, at first sight, like unhealthy maccaroni. On a nearer inspection these were found to be Tapeworms, extracted from the internal mechanism of certain ladies and gentlemen who were delicately referred to, on the bottles, by initial letters. Doctor Gardner's[8] medicine had effected these wonderful results; but, the Doctor, probably apprehensive that his patients might "blush to find it fame,"[9] enshrined them in his museum, under a thin cloud of mystery. We have a lively remembrance of a white basin, which, in the days of our boyhood, remained for eight or ten years, in a conspicuous part of the museum, and was supposed to contain a specimen so recent that there had not yet been time for its more elaborate preservation. It bore, as we remember, the label, "This singular creature, with ears like a mouse, was last week found destroying the inside of Mr. O – in the City Road." But, this was an encroachment on the province of the legitimate Tapeworms. That species were all alike except in length. The smallest, according to the labels, measured, to the best of our recollection, about two hundred yards.

If, in any convenient part of the United Kingdom (we suggest the capital as the centre of resort), a similar museum could be established, for the destruction and exhibition of the Red Tapeworms with which the British public are so sorely afflicted, there can be no doubt that it would be, at once, a vast national benefit, and a curious national spectacle. Nor can there be a doubt that the people in general would cheerfully contribute to the support of such an establishment. The labels might be neatly and legibly written, according to the precedent we have mentioned. "The Right Honourable Mr. X – from the Exchequer. Seven thousand yards." "Earl Y – from the Colonial Office. Half as long again." "Lord Z – from the Woods and Forests. The longest ever known." "This singular creature," – not mentioning its ears – "was found destroying the patience of Mr. John B – in the House of Commons." If it were practicable to open such an Institution before the departure of All Nations (which can scarcely be hoped) it might be desirable to translate these abstracts into a variety of languages, for the wider understanding of one of our most agreeable and improving sights.

A Monument of French Folly

First published in *Household Words*, 8 March 1851, and subsequently in *Reprinted Pieces* from which this text is reproduced. This article might be compared with that jointly written by Dickens and Wills, 'The Heart of Mid-London', which sought to draw attention to the insanitary conditions.

It was profoundly observed by a witty member of the Court of Common Council, in Council assembled in the City of London, in the year of our Lord one thousand eight hundred and fifty, that the French are a frog-eating people, who wear wooden shoes.

We are credibly informed, in reference to the nation whom this choice spirit so happily disposed of, that the caricatures and stage representations which were current in England some half a century ago, exactly depict their present condition. For example, we understand that every Frenchman, without exception, wears a pigtail and curl-papers. That he is extremely sallow, thin, long-faced, and lantern-jawed. That the calves of his legs are invariably undeveloped; that his legs fail at the knees, and that his shoulders are always higher than his ears. We are likewise assured that he rarely tastes any food but soup maigre, and an onion; that he always says, "By Gar! Aha! Vat you tell me, sare?" at the end of every sentence he utters; and that the true generic name of his race is the Mounseers, or the Parly-voos. If he be not a dancing-master, or a barber, he must be a cook; since no other trades but those three are congenial to the tastes of the people, or permitted by the Institutions of the country. He is a slave, of course. The ladies of France (who are also slaves) invariably have their heads tied up in Belcher handkerchiefs,[1] wear long earrings, carry tambourines, and beguile the weariness of their yoke by singing in head voices through their noses – principally to barrel-organs.

It may be generally summed up, of this inferior people, that they have no idea of anything.

Of a great Institution like Smithfield, they are unable to form the least conception. A Beast Market in the heart of Paris would be regarded an impossible nuisance. Nor have they any notion of slaughter-houses in the midst of a city. One of these benighted frog-eaters would scarcely understand your meaning, if you told him of the existence of such a British bulwark.

427

It is agreeable, and perhaps pardonable, to indulge in a little self-complacency when our right to it is thoroughly established. At the present time, to be rendered memorable by a final attack on that good old market which is the (rotten) apple of the Corporation's eye, let us compare ourselves, to our national delight and pride as to these two subjects of slaughter-house and beast-market, with the outlandish foreigner.

The blessings of Smithfield are too well understood to need recapitulation; all who run (away from mad bulls and pursuing oxen) may read. Any market-day they may be beheld in glorious action. Possibly the merits of our slaughter-houses are not yet quite so generally appreciated.

Slaughter-houses, in the large towns of England, are always (with the exception of one or two enterprising towns) most numerous in the most densely crowded places, where there is the least circulation of air. They are often underground, in cellars; they are sometimes in close back yards; sometimes (as in Spitalfields) in the very shops where the meat is sold. Occasionally, under good private management, they are ventilated and clean. For the most part, they are unventilated and dirty; and, to the reeking walls, putrid fat and other offensive animal matter clings with a tenacious hold. The busiest slaughter-houses in London are in the neighbourhood of Smithfield, in Newgate Market, in Whitechapel, in Newport Market, in Leadenhall Market, in Clare Market. All these places are surrounded by houses of a poor description, swarming with inhabitants. Some of them are close to the worst burial-grounds in London. When the slaughter-house is below the ground, it is a common practice to throw the sheep down areas, neck and crop – which is exciting, but not at all cruel. When it is on the level surface, it is often extremely difficult of approach. Then, the beasts have to be worried, and goaded, and pronged, and tail-twisted, for a long time before they can be got in – which is entirely owing to their natural obstinacy. When it is not difficult of approach, but is in a foul condition, what they see and scent makes them still more reluctant to enter – which is their natural obstinacy again. When they do get in at last, after no trouble and suffering to speak of (for there is nothing in the previous journey into the heart of London, the night's endurance in Smithfield, the struggle out again, among the crowded multitude, the coaches, carts, waggons, omnibuses, gigs, chaises, phaetons, cabs, trucks, dogs, boys, whoopings, roarings, and ten thousand other distractions), they are represented to be in a most unfit state to be killed, according to microscopic examinations made of their fevered blood by one of the most distinguished physiologists in the world, PROFESSOR OWEN[2] – but that's humbug. When they *are* killed, at last, their reeking carcases are hung in impure air, to become, as

428

the same Professor will explain to you, less nutritious and more unwholesome – but he is only an *un*common counsellor, so don't mind *him*. In half a quarter of a mile's length of Whitechapel, at one time, there shall be six hundred newly slaughtered oxen hanging up, and seven hundred sheep – but the more the merrier – proof of prosperity. Hard by Snow Hill and Warwick Lane, you shall see the little children, inured to sights of brutality from their birth, trotting along the alleys, mingled with troops of horribly busy pigs, up to their ankles in blood – but it makes the young rascals hardy. Into the imperfect sewers of this overgrown city, you shall have the immense mass of corruption, engendered by these practices, lazily thrown out of sight, to rise, in poisonous gases, into your house at night, when your sleeping children will most readily absorb them, and to find its languid way, at last, into the river that you drink – but the French are a frog-eating people who wear wooden shoes, and it's O the roast beef of England, my boy, the jolly old English roast beef.

It is quite a mistake – a new-fangled notion altogether – to suppose that there is any natural antagonism between putrefaction and health. They know better than that, in the Common Council. You may talk about Nature, in her wisdom, always warning man through his sense of smell, when he draws near to something dangerous; but that won't go down in the City. Nature very often don't mean anything. Mrs. Quickly says that prunes are ill for a green wound;[3] but whosoever says that putrid animal substances are ill for a green wound, or for robust vigour, or for anything or for anybody, is a humanity-monger and a humbug. Britons never, never, never, &c., therefore. And prosperity to cattle-driving, cattle-slaughtering, bone-crushing, blood-boiling, trotter-scraping, tripe-dressing, paunch-cleaning, gut-spinning, hide-preparing, tallow-melting, and other salubrious proceedings, in the midst of hospitals, churchyards, workhouses, schools, infirmaries, refuges, dwellings, provision-shops, nurseries, sick-beds, every stage and baiting-place in the journey from birth to death!

These *un*common counsellors, your Professor Owens and fellows, will contend that to tolerate these things in a civilised city, is to reduce it to a worse condition than BRUCE found to prevail in ABYSSINIA.[4] For there (say they) the jackals and wild dogs came at night to devour the offal; whereas, here there are no such natural scavengers, and quite as savage customs. Further, they will demonstrate that nothing in Nature is intended to be wasted, and that besides the waste which such abuses occasion in the articles of health and life – main sources of the riches of any community – they lead to a prodigious waste of changing matters, which might, with proper preparation, and under scientific direction, be safely applied to the increase of the fertility of the land. Thus (they argue) does Nature ever avenge infractions of her beneficent laws, and so surely as Man is determined to warp any of her blessings into curses, shall they become curses, and shall he suffer heavily. But this is cant. Just as it is cant of the worst description to say to the London Corporation, "How can you exhibit to the people so plain a spectacle of dishonest equivocation, as to claim the right of holding a market in the midst of the great city, for one of your vested privileges, when you know that when your last market holding charter was granted to you by King Charles the First,[5] Smithfield stood IN THE SUBURBS OF LONDON, and is in that very charter so described in those five words?" – which is certainly true, but has nothing to do with the question.

Now to the comparison, in these particulars of civilisation, between the capital of England, and the capital of that frog-eating and wooden-shoe wearing country, which the illustrious Common Councilman so sarcastically settled.

In Paris, there is no Cattle Market. Cows and calves are sold within the city, but the Cattle Markets are at Poissy,[6] about thirteen miles off, on a line of railway; and at Sceaux, about five miles off. The Poissy market is held every Thursday; the Sceaux market, every Monday. In Paris, there are no slaughter-houses, in our acceptation of the term. There are five public Abattoirs – within the walls, though in the suburbs – and in these all the slaughtering for the city must be performed. They are managed by a Syndicat or Guild of Butchers, who confer with the Minister of the Interior on all matters affecting the trade, and who are consulted when any new regulations are contemplated for its government. They are, likewise, under the vigilant superintendence of the police. Every butcher must be licensed: which proves him at once to be a slave, for we don't license butchers in England – we only license apothecaries, attorneys, post-masters, publicans, hawkers, retailers of tobacco, snuff, pepper, and vinegar – and one or two other little trades, not worth mentioning. Every arrangement in connexion with the slaughtering and sale of meat, is matter of strict police regulation. (Slavery again, though we certainly have a general sort of Police Act here.)

But, in order that the reader may understand what a monument of folly these frog-eaters have raised in their abattoirs and cattle-markets, and may compare it with what common counselling has done for us all these years, and would still do but for the innovating spirit of the times, here follows a short account of a recent visit to these places:

It was as sharp a February morning as you would desire to feel at your fingers' ends when I turned out – tumbling over a chiffonier with his little basket and rake, who was picking up the bits of coloured paper that had been swept out, over-night, from a Bon-Bon shop – to take the Butchers' Train to Poissy. A cold, dim light just touched the high roofs of the Tuileries which have seen such changes, such distracted crowds, such riot and bloodshed; and they looked as calm, and as old, all covered with white frost, as the very Pyramids. There was not light enough, yet, to strike upon the towers of Notre Dame across the water; but I thought of the dark pavement of the old Cathedral as just beginning to be streaked with grey; and of the lamps in the "House of God," the Hospital close to it, burning low and being quenched; and of the keeper of the Morgue going about with a fading lantern, busy in the arrangement of his terrible waxwork for another sunny day.

The sun was up, and shining merrily when the butchers and I, announcing our departure with an engine shriek to sleepy Paris, rattled away for the Cattle Market. Across the country, over the Seine, among a forest of scrubby trees – the hoar frost lying cold in shady places, and glittering in the light – and here we are at Poissy! Out leap the butchers, who have been chattering all the way like madmen, and off they straggle for the Cattle Market (still chattering, of course, incessantly), in hats and caps of all shapes, in coats and blouses, in calf-skins, cow-skins, horse-skins, furs, shaggy mantles, hairy coats, sacking, baize, oil-skin, anything you please that will keep a man and a butcher warm, upon a frosty morning.

Many a French town have I seen, between this spot of ground and Strasburgh or Marseilles, that might sit for your picture, little Poissy! Barring the details of your old church, I know you well, albeit we make acquaintance, now, for the first time. I know your narrow, straggling, winding streets, with a kennel in the midst, and lamps slung across. I know your picturesque street-corners, winding up-hill Heaven knows why or where! I know your tradesmen's inscriptions, in letters not quite fat enough; your barbers' brazen basins dangling over little shops; your Cafés and Estaminets, with cloudy bottles of stale syrup in the windows, and pictures of crossed billiard cues outside. I know this identical grey horse with his tail rolled up in a knot like the "back hair" of an untidy woman, who won't be shod, and who makes himself heraldic by clattering across the street on his hind-legs, while twenty voices shriek and growl at him as a Brigand, an accursed Robber, and an everlastingly-doomed Pig. I know your sparkling town-fountain, too, my Poissy, and am glad to see it near a cattle-market, gushing so freshly, under the auspices of a gallant little sublimated Frenchman[7] wrought in metal, perched upon the top. Through all the land of France I know this unswept room at The Glory, with its peculiar smell of beans and coffee, where the butchers crowd about the stove, drinking the thinnest of wine from the smallest of tumblers; where the thickest of coffee-cups mingle with the longest of loaves, and the weakest of lump sugar; where Madame at the counter easily acknowledges the homage of all entering and departing butchers; where the billiard-table is covered up in the midst like a great bird-cage – but the bird may sing by-and-by!

A bell! The Calf Market! Polite departure of butchers. Hasty payment and departure on the part of amateur Visitor. Madame reproaches Ma'amselle for too fine a susceptibility in reference to the devotion of a Butcher in a bear-skin. Monsieur, the landlord of The Glory, counts a double handful of sous, without an unobliterated inscription, or an undamaged crowned head, among them.

There is little noise without, abundant space, and no confusion. The open area devoted to the market is divided into three portions: the Calf Market, the Cattle Market, the Sheep Market. Calves at eight, cattle at ten, sheep at mid-day. All is very clean.

The Calf Market is a raised platform of stone, some three or four feet high, open on all sides, with a lofty over-spreading roof, supported on stone columns, which give it the appearance of a sort of vineyard from Northern Italy. Here, on the raised pavement, lie innumerable calves, all bound hind-legs and fore-legs together, and all trembling violently – perhaps with cold, perhaps with fear, perhaps with pain; for this mode of tying, which seems to be an absolute superstition with the peasantry, can hardly fail to cause great suffering. Here they lie patiently in rows, among the straw, with their stolid faces and inexpressive eyes, superintended by men and women, boys and girls; here they are inspected by our friends, the butchers, bargained for, and bought. Plenty of time; plenty of room; plenty of good humour. "Monsieur François in the bear-skin, how do you do, my friend? You come from Paris by the train? The fresh air does you good. If you are in want of three or four fine calves this market morning, my angel, I, Madame Doche, shall be happy to deal with you. Behold these calves, Monsieur François! Great Heaven, you are doubtful! Well, sir, walk round and look about you. If you find better for the money, buy them. If not, come to me!" Monsieur François goes his way leisurely, and keeps a wary eye upon the stock. No other butcher jostles Monsieur François; Monsieur François jostles no other butcher. Nobody is flustered and aggravated. Nobody is savage. In the midst of the country blue frocks and red handker-chiefs, and the butchers' coats, shaggy, furry, and hairy: of calf-skin, cow-skin, horse-skin, and bear-skin: towers a cocked hat and a blue cloak. Slavery! For *our* Police wear great-coats and glazed hats.

But now the bartering is over, and the calves are sold. "Ho! Gregoire, Antoine, Jean, Louis! Bring up the carts, my children! Quick, brave infants! Hola! Hi!"

The carts, well littered with straw, are backed up to the edge of the raised pavement, and various hot infants carry calves upon their heads, and dexterously pitch them in, while other hot infants, standing in the carts, arrange the calves, and pack them carefully in straw. Here is a promising young calf, not sold, whom Madame Doche unbinds. Pardon me, Madame Doche, but I fear this mode of tying the four legs of a quadruped together, though strictly à la mode, is not quite right. You observe, Madame Doche, that the cord leaves deep indentations in the skin, and that the animal is so cramped at first as not to know, or even remotely suspect that he *is* unbound, until you are so obliging as to kick him, in your delicate little way, and pull his tail like a bell-rope. Then, he staggers to his knees, not being able to stand, and stumbles about like a drunken calf, or the horse at Franconi's,[8] whom you may have seen, Madame Doche, who is supposed to have been mortally wounded in battle. But what is this rubbing against me, as I apostrophise Madame Doche? It is another heated infant with a calf upon his head. "Pardon, Monsieur, but will you have the politeness to allow me to pass?" "Ah, sir, willingly. I am vexed to obstruct the way." On he staggers, calf and all, and makes no allusion whatever either to my eyes or limbs.

Now, the carts are all full. More straw, my Antoine, to shake over these top rows; then, off we will clatter, rumble, jolt, and rattle, a long row of us, out of the first town-gate, and out at the second town-gate, and past the empty sentry-box, and the little thin square bandbox of a guardhouse, where nobody seems to live: and away for Paris, by the paved road, lying, a straight straight line, in the long long avenue of trees. We can neither choose our road, nor our pace, for that is all prescribed to us. The public convenience demands that our carts should get to Paris by such a route, and no other (Napoleon had leisure to find that out, while he had a little war with the world upon his hands), and woe betide us if we infringe orders.

Droves of oxen stand in the Cattle Market, tied to iron bars fixed into posts of granite. Other droves advance slowly down the long avenue, past the second town-gate, and the first town-gate, and the sentry-box, and the bandbox, thawing the morning with their smoky breath as they come along. Plenty of room; plenty of time. Neither man nor beast is driven out of his wits by coaches, carts, waggons, omnibuses, gigs, chaises, phaetons, cabs, trucks, boys, whoopings, roarings, and multitudes. No tail-twisting is necessary – no iron pronging is necessary. There are no iron prongs here.

The market for cattle is held as quietly as the market for calves. In due time, off the cattle go to Paris; the drovers can no more choose their road, nor their time, nor the numbers they shall drive, than they can choose their hour for dying in the course of nature.

Sheep next. The sheep-pens are up here, past the Branch Bank of Paris established for the convenience of the butchers, and behind the two pretty fountains they are making in the Market. My name is Bull: yet I think I should like to see as good twin fountains – not to say in Smithfield, but in England anywhere. Plenty of room; plenty of time. And here are sheep-dogs, sensible as ever, but with a certain French air about them – not without a suspicion of dominoes – with a kind of flavour of moustache and beard – demonstrative dogs, shaggy and loose where an English dog would be tight and close – not so troubled with business calculations as our English drovers' dogs, who have always got their sheep upon their minds, and think about their work, even resting, as you may see by their faces; but dashing, showy, rather unreliable dogs: who might worry me instead of their legitimate charges if they saw occasion – and might see it somewhat suddenly.

The market for sheep passes off like the other two; and away they go, by *their* allotted road to Paris. My way being the Railway, I make the best of it at twenty miles an hour; whirling through the now high-lighted landscape; thinking that the inexperienced green buds will be wishing, before long, they had not been tempted to come out so soon; and wondering who lives in this or that château, all window and lattice, and what the family may have for breakfast this sharp morning.

After the Market comes the Abattoir. What abattoir shall I visit first? Montmartre is the largest. So I will go there.

The abattoirs are all within the walls of Paris, with an eye to the receipt of the octroi duty; but they stand in open places in the suburbs, removed from the press and bustle of the city. They are managed by the Syndicat or Guild of Butchers, under the inspection of the Police. Certain smaller items of the revenue derived from them are in part retained by the Guild for the payment of their expenses, and in part devoted by it to charitable purposes in connexion with the trade. They cost six hundred and eighty thousand pounds; and they return to the city of Paris an interest on that outlay, amounting to nearly six and a-half per cent.

Here, in a sufficiently dismantled space is the Abattoir of Montmartre, covering nearly nine acres of ground, surrounded by a high wall, and looking from the outside like a cavalry barrack. At the iron gates is a small functionary in a large cocked hat. "Monsieur desires to see the abattoir? Most certainly." State being inconvenient in private transactions, and Monsieur being already aware of the cocked hat, the functionary puts it into a little official bureau which it almost fills, and accompanies me in the modest attire – as to his head – of ordinary life.

Many of the animals from Poissy have come here. On the arrival of each drove, it was turned into yonder ample space, where each butcher who had bought, selected his own purchases. Some, we see now, in these long perspectives of stalls with a high overhanging roof of wood and open tiles rising above the walls. While they rest here, before being slaughtered, they are required to be fed and watered, and the stalls must be kept clean. A stated amount of fodder must always be ready in the loft above; and the supervision is of the strictest kind. The same regulations apply to sheep and calves; for which, portions of these perspectives are strongly railed off. All the buildings are of the strongest and most solid description.

After traversing these lairs, through which, besides the upper provision for ventilation just mentioned, there may be a thorough current of air from opposite windows in the side walls, and from doors at either end, we traverse the broad, paved, court-yard until we come to the slaughter-houses. They are all exactly alike, and adjoin each other, to the number of eight or nine together, in blocks of solid building. Let us walk into the first.

It is firmly built and paved with stone. It is well lighted, thoroughly aired, and lavishly provided with fresh water. It has two doors opposite each other; the first, the door by which I entered from the main yard; the second, which is opposite, opening on another smaller yard, where the sheep and calves are killed on benches. The pavement of that yard, I see, slopes downward to a gutter, for its being more easily cleansed. The slaughter-house is fifteen feet high, sixteen feet and a-half wide, and thirty-three feet long. It is fitted with a powerful windlass, by which one man at the handle can bring the head of an ox down to the ground to receive the blow from the pole-axe that is to fell him – with the means of raising the carcass and keeping it suspended during the after-operation of dressing – and with hooks on which carcasses can hang, when completely prepared, without touching the walls. Upon the pavement of this first stone chamber, lies an ox scarcely dead. If I except the blood draining from him, into a little stone well in a corner of the pavement, the place is free from offence as the Place de la Concorde. It is infinitely purer and cleaner, I know, my friend the functionary, than the Cathedral of Notre Dame. Ha, ha! Monsieur is pleasant, but, truly, there is reason, too, in what he says.

I look into another of these slaughter-houses. "Pray enter," says a gentleman in bloody boots. "This is a calf I have killed this morning. Having a little time upon my hands, I have cut and punctured this lace pattern in the coats of his stomach. It is pretty enough. I did it to divert myself." – "It is beautiful, Monsieur, the slaughterer!" He tells me I have the gentility to say so.

I look into rows of slaughter-houses. In many, retail dealers, who have come here for the purpose, are making bargains for meat. There is killing enough, certainly, to satiate an unused eye; and there are steaming carcasses enough, to suggest the expediency of a fowl and salad for dinner; but everywhere, there is an orderly, clean, well-systematised routine of work in progress – horrible work at the best, if you please; but so much the greater reason why it should be made the best of. I don't know (I think I have observed, my name is Bull) that a Parisian of the lowest order is particularly delicate, or that his nature is remarkable for an infinitesimal infusion of ferocity; but I do know, my potent, grave, and common counselling Signors, that he is forced, when at this work, to submit himself to a thoroughly good system, and to make an Englishman very heartily ashamed of you.

Here, within the walls of the same abattoir, in other roomy and commodious buildings, are a place for converting the fat into tallow and packing it for market – a place for cleansing and scalding calves' heads and sheep's feet – a place for preparing tripe – stables and coach-houses for the butchers – innumerable conveniences, aiding in the diminution of offensiveness to its lowest possible point, and the raising of cleanliness and supervision to their highest. Hence, all the meat that goes out of the gate is sent away in clean covered carts. And if every trade connected with the slaughtering of animals were obliged by law to be carried on in the same place, I doubt, my friend, now reinstated in the cocked hat (whose civility these two francs imperfectly acknowledge, but appear munificently to repay), whether there could be better regulations than those which are carried out at the Abattoir of Montmartre. Adieu, my friend, for I am away to the other side of Paris, to the Abattoir of Grenelle! And there I find exactly the same thing on a smaller scale, with the addition of a magnificent Artesian well, and a different sort of conductor, in the person of a neat little woman with neat little eyes, and a neat little voice, who picks her neat little way among the bullocks in a very neat little pair of shoes and stockings.

Such is the Monument of French Folly which a foreigneering people have erected, in a national hatred and antipathy for common counselling wisdom. That wisdom, assembled in the City of London, having distinctly refused, after a debate of three days long, and by a majority of nearly seven to one, to associate itself with any Metropolitan Cattle-Market unless it be held in the midst of the City, it follows that we shall lose the inestimable advantages of common counselling protection, and be thrown, for a market, on our own wretched resources. In all human probability we shall thus come, at last, to erect a monument of folly very like this French monument. If that be done, the consequences are obvious. The leather trade will be ruined, by the introduction of American timber, to be manufactured into shoes for the fallen English; the Lord Mayor will be required, by the popular voice, to live entirely on frogs; and both these changes will (how, is not at present quite clear, but certainly somehow or other) fall on that unhappy landed interest which is always being killed, yet is always found to be alive – and kicking.

Trading in Death

First published in *Household Words*, 27 November 1852, from which this text is reproduced. Dickens wrote to Miss Burdett Coutts on 2 November 1852: 'I am quite vexed about the State Funeral. I think it is altogether wrong as regards the memory of the Duke, and at least equally wrong in the Court estimate it implies of the People. The nonsense of the Herald's College and Lord Chamberlain's absurdities keep his own soldiers away; the only real links of sympathy the public could have found in it are carefully filed off; and a vulgar holiday, with a good deal of business for the thieves and the public houses, will be the chief result.'

Several years have now elapsed since it began to be clear to the comprehension of most rational men, that the English people had fallen into a condition much to be regretted, in respect of their Funeral customs. A system of barbarous show and expense was found to have gradually erected itself above the grave, which, while it could possibly do no honor to the memory of the dead, did great dishonor to the living, as inducing them to associate the most solemn of human occasions with unmeaning mummeries, dishonest debt, profuse waste, and bad example in an utter oblivion of responsibility. The more the subject was examined, and the lower the investigation was carried, the more monstrous (as was natural) these usages appeared to be, both in themselves and in their consequences. No class of society escaped. The competition among the middle classes for superior gentility in Funerals – the gentility being estimated by the amount of ghastly folly in which the undertaker was permitted to run riot – descended even to the very poor: to whom the cost of funeral customs was so ruinous and so disproportionate to their means, that they formed Clubs among themselves to defray such charges. Many of these Clubs, conducted by designing villains who preyed upon the general infirmity, cheated and wronged the poor, most cruelly; others, by presenting a new class of temptations to the wickedest natures among them, led to a new class of mercenary murders, so abominable in their iniquity, that language cannot stigmatise them with sufficient severity. That nothing might be wanting to complete the general depravity, hollowness, and falsehood, of this state of things, the absurd fact came to light, that innumerable harpies assumed the titles of furnishers of Funerals, who possessed no Funeral furniture whatever, but who formed a long file of middlemen between the chief mourner and the real tradesman, and who hired out the trappings from one to another – passing them on like water-buckets at a fire – every one of them charging his enormous percentage on his share of the "black job." Add to all this, the demonstration, by the simplest and plainest practical science, of the terrible consequences to the living, inevitably resulting from the practice of burying the dead in the midst of crowded towns; and the exposition of a system of indecent horror, revolting to our nature and disgraceful to our age and nation, arising out of the confined limits of such burial-grounds, and the avarice of their proprietors; and the culminating point of this gigantic mockery is at last arrived at.

Out of such almost incredible degradation, saving that the proof of it is too easy, we are still very slowly and feebly emerging. There are now, we confidently hope, among the middle classes, many, who having made themselves acquainted with these evils through the parliamentary papers in which they are described, would be moved by no human consideration to perpetuate the old bad example; but who will leave it as their solemn injunction on their nearest and dearest survivors, that they shall not, in their death, be made the instruments of infecting, either the minds or the bodies of their fellow-creatures. Among persons of note, such examples have not been wanting. The late Duke of Sussex[1] did a national service when he desired to be laid, in the equality of death, in the cemetery of Kensal Green,[2] and not with the pageantry of a State Funeral in the Royal vault at Windsor. Sir Robert Peel[3] requested to be buried at Drayton. The late Queen Dowager[4] left a pattern to every rank in these touching and admirable words. "I die in all humility, knowing well that we are all alike before the Throne of God; and I request, therefore, that my mortal remains be conveyed to the grave without any pomp or state. They are to be removed to St. George's Chapel, Windsor, where I request to have as private and quiet a funeral as possible. I particularly desire not to be laid out in state. I die in peace and wish to be carried to the tomb in peace, and free from the vanities and pomp of this world. I request not to be dissected or embalmed, and desire to give as little trouble as possible."

With such precedents and such facts fresh in the general knowledge, and at this transition-time in so serious a chapter of our social history, the obsolete custom of a State Funeral has been revived, in miscalled "honor" of the late Duke of Wellington.[5] To whose glorious memory be all true honor while England lasts!

We earnestly submit to our readers that there is, and that there can be, no kind of honor in such a revival; that the more truly great the man, the more truly little the ceremony; and that it has been, from first to last, a pernicious instance and encouragement of the demoralising practice of trading in Death.

It is within the knowledge of the whole public, of all diversities of political opinion, whether or no any of the Powers that be, have traded in this Death – have saved it up, and petted it, and made the most of it, and reluctantly let it go. On that aspect of the question we offer no further remark.

But, of the general trading spirit which, in its inherent emptiness and want of consistency and reality, the long-deferred State Funeral has appropriately awakened, we will proceed to furnish a few instances all faithfully copied from the advertising columns of The Times.

First, of seats and refreshments. Passing over that desirable first-floor where a party could be accommodated with "the use of a piano"; and merely glancing at the decorous daily announcement of "The Duke of Wellington Funeral Wine," which was in such high demand that immediate orders were necessary; and also "The Duke of Wellington Funeral Cake," which "delicious article" could only be had of such a baker; and likewise "The Funeral Life Preserver," which could only be had of such a tailor; and further "the celebrated lemon biscuits," at one and fourpence per pound, which were considered by the manufacturer as the only infallible assuagers of the national grief; let us pass in review some dozen of the more eligible opportunities the public had of profiting by the occasion.

LUDGATE HILL. – The fittings and arrangements for viewing this grand and solemnly imposing procession are now completed at this establishment, and those who are desirous of obtaining a fine and extensive view, combined with every personal convenience and comfort, will do well to make immediate inspection of the SEATS now remaining on hand.

FUNERAL, including Beds the night previous. – To be LET, a SECOND FLOOR, of three rooms, two windows, having a good view of the procession. Terms, including refreshment, 10 guineas. Single places, including bed and breakfast, from 15s.

THE DUKE'S FUNERAL. – A first-rate VIEW for 15 persons, also good clean beds and a sitting-room on reasonable terms.

SEATS and WINDOWS to be LET, in the best part of the Strand, a few doors from Coutts's banking-house. First floor windows, £8 each; second floor, £5 10s. each; third floor, £3 10s. each; two plate-glass shop windows, £7 each.

SEATS to VIEW the DUKE of WELLINGTON'S FUNERAL. Best position of all the route, no obstruction to the view. Apply Old Bailey. N.B. From the above position you can nearly see to St. Paul's and to Temple-bar.

FUNERAL of the late Duke of WELLINGTON. – To be LET, a SECOND FLOOR, two windows, firing and every convenience. Terms moderate for a party. Also a few seats in front, one guinea each. Commanding a view from Piccadilly to Pall-mall.

FUNERAL of the DUKE of WELLINGTON. – The FIRST and SECOND FLOORS to be LET, either by the room or window, suited to gentlemen's families, for whom every comfort and accommodation will be provided, and commanding the very best view of this imposing spectacle. The ground floor is also fitted up with commodious seats, ranging in price from one guinea. Apply on the premises.

THE DUKE'S FUNERAL. – Terms very moderate. – TWO FIRST FLOOR ROOMS, with balcony and private entrance out of the Strand. The larger room capable of holding 15 persons. The small room to be let for eight guineas.

THE DUKE'S FUNERAL. – To be LET, a SHOP WINDOW, with seats erected for about 30, for 25 guineas. Also a Furnished First Floor, with two large windows. One of the best views in the whole range from Temple-bar to St. Paul's. Price 35 guineas. A few single seats one guinea each.

THE FUNERAL PROCESSION of the DUKE of WELLINGTON. – Cockspur-street, Charing-cross, decidedly the best position in the whole route, a few SEATS still DISENGAGED, which will be offered at reasonable prices. An early application is requisite, as they are fast filling up. Also a few places on the roof. A most excellent view.

FUNERAL of the Late DUKE of WELLINGTON. – To be LET, in the best part of the Strand, a SECOND FLOOR, for £10; a Third Floor, £7 10s., containing two windows in each; front seats in shop, at one guinea.

THE DUKE'S FUNERAL. – To be LET, for 25 guineas to a genteel family, in one of the most commanding situations in the line of route, a FIRST FLOOR, with safe balcony, and ante-room. Will accommodate 20 persons, with an uninterrupted and extensive view for all. For a family of less number a reduction will be made. Every accommodation will be afforded.

But above all let us not forget the

NOTICE TO CLERGYMEN. – T. C. Fleet-street, has reserved for clergymen exclusively, *upon condition only that they appear in their surplices*, FOUR FRONT SEATS, at £1 each; four second tier, at 15s. each; four third tier, at 12s. 6d.; four fourth tier, at 10s.; four fifth tier, at 7s. 6d.; and four sixth tier, at 5s. All the other seats are respectively 40s., 30s., 20s., 15s., 10s.

The anxiety of this enterprising tradesman to get up a reverend tableau in his shop-window of four-and-twenty clergymen all on six rows, is particularly commendable, and appears to us to shed a remarkable grace on the solemnity.

These few specimens are collected at random from scores upon scores of such advertisements, mingled with descriptions of non-existent ranges of view, and with invitations to a few agreeable gentlemen who are wanted to complete a little assembly of kindred souls, who have laid in abundance of "refreshments, wines, spirits, provisions, fruit, plate, glass, china," and other light matters too numerous to mention, and who keep "good fires." On looking over them we are constantly startled by the words in large capitals, "WOULD TO GOD NIGHT OR BLUCHER[6] WERE COME!" which, referring to a work of art, are relieved by a legend setting forth how the lamented hero observed of it, "in his characteristic manner, 'Very good; very good indeed.'" O Art! *You* too trading in Death!

Then, autographs fall into their place in the State Funeral train. The sanctity of a seal, or the confidence of a letter, is a meaningless phrase that has no place in the vocabulary of the Traders in Death. Stop, trumpets, in the Dead March, and blow to the world how characteristic we autographs are!

WELLINGTON AUTOGRAPHS. – TWO consecutive LETTERS of the DUKE'S (1843) highly characteristic and authentic, with the Correspondence, &c. that elicited them, the whole forming quite a literary curiosity, for £15.

WELLINGTON AUTOGRAPHS. – To be DISPOSED OF, TWO AUTOGRAPH LETTERS of the DUKE of WELLINGTON, one dated Walmer Castle, 9th October, 1834, the other London, 17th May, 1843, with their post-marks and seals.

WELLINGTON. – THREE original NOTES, averaging 2¼ pages each, (not lithographs,) seal, and envelopes, to be SOLD. Supposed to be the most characteristic of his Grace yet published. The highest sum above £30 for the two, or £20 for the one, which is distinct, will be accepted.

TO BE DISPOSED OF, by a retired officer, FIVE LETTERS and NOTES of the late HERO – three when Sir A. Wellesley. Also a large Envelope. All with seals. Apply personally, or by letter.

THE DUKE'S LETTERS. – TWO highly interesting LETTERS, authentic, and relating to a most amusing and characteristic circumstance, to be SOLD.

THE DUKE of WELLINGTON. – AUTOGRAPH LETTER to a lady, with seal and envelope. This is quite in the Duke's peculiar style, and will be parted with for the highest offer. Apply — where the letter can be seen.

F.M. the DUKE of WELLINGTON. – To be SOLD, by a member of the family, to whom it was written, an ORIGINAL AUTOGRAPH LETTER of the late Duke of Wellington, on military affairs, six pages long, in the best preservation. Price £30.

FIELD-MARSHAL the DUKE of WELLINGTON'S AUTOGRAPH. – A highly characteristic LETTER of the DUKE'S for DISPOSAL, wherein he alludes to his living 100 years, date 1847, with envelope. Seal, with crest perfect. £10 will be taken.

DUKE of WELLINGTON. – An AUTOGRAPH LETTER of the DUKE, written immediately after the death of the Duchess in 1831, is for SALE; also Two Autograph Envelopes franked and sealed.

DUKE of WELLINGTON. – AUTOGRAPH BUSINESS LETTER, envelope, seal, post-mark, &c. complete. Style courteous and highly characteristic. Will be shown by the party and at the place addressed. Price £15.

FIELD-MARSHAL the DUKE of WELLINGTON. – TWO AUTO-GRAPH LETTERS of His Grace, one written in his 61st, the other in his 72d year, both first-rate specimens of his characteristic graphic style, and on an important subject, to be SOLD. Their genuineness can be fully proved.

THE DUKE of WELLINGTON. – A very curious DOCUMENT, partly printed, and the rest written by His Grace to a lady. This is well worthy of a place in the cabinet of the curious. There is nothing like it. Highest offer will be taken.

TO be SOLD, SIX AUTOGRAPH LETTERS from F.M. the Duke of WELLINGTON, with envelopes and seals, which have been most generously given to aid a lady in distressed circumstances.

THE DUKE of WELLINGTON. – A lady has in her possession a LETTER, written by his Grace on the 18th of June, in the present year, and will be happy to

DISPOSE OF the same. The letter is rendered more valuable by its being written on the last anniversary which his Grace was spared to celebrate. The letter bears date from Apsley House, with perfect envelope and seal.

A CLERGYMAN has TWO LETTERS, with Envelopes, addressed to him by the late DUKE, and bearing striking testimony to the extent of his Grace's private charities, to be DISPOSED OF at the highest offer (for one or both) received by the 18th instant. The offers may be contingent on further particulars being satisfactory.

THE DUKE of WELLINGTON. – A widow, in deep distress, has in her possession an AUTOGRAPH LETTER of his Grace the Duke of WELLING-TON, written in 1830, enclosed and directed in an envelope, and sealed with his ducal coronet, which she would be happy to PART WITH for a trifle.

VALUABLE AUTOGRAPH NOTE of the late Duke of WELLINGTON, dated March 27, 1850, to be SOLD, for £20, by the gentleman to whom it was addressed, together with envelope, perfect impression of Ducal seal, and Knightsbridge post-mark distinct. The whole in excellent preservation. A better specimen of the noble Duke's handwriting and highly characteristic style cannot be seen.

ONE of the last LETTERS of the DUKE of WELLINGTON for DIS-POSAL, dated from Walmer Castle within a day or two of his death, highly characteristic, with seal and post-marks distinct. This being probably the last letter written by the late Duke its interest as a relic must be greatly enhanced. The highest offer accepted. May be seen on application.

THE GREAT DUKE. – A LETTER of the GREAT HERO, dated March 27, 1851, to be SOLD. Also a beautiful Letter from Jenny Lind, dated June 20, 1852. The highest offer will be accepted. Address with offers of price.

Miss Lind's autograph would appear to have lingered in the shade until the Funeral Train came by, when it modestly stepped into the procession and took a conspicuous place. We are in doubt which to admire most; the ingenuity of this little stroke of business; or the affecting delicacy that sells "probably the last letter written by the late Duke" before the aged hand that wrote it under some manly sense of duty, is yet withered in its grave; or the piety of that excellent clergyman – did he appear in his surplice in the front row of T. C.'s shop-window? – who is so anxious to sell "striking testimony to the extent of His Grace's private charities;" or the generosity of that Good Samaritan who poured "six letters with envelopes and seals" into the wounds of the lady in distressed circumstances.

Lastly come the relics – precious remembrances worn next to the bereaved heart, like Hardy's miniature of Nelson, and never to be wrested from the advertisers but with ready money.

MEMENTO of the late DUKE of WELLINGTON. – To be DISPOSED OF, a LOCK of the late illustrious DUKE'S HAIR. Can be guaranteed. The highest offer will be accepted. Apply by letter prepaid.

THE DUKE of WELLINGTON. – A LOCK of HAIR of the late Duke of WELLINGTON to be DISPOSED OF, now in the possession of a widow lady. Cut off the morning the Queen was crowned. Apply by letter post paid.

VALUABLE RELIC of the late DUKE of WELLINGTON. – A lady, having in her possession a quantity of the late illustrious DUKE'S HAIR, cut in 1841, is willing to PART WITH a portion of the same for £25. Satisfactory proof will be given of its identity, and of how it came into the owner's possession, on application by letter, pre-paid.

RELIC of the DUKE of WELLINGTON for SALE. – The son of the late well-known haircutter to his Grace the late Duke of Wellington, at Strathfieldsaye, has a small quantity of HAIR, that his father cut from the Duke's head, which he is willing to DISPOSE OF. Any one desirous of possessing such a relic of England's hero are requested to make their offer for the same, by letter.

RELICS of the late DUKE of WELLINGTON. – For SALE, a WAIST-COAT, in good preservation, worn by his Grace some years back, which can be well authenticated as such.

Next, a very choice article – quite unique – the value of which may be presumed to be considerably enhanced by the conclusive impossibility of its being doubted in the least degree by the most suspicious mind.

A MEMENTO of the DUKE of WELLINGTON. – La Mort de Napoleon. Ode d'Alexandre Manzoni,[7] avec la Traduction en Français, par Edmond Angelini, de Venise. – A book, of which the above is the title, was torn up by the Duke and thrown by him from the carriage, in which he was riding, as he was passing through Kent: the pieces of the book were collected and put together by a person who saw the Duke tear it and throw the same away. Any person desirous of obtaining the above memento will be communicated with.

Finally, a literary production of astonishing brilliancy and spirit; without which, we are authorised to state, no nobleman's or gentleman's library can be considered complete.

DUKE of WELLINGTON and SIR R. PEEL. – A talented, interesting, and valuable WORK, on Political Economy and Free Trade, was published in 1830, and immediately bought up by the above statesmen, except one copy, which is now for DISPOSAL. Apply by letter only.

Here, for the reader's sake, we terminate our quotations. They might easily have been extended through the whole of the present number of this Journal.

We believe that a State Funeral at this time of day – apart from the mischievously confusing effect it has on the general mind, as to the necessary union of funeral expense and pomp with funeral respect, and the consequent injury it may do to the cause of a great reform most necessary for the benefit of all classes of society – is, in itself, so plainly a pretence of being what it is not: is so unreal, such a substitution of the form for the substance: is so cut and dried, and stale: is such a palpably got up theatrical trick: that it puts the dread solemnity of death to flight, and encourages these shameless traders in their dealings on the very coffin-lid of departed greatness. That private letters and other memorials of the great Duke of Wellington would still have been advertised and sold, though he had been laid in his grave amid the silent respect of the whole country with the simple honors of a military commander, we do not doubt; but that, in that case, the traders would have been discouraged from holding anything like this Public Fair and Great Undertakers' Jubilee over his remains, we doubt as little. It is idle to attempt to connect the frippery of the Lord Chamberlain's Office and the Herald's College, with the awful passing away of that vain shadow in which man walketh and disquieteth himself in vain.[8] There is a great gulf set between the two which is set there by no mortal hands, and cannot by mortal hands be bridged across. Does any one believe that, otherwise, "the Senate" would have been "mourning its hero" (in the likeness of a French Field-Marshal) on Tuesday evening, and that the same Senate would have been in fits of laughter with Mr. Hume[9] on Wednesday afternoon when the same hero was still in question and unburied?

The mechanical exigencies of this journal render it necessary for these remarks to be written on the evening of the State Funeral. We have already indicated in these pages that we consider the State Funeral a mistake, and we hope temperately to leave the question here for temperate consideration. It is easy to imagine how it may have done much harm, and it is hard to imagine how it can have done any good. It is only harder to suppose that it can have afforded a grain of satisfaction to the immediate descendants of the great Duke of Wellington, or that it can reflect the faintest ray of lustre on so bright a name. If it were assumed that such a ceremonial was the general desire of the English people, we would reply that that assumption was founded on a misconception of the popular character, and on a low estimate of the general sense; and that the sooner both were better appreciated in high places, the better it could not fail to be for us all. Taking for granted at this writing, what we hope may be assumed without any violence to the truth; namely, that the ceremonial was in all respects well conducted, and that the English people sustained throughout, the high character they have nobly earned, to the shame of their silly detractors among their own countrymen; we must yet express our hope that State Funerals in this land went down to their tomb, most fitly, in the tasteless and tawdry Car[10] that nodded and shook through the streets of London on the eighteenth of November, eighteen hundred and fifty-two. And sure we are, with large consideration for opposite opinions, that when History shall rescue that very ugly machine – worthy to pass under decorated Temple Bar, as decorated Temple Bar was worthy to receive it – from the merciful shadows of obscurity, she will reflect with amazement – remembering his true, manly, modest, self-contained, and genuine character – that the man who, in making it the last monster of its race, rendered his last enduring service to the country he had loved and served so faithfully, was Arthur Duke of Wellington.

Proposals for Amusing Posterity

First published in *Household Words*, 12 February 1853, from which this text is reproduced. Dickens was thinking about this article as early as 22 August 1851 when he wrote to Wills: 'I want a great paper done, on the distribution of Titles in England. It would be a very remarkable thing to take the list of the House of Peers, the list of Baronets and Knights and (without personality) divide the more recent titles into classes and ascertain what they were given *for*. How many chemists, how many men of science, how many writers, how many aldermen.'

Posterity, that ancient personage yet unborn, is at times a topic of much speculation with me. I consider him in a variety of lights, and represent him to myself in many odd humours, but principally in those with which he is likely to regard the present age. I am particularly fond of inquiring whether we contribute our share towards the entertainment and diversion of the old gentleman. It is important that we should, for all work and no play would make even Posterity a dull boy.

And, good Heaven, to think of the amount of work he will have to get through! Only to read all those books, to contemplate all those pictures and statues, and to listen to all that music, so generously bequeathed to him by crowds of admiring legatees through many generations, will be no slight labor. I doubt if even the poetry written expressly for his perusal would not be sufficient to addle any other head. The prodigious spaces of time that his levees will occupy, are overwhelming to think of: for how else can he ever receive those hosts of ladies and gentlemen who have been resolved and determined to go down to him! Then the numbers of ingenious inventions he will have to test, prove, and adopt, from the perpetual motion to the long range, will necessarily consume some of the best years of his life. In hearing Appeals, though the claims of the Appellants will be in every case as clear as crystal, it will be necessary for him to sit as long as twenty Chancellors, though each sat on the woolsack twenty years. The mere rejection of those swindlers in the various arts and sciences who basely witnessed any appreciation of their works, and the folding to his bosom of those worthies whom mankind were in a combination to discard, will take time. It is clear that it is reserved for Posterity to be, in respect of his labors, immeasurably more than the Hercules of the future.

Hence, it is but moderately considerate to have an eye to the amusement of this industrious person. If he *must* be so overworked, let us at least do something to entertain him – something even over and above those books of poetry and prose, those pictures and statues, and that music, for which he will have an unbounded relish, but perhaps a relish (so I venture to conceive) of a pensive rather than an exhilarating kind.

These are my reflections when I consider the present time with a reference to Posterity. I am sorry to say that I don't think we do enough to make him smile. It appears to me that we might tickle him a little more. I will suggest one or two odd notions – somewhat far-fetched and fantastic, I allow, but they may serve the purpose – of the kind of practical humour that might seem droll to Posterity.

If we had had, in this time of ours, two great commanders – say one by land and one by sea; one dying in battle (or what was left of him, for we will suppose him to have lost an arm and an eye or so before), and one living to old age – it might be a jest for Posterity if we choked our towns with bad Statues to one of the two, and utterly abandoned and deserted the memory of the other. We might improve on this conceit. If we laid those two imaginary great men side by side in Saint Paul's cathedral and then laid side by side in the advertising columns of our public newspapers, two appeals respecting two Memorials, one to each of them; and if we so carried on the joke as that the Memorial to the one should be enormously rich, and the Memorial to the other, miserably poor – as that the subscriptions to the one should include the names of three-fourths of the grandees of the land, and the subscriptions to the other but a beggarly account of rank and file – as that the one should leap with ease into a magnificent endowment, and the other crawl and stagger as a pauper provision for the dead Admiral's daughter – if we could only bring the joke, as Othello says,

" – to this extent, no more;"[1]

I think it might amuse Posterity a good deal.

The mention of grandees brings me to my next proposal. It would involve a change in the present mode of bestowing public honours and titles in England; but, encouraged by the many examples we have before us of disinterested magnanimity in favour of Posterity, we might perhaps be animated to try it.

I will assume that among the books in that very large library (for the most part quite unknown at the present benighted time) which will infallibly become the rich inheritance of Posterity, there will be found a history of England. From that record, Posterity will learn the origin of many noble families and noble titles. Now the jest I have in my mind, is this. If we could so arrange matters as that that privileged class should be always with great jealousy preserved, and hedged round by a barrier of buckram and a board of green cloth, which only a few generals, a few great capitalists, and a few lawyers, should be allowed to scale – the latter not in a very creditable manner until within the last few generations: as our amiable friend Posterity will find when he looks back for the date at which Chief Justices and Puisne Judges[2] began to be men of undoubted freedom, honor, and independence – if such privileged class were always watched and warded and limited, and fended off, in the manner of hundreds of years ago, and never adapted to the altered circumstances of the time; and if it were in practice set up and maintained as having been, from Genesis thenceforward, endowed with a superior natural instinct for noble ruling and governing and Cabinet-making, as triumphantly shown in the excellent condition of the whole machinery of Government, of every public office, every dockyard, every ship, every diplomatic relation, and particularly every colony – I think there would be a self-evident pleasantry in this that would make Posterity chuckle. The present British practice being, as we all know, widely different, we should have many changes to make before we could hand down this amusing state of things. For example, it would be necessary to limit the great Jenner or Vaccination Dukedom and endowment, at present so worthily represented in the House of Lords, by the noble and scientific Duke who will no doubt be called upon (some day or other) to advise Her Majesty in the formation of a Ministry. The Watt or Steam-Engine peerage would also require to be gradually abolished. So would the Iron-Road Earldom, the Tubular Bridge Baronetcy, the Faraday Order of Merit, the Electric Telegraph Garter,[3] the titles at present held by distinguished writers on literary grounds alone, and the similar titles held by painters; – though it might point the joke to make a few Academicians equal in rank to an alderman. But, the great practical joke once played off, of entirely separating the ennobled class from the various orders of men who attain to social distinction by making their country happier, better, and more illustrious among nations, we might be comfortably sure, as it seems to me – and as I now humbly submit – of having done something to amuse Posterity.

Another thing strikes me. Our venerable friend will find in that English history of his, that, in comparatively barbarous times, when the Crown was poor, it did anything for money – commuted murder, or anything else – and that, partly of this desperate itching for gold, and partly of partial laws in favor of the feudal rich, a most absurd and obsolete punishment, called punishment by fine, had its birth. Now, it appears to me, always having an eye on the entertainment of Posterity, that if while we proclaimed the laws to be equal against all offenders, we would only preserve this obsolete punishment by fine – of course no punishment whatever to those who have money – say in a very bad class of cases such as gross assaults, we should certainly put Posterity on the broad grin. Why, we might then even come to this. A "captain" might be brought up to a Police Office, charged with caning a young woman for an absolutely diabolical reason; and the offence being proved, the "captain" might, as a great example of the equality of the law (but by no fault in the magistrate, he having no alternative), be fined fifty shillings, and might take a full purse from his pocket and offer, if that were all, to make it pounds. And what a joke *that* would be for Posterity! To be done in the face of day, in the first city upon earth, in the year one thousand eight hundred and fifty-three!

Or, we might have our laws regarding this same offence of assault in such a facetious state as to empower a workhouse nurse within two hours' walk of the capital, slowly to torture a child with fire, and afterwards to walk off from the law's presence scot free of all pains and penalties, but a fortnight's imprisonment! And we might so carry out this joke to the uttermost as that the forlorn child should happily die and rot, and the barbarous nurse be *then* committed for trial; her horrible offence being legally measured by that one result or its absence, and not by the agony it caused, and the awful cruelty it shewed. And all this time (to make the pleasantry the greater), we might have all manner of watch-towers, in measurement as near as possible of the altitude of the Tower of Babel when it was overthrown, erected in all parts of the kingdom, with all sorts and conditions of men and women perched on plaforms thereupon, looking out for any grievance afar off, East, West, North, and South, night and day. So should that tender nurse return, gin-solaced, to her ministration upon babies (imagine the dear matron's antecedents, all ye mothers!), and so should Posterity be made to laugh, though bitterly!

Indeed, I think Posterity would have such an indifferent appreciation of this last joke, on account of its intensely practical character, that it might require another to relieve it. And I would suggest that if a body of gentlemen possessing their full phrenological share of the combative and antagonistic organs, could only be induced to form themselves into a society for declaiming about Peace, with a very considerable War-Whoop against all non-declaimers; and if they could only be prevailed upon to sum up eloquently the many unspeakable miseries and horrors of War, and to present them to their own country as a conclusive reason for its being undefended against War, and becoming the prey of the first despot who might choose to inflict those miseries and horrors upon it, – why then I really believe we should have got to the very best joke we could hope to have in our whole Complete Jest-Book for Posterity, and might fold our arms and rest convinced that we had done enough for that discerning patriarch's amusement.

On Strike

First published in *Household Words*, 11 February 1854, from which this text is reproduced. Dickens and Wills travelled to Preston on 28 January 1854, and stayed for two days. Dickens wrote to Forster on 29 January: 'I am afraid I shall not be able to get much here. Except the crowd at the street-corner reading the placards pro and con; and the cold absence of smoke from the mill-chimneys; there is very little within the streets to make the town remarkable . . . It is a nasty place (I thought it was a model town).' On the historical and literary contexts of the Preston Strike, see R. D. Butterworth, 'Dickens the Journalist: The Preston Strike and "On Strike"' in *The Dickensian*, 1993, pp. 129–38; and G. D. Carnall, 'Dickens, Mrs. Gaskell and the Preston Strike', *Victorian Studies* 8 (1964), pp. 31–48.

Travelling down to Preston a week from this date, I chanced to sit opposite to a very acute, very determined, very emphatic personage, with a stout railway rug so drawn over his chest that he looked as if he were sitting up in bed with his great-coat, hat, and gloves on, severely contemplating your humble servant from behind a large blue and grey checked counterpane. In calling him emphatic, I do not mean that he was warm; he was coldly and bitingly emphatic as a frosty wind is.

"You are going through to Preston, sir?" says he, as soon as we were clear of the Primrose Hill tunnel.

The receipt of his question was like the receipt of a jerk of the nose; he was so short and sharp.

"Yes."

"This Preston strike is a nice piece of business!" said the gentleman. "A pretty piece of business!"

"It is very much to be deplored," said I, "on all accounts."

"They want to be ground. That's what they want, to bring 'em to their senses," said the gentleman; whom I had already began to call in my own mind Mr. Snapper, and whom I may as well call by that name here as by any other.

I deferentially enquired, who wanted to be ground?

"The hands," said Mr. Snapper. "The hands on strike, and the hands who help 'em."

I remarked that if that was all they wanted, they must be a very unreasonable people, for surely they had had a little grinding, one way and another, already. Mr. Snapper eyed me with sternness, and after opening and shutting his leathern-gloved hands several times outside his counterpane, asked me abruptly, "Was I a delegate?"

I set Mr. Snapper right on that point, and told him I was no delegate.

"I am glad to hear it," said Mr. Snapper. "But a friend to the Strike, I believe?"

"Not at all," said I.

"A friend to the Lock-out?" pursued Mr. Snapper.

"Not in the least," said I.

Mr. Snapper's rising opinion of me fell again, and he gave me to understand that a man *must* either be a friend to the Masters or a friend to the Hands.

"He may be a friend to both," said I.

Mr. Snapper didn't see that; there was no medium in the Political Economy of the subject. I retorted on Mr. Snapper, that Political Economy was a great and useful science in its own way and its own place; but that I did not transplant my definition of it from the Common Prayer Book, and make it a great king above all gods. Mr. Snapper tucked himself up as if to keep me off, folded his arms on the top of his counterpane, leaned back, and looked out of window.

"Pray what would you have, sir," enquired Mr. Snapper, suddenly withdrawing his eyes from the prospect to me, "in the relations between Capital and Labor, *but* Political Economy?"

I always avoid the stereotyped terms in these discussions as much as I can, for I have observed, in my little way, that they often supply the place of sense and moderation. I therefore took my gentleman up with the words employers and employed, in preference to Capital and Labor.

"I believe," said I, "that into the relations between employers and employed, as into all the relations of this life, there must enter something of feeling and sentiment; something of mutual explanation, forbearance, and consideration; something which is not to be found in Mr. McCulloch's dictionary,[1] and is not exactly stateable in figures; otherwise those relations are wrong and rotten at the core and will never bear sound fruit."

Mr. Snapper laughed at me. As I thought I had just as good reason to laugh at Mr. Snapper, I did so, and we were both contented.

"Ah!" said Mr. Snapper, patting his counterpane with a hard touch. "You know very little of the improvident and unreasoning habits of the common people, *I* see."

"Yet I know something of those people, too," was my reply. "In fact,

Mr. —," I had so nearly called him Snapper! "in fact, sir, I doubt the existence at this present time of many faults that are merely class faults. In the main, I am disposed to think that whatever faults you may find to exist, in your own neighbourhood for instance, among the hands, you will find tolerably equal in amount among the masters also, and even among the classes above the masters. They will be modified by circumstances, and they will be the less excusable among the better-educated, but they will be pretty fairly distributed. I have a strong expectation that we shall live to see the conventional adjectives now apparently inseparable from the phrases working people and lower orders, gradually fall into complete disuse for this reason."

"Well, but we began with strikes," Mr. Snapper observed impatiently. "The masters have never had any share in strikes."

"Yet I have heard of strikes once upon a time in that same county of Lancashire," said I, "which were not disagreeable to some masters when they wanted a pretext for raising prices."

"Do you mean to say those masters had any hand in getting up those strikes?" asked Mr. Snapper.

"You will perhaps obtain better information among persons engaged in some Manchester branch trades, who have good memories," said I.

Mr. Snapper had no doubt, after this, that I thought the hands had a right to combine.[2]

"Surely," said I. "A perfect right to combine in any lawful manner. The fact of their being able to combine and accustomed to combine may, I can easily conceive, be a protection to them. The blame even of this business is not all on one side. I think the associated Lock-out was a grave error. And when you Preston masters —"[3]

"*I* am not a Preston master," interrupted Mr. Snapper.

"When the respectable combined body of Preston masters," said I, "in the beginning of this unhappy difference, laid down the principle that no man should be employed henceforth who belonged to any combination – such as their own – they attempted to carry with a high hand a partial and unfair impossibility, and were obliged to abandon it. This was an unwise proceeding, and the first defeat."

Mr. Snapper had known, all along, that I was no friend to the masters.

"Pardon me," said I, "I am unfeignedly a friend to the masters, and have many friends among them."

"Yet you think these hands in the right?" quoth Mr. Snapper.

"By no means," said I; "I fear they are at present engaged in an unreasonable struggle, wherein they began ill and cannot end well."

Mr. Snapper, evidently regarding me as neither fish, flesh, nor fowl, begged to know after a pause if he might enquire whether I was going to Preston on business?

Indeed I was going there, in my unbusinesslike manner, I confessed, to look at the strike.

"To look at the strike!" echoed Mr. Snapper, fixing his hat on firmly with both hands. "To look at it! Might I ask you now, with what object you are going to look at it?"

"Certainly," said I, "I read, even in liberal pages, the hardest Political Economy – of an extraordinary description too sometimes, and certainly not to be found in the books – as the only touchstone of this strike. I see, this very day, in a to-morrow's liberal paper, some astonishing novelties in the politico-economical way, showing how profits and wages have no connexion whatever; coupled with such references to these hands as might be made by a very irascible General to rebels and brigands in arms. Now, if it be the case that some of the highest virtues of the working people still shine through them brighter than ever in their conduct of this mistake of theirs, perhaps the fact may reasonably suggest to me – and to others besides me – that there is some little thing wanting in the relations between them and their employers, which neither political economy nor Drum-head[4] proclamation writing will altogether supply, and which we cannot too soon or too temperately unite in trying to find out."

Mr. Snapper, after again opening and shutting his gloved hands several times, drew the counterpane higher over his chest, and went to bed in disgust. He got up at Rugby, took himself and counterpane into another carriage, and left me to pursue my journey alone.

When I got to Preston, it was four o'clock in the afternoon. The day being Saturday and market-day, a foreigner might have expected, from among so many idle and not over-fed people as the town contained, to find a turbulent, ill-conditioned crowd in the streets. But, except for the cold smokeless factory chimnies, the placards at the street corners, and the groups of working people attentively reading them, nor foreigner nor Englishman could have had the least suspicion that there existed any interruption to the usual labours of the place. The placards thus perused were not remarkable for their logic certainly, and did not make the case particularly clear; but, considering that they emanated from, and were addressed to, people who had been out of employment for three-and-twenty consecutive weeks, at least they had little passion in them, though they had not much reason. Take the worst I could find:

"Friends and Fellow Operatives,

"Accept the grateful thanks of twenty thousand struggling Operatives, for the help you have showered upon Preston since the present contest commenced.

"Your kindness and generosity, your patience and long-continued support deserve every praise, and are only equalled by the heroic and determined perseverance of the outraged and insulted factory workers of Preston, who have been struggling for some months, and are, at this inclement season of the year, bravely battling for the rights of themselves and the whole toiling community.

"For many years before the strike took place at Preston, the Operatives were the down trodden and insulted serfs of their Employers, who in times of good trade and general prosperity, wrung from their labour a California of gold, which is now being used to crush those who created it, still lower and lower in the scale of civilisation. This has been the result of our commercial prosperity! — *more wealth for the rich and more poverty for the Poor!* Because the workpeople of Preston protested against this state of things, — because they combined in a fair and legitimate way for the purpose of getting a reasonable share of the reward of their own labour, the *fair dealing* Employers of Preston, to their eternal shame and disgrace *locked up* their Mills, and at one fell swoop deprived, as they thought, from twenty to thirty thousand human beings of the means of existence. Cruelty and tyranny always defeat their own object; it was so in this case, and to the honour and credit of the working classes of this country, we have to record, that, those whom the rich and wealthy sought to destroy, the poor and industrious have protected from harm. This love of justice and hatred of wrong, is a noble feature in the character and disposition of the working man, and gives us hope that in the future, this world will become what its great architect intended, not a place of sorrow, toil, oppression and wrong, but the dwelling place and the abode of peace, plenty, happiness and love, where avarice and all the evil passions engendered by the present system of fraud and injustice shall not have a place.

"The earth was not made for the misery of its people; intellect was not given to man to make himself and fellow creatures unhappy. No, the fruitfulness of the soil and the wonderful inventions — the result of mind — all proclaim that these things were bestowed upon us for our happiness and well-being, and not for the misery and degradation of the human race.

"It may serve the manufacturers and all who run away with the lion's share of labour's produce, to say that the *impartial* God intended that there should be a *partial* distribution of his blessings. But we know that it is against nature to believe, that those who plant and reap all the grain, should not have enough to make a mess of porridge; and we know that those who weave all the cloth should not want a yard to cover their persons, whilst those who never wove an inch have more calico, silks and satins, than would serve the reasonable wants of a dozen working men and their families.

"This system of giving everything to the few, and nothing to the many, has lasted long enough, and we call upon the working people of this country to be determined to establish a new and improved system – a system that shall give to all who labour, a fair share of those blessings and comforts which their toil produce; in short, we wish to see that divine precept enforced, which says, 'Those who will not work, shall not eat.'

"The task is before you, working men; if you think the good which would result from its accomplishment, is worth struggling for, set to work and cease not, until you have obtained the *good time coming*, not only for the Preston Operatives, but for yourselves as well.

"*By Order of the Committee.*

"*Murphy's Temperance Hotel, Chapel Walks,*
"*Preston, January 24th, 1854.*"

It is a melancholy thing that it should not occur to the Committee to consider what would become of themselves, their friends, and fellow operatives, if those calicoes, silks, and satins, were *not* worn in very large quantities; but I shall not enter into that question. As I had told my friend Snapper, what I wanted to see with my own eyes, was, how these people acted under a mistaken impression, and what qualities they showed, even at that disadvantage, which ought to be the strength and peace – not the weakness and trouble – of the community. I found, even from this literature, however, that all masters were not indiscriminately unpopular. Witness the following verses from the New Song of the Preston Strike:

"There's Henry Hornby, of Blackburn, he is a jolly brick,
He fits the Preston masters nobly, and is very bad to trick;
He pays his hands a good price, and I hope he will never sever,
So we'll sing success to Hornby and Blackburn for ever.

"There is another gentleman, I'm sure you'll all lament,
In Blackburn for him they're raising a monument,
You know his name, 'tis of great fame, it was late Eccles of honour,
May Hopwood, and Sparrow, and Hornby live for ever.

"So now it is time to finish and end my rhyme,
We warn these Preston Cotton Lords to mind for future time.
With peace and order too I hope we shall be clever,

We sing success to Stockport and Blackburn for ever.
"Now, lads, give your minds to it."

The balance sheet of the receipts and expenditure for the twenty-third week of the strike was extensively posted. The income for that week was two thousand one hundred and forty pounds odd. Some of the contributors were poetical. As,

"Love to all and peace to the dead,
May the poor now in need never want bread –

three-and-sixpence." The following poetical remonstrance was appended to the list of contributions from the Gorton[5] district.

"Within these walls the lasses fair
Refuse to contribute their share,
Careless of duty – blind to fame,
For shame, ye lasses, oh! for shame!
Come, pay up, lasses, think what's right,
Defend your trade with all your might;
For if you don't the world will blame,
And cry, ye lasses, oh, for shame!
Let's hope in future all will pay,
That Preston folks may shortly say –
That by your aid they have obtain'd
The greatest victory ever gained."

Some of the subscribers veiled their names under encouraging sentiments, as Not tired yet, All in a mind, Win the day, Fraternity, and the like. Some took jocose appellations, as A stunning friend, Two to one Preston wins, Nibbling Joe, and The Donkey Driver. Some expressed themselves through their trades, as Cobbler Dick, sixpence, The tailor true, sixpence, Shoemaker, a shilling, The chirping blacksmith, sixpence, and A few of Maskery's most feeling coachmakers, three and threepence. An old balance sheet for the fourteenth week of the Strike was headed with this quotation from MR. CARLYLE,[6] "Adversity is sometimes hard upon a man; but for one man who can stand prosperity, there are a hundred that will stand adversity." The Elton district prefaced its report with these lines:

"Oh! ye who start a noble scheme,
For general good designed;
Ye workers in a cause that tends
To benefit your kind!

Mark out the path ye fain would tread,
    The game ye mean to play;
And if it be an honest one,
    Keep stedfast in your way!

"Although you may not gain at once
    The points ye most desire;
Be patient – time can wonders work;
    Plod on, and do not tire:
Obstructions, too, may crowd your path,
    In threatening, stern array;
Yet flinch not! fear not! they may prove
    Mere shadows in your way.

"Then, while there's work for you to do,
    Stand not despairing by,
Let 'forward' be the move ye make,
    Let 'onward' be your cry;
And when success has crowned your plans,
    'Twill all your pains repay,
To see the good your labour's done –
    Then droop not on your way."

In this list, "Bear ye one another's burthens," sent one Pound fifteen. "We'll stand to our text, see that ye love one another," sent nineteen shillings. "Christopher Hardman's men again, they say they can always spare one shilling out of ten," sent two-and-sixpence. The following masked threats were the worst feature in any bill I saw:–

"If that fiddler at Uncle Tom's Cabin blowing room does not pay, Punch will set his legs straight.

"If that drawer at card side and those two slubbers do not pay, Punch will say something about their bustles.

"If that winder[7] at last shift does not pay next week, Punch will tell about her actions."

But, on looking at this bill again, I found that it came from Bury and related to Bury, and had nothing to do with Preston. The Masters' placards were not torn down or disfigured, but were being read quite as attentively as those on the opposite side.

That evening, the Delegates from the surrounding districts were coming in, according to custom, with their subscription lists for the week just closed. These delegates meet on Sunday as their only day of leisure; when they have made their reports, they go back to their homes and their Monday's work. On Sunday morning, I repaired to the Delegates' meeting.

These assemblages take place in a cockpit, which, in the better times of our fallen land, belonged to the late Lord Derby for the purposes of the intellectual recreation implied in its name. I was directed to the cockpit up a narrow lane, tolerably crowded by the lower sort of working people. Personally, I was quite unknown in the town, but every one made way for me to pass, with great civility, and perfect good humour. Arrived at the cockpit door, and expressing my desire to see and hear, I was handed through the crowd, down into the pit, and up again, until I found myself seated on the topmost circular bench, within one of the secretary's table, and within three of the chairman. Behind the chairman was a great crown on the top of a pole, made of parti-coloured calico, and strongly suggestive of May-day. There was no other symbol or ornament in the place.

It was hotter than any mill or factory I have ever been in; but there was a stove down in the sanded pit, and delegates were seated close to it, and one particular delegate often warmed his hands at it, as if he were chilly. The air was so intensely close and hot, that at first I had but a confused perception of the delegates down in the pit, and the dense crowd of eagerly listening men and women (but not very many of the latter) filling all the benches and choking such narrow standing-room as there was. When the atmosphere cleared a little on better acquaintance, I found the question under discussion to be, Whether the Manchester Delegates in attendance from the Labor Parliament, should be heard?

If the Assembly, in respect of quietness and order, were put in comparison with the House of Commons, the Right Honorable the Speaker himself[8] would decide for Preston. The chairman was a Preston weaver, two or three and fifty years of age, perhaps; a man with a capacious head, rather long dark hair growing at the sides and back, a placid attentive face, keen eyes, a particularly composed manner, a quiet voice, and a persuasive action of his right arm. Now look'ee heer my friends. See what t' question is. T' question is, sholl these heer men be heerd. Then 't cooms to this, what ha' these men got t' tell us? Do they bring mooney? If they bring mooney t'ords t' expences o' this strike, they're welcome. For, Brass, my friends, is what we want, and what we must ha' (hear hear hear!). Do they coom to us wi' any suggestion for the conduct of this strike? If they do, they're welcome. Let 'em give us their advice and we will hearken to 't. But, if these men coom heer, to tell us what t' Labor Parliament is, or what Ernest

Jones's[9] opinions is, or t' bring in politics and differences amoong us when what we want is 'armony, brotherly love, and con-cord; then I say t' you, decide for yoursel' carefully, whether these men ote to be heerd in this place. (Hear hear hear! and No no no!) Chairman sits down, earnestly regarding delegates, and holding both arms of his chair. Looks extremely sensible; his plain coarse working man's shirt collar easily turned down over his loose Belcher neckerchief. Delegate who has moved that Manchester delegates be heard, presses motion – Mr. Chairman, will that delegate tell us, as a man, that these men have anything to say concerning this present strike and lock-out, for we have a deal of business to do, and what concerns this present strike and lock-out is our business and nothing else is. (Hear hear hear!) – Delegate in question will not compromise the fact; these men want to defend the Labor Parliament from certain charges made against them. – Very well, Mr. Chairman, Then I move as an amendment that you do not hear these men now, and that you proceed wi' business – and if you don't I'll look after you, I tell you that. (Cheers and laughter) – Coom lads, prove 't then! – Two or three hands for the delegates; all the rest for the business. Motion lost, amendment carried, Manchester deputation not to be heard.

But now, starts up the delegate from Throstletown,[10] in a dreadful state of mind. Mr. Chairman, I hold in my hand a bill; a bill that requires and demands explanation from you, sir; an offensive bill; a bill posted in my town of Throstletown without my knowledge, without the knowledge of my fellow delegates who are here beside me; a bill purporting to be posted by the authority of the massed committee, sir, and of which my fellow delegates and myself were kept in ignorance. Why are we to be slighted? Why are we to be insulted? Why are we to be meanly stabbed in the dark? Why is this assassin-like course of conduct to be pursued towards us? Why is Throstletown, which has nobly assisted you, the operatives of Preston, in this great struggle, and which has brought its contributions up to the full sevenpence a loom, to be thus degraded, thus aspersed, thus traduced, thus despised, thus outraged in its feelings by un-English and unmanly conduct? Sir, I hand you up that bill, and I require of you, sir, to give me a satisfactory explanation of that bill. And I have that confidence in your known integrity, sir, as to be sure that you will give it, and that you will tell us who is to blame, and that you will make reparation to Throstletown for this scandalous treatment. Then, in hot blood, up starts Gruffshaw[11] (professional speaker) who is somehow responsible for this bill. O my friends, but explanation is required here! O my friends, but it is fit and right that you should have the dark ways of the real traducers and apostates, and the real un-English stabbers, laid bare before you. My friends when this dark conspiracy first began – But here the persuasive right hand of the chairman falls gently on Gruffshaw's shoulder. Gruffshaw stops in full boil. My friends, these are hard words of my friend Gruffshaw, and this is not the business – No more it is, and once again, sir, I, the delegate who said I would look after you, do move that you proceed to business! – Preston has not the strong relish for personal altercation that Westminster hath. Motion seconded and carried, business passed to, Gruffshaw dumb.

Perhaps the world could not afford a more remarkable contrast than between the deliberate collected manner of these men proceeding with their business, and the clash and hurry of the engines among which their lives are passed. Their astonishing fortitude and perseverance; their high sense of honor among themselves; the extent to which they are impressed with the responsibility that is upon them of setting a careful example, and keeping their order out of any harm and loss of reputation; the noble readiness in them to help one another, of which most medical practitioners and working clergymen can give so many affecting examples; could scarcely ever be plainer to an ordinary observer of human nature than in this cockpit. To hold, for a minute, that the great mass of them were not sincerely actuated by the belief that all these qualities were bound up in what they were doing, and that they were doing right, seemed to me little short of an impossibility. As the different delegates (some in the very dress in which they had left the mill last night) reported the amounts sent from the various places they represented, this strong faith on their parts seemed expressed in every tone and every look that was capable of expressing it. One man was raised to enthusiasm by his pride in bringing so much; another man was ashamed and depressed because he brought so little; this man triumphantly made it known that he could give you, from the store in hand, a hundred pounds in addition next week, if you should want it; and that man pleaded that he hoped his district would do better before long; but I could as soon have doubted the existence of the walls that enclosed us, as the earnestness with which they spoke (many of them referring to the children who were to be born to labor after them) of "this great, this noble, gallant, godlike struggle." Some designing and turbulent spirits among them, no doubt there are; but I left the place with a profound conviction that their mistake is generally an honest one, and that it is sustained by the good that is in them, and not by the evil.

Neither by night nor by day was there any interruption to the peace of the streets. Nor was this an accidental state of things, for the police records of the town are eloquent to the same effect. I traversed the streets very much, and was, as a stranger, the subject of a little curiosity among the idlers; but I met with no rudeness or ill-temper. More than once, when I was looking at the printed balance-sheets to which I have referred, and could not quite comprehend the setting forth of the figures, a bystander of the working class interposed with his explanatory forefinger and helped me out. Although the pressure in the cockpit on Sunday was excessive, and the heat of the room obliged me to make my way out as I best could before the close of the proceedings, none of the people whom I put to inconvenience showed the least impatience; all helped me, and all cheerfully acknowledged my word of apology as I passed. It is very probable, notwithstanding, that they may have supposed from my being there at all – I and my companion were the only persons present, not of their own order – that I was there to carry what I heard and saw to the opposite side; indeed one speaker seemed to intimate as much.

On the Monday at noon, I returned to this cockpit, to see the people paid. It was then about half filled, principally with girls and women. They were all seated, waiting, with nothing to occupy their attention; and were just in that state when the unexpected appearance of a stranger differently dressed from themselves, and with his own individual peculiarities of course, might, without offence, have had something droll in it even to more polite assemblies. But I stood there, looking on, as free from remark as if I had come to be paid with the rest. In the place which the secretary had occupied yesterday, stood a dirty little common table, covered with five-penny piles of halfpence. Before the paying began, I wondered who was going to receive these very small sums; but when it did begin, the mystery was soon cleared up. Each of these piles was the change for sixpence, deducting a penny. All who were paid, in filing round the building to prevent confusion, had to pass this table on the way out; and the greater part of the unmarried girls stopped here, to change, each a sixpence, and subscribe her weekly penny in aid of the people on strike who had families. A very large majority of these girls and women were comfortably dressed in all respects, clean, wholesome and pleasant-looking. There was a prevalent neatness and cheerfulness, and an almost ludicrous absence of anything like sullen discontent.

Exactly the same appearances were observable on the same day, at a not numerously attended open air meeting in "Chadwick's Orchard"[12] – which blossoms in nothing but red bricks. Here, the chairman of yesterday presided in a cart, from which speeches were delivered. The proceedings commenced with the following sufficiently general and discursive hymn, given out by a workman from Burnley, and sung in long metre by the whole audience:

464

> "Assembled beneath thy broad blue sky,
> To thee, O God, thy children cry.
> Thy needy creatures on Thee call,
> For thou art great and good to all.
>
> "Thy bounty smiles on every side,
> And no good thing hast thou denied;
> But men of wealth and men of power,
> Like locusts, all our gifts devour.
>
> "Awake, ye sons of toil! nor sleep
> While millions starve, while millions weep;
> Demand your rights; let tyrants see
> You are resolved that you'll be free."

Mr. Hollins's Sovereign Mill was open all this time. It is a very beautiful mill, containing a large amount of valuable machinery, to which some recent ingenious improvements have been added. Four hundred people could find employment in it; there were eighty-five at work, of whom five had "come in" that morning. They looked, among the vast array of motionless power-looms, like a few remaining leaves in a wintry forest. They were protected by the police (very prudently not obtruded on the scenes I have described), and were stared at every day when they came out, by a crowd which had never been large in reference to the numbers on strike, and had diminished to a score or two. One policeman at the door sufficed to keep order then. These eighty-five were people of exceedingly decent appearance, chiefly women, and were evidently not in the least uneasy for themselves. I heard of one girl among them, and only one, who had been hustled and struck in a dark street.

In any aspect in which it can be viewed, this strike and lock-out is a deplorable calamity. In its waste of time, in its waste of a great people's energy, in its waste of wages, in its waste of wealth that seeks to be employed, in its encroachment on the means of many thousands who are laboring from day to day, in the gulf of separation it hourly deepens between those whose interests must be understood to be identical or must be destroyed, it is a great national affliction. But, at this pass, anger is of no use, starving out is of no use – for what will that do, five years hence, but overshadow all the mills in England with the growth of a bitter remembrance? – political economy is a mere skeleton unless it has a little human covering and filling out, a little human bloom upon it, and a little human warmth in it. Gentlemen are found, in great manufacturing towns, ready enough to extol imbecile mediation with dangerous madmen abroad; can none of them be brought to think of authorised mediation and explanation at home? I do not suppose that such a knotted difficulty as this, is to be at all untangled by a morning-party in the Adelphi;[13] but I would entreat both sides now so miserably opposed, to consider whether there are no men in England, above suspicion, to whom they might refer the matters in dispute, with a perfect confidence above all things in the desire of those men to act justly, and in their sincere attachment to their countrymen of every rank and to their country. Masters right, or men right; masters wrong, or men wrong; both right, or both wrong; there is certain ruin to both in the continuance or frequent revival of this breach. And from the ever-widening circle of their decay, what drop in the social ocean shall be free!

To Working Men

First published in *Household Words*, 7 October 1854, from which this text is reproduced. Dickens wrote to Wills on 25 September 1854: 'I am really quite shocked and ashamed on looking at the new No. to find nothing in it appropriate to the memorable time. I have written a little paper To Working Men which I hope may do good.' For Dickens's passionate defence of the fervid tone of his article, see his letter to Miss Burdett Coutts on 26 October 1854, Pilgrim *Letters*.

It behoves every journalist, at this time when the memory of an awful pestilence[1] is fresh among us, and its traces are visible at every turn in various affecting aspects of poverty and desolation, which any of us can see who are not purposely blind, to warn his readers, whatsoever be their ranks and conditions, that unless they set themselves in earnest to improve the towns in which they live, and to amend the dwellings of the poor, they are guilty, before GOD, of wholesale murder.

The best of our journals have so well remembered their responsibility in this respect, and have so powerfully presented the truth to the general conscience, that little remains to be written on the urgent subject. But we would carry a forcible appeal made by our contemporary the *Times* to the working people of England a little further, and implore them – with a view to their future avoidance of a fatal old mistake – to beware of being led astray from their dearest interests, by high political authorities on the one hand, no less than by sharking mountebanks on the other. The noble lord, and the right honourable baronet, and the honourable gentleman, and the honourable and learned gentleman, and the honourable and gallant gentleman, and the whole of the honourable circle, have, in their contests for place, power, and patronage, loaves and fishes, distracted the working man's attention from his first necessities, quite as much as the broken creature – once a popular Misleader – who is now sunk in hopeless idiotcy in a madhouse. To whatsoever shadows these may offer in lieu of substances, it is now the first duty of The People to be resolutely blind and deaf; firmly insisting, above all things, on their and their children's right to every means of life and health that Providence has afforded for all, and firmly refusing to allow their name to be taken in vain for any purpose, by any party, until their homes are purified and the amplest means of cleanliness and decency are secured to them.

We may venture to remark that this most momentous of all earthly questions is one we are not now urging for the first time. Long before this Journal[2] came into existence, we systematically tried to turn Fiction to the good account of showing the preventible wretchedness and misery in which the mass of the people dwell, and of expressing again and again the conviction, founded upon observation, that the reform of their habitations must precede all other reforms; and that without it, all other reforms must fail. Neither Religion nor Education will make any way, in this nineteenth century of Christianity, until a Christian government shall have discharged its first obligation, and secured to the people Homes, instead of polluted dens.

Now, any working man of common intelligence knows perfectly well, that one session of parliament zealously devoted to this object would secure its attainment. If he do not also know perfectly well that a government or a parliament will of itself originate nothing to save his life, he may know it by instituting a very little inquiry. Let him inquire what either power has done to better his social condition, since the last great outbreak of disease five years ago.[3] Let him inquire what amount of attention from government, and what amount of attendance in parliament, the question of that condition has ever attracted, until one night in this last August, when it became a personal question and a facetious question, and when Lord Seymour,[4] the member for Totnes, exhibited his fitness for ever having been placed at the head of a great public department by cutting jokes, which were received with laughter, on the subject of the pestilence then raging. If the working man, on such a review of plain facts, be satisfied that without his own help he will not be helped, but will be pitilessly left to struggle at unnatural odds with disease and death; then let him bestir himself to set so monstrous a wrong right, and let him – for the time at least – dismiss from his mind all other public questions, as straws in the balance. The glorious right of voting for Lord This (say Seymour, for instance) or Sir John That; the intellectual state of Abyssinia; the endowment of the College of Maynooth;[5] the paper duty; the newspaper duty; the five per cent.; the twenty-five per cent.; the ten thousand hobby-horses that are exercised before him, scattering so much dust in his eyes that he cannot see his own hearth, until the cloud is suddenly fanned away by the wings of the Angel of Death: all these distractions let him put aside, holding steadily to one truth – "Waking and sleeping, I and mine are slowly poisoned. Imperfect development and premature decay are the lot of those who are dear to me as my life. I bring children into the world to suffer unnaturally, and to die when my Merciful Father would have them live. The beauty of infancy is blotted out from my sight, and in its stead sickliness and pain look at me from the wan mother's knee. Shameful deprivation of the commonest appliances, distinguishing the lives of human beings from the lives of beasts, is my inheritance. My family is one of tens of thousands of families who are set aside as food for pestilence." And let him then, being made in the form of man, resolve, "I will not bear it, and it shall not be!"

If working men will be thus true to themselves and one another, there never was a time when they had so much just sympathy and so much ready help at hand. The whole powerful middle-class of this country, newly smitten with a sense of self-reproach – far more potent with it, we fully believe, than the lower motives of self-defence and fear – is ready to join them. The utmost power of the press is eager to assist them. But the movement, to be irresistible, must originate with themselves, the suffering many. Let *them* take the initiative, and call the middle-class to unite with them: which they will do, heart and soul! Let the working people, in the metropolis, in any one great town, but turn their intelligence, their energy, their numbers, their power of union, their patience, their perseverance, in this straight direction in earnest – and by Christmas, they shall find a government in Downing Street and a House of Commons within hail of it, possessing not the faintest family resemblance to the Indifferents and Incapables last heard of in that slumberous neighbourhood.

It is only through a government so acted upon and so forced to acquit itself of its first responsibility, that the intolerable ills arising from the present nature of the dwellings of the poor can be remedied. A Board of Health can do much, but not near enough. Funds are wanted, and great powers are wanted; powers to over-ride little interests for the general good; powers to coerce the ignorant, obstinate, and slothful, and to punish all who, by any infraction of necessary laws, imperil the public health. The working people and the middle-class thoroughly resolved to have such laws, there is no more choice left to all the Red Tape in Britain as to the form in which it shall tie itself next, than there is option in the barrel of a barrel-organ what tune it shall play.

But, though it is easily foreseen that such an alliance must soon incalculably mitigate, and in the end annihilate, the dark list of calamities resulting from sinful and cruel neglect which the late visitation has – unhappily not for the first time – unveiled; it is impossible to set limits to the happy issues that would flow from it. A better understanding between the two great divisions of society, a habit of kinder and nearer approach, an increased respect and trustfulness on both sides, a gently corrected method in each of considering the views of the other, would lead to such blessed improvements and interchanges among us, that even our narrow wisdom might within the compass of a short time learn to bless the sickly year in which so much good blossomed out of evil.

In the plainest sincerity, in affectionate sympathy, in the ardent desire of our heart to do them some service, and to see them take their place in the system which should bind us all together, and bring home, to us all, the happiness of which our necessarily varied conditions are all susceptible, we submit these few words to the working men. The time is ripe for every one of them to raise himself and those who are dear to him, at no man's cost, with no violence or injustice, with cheerful help and support, with lasting benefit to the whole community. Even the many among them at whose fire-sides there will be vacant seats this winter, we address with hope. However hard the trial and heavy the bereavement, there is a far higher consolation in striving for the life that is left, than in brooding with sullen eyes beside the grave.

Insularities

First published in *Household Words*, 19 January 1856, from which this text is reproduced.

It is more or less the habit of every country – more or less commendable in every case – to exalt itself and its institutions above every other country, and be vain-glorious. Out of the partialities thus engendered and maintained, there has arisen a great deal of patriotism, and a great deal of public spirit. On the other hand, it is of paramount importance to every nation that its boastfulness should not generate prejudice, conventionality, and a cherishing of unreasonable ways of acting and thinking, which have nothing in them deserving of respect, but are ridiculous or wrong.

We English people, owing in a great degree to our insular position, and in a small degree to the facility with which we have permitted electioneering lords and gentlemen to pretend to think for us, and to represent our weaknesses to us as our strength, have been in particular danger of contracting habits which we will call for our present purpose, Insularities. Our object in this paper, is to string together a few examples.

On the continent of Europe, generally, people dress according to their personal convenience and inclinations. In that capital which is supposed to set the fashion in affairs of dress, there is an especial independence in this regard. If a man in Paris have an idiosyncrasy on the subject of any article of attire between his hat and his boots, he gratifies it without the least idea that it can be anybody's affair but his; nor does anybody else make it his affair. If, indeed, there be anything obviously convenient or tasteful in the peculiarity, then it soon ceases to be a peculiarity, and is adopted by others. If not, it is let alone. In the meantime, the commonest man in the streets does not consider it at all essential to his character as a true Frenchman, that he should howl, stare, jeer, or otherwise make himself offensive to the author of the innovation. That word has ceased to be Old Boguey[1] to him since he ceased to be a serf, and he leaves the particular sample of innovation to come in or go out upon its merits.

Our strong English prejudice against anything of this kind that is new to the eye, forms one of our decided insularities. It is disappearing before the extended knowledge of other countries consequent upon steam and

471

electricity, but it is not gone yet. The hermetically-sealed, black, stiff, chimney-pot, a foot and a half high, which we call a hat, is generally admitted to be neither convenient nor graceful; but, there are very few middle-aged gentlemen within two hours' reach of the Royal Exchange,[2] who would bestow their daughters on wide-awakes,[3] however estimable the wearers. Smith Payne and Smith, or Ransom and Co.,[4] would probably consider a run upon the house not at all unlikely, in the event of their clerks coming to business in caps, or with such felt-fashions on their heads as didn't give them the headache, and as they could wear comfortably and cheaply. During the dirt and wet of at least half the year in London, it would be a great comfort and a great saving of expense to a large class of persons, to wear the trousers gathered up about the leg, as a Zouave[5] does, with a long gaiter below – to shift which, is to shift the whole mud-incumbered part of the dress, and to be dry, and clean directly. To such clerks, and others with much out-door work to do, as could afford it, Jack-boots, a much more costly article, would, for similar reasons, be excellent wear. But what would Griggs and Bodger[6] say to Jack-boots? They would say, "This sort of thing, sir, is not the sort of thing the house has been accustomed to, you will bring the house into the Gazette,[7] you must ravel out four inches of trousers daily, sir, or you must go."

Some years ago, we, the writer, not being in Griggs and Bodger's, took the liberty of buying a great-coat which we saw exposed for sale in the Burlington Arcade, London, and which appeared to be in our eyes the most sensible great-coat we had ever seen. Taking the further liberty to wear this great-coat after we had bought it, we became a sort of Spectre, eliciting the wonder and terror of our fellow creatures as we flitted along the streets. We accompanied the coat to Switzerland for six months; and, although it was perfectly new there, we found it was not regarded as a portent of the least importance. We accompanied it to Paris for another six months; and, although it was perfectly new there too, nobody minded it. This coat so intolerable to Britain, was nothing more nor less than the loose wide-sleeved mantle, easy to put on, easy to put off, and crushing nothing beneath it, which everybody now wears.

During hundreds of years, it was the custom in England to wear beards. It became, in course of time, one of our Insularities to shave close. Whereas, in almost all the other countries of Europe, more or less of moustache and beard was habitually worn, it came to be established in this speck of an island, as an Insularity from which there was no appeal, that an Englishman, whether he liked it or not, must hew, hack, and rasp his chin and upper lip daily. The inconvenience of this infallible test of British respectability was so widely felt, that fortunes were made by razors, razor-strops, hones, pastes, shaving-soaps, emollients for the soothing of the tortured skin, all sorts of contrivances to lessen the misery of the shaving process and diminish the amount of time it occupied. This particular Insularity even went some miles further on the broad highway of Nonsense than other Insularities; for it not only tabooed unshorn civilians, but claimed for one particular and very limited military class the sole right to dispense with razors as to their upper lips. We ventured to suggest in this journal that the prohibition was ridiculous, and to show some reasons why it was ridiculous. The Insularity having no sense in it, has since been losing ground every day.

One of our most remarkable Insularities is a tendency to be firmly persuaded that what is not English is not natural. In the Fine Arts department of the French Exhibition,[8] recently closed, we repeatedly heard, even from the more educated and reflective of our countrymen, that certain pictures which appeared to possess great merit – of which not the lowest item was, that they possessed the merit of a vigorous and bold Idea – were all very well, but were "theatrical." Conceiving the difference between a dramatic picture and a theatrical picture, to be, that in the former case a story is strikingly told, without apparent consciousness of a spectator, and that in the latter case the groups are obtrusively conscious of a spectator, and are obviously dressed up, and doing (or not doing) certain things with an eye to the spectator, and not for the sake of the story; we sought in vain for this defect. Taking further pains then, to find out what was meant by the term theatrical, we found that the actions and gestures of the figures were not English. That is to say, – the figures expressing themselves in the vivacious manner natural in a greater or less degree to the whole great continent of Europe, were overcharged and out of the truth, because they did not express themselves in the manner of our little Island – which is so very exceptional, that it always places an Englishman at a disadvantage, out of his own country, until his fine sterling qualities shine through his external formality and constraint. Surely nothing can be more unreasonable, say, than that we should require a Frenchman of the days of Robespierre, to be taken out of his jail to the guillotine with the calmness of Clapham or the respectability of Richmond Hill,[9] after a trial at the Central Criminal Court in eighteen hundred and fifty-six. And yet this exactly illustrates the requirement of the particular Insularity under consideration.

When shall we get rid of the Insularity of being afraid to make the most of small resources, and the best of scanty means of enjoyment? In Paris (as in innumerable other places and countries) a man who has six square feet of yard, or six square feet of housetop, adorns it in his own poor way, and sits there in the fine weather because he likes to do it, because he chooses to do it, because he has got nothing better of his own, and has never been laughed out of the enjoyment of what he has got. Equally, he will sit at his door, or in his balcony, or out on the pavement, because it is cheerful and pleasant and he likes to see the life of the city. For the last seventy years his family have not been tormenting their lives with continual enquiries and speculations whether other families, above and below, to the right and to the left, over the way and round the corner, would consider these recreations genteel, or would do the like, or would not do the like. That abominable old Tyrant, Madame Grundy,[10] has never been of his acquaintance. The result is, that, with a very small income and in a very dear city, he has more innocent pleasure than fifty Englishmen of the same condition; and is distinctly, in spite of our persuasion to the contrary (another Insularity!) a more domestic man than the Englishman, in regard of his simple pleasures being, to a much greater extent, divided with his wife and children. It is a natural consequence of their being easy and cheap, and profoundly independent of Madame Grundy.

But, this Insularity rests, not to the credit of England, on a more palpable foundation than perhaps any other. The old school of Tory writers did so pertinaciously labor to cover all easily available recreations and cheap reliefs from the monotony of common life, with ridicule and contempt, that great numbers of the English people got scared into being dull, and are only now beginning to recover their courage. The object of these writers, when they had any object beyond an insolent disparagement of the life-blood of the nation, was to jeer the weaker members of the middle class into making themselves a poor fringe on the skirts of the class above them, instead of occupying their own honest, honorable, independent place. Unfortunately they succeeded only too well, and to this grievous source may be traced many of our present political ills. In no country but England have the only means and scenes of relaxation within the reach of some million or two of people been systematically lampooned and derided. This disgraceful Insularity exists no longer. Still, some weak traces of its contemptuous spirit may occasionally be found, even in very unlikely places. The accomplished Mr. Macaulay, in the third volume of his brilliant History, writes loftily about "the thousands of clerks and milliners who are now thrown into raptures by the sight of Loch Katrine and Loch Lomond."[11] No such responsible gentleman, in France or Germany, writing history – writing anything – would think it fine to sneer at any inoffensive and useful class of his fellow subjects. If the clerks and milliners – who pair off arm in arm, by thousands, for Loch Katrine and Loch Lomond, to celebrate the Early

Closing Movement,[12] we presume – will only imagine their presence poisoning those waters to the majestic historian as he roves along the banks, looking for Whig Members of Parliament to sympathise with him in admiration of the beauties of Nature, we think they will be amply avenged in the absurdity of the picture.

Not one of our Insularities is so astonishing in the eyes of an intelligent foreigner, as the Court Newsman. He is one of the absurd little obstructions perpetually in the way of our being understood abroad. The quiet greatness and independence of the national character seems so irreconcileable with its having any satisfaction in the dull slipslop about the slopes and the gardens, and about the Prince Consort's going a-hunting and coming back to lunch, and about Mr. Gibbs[13] and the ponies, and about the Royal Highnesses on horseback and the Royal infants taking carriage exercise, and about the slopes and the gardens again, and the Prince Consort again, and Mr. Gibbs and the ponies again, and the Royal Highnesses on horseback again, and the Royal infants taking carriage exercise again, and so on for every day in the week and every week in the year, that in questions of importance the English as a people, really miss their just recognition. Similar small beer is chronicled with the greatest care about the nobility in their country-houses. It is in vain to represent that the English people don't care about these insignificant details, and don't want them; that aggravates the misunderstanding. If they don't want them, why do they have them? If they feel the effect of them to be ridiculous, why do they consent to be made ridiculous? If they can't help it, why, then the bewildered foreigner submits that he was right at first, and that it is not the English people that is the power, but Lord Aberdeen, or Lord Palmerston, or Lord Aldborough,[14] or Lord Knowswhom.

It is an Insularity well worth general consideration and correction, that the English people are wanting in self-respect. It would be difficult to bear higher testimony to the merits of the English aristocracy than they themselves afford in not being very arrogant or intolerant, with so large a public always ready to abase themselves before titles. On all occasions, public and private, where the opportunity is afforded, this readiness is to be observed. So long as it obtains so widely, it is impossible that we should be justly appreciated and comprehended, by those who have the greatest part in ruling us. And thus it happens that now we are facetiously pooh-poohed by our Premier[15] in the English capital, and now the accredited representatives of our arts and sciences are disdainfully slighted by our Ambassador in the French capital,[16] and we wonder to find ourselves in such curious and disadvantageous comparison with the people of other countries. Those people may, through many causes, be less fortunate and less free; but, they have more social self-respect: and that self-respect must, through all their changes, be deferred to, and will assert itself. We apprehend that few persons are disposed to contend that Rank does not receive its due share of homage on the continent of Europe; but, between the homage it receives there, and the homage it receives in our island, there is an immense difference. Half a dozen dukes and lords, at an English county ball, or public dinner, or any tolerably miscellaneous gathering, are painful and disagreeable company; not because they have any disposition unduly to exalt themselves, or are generally otherwise than cultivated and polite gentlemen, but, because too many of us are prone to twist ourselves out of shape before them, into contortions of servility and adulation. Elsewhere, Self-respect usually steps in to prevent this; there is much less toadying and tuft-hunting; and the intercourse between the two orders is infinitely more agreeable to both, and far more edifying to both.

It is one of our Insularities, if we have a royal or titled visitor among us, to use expressions of slavish adulation in our public addresses that have no response in the heart of any breathing creature, and to encourage the diffusion of details respecting such visitor's devout behaviour at church, courtly behaviour in reception-rooms, decent behaviour at dinner-tables, implying previous acquaintance with the uses of knife, fork, spoon, and wine-glass, – which would really seem to denote that we had expected Orson.[17] These doubtful compliments are paid nowhere else, and would not be paid by us if we had a little more self-respect. Through our intercourse with other nations, we cannot too soon import some. And when we have left off representing, fifty times a day, to the King of Brentford and the Chief Tailor of Tooley Street,[18] that their smiles are necessary to our existence, those two magnificent persons will begin to doubt whether they really are so, and we shall have begun to get rid of another Insularity.

The Demeanour of Murderers

First published in *Household Words*, 14 June 1856, from which this text is reproduced.

The recent trial[1] of the greatest villain that ever stood in the Old Bailey dock, has produced the usual descriptions inseparable from such occasions. The public has read from day to day of the murderer's complete self-possession, of his constant coolness, of his profound composure, of his perfect equanimity. Some describers have gone so far as to represent him, occasionally rather amused than otherwise by the proceedings; and all the accounts that we have seen, concur in more or less suggesting that there is something admirable, and difficult to reconcile with guilt, in the bearing so elaborately set forth.

As whatever tends, however undesignedly, to insinuate this uneasy sense of incongruity into any mind, and to invest so abhorrent a ruffian with the slightest tinge of heroism, must be prejudicial to the general welfare, we revive the detestable subject with the hope of showing that there is nothing at all singular in such a deportment, but that it is always to be looked for and counted on, in the case of a very wicked murderer. The blacker the guilt, the stronger the probability of its being thus carried off.

In passing, we will express an opinion that Nature never writes a bad hand. Her writing, as it may be read in the human countenance, is invariably legible, if we come at all trained to the reading of it. Some little weighing and comparing are necessary. It is not enough in turning our eyes on the demon in the Dock, to say he has a fresh color, or a high head, or a bluff manner, or what not, and therefore he does not look like a murderer, and we are surprised and shaken. The physiognomy and conformation of the Poisoner whose trial occasions these remarks, were exactly in accordance with his deeds; and every guilty consciousness he had gone on storing up in his mind, had set its mark upon him.

We proceed, within as short a compass as possible, to illustrate the position we have placed before our readers in the first paragraph of this paper.

The Poisoner's demeanour was considered exceedingly remarkable, because of his composure under trial, and because of the confident expectation of acquittal which he professed to the last, and under the influence of which he, at various times during his incarceration, referred to the plans he entertained for the future when he should be free again.

Can any one, reflecting on the matter for five minutes, suppose it possible – we do not say probable, but possible – that in the breast of this Poisoner there were surviving, in the days of his trial, any lingering traces of sensibility, or any wrecked fragment of the quality which we call sentiment? Can the profoundest or the simplest man alive, believe that in such a heart there could have been left, by that time, any touch of Pity? An objection to die, and a special objection to be killed, no doubt he had; and with that objection very strong within him for divers very weighty reasons, he was – *not* quite composed. Distinctly *not* quite composed, but, on the contrary, very restless. At one time, he was incessantly pulling on and pulling off his glove; at another time, his hand was constantly passing over and over his face; and the thing most instanced in proof of his composure, the perpetual writing and scattering about of little notes, which, as the verdict drew nearer and nearer, thickened from a sprinkling to a heavy shower, is in itself a proof of miserable restlessness. Beyond this emotion, which any lower animal would have, with an apprehension on it of a similar fate, what was to be expected from such a creature but insensibility? I poison my friend in his drink, and I poison my friend in his bed, and I poison my wife, and I poison her memory, and do you look to ME, at the end of such a career as mine, for sensibility? I have not the power of it even in my own behalf, I have lost the manner of it, I don't know what it means, I stand contemptuously wondering at you people here when I see you moved by this affair. In the Devil's name, man, have you heard the evidence of that chambermaid, whose tea I should like to have the sweetening of? Did you hear her describe the agonies in which my friend expired? Do you know that it was my trade to be learned in poisons, and that I foresaw all that, and considered all that, and knew, when I stood at his bedside looking down upon his face turned to me for help on its road to the grave through the frightful gate then swinging on its hinges, that in so many hours or minutes all those horrors would infallibly ensue? Have you heard that, after my poisonings, I have had to face the circumstances out, with friends and enemies, doctors, undertakers, all sorts of men, and have uniformly done it; and do you wonder that I face it out with you? Why not? What right or reason can you have to expect anything else of me? Wonder! You might wonder, indeed, if you saw me moved, here now before you. If I had any natural human feeling for my face to express, do you imagine that those medicines of my prescribing and administering would ever have been taken from my hand? Why, man, my demeanour at this bar is the natural companion of my crimes, and, if it were a tittle different from what it is, you might even begin reasonably to doubt whether I had ever committed them!

The Poisoner had a confident expectation of acquittal. We doubt as little that he really had some considerable hope of it, as we do that he made a pretence of having more than he really had. Let us consider, first, if it be wonderful that he should have been rather sanguine. He had poisoned his victims according to his carefully-laid plans; he had got them buried out of his way; he had murdered, and forged, and yet kept his place as a good fellow and a sporting character; he had made a capital friend of the coroner, and a serviceable traitor of the postmaster; he was a great public character, with a special Act of Parliament for his trial; the choice spirits of the Stock Exchange were offering long odds in his favor, and, to wind up all, here was a tip-top Counsellor bursting into tears for him, saying to the jury, three times over, "You dare not, you dare not, you dare not!" and bolting clean out of the court to declare his belief that he was innocent. With all this to encourage him, with his own Derby-day division of mankind into knaves and fools, and with his own secret knowledge of the difficulties and mysteries with which the proof of Poison had been, in the manner of the Poisoning, surrounded, it would have been strange indeed if he were not borne up by some idea of escape. But, why should he have professed himself to have more hope of escape than he really entertained? The answer is, because it belongs to that extremity, that the villain in it should not only declare a strong expectation of acquittal himself, but should try to infect all the people about him with it. Besides having an artful fancy (not wholly without foundation) that he disseminates by that means an impression that he is innocent; to surround himself in his narrowed world with this fiction is, for the time being, to fill the jail with a faintly rose-coloured atmosphere, and to remove the gallows to a more agreeable distance. Hence, plans are laid for the future, communicated with an engaging candor to turnkeys, and discussed in a reliant spirit. Even sick men and women, over whom natural death is impending, constantly talk with those about them on precisely the same principle.

It may be objected that there is some slight ingenuity in our endeavours to resolve the demeanour of this Poisoner into the same features as the demeanour of every other very wicked and very hardened criminal in the same strait, but that a parallel would be better than argument. We have no difficulty in finding a parallel; we have no difficulty in finding scores, beyond the almost insuperable difficulty of finding, in the criminal records, as deeply-dyed a murderer. To embarrass these remarks, however, with references to cases that have passed out of the general memory, or have never been widely known, would be to render the discussion very irksome. We will confine ourselves to a famous instance. We will not even ask if it be so long ago since RUSH[2] was tried, that *his* demeanour is forgotten. We will call THURTELL[3] into court, as one of the murderers best remembered in England.

With the difference that the circumstances of Thurtell's guilt are not comparable in atrocity with those of the Poisoner's, there are points of strong resemblance between the two men. Each was born in a fair station, and educated in conformity with it; each murdered a man with whom he had been on terms of intimate association, and for whom he professed a friendship at the time of the murder; both were members of that vermin-race of outer betters and blacklegs, of whom some worthy samples were presented on both trials, and of whom, as a community, mankind would be blessedly rid, if they could all be, once and for ever, knocked on the head at a blow. Thurtell's demeanour was exactly that of the Poisoner's. We have referred to the newspapers of his time, in aid of our previous knowledge of the case; and they present a complete confirmation of the simple fact for which we contend. From day to day, during his imprisonment before his trial, he is described as "collected and resolute in his demeanour," as "rather mild and conciliatory in his address," as being visited by "friends whom he receives with cheerfulness," as "remaining firm and unmoved," as "increasing in confidence as the day which is to decide his fate draws nigh," as "speaking of the favourable result of the trial with his usual confidence." On his trial, he looks "particularly well and healthy." His attention and composure are considered as wonderful as the Poisoner's; he writes notes as the Poisoner did; he watches the case with the same cool eye; he "retains that firmness for which, from the moment of his apprehension, he has been distinguished;" he "carefully assorts his papers on a desk near him;" he is (in this being singular) his own orator, and makes a speech in the manner of Edmund Kean,[4] on the whole not very unlike that of the leading counsel for the Poisoner, concluding, as to his own innocence, with a So help me God! Before his trial, the Poisoner says he will be at the coming race for the Derby. Before his trial, Thurtell says, "that after his acquittal he will visit his father, and will propose to him to advance the portion which he intended for him, upon which he will reside abroad." (So Mr. Manning[5] observed, under similar circumstances, that when all that nonsense was over, and the thing wound up, he had an idea of establishing himself in the West Indies.) When the Poisoner's trial is yet to last another day or so, he enjoys his half-pound of steak and his tea, wishes his best friends may sleep as he does, and fears the grave "no more than his bed." (See the Evening Hymn for a Young Child.⁶) When Thurtell's trial is yet to last another day or so, he takes his cold meat, tea, and coffee, and "enjoys himself with great comfort;" also, on the morning of his execution, he wakes from as innocent a slumber as the Poisoner's, declaring that he has had an excellent night, and that he hasn't dreamed "about this business." Whether the parallel will hold to the last, as to "feeling very well and very comfortable," as to "the firm step and perfect calmness," as to "the manliness and correctness of his general conduct," as to "the countenance unchanged by the awfulness of the situation" – not to say as to bowing to a friend, from the scaffold "in a friendly but dignified manner" – our readers will know for themselves when we know too.

It is surely time that people who are not in the habit of dissecting such appearances, but who are in the habit of reading about them, should be helped to the knowledge that, in the worst examples they are the most to be expected, and the least to be wondered at. That, there is no inconsistency in them, and no fortitude in them. That, there is nothing in them but cruelty and insensibility. That, they are seen, because the man is of a piece with his misdeeds; and that it is not likely that he ever could have committed the crimes for which he is to suffer, if he had not this demeanour to present, in standing publicly to answer for them.

Nobody, Somebody, and Everybody

First published in *Household Words*, 30 August 1856, from which this text is reproduced.

The power of Nobody is becoming so enormous in England, and he alone is responsible for so many proceedings, both in the way of commission and omission; he has so much to answer for, and is so constantly called to account; that a few remarks upon him may not be ill-timed.

The hand which this surprising person had in the late war[1] is amazing to consider. It was he who left the tents behind, who left the baggage behind, who chose the worst possible ground for encampments, who provided no means of transport, who killed the horses, who paralysed the commissariat, who knew nothing of the business he professed to know and monopolised, who decimated the English army. It was Nobody who gave out the famous unroasted coffee, it was Nobody who made the hospitals more horrible than language can describe, it was Nobody who occasioned all the dire confusion of Balaklava harbor, it was even Nobody who ordered the fatal Balaklava cavalry charge.[2] The non-relief of Kars[3] was the work of Nobody, and Nobody has justly and severely suffered for that infamous transaction.

It is difficult for the mind to span the career of Nobody. The sphere of action opened to this wonderful person, so enlarges every day, that the limited faculties of Anybody are too weak to compass it. Yet, the nature of the last tribunal expressly appointed for the detection and punishment of Nobody may, as a part of his stupendous history, be glanced at without winking.

At the Old Bailey, when a person under strong suspicion of mal-practices is tried, it is the custom (the rather as the strong suspicion has been found, by a previous enquiry, to exist), to conduct the trial on stringent principles, and to confide it to impartial hands. It has not yet become the practice of the criminal, or even of the civil courts – but they, indeed, are constituted for the punishment of Somebody – to invite the prisoner's or defendant's friends to talk the matter over with him in a cosy, tea-and-muffin sort of way, and make out a verdict together, that shall be what a deposed iron king[4] called making things "pleasant." But, when Nobody was shown within these few weeks to have occasioned intolerable misery and loss in the late war, and to have incurred a vast amount of guilt in bringing to pass results which all morally sane persons can understand to be fraught with fatal consequences, far beyond present calculation, this cosy course of proceeding was the course pursued. My Lord, intent upon establishing the responsibility of Nobody, walked into court as he would walk into a ball-room; and My Lord's friends and admirers toadied and fawned upon him in court, as they would toady him and fawn upon him in the other assembly. My Lord carried his head very high, and took a mighty great tone with the common people; and there was no question as to anything My Lord did or said, and Nobody got triumphantly fixed. Ignorance enough and incompetency enough to bring any country that the world has ever seen to defeat and shame, and to lay any head that ever was in it low, were proved beyond question; but, My Lord cried, "On Nobody's eyes be it!" and My Lord's impaneled chorus cried, "There is no impostor but Nobody; on him be the shame and blame!"

Surely, this is a rather wonderful state of things to be realising itself so long after the Flood, in such a country as England. Surely, it suggests to us with some force, that wherever this ubiquitous Nobody is, there mischief is and there danger is. For, it is especially to be borne in mind that wherever failure is accomplished, there Nobody lurks. With success, he has nothing to do. That is Everybody's business, and all manner of improbable people will invariably be found at the bottom of it. But, it is the great feature of the present epoch that all public disaster in the United Kingdom of Great Britain and Ireland is assuredly, and to a dead certainty, Nobody's work.

We have, it is not to be denied, punished Nobody, with exemplary rigor. We have, as a nation, allowed ourselves to be deluded by no influences or insolences of office or rank, but have dealt with Nobody in a spirit of equal and uncompromising justice that has moved the admiration of the world. I have had some opportunities of remarking, out of England, the impression made on other peoples by the stern Saxon spirit with which, the default proved and the wrong done, we have tracked down and punished the defaulter and wrong-doer. And I do here declare my solemn belief, founded on much I have seen, that the remembrance of our frightful failures within the last three years, and of our retaliation upon Nobody, will be more vivid and potent in Europe (mayhap in Asia, too, and in America) for years upon years to come than all our successes since the days of the Spanish Armada.

In civil matters we have Nobody equally active. When a civil office breaks down, the break-down is sure to be in Nobody's department. I entreat on my reader, dubious of this proposition, to wait until the next break-down (the reader is certain not to have to wait long), and to observe, whether or no, it is in Nobody's department. A dispatch of the greatest moment is sent to a minister abroad, at a most important crisis; Nobody reads it. British subjects are affronted in a foreign territory; Nobody interferes. Our own loyal fellow-subjects, a few thousand miles away, want to exchange political, commercial, and domestic intelligence with us; Nobody stops the mail. The government, with all its mighty means and appliances, is invariably beaten and outstripped by private enterprise; which we all know to be Nobody's fault. Something will be the national death of us, some day; and who can doubt that Nobody will be brought in Guilty?

Now, might it not be well, if it were only for the novelty of the experiment, to try Somebody a little? Reserving Nobody for statues, and stars and garters, and batons, and places and pensions without duties, what if we were to try Somebody for real work? More than that, what if we were to punish Somebody with a most inflexible and grim severity, when we caught him pompously undertaking in holiday-time to do work, and found him, when the working-time came, altogether unable to do it?

Where do I, as an Englishman, want Somebody? Before high Heaven, I want him everywhere! I look round the whole dull horizon, and I want Somebody to do work while the Brazen Head, already hoarse with crying "Time is!" passes into the second warning, "Time was!" I don't want Somebody to let off Parliamentary penny crackers against evils that need to be stormed by the thunderbolts of Jove. I don't want Somebody to sustain, for Parliamentary and Club entertainment, and by the desire of several persons of distinction, the character of a light old gentleman, or a fast old gentleman, or a debating old gentleman, or a dandy old gentleman, or a free-and-easy old gentleman, or a capital old gentleman considering his years. I want Somebody to be clever in doing the business, not clever in evading it. The more clever he is in the latter quality (which has been the making of Nobody), the worse I hold it to be for me and my children and for all men and their children. I want Somebody who shall be no fiction; but a capable, good, determined workman. For, it seems to me that from the moment when I accept Anybody in a high place, whose function in that place is to exchange winks with me instead of doing the serious deeds that belong to it, I set afloat a system of false pretence and general swindling, the taint of which soon begins to manifest itself in every department of life, from Newgate[5] to the Court of Bankruptcy, and thence to the highest Court of Appeal. For this reason, above all others, I want to see the working Somebody in every responsible position which the winking Somebody and Nobody now monopolise between them.

And this brings me back to Nobody; to the great irresponsible, guilty, wicked, blind giant of this time. O friends, countrymen, and lovers, look at that carcase smelling strong of prussic acid, (drunk out of a silver milkpot, which was a part of the plunder, or as the less pernicious thieves call it, the swag), cumbering Hampstead Heath by London town![6] Think of the history of which that abomination is at once the beginning and the end; of the dark social scenes daguerreotyped[7] in it; and of the Lordship of your Treasury to which Nobody, driving a shameful bargain, raised this creature when he was alive. Follow the whole story, and finish by listening to the parliamentary lawyers as they tell you that Nobody knows anything about it; that Nobody is entitled (from the attorney point of view) to believe that there ever was such a business at all; that Nobody can be allowed to demand, for decency's sake, the swift expulsion from the lawmaking body of the surviving instrument in the heap of crime; that such expulsion is, in a word, just Nobody's business, and must at present be constitutionally left to Nobody to do.

There is a great fire raging in the land, and – by all the polite precedents and prescriptions! – you shall leave it to Nobody to put it out with a squirt, expected home in a year or so. There are inundations bursting on the valleys, and – by the same precedents and prescriptions! – you shall trust to Nobody to bale the water out with a bottomless tin kettle. Nobody being responsible to you for his perfect success in these little feats, and you confiding in him, you shall go to Heaven. Ask for Somebody in his stead, and you shall go in quite the contrary direction.

And yet, for the sake of Everybody, give me Somebody! I raise my voice in the wilderness for Somebody. My heart, as the ballad says, is sore for Somebody.[8] Nobody has done more harm in this single generation than Everybody can mend in ten generations. Come, responsible Somebody; accountable Blockhead, come!

The Murdered Person

First published in *Household Words*, 11 October 1856, from which this text is reproduced.

In an early number of this journal,[1] we made some reference to the fact that in the highly improving accounts which are given to the public of the last moments of murderers, the murdered person may be usually observed to be entirely dismissed from the moral discourses with which the murderer favors his admiring audience, except as an incidental and tributary portion of his own egotistical story.

To what lengths this dismissal of the very objectionable personage who persisted in tempting the Saint in the condemned cell to murder him, may be carried, we have had a recent opportunity of considering, in the case of the late lamented MR. DOVE.[2] That amiable man, previous to taking the special express-train to Paradise which is vulgarly called the Gallows, indited a document wherein he made it manifest to all good people that the mighty and beneficent Creator of the vast Universe had specially wrought to bring it about that he should cruelly and stealthily torture, torment, and by inches slay, a weak sick woman, and that woman his wife, in order that he, Dove, as with the wings of a Dove[3] (a little blood-stained or so, but that's not much) should be put in the way of ascending to Heaven.

Frightful as this statement is, and sickening as one would suppose it must be, to any mind capable of humbly and reverentially approaching at an inconceivable distance the idea of the Divine Majesty, there it stands in the printed records of the day: a part of the Gaol Court-Newsman's account of the visitors whom the chosen vessel received in his cell, of his proposing to sing hymns in chorus in the night season, and of the "Prison Philanthropist" declaring him to be a pattern penitent.

Now, to the Prison Philanthropist we concede all good intentions. We take it for granted that the venerable gentleman did not confer his alliterative title on himself, and that he is no more responsible for it, than a public-house is for its sign, or a ship for her figure-head. Yet, holding this horrible confusion of mind on the part of the inhuman wretch to whom he devoted so much humanity, to be shocking in itself and widely perilous in its influences, we plainly avow that we for our part cannot accept good intentions as any set-off against the production of such a mental state, and that we think the condemned cells everywhere (left to their appointed ministers of religion who are very rarely deficient in kindness and zeal) would be better without such philanthropy. What would the Home Secretary say to Professor Holloway,[4] if that learned man applied for free admission to the condemned cells throughout England, in order that he might with his ointment anoint the throats of the convicts about to be hanged, so that under the influences of the application their final sensations should be of a mild tickling? What would the Home Secretary reply to the august members of the Hygeian Council of the British College of Health, if they made a similar request, with a view to the internal exhibition for a similar purpose of that great discovery, Morrison's pills?[5] Even if some regular medical hand of eminence were to seek the same privilege, with a view to a drugging within the limits of the pharmacopœia – say for the philanthropic purpose of making the patient maudlin drunk with opium and peppermint, and sending him out of this world with a leer – how would the Home Secretary receive that edifying proposal? And is there nothing of greater moment involved in this revolting conceit, setting its heel on the murdered body, and daring eternity on the edge of the murderer's grave?

Pursue this advance made by the late Mr. Dove on the usual calm dismissal of the murdered person, and see where it ends. There are sent into this world two human creatures: one, a highly interesting individual in whom Providence is much concerned – Mr. Dove: one, a perfectly uninteresting individual of no account whatever, here or hereafter – Mrs. Dove. Mr. Dove being expressly wanted in the regions of the blessed, Mrs. Dove is delivered over to him, soul and body, to ensure his presence there, and provide against disappointment. There is no escape from this appalling, this impious conclusion. The special Gaol-Call which was wanting to, and was found by, Mr. Dove who is hanged, was wanting to, and was not found by, Mrs. Dove who is poisoned. Thus, the New Drop usurps the place of the Cross; and Saint John Ketch[6] is preached to the multitude as the latest and holiest of the Prophets!

Our title is so associated with the remembrance of this exhibition, that we have been led into the present comments on it. But, the purpose with which we adopted the title was rather to illustrate the general prevalence of the practice of putting the murdered person out of the question, and the extensive following which the custom of criminals has found outside the gaols.

Two noble lords at loggerheads, each of whom significantly suggests that he thinks mighty little of the capabilities of the other, are blamed for certain disasters which did undoubtedly befall, under their distinguished administration of military affairs. They demand enquiry.[7] A Board of their particular friends and admirers is appointed "to enquire" – much as its members might leave their cards for the noble lords with that inscription. The enquiry is in the first instance directed by one of the noble lords to the question – not quite the main question at issue – whether the Board can muzzle the Editor of the Times?[8] The Board have the best will in the world to do it, but, finding that the Editor declines to be muzzled, perforce confess their inability to muzzle him. The enquiry then proceeds into anything else that the noble lords like, and into nothing else that the noble lords don't like. It ends in eulogiums on the soldierly qualities and conduct of both lords, and clearly shows their fitness for command to have been so completely exemplified, in failing, that the inference is, if they had succeeded they would have failed. The compliments ended, the Board breaks up (the best thing it could possibly do, and the only function it is fit for), the noble lords are decorated, and there is an end of the matter.

How like the case of the late Mr. Dove! The murdered person – by name the wasted forces and resources of England – is not to be thought of; or, if thought of, is only to be regarded as having been expressly called into being for the noble lords to make away with, and mount up to the seventh Heaven of merit upon. The President of the Board (answering to the Prison Philanthropist) sings pæans in the dark to any amount, and the only thing wanting in the parallel, is, the finishing hand of Mr. Calcraft.[9]

Let us pass to another instance. The Law of Divorce is in such condition that from the tie of marriage there is no escape to be had, no absolution to be got, except under certain proved circumstances not necessary to enter upon here, and then only on payment of an enormous sum of money. Ferocity, drunkenness, flight, felony, madness, none of these will break the chain, without the enormous sum of money. The husband who, after years of outrage, has abandoned his wife, may at any time claim her for his property and seize the earnings on which she subsists. The most profligate of women, an intolerable torment, torture, and shame to her husband, may nevertheless, unless he be a very rich man, insist on remaining handcuffed to him, and dragging him away from any happier alliance, from youth to old age and death. Out of this condition of things among the common people, out of the galling knowledge of the impossibility of relief – aggravated, in cottages and single rooms, to a degree not easily imaginable by ill-assorted couples who live in houses of many chambers, and who, both at home and abroad, can keep clear of each other and go their respective ways – vices and crimes arise which no one with open eyes and any fair experience of the people can fail often to trace, from the Calendars of Assizes, back to this source. It is proposed a little to relax the severity of a thraldom prolonged beyond the bounds of morality, justice, and sense, and to modify the law. Instantly the singing of pæans begins, and the murdered person disappears! Authorities, lay and clerical, rise in their parliamentary places to deliver panegyrics on Marriage as an Institution (which nobody disputes to be just); they have much to relate concerning what the Fathers thought of it, and what was written, said, and done about it hundreds of years before these evils were; they set up their fancy whipping-tops, and whip away; they utter homilies without end upon the good side of the question, which is in no want of them; but, from their exalted state of vision the murdered person utterly vanishes. The tortures and wrongs of the sufferer have no place in their speeches. They felicitate themselves, like the murderers, on their own glowing state of mind, and they mount upon the mangled creature to deliver their orations, much as the Duke's man in the sham siege took his post on the fallen governor of Barataria.[10]

So in the case of overstrained Sunday observance, and denial of innocent popular reliefs from labour. The murdered person – the consumptive, scrofulous, ricketty worker in unwholesome places, the wide prevalence of whose reduced physical condition has rendered it necessary to lower the standard of health and strength for recruiting into the army, and caused its ranks to be reinforced in the late war by numbers of poor creatures notoriously in an unserviceable bodily state – the murdered person, in this phase of his ubiquity, is put out of sight, as a matter of course. We have flaming and avenging speeches made, as if a bold peasantry, their country's pride, models of cheerful health and muscular development, were in every hamlet, town, and city, once a week ardently bent upon the practice of asceticism and the renunciation of the world; but, the murdered person, Legion, who cannot at present by any means be got at once a week, and who does nothing all that day but gloom and grumble and deteriorate, is put out of sight as if none of us had ever heard of him! What is it to the holders forth, that wherever we live, or wherever we go, we see him, and see him with so much pity and dismay that we want to make him better by other human means than those which have missed him? To get rid of his memory, in the murdering way, and vaunt ourselves instead, is much easier.

Bankrupts are declared, greedy speculators smash, and bankers break. Who does not hear of the reverses of those unfortunate gentlemen; of the disruption of their establishments; of their wives being reduced to live upon their settlements; of the sale of their horses, equipages, pictures, wines; of the mighty being fallen, and of their magnanimity under their reverses?

But, the murdered person, the creditor, investor, depositor, the cheated and swindled under whatsoever name, whose mind does he trouble? The mind of the fraudulent firm? Enquire at the House of Detention, Clerkenwell, London, and you will find that the last great fraudulent firm was no more troubled about *him*, than Mr. Dove or Mr. Palmer[11] was by the client whom he "did for," in the way of his different line of business.

And, lastly, get an order of admission to SIR CHARLES BARRY'S palace[12] any night in the session, and you will observe the murdered person to be as comfortably stowed away as he ever is at Newgate. What In said to Out in eighteen hundred and thirty-five, what Out retorted upon In in eighteen hundred and forty-seven, why In would have been Out in eighteen hundred and fifty-four but for Out's unparalleled magnanimity in not coming in, this, with all the contemptible ins and outs of all the Innings and Outings, shall be discoursed upon, with abundance of hymns and pæans on all sides, for six months together. But, the murdered old gentleman TIME, and the murdered matron, BRITANNIA, shall no more come in question than the murdered people do in the cells of the penitents – unless indeed they are reproduced, as in the odious case with which we began, to show that they were expressly created for the exaltation of the speech-makers.

The Best Authority

First published in *Household Words*, 20 June 1857, from which this text is reproduced.

I wish he was not so ubiquitous.

I wish he was not always having people to dine with him, into whom he crams all manner of confidences, and who come from his too hospitable board to harass my soul with special intelligence (which is never true), upon all the subjects that arise in Europe, Asia, Africa, and America. I wish to Heaven he would dine out!

Yet, that is a weak wish, because he does dine out. He makes a habit of dining out. He is always dining out. How could I be the confused, perplexed, benighted wretch I am, but for everybody I know, meeting him at dinner everywhere, and receiving information from him which they impart to me? I wish he would hold his tongue!

Yet, that is another weak wish, because when he does hold his tongue, I am none the better for it. His silence is used against me. If I mention to my friend, Pottington, any little scrap of fact of which in my very humble way I may have become possessed, Pottington says, that's very odd, he hardly thinks it can be, he will tell me why; dining yesterday at Croxford's[1] he happened to sit next to the Best Authority, and had a good deal of talk with him, and yet he never said a word to lead him to suppose –

This brings me to inquire how does it happen that everybody always sits next him? At a dinner of eighteen persons, I have known seventeen sit next him. Nay, at a public dinner of one hundred and thirty, I have known one hundred and twenty-nine sit next him. How is it done? In his ardent desire to impart special intelligence to his fellow-men, does he shift his position constantly, and sit upon all the chairs in the social circle successively? If he does so, it is obvious that he has no moral right to represent to each individual member of the company that his communication is of an exclusive character, and that he is impelled to it by strong personal consideration and respect. Yet I find that he invariably makes some such representation. I augur from this, that he is a deceiver.

What is his calling in life, that it leaves him so much time upon his hands? He is always at all the clubs – must spend a respectable income in annual club subscriptions alone. He is always in all the streets, and is met in the market-places by all sorts and conditions of men. Who is his bootmaker? Who cuts his corns? He is always going up and down the pavements, and must have corns of a prodigious size.

I object to his being addicted to compliments and flattery. I boldly publish this accusation against him, because I have several respected friends who would scorn to compliment themselves, whom he is always complimenting. For example. He meets my dear Flounceby (whom I regard as a brother), at a mutual friend's – there again! He is mutual friends with everybody! – and I find that he prefaces his communications to Flounceby, with such expressions as these: "Mr. Flounceby, I do not wish what I am about to mention, to go any further; it is a matter of some little delicacy which I should not consider myself justified in speaking of to general society; but, knowing your remarkable powers, your delicate discrimination, and great discretion," etc. All of which, my dear Flounceby, in the modest truthfulness of his nature, feels constrained to repeat to me! This is the Best Authority's didactic style; but, I observe him also, by incidental strokes, artfully to convey complimentary touches of character into casual dialogue. As when he remarks, in reference to some handsome reticence on my friend's part, "Ah Flounceby! Your usual reserve in committing others!" Or, "Your expressive eye, my dear Mr. Flounceby, discloses what your honourable tongue would desire to conceal!" And the like. All of which, Flounceby, in his severe determination to convey to me the truth, the whole truth, and nothing but the truth, repeats, with evident pain to his modesty.

Is he a burglar, or of the swell mob? I do not accuse him of occupying either position (which would be libellous), but I ask for information. Because my mind is tormented by his perpetually getting into houses into which he would seem to have no lawful open way, and by his continually diving into people's pocket-books in an otherwise inexplicable manner. In respect of getting into the Queen's Palace, the Boy Jones[2] was a fool to him. He knows everything that takes place there. On a late auspicious occasion when the nation was hourly expecting to be transported with joy for the ninth time, it is surprising what he knew on the question of Chloroform. Now, Doctor Locock[3] is known to be the most trustworthy even of doctors; and Her Majesty's self-reliance and quiet force of character have passed into an axiom. I want to know, therefore, How, When, Where, and From Whom, did the Best Authority acquire all that chloroform information which he was, for months, prowling about all the clubs, going up and down all the streets, having all London to dine with him, and going out to dine with all London, for the express purpose of diffusing? I hope society does not demand that I should be slowly bothered to death by any man, without demanding this much satisfaction. How did he come by his intelligence, I ask? The Best Authority must have had an authority. Let it be produced.

I have mentioned the pocket-books in which he deciphers secret entries; many of them written, probably, in invisible ink, for they are non-existent even to the owner's eyes. How does he come by all the ambassadors' letter-bags, and by all the note-books of all the judges? Who gave him all the little scraps of paper that the late Mr. Palmer[4] wrote and handed about in the course of his protracted trial? He tells all sorts of people what was in them all; he must have seen them, surely. Who made out for him the accounts of this journal? Who calculated for him the sum total of profit? And when will it be quite convenient to him to name an early day for handing over to the Conductor[5] the very large balance, with several ciphers at the end of it, which clearly must be owing the said Conductor, as he has never laid hands on it yet?

How did he get into the Russian lines? He was always there; just as he was always in the English camp, and always coming home to put Mr. Russell[6] right, and going back again. It was he who found out that the Commissariat wouldn't give the *Times* rations of pork, and that the porkless *Times* would never afterwards leave the Commissariat alone. Had he known much of the Russian leaders before the war, that he began to talk of them so familiarly by their surnames as soon as the first gun was fired? Will any of us ever forget while memory holds her seat in these distracted globes, our aching heads, what we suffered from this man in connexion with the Redan?[7] Can the most Christian of us ever forgive the lies he told us about the Malakhoff?[8] I might myself overlook even those injuries, but for his having put so many people up to making plans of that detested fortress, on tablecloths, with salt-spoons, forks, dessert-dishes, nut-crackers, and wine-glasses. Which frightful persecution, a thousand times inflicted on me, upon his authority – the best – I hereby swear never to condone! Never shall the Sapping and Mining knowledge, stamped in characters of lead upon this burning brow, remain with me but as a dreadful injury stimulating me to devote the residue of my life to vengeance on the Best Authority. If I could have his blood, I would! I avow it, in fell remembrance of the baying hounds of Boredom with which he hunted me in the days of the Russian war.

Will he, on this public challenge, stand forward foot to foot against me, his mortal enemy, and declare how he can justify his behaviour? Why am I, a free-born Briton, who never, never will – or rather who never, never would, if I could help it – why am I to truckle to this tyrant all the days of my life? Why is the Best Authority, Gesler-like,[9] to set his hat upon a pole in the épergne of every dinner table, in the hall of every club-house, in the stones of every street, and, violating the Charter proclaimed by the Guardian Angels who sang that strain, to demand me for his slave? What does he mean by his unreasonable requirement that I shall make over my five senses to him? Who is he that he is to absorb my entity into his non-entity? And are not these his appetites? I put it to Flounceby.

Flounceby is rather an obstinate character (Mrs. Flounceby says the most obstinate of men; but, that may be her impulsive way of expressing herself), and will argue with you on any point, for any length of time you like – or don't like. He is certain to beat you, too, by a neat method he has of representing you to have said something which you never did say, or so much as think of, and then indignantly contradicting it. No further back than within this month, Flounceby was holding forth at a great rate on the most argumentative question of all questions – which every question is with him, and therefore I simply mean any question – and had made out his case entirely to his own satisfaction, and was pounding his dinner-company of six with it, as if they were plastic metal, and he and the question were the steam-hammer; when an unknown man of faint and fashionable aspect (one of the six) slided out from under the hammer without any apparent effort, and flatly denied Flounceby's positions, one and all, "on the best authority." If he had contested them on any ground of faith, reason, probability, or analogy, Flounceby would have pinned him like a bull-dog; but, the mere mention of the Best Authority (it was a genteel question in its bearings) instantly laid Flounceby on his back. He turned pale, trembled, and gave in. It happened, however, as it always does at Flounceby's, that the next most argumentative question of questions came on immediately afterwards. Upon that point I, deriving courage from the faint and fashionable man, who by the way from the moment of his victory, retired, like Iago, and word spake never more[10] – opposed myself to Flounceby. I had not been rolled and flattened under the steam-hammer two minutes, when Flounceby, throwing the machinery out of gear, gave me one final crush from the Best Authority, and left me for dead. Goaded to distraction by the anonymous oppressor, I wildly cried that I cared nothing for the Best Authority. A shudder went round the table, and all present shrank from me, as if I had distinctly made the one greatest and most audacious denial of which humanity is capable.

Still goaded by this oppressor – always goaded by this oppressor – I ask, Who is he? Whence does he come when he goes out to dinner; where does he give those dinners at which so many people dine? Was he enrolled in the last census? Does he bear his part in the light burdens of the country?

Is he assessed to the equitable income-tax? I call upon the Best Authority to stand forth.

On more than one occasion I have thought I had him. In that portion of Pall Mall, London, which is bounded on the east by the Senior United Service Club House, and on the west by the Carlton Club House – a miasmatic spot, in which I suppose more boredom to be babbled daily, than in any two thousand square miles on the surface of the earth – into that dismal region I had sometimes tracked the despot, and there lost him. One day, upon the steps of the Athenæum, of which eminent institution I have the honour to be a member, I found a fellow-member, Mr. Prowler, of the Royal Society of Arts, lying in wait, under the portico, to pour a drop of special information into the ear of every man and brother who approached the temple. Mr. Prowler is a grave and secret personage, always specially informed, who whispers his way through life; incessantly acting Midas to everybody else's Reed.[11] He goes about, like a lukewarm draught of air, breathing intelligence into the ears of his fellow-men, and passing on. He had often previously brought me into trouble, and caused me to be covered with confusion and shame. On this occasion the subject-matter of his confidence was – if I may be allowed the expression – so much more than usually impossible that I took the liberty to intimate my sense of its irreconcilability with all laws human and divine, and to ask him from whom he had his information? He replied, from the Best Authority; at the same time implying, with a profound and portentous movement of his head, that that mysterious Being had just gone in. I thought the hour was come – rushed into the hall – and found nobody there, but a weak old gentleman, to all appearance harmlessly idiotic, who was drying his pocket-handkerchief before the fire, and gazing over his shoulder at two graceful leathern institutions, in the form of broken French bedsteads without the pole, which embellish that chaste spot and invite to voluptuous repose.

On another occasion, I was so near having my hand at my enemy's throat and he so unaccountably eluded me, that a brief recital of the circumstances may aptly close this paper. The pursuit and escape occurred at the Reform Club, of which eminent Institution likewise, I have the honour to be a member. As I know the Best Authority to pervade that building constantly, my eye had frequently sought him, with a vague sense of the supernatural and an irresistible feeling of dread, in the galleries overhanging the hall where I had but too often heard him quoted. No trace of his form, however, had revealed itself to me. I had frequently been close upon him; I had heard of him as having "just gone down to the House," or "just come up"; but, between us there had been a void. I should explain that in the palatial establishment of which I write, there is a dreadful little vault on the left of the Hall, where we hang up our hats and coats; the gloom and closeness of which vault, shade the imagination. I was crossing the Hall to dinner, in the height of the then Session of Parliament, when my distinguished friend, O' Boodleom[12] (Irish Member), being disappointed of a man of title, whom he was waiting to stun with a piece of information which he had just telegraphed to Erin, did me the honour to discharge that weapon upon me. As I had every conceivable reason to know that it could not possibly be correct, I deferentially asked O'Boodleom from whom he had received it? "Bedad, sir," says he – and, knowing his sensitive bravery, I really felt grateful to him, for not saying, "Blood, sir!" – "Bedad, sir," says he, "I had it, a while ago, from the Best Authority, and he's at this moment hanging up the entire of his coat and umberreller in the vault." I dashed into the vault, and seized (as I fondly thought) the Best Authority, to cope with him at last in the death-struggle. It was only my cousin Cackles, admitted on all hands to be the most amiable ass alive, who inoffensively asked me if I had heard the news?

The Best Authority was gone! How gone, whither gone, I am in no condition to say. I again, therefore, raise my voice, and call upon him to stand forward and declare himself.

AMUSEMENTS OF THE PEOPLE

The Amusements of the People

First published in two parts in *Household Words*, 30 March and 13 April 1850, from which this text is reproduced. Dickens wrote to William Brown on 1 August 1853: 'The more I look about me the more convinced I become, that if we would only condescend to amuse our people a little more, they would drink and do worse a good deal less.'

As one half of the world is said not to know how the other half lives, so it may be affirmed that the upper half of the world neither knows nor greatly cares how the lower half amuses itself. Believing that it does not care, mainly because it does not know, we purpose occasionally recording a few facts on this subject.

The general character of the lower class of dramatic amusements is a very significant sign of a people, and a very good test of their intellectual condition. We design to make our readers acquainted in the first place with a few of our experiences under this head in the metropolis.

It is probable that nothing will ever root out from among the common people an innate love they have for dramatic entertainment in some form or other. It would be a very doubtful benefit to society, we think, if it could be rooted out. The Polytechnic Institution in Regent Street,[1] where an infinite variety of ingenious models are exhibited and explained, and where lectures comprising a quantity of useful information on many practical subjects are delivered, is a great public benefit and a wonderful place, but we think a people formed *entirely* in their hours of leisure by Polytechnic Institutions would be an uncomfortable community. We would rather not have to appeal to the generous sympathies of a man of five-and-twenty, in respect of some affliction of which he had had no personal experience, who had passed all his holidays, when a boy, among cranks and cogwheels. We should be more disposed to trust him if he had been brought into occasional contact with a Maid and a Magpie;[2] if he had made one or two diversions into the Forest of Bondy;[3] or had even gone the length of a Christmas Pantomime. There is a range of imagination in most of us, which no amount of steam-engines will satisfy; and which The-great-exhibition-of-the-works-of-industry-of-all-nations, itself, will probably leave unappeased. The lower we go, the more natural it is that the best-relished provision for this should be found in dramatic entertainments; as at once the most obvious, the least troublesome, and the most real, of all escapes out of the literal world. JOE WHELKS, of the New Cut, Lambeth,[4] is not much of a reader, has no great store of books, no very commodious room to read in, no very decided inclination to read, and no power at all of presenting vividly before his mind's eye what he reads about. But put Joe in the gallery of the Victoria Theatre;[5] show him doors and windows in the scene that will open and shut, and that people can get in and out of; tell him a story with these aids, and by the help of live men and women dressed up, confiding to him their innermost secrets, in voices audible half a mile off; and Joe will unravel a story through all its entanglements, and sit there as long after midnight as you have anything left to show him. Accordingly, the Theatres to which Mr. Whelks resorts, are always full; and whatever changes of fashion the drama knows elsewhere, it is always fashionable in the New Cut.

The question, then, might not unnaturally arise, one would suppose, whether Mr. Whelks's education is at all susceptible of improvement, through the agency of his theatrical tastes. How far it is improved at present, our readers shall judge for themselves.

In affording them the means of doing so, we wish to disclaim any grave imputation on those who are concerned in ministering to the dramatic gratification of Mr. Whelks. Heavily taxed, wholly unassisted by the State, deserted by the gentry, and quite unrecognised as a means of public instruction, the higher English Drama has declined. Those who would live to please Mr. Whelks, must please Mr. Whelks to live. It is not the Manager's province to hold the Mirror up to Nature,[6] but to Mr. Whelks – the only person who acknowledges him. If, in like manner, the actor's nature, like the dyer's hand,[7] becomes subdued to what he works in, the actor can hardly be blamed for it. He grinds hard at his vocation, is often steeped in direful poverty, and lives, at the best, in a little world of mockeries. It is bad enough to give away a great estate six nights a-week, and want a shilling; to preside at imaginary banquets, hungry for a mutton chop; to smack the lips over a tankard of toast and water, and declaim about the mellow produce of the sunny vineyard on the banks of the Rhine; to be a rattling young lover, with the measles at home; and to paint sorrow over, with burnt cork and rouge; without being called upon to despise his vocation too. If he can utter the trash to which he is condemned, with any relish, so much the better for him, Heaven knows; and peace be with him!

A few weeks ago, we went to one of Mr. Whelks's favourite Theatres, to see an attractive Melo-Drama[8] called MAY MORNING, or THE MYSTERY OF 1715, AND THE MURDER! We had an idea that the former of these titles might refer to the month in which either the mystery or the murder happened, but we found it to be the name of the heroine, the pride of Keswick Vale; who was "called May Morning" (after a common custom among the English Peasantry) "from her bright eyes and merry laugh." Of this young lady, it may be observed, in passing, that she subsequently sustained every possible calamity of human existence, in a white muslin gown with blue tucks; and that she did every conceivable and inconceivable thing with a pistol, that could anyhow be effected by that description of fire-arms.

The Theatre was extremely full. The prices of admission were, to the boxes, a shilling; to the pit, sixpence; to the gallery, threepence. The gallery was of enormous dimensions (among the company, in the front row, we observed Mr. Whelks); and overflowing with occupants. It required no close observation of the attentive faces, rising one above another, to the very door in the roof, and squeezed and jammed in, regardless of all discomforts, even there, to impress a stranger with a sense of its being highly desirable to lose no possible chance of effecting any mental improvement in that great audience.

The company in the pit were not very clean or sweet-savoured, but there were some good-humoured young mechanics among them, with their wives. These were generally accompanied by "the baby," insomuch that the pit was a perfect nursery. No effect made on the stage was so curious, as the looking down on the quiet faces of these babies fast asleep, after looking up at the staring sea of heads in the gallery. There were a good many cold fried soles in the pit, besides; and a variety of flat stone bottles, of all portable sizes.

The audience in the boxes was of much the same character (babies and fish excepted) as the audience in the pit. A private in the Foot Guards sat in the next box; and a personage who wore pins on his coat instead of buttons, and was in such a damp habit of living as to be quite mouldy, was our nearest neighbour. In several parts of the house we noticed some young pickpockets of our acquaintance; but as they were evidently there as private individuals, and not in their public capacity, we were little disturbed by their presence. For we consider the hours of idleness passed by this class of society as so much gain to society at large; and we do not join in a whimsical sort of lamentation that is generally made over them, when they are found to be unoccupied.

As we made these observations the curtain rose, and we were presently in possession of the following particulars.

Sir George Elmore, a melancholy Baronet with every appearance of being in that advanced stage of indigestion in which Mr. Morrison's patients usually are, when they happen to hear through Mr. Moat, of the surprising effects of his Vegetable Pills, was found to be living in a very large castle, in the society of one round table, two chairs, and Captain George Elmore, "his supposed son, the Child of Mystery, and the Man of Crime." The Captain, in addition to an undutiful habit of bullying his father on all occasions, was a prey to many vices: foremost among which may be mentioned his desertion of his wife, "Estella de Neva, a Spanish lady," and his determination unlawfully to possess himself of May Morning; M. M. being then on the eve of marriage to Will Stanmore, a cheerful sailor, with very loose legs.

The strongest evidence, at first, of the Captain's being the Child of Mystery and the Man of Crime was deducible from his boots, which, being very high and wide, and apparently made of sticking-plaister, justified the worst theatrical suspicions to his disadvantage. And indeed he presently turned out as ill as could be desired: getting into May Morning's Cottage by the window after dark; refusing to "unhand" May Morning when required to do so by that lady; waking May Morning's only surviving parent, a blind old gentleman with a black ribbon over his eyes, whom we shall call Mr. Stars, as his name was stated in the bill thus * * * * * *; and showing himself desperately bent on carrying off May Morning by force of arms. Even this was not the worst of the Captain; for, being foiled in his diabolical purpose – temporarily by means of knives and pistols, providentially caught up and directed at him by May Morning, and finally, for the time being, by the advent of Will Stanmore – he caused one Slink, his adherent, to denounce Will Stanmore as a rebel, and got that cheerful mariner carried off, and shut up in prison. At about the same period of the Captain's career, there suddenly appeared in his father's castle, a dark complexioned lady of the name of Manuella, "a Zingara Woman from the Pyrenean Mountains; the Wild Wanderer of the Heath, and the Pronouncer of the Prophecy," who threw the melancholy baronet, his supposed father, into the greatest confusion by asking him what he had upon his conscience, and by pronouncing mysterious rhymes concerning the Child of Mystery and the Man of Crime, to a low trembling of fiddles. Matters were in this state when the Theatre resounded with applause, and Mr. Whelks fell into a fit of unbounded enthusiasm, consequent on the entrance of "Michael the Mendicant."

At first we referred something of the cordiality with which Michael the Mendicant was greeted, to the fact of his being "made up" with an excessively dirty face, which might create a bond of union between himself and a large majority of the audience. But it soon came out that Michael the Mendicant had been hired in old time by Sir George Elmore, to murder his (Sir George Elmore's) elder brother – which he had done; notwithstanding which little affair of honour, Michael was in reality a very good fellow; quite a tender-hearted man; who, on hearing of the Captain's determination to settle Will Stanmore, cried out, "What! more bel-ood!" and fell flat – overpowered by his nice sense of humanity. In like manner, in describing that small error of judgment into which he had allowed himself to be tempted by money, this gentleman exclaimed, "I ster-ruck him down, and fel-ed in er-orror!" and further he remarked, with honest pride, "I have liveder as a beggar – a roadersider vaigerant, but no ker-rime since then has stained these hands!" All these sentiments of the worthy man were hailed with showers of applause; and when, in the excitement of his feelings on one occasion, after a soliloquy, he "went off" *on his back*, kicking and shuffling along the ground, after the manner of bold spirits in trouble, who object to be taken to the station-house, the cheering was tremendous.

And to see how little harm he had done, after all! Sir George Elmore's elder brother was NOT dead. Not he! He recovered, after this sensitive creature had "fel-ed in er-orror," and, putting a black ribbon over his eyes to disguise himself, went and lived in a modest retirement with his only child. In short, Mr. Stars was the identical individual! When Will Stanmore turned out to be the wrongful Sir George Elmore's son, instead of the Child of Mystery and the Man of Crime, who turned out to be Michael's son (a change having been effected, in revenge, by the lady from the Pyrenean Mountains, who became the Wild Wanderer of the Heath, in consequence of the wrongful Sir George Elmore's perfidy to her and desertion of her), Mr. Stars went up to the Castle, and mentioned to his murdering brother how it was. Mr. Stars said it was all right; he bore no malice; he had kept out of the way, in order that his murdering brother (to whose numerous virtues he was no stranger) might enjoy the property; and now he would propose that they should make it up and dine together. The murdering brother immediately consented, embraced the Wild Wanderer, and it is supposed sent instructions to Doctors' Commons[9] for a license to marry her. After which, they were all very comfortable indeed. For it is not much to try to murder your brother for the sake of his property, if you only suborn such a delicate assassin as Michael the Mendicant!

All this did not tend to the satisfaction of the Child of Mystery and Man of Crime, who was so little pleased by the general happiness, that he shot Will Stanmore, now joyfully out of prison and going to be married directly to May Morning, and carried off the body, and May Morning to boot, to a lone hut. Here, Will Stanmore, laid out for dead at fifteen minutes past twelve, P.M., arose at seventeen minutes past, infinitely fresher than most daisies, and fought two strong men single-handed. However, the Wild Wanderer, arriving with a party of male wild wanderers, who were always at her disposal – and the murdering brother arriving arm-in-arm with Mr. Stars – stopped the combat, confounded the Child of Mystery and Man of Crime, and blessed the lovers.

The adventures of RED RIVEN THE BANDIT concluded the moral lesson of the evening. But, feeling by this time a little fatigued, and believing that we already discerned in the countenance of Mr. Whelks a sufficient confusion between right and wrong to last him for one night, we retired: the rather as we intended to meet him, shortly, at another place of dramatic entertainment for the people.

[13 April 1850]

Mr. Whelks being much in the habit of recreating himself at a class of theatres called "Saloons," we repaired to one of these, not long ago, on a Monday evening; Monday being a great holiday-night with Mr. Whelks and his friends.

The Saloon in question[10] is the largest in London (that which is known as the Eagle, in the City Road,[11] should be excepted from the generic term, as not presenting by any means the same class of entertainment), and is situate not far from Shoreditch Church. It announces "The People's Theatre," as its second name. The prices of admission are, to the boxes, a shilling; to the pit, sixpence; to the lower gallery, fourpence; to the upper gallery and back seats, threepence. There is no half-price. The opening piece on this occasion was described in the bills as "The greatest hit of the season, the grand new legendary and traditionary drama, combining supernatural agencies with historical facts, and identifying extraordinary superhuman causes with material, terrific, and powerful effects." All the queen's horses[12] and all the queen's men could not have drawn Mr. Whelks into the place like this description. Strengthened by lithographic representations of the principal superhuman causes, combined with the most popular of the material, terrific, and powerful effects, it became irresistible. Consequently, we had already failed, once, in finding six square inches of room within the walls, to stand upon; and when we now paid our money for a little stage box, like a dry shower-bath, we did so in the midst of a stream of people who persisted on paying theirs for other parts of the house in despite of the representations of the Money-taker that it was "very full, everywhere."

The outer avenues and passages of the People's Theatre bore abundant testimony to the fact of its being frequented by very dirty people. Within, the atmosphere was far from odoriferous. The place was crammed to excess, in all parts. Among the audience were a large number of boys and youths, and a great many very young girls grown into bold women before they had well ceased to be children. These last were the worst features of the whole crowd and were more prominent there than in any other sort of public assembly that we know of, except at a public execution. There was no drink supplied, beyond the contents of the porter-can (magnified in its dimensions, perhaps), which may be usually seen traversing the galleries of the largest Theatres as well as the least, and which was here seen everywhere. Huge ham sandwiches, piled on trays like deals in a timber-yard, were handed about for sale to the hungry; and there was no stint of oranges, cakes, brandy-balls, or other similar refreshments. The Theatre was capacious, with a very large, capable stage, well lighted, well appointed, and managed in a business-like, orderly manner in all respects; the perform-ances had begun so early as a quarter past six, and had been then in progress for three-quarters of an hour.

It was apparent here, as in the theatre we had previously visited, that one of the reasons of its great attraction was its being directly addressed to the common people, in the provision made for their seeing and hearing. Instead of being put away in a dark gap in the roof of an immense building, as in our once National Theatres, they were here in possession of eligible points of view, and thoroughly able to take in the whole performance. Instead of being at a great disadvantage in comparison with the mass of the audience, they were here *the* audience, for whose accommodation the place was made. We believe this to be one great cause of the success of these speculations. In whatever way the common people are addressed, whether in churches, chapels, schools, lecture-rooms, or theatres, to be successfully addressed they must be directly appealed to. No matter how good the feast, they will not come to it on mere sufferance. If, on looking round us, we find that the only things plainly and personally addressed to them, from quack medicines upwards, be bad or very defective things, – so much the worse for them and for all of us, and so much the more unjust and absurd the system which has haughtily abandoned a strong ground to such occupation.

We will add that we believe these people have a right to be amused. A great deal that we consider to be unreasonable, is written and talked about not licensing these places of entertainment. We have already intimated that we believe a love of dramatic representations to be an inherent principle in human nature. In most conditions of human life of which we have any knowledge, from the Greeks to the Bosjesmen,[13] some form of dramatic representation has always obtained.* We have a vast respect for county magistrates, and for the lord chamberlain; but we render greater deference to such extensive and immutable experience, and think it will outlive the whole existing court and commission. We would assuredly not bear harder on the fourpenny theatre, than on the four shilling theatre, or the four guinea theatre; but we would decidedly interpose to turn to some wholesome account the means of instruction which it has at command, and we would make that office of Dramatic Licenser, which, like many other offices, has become a mere piece of Court favour and dandy conventionality, a real, responsible, educational trust.[15] We would have it exercise a sound supervision over the lower drama, instead of stopping the career of a real work of art, as it did in the case of Mr. Chorley's play[16] at the Surrey Theatre, but a few weeks since, for a sickly point of form.

To return to Mr. Whelks. The audience, being able to see and hear, were very attentive. They were so closely packed, that they took a little time in settling down after any pause; but otherwise the general disposition was to lose nothing, and to check (in no choice language) any disturber of the business of the scene.

On our arrival, Mr. Whelks had already followed Lady Hatton the Heroine (whom we faintly recognised as a mutilated theme of the late THOMAS INGOLDSBY[17]) to the "Gloomy Dell and Suicide's Tree," where Lady H. had encountered the "apparition of the dark man of doom," and heard the "fearful story of the Suicide." She had also "signed the compact in her own Blood"; beheld "the Tombs rent asunder"; seen "skeletons start from their graves, and gibber Mine, mine, for ever!" and undergone all these little experiences (each set forth in a separate line in the bill) in the compass of one act. It was not yet over, indeed, for we found a remote king of England of the name of "Enerry," refreshing himself with the spectacle of a dance in a Garden, which was interrupted by the "thrilling appearance of the Demon." This "superhuman cause" (with black eyebrows slanting up into his temples, and red-foil cheekbones,) brought the Drop-Curtain down as we took possession of our Shower-Bath.

---

* In the remote interior of Africa, and among the North American Indians, this truth is exemplified in an equally striking manner. Who that saw the four grim, stunted, abject Bush-people at the Egyptian Hall – with two natural actors among them out of that number, one a male and the other a female – can forget how something human and imaginative gradually broke out in the little ugly man, when he was roused from crouching over the charcoal fire, into giving a dramatic representation of the tracking of a beast, the shooting of it with poisoned arrows, and the creature's death?[14]

It seemed, on the curtain's going up again, that Lady Hatton had sold herself to the Powers of Darkness, on very high terms, and was now overtaken by remorse, and by jealousy too; the latter passion being excited by the beautiful Lady Rodolpha, ward to the king. It was to urge Lady Hatton on to the murder of this young female (as well as we could make out, but both we and Mr. Whelks found the incidents complicated) that the Demon appeared "once again in all his terrors." Lady Hatton had been leading a life of piety, but the Demon was not to have his bargain declared off, in right of any such artifices, and now offered a dagger for the destruction of Rodolpha. Lady Hatton hesitating to accept this trifle from Tartarus,[18] the Demon, for certain subtle reasons of his own, proceeded to entertain her with a view of the "gloomy court-yard of a convent," and the apparitions of the "Skeleton Monk," and the "King of Terrors." Against these super-human causes, another superhuman cause, to wit, the ghost of Lady H.'s mother came into play, and greatly confounded the Powers of Darkness, by waving the "sacred emblem" over the head of the else devoted Rodolpha, and causing her to sink unto the earth. Upon this the Demon, losing his temper, fiercely invited Lady Hatton to "Be-old the tortures of the damned!" and straightway conveyed her to a "grand and awful view of Pandemonium, and Lake of Transparent Rolling Fire," whereof, and also of "Prometheus chained, and the Vulture gnawing at his liver,"[19] Mr. Whelks was exceedingly derisive.

The Demon still failing, even there, and still finding the ghost of the old lady greatly in his way, exclaimed that these vexations had such a remarkable effect upon his spirit as to "sear his eyeballs," and that he must go "deeper down," which he accordingly did. Hereupon it appeared that it was all a dream on Lady Hatton's part, and that she was newly married and uncom-monly happy. This put an end to the incongruous heap of nonsense, and set Mr. Whelks applauding mightily; for, except with the lake of transparent rolling fire (which was not half infernal enough for him), Mr. Whelks was infinitely contented with the whole of the proceedings.

Ten thousand people, every week, all the year round, are estimated to attend this place of amusement. If it were closed to-morrow – if there were fifty such, and they were all closed to-morrow – the only result would be to cause that to be privately and evasively done, which is now publicly done; to render the harm of it much greater, and to exhibit the suppressive power of the law in an oppressive and partial light. The people who now resort here, *will be* amused somewhere. It is of no use to blink that fact, or to make pretences to the contrary. We had far better apply ourselves to improving the character of their amusement. It would not be exacting much, or exacting anything very difficult, to require that the pieces represented in these Theatres should have, at least, a good, plain, healthy purpose in them.

To the end that our experiences might not be supposed to be partial or unfortunate, we went, the very next night, to the Theatre where we saw MAY MORNING, and found Mr. Whelks engaged in the study of an "Original old English Domestic and Romantic Drama," called "EVA THE BETRAYED, or THE LADYE OF LAMBYTHE." We proceed to develop the incidents which gradually unfolded themselves to Mr. Whelks's understanding.

One Geoffrey Thornley the younger, on a certain fine morning, married his father's ward, Eva the Betrayed, the Ladye of Lambythe. She had become the betrayed, in right – or in wrong – of designing Geoffrey's machinations; for that corrupt individual, knowing her to be under promise of marriage to Walter More, a young mariner (of whom he was accustomed to make slighting mention as "a minion"), represented the said More to be no more, and obtained the consent of the too trusting Eva to their immediate union.

Now, it came to pass, by a singular coincidence, that on the identical morning of the marriage, More came home, and was taking a walk about the scenes of his boyhood – a little faded since that time – when he rescued "Wilbert the Hunchback" from some very rough treatment. This misguided person, in return, immediately fell to abusing his preserver in round terms, giving him to understand that he (the preserved) hated "manerkind, wither two eckerceptions," one of them being the deceiving Geoffrey, whose retainer he was, and for whom he felt an unconquerable attachment; the other, a relative, whom, in a similar redundancy of emphasis, adapted to the requirements of Mr. Whelks, he called his "assister." This misanthrope also made the cold-blooded declaration, "There was a timer when I loved my fellow keretures, till they deserpised me. Now, I live only to witness man's disergherace and woman's misery!" In furtherance of this amiable purpose of existence, he directed More to where the bridal procession was coming home from church, and Eva recognised More, and More reproached Eva, and there was a great to-do, and a violent struggling, before certain social villagers who were celebrating the event with morris-dances. Eva was borne off in a tearing condition, and the bill very truly observed that the end of that part of the business was "despair and madness."

Geoffrey, Geoffrey, why were you already married to another! Why could you not be true to your lawful wife Katherine, instead of deserting her, and leaving her to come tumbling into public-houses (on account of weakness) in search of you! You might have known what it would end in,

Geoffrey Thornley! You might have known that she would come up to your house on your wedding day with her marriage-certificate in her pocket, determined to expose you. You might have known beforehand, as you now very composedly observe, that you would have "but one course to pursue." That course clearly is to wind your right hand in Katherine's long hair, wrestle with her, stab her, throw down the body behind the door (cheers from Mr. Whelks), and tell the devoted Hunchback to get rid of it. On the devoted Hunchback's finding that it is the body of his "assister," and taking her marriage-certificate from her pocket and denouncing you, of course you have still but one course to pursue, and that is to charge the crime upon him, and have him carried off with all speed into the "deep and massive dungeons beneath Thornley Hall."

More having, as he was rather given to boast, "a goodly vessel on the lordly Thames," had better have gone away with it, weather permitting, than gone after Eva. Naturally, he got carried down to the dungeons, too, for lurking about, and got put into the next dungeon to the Hunchback, then expiring from poison. And there they were, hard and fast, like two wild beasts in dens, trying to get glimpses of each other through the bars, to the unutterable interest of Mr. Whelks.

But when the Hunchback made himself known, and when More did the same; and when the Hunchback said he had got the certificate which rendered Eva's marriage illegal; and when More raved to have it given to him, and when the Hunchback (as having some grains of misanthropy in him to the last) persisted in going into his dying agonies in a remote corner of his cage, and took unheard-of trouble not to die anywhere near the bars that were within More's reach; Mr. Whelks applauded to the echo. At last the Hunchback was persuaded to stick the certificate on the point of a dagger, and hand it in; and that done, died extremely hard, knocking himself violently about, to the very last gasp, and certainly making the most of all the life that was in him.

Still, More had yet to get out of his den before he could turn this certificate to any account. His first step was to make such a violent uproar as to bring into his presence a certain "Norman Free Lance" who kept watch and ward over him. His second, to inform this warrior, in the style of the Polite Letter-Writer, that "circumstances had occurred" rendering it necessary that he should be immediately let out. The warrior declining to submit himself to the force of these circumstances, Mr. More proposed to him, as a gentleman and a man of honour, to allow him to step out into the gallery, and there adjust an old feud subsisting between them, by single combat. The unwary Free Lance, consenting to this reasonable proposal, was shot from behind by the comic man, whom he bitterly designated as "a snipe" for that action, and then died exceedingly game.

All this occurred in one day – the bridal day of the Ladye of Lambythe; and now Mr. Whelks concentrated all his energies into a focus, bent forward, looked straight in front of him, and held his breath. For, the night of the eventful day being come, Mr. Whelks was admitted to the "bridal chamber of the Ladye of Lambythe," where he beheld a toilet table, and a particularly large and desolate four-post bedstead. Here the Ladye, having dismissed her bridesmaids, was interrupted in deploring her unhappy fate, by the entrance of her husband; and matters, under these circumstances, were proceeding to very desperate extremities, when the Ladye (by this time aware of the existence of the certificate) found a dagger on the dressing-table, and said, "Attempt to enfold me in thy pernicious embrace, and this poignard —!" etc. He did attempt it, however, for all that, and he and the Ladye were dragging one another about like wrestlers, when Mr. More broke open the door, and entering with the whole domestic establishment and a Middlesex magistrate, took him into custody and claimed his bride.

It is but fair to Mr. Whelks to remark on one curious fact in this entertainment. When the situations were very strong indeed, they were very like what some favourite situations in the Italian Opera would be to a profoundly deaf spectator. The despair and madness at the end of the first act, the business of the long hair, and the struggle in the bridal chamber, were as like the conventional passion of the Italian singers, as the orchestra was unlike the opera band, or its "hurries"[20] unlike the music of the great composers. So do extremes meet; and so is there some hopeful congeniality between what will excite Mr. Whelks, and what will rouse a Duchess.

Some Account of an Extraordinary Traveller

First published in *Household Words*, 20 April 1850, from which this text is reproduced. On 16 December 1848, Dickens published a review in *The Examiner* of John Banvard's 'Mississippi', one of the panoramas featured here.

No longer ago than this Easter time last past, we became acquainted with the subject of the present notice. Our knowledge of him is not by any means an intimate one, and is only of a public nature. We have never interchanged any conversation with him, except on one occasion when he asked us to have the goodness to take off our hat, to which we replied "Certainly."

MR. BOOLEY was born (we believe) in Rood Lane, in the City of London. He is now a gentleman advanced in life, and has for some years resided in the neighbourhood of Islington. His father was a wholesale grocer (perhaps) and he was (possibly) in the same way of business; or he may, at an early age, have become a clerk in the Bank of England or in a private bank, or in the India House. It will be observed that we make no pretence of having any information in reference to the private history of this remarkable man, and that our account of it must be received as rather speculative than authentic.

In person Mr. Booley is below the middle size, and corpulent. His countenance is florid, he is perfectly bald, and soon hot; and there is a composure in his gait and manner, calculated to impress a stranger with the idea of his being, on the whole, an unwieldy man. It is only in his eye that the adventurous character of Mr. Booley is seen to shine. It is a moist, bright eye, of a cheerful expression, and indicative of keen and eager curiosity.

It was not until late in life that Mr. Booley conceived the idea of entering on the extraordinary amount of travel he has since accomplished. He had attained the age of sixty-five before he left England for the first time. In all the immense journeys he has since performed, he has never laid aside the English dress, nor departed in the slightest degree from English customs. Neither does he speak a word of any language but his own.

Mr. Booley's powers of endurance are wonderful. All climates are alike to him. Nothing exhausts him; no alternations of heat and cold appear to have the least effect upon his hardy frame. His capacity of travelling, day and night, for thousands of miles, has never been approached by any traveller of whom we have any knowledge through the help of books. An intelligent Englishman may have occasionally pointed out to him objects and scenes of interest; but otherwise he has travelled alone and unattended. Though remarkable for personal cleanliness, he has carried no luggage; and his diet has been of the simplest kind. He has often found a biscuit, or a bun, sufficient for his support over a vast tract of country. Frequently, he has travelled hundreds of miles, fasting, without the least abatement of his natural spirits. It says much for the Total Abstinence cause, that Mr. Booley has never had recourse to the artificial stimulus of alcohol, to sustain him under his fatigues.

His first departure from the sedentary and monotonous life he had hitherto led, strikingly exemplifies, we think, the energetic character, long suppressed by that unchanging routine. Without any communication with any member of his family – Mr. Booley has never been married, but has many relations – without announcing his intention to his solicitor, or banker, or any person entrusted with the management of his affairs, he closed the door of his house behind him at one o'clock in the afternoon of a certain day, and immediately proceeded to New Orleans, in the United States of America.

His intention was to ascend the Mississippi and Missouri rivers, to the base of the Rocky Mountains. Taking his passage in a steamboat without loss of time, he was soon upon the bosom of the Father of Waters, as the Indians call the mighty stream which, night and day, is always carrying huge instalments of the vast continent of the New World down into the sea.

Mr. Booley found it singularly interesting to observe the various stages of civilisation obtaining on the banks of these mighty rivers. Leaving the luxury and brightness of New Orleans – a somewhat feverish luxury and brightness, he observed, as if the swampy soil were too much enriched in the hot sun with the bodies of dead slaves – and passing various towns in every stage of progress, it was very curious to observe the changes of civilisation and of vegetation too. Here, while the doomed negro race were working in the plantations, while the republican overseer looked on, whip in hand, tropical trees were growing, beautiful flowers in bloom; the alligator, with his horribly sly face, and his jaws like two great saws, was basking on the mud; and the strange moss of the country was hanging in wreaths and garlands on the trees, like votive offerings. A little farther towards the west, and the trees and flowers were changed, the moss was gone, younger infant towns were rising, forests were slowly disappearing, and the trees, obliged to aid in the destruction of their kind, fed the heavily-breathing monster that came clanking up those solitudes laden with the pioneers of the advancing human army. The river itself, that moving highway, showed him every kind of floating contrivance, from the lumbering flat-bottomed boat, and the raft of logs, upward to the steamboat, and downward to the poor Indian's frail canoe. A winding thread through the enormous range of country, unrolling itself before the wanderer like the magic skein in the story, he saw it tracked by wanderers of every kind, roaming from the more settled world, to those first nests of men. The floating theatre, dwelling-house, hotel, museum, shop; the floating mechanism for screwing the trunks of mighty trees out of the mud, like antediluvian teeth; the rapidly-flowing river, and the blazing woods; he left them all behind – town, city, and log-cabin, too; and floated up into the prairies and savannahs, among the deserted lodges of tribes of savages, and among their dead, lying alone on little wooden stages with their stark faces upward towards the sky. Among the blazing grass, and herds of buffaloes and wild horses, and among the wigwams of the fast-declining Indians, he began to consider how, in the eternal current of progress setting across this globe in one unchangeable direction, like the unseen agency that points the needle to the Pole, the Chiefs who only dance the dances of their fathers, and will never have a new figure for a new tune, and the Medicine men who know no Medicine but what was Medicine a hundred years ago, must be surely and inevitably swept from the earth, whether they be Choctawas,[1] Mandans,[2] Britons, Austrians, or Chinese.

He was struck, too, by the reflection that savage nature was not by any means such a fine and noble spectacle as some delight to represent it. He found it a poor, greasy, paint-plastered, miserable thing enough; but a very little way above the beasts in most respects; in many customs a long way below them. It occurred to him that the "Big Bird," or the "Blue Fish," or any of the other Braves, was but a troublesome braggart after all; making a mighty whooping and halloaing about nothing particular, doing very little for science, not much more than the monkeys for art, scarcely anything worth mentioning for letters, and not often making the world greatly better than he found it. Civilisation, Mr. Booley concluded, was, on the whole, with all its blemishes, a more imposing sight, and a far better thing to stand by.

Mr. Booley's observations of the celestial bodies, on this voyage, were principally confined to the discovery of the alarming fact, that light had altogether departed from the moon; which presented the appearance of a white dinner-plate. The clouds, too, conducted themselves in an extraordinary manner, and assumed the most eccentric forms, while the sun rose and set in a very reckless way. On his return to his native country, however, he had the satisfaction of finding all these things as usual.

It might have been expected that at his advanced age, retired from the active duties of life, blessed with a competency, and happy in the affections of his numerous relations, Mr. Booley would now have settled himself down, to muse, for the remainder of his days, over the new stock of experience thus acquired. But travel had whetted, not satisfied, his appetite; and remembering that he had not seen the Ohio River, except at the point of its junction with the Mississippi, he returned to the United States, after a short interval of repose, and appearing suddenly at Cincinnati, the queen City of the West, traversed the clear waters of the Ohio to its Falls. In this expedition he had the pleasure of encountering a party of intelligent workmen from Birmingham who were making the same tour. Also his nephew Septimus, aged only thirteen. This intrepid boy had started from Peckham, in the old country, with two and sixpence sterling in his pocket; and had, when he encountered his uncle at a point of the Ohio River, called Snaggy Bar, still one shilling of that sum remaining!

Again at home, Mr. Booley was so pressed by his appetite for knowledge as to remain at home only one day. At the expiration of that short period, he actually started for New Zealand.

It is almost incredible that a man in Mr. Booley's station of life, however adventurous his nature, and however few his artificial wants, should cast himself on a voyage of thirteen thousand miles from Great Britain with no other outfit than his watch and purse, and no arms but his walking-stick. We are, however, assured on the best authority, that thus he made the passage out, and thus appeared, in the act of wiping his smoking head with his pocket-handkerchief, at the entrance to Port Nicholson in Cook's Straits: with the very spot within his range of vision, where his illustrious predecessor, Captain Cook, so unhappily slain at Owyhee,[3] once anchored.

After contemplating the swarms of cattle maintained on the hills in this neighbourhood, and always to be found by the stockmen when they are wanted, though nobody takes any care of them – which Mr. Booley considered the more remarkable, as their natural objection to be killed might be supposed to be augmented by the beauty of the climate – Mr. Booley proceeded to the town of Wellington. Having minutely examined it in every point, and made himself perfect master of the whole natural history and process of manufacture of the flax-plant, with its splendid yellow blossoms, he repaired to a Native Pa, which, unlike the Native Pa to which he was accustomed, he found to be a town, and not a parent. Here he observed a chief with a long spear, making every demonstration of spitting a visitor, but really giving him the Maori or welcome – a word Mr. Booley is inclined to derive from the known hospitality of our English Mayors – and here also he observed some Europeans rubbing noses, by way of shaking hands, with the aboriginal inhabitants. After participating in an affray between the natives and the English soldiers in which the former were defeated with great loss, he plunged into the Bush, and there camped out for some months, until he had made a survey of the whole country.

While leading this wild life, encamped by night near a stream for the convenience of water in a Ware, or hut, built open in the front, with a roof sloping backward to the ground, and made of poles, covered and enclosed with bark or fern, it was Mr. Booley's singular fortune to encounter Miss Creeble, of The Misses Creebles' Boarding and Day Establishment for Young Ladies, Kennington Oval, who, accompanied by three of her young ladies in search of information, had achieved this marvellous journey, and was then also in the Bush. Miss Creeble having very unsettled opinions on the subject of gunpowder, was afraid that it entered into the composition of the fire before the tent, and that something would presently blow up or go off. Mr. Booley, as a more experienced traveller, assuring her that there was no danger; and calming the fears of the young ladies, an acquaintance commenced between them. They accomplished the rest of their travels in New Zealand together, and the best understanding prevailed among the little party. They took notice of the trees, as the Kaikatea, the Kauri, the Ruta, the Pukatea, the Hinau, and the Tanakaka – names which Miss Creeble had a bland relish in pronouncing. They admired the beautiful, aborescent, palm-like fern, abounding everywhere, and frequently exceeding thirty feet in height. They wondered at the curious owl, who is supposed to demand "More Pork!" wherever he flies, and whom Miss Creeble termed "an admonition of Nature against greediness!" And they contemplated some very rampant natives of cannibal propensities. After many pleasing and instructive vicissitudes, they returned to England in company, where the ladies were safely put into a hackney cabriolet by Mr. Booley, in Leicester Square, London.

And now, indeed, it might have been imagined that that roving spirit, tired of rambling about the world, would have settled down at home in peace and honor. Not so. After repairing to the tubular bridge across the Menai Straits,[4] and accompanying Her Majesty on her visit to Ireland (which he characterised as "a magnificent Exhibition"), Mr. Booley, with his usual absence of preparation, departed for Australia.

Here again, he lived out in the Bush, passing his time chiefly among the working-gangs of convicts who were carrying timber. He was much impressed by the ferocious mastiffs chained to barrels, who assist the sentries in keeping guard over those misdoers. But he observed that the atmosphere in this part of the world, unlike the descriptions he had read of it, was extremely thick, and that objects were misty, and difficult to be discerned. From a certain unsteadiness and trembling, too, which he frequently remarked on the face of Nature, he was led to conclude that this part of the globe was subject to convulsive heavings and earthquakes. This caused him to return with some precipitation.

Again at home, and probably reflecting that the countries he had hitherto visited were new in the history of man, this extraordinary traveller resolved to proceed up the Nile to the second cataract.[5] At the next performance of the great ceremony of "opening the Nile," at Cairo, Mr. Booley was present.

Along that wonderful river, associated with such stupendous fables, and with a history more prodigious than any fancy of man, in its vast and gorgeous facts; among temples, palaces, pyramids, colossal statues, crocodiles, tombs, obelisks, mummies, sand and ruin; he proceeded, like an opium-eater in a mighty dream. Thebes rose before him. An avenue of two hundred sphinxes, with not a head among them, – one of six or eight, or ten such avenues, all leading to a common centre – conducted to the Temple of Carnak: its walls, eighty feet high and twenty-five feet thick, a mile and three-quarters in circumference; the interior of its tremendous hall, occupying an area of forty-seven thousand square feet, large enough to hold four Great Christian churches, and yet not more than one-seventh part of the entire ruin. Obelisks he saw, thousands of years of age, as sharp as if the chisel had cut their edges yesterday; colossal statues fifty-two feet high, with "little" fingers five feet and a half long; a very world of ruins, that were marvellous old ruins in the days of Herodotus;[6] tombs cut high up in the rock, where European travellers live solitary, as in stony crows' nests, burning mummied Thebans, gentle and simple – of the dried blood-royal maybe – for their daily fuel, and making articles of furniture of their dusty coffins. Upon the walls of temples, in colors fresh and bright as those of yesterday, he read the conquests of great Egyptian monarchs; upon the tombs of humbler people in the same blooming symbols, he saw their ancient way of working at their trades, of riding, driving, feasting, playing games; of marrying and burying, and performing on instruments, and singing songs, and healing by the power of animal magnetism, and performing all the occupations of life. He visited the quarries of Silsileh, whence nearly all the red stone used by the ancient Egyptian architects and sculptors came; and there beheld enormous single-stoned colossal figures, nearly finished – redly snowed up, as it were, and trying hard to break out – waiting for the finishing touches, never to be given by the mummied hands of thousands of years ago. In front of the temple of Abou Simbel, he saw gigantic figures sixty feet in height and twenty-one across the shoulders, dwarfing live men on camels down to pigmies. Elsewhere he beheld complacent monsters tumbled down like ill-used Dolls of a Titanic make, and staring with stupid benignity at the arid earth whereon their huge faces rested. His last look of that amazing land was at the Great Sphinx, buried in the sand – sand in its eyes, sand in its ears, sand drifted on its broken nose, sand lodging, feet deep, in the ledges of its head – struggling out of a wide sea of sand, as if to look hopelessly forth for the ancient glories once surrounding it.

In this expedition, Mr. Booley acquired some curious information in reference to the language of hieroglyphics. He encountered the Simoon[7] in the Desert, and lay down, with the rest of his caravan until it had passed over. He also beheld on the horizon some of those stalking pillars of sand, apparently reaching from earth to heaven, which, with the red sun shining through them, so terrified the Arabs attendant on Bruce,[8] that they fell prostrate, crying that the Day of Judgment was come. More Copts, Turks, Arabs, Fellahs, Bedouins, Mosques, Mamelukes, and Moosulmen[9] he saw, than we have space to tell. His days were all Arabian Nights, and he saw wonders without end.

This might have satiated any ordinary man, for a time at least. But Mr. Booley, being no ordinary man, within twenty-four hours of his arrival at home was making the overland journey to India.

He has emphatically described this, as "a beautiful piece of scenery," and "a perfect picture." The appearance of Malta and Gibraltar he can never sufficiently commend. In crossing the desert from Grand Cairo to Suez he was particularly struck by the undulations of the Sandscape (he preferred that word to Landscape, as more expressive of the region), and by the incident of beholding a caravan upon its line of march; a spectacle which in the remembrance always affords him the utmost pleasure. Of the stations on the desert, and the cinnamon gardens of Ceylon, he likewise entertains a lively recollection. Calcutta he praises also; though he has been heard to observe that the British military at that seat of Government were not as well proportioned as he could desire the soldiers of his country to be; and that the breed of horses there in use was susceptible of some improvement.

Once more in his native land, with the vigor of his constitution unimpaired by the many toils and fatigues he had encountered, what had Mr. Booley now to do, but, full of years and honor, to recline upon the grateful appreciation of his Queen and country, always eager to distinguish peaceful merit? What had he now to do, but to receive the decoration ever ready to be bestowed, in England, on men deservedly distinguished, and to take his place among the best? He had this to do. He had yet to achieve the most astonishing enterprise for which he was reserved. In all the countries he had yet visited, he had seen no frost and snow. He resolved to make a voyage to the ice-bound arctic regions.

In pursuance of this surprising determination, Mr. Booley accompanied the expedition under Sir James Ross, consisting of Her Majesty's ships the Enterprise and Investigator, which sailed from the River Thames on the 12th of May 1848, and which, on the 11th of September, entered Port Leopold Harbor.[10]

In this inhospitable region, surrounded by eternal ice, cheered by no glimpse of the sun, shrouded in gloom and darkness, Mr. Booley passed the entire winter. The ships were covered in, and fortified all round with walls of ice and snow; the masts were frozen up; hoar frost settled on the yards, tops, shrouds, stays, and rigging; around, in every direction, lay an interminable waste, on which only the bright stars, the yellow moon, and the vivid Aurora Borealis looked, by night or day.

And yet the desolate sublimity of this astounding spectacle was broken in a pleasant and surprising manner. In the remote solitude to which he had penetrated, Mr. Booley (who saw no Esquimaux during his stay, though he looked for them in every direction) had the happiness of encountering two Scotch gardeners; several English compositors, accompanied by their wives; three brass founders from the neighbourhood of Long Acre, London; two coach painters, a gold-beater and his only daughter, by trade a stay-maker; and several other working-people from sundry parts of Great Britain who had conceived the extraordinary idea of "holiday-making" in the frozen wilderness. Hither, too, had Miss Creeble and her three young ladies penetrated: the latter attired in braided peacoats of a comparatively light material; and Miss Creeble defended from the inclemency of a Polar Winter by no other outer garment than a wadded Polka-jacket.[11] He found this courageous lady in the act of explaining, to the youthful sharers of her toils, the various phases of nature by which they were surrounded. Her explanations were principally wrong, but her intentions always admirable.

Cheered by the society of these fellow-adventurers, Mr. Booley slowly glided on into the summer season. And now, at midnight, all was bright and shining. Mountains of ice, wedged and broken into the strangest forms – jagged points, spires, pinnacles, pyramids, turrets, columns in endless succession and in infinite variety, flashing and sparkling with ten thousand hues, as though the treasures of the earth were frozen up in all that water

– appeared on every side. Masses of ice, floating and driving hither and thither, menaced the hardy voyagers with destruction; and threatened to crush their strong ships, like nutshells. But, below those ships was clear sea-water, now; the fortifying walls were gone; the yards, tops, shrouds and rigging, free from that hoary rust of long inaction, showed like themselves again; and the sails, bursting from the masts, like foliage which the welcome sun at length developed, spread themselves to the wind, and wafted the travellers away.

In the short interval that has elapsed since his safe return to the land of his birth, Mr. Booley has decided on no new expedition; but he feels that he will yet be called upon to undertake one, perhaps of greater magnitude than any he has achieved, and frequently remarks, in his own easy way, that he wonders where the deuce he will be taken to next! Possessed of good health and good spirits, with powers unimpaired by all he has gone through, and with an increase of appetite still growing with what it feeds on, what may not be expected yet from this extraordinary man!

It was only at the close of Easter week that, sitting in an armchair, at a private club called the Social Oysters, assembling at Highbury Barn, where he is much respected, this indefatigable traveller expressed himself in the following terms:

"It is very gratifying to me," said he, "to have seen so much at my time of life, and to have acquired a knowledge of the countries I have visited, which I could not have derived from books alone. When I was a boy, such travelling would have been impossible, as the gigantic-moving-panorama or diorama mode of conveyance, which I have principally adopted (all my modes of conveyance have been pictorial), had then not been attempted.[12] It is a delightful characteristic of these times, that new and cheap means are continually being devised for conveying the results of actual experience to those who are unable to obtain such experiences for themselves; and to bring them within the reach of the people – emphatically of the people; for it is they at large who are addressed in these endeavours, and not exclusive audiences. Hence," said Mr. Booley, "even if I see a run on an idea, like the panorama one, it awakens no ill-humour within me, but gives me pleasant thoughts. Some of the best results of actual travel are suggested by such means to those whose lot it is to stay at home. New worlds open out to them, beyond their little worlds, and widen their range of reflection, information, sympathy, and interest. The more man knows of man, the better for the common brotherhood among us all. I shall, therefore," said Mr. Booley, "now propose to the Social Oysters, the healths of Mr. Banvard, Mr. Brees, Mr. Phillips, Mr. Allen, Mr. Prout, Messrs. Bonomi, Fahey, and

Warren, Mr. Thomas Grieve, and Mr. Burford.[13] Long life to them all, and
more power to their pencils!"

The Social Oysters having drunk this toast with acclamation, Mr. Booley
proceeded to entertain them with anecdotes of his travels. This he is in the
habit of doing after they have feasted together, according to the manner of
Sinbad the Sailor – except that he does not bestow upon the Social Oysters
the munificent reward of one hundred sequins per night, for listening.

Old Lamps for New Ones

First published in *Household Words*, 15 June 1850, from which this text is reproduced. On 30 May 1850, Dickens wrote to Daniel Maclise,[1] one of the painters mentioned in the article, and explained himself: 'I feel sure you will see nothing in it but what is fair public satire on a point that opens very serious social considerations. If such things were allowed to sweep on, without some vigorous protest, three fourths of this Nation would be under the feet of Priests in ten years.' For further background, see Leonee Ormond, 'Dickens and Painting: Contemporary Art,' *The Dickensian*, 80 (1984), p. 21.

The magician in *Aladdin* may possibly have neglected the study of men, for the study of alchemical books; but it is certain that in spite of his profession he was no conjuror. He knew nothing of human nature, or the everlasting set of the current of human affairs. If, when he fraudulently sought to obtain possession of the wonderful Lamp, and went up and down, disguised, before the flying-palace, crying New Lamps for Old ones, he had reversed his cry, and made it Old Lamps for New ones, he would have been so far before his time as to have projected himself into the nineteenth century of our Christian Era.

This age is so perverse, and is so very short of faith – in consequence, as some suppose, of there having been a run on that bank for a few generations – that a parallel and beautiful idea, generally known among the ignorant as the young England hallucination, unhappily expired before it could run alone, to the great grief of a small but a very select circle of mourners. There is something so fascinating, to a mind capable of any serious reflection, in the notion of ignoring all that has been done for the happiness and elevation of mankind during three or four centuries of slow and dearly-bought amelioration, that we have always thought it would tend soundly to the improvement of the general public, if any tangible symbol, any outward and visible sign, expressive of that admirable conception, could be held up before them. We are happy to have found such a sign at last; and although it would make a very indifferent sign, indeed, in the Licensed Victualling sense of the word, and would probably be rejected with contempt and horror by any Christian publican, it has our warmest philosophical appreciation.

In the fifteenth century, a certain feeble lamp of art arose in the Italian town of Urbino. This poor light, Raphael Sanzio by name, better known to a few miserably mistaken wretches in these later days, as Raphael (another burned at the same time called Titian), was fed with a preposterous idea of Beauty – with a ridiculous power of etherealising, and exalting to the very Heaven of Heavens, what was most sublime and lovely in the expression of the human face divine on Earth – with the truly contemptible conceit of finding in poor humanity the fallen likeness of the angels of God, and raising it up again to their pure spiritual condition. This very fantastic whim effected a low revolution in Art, in this wise, that Beauty came to be regarded as one of its indispensable elements. In this very poor delusion, artists have continued until this present nineteenth century, when it was reserved for some bold aspirants to "put it down."

The pre-Raphael Brotherhood,[2] Ladies and Gentlemen, is the dread Tribunal which is to set this matter right. Walk up, walk up; and here, conspicuous on the wall of the Royal Academy of Art in England, in the eighty-second year of their annual exhibition, you shall see what this new Holy Brotherhood, this terrible Police that is to disperse all Post-Raphael offenders, has been and done!

You come – in this Royal Academy Exhibition, which is familiar with the works of Wilkie, Collins, Etty, Eastlake, Mulready, Leslie, Maclise, Turner, Stanfield, Landseer, Roberts, Danby, Creswick, Lee, Webster, Herbert, Dyce, Cope, and others who would have been renowned as great masters in any age or country – you come, in this place, to the contemplation of a Holy Family. You will have the goodness to discharge from your minds all Post-Raphael ideas, all religious aspirations, all elevating thoughts; all tender, awful, sorrowful, ennobling, sacred, graceful, or beautiful associations; and to prepare yourselves, as befits such a subject – pre-Raphaelly considered – for the lowest depths of what is mean, odious, repulsive, and revolting.

You behold the interior of a carpenter's shop.[3] In the foreground of that carpenter's shop is a hideous, wry-necked, blubbering red-headed boy, in a bed-gown, who appears to have received a poke in the hand from the stick of another boy with whom he has been playing in an adjacent gutter, and to be holding it up for the contemplation of a kneeling woman, so horrible in her ugliness, that (supposing it were possible for any human creature to exist for a moment with that dislocated throat) she would stand out from the rest of the company as a Monster, in the vilest cabaret in France, or the lowest gin-shop in England. Two almost naked carpenters, master and journeyman, worthy companions of this agreeable female, are working at their trade; a boy, with some small flavour of humanity in him, is entering with a vessel of water; and nobody is paying any attention to a snuffy old woman who seems to have mistaken that shop for the tobacconist's next door, and to be hopelessly waiting at the counter to be served with half an ounce of her favourite mixture. Wherever it is possible to express ugliness of feature, limb, or attitude, you have it expressed. Such men as the carpenters might be undressed in any hospital where dirty drunkards, in a high state of varicose veins are received. Their very toes have walked out of Saint Giles's.[4]

This, in the nineteenth century, and in the eighty-second year of the annual exhibition of the National Academy of Art, is the Pre-Raphael representation to us, Ladies and Gentlemen, of the most solemn passage which our minds can ever approach. This, in the nineteenth century, and in the eighty-second year of the annual exhibition of the National Academy of Art, is what Pre-Raphael Art can do to render reverence and homage to the faith in which we live and die! Consider this picture well. Consider the pleasure we should have in a similar Pre-Raphael rendering of a favourite horse, or dog, or cat; and, coming fresh from a pretty considerable turmoil about "desecration" in connexion with the National Post Office, let us extol this great achievement, and commend the National Academy.

In further considering this symbol of the great retrogressive principle, it is particularly gratifying to observe that such objects as the shavings which are strewn on the carpenter's floor are admirably painted; and that the Pre-Raphael Brother is indisputably accomplished in the manipulation of his art. It is gratifying to observe this, because the fact involves no low effort at notoriety; everybody knowing that it is by no means easier to call attention to a very indifferent pig with five legs than to a symmetrical pig with four. Also, because it is good to know that the National Academy thoroughly feels and comprehends the high range and exalted purposes of art; distinctly perceives that art includes something more than the faithful portraiture of shavings, or the skilful colouring of drapery – imperatively requires, in short, that it shall be informed with mind and sentiment; will on no account reduce it to a narrow question of trade-juggling with a palette, palette-knife, and paint-box. It is likewise pleasing to reflect that the great educational establishment foresees the difficulty into which it would be led, by attaching greater weight to mere handicraft, than to any other consideration – even to considerations of common reverence or decency; which absurd principle in the event of a skilful painter of the figure becoming a very little more perverted in his taste, than certain skilful painters are just now, might place Her Gracious Majesty in a very painful position, one of these fine Private View Days.

Would it were in our power to congratulate our readers on the hopeful prospects of the great retrogressive principle, of which this thoughtful picture is the sign and emblem! Would that we could give our readers encouraging assurance of a healthy demand for Old Lamps in exchange for New ones, and a steady improvement in the Old Lamp Market! The perversity of mankind is such, and the untoward arrangements of Providence are such, that we cannot lay that flattering unction to their souls. We can only report what Brotherhoods, stimulated by this sign, are forming; and what opportunities will be presented to the people, if the people will but accept them.

In the first place, the Pre-Perspective Brotherhood will be presently incorporated, for the subversion of all known rules and principles of perspective. It is intended to swear every P.P.B. to a solemn renunciation of the art of perspective on a soup-plate of the willow pattern; and we may expect, on the occasion of the eighty-third annual exhibition of the Royal Academy of Art in England, to see some pictures by this pious Brotherhood, realising Hogarth's idea of a man on a mountain several miles off, lighting his pipe at the upper window of a house in the foreground.[5] But we are informed that every brick in the house will be a portrait; that the man's boots will be copied with the utmost fidelity from a pair of Bluchers[6] sent up out of Northamptonshire for the purpose; and that the texture of his hands (including four chilblains, a whitlow, and ten dirty nails) will be a triumph of the painter's art.

A Society, to be called the Pre-Newtonian Brotherhood, was lately projected by a young gentleman, under articles to a Civil Engineer, who objected to being considered bound to conduct himself according to the laws of gravitation. But this young gentleman, being reproached by some aspiring companions with the timidity of his conception, has abrogated that idea in favour of a Pre-Galileo Brotherhood now flourishing, who distinctly refuse to perform any annual revolution round the sun, and have arranged that the world shall not do so any more. The course to be taken by the Royal Academy of Art in reference to this Brotherhood is not yet decided upon; but it is whispered that some other large educational Institutions in the neighbourhood of Oxford are nearly ready to pronounce in favour of it.

Several promising students connected with the Royal College of Surgeons have held a meeting, to protest against the circulation of the blood, and to pledge themselves to treat all the patients they can get, on principles condemnatory of that innovation. A Pre-Harvey Brotherhood[7] is the result, from which a great deal may be expected – by the undertakers.

In Literature, a very spirited effort has been made, which is no less than the formation of a P.G.A.P.C.B., or Pre-Gower[8] and Pre-Chaucer Brotherhood, for the restoration of the ancient English style of spelling, and the weeding out from all libraries, public and private, of those and all later pretenders, particularly a person of loose character named Shakespeare. It having been suggested, however, that this happy idea could scarcely be considered complete while the art of printing was permitted to remain unmolested, another society, under the name of the Pre-Laurentius[9] Brotherhood, has been established in connexion with it, for the abolition of all but manuscript books. These Mr. Pugin[10] has engaged to supply, in characters that nobody on earth shall be able to read. And it is confidently expected by those who have seen the House of Lords, that he will faithfully redeem his pledge.

In Music, a retrogressive step, in which there is much hope, has been taken. The P.A.B., or Pre-Agincourt Brotherhood has arisen, nobly devoted to consign to oblivion Mozart, Beethoven, Handel, and every other such ridiculous reputation, and to fix its Millennium (as its name implies) before the date of the first regular musical composition known to have been achieved in England. As this Institution has not yet commenced active operations, it remains to be seen whether the Royal Academy of Music will be a worthy sister of the Royal Academy of Art, and admit this enterprising body to its orchestra. We have it on the best authority, that its compositions will be quite as rough and discordant as the real old original – that it will be, in a word, exactly suited to the pictorial Art we have endeavoured to describe. We have strong hopes, therefore, that the Royal Academy of Music, not wanting an example, may not want courage.

The regulation of social matters, as separated from the Fine Arts, has been undertaken by the Pre-Henry-the-Seventh Brotherhood,[11] who date from the same period as the Pre-Raphael Brotherhood. This Society, as cancelling all the advances of nearly four hundred years, and reverting to one of the most disagreeable periods of English History, when the Nation was yet very slowly emerging from barbarism, and when gentle female foreigners, come over to be the wives of Scottish Kings, wept bitterly (as well they might) at being left alone among the savage Court, must be regarded with peculiar favour. As the time of ugly religious caricatures (called mysteries), it is thoroughly Pre-Raphael in its spirit; and may be deemed the twin brother to that great society. We should be certain of the

Plague among many other advantages, if this Brotherhood were properly encouraged.

All these Brotherhoods, and any other society of the like kind, now in being or yet to be, have at once a guiding star, and a reduction of their great ideas to something palpable and obvious to the senses, in the sign to which we take the liberty of directing their attention. We understand that it is in the contemplation of each Society to become possessed, with all convenient speed, of a collection of such pictures; and that once, every year, to wit, upon the first of April, the whole intend to amalgamate in a high festival, to be called the Convocation of Eternal Boobies.

The Ghost of Art

First published in *Household Words*, 20 July 1850, and subsequently included in *Reprinted Pieces* from which this text is taken.

I am a bachelor, residing in rather a dreary set of chambers in the Temple.[1] They are situated in a square court of high houses, which would be a complete well, but for the want of water and the absence of a bucket. I live at the top of the house, among the tiles and sparrows. Like the little man in the nursery-story,[2] I live by myself, and all the bread and cheese I get – which is not much – I put upon a shelf. I need scarcely add, perhaps, that I am in love, and that the father of my charming Julia objects to our union.

I mention these little particulars as I might deliver a letter of introduction. The reader is now acquainted with me, and perhaps will condescend to listen to my narrative.

I am naturally of a dreamy turn of mind; and my abundant leisure – for I am called to the Bar – coupled with much lonely listening to the twittering of sparrows, and the pattering of rain, has encouraged that disposition. In my "top set" I hear the wind howl on a winter night, when the man on the ground floor believes it is perfectly still weather. The dim lamps with which our Honourable Society[3] (supposed to be as yet unconscious of the new discovery called Gas[4]) make the horrors of the staircase visible, deepen the gloom which generally settles on my soul when I go home at night.

I am in the Law, but not of it. I can't exactly make out what it means. I sit in Westminster Hall sometimes (in character) from ten to four; and when I go out of Court, I don't know whether I am standing on my wig or my boots.

It appears to me (I mention this in confidence) as if there were too much talk and too much law – as if some grains of truth were started overboard into a tempestuous sea of chaff.

All this may make me mystical. Still, I am confident that what I am going to describe myself as having seen and heard, I actually did see and hear.

It is necessary that I should observe that I have a great delight in pictures. I am no painter myself, but I have studied pictures and written about them.

I have seen all the most famous pictures in the world; my education and reading have been sufficiently general to possess me beforehand with a knowledge of most of the subjects to which a Painter is likely to have recourse; and, although I might be in some doubt as to the rightful fashion of the scabbard of King Lear's sword, for instance, I think I should know King Lear tolerably well, if I happened to meet with him.

I go to all the Modern Exhibitions every season, and of course I revere the Royal Academy. I stand by its forty Academical articles almost as firmly as I stand by the thirty-nine Articles of the Church of England.[5] I am convinced that in neither case could there be, by any rightful possibility, one article more or less.

It is now exactly three years – three years ago, this very month – since I went from Westminster to the Temple, one Thursday afternoon, in a cheap steamboat. The sky was black, when I imprudently walked on board. It began to thunder and lighten immediately afterwards, and the rain poured down in torrents. The deck seeming to smoke with the wet, I went below; but so many passengers were there, smoking too, that I came up again, and buttoning my pea-coat, and standing in the shadow of the paddle-box, stood as upright as I could, and made the best of it.

It was at this moment that I first beheld the terrible Being, who is the subject of my present recollections.

Standing against the funnel, apparently with the intention of drying himself by the heat as fast as he got wet, was a shabby man in threadbare black, and with his hands in his pockets, who fascinated me from the memorable instant when I caught his eye.

Where had I caught that eye before? Who was he? Why did I connect him, all at once, with the Vicar of Wakefield, Alfred the Great, Gil Blas, Charles the Second, Joseph and his Brethren, the Fairy Queen, Tom Jones, the Decameron of Boccaccio, Tam O'Shanter, the Marriage of the Doge of Venice with the Adriatic, and the Great Plague of London?[6] Why, when he bent one leg, and placed one hand upon the back of the seat near him, did my mind associate him wildly with the words, "Number one hundred and forty-two, Portrait of a gentleman?" Could it be that I was going mad?

I looked at him again, and now I could have taken my affidavit that he belonged to the Vicar of Wakefield's family. Whether he was the Vicar, or Moses, or Mr. Burchill, or the Squire, or a conglomeration of all four, I knew not; but I was impelled to seize him by the throat, and charge him with being, in some fell way, connected with the Primrose blood.[7] He looked up at the rain, and then – oh Heaven! – he became St. John. He folded his arms, resigning himself to the weather, and I was frantically inclined to address him as the Spectator, and firmly demand to know what he had done with Sir Roger de Coverley.[8]

The frightful suspicion that I was becoming deranged, returned on me with redoubled force. Meantime, this awful stranger, inexplicably linked to my distress, stood drying himself at the funnel; and ever, as the steam rose from his clothes, diffusing a mist around him, I saw through the ghostly medium all the people I have mentioned, and a score more, sacred and profane.

I am conscious of a dreadful inclination that stole upon me, as it thundered and lightened, to grapple with this man, or demon, and plunge him over the side. But I constrained myself – I know not how – to speak to him, and in a pause of the storm, I crossed the deck, and said:

"What are you?"

He replied, hoarsely, "A Model."

"A what?" said I.

"A Model," he replied. "I sets to the profession for a bob a-hour." (All through this narrative I give his own words, which are indelibly imprinted on my memory.)

The relief which this disclosure gave me, the exquisite delight of the restoration of my confidence in my own sanity, I cannot describe. I should have fallen on his neck, but for the consciousness of being observed by the man at the wheel.

"You then," said I, shaking him so warmly by the hand, that I wrung the rain out of his coat-cuff, "are the gentleman whom I have so frequently contemplated, in connexion with a high-backed chair with a red cushion, and a table with twisted legs."

"I am that Model," he rejoined moodily, "and I wish I was anything else."

"Say not so," I returned. "I have seen you in the society of many beautiful young women;" as in truth I had, and always (I now remember) in the act of making the most of his legs.

"No doubt," said he. "And you've seen me along with warses of flowers, and any number of table-kivers,[9] and antique cabinets, and warious gammon."

"Sir?" said I.

"And warious gammon," he repeated, in a louder voice. "You might have seen me in armour, too, if you had looked sharp. Blessed if I ha'n't stood in half the suits of armour as ever came out of Pratt's shop: and sat, for weeks together, a-eating nothing, out of half the gold and silver dishes as has ever been lent for the purpose out of Storrses, and Mortimerses, or Garrardses, and Davenportseseses."[10]

Excited, as it appeared, by a sense of injury, I thought he would never have found an end for the last word. But at length it rolled sullenly away with the thunder.

"Pardon me," said I, "you are a well-favoured, well-made man, and yet – forgive me – I find, on examining my mind, that I associate you with – that my recollection indistinctly makes you, in short – excuse me – a kind of powerful monster."

"It would be a wonder if it didn't," he said. "Do you know what my points are?"

"No," said I.

"My throat and my legs," said he. "When I don't set for a head, I mostly sets for a throat and a pair of legs. Now, granted you was a painter, and was to work at my throat for a week together, I suppose you'd see a lot of lumps and bumps there, that would never be there at all, if you looked at me, complete, instead of only my throat. Wouldn't you?"

"Probably," said I, surveying him.

"Why, it stands to reason," said the Model. "Work another week at my legs, and it'll be the same thing. You'll make 'em out as knotty and as knobby, at last, as if they was the trunks of two old trees. Then, take and stick my legs and throat on to another man's body, and you'll make a reg'lar monster. And that's the way the public gets their reg'lar monsters, every first Monday in May, when the Royal Academy Exhibition opens."

"You are a critic," said I, with an air of deference.

"I'm in an uncommon ill humour, if that's it," rejoined the Model, with great indignation. "As if it warn't bad enough for a bob a-hour, for a man to be mixing himself up with that there jolly old furniter that one 'ud think the public know'd the wery nails in by this time – or to be putting on greasy old 'ats and cloaks, and playing tambourines in the Bay o' Naples, with Wesuvius a smokin' according to pattern in the background, and the wines a bearing wonderful in the middle distance – or to be unpolitely kicking up his legs among a lot o' gals, with no reason whatever in his mind, but to show 'em – as if this warn't bad enough, I'm to go and be thrown out of employment too!"

"Surely no!" said I.

"Surely yes," said the indignant Model. "BUT I'LL GROW ONE."

The gloomy and threatening manner in which he muttered the last words, can never be effaced from my remembrance. My blood ran cold.

I asked of myself, what was it that this desperate Being was resolved to grow. My breast made no response.

I ventured to implore him to explain his meaning. With a scornful laugh, he uttered this dark prophecy:

"I'LL GROW ONE. AND, MARK MY WORDS, IT SHALL HAUNT YOU!"

We parted in the storm, after I had forced half-a-crown on his acceptance, with a trembling hand. I conclude that something supernatural happened to the steamboat, as it bore his reeking figure down the river; but it never got into the papers.

Two years elapsed, during which I followed my profession without any vicissitudes; never holding so much as a motion, of course. At the expiration of that period, I found myself making my way home to the Temple, one night, in precisely such another storm of thunder and lightning as that by which I had been overtaken on board the steamboat – except that this storm, bursting over the town at midnight, was rendered much more awful by the darkness and the hour.

As I turned into my court, I really thought a thunderbolt would fall, and plough the pavement up. Every brick and stone in the place seemed to have an echo of its own for the thunder. The waterspouts were overcharged, and the rain came tearing down from the house-tops as if they had been mountain-tops.

Mrs. Parkins, my laundress – wife of Parkins the porter, then newly dead of a dropsy – had particular instructions to place a bedroom candle and a match under the staircase lamp on my landing, in order that I might light my candle there, whenever I came home. Mrs. Parkins invariably disregarding all instructions, they were never there. Thus it happened that on this occasion I groped my way into my sitting-room to find the candle, and came out to light it.

What were my emotions when, underneath the staircase lamp, shining with wet as if he had never been dry since our last meeting, stood the mysterious Being whom I had encountered on the steamboat in a thunderstorm, two years before! His prediction rushed upon my mind, and I turned faint.

"I said I'd do it," he observed, in a hollow voice, "and I have done it. May I come in?"

"Misguided creature, what have you done?" I returned.

"I'll let you know," was his reply, "if you'll let me in."

Could it be murder that he had done? And had he been so successful that he wanted to do it again, at my expense?

I hesitated.

"May I come in?" said he.

I inclined my head, with as much presence of mind as I could command, and he followed me into my chambers. There, I saw that the lower part of his face was tied up, in what is commonly called a Belcher handkerchief. He slowly removed this bandage, and exposed to view a long dark beard, curling over his upper lip, twisting about the corners of his mouth, and hanging down upon his breast.

"What is this?" I exclaimed involuntarily, "and what have you become?"

"I am the Ghost of Art!" said he.

The effect of these words, slowly uttered in the thunderstorm at midnight, was appalling in the last degree. More dead than alive, I surveyed him in silence.

"The German taste[11] came up," said he, "and threw me out of bread. I am ready for the taste now."

He made his beard a little jagged with his hands, folded his arms, and said,

"Severity!"

I shuddered. It was so severe.

He made his beard flowing on his breast, and, leaning both hands on the staff of a carpet-broom which Mrs. Parkins had left among my books, said: "Benevolence."

I stood transfixed. The change of sentiment was entirely in the beard. The man might have left his face alone, or had no face. The beard did everything.

He lay down, on his back, on my table, and with that action of his head threw up his beard at the chin.

"That's death!" said he.

He got off my table and, looking up at the ceiling, cocked his beard a little awry; at the same time making it stick out before him.

"Adoration, or a vow of vengeance," he observed.

He turned his profile to me, making his upper lip very bulky with the upper part of his beard.

"Romantic character," said he.

He looked sideways out of his beard, as if it were an ivy-bush. "Jealousy," said he. He gave it an ingenious twist in the air, and informed me that he was carousing. He made it shaggy with his fingers and it was Despair; lank – and it was avarice; tossed it all kinds of ways – and it was rage. The beard did everything.

"I am the Ghost of Art," said he. "Two bob a-day now, and more when it's longer! Hair's the true expression. There is no other. I SAID I'D GROW IT, AND I'VE GROWN IT, AND IT SHALL HAUNT YOU!"

He may have tumbled down-stairs in the dark, but he never walked down or ran down. I looked over the banisters, and I was alone with the thunder.

Need I add more of my terrific fate? IT HAS haunted me ever since. It glares upon me from the walls of the Royal Academy, (except when MACLISE subdues it to his genius,) it fills my soul with terror at the British Institution, it lures young artists on to their destruction. Go where I will, the Ghost of Art, eternally working the passions in hair, and expressing everything by beard, pursues me. The prediction is accomplished, and the victim has no rest.

Epsom

First published in *Household Words*, 7 June 1851, this paper was written in collaboration with W. H. Wills. The text reproduced here is that published in *The Uncollected Writings of Charles Dickens*. Harry Stone suggests that Dickens was responsible for the portion from 'On that great occasion' to the conclusion.

A straggling street, an undue proportion of inns, a large pond, a pump, and a magnificent brick clock case, make up – with a few more touches not necessary to be given here – the picture of the metropolis of English racing, and the fountain of Epsom salts. For three hundred and sixty-four days in the year a cannon-ball might be fired from one end of Epsom to the other without endangering human life. On the three hundred and sixty-fifth, or Derby Day,[1] a population surges and rolls, and scrambles through the place, that may be counted in millions.

Epsom during the races, and Epsom at any other time, are things as unlike as the Desert of Saharah and the interior of the Palace of Glass in Hyde Park.[2] We intend, for the edification of the few who know Epsom races only by name, and for the amusement (we hope) of the many who have sported over its Downs during the races, to give some account of Epsom under both aspects.

Our graver readers need not be alarmed – we know little of horses; and, happily, for ourselves, nothing of sporting; but, believing in the dictum of the Natural History chapters of the Universal Spelling Book that the "horse is a noble animal," and that he is nowhere so noble, so well bred, so handsome, so tractable, so intelligent, so well cared for, and so well appreciated, as in this country; and that, in consequence of the national fondness for races his breed has been improved until he has attained his present excellency – believing all this, we think it quite possible to do him justice, without defiling the subject with any allusion to the knavery to which he, sometimes, innocently gives rise. Those who practise it are his vulgar parasites; for the owners of race-horses number among them the highest and most honourable names in the country.

Financially, the subject is not unworthy of notice. Racers give employment to thousands. According to Captain Rous, there are upwards of two hundred thorough-bred stallions, and one thousand one hundred brood mares, which produce about eight hundred and thirty foals annually: of these there are generally three in the first class of race-horses, seven in the second class; and they descend gradually in the scale to the amount of four hundred and eighty, one half of which never catch the judge's eye; the remainder are either not trained, or are found unworthy at an early period.

The number of race-courses is one hundred and eleven; of which three are in Ireland, and six in Scotland.

It is Monday – the Monday before the Derby Day, and a railway takes us, in less than an hour, from London Bridge to the capital of the racing world, close to the abode of its Great Man, who is – need we add! – the Clerk of the Epsom Course. It is, necessarily, one of the best houses in the place; being – honour to literature – a flourishing bookseller's shop. We are presented to the official. He kindly conducts us to the Downs, to show how the horses are temporarily stabled; to initiate us into some of the mysteries of the "field;" to reveal to us, in fact, the private life of the race-horse.

We arrive at a neat farm-house, with more outbuildings than are usually seen appended to so modest a homestead. A sturdy, well-dressed, well-mannered, purpose-like, sensible-looking man, presents himself. He has a Yorkshire accent. A few words pass between him and the Clerk of the Course, in which we hear the latter asseverate with much emphasis that we are, in a sporting sense, quite artless – we rather think "green," was the exact expression – that we never bet a shilling, and are quite incapable, if even willing, to take advantage of any information, or of any inspection vouchsafed to us. Mr. Filbert (the trainer) hesitates no longer. He moves his hat with honest politeness; bids us follow him, and lays his finger on the latch of a stable.

The trainer opens the door with one hand; and, with a gentleman-like wave of the other, would give us the precedence. We hesitate. We would rather not go in first. We acknowledge an enthusiastic admiration for the race-horse; but at the very mention of a race-horse, the stumpy animal whose portrait headed our earliest lesson of equine history, in the before-quoted "Universal Spelling Book," vanishes from our view, and the animal described in the Book of Job[3] prances into our mind's eye: "The glory of his nostril is terrible. He mocketh at fear and is not affrighted. He swalloweth the ground with the fierceness of his rage." To enjoy, therefore, a fine racer – not as one does a work of art – we like the point of sight to be the point of distance. The safest point, in case of accident (say, for instance, a sudden striking-out of the hinder hoofs), we hold to be the vanishing point – a point by no means attainable on the inside of that contracted kind of stable known as a "loose box."

The trainer evidently mistakes our fears for modesty. We boldly step forward to the outer edge of the threshold, but uncomfortably close to the hind-quarters of Pollybus, a "favourite" for the Derby. When we perceive that he has neither bit nor curb; nor bridle, nor halter; that he is being "rubbed down" by a small boy, after having taken his gallops; that there is nothing on earth — except the small boy — to prevent his kicking, or plunging, or biting, or butting his visitors to death; we breathe rather thickly. When the trainer exclaims, "Shut the door, Sam!" and the little groom does his master's bidding, and boxes us up, we desire to be breathing the fresh air of the Downs again.

"Bless you, sir!" says our good-tempered informant, when he sees us shrink away from Pollybus, changing sides at a signal from his cleaner; "these horses" (we look round, and for the first time perceive, with a tremor, the heels of another high-mettled racer protruding from an adjoining stall) "these horses are as quiet as you are; and — I say it without offence — just as well behaved. It is quite laughable to hear the notions of people who are not used to them. They are the gentlest and most tractable creeturs in creation. Then, as to shape and symmetry, is there anything like them?"

We acknowledge that Pretty Perth — the mare in the adjoining box — could hardly be surpassed for beauty.

"Ah, *can* you wonder at noblemen and gentlemen laying out their twenty and thirty thousand a year on them?"

"So much?"

"Why, my gov'nor's stud costs us five-and-twenty thousand a year, one year with another. — There's an eye, sir!"

The large, prominent, but mild optics of Pretty Perth are at this moment turned full upon us. Nothing, certainly, can be gentler than the expression that beams from them. She is "taking," as Mr. Filbert is pleased to say, "measure of us." She does not stare vulgarly, or peer upon us a half-bred indifference; but, having duly and deliberately satisfied her mind respecting our external appearance, allows her attention to be leisurely diverted to some oats with which the boy had just supplied the manger.

"It is all a mistake," continues Mr. Filbert, commenting on certain vulgar errors respecting race-horses; "thorough-breds are not nearly so rampagious as mongrels and half-breds. The two horses in this stall are gentlefolks, with as good blood in their veins as the best nobleman in the land. They would be just as back'ard in doing anything unworthy of a lady or gentleman, as any lord or lady in St. James's[4] – such as kicking, or rearing, or shying, or biting. The pedigree of every horse that starts in any great race, is to be traced as regularly up to James the First's Arabian, or to Cromwell's White Turk, or to the Darley or Godolphin barbs, as your great English families are to the Conqueror. The worst thing they will do, is running away now and then with their jockeys. And what's that? Why, only the animal's animal-spirit running away with *him*. They are not," adds Mr. Filbert, with a merry twinkle in his eye, "the only young bloods that are fond of going too fast."

To our question whether he considers that a race-horse *could* go too fast, Mr. Filbert gives a jolly negative, and remarks that it is all owing to high feeding and fine air; "for, mind you, horses get much better air to breathe than men do, and more of it."

All this while the two boys are sibillating lustily while rubbing and polishing the coats of their horses; which are as soft as velvet, and much smoother. When the little grooms come to the fetlock and pastern, the chamois-leather they have been using is discarded as too coarse and rough, and they rub away down to the hoofs with their sleek and plump hands. Every wish they express, either in words or by signs, is cheerfully obeyed by the horse. The terms the quadruped seems to be on with the small biped, are those of the most easy and intimate friendship. They thoroughly understand one another. We feel a little ashamed of our mistrust of so much docility, and leave the stable with much less awe of a race-horse than we entered it.

"And now, Mr. Filbert, one delicate question – What security is there against these horses being drugged, so that they may lose a race?"

Mr. Filbert halts, places his legs apart, and his arms akimbo, and throws into his reply a severe significance, mildly tinged with indignation. He commences with saying, "I'll tell you where it is: – there is a deal more said about foul play and horses going amiss, than there need be."

"Then the boys are never heavily bribed?"

"Heavily bribed, Sir!" Mr. Filbert contracts his eyes, but sharpens up their expression, to look the suspicion down. "Bribed! – it may not be hard to bribe a man, but it's not so easy to bribe a boy. What's the use of a hundred-pound note to a child of ten or twelve year old? Try him with a pen'north of apples, or a slice of pudding, and you have a better chance; though I would not give you the price of a sugar-stick for it. Nine out of ten of these lads would not have a hair of their horse's tail ruffled if they could help it; much more any such harm as drugs or downright poison. The boy and the horse are so fond of one another, that a racing stable is a regular happy family of boys and horses. When the foal is first born, it is turned loose into the paddock; and if his mother don't give him enough milk, the cow makes up the deficiency. He scampers about in this way for about a year: then he is 'taken up;' that is, bitted, and backed by a 'dumb-jockey' – a cross of wood made for the purpose. When he has got a little used to that, we try him with a speaking jockey – a child some seven or eight years old, who has been born, like the colt, in the stables. From that time till the horse retires from the turf, the two are inseparable. They eat, drink, sleep, go out and come in together. Under the directions of the trainer, the boy tells the horse what to do, and he does it; for he knows that he is indebted to the boy for everything he gets. When he is hungry, it is the boy that gives him his corn; when he is thirsty, the boy hands him his water; if he gets a stone in his foot, the boy picks it out. By the time the colt is old enough to run, he and the boy have got to like one another so well that they fret to be away from one another. As for bribing! Why, you may as well try to bribe the horse to poison the boy, as the boy to let the horse be injured."

"But the thing *has* happened, Mr. Filbert?"

"Not so much as is talked about. Sometimes a likely foal is sent to a training stable, and cracked up as something wonderful. He is entered to run. On trial, he turns out to be next to nothing; and the backers, to save their reputation, put it about, that the horse was played tricks with. There is hardly a great race, but you hear something about horses going amiss by foul play."

"Do many of these boys become jockeys?"

"Mostly. Some of them are jockeys already, and ride 'their own' horses, as they call them. Here comes one."

A miniature man, with a horsewhip neatly twisted round the crop or handle, opens the gate.

"Well, Tommy, how are you, Tommy?"

"Well, Sir, bobbish. Fine day, Mr. Filbert."

Although Mr. Filbert tells us in a whisper that Tommy is only twelve next birth-day, Tommy looks as if he had entered far into his teens. His dress is deceptive. Light trousers terminating in buttons, laced shoes, long striped waistcoat, a cut-away coat, a coloured cravat, a collar to which juveniles aspire under the name of "stick-ups," and a Paris silk hat, form his equipment.

"Let's see, Tommy; what stakes did you win last?"

Tommy flicks, with the end of his whip-crop, a speck of dirt from the toe of his "off" shoe, and replies carelessly, "The Great Northamptonshire upon Valentine. But then, I have won a many smaller stakes, you know, Mr. Filbert."

Are there many jockeys so young as Tommy?

"Not many so young," says Tommy, tying a knot in his whip thong, "but a good many smaller." Tommy then walks across the straw-yard to speak to some stable friend he has come to see. Tommy has not only the appearance, but the manners of a man.

"That boy will be worth money," says Mr. Filbert. "It is no uncommon thing for a master to give a lad like that a hundred pound when he wins a race. As he can't spend it in hard-bake, or ginger-beer, or marbles, (the young rogue *does*, occasionally, get rid of a pound or two in cigars,) he saves it. I have known a racing-stable lad begin the world at twenty, with from three to four thousand pound."

Tommy is hopping back over the straw, as if he had forgotten something. "O, I beg your pardon for not asking before," he says, "but – how does Mrs. Filbert find herself?"

"Quite well, thank you, Tommy." Tommy says he is glad to hear it, and walks off like a family-man.

Our interview with Mr. Filbert is finished, and we pace towards the race-course with its indefatigable clerk. Presently, he points to a huge white object that rears its leaden roof on the apex of the highest of the "Downs." It is the Grand Stand. It is so extensive, so strong, and so complete, that it seems built for eternity, instead of for busy use during one day in the year, and for smaller requisition during three others. Its stability is equal to St. Paul's or the Memnonian Temple. Our astonishment, already excited, is increased when our cicerone tells us that he pays as rent, and in subscriptions to stakes to be run for, nearly two thousand pounds per annum for that stand. Expecting an unusually great concourse of visitors this year, he has erected a new wing, extended the betting enclosure, and fitted up two apartments for the exclusive use of ladies.

Here we are! Let us go into the basement. First into the weighing-house, where the jockeys "come to scale" after each race. We then inspect the offices for the Clerk of the Course himself; wine-cellars, beer-cellars, larders, sculleries, and kitchens, all as gigantically appointed, and as copiously furnished as if they formed part of an Ogre's Castle. To furnish the refreshment-saloon, the Grand Stand has in store two thousand four hundred tumblers, one thousand two hundred wine-glasses, three thousand plates and dishes, and several of the most elegant vases we have seen out of the Glass Palace, decorated with artificial flowers. An exciting odour of cookery meets us in our descent. Rows of spits are turning rows of joints before blazing walls of fire. Cooks are trussing fowls; confectioners are making jellies; kitchen-maids are plucking pigeons; huge crates of boiled tongues are being garnished on dishes. One hundred and thirty legs of lamb, sixty-five saddles of lamb, and one hundred and thirty shoulders of lamb; in short, a whole flock of sixty-five lambs have to be roasted, and dished, and garnished, by the Derby Day. Twenty rounds of beef, four hundred lobsters, one hundred and fifty tongues, twenty fillets of veal, one hundred sirloins of beef, five hundred spring chickens, three hundred and fifty pigeon-pies; a countless number of quartern loaves, and an incredible quantity of ham have to be cut up into sandwiches; eight hundred eggs have got to be boiled for the pigeon-pies and salads. The forests of lettuces, the acres of cress, and beds of radishes, which will have to be chopped up; the gallons of "dressing" that will have to be poured out and converted into salads for the insatiable Derby Day, will be best understood by a memorandum from the chief of that department to the *chef-de-cuisine*, which happened, accidentally, to fall under our notice: "Pray don't forget a large tub and a birch-broom for mixing the salad!"

We are preparing to ascend, when we hear the familiar sound of a printing machine. Are we deceived? O, no! The Grand Stand is like the kingdom of China – self-supporting, self-sustaining. It scorns foreign aid; even to the printing of the Racing Lists. This is the source of the innumerable cards with which hawkers persecute the sporting world on its way to the Derby, from the Elephant and Castle to the Grand Stand. "Dorling's list! Dorling's correct list! with the names of the horses, and colours of the riders!"

We are now in the hall. On our left, are the parlours, – refreshment-rooms specially devoted to the Jockey Club; on our right, a set of seats, reserved, from the days of Flying Childers, for the members of White's Club-house.

We step out upon the lawn; in the midst is the betting-ring, where sums of money of fabulous amounts change hands. The following salutary notice, respecting too numerous a class of characters, is printed on the admission card:–

"The Lessee of the Epsom Grand Stand hereby gives notice that no person guilty of any malpractices, or notoriously in default in respect of stakes, forfeits, or bets lost upon horse-racing, will be admitted within the Grand Stand or its enclosure during any race meetings at Epsom; and if any such person should gain admittance therein or thereupon, he will be expelled, upon his presence being pointed out to the Stewards for the time being, or to the Clerk of the Course."

The first floor is entirely occupied with a refreshment-room and a police court. Summary justice is the law of the Grand Stand. Two magistrates sit during the races. Is a pickpocket detected, a thimble-rigger[5] caught, a policeman assaulted? The delinquent is brought round to the Grand Stand, to be convicted, sentenced, and imprisoned in as short a time as it takes to run a mile race.

The sloping roof is covered with lead, in steps; the spectator from that point has a bird's-eye view of the entire proceedings, and of the surrounding country, which is beautifully picturesque. When the foreground of the picture is brightened and broken by the vast multitude that assembles here upon the Derby Day, it presents a whole which has no parallel in the world.

On that great occasion, an unused spectator might imagine that all London turned out. There is little perceptible difference in the bustle of its crowded streets, but all the roads leading to Epsom Downs are so thronged and blocked by every description of carriage that it is marvellous to consider how, when, and where, they were all made – out of what possible wealth they are all maintained – and by what laws the supply of horses is kept equal to the demand. Near the favourite bridges, and at various leading points of the leading roads, clusters of people post themselves by nine o'clock, to see the Derby people pass. Then come flitting by, barouches, phætons, broughams, gigs, four-wheeled chaises, four-in-hands, Hansom cabs, cabs of lesser note, chaise-carts, donkey-carts, tilted vans[6] made arborescent with green boughs and carrying no end of people, and a cask of beer, – equestrians, pedestrians, horse-dealers, gentlemen, notabilities, and swindlers, by tens of thousands – gradually thickening and accumulating, until, at last, a mile short of the turnpike, they become wedged together, and are very slowly filtered through layers of policemen, mounted and a-foot, until, one by one, they pass the gate and skurry down the hill beyond. The most singular combinations occur in these turnpike stoppages and presses. Four-in-hand leaders look affectionately over the shoulders of ladies, in bright shawls, perched in gigs; poles of carriages appear, uninvited, in the midst of social parties in phætons; little, fast, short-stepping ponies run up carriage-wheels before they can be stopped, and hold on behind like footmen. Now, the gentleman who is unaccustomed to public driving, gets into astonishing perplexities. Now, the Hansom cab whisks craftily in and out, and seems occasionally to fly over a waggon or so. Now the postboy on a jobbing [jibbing?] or a shying horse, curses the evil hour of his birth, and is ingloriously assisted by the shabby hostler [ostler?] out of place, who is walking down with seven shabby companions more or less equine, open to the various chances of the road. Now, the air is fresh, and the dust flies thick and fast. Now, the canvas-booths upon the course are seen to glisten and flutter in the distance. Now, the adventurous vehicles make cuts across, and get into ruts and gravel-pits. Now, the heather in bloom is like a field of gold,[7] and the roar of voices is like a wind. Now, we leave the hard road and go smoothly rolling over the soft green turf, attended by an army of unfortunate [importunate?][8] worshippers in red jackets and stable-jackets, who make a very Juggernaut-car[9] of our equipage, and now breathlessly call us "My Lord," and now, "your Honor." Now, we pass the outer settlements of tents where pots and kettles are – where gipsy children are – where airy stabling is – where tares for horses may be bought – where water, water, water, is proclaimed – where the Tumbler in an old pea-coat, with a spangled fillet round his head, eats oysters, while his wife takes care of the golden globes, and the knives, and also of the starry little boy, their son, who lives principally upside-down. Now, we pay our one pound at the barrier, and go faster on, still Juggernaut-wise, attended by our devotees, until at last we are drawn, and rounded, and backed, and sidled, and cursed, and complimented, and vociferated into a station on the hill opposite the Grand Stand, where we presently find ourselves on foot, much bewildered, waited on by five respectful persons, who *will* brush us all at once.

Well, to be sure, there never was such a Derby Day, as this present Derby Day! Never, to be sure, were there so many carriages, so many fours, so many twos, so many ones, so many horsemen, so many people who have come down by "rail," so many fine ladies in so many broughams, so many of Fortnum and Mason's[10] hampers, so much ice and champagne! If I were on the turf, and had a horse to enter for the Derby, I would call that horse Fortnum and Mason, convinced that with that name he would beat the field. Public opinion would bring him in somehow. Look where I will – in some connexion with the carriages – made fast upon the top, or occupying the box, or tied up behind, or dangling below, or peeping out of window – I see Fortnum and Mason. And now, Heavens! all the hampers fly wide open, and the green Downs burst into a blossom of lobster-salad!

As if the great Trafalgar signal had been suddenly displayed from the top of the Grand Stand, every man proceeds to "do his duty."[11] The weaker spirits, who were ashamed to set the great example, follow it instantly, and all around me there are table-cloths, pies, chickens, hams, tongues, rolls, lettuces, radishes, shell-fish, broad-bottomed bottles, clinking glasses, and carriages turned inside out. Amidst the hum of voices a bell rings. What's that? What's the matter? They are clearing the course. Never mind. Try the pigeon-pie. A roar. What's the matter? It's only the dog upon the course. Is that all? Glass of wine. Another roar. What's that? It's only the man who wants to cross the course, and is intercepted, and brought back. Is that all? I wonder whether it is always the same dog and the same man, year after year! A great roar. What's the matter? By Jupiter, they are going to start.

A deeper hum and a louder roar. Everybody standing on Fortnum and Mason. Now they're off! No. *Now* they're off! No. *Now* they're off. No. *Now* they are! Yes!

There they go! Here they come! Where? Keep your eye on Tattenham Corner, and you'll see 'em coming round in half a minute. Good gracious, look at the Grand Stand, piled up with human beings to the top, and at the wonderful effect of changing light as all their faces and uncovered heads turn suddenly this way! Here they are! Who is? The horses! Where? Here they come! Green first. No: Red first. No: Blue first. No: the Favorite first. Who says so? Look! Hurrah! Hurrah! All over. Glorious race. Favorite wins! Two hundred thousand pounds lost and won. You don't say so? Pass the pie!

Now, the pigeons fly away with the news. Now, every one dismounts from the top of Fortnum and Mason, and falls to work with greater earnestness than before, on carriage boxes, sides, tops, wheels, steps, roofs, and rumbles. Now, the living stream upon the course, dammed for a little while at one point, is released, and spreads like parti-colored grain. Now, the roof of the Grand Stand is deserted. Now, rings are formed upon the course, where strong men stand in pyramids on one another's heads; where the Highland lady dances; where the Devonshire Lad sets-to with the Bantam;[12] where the Tumbler throws the golden globes about, with the starry little boy tied round him in a knot.

Now, all the variety of human riddles who propound themselves on race-courses, come about the carriages, to be guessed. Now, the gipsy woman, with the flashing red or yellow handkerchief about her head, and the strange silvery-hoarse voice, appears, "My pretty gentleman, to tell your fortin, Sir; for you have a merry eye, my gentleman, and surprises is in store; for you're connected with a dark lady as loves you better than you love a kiss in a dark corner when the moon's a-shining; for you have a lively 'art, my gentleman, and you shall know her secret thoughts, and the first and last letters of her name, my pretty gentleman, if you will cross your poor gipsy's hand with a little bit of silver, for the luck of the fortin as the gipsy will read true, from the lines of your hand, my gentleman, both as to what is past, and present, and to come." Now, the Ethiopians,[13] looking unutterably hideous in the sunlight, play old banjoes and bones,[14] on which no man could perform ten years ago, but which, it seems, any

543

man may play now, if he will only blacken his face, put on a crisp wig, a white waistcoat and wristbands, a large white tie, and give his mind to it. Now, the sickly-looking ventriloquist, with an anxious face (and always with a wife in a shawl) teaches the alphabet to the puppet pupil, whom he takes out of his pocket. Now, my sporting gentlemen, you may ring the Bull,[15] the Bull, the Bull; you may ring the Bull! Now, try your luck at the knock-em-downs,[16] my Noble Swells – twelve heaves for sixpence, and a pincushion in the centre, worth ten times the money! Now the Noble Swells take five shillings' worth of "heaves", and carry off a halfpenny wooden pear in triumph. Now, it hails, as it always does hail, formidable wooden truncheons round the heads, bodies, and shins of the proprietors of the said knock-em-downs, whom nothing hurts. Now, inscrutable creatures, in smock frocks, beg for bottles. Now, a coarse vagabond, or idiot, or a compound of the two, never beheld by mortal off a race-course, hurries about, with ample skirts and a tattered parasol, counterfeiting a woman. Now, a shabby man, with an overhanging forehead, and a slinking eye, produces a small board, and invites your attention to something novel and curious – three thimbles and one little pea – with a one, two, three, – and a two, three, one, – and a one – and a two – in the middle – right hand, left hand – go you any bet from a crown to five sovereigns you don't lift the thimble the pea's under! Now, another gentleman (with a stick) much interested in the experiment, will "go" two sovereigns that he does lift the thimble, provided strictly, that the shabby man holds his hand still, and don't touch 'em again. Now, the bet's made, and the gentleman with the stick, lifts obviously the wrong thimble, and loses. Now, it is as clear as day to an innocent bystander, that the loser must have won if he had not blindly lifted the wrong thimble – in which he is strongly confirmed by another gentleman with a stick, also much interested, who proposes to "go him" halves – a friendly sovereign to *his* sovereign – against the bank. Now, the innocent agrees, and loses; – and so the world turns round bringing innocents with it in abundance, though the three confederates are wretched actors, and could live by no other trade if they couldn't do it better.

Now, there is another bell, and another clearing of the course, and another dog, and another man, and another race. Now, there are all these things all over again. Now, down among the carriage-wheels and poles, a scrubby growth of drunken postboys and the like has sprung into existence, like weeds among the many-colored flowers of fine ladies in broughams, and so forth. Now, the drinking-booths are all full, and tobacco-smoke is abroad, and an extremely civil gentleman confidentially proposes roulette.

And now, faces begin to be jaded, and horses are harnessed, and wherever the old grey-headed beggarman goes, he gets among traces and splinter-bars,[17] and is roared at.

So now we are on the road again, going home. Now, there are longer stoppages than in the morning; for we are a dense mass of men and women, wheels, horses, and dust. Now, all the houses on the road seem to be turned inside out, like the carriages on the course, and the people belonging to the houses, like the people belonging to the carriages, occupy stations which they never occupy at another time – on leads,[18] on housetops, on out-buildings, at windows, in balconies, in doorways, in gardens. Schools are drawn out to see the company go by. The academies for young gentlemen favor us with dried peas; the Establishments for Young Ladies (into which sanctuaries many wooden pears are pitched), with bright eyes. We become sentimental, and wish we could marry Clapham.[19] The crowd thickens on both sides of the road. All London appears to have come out to see us. It is like a triumphant entry – except that, on the whole, we rather amuse than impress the populace. There are little love-scenes among the chestnut trees by the roadside – young gentlemen in gardens resentful of glances at young ladies from coach-tops – other young gentlemen in other gardens, minding young ladies, whose arms seem to be trained like the vines. There are good family pictures – stout fathers and jolly mothers – rosy cheeks squeezed in between the rails – and infinitesimal jockeys winning in canters on walking-sticks. There are smart maid-servants among the grooms at stable-doors, where Cook looms large and glowing. There is plenty of smoking and drinking among the tilted vans and at the public-houses, and some singing, but general order and good-humour. So, we leave the gardens and come into the streets, and if we there encounter a few ruffians throwing flour and chalk about, we know them for the dregs and refuse of a fine, trustworthy people, deserving of all confidence and honor.

And now we are at home again – far from absolutely certain of the name of the winner of the Derby – knowing nothing whatever about any other race of the day – still tenderly affected by the beauty of Clapham – and thoughtful over the ashes of Fortnum and Mason.

Betting-Shops

First published in *Household Words*, 26 June 1852, from which this text is reproduced.

In one sporting newspaper for Sunday, June the fourteenth, there are nine-and-twenty advertisements from Prophets, who have wonderful information to give – for a consideration ranging from one pound one, to two-and-sixpence – concerning every "event" that is to come off upon the Turf. Each of these Prophets has an unrivalled and unchallengeable "Tip," founded on amazing intelligence communicated to him by illustrious unknowns (traitors of course, but that is nobody's business) in all the racing stables. Each, is perfectly clear that his enlightened patrons and correspondents *must* win; and each, begs to guard a too-confiding world against relying on the other. They are all philanthropists. One Sage announces "that when he casts his practised eye on the broad surface of struggling society, and witnesses the slow and enduring perseverance of some, and the infatuous rush of the many who are grappling with a cloud, he is led with more intense desire to hold up the lamp of light to all." He is also much afflicted, because "not a day passes, without his witnessing the public squandering away their money on worthless rubbish." Another, heralds his re-appearance among the lesser stars of the firmament with the announcement, "Again the Conquering Prophet comes!" Another moralist intermingles with his "Pick," and "Tip," the great Christian precept of the New Testament. Another, confesses to a small recent mistake which has made it "a disastrous meeting for us," but considers that excuses are unnecessary (after making them), for, "surely, after the unprecedented success of the proofs he has lately afforded of his capabilities in fishing out the most carefully-hidden turf secrets, he may readily be excused one blunder." All the Prophets write in a rapid manner, as receiving their inspiration on horseback, and noting it down, hot and hot, in the saddle, for the enlightenment of mankind and the restoration of the golden age.

This flourishing trade is a melancholy index to the round numbers of human donkeys who are everywhere browzing about. And it is worthy of remark that the great mass of disciples were, at first, undoubtedly to be found among those fast young gentlemen, who are so excruciatingly knowing that they are not by any means to be taken in by Shakespeare, or any sentimental gammon of that sort. To us, the idea of this would-be keen race being preyed upon by the whole Betting-Book of Prophets, is one of the most ludicrous pictures the mind can imagine; while there is a just and pleasant retribution in it which would awaken in us anything but animosity towards the Prophets, if the mischief ended here.

But, the mischief has the drawback that it does not end here. When there are so many Picks and Tips to be had, which will, of a surety, pick and tip their happy owners into the lap of Fortune, it becomes the duty of every butcher's boy and errand lad who is sensible of what is due to himself, immediately to secure a Pick and Tip of the cheaper sort, and to go in and win. Having purchased the talisman from the Conquering Prophet, it is necessary that the noble sportsman should have a handy place provided for him, where lists of the running horses and of the latest state of the odds, are kept, and where he can lay out his money (or somebody else's) on the happy animals at whom the Prophetic eye has cast a knowing wink. Presto! Betting-shops spring up in every street! There is a demand at all the brokers' shops for old, fly-blown, coloured prints of race-horses, and for any odd folio volumes that have the appearance of Ledgers. Two such prints in any shop-window, and one such book on any shop-counter, will make a complete Betting-office, bank, and all.

The Betting-shop may be a Tobacconist's, thus suddenly transformed; or it may be nothing but a Betting-shop. It may be got up cheaply, for the purposes of Pick and Tip investment, by the removal of the legitimate counter, and the erection of an official partition and desk in one corner; or, it may be wealthy in mahogany fittings, French polish, and office furniture. The presiding officer, in an advanced stage of shabbiness, may be accidentally beheld through the little window – whence from the inner mysteries of the Temple, he surveys the devotees before entering on business – drinking gin with an admiring client; or he may be a serenely condescending gentleman of Government Office appearance, who keeps the books of the establishment with his glass in his eye. The Institution may stoop to bets of single shillings, or may reject lower ventures than half-crowns, or may draw the line of demarcation between itself and the snobs at five shillings, or seven-and-sixpence, or half-a-sovereign, or even (but very rarely indeed), at a pound. Its note of the little transaction may be a miserable scrap of limp pasteboard with a wretchedly printed form, worse filled up; or, it may be a genteelly tinted card, addressed "To the Cashier of the Aristocratic Club," and authorising that important officer to pay the bearer two pounds fifteen shillings, if Greenhorn wins the Fortunatus's Cup; and to be very particular to pay it the day after the race. But, whatever the Betting-shop be, it has only to be somewhere – anywhere, so people pass and repass – and the rapid youth of England, with its slang intelligence perpetually broad awake and its weather eye continually open, will walk in and deliver up its money, like the helpless Innocent that it is.

> Pleased to the last, it thinks its wager won,
> And licks the hand by which it's surely Done![1]

We cannot represent the head quarters of Household Words as being situated peculiarly in the midst of these establishments, for, they pervade the whole of London and its suburbs. But, our neighbourhood[2] yields an abundant crop of Betting-shops, and we have not to go far to know something about them. Passing the other day, through a dirty thoroughfare, much frequented, near Drury Lane Theatre, we found that a new Betting-shop had suddenly been added to the number under the auspices of Mr. Cheerful.

Mr. Cheerful's small establishment was so very like that of the apothecary in Romeo and Juliet,[3] unfurnished, and hastily adapted to the requirements of secure and profitable investment, that it attracted our particular notice. It burst into bloom, too, so very shortly before the Ascot Meeting, that we had our suspicions concerning the possibility of Mr. Cheerful having devised the ingenious speculation of getting what money he could, up to the day of the race, and then – if we may be allowed the harsh expression – bolting. We had no doubt that investments would be made with Mr. Cheerful, notwithstanding the very unpromising appearance of his establishment; for, even as we were considering its exterior from the opposite side of the way (it may have been opened that very morning), we saw two newsboys, an incipient baker, a clerk, and a young butcher, go in, and transact business with Mr. Cheerful in a most confiding manner.

We resolved to lay a bet with Mr. Cheerful, and see what came of it. So we stepped across the road into Mr. Cheerful's Betting-shop, and, having glanced at the lists hanging up therein, while another noble sportsman (a boy with a blue bag) laid another bet with Mr. Cheerful, we expressed our desire to back Tophana for the Western Handicap, to the spirited amount of half-a-crown. In making this advance to Mr. Cheerful, we looked as knowing on the subject, both of Tophana and the Western Handicap, as it was in us to do: though, to confess the humiliating truth, we neither had, nor have, the least idea in connexion with those proper names, otherwise than as we suppose Tophana to be a horse, and the Western Handicap an aggregate of stakes. It being Mr. Cheerful's business to be grave and ask no questions, he accepted our wager, booked it, and handed us over his railed desk the dirty scrap of pasteboard, in right of which we were to claim – the day after the race; we were to be very particular about that – seven-and-sixpence sterling, if Tophana won. Some demon whispering us that here was an opportunity of discovering whether Mr. Cheerful had a good bank of silver in the cash-box, we handed in a sovereign. Mr. Cheerful's head immediately slipped down behind the partition, investigating imaginary drawers; and Mr. Cheerful's voice was presently heard to remark, in a stifled manner, that all the silver had been changed for gold that morning. After which, Mr. Cheerful reappeared in the twinkling of an eye, called in from a parlour the sharpest small boy ever beheld by human vision, and dispatched him for change. We remarked to Mr. Cheerful that if he would obligingly produce half-a-sovereign (having so much gold by him) we would increase our bet, and save him trouble. But, Mr. Cheerful, sliding down behind the partition again, answered that the boy was gone, now – trust him for that; he had vanished the instant he was spoken to – and it was no trouble at all. Therefore, we remained until the boy came back, in the society of Mr. Cheerful, and of an inscrutable woman who stared out resolutely into the street, and was probably Mrs. Cheerful. When the boy returned, we thought we once saw him faintly twitch his nose while we received our change, as if he exulted over a victim; but, he was so miraculously sharp, that it was impossible to be certain.

The day after the race, arriving, we returned with our document to Mr. Cheerful's establishment, and found it in great confusion. It was filled by a crowd of boys, mostly greasy, dirty, and dissipated; and all clamouring for Mr. Cheerful. Occupying Mr. Cheerful's place, was the miraculous boy; all alone, and unsupported, but not at all disconcerted. Mr. Cheerful, he said, had gone out on "'tickler bizniz" at ten o'clock in the morning, and wouldn't be back till late at night. Mrs. Cheerful was gone out of town for her health, till the winter. Would Mr. Cheerful be back to-morrow? cried the crowd. "He won't be *here*, to-morrow," said the miraculous boy. "Coz it's Sunday, and he always goes to church, a' Sunday." At this, even the losers laughed. "Will he be here a' Monday, then?" asked a desperate young green-grocer. "A' Monday?" said the miracle, reflecting. "No, I don't think he'll be here, a' Monday, coz he's going to a sale a' Monday." At this, some of the boys taunted the unmoved miracle with meaning "a sell instead of a sale," and others swarmed over the whole place, and some laughed, and some swore, and one errand boy, discovering the book – the only thing Mr. Cheerful had left behind him – declared it to be a "stunning good 'un." We took the liberty of looking over it, and found it so. Mr. Cheerful had received about seventeen pounds, and, even if he had paid his losses, would have made a profit of between eleven and twelve pounds. It is scarcely necessary to add that Mr. Cheerful has been so long detained at the sale that he has never come back. The last time we loitered past his late establishment (over which is inscribed Boot and Shoe Manufactory), the dusk of evening was closing in, and a young gentleman from New Inn was making some rather particular enquiries after him of a dim and dusty man who held the door a very little way open, and knew nothing about anybody, and less than nothing (if possible) about Mr. Cheerful. The handle of the lower door-bell was most significantly pulled out to its utmost extent, and left so, like an Organ stop in full action. It is to be hoped that the poor gull who had so frantically rung for Mr. Cheerful, derived some gratification from that expenditure of emphasis. He will never get any other, for his money.

But the public in general are not to be left a prey to such fellows as Cheerful. O, dear no! We have better neighbours than *that*, in the Betting-shop way. Expressly for the correction of such evils, we have The Tradesmen's Moral Associative Betting Club; the Prospectus of which Institution for the benefit of tradesmen (headed in the original with a racing woodcut), we here faithfully present without the alteration of a word.

"The Projectors of the Tradesmen's Moral Associative Betting Club, in announcing an addition to the number of Betting Houses in the Metropolis, beg most distinctly to state that they are not actuated by a feeling of rivalry towards old established and honourably conducted places of a similar nature, but in a spirit of fair competition, ask for the support of the public, guaranteeing to them more solid security for the investment of their monies, than has hitherto been offered.

"The Tradesmen's Moral Associative Betting Club is really what its name imports, viz., an Association of Tradesmen, persons in business, who witnessing the robberies hourly inflicted upon the humbler portion of the sporting public, by parties bankrupts alike in character and property, have come to the conclusion that the establishment of a club wherein their fellow-tradesmen, and the speculator of a few shillings, may invest their money with assured consciousness of a fair and honourable dealing, will be deemed worthy of public support.

"The Directors of this establishment feel that much of the odium attached to Betting Houses (acting to the prejudice of those which have striven hard by honourable means to secure public confidence), has arisen from the circumstance, that many offices have been fitted up in a style of gaudy imitative magnificence, accompanied by an expense, which, if defrayed, is obviously out of keeping with the profits of a legitimate concern. Whilst, in singular contrast, others have presented such a poverty stricken appearance, that it is evident the design of the occupant was only to receive money of *all*, and terminate in paying *none*.

"Avoiding these extremes of appearance, and with a determination never to be induced to speculate to an extent, that may render it even probable that we shall be unable 'to pay the day after the race.'

"The business of the club will be carried on at the house of a highly respectable and well-known tradesman, situate in a central locality, the existence of an agreement with whom, on the part of the directors, forms the strongest possible guarantee of our intention to keep faith with the public.

"The market odds will be laid on all events, and every ticket issued be signed by the director only, the monies being invested," &c. &c.

After this, Tradesmen are quite safe in laying out their money on their favourite horses. And their families, like the people in old fireside stories, will no doubt live happy ever afterwards!

Now, it is unquestionable that this evil has risen to a great height, and that it involves some very serious social considerations. But, with all respect for opinions which we do not hold, we think it a mistake to cry for legislative interference in such a case. In the first place, we do not think it wise to exhibit a legislature which has always cared so little for the amusements of the people, in repressive action only. If it had been an educational legislature, considerate of the popular enjoyments, and sincerely desirous to advance and extend them during as long a period as it has been exactly the reverse, the question might assume a different shape; though, even then, we should greatly doubt whether the same notion were not a shifting of the real responsibility. In the second place, although it is very edifying to have honorable members, and right honorable members, and honorable and learned members, and what not, holding forth in their places upon what is right, and what is wrong, and what is true, and what is false – among the people – we have that audacity in us that we do not admire the present Parliamentary standard and balance of such questions; and we believe that if those be not scrupulously just, Parliament cannot invest itself with much moral authority. Surely the whole country knows that certain chivalrous public Prophets have been, for a pretty long time past, advertising their Pick and Tip in all directions, pointing out the horse which was to make everybody's fortune! Surely we all know, howsoever our political opinions may differ, that more than one of them "casting his practised eye," exactly like the Prophet in the sporting paper, "on the broad surface of struggling society," has been possessed by the same "intense desire to hold up the lamp of light to all," and has solemnly known by the lamp of light that Black was the winning horse – until his Pick and Tip was purchased; when he suddenly began to think it might be White, or even Brown, or very possibly Grey. Surely, we all know, however reluctant we may be to admit it, that this has tainted and confused political honesty; that the Elections before us, and the whole Government of the country, are at present a great reckless Betting-shop, where the Prophets have pocketed their own predictions after playing fast and loose with their patrons as long as they could; and where, casting their practised eyes over things in general, they are now backing anything and everything for a chance of winning!

No. If the legislature took the subject in hand it would make a virtuous demonstration, we have no doubt, but it would not present an edifying spectacle. Parents and employers must do more for themselves. Every man should know something of the habits and frequentings of those who are placed under him; and should know much, when a new class of temptation thus presents itself. Apprentices are, by the terms of their indentures, punishable for gaming; it would do a world of good, to get a few score of that class of noble sportsmen convicted before magistrates, and shut up in the House of Correction, to Pick a little oakum, and Tip a little gruel into their silly stomachs. Betting clerks, and betting servants of all grades, once detected after a grave warning, should be firmly dismissed. There are plenty of industrious and steady young men to supply their places. The police should receive instructions by no means to overlook any gentleman of established bad reputation – whether "wanted" or not – who is to be found connected with a Betting-shop. It is our belief that several eminent characters could be so discovered. These precautions; always supposing parents and employers resolute to discharge their own duties instead of vaguely delegating them to a legislature they have no reliance on; would probably be sufficient. Some fools who are under no control, will always be found wandering away to ruin; but, the greater part of that extensive department of the commonalty *are* under some control, and the great need is, that it be better exercised.

The Spirit Business

First published in *Household Words*, 7 May 1853, from which this text is reproduced.

Persons of quality, and others, who visit the various "gifted media" now in London, or receive those supernaturally endowed ladies at their own houses, may be glad to hear how the spirit business has been doing in America. Two numbers of *The Spiritual Telegraph*[1], a newspaper published in New York, and "devoted to the illustration of spiritual intercourse," having fallen into our hands, we are happy to have some means from head-quarters of gratifying the laudable curiosity of these philosophical inquirers.

In the first place, it is gratifying to know that the second volume of that admirable publication, *The Shekinah*,[2] was advertised last Fall, containing "Psychometrical sketches of living characters given by a lady while in the waking state, who derives her impressions by holding a letter from the unknown person against her forehead." To this remarkable journal, "several distinguished minds in Europe are expected to contribute occasionally." It appears, however, scarcely to meet with sufficient terrestrial circulation; the editor being under the necessity of inquiring in capitals, "SHALL IT HAVE A PATRONAGE WORTHY OF ITS OBJECTS AND ITS CHARACTER?" We also observe with pleasure the publication of a fourth edition of "The Pilgrimage of Thomas Paine[3] and others, to the sixth circle in the Spirit World, by the Reverend Charles Hammond, Medium, written by the spirit of Thomas Paine without Volition on the part of the medium."

Also the following publications: "A Chart exhibiting an outline of progressive history, and approaching destiny of the race. A. J. D. Can be sent by mail." "The Philosophy of Spiritual Intercourse. Light from the Spirit World, comprising a Series of Articles on the Condition of Spirits and the development of mind in the Rudimental and Second Spheres; being written by the controul of Spirits." We are further indebted to a gentleman – we presume a mortal – of the name of Coggshall, for "The Signs of the Times, comprising a History of the Spirit Rappings in Cincinnati and other places." The Reverend Adin Ballou has been so obliging as to favour the world with his "Spirit Manifestations;" and a Medium, of the gentle name of Ambler, has produced the "Spiritual Teacher," from the dictation of a little knot of choice spirits of the sixth circle.

As a counterpoise to the satisfaction these spiritual literary announcements are calculated to inspire, we regret to perceive that some men have been at their old work of blinking at the light. This melancholy fact is made known to us through the "medium" of a paragraph, headed "BEHIND THE DOOR;" from which we learn with indignation that "a good Presbyterian brother in Newtown, Conn.": with that want of moral courage which is unhappily characteristic of the man, is accustomed to read *The Telegraph* in that furtive situation, bringing down upon himself the terrible apostrophe, "Read on, brother, until thy spirit shall receive strength sufficient to enable thee to crawl from thy hiding-place." On the other hand it is a consolation to know that "we have, out in Ohio, a little girl who writes fonography[4] interspersed with celestial characters." We have also "Mrs. S., a gifted friend," who writes, "I may at some future time draw upon the storehouse of memory for some Spiritual facts which have long slumbered there; fearing the scoff of the skeptic has hitherto kept me silent, but I believe there is a time now dawning upon us when we shall no longer hide the light given us, under a bushel." This gifted lady is supplied with a number of papers, but has none that she greets so cordially as *The Telegraph*, which is "loaned" her by a friend. "It ministers," says she, modestly, "to my spiritual and higher nature which craves a kindred aliment, and which, in past years, has nearly starved on the husks and verbiage dressed up by the sensuous and unbelieving in spiritual illumination." Mrs. Fish and the Misses Fox[5] were, at the date of these advices, to be heard of, we rejoice to state, at number seventy-eight, West Twenty-Sixth Street, where those estimable ladies "entertain strangers" on three evenings in the week from eight to ten. The enlarged liberality of Mr. Partridge, who addressed THE NEW YORK CONFERENCE FOR THE INVESTIGATION OF SPIRITUAL PHENOMENA, is worthy of all imitation, and proves him to be game indeed. Mr. P. was of opinion, when last heard of, that "the Devil should have his due," and that if he (the Devil) were found engaged in the spirit business, then let them "stretch forth the right hand of fellowship, and let joy resound through earth and heaven at the conversion of the Prince of Evil."

The following explicit and important communications had been received from spirits – the exalted and improving character of the announcements, evidently being a long way beyond mortality, and requiring special spiritual revelation.

FROM A SPIRIT, BY NAME JOHN COLLINSWORTH

"Who can say it, 'I am free as God made'? My dear friends, it is sometimes very difficult to express our sentiments in words. What matter who speak so long as you feel a witness in your own souls, that what is said, is said to benefit mankind and advance the truth. Why, my dear friends, my soul is filled with love towards you. I daily lift my desires to the Divine Giver of every good thing for your welfare and eternal happiness in the life to come. I will strive to watch over you as a circle."

FROM A SPIRIT, BY NAME ANN BILLINGS

"I have long taken a deep interest in the progress of this circle. I have called a circle together, and now imagine your guardian spirits assembled in a circle encircling your circle, willing and anxious to gratify your every wish; you must suspend your judgment and wait patiently for further developments, which will set believers right."

FROM AN ANONYMOUS SPIRIT, PRESUMED TO BE OF THE QUAKER PERSUASION

"Dear John, it is a pleasure to address thee now and then, after a lapse of many years. This new mode of conversing is no less interesting to thy mother than to thee. It greatly adds to the enjoyment and happiness of thy friends here to see thee happy, looking forward with composure to the change from one sphere to another."

FROM A SPIRIT, BY NAME LORENZO DOW

"I will add a little to what has already been said. Keep calm – let skeptics scoff – bigots rave – the press ridicule – keep an eye on the pulpit, there will be a mighty onslaught by the clergy soon; hew straight, keep cool, and welcome them into your ranks."

Upon the general question we observe that an eminent man with the singular title of Bro Hewitt attended a meeting at Boston, where there was some speaking from, or through, the mediums, which, "although not according to the common rules or order of speaking, was nevertheless of an interesting character in its thought, as well as in the novelty of its method. Two young men were the speaking mediums alluded to, who have never spoken in public before they were thus moved to do it." Bro Hewitt does not mention, that the spirits began this particular revelation with the startling and novel declaration that they were unaccustomed to public speaking; but it appears probable. The spirits were assailed (as was only to be expected), by the Boston press, and Bro Hewitt is of opinion that "such a tissue of falsehood, slang, and abuse, was never before expressed in so eminently laconic and classic a style since Protestant Methodism began with S. F. Norris." At the Boston Melodeon,[6] a large audience had assembled to hear Theodore Parker; but in lieu of that inspired person, "the desk was supplied by the celebrated Andrew Jackson Davis." One lady was much surprised to find this illustrious individual so young; he being only twenty-five and having a higher forehead than Mr. Sunderland,[7] the mesmeriser; but wearing "a similarly savage-looking beard and moustache." His text was "All the World's a Stage"; and he merely "wished to propose a new philosophy, which, unlike the theology of the Testaments should be free from inconsistencies, and tend to perfect harmony." Our game friend Partridge had remarked in solemn conference that "some seek to protect themselves from conflicting communications, by refusing to hearken to any spirit unless he claims to hail from the sixth or seventh sphere." Mr. Thomas Hutching, "a venerable Peracher," whatever that may be, "of forty years' standing," had been "overwhelmed" by the rapping medium, Mrs. Fish; and the venerable Peracher had not recovered when last heard of. The Reverend Charles Hammond, medium, had communicated the following important facts: "I. All spirits are good and not evil. There is no evil spirit on earth or in this sphere. God nor nature never made an evil spirit. II. There is no condition of spirit lower than the rudimental. Earth has the lowest order, and the darkest sphere. Hell is not a correct word to convey the proper idea of the comparative condition of spirits in different circles. And III. A circle is not a space but a development," – which piece of information we particularly recommend to the reader's consideration as likely to do him good.

We find that our American friends, with that familiar nomenclature which is not uncommon among them, have agreed to designate one branch of the spiritual proceedings as "Tippings." We did at first suppose this expressive word to be of English growth, and to refer to the preliminary "tipping" of the medium, which is found to be indispensable to the entertainments on this side of the Atlantic. We have discovered, however, that it denotes the spiritual movements of the tables and chairs, and of a mysterious piece of furniture called a "stand," which appears to be in every apartment. The word has passed into current use, insomuch that one correspondent writes: "The other evening, as myself and a party of friends were entertaining ourselves with the tippings," – and so on.

And now for a few individual cases of spiritual manifestation: –

There was a horrible medium down in Philadelphia, who recorded of herself, "Whenever I am passive, day or night, my hand writes." This appalling author came out under the following circumstances: – "A pencil and paper were lying on the table. The pencil came into my hand; my fingers were clenched on it! An unseen iron grasp compressed the tendons of my arms – my hand was flung violently forward on the paper, and I wrote meaning sentences without any intention, or knowing what they were to be." The same prolific person presently inquires, "Is this Insanity?" To which we take the liberty of replying, that we rather think it is.

R. B. Barker had been subject to a good deal of "telegraphing by the spirits." The death of U. J. had been predicted to him, and a fluttering of ethereal creatures, resembling pigeons, had taken place in his bedroom. After this supernatural poultry took flight, U. J. died. Other circumstances had occurred to R. B. Barker, "which he might relate," but which were "of such a nature as to preclude exposure" at that present writing.

D. J. Mandell had had the following experience. "I was invited to conduct a sitting at a neighbour's, with reference to affording an opportunity to a young clergyman to witness something of the manifestations. A name was here spelled out which none of the family recognised, and of which the said young clergyman at first denied any knowledge. I called for a message, and this was given: 'Believe this is spiritual.' Thinking it singular that no relative of the family, and especially that no one whom the young minister could remember, should announce himself, I inquired if the spirit of any of his friends were present. Almost before the response could be given, he spoke sharply, and said, 'I wish not to hear from any of my friends through any such means.' I found there was considerable pride and prejudice aboard the little man, and pretty strongly suspected that there was more in the announcement of that name than he was willing to acknowledge. After considerable conversation, direct and indirect, he confessed to a knowledge of the person whose name had been given as aforesaid: it was that of a black barber who had died some time before, and who, during his life-time, had resided in the clergyman's native village. The latter had been well acquainted with him, but despised him; and, from what I could make out of the manifestation, take it all in all, I judged that his spiritual friends were present to communicate with him; but perceiving his strong repugnance to hear from his friends through the tippings, they had resolved to shock his self-complacency by putting forward the very one whom he detested most."

The following state, described by a gentleman who withholds his name, appears to us to indicate a condition, as to spirits, which is within the experience of many persons. To point our meaning we italicise a few words:

"On the evening of the fifteenth instant, at the residence of Dr. Hallock, I was directed through the raps (a medium being present), to go to the residence of Dr. Gray, and sit in a circle to be convened for the purpose of seeing an exhibition of spirit lights. As I had no other invitation I felt exceeding delicate about complying. I mentioned this to the power that was giving the direction, and added, as an additional excuse, *that my attendance there on an occasion long gone by had left an unfavourable impression.* Still I was directed to go. On arriving at Dr. Gray's, I explained the occasion of my presence, and was admitted to the circle. Being desirous that my influence should not mar the harmony of the company, I put forth a strong effort of the will to induce a passiveness in my nervous system; and, in order that I might not be deceived as to my success, *resigned myself to sleep.* .... *I suppose I was unconscious for thirty minutes.*" After this, the seer had a vision of stalks and leaves, "a large species of fruit, somewhat resembling a pine-apple," and "a nebulous column, somewhat resembling the milky way," which nothing but spirits could account for, and from which nothing but soda-water, or time, is likely to have recovered him. We believe this kind of manifestation is usually followed by a severe headache next morning, attended by some degree of thirst.

A spiritualist residing at Troy, communicates the case of a lady, which appears to us to be of a nature closely resembling the last. "A lady − the wife of a certain officer in a Presbyterian church − who is a partial believer in spiritual manifestations, *was so far under the influence of spirits,* that her hands were moved, and made to perform some very singular gestures. This new mode of doing business was not very pleasing to the lady, and caused her to be a little frightened. One day, seeing their clergyman, Dr. — passing, the latter was invited in to witness the phenomena, and to render assistance, if possible. As the Doctor entered the room, the lady shook hands with him cordially, but found it easier to commence than to leave off. After shaking hands for some time, the hands commenced patting the Doctor on the shoulders, head, and ears, to the confusion of both parties. The Doctor then advised that the hands be immersed in cold water, with a view to disengage the electricity, of which he said the lady was overcharged. When the water was procured the motion of the hands became more violent, and manifested a repugnance to the water-cure. With a little assistance, however, the hands were finally immersed, when they at once commenced throwing the water so plentifully over the Doctor's head and shoulders, that he was compelled to beat a hasty retreat, carrying with him the marks of water-baptism at spirit hands. It is hoped that the Doctor, after this experience in the Spiritual electrical-fountain-bath will have a little more charity for his rapping sisters, as he terms them, and not again assail them from the pulpit as void of common sense."

It certainly is very extraordinary that, with such lights as these, any men can assail their rapping and tipping brothers and sisters, from any sort of pulpit, as void of common sense. The spirit business cannot fail to be regarded by all dispassionate persons as the last great triumph of common sense.

These extracts, which we might extend through several pages, will quite dispose of the objection that there is any folly or stupidity among the patrons of the spirit business. As a proof that they are equally free from self-conceit, and that that little weakness in human nature has nothing to do with the success of the trade, and is not at all consulted by the dealers, we will come home to England for a concluding testimony borne by Mr. Robert Owen.[8] This gentleman, in a conversation with the spirits of his deceased wife and youngest daughter, inquired what object they had in view in favouring him with their company? "Answer. To reform the world. Question. Can *I* materially promote this object? Answer. You can assist in promoting it. Question. Shall *I* be aided by the spirits to enable me to succeed? Answer. Yes. Question. Shall *I* devote the remainder of my life to this mission? Answer. Yes. Question. Shall *I* hold a public meeting to announce to the world these proceedings; or shall they be made known through the British Parliament? Answer. Through the British Parliament. Question. Shall *I* also apply for an investigation of this subject to the Congress of the United States? Answer. Yes." This naturally brought up the spirit of Benjamin Franklin, of whom Mr. Owen inquired, "Have *I* been assisted in my writings for the public, by any particular spirit? Answer. Yes. Question. What spirit? Answer. G O D. (This reply was made in such a manner as to create a peculiarly awful impression on those present.) Question. Shall *I* continue to be assisted by the same spirit? Answer. Yes."

We have inquired of Dr. Conolly,[9] and are informed that there are several philosophers now resident at Hanwell, Middlesex, and also in Saint George's Fields, Southwark, who, without any tippings or rappings, find themselves similarly inspired. But those learned prophets cry aloud in their wards, and no man regardeth them; which brings us to the painful conclusion, that in the Spirit business, as in most other trades, there are some bankruptcies.

The Noble Savage

First published in *Household Words*, 11 June 1853, and subsequently in *Reprinted Pieces* from which this text is taken. On the background to the exhibiting 'savages' in Britain in the nineteenth century, see Altick, *The Shows of London*.

To come to the point at once, I beg to say that I have not the least belief in the Noble Savage. I consider him a prodigious nuisance, and an enormous superstition. His calling rum fire-water, and me a pale face, wholly fail to reconcile me to him. I don't care what he calls me. I call him a savage, and I call a savage a something highly desirable to be civilised off the face of the earth. I think a mere gent (which I take to be the lowest form of civilisation) better than a howling, whistling, clucking, stamping, jumping, tearing savage. It is all one to me, whether he sticks a fish-bone through his visage, or bits of trees through the lobes of his ears, or bird's feathers in his head; whether he flattens his hair between two boards, or spreads his nose over the breadth of his face, or drags his lower lip down by great weights, or blackens his teeth, or knocks them out, or paints one cheek red and the other blue, or tattoos himself, or oils himself, or rubs his body with fat, or crimps it with knives. Yielding to whichsoever of these agreeable eccentricities, he is a savage – cruel, false, thievish, murderous; addicted more or less to grease, entrails, and beastly customs; a wild animal with the questionable gift of boasting; a conceited, tiresome, bloodthirsty, mono-tonous humbug.

Yet it is extraordinary to observe how some people will talk about him, as they talk about the good old times; how they will regret his disappearance, in the course of this world's development, from such and such lands where his absence is a blessed relief and an indispensable preparation for the sowing of the very first seeds of any influence that can exalt humanity; how, even with the evidence of himself before them, they will either be determined to believe, or will suffer themselves to be persuaded into believing, that he is something which their five senses tell them he is not.

There was Mr. Catlin, some few years ago, with his Ojibbeway Indians.[1] Mr. Catlin was an energetic, earnest man, who had lived among more tribes of Indians than I need reckon up here, and who had written a picturesque and glowing book about them. With his party of Indians squatting and spitting on the table before him, or dancing their miserable jigs after their own dreary manner, he called, in all good faith, upon his civilised audience to take notice of their symmetry and grace, their perfect limbs, and the exquisite expression of their pantomine; and his civilised audience, in all good faith, complied and admired. Whereas, as mere animals, they were wretched creatures, very low in the scale and very poorly formed; and as men and women possessing any power of truthful dramatic expression by means of action, they were no better than the chorus at an Italian Opera in England – and would have been worse if such a thing were possible.

Mine are no new views of the noble savage. The greatest writers on natural history found him out long ago. BUFFON[2] knew what he was, and showed why he is the sulky tyrant that he is to his women, and how it happens (Heaven be praised!) that his race is spare in numbers. For evidence of the quality of his moral nature, pass himself for a moment and refer to his "faithful dog." Has he ever improved a dog, or attached a dog, since his nobility first ran wild in woods, and was brought down (at a very long shot) by POPE?[3] Or does the animal that is the friend of man always degenerate in his low society?

It is not the miserable nature of the noble savage that is the new thing; it is the whimpering over him with maudlin admiration, and the affecting to regret him, and the drawing of any comparison of advantage between the blemishes of civilisation and the tenor of his swinish life. There may have been a change now and then in those diseased absurdities, but there is none in him.

Think of the Bushmen.[4] Think of the two men and the two women who have been exhibited about England for some years. Are the majority of persons – who remember the horrid little leader of that party in his festering bundle of hides, with his filth and his antipathy to water, and his straddled legs, and his odious eyes shaded by his brutal hand, and his cry of "Qu-u-u-u-aaa!" (Bosjesman for something desperately insulting, I have no doubt) – conscious of an affectionate yearning towards that noble savage, or is it idiosyncratic in me to abhor, detest, abominate, and abjure him? I have no reserve on this subject, and will frankly state that, setting aside that stage of the entertainment when he counterfeited the death of some creature he had shot, by laying his head on his hand and shaking his left leg – at which time I think it would have been justifiable homicide to slay him – I have never seen that group sleeping, smoking, and expectorating round their brazier, but I have sincerely desired that something might happen to the charcoal smouldering therein, which would cause the immediate suffocation of the whole of the noble strangers.

There is at present a party of Zulu Kaffirs exhibiting at the St. George's Gallery, Hyde Park Corner, London.[5] These noble savages are represented in a most agreeable manner; they are seen in an elegant theatre, fitted with appropriate scenery of great beauty, and they are described in a very sensible and unpretending lecture, delivered with a modesty which is quite a pattern to all similar exponents. Though extremely ugly, they are much better shaped than such of their predecessors as I have referred to; and they are rather picturesque to the eye, though far from odoriferous to the nose. What a visitor left to his own interpretings and imaginings might suppose these noblemen to be about, when they give vent to that pantomimic expression which is quite settled to be the natural gift of the noble savage, I cannot possibly conceive; for it is so much too luminous for my personal civilisation that it conveys no idea to my mind beyond a general stamping, ramping, and raving, remarkable (as everything in savage life is) for its dire uniformity. But let us – with the interpreter's assistance, of which I for one stand so much in need – see what the noble savage does in Zulu Kaffirland.

The noble savage sets a king to reign over him, to whom he submits his life and limbs without a murmur or question, and whose whole life is passed chin deep in a lake of blood; but who, after killing incessantly, is in his turn killed by his relations and friends, the moment a grey hair appears on his head. All the noble savage's wars with his fellow-savages (and he takes no pleasure in anything else) are wars of extermination – which is the best thing I know of him, and the most comfortable to my mind when I look at him. He has no moral feelings of any kind, sort, or description; and his "mission" may be summed up as simply diabolical.

The ceremonies with which he faintly diversifies his life are, of course, of a kindred nature. If he wants a wife he appears before the kennel of the gentleman whom he has selected for his father-in-law, attended by a party of male friends of a very strong flavour, who screech and whistle and stamp an offer of so many cows for the young lady's hand. The chosen father-in-law – also supported by a high-flavoured party of male friends – screeches, whistles, and yells (being seated on the ground, he can't stamp) that there never was such a daughter in the market as his daughter, and that he must have six more cows. The son-in-law and his select circle of backers screech, whistle, stamp, and yell in reply, that they will give three more cows. The father-in-law (an old deluder, overpaid at the beginning) accepts four, and rises to bind the bargain. The whole party, the young lady included, then falling into epileptic convulsions, and screeching, whistling, stamping, and yelling together – and nobody taking any notice of the young lady (whose charms are not to be thought of without a shudder) – the noble savage is considered married, and his friends make demoniacal leaps at him by way of congratulation.

When the noble savage finds himself a little unwell, and mentions the circumstance to his friends, it is immediately perceived that he is under the influence of witchcraft. A learned personage, called an Imyanger or Witch Doctor, is immediately sent for to Nooker the Umtargartie, or smell out the witch. The male inhabitants of the kraal being seated on the ground, the learned doctor, got up like a grizzly bear, appears, and administers a dance of a most terrific nature, during the exhibition of which remedy he incessantly gnashes his teeth, and howls: – "I am the original physician to Nooker the Umtargartie. Yow yow yow! No connexion with any other establishment. Till till till! All other Umtargarties are feigned Umtargarties, Boroo Boroo! but I perceive here a genuine and real Umtargartie, Hoosh Hoosh Hoosh! in whose blood I, the original Imyanger and Nookerer, Blizzerum Boo! will wash these bear's claws of mine. O yow yow yow!" All this time the learned physician is looking out among the attentive faces for some unfortunate man who owes him a cow, or who has given him any small offence, or against whom, without offence, he has conceived a spite. Him he never fails to Nooker as the Umtargartie, and he is instantly killed. In the absence of such an individual, the usual practice is to Nooker the quietest and most gentlemanly person in company. But the nookering is invariably followed on the spot by the butchering.

Some of the noble savages in whom Mr. Catlin was so strongly interested, and the diminution of whose numbers, by rum and small-pox, greatly affected him, had a custom not unlike this, though much more appalling and disgusting in its odious details.

The women being at work in the fields, hoeing the Indian corn, and the noble savage being asleep in the shade, the chief has sometimes the condescension to come forth, and lighten the labour by looking at it. On these occasions, he seats himself in his own savage chair, and is attended by his shield-bearer: who holds over his head a shield of cowhide – in shape like an immense mussel shell – fearfully and wonderfully, after the manner of a theatrical supernumerary. But lest the great man should forget his greatness in the contemplation of the humble works of agriculture, there suddenly rushes in a poet, retained for the purpose, called a Praiser. This literary gentleman wears a leopard's head over his own, and a dress of tigers' tails; he has the appearance of having come express on his hind legs from the Zoological Gardens; and he incontinently strikes up the chief's praises, plunging and tearing all the while. There is a frantic wickedness in this brute's manner of worrying the air, and gnashing out, "O what a delightful chief he is! O what a delicious quantity of blood he sheds! O how majestically he laps it up! O how charmingly cruel he is! O how he tears the flesh of his enemies and crunches the bones! O how like the tiger and the leopard and the wolf and the bear he is! O, row row row row, how fond I am of him!" which might tempt the Society of Friends to charge at a hand-gallop into the Swartz-Kop location and exterminate the whole kraal.

When war is afoot among the noble savages – which is always – the chief holds a council to ascertain whether it is the opinion of his brothers and friends in general that the enemy shall be exterminated. On this occasion, after the performance of an Umsebeuza, or war song, – which is exactly like all the other songs, – the chief makes a speech to his brothers and friends, arranged in single file. No particular order is observed during the delivery of this address, but every gentleman who finds himself excited by the subject, instead of crying "Hear, hear!" as is the custom with us, darts from the rank and tramples out the life, or crushes the skull, or mashes the face, or scoops out the eyes, or breaks the limbs, or performs a whirlwind of atrocities on the body, of an imaginary enemy. Several gentlemen becoming thus excited at once, and pounding away without the least regard to the orator, that illustrious person is rather in the position of an orator in an Irish House of Commons. But several of these scenes of savage life bear a strong generic resemblance to an Irish election, and I think would be extremely well received and understood at Cork.

In all these ceremonies the noble savage holds forth to the utmost possible extent about himself; from which (to turn him to some civilised account) we may learn, I think, that as egotism is one of the most offensive and contemptible littlenesses a civilised man can exhibit, so it is really incompatible with the interchange of ideas; inasmuch as if we all talked about ourselves we should soon have no listeners, and must be all yelling and screeching at once on our own separate accounts: making society hideous. It is my opinion that if we retained in us anything of the noble savage, we could not get rid of it too soon. But the fact is clearly otherwise. Upon the wife and dowry question, substituting coin for cows, we have assuredly nothing of the Zulu Kaffir left. The endurance of despotism is one great distinguishing mark of a savage always. The improving world has quite got the better of that too. In like manner, Paris is a civilised city, and the Théâtre Français a highly civilised theatre; and we shall never hear, and never have heard in these later days (of course) of the Praiser *there*. No, no, civilised poets have better work to do. As to Nookering Umtargarties, there are no pretended Umtargarties in Europe, and no European powers to Nooker them; that would be mere spydom, subordination, small malice, superstition, and false pretence. And as to private Umtargarties are we not in the year eighteen hundred and fifty-three, with spirits rapping at our doors?

To conclude as I began. My position is, that if we have anything to learn from the Noble Savage, it is what to avoid. His virtues are a fable; his happiness is a delusion; his nobility, nonsense. We have no greater justification for being cruel to the miserable object, than for being cruel to a WILLIAM SHAKESPEARE or an ISAAC NEWTON; but he passes away before an immeasurably better and higher power than ever ran wild in any earthly woods, and the world will be all the better when his place knows him no more.

Frauds on the Fairies

First published in *Household Words*, 1 October 1853, from which this text is reproduced. Dickens wrote to Wills on 27 July 1853, with an idea for an article: 'Half playfully and half seriously, I mean to protest most strongly against alteration – for any purpose of the beautiful little stories which are so tenderly and humanly useful to us in these times when the world is too much with us early and late; and then to re-write Cinderella according to Total-Abstinence, Peace Society, and Bloomer principles,' social movements which advocated teetotalism, pacifism and feminism, respectively. Once the article – which he himself thought 'ADMIR-ABLE. Both merry and wise' – was completed, he wrote to Miss Burdett Coutts on 18 September 1853: '*Frauds on the Fairies*, I think will amuse you, and enlist you on my side – which is for a little more fancy among children and a little less fact.' Dickens had little tolerance for the Total Abstinence movement, and attacked it elsewhere in his journalism. See, for instance, 'Whole Hogs', *Household Words*, 23 August 1851, and 'The Great Baby', *Household Words*, 4 August 1855.

We may assume that we are not singular in entertaining a very great tenderness for the fairy literature of our childhood. What enchanted us then, and is captivating a million of young fancies now, has, at the same blessed time of life, enchanted vast hosts of men and women who have done their long day's work, and laid their grey heads down to rest. It would be hard to estimate the amount of gentleness and mercy that has made its way among us through these slight channels. Forbearance, courtesy, consideration for the poor and aged, kind treatment of animals, the love of nature, abhorrence of tyranny and brute force – many such good things have been first nourished in the child's heart by this powerful aid. It has greatly helped to keep us, in some sense, ever young, by preserving through our worldly ways one slender track not overgrown with weeds, where we may walk with children, sharing their delights.

In an utilitarian age, of all other times, it is a matter of grave importance that Fairy tales should be respected. Our English red tape is too magnificently red ever to be employed in the tying up of such trifles, but every one who has considered the subject knows full well that a nation without fancy, without some romance, never did, never can, never will, hold a great place under the sun. The theatre, having done its worst to destroy these admirable fictions – and having in a most exemplary manner destroyed itself, its artists, and its audiences, in that perversion of its duty – it becomes doubly important that the little books themselves, nurseries of fancy as they are, should be preserved. To preserve them in their usefulness, they must be as much preserved in their simplicity, and purity, and innocent extravagance, as if they were actual fact. Whosoever alters them to suit his own opinions, whatever they are, is guilty, to our thinking, of an act of presumption, and appropriates to himself what does not belong to him.

We have lately observed, with pain, the intrusion of a Whole Hog of unwieldy dimensions into the fairy flower garden. The rooting of the animal among the roses would in itself have awakened in us nothing but indignation; our pain arises from his being violently driven in by a man of genius, our own beloved friend, Mr. George Cruikshank.[1] That incomparable artist is, of all men, the last who should lay his exquisite hand on fairy text. In his own art he understands it so perfectly, and illustrates it so beautifully, so humorously, so wisely, that he should never lay down his etching needle to "edit" the Ogre, to whom with that little instrument he can render such extraordinary justice. But, to "editing" Ogres, and Hop-o'-my-thumbs, and their families, our dear moralist has in a rash moment taken, as a means of propagating the doctrines of Total Abstinence, Prohibition of the sale of spirituous liquors, Free Trade, and Popular Education. For the introduction of these topics, he has altered the text of a fairy story; and against his right to do any such thing we protest with all our might and main. Of his likewise altering it to advertise that excellent series of plates, "The Bottle," we say nothing more than that we foresee a new and improved edition of Goody Two Shoes, edited by E. Moses and Son; of the Dervish with the box of ointment, edited by Professor Holloway; and of Jack and the Beanstalk, edited by Mary Wedlake, the popular authoress of Do you bruise your oats yet.[2]

Now, it makes not the least differences to our objection whether we agree or disagree with our worthy friend, Mr. Cruikshank, in the opinions he interpolates upon an old fairy story. Whether good or bad in themselves, they are, in that relation, like the famous definition of a weed; a thing growing up in a wrong place. He had no greater moral justification in altering the harmless little books than we should have in altering his best etchings. If such a precedent were followed we must soon become disgusted with the old stories into which modern personages so obtruded themselves, and the stories themselves must soon be lost. With seven Blue Beards in the field, each coming at a gallop from his own platform mounted on a foaming hobby, a generation or two hence would not know which was which, and the great original Blue Beard would be confounded with the counterfeits. Imagine a Total abstinence edition of *Robinson Crusoe*, with the rum left out. Imagine a Peace edition, with the gunpowder left out, and the rum left in. Imagine a Vegetarian edition, with the goat's flesh left out. Imagine a Kentucky edition, to introduce a flogging of that 'tarnal old nigger Friday, twice a week. Imagine an Aborigines Protection Society edition, to deny the cannibalism and make Robinson embrace the amiable savages whenever they landed. Robinson Crusoe would be "edited" out of his island in a hundred years, and the island would be swallowed up in the editorial ocean.

Among the other learned professions we have now the Platform profession, chiefly exercised by a new and meritorious class of commercial travellers who go about to take the sense of meetings on various articles: some, of a very superior description: some, not quite so good. Let us write the story of Cinderella, "edited" by one of these gentlemen, doing a good stroke of business, and having a rather extensive mission.

Once upon a time, a rich man and his wife were the parents of a lovely daughter. She was a beautiful child, and became, at her own desire, a member of the Juvenile Bands of Hope when she was only four years of age. When this child was only nine years of age her mother died, and all the Juvenile Bands of Hope in her district – the Central district, number five hundred and twenty-seven – formed in a procession of two and two, amounting to fifteen hundred, and followed her to the grave, singing chorus Number forty-two, "O come," etc. This grave was outside the town, and under the direction of the Local Board of Health, which reported at certain stated intervals to the General Board of Health, Whitehall.

The motherless little girl was very sorrowful for the loss of her mother, and so was her father too, at first; but, after a year was over, he married again – a very cross widow lady, with two proud tyrannical daughters as cross as herself. He was aware that he could have made his marriage with this lady a civil process by simply making a declaration before a Registrar; but he was averse to this course on religious grounds, and, being a member of the Montgolfian persuasion,[3] was married according to the ceremonies of that respectable church by the Reverend Jared Jocks, who improved the occasion.

He did not live long with his disagreeable wife. Having been shamefully accustomed to shave with warm water instead of cold, which he ought to have used (see Medical Appendix B. and C.), his undermined constitution could not bear up against her temper, and he soon died. Then, this orphan was cruelly treated by her stepmother and the two daughters, and was forced to do the dirtiest of the kitchen work; to scour the saucepans, wash the dishes, and light the fires – which did not consume their own smoke, but emitted a dark vapour prejudicial to the bronchial tubes. The only warm place in the house where she was free from ill-treatment was the kitchen chimney-corner; and as she used to sit down there, among the cinders, when her work was done, the proud fine sisters gave her the name of Cinderella.

About this time, the King of the land, who never made war against anybody, and allowed everybody to make war against him – which was the reason why his subjects were the greatest manufacturers on earth, and always lived in security and peace – gave a great feast, which was to last two days. This splendid banquet was to consist entirely of artichokes and gruel; and from among those who were invited to it, and to hear the delightful speeches after dinner, the King's son was to choose a bride for himself. The proud fine sisters were invited, but nobody knew anything about poor Cinderella, and she was to stay at home.

She was so sweet-tempered, however, that she assisted the haughty creatures to dress, and bestowed her admirable taste upon them as freely as if they had been kind to her. Neither did she laugh when they broke seventeen stay-laces in dressing; for, although she wore no stays herself, being sufficiently acquainted with the anatomy of the human figure to be aware of the destructive effects of tight-lacing, she always reserved her opinions on that subject for the Regenerative Record (price three halfpence in a neat wrapper), which all good people take in, and to which she was a Contributor.

At length the wished-for moment arrived, and the proud fine sisters swept away to the feast and speeches, leaving Cinderella in the chimney-corner. But, she could always occupy her mind with the general question of the Ocean Penny Postage, and she had in her pocket an unread Oration on that subject, made by the well-known Orator, Nehemiah Nicks. She was lost in the fervid eloquence of that talented Apostle when she became aware of the presence of one of those female relatives which (it may not be generally known) it is not lawful for a man to marry. I allude to her grandmother.

"Why so solitary, my child?" said the old lady to Cinderella.

"Alas, grandmother," returned the poor girl, "my sisters have gone to the feast and speeches, and here sit I in the ashes, Cinderella!"

"Never," cried the old lady with animation, "shall one of the Band of Hope despair! Run into the garden, my dear, and fetch me an American Pumpkin! American, because in some parts of that independent country, there are prohibitory laws against the sale of alcoholic drinks in any form. Also; because America produced (among many great pumpkins) the glory of her sex, Mrs. Colonel Bloomer.[4] None but an American Pumpkin will do, my child."

Cinderella ran into the garden, and brought the largest American Pumpkin she could find. This virtuously democratic vegetable her grandmother immediately changed into a splendid coach. Then, she sent her for six mice from the mouse-trap, which she changed into prancing horses, free from the obnoxious and oppressive post-horse duty. Then, to the rat-trap in the stable for a rat, which she changed to a state-coachman, not amenable to the iniquitous assessed taxes. Then, to look behind a watering-pot for six lizards, which she changed into six footmen, each with a petition in his hand ready to present to the Prince, signed by fifty thousand persons, in favour of the early closing movement.

"But grandmother," said Cinderella, stopping in the midst of her delight, and looking at her clothes, "how can I go to the palace in these miserable rags?"

"Be not uneasy about that, my dear," returned her grandmother.

Upon which the old lady touched her with her wand, her rags disappeared, and she was beautifully dressed. Not in the present costume of the female sex, which has been proved to be at once grossly immodest and absurdly inconvenient, but in rich sky-blue satin pantaloons gathered at the ankle, a puce-coloured satin pelisse sprinkled with silver flowers, and a very broad Leghorn hat. The hat was chastely ornamented with a rainbow-coloured ribbon hanging in two bell-pulls down the back; the pantaloons were ormamented with a golden stripe; and the effect of the whole was unspeakably sensible, feminine, and retiring. Lastly, the old lady put on Cinderella's feet a pair of shoes made of glass: observing that but for the abolition of the duty on that article, it never could have been devoted to such a purpose; the effect of all such taxes being to cramp invention, and embarrass the producer, to the manifest injury of the consumer. When the old lady had made these wise remarks, she dismissed Cinderella to the feast and speeches, charging her by no means to remain after twelve o'clock at night.

The arrival of Cinderella at the Monster Gathering produced a great excitement. As a delegate from the United States had just moved that the King do take the chair, and as the motion had been seconded and carried unanimously, the King himself could not go forth to receive her. But His Royal Highness the Prince (who was to move the second resolution), went to the door to hand her from her carriage. This virtuous Prince, being completely covered from head to foot with Total Abstinence Medals, shone as if he were attired in complete armour; while the inspiring strains of the Peace Brass Band in the gallery (composed of the Lambkin Family, eighteen in number, who cannot be too much encouraged) awakened additional enthusiasm.

The King's son handed Cinderella to one of the reserved seats for pink tickets, on the platform, and fell in love with her immediately. His appetite deserted him; he scarcely tasted his artichokes, and merely trifled with his gruel. When the speeches began, and Cinderella, wrapped in the eloquence of the two inspired delegates who occupied the entire evening in speaking to the first Resolution, occasionally cried, "Hear, hear!" the sweetness of her voice completed her conquest of the Prince's heart. But, indeed the whole male portion of the assembly loved her – and doubtless would have done so, even if she had been less beautiful, in consequence of the contrast which her dress presented to the bold and ridiculous garments of the other ladies.

At a quarter before twelve the second inspired delegate having drunk all the water in the decanter, and fainted away, the King put the question, "That this meeting do now adjourn until to-morrow." Those who were of that opinion holding up their hands, and then those who were of the contrary, theirs, there appeared an immense majority in favour of the resolution, which was consequently carried. Cinderella got home in safety, and heard nothing all that night, or all next day, but the praises of the unknown lady with the sky-blue satin pantaloons.

When the time for the feast and speeches came round again, the cross stepmother and the proud fine daughters went out in good time to secure their places. As soon as they were gone, Cinderella's grandmother returned and changed her as before. Amid a blast of welcome from the Lambkin family, she was again handed to the pink seat on the platform by His Royal Highness.

This gifted Prince was a powerful speaker, and had the evening before him. He rose at precisely ten minutes before eight, and was greeted with tumultuous cheers and waving of handkerchiefs. When the excitement had in some degree subsided, he proceeded to address the meeting: who were never tired of listening to speeches, as no good people ever are. He held them enthralled for four hours and a quarter. Cinderella forgot the time, and hurried away so when she heard the first stroke of twelve, that her beautiful dress changed back to her old rags at the door, and she left one of her glass shoes behind. The Prince took it up, and vowed – that is, made a declaration before a magistrate; for he objected on principle to the multiplying of oaths – that he would only marry the charming creature to whom that shoe belonged.

He accordingly caused an advertisement to that effect to be inserted in all the newspapers; for, the advertisement duty, an impost most unjust in principle and most unfair in operation, did not exist in that country; neither was the stamp on newspapers known in that land – which had as many newspapers as the United States, and got as much good out of them. Innumerable ladies answered the advertisement and pretended that the shoe was theirs; but, every one of them was unable to get her foot into it. The proud fine sisters answered it, and tried their feet with no greater success. Then, Cinderella, who had answered it too, came forward amidst their scornful jeers, and the shoe slipped on in a moment. It is a remarkable tribute to the improved and sensible fashion of the dress her grandmother had given her, that if she had not worn it the Prince would probably never have seen her feet.

The marriage was solemnised with great rejoicing. When the honeymoon was over, the King retired from public life, and was succeeded by the Prince. Cinderella, being now a queen, applied herself to the government of the country on enlightened, liberal, and free principles. All the people who ate anything she did not eat, or who drank anything she did not drink, were imprisoned for life. All the newspaper offices from which any doctrine proceeded that was not her doctrine, were burnt down. All the public speakers proved to demonstration that if there were any individual on the face of the earth who differed from them in anything, that individual was a designing ruffian and an abandoned monster. She also threw open the right of voting, and of being elected to public offices, and of making the laws, to the whole of her sex; who thus came to be always gloriously occupied with public life and whom nobody dared to love. And they all lived happily ever afterwards.

Frauds on the Fairies once permitted, we see little reason why they may not come to this, and great reason why they may. The Vicar of Wakefield was wisest when he was tired of being always wise.[5] The world is too much with us, early and late.[6] Leave this precious old escape from it, alone.

Gaslight Fairies

First published in *Household Words*, 10 February 1855, from which this text is reproduced.

Fancy an order for five-and-thirty Fairies! Imagine a mortal in a loose-sleeved great coat, with the mud of London streets upon his legs, commercially ordering, in the common-place, raw, foggy forenoon, "five-and-thirty more Fairies"! Yet I, the writer, heard the order given. "Mr. Vernon, let me have five-and-thirty more Fairies to-morrow morning – and take care they are good ones."

Where was it that, towards the close of the year one thousand eight hundred and fifty-four, on a dark December morning, I overheard this astonishing commission given to Mr. Vernon, and by Mr. Vernon accepted without a word of remonstrance and entered in a note-book? It was in a dark, deep gulf of a place, hazy with fog – at the bottom of a sort of immense well without any water in it; remote crevices and chinks of daylight faintly visible on the upper rim; dusty palls enveloping the sides; gas flaring at my feet; hammers going, in invisible workshops; groups of people hanging about, trying to keep their toes and fingers warm, what time their noses were dimly seen through the smoke of their own breath. It was in the strange conventional world where the visible people only, never advance; where the unseen painter learns and changes; where the unseen tailor learns and changes; where the unseen mechanist adapts to his purpose the striding ingenuity of the age; where the electric light comes, in a box that is carried under a man's arm; but, where the visible flesh and blood is so persistent in one routine that, from the waiting-woman's apron-pockets (with her hands in them), upward to the smallest retail article in the "business" of mad Lear with straws in his wig, and downward to the last scene but one of the panto-mime, where, for about one hundred years last past, all the characters have entered groping, in exactly the same way, in identically the same places, under precisely the same circumstances, and without the smallest reason – I say, it was in that strange world where the visible population have so completely settled their so-potent art, that when I pay my money at the door I know beforehand everything than can possibly happen to me, inside. It was in the Theatre, that I heard this order given for five-and-thirty Fairies.

And hereby hangs a recollection, not out of place, though not of a Fairy. Once, on just such another December morning, I stood on the same dusty boards, in the same raw atmosphere, intent upon a pantomine-rehearsal. A massive giant's castle arose before me, and the giant's body-guard marched in to comic music; twenty grotesque creatures, with little arms and legs, and enormous faces moulded into twenty varieties of ridiculous leer. One of these faces in particular – an absurdly radiant face, with a wink upon it, and its tongue in its cheek – elicited much approving notice from the authorities, and a ready laugh from the orchestra, and was, for a full half minute, a special success. But, it happened that the wearer of the beaming visage carried a banner; and, not to turn a banner as a procession moves, so as always to keep its decorated side towards the audience, is one of the deadliest sins a banner-bearer can commit. This radiant goblin, being half-blinded by his mask, and further disconcerted by partial suffocation, three distinct times omitted the first duty of man, and petrified us by displaying, with the greatest ostentation, mere sackcloth and timber, instead of the giant's armorial bearings. To crown which offence he couldn't hear when he was called to, but trotted about in his richest manner, unconscious of threats and imprecations. Suddenly, a terrible voice was heard above the music, crying, "Stop!" Dead silence, and we became aware of Jove in the boxes. "Hatchway," cried Jove to the director, "who is that man? Show me that man." Hereupon Hatchway (who had a wooden leg), vigorously apostrophising the defaulter as an "old beast," stumped straight up to the body-guard now in line before the castle, and taking the radiant countenance by the nose, lifted it up as if it were a saucepan-lid, and disclosed below, the features of a bald, superannuated, aged person, very much in want of shaving, who looked in the forlornest way at the spectators, while the large face aslant on the top of his head mocked him. "What! It's *you*, is it?" said Hatchway, with dire contempt. "I thought it was you." "I knew it was that man!" cried Jove. "I told you yesterday, Hatchway, he was not fit for it. Take him away, and bring another!" He was ejected with every mark of ignominy, and the inconstant mask was just as funny on another man's shoulders immediately afterwards. To the present day, I never see a very comic pantomime-mask but I wonder whether this wretched old man can possibly have got behind it; and I never think of him as dead and buried (which is far more likely), but I make that absurd countenance a part of his mortality, and picture it to myself as gone the way of all the winks in the world.

Five-and-thirty more Fairies, and let them be good ones. I saw them next day. They ranged from an anxious woman of ten, learned in the prices of victual and fuel, up to a conceited young lady of five times that age, who always persisted in standing on one leg longer than was necessary, with the determination (as I was informed), "to make a Part of it." This Fairy was of long theatrical descent – centuries, I believe – and had never had an ancestor who was entrusted to communicate one word to a British audience. Yet, the whole race had lived and died with the fixed idea of "making a Part of it"; and she, the last of the line, was still unchangeably resolved to go down on one leg to posterity. Her father had fallen a victim to the family ambition; having become in course of time so extremely difficult to "get off," as a villager, seaman, smuggler, or what not, that it was at length considered unsafe to allow him to "go on." Consequently, those neat confidences with the public in which he had displayed the very acmé of his art – usually consisting of an explanatory tear, or an arch hint in dumb show of his own personal determination to perish in the attempt then on foot – were regarded as superfluous, and came to be dispensed with, exactly at the crisis when he himself foresaw that he would "be put into Parts" shortly. I had the pleasure of recognising in the character of an Evil Spirit of the Marsh, overcome by this lady with one (as I should else have considered purposeless) poke of a javelin, an actor whom I had formerly encountered in the provinces under circumstances that had fixed him agreeably in my remembrance. The play represented to a nautical audience, was Hamlet; and this gentleman having been killed with much credit as Polonius, reappeared in the part of Osric: provided against recognition by the removal of his white wig, and the adjustment round his waist of an extremely broad belt and buckle. He was instantly recognised, notwithstanding these artful precautions, and a solemn impression was made upon the spectators for which I could not account, until a sailor in the Pit drew a long breath, said to himself in a deep voice, "Blowed if here an't another Ghost!" and composed himself to listen to a second communication from the tomb. Another personage whom I recognised as taking refuge under the wings of Pantomime (she was not a Fairy, to be sure, but she kept the cottage to which the Fairies came, and lived in a neat upper bedroom, with her legs obviously behind the street door), was a country manager's wife – a most estimable woman of about fifteen stone, with a larger family than I had ever been able to count: whom I had last seen in Lincolnshire, playing Juliet, while her four youngest children (and nobody else) were in the boxes – hanging out of window, as it were, to trace with their forefingers the pattern on the front, and making all Verona uneasy by their imminent peril of falling into the Pit. Indeed, I had seen this excellent woman in the whole round of Shakesperian beauties, and had much admired her way of getting through the text. If anybody made any remark to her, in reference to which any sort of answer occurred to her mind, she made that answer; otherwise, as a character in the drama, she preserved an impressive silence, and, as an individual, was heard to murmur to the unseen person next in order of appearance, "Come on!" I found her, now, on good motherly terms with the Fairies, and kindly disposed to chafe and warm the fingers of the younger of that race. Out of Fairy-land, I suppose that so many shawls and bonnets of a peculiar limpness were never assembled together. And, as to shoes and boots, I heartily wished that "the good people" were better shod, or were as little liable to take cold as in the sunny days when they were received at Court as Godmothers to Princesses.

Twice a-year, upon an average, these gaslight Fairies appear to us; but, who knows what becomes of them at other times? You are sure to see them at Christmas, and they may be looked for hopefully at Easter; but, where are they through the eight or nine long intervening months? They cannot find shelter under mushrooms, they cannot live upon dew; unable to array themselves in supernatural green, they must even look to Manchester for cotton stuffs to wear. When they become visible, you find them a traditionary people, with a certain conventional monotony in their proceedings which prevents their surprising you very much, save now and then when they appear in company with Mr. Beverley.[1] In a general way, they have been sliding out of the clouds, for some years, like barrels of beer delivering at a public-house. They sit in the same little rattling stars, with glorious corkscrews twirling about them and never drawing anything, through a good many successive seasons. They come up in the same shells out of the same three rows of gauze water (the little ones lying down in front, with their heads diverse ways); and you resign yourself to what must infallibly take place when you see them armed with garlands. You know all you have to expect of them by moonlight. In the glowing day, you are morally certain that the gentleman with the muscular legs and the short tunic (like the Bust at the Hairdresser's, completely carried out), is coming, when you see them "getting over" to one side, while the surprising phenomenon is presented on the landscape of a vast mortal shadow in a hat of the present period, violently directing them so to do. You are acquainted with all these peculiarities of the gaslight Fairies, and you know by heart everything that they will do with their arms and legs, and when they will do it. But, as to the same good people in their invisible condition, it is a hundred to one that you know nothing, and never think of them.

I began this paper with, perhaps, the most curious trait, after all, in the history of the race. They are certain to be found when wanted. Order Mr.

Vernon to lay on a hundred and fifty gaslight Fairies next Monday morning, and they will flow into the establishment like so many feet of gas. Every Fairy can bring other Fairies; her sister Jane, her friend Matilda, her friend Matilda's friend, her brother's young family, her mother – if Mr. Vernon will allow that respectable person to pass muster. Summon the Fairies, and Drury Lane, Soho, Somers' Town,[2] and the neighbourhood of the obelisk in St. George's Fields,[3] will become alike prolific in them. Poor, good-humoured, patient, fond of a little self-display, perhaps, (sometimes, but far from always), they will come trudging through the mud, leading brother and sister lesser Fairies by the hand, and will hover about in the dark stage-entrances, shivering and chattering in their shrill way, and earning their little money hard, idlers and vagabonds though we may be pleased to think them. I wish, myself, that we were not so often pleased to think ill of those who minister to our amusement. I am far from having satisfied my heart that either we or they are a bit the better for it.

Nothing is easier than for any one of us to get into a pulpit, or upon a tub, or a stump, or a platform, and blight (so far as with our bilious and complacent breath we can), any class of small people we may choose to select. But, it by no means follows that because it is easy and safe, it is right. Even these very gaslight Fairies, now. Why should I be bitter on them because they are shabby personages, tawdrily dressed for the passing hour, and then to be shabby again? I have known very shabby personages indeed – the shabbiest I ever heard of – tawdrily dressed for public performances of other kinds, and performing marvellously ill too, though transcendently rewarded: yet whom none disparaged! In even-handed justice, let me render these little people their due.

Ladies and Gentlemen. Whatever you may hear to the contrary (and may sometimes have a strange satisfaction in believing), there is no lack of virtue and modesty among the Fairies. All things considered, I doubt if they be much below our own high level. In respect of constant acknowledgment of the claims of kindred, I assert for the Fairies, that they yield to no grade of humanity. Sad as it is to say, I have known Fairies even to fall, through this fidelity of theirs. As to young children, sick mothers, dissipated brothers, fathers unfortunate and fathers undeserving, Heaven and Earth, how many of these have I seen clinging to the spangled skirts, and contesting for the nightly shilling or two, of one little lop-sided, weak-legged Fairy!

Let me, before I ring the curtain down on this short piece, take a single Fairy, as Sterne took his Captive,[4] and sketch the Family-Picture. I select Miss Fairy, aged three-and-twenty, lodging within cannon range of Waterloo Bridge, London – not alone, but with her mother, Mrs. Fairy, disabled by chronic rheumatism in the knees; and with her father, Mr. Fairy, principally employed in lurking about a public-house, and waylaying the theatrical profession for twopence wherewith to purchase a glass of old ale, that he may have something warming on his stomach (which has been cold for fifteen years); and with Miss Rosina Fairy, Miss Angelica Fairy and Master Edmund Fairy, aged respectively, fourteen, ten, and eight. Miss Fairy has an engagement of twelve shillings a week – sole means of preventing the Fairy family from coming to a dead lock. To be sure, at this time of year the three young Fairies have a nightly engagement to come out of a Pumpkin as French soldiers; but, its advantage to the housekeeping is rendered nominal, by that dreadful old Mr. Fairy's making it a legal formality to draw the money himself every Saturday – and never coming home until his stomach is warmed, and the money gone. Miss Fairy is pretty too, makes up very pretty. This is a trying life at the best, but very trying at the worst. And the worst is, that that always beery old Fairy, the father, hovers about the stage-door four or five nights a week, and gets his cronies among the carpenters and footmen to carry in messages to his daughter (he is not admitted himself), representing the urgent coldness of his stomach and his parental demand for twopence; failing compliance with which, he creates disturbances; and getting which, he becomes maudlin and waits for the manager, to whom he represents with tears that his darling child and pupil, the pride of his soul, is "kept down in the Theatre." A hard life this for Miss Fairy, I say, and a dangerous! And it is good to see her, in the midst of it, so watchful of Rosina Fairy, who otherwise might come to harm one day. A hard life this, I say again, even if John Kemble Fairy,[5] the brother, who sings a good song, and when he gets an engagement always disappears about the second week or so and is seen no more, had not a miraculous property of turning up on a Saturday without any heels to his boots, firmly purposing to commit suicide, unless bought off with half-a-crown. And yet – so curious is the gaslighted atmosphere in which these Fairies dwell! – through all the narrow ways of such an existence, Miss Fairy never relinquishes the belief that that incorrigible old Fairy, the father, is a wonderful man! She is immovably convinced that nobody ever can, or ever could, approach him in Rolla.[6] She has grown up in this conviction, will never correct it, will die in it. If, through any wonderful turn of fortune, she were to arrive at the emolument and dignity of a Free Benefit to-morrow, she would "put up" old Fairy, red nosed, stammering and imbecile – with delirium tremens shaking his very buttons off – as the noble Peruvian, and would play Cora herself, with a profound belief in his taking the town by storm at last.

Well-Authenticated Rappings

First published in *Household Words*, 20 February 1858, from which this text is reproduced.

The writer, who is about to record three spiritual experiences of his own in the present truthful article, deems it essential to state that, down to the time of his being favored therewith, he had not been a believer in rappings, or tippings. His vulgar notions of the spiritual world, represented its inhabitants as probably advanced, even beyond the intellectual supremacy of Peckham or New York; and it seemed to him, considering the large amount of ignorance, presumption, and folly with which this earth is blessed, so very unnecessary to call in immaterial Beings to gratify mankind with bad spelling and worse nonsense, that the presumption was strongly against those respected films taking the trouble to come here, for no better purpose than to make supererogatory idiots of themselves.

This was the writer's gross and fleshy state of mind at so late a period as the twenty-sixth of December last. On that memorable morning, at about two hours after day-light, – that is to say, at twenty minutes before ten by the writer's watch, which stood on a table at his bedside, and which can be seen at the publishing-office, and identified as a demi-chronometer made by B AUTTE of Geneva, and numbered 67,709 – on that memorable morning, at about two hours after daylight, the writer, starting up in bed with his hand to his forehead, distinctly felt seventeen heavy throbs or beats in that region. They were accompanied by a feeling of pain in the locality, and by a general sensation not unlike that which is usually attendant on biliousness. Yielding to a sudden impulse, the writer asked:

"What is this?"

The answer immediately returned (in throbs or beats upon the forehead) was, "Yesterday."

The writer then demanded, being as yet but imperfectly awake:

"What was yesterday?"

Answer: "Christmas Day."

The writer, being now quite come to himself, inquired, "Who is the Medium in this case?"

Answer: "Clarkins."

579

Question: "Mrs. Clarkins, or Mr. Clarkins?"

Answer: "Both."

Question: "By Mr., do you mean Old Clarkins, or Young Clarkins?"

Answer: "Both."

Now, the writer had dined with his friend Clarkins (who can be appealed to, at the State-Paper Office) on the previous day, and spirits had actually been discussed at that dinner, under various aspects. It was in the writer's remembrance, also, that both Clarkins Senior and Clarkins Junior had been very active in such discussion, and had rather pressed it on the company. Mrs. Clarkins too had joined in it with animation, and had observed, in a joyous if not an exuberant tone, that it was "only once a year."

Convinced by these tokens that the rapping was of spiritual origin, the writer proceeded as follows:

"Who are you?"

The rapping on the forehead was resumed, but in a most incoherent manner. It was for some time impossible to make sense of it. After a pause, the writer (holding his head) repeated the inquiry in a solemn voice, accompanied with a groan:

"Who ARE you?"

Incoherent rappings were still the response.

The writer then asked, solemnly as before, and with another groan:

"What is your name?"

The reply was conveyed in a sound exactly resembling a loud hiccough. It afterwards appeared that this spiritual voice was distinctly heard by Alexander Pumpion, the writer's footboy (seventh son of Widow Pumpion, mangler), in an adjoining chamber.

Question: "Your name cannot be Hiccough? Hiccough is not a proper name?"

No answer being returned, the writer said: "I solemnly charge you, by our joint knowledge of Clarkins the Medium – of Clarkins Senior, Clarkins Junior, and Clarkins Mrs. – to reveal your name!"

The reply rapped out with extreme unwillingness, was, "Sloe-Juice, Logwood, Blackberry."

This appeared to the writer sufficiently like a parody on Cobweb, Moth, and Mustard-Seed, in the Midsummer Night's Dream, to justify the retort:

"*That* is not your name?"

The rapping spirit admitted, "No."

"Then what do they generally call you?"

A pause.

"I ask you, what do they generally call you?"

The spirit, evidently under coercion, responded, in a most solemn manner. "Port!"

This awful communication caused the writer to lie prostrate, on the verge of insensibility, for a quarter of an hour: during which the rappings were continued with violence, and a host of spiritual appearances passed before his eyes, of a black hue, and greatly resembling tadpoles endowed with the power of occasionally spinning themselves out into musical notes as they swam down into space. After contemplating a vast Legion of these appearances, the writer demanded of the rapping spirit:

"How am I to present you to myself? What, upon the whole, is most like you?"

The terrific reply was, "Blacking."

As soon as the writer could command his emotion, which was now very great, he inquired:

"Had I better take something?"

Answer: "Yes."

Question: "Can I write for something?"

Answer: "Yes."

A pencil and a slip of paper which were on the table at the bedside immediately bounded into the writer's hand, and he found himself forced to write (in a curiously unsteady character and all down-hill, whereas his own writing is remarkably plain and straight) the following spiritual note.

"Mr. C. D. S. Pooney presents his compliments to Messrs. Bell and Company, Pharmaceutical chemists, Oxford Street, opposite to Portland Street, and begs them to have the goodness to send him by Bearer a five-grain genuine blue pill and a genuine black draught[1] of corresponding power."

But, before entrusting this document to Alexander Pumpion (who unfortunately lost it on his return, if he did not even lay himself open to the suspicion of having wilfully inserted it into one of the holes of a perambulating chesnut-roaster, to see how it would flare), the writer resolved to test the rapping spirit with one conclusive question. He therefore asked, in a slow and impressive voice:

"Will these remedies make my stomach ache?"

It is impossible to describe the prophetic confidence of the reply. "YES." The assurance was fully borne out by the result, as the writer will long remember; and after this experience it were needless to observe that he could no longer doubt.

The next communication of a deeply interesting character with which the writer was favored, occurred on one of the leading lines of railway.

The circumstances under which the revelation was made to him – on the second day of January in the present year – were these: He had recovered from the effects of the previous remarkable visitation, and had again been partaking of the compliments of the season. The preceding day had been passed in hilarity. He was on his way to a celebrated town, a well-known commercial emporium where he had business to transact, and had lunched in a somewhat greater hurry than is usual on railways, in consequence of the train being behind time. His lunch had been very reluctantly administered to him by a young lady behind a counter. She had been much occupied at the time with the arrangement of her hair and dress, and her expressive countenance had denoted disdain. It will be seen that this young lady proved to be a powerful Medium.

The writer had returned to the first-class carriage in which he chanced to be travelling alone, the train had resumed its motion, he had fallen into a doze, and the unimpeachable watch already mentioned recorded forty-five minutes to have elapsed since his interview with the Medium, when he was aroused by a very singular musical instrument. This instrument, he found to his admiration not unmixed with alarm, was performing in his inside. Its tones were of a low and rippling character, difficult to describe; but, if such a comparison may be admitted, resembling a melodious heart-burn. Be this as it may, they suggested that humble sensation to the writer.

Concurrently with his becoming aware of the phenomenon in question, the writer perceived that his attention was being solicited by a hurried succession of angry raps in the stomach, and a pressure on the chest. A sceptic no more, he immediately communed with the spirit. The dialogue was as follows:

Question: "Do I know your name?"

Answer: "*I* should think so!"

Question: "Does it begin with a P?"

Answer (second time): "*I* should think so!"

Question: "Have you two names, and does each begin with a P?"

Answer (third time): "*I* should think so!"

Question: "I charge you to lay aside this levity, and inform me what you are called."

The spirit, after reflecting for a few seconds, spelt out P. O. R. K. The musical instrument then performed a short and fragmentary strain. The spirit then recommenced, and spelt out the word "P. I. E."

Now, this precise article of pastry, this particular viand or comestible, actually had formed – let the scoffer know – the staple of the writer's lunch, and actually had been handed to him by the young lady whom he now knew to be a powerful Medium! Highly gratified by the conviction thus forced upon his mind that the knowledge with which he conversed was not of this world, the writer pursued the dialogue.

Question: "They call you Pork Pie?"

Answer: "Yes."

Question (which the writer timidly put, after struggling with some natural reluctance),

"Are you, in fact, Pork Pie?"

Answer: "Yes."

It were vain to attempt a description of the mental comfort and relief which the writer derived from this important answer. He proceeded:

Question: "Let us understand each other. A part of you is Pork, and a part of you is Pie?"

Answer: "Exactly so."

Question: "What is your Pie-part made of?"

Answer: "Lard." Then came a sorrowful strain from the musical instrument. Then the word "Dripping."

Question: "How am I to present you to my mind? What are you most like?"

Answer (very quickly): "Lead."

A sense of despondency overcame the writer at this point. When he had in some measure conquered it, he resumed:

Question: "Your other nature is a Porky nature. What has that nature been chiefly sustained upon?"

Answer (in a sprightly manner): "Pork, to be sure!"

Question: "Not so. Pork is not fed upon Pork?"

Answer: "Isn't it, though!"

A strange internal feeling, resembling a flight of pigeons, seized upon the writer. He then became illuminated in a surprising manner, and said:

"Do I understand you to hint that the human race, incautiously attacking the indigestible fortresses called by your name, and not having time to storm them, owing to the great solidity of their almost impregnable walls, are in the habit of leaving much of their contents in the hands of the Mediums, who with such pig nourish the pigs of future pies?"

Answer: "That's it!"

Question: "Then to paraphrase the words of our immortal bard —"

Answer (interrupting):

> "The same pork in its time, makes many pies,
>   Its least being seven pasties."

The writer's emotion was profound. But, again desirous still further to try the Spirit, and to ascertain whether, in the poetic phraseology of the advanced seers of the United States, it hailed from one of the inner and more elevated circles, he tested its knowledge with the following.

Question: "In the wild harmony of the musical instrument within me, of which I am again conscious, what other substances are there airs of, besides those you have mentioned?"

Answer: "Cape. Gamboge.[2] Camomile. Treacle. Spirits of wine. Distilled Potatoes."

Question: "Nothing else?"

Answer: "Nothing worth mentioning."

Let the scorner tremble and do homage; let the feeble sceptic blush! The writer at his lunch had demanded of the powerful Medium, a glass of Sherry, and likewise a small glass of Brandy. Who can doubt that the articles of commerce indicated by the Spirit were supplied to him from that source under those two names?

One other instance may suffice to prove that experiences of the foregoing nature are no longer to be questioned, and that it ought to be made capital to attempt to explain them away. It is an exquisite case of Tipping.

The writer's Destiny had appointed him to entertain a hopeless affection for Miss L. B., of Bungay, in the county of Suffolk. Miss L. B. had not, at the period of the occurrence of the Tipping, openly rejected the writer's offer of his hand and heart; but it has since seemed probable that she had been withheld from doing so, by filial fear of her father, Mr. B., who was favourable to the writer's pretensions. Now, mark the Tipping. A young man, obnoxious to all well-constituted minds (since married to Miss L. B.), was visiting at the house. Young B., was also home from school. The writer was present. The family party were assembled about a round table. It was the spiritual time of twilight in the month of July. Objects could not be discerned with any degree of distinctness. Suddenly, Mr. B. whose senses had been lulled to repose, infused terror into all our breasts, by uttering a passionate roar or ejaculation. His words (his education was neglected in his youth) were exactly these: "Damme, here's somebody a shoving of a letter into my hand, under my own mahogany!" Consternation seized the assembled group. Mrs. B. augmented the prevalent dismay by declaring that somebody had been softly treading on her toes, at intervals, for half-an-hour. Greater consternation seized the assembled group. Mr. B. called for lights. Now, mark the Tipping. Young B. cried (I quote his expressions accurately), "It's the spirits, father! They've been at it with me this last fortnight." Mr. B. demanded with irascibility, "What do you mean, sir? What have they been at?" Young B. replied, "Wanting to make a regular Post-office of me, father. They're always handing impalpable letters to me, father. A letter must have come creeping round to you by mistake. I must be a Medium, father. O here's a go!" cried young B. "If I an't a jolly Medium!" The boy now became violently convulsed, spluttering exceedingly, and jerking out his legs and arms in a manner calculated to cause me (and which did cause me) serious inconvenience; for, I was supporting his respected mother within range of his boots, and he conducted himself like a telegraph before the invention of the electric one. All this time Mr. B. was looking about under the table for the letter, while the obnoxious young man, since married to Miss L. B., protected that young lady in an obnoxious manner. "O here's a go!" Young B. continued to cry without intermission, "If I an't a jolly Medium, father! Here's a go! There'll be a Tipping presently, father. Look out for the table!" Now mark the Tipping. The table tipped so violently as to strike Mr. B. a good half-dozen times on his bald head while he was looking under it; which caused Mr. B. to come out with great agility, and rub it with much tenderness (I refer to his head), and to imprecate it with much violence (I refer to the table). I observed that the tipping of the table was uniformly in the direction of the magnetic current; that is to say, from south to north, or from young B. to Mr. B. I should have made some further observations on this deeply interesting point, but that the table suddenly revolved, and tipped over on myself, bearing me to the ground with a force increased by the momentum imparted to it by young B., who came over with it in a state of mental exaltation, and could not be displaced for some time. In the interval, I was aware of being crushed by his weight and the table's, and also of his constantly calling out to his sister and the obnoxious young man, that he foresaw there would be another Tipping presently.

None such, however, took place. He recovered after taking a short walk with them in the dark, and no worse effects of the very beautiful experience with which we had been favoured, were perceptible in him during the rest of the evening, than a slight tendency to hysterical laughter, and a noticeable attraction (I might almost term it fascination) of his left hand, in the direction of his heart or waistcoat-pocket.

Was this, or was it not a case of Tipping? Will the sceptic and the scoffer reply?

Please to Leave Your Umbrella

First published in *Household Words*, 1 May 1858, from which this text is reproduced.

I made a visit the other day to the Palace at Hampton Court.[1] I may have had my little reason for being in the best of humours with the Palace at Hampton Court; but that little reason is neither here (ah! I wish it were here!) nor there.

In the readiest of moods for complying with any civil request, I was met, in the entrance-hall of the public apartments at Hampton Court, by the most obliging of policemen, who requested me to leave my umbrella in his custody at the foot of the stairs. "Most willingly," said I, "for my umbrella is very wet." So the policeman hung it on a rack, to drip on the stone floor with the sound of an irregular clock, and gave me a card of authority to reclaim it when I should come out again. Then, I went prosperously through the long suites of deserted rooms, now looking at the pictures, and now leaning over the broad old window-seats and looking down into the rainy old gardens, with their formal gravel walks, clipped trees, and trim turf banks – gardens with court-suits on. There was only one other visitor (in very melancholy boots) at Hampton Court that blessed day: who soon went his long grave way, alternately dark in the piers and light in the windows, and was seen no more.

"I wonder," said I, in the manner of the Sentimental Journeyer,[2] "I wonder, Yorick, whether, with this little reason in my bosom, I should ever want to get out of these same interminable suites of rooms, and return to noise and bustle! It seems to me that I could stay here very well until the grisly phantom on the pale horse came at a gallop up the staircase, seeking me. My little reason should make of these queer dingy closet-rooms, these little corner chimney-pieces tier above tier, this old blue china of squat shapes, these dreary old state bedsteads with attenuated posts, nay, dear Yorick," said I, stretching forth my hand towards a stagnant pool of blacking in a frame, "should make, even of these very works of art, an encompassing universe of beauty and happiness. The fountain in the staid red and white courtyard without (for we had turned that angle of the building), would never fall too monotonously on my ear, the four chilled sparrows now fluttering on the brink of its basin would never chirp a wish for change of weather, no bargeman on the rain-speckled river; no wayfarer rain-belated under the leafless trees in the park, would ever come into my fancy as examining in despair those swollen clouds, and vainly peering for a ray of sunshine. I and my little reason, Yorick, would keep house here, all our lives, in perfect contentment; and when we died, our ghosts should make of this dull Palace the first building ever haunted happily!"

I had got thus far in my adaptation of the *Sentimental Journey* when I was recalled to my senses by the visible presence of the Blacking which I just now mentioned. "Good Heaven!" I cried, with a start; "now I think of it, what a number of articles that policeman below-stairs required me to leave with him!"

"Only an umbrella. He said no more than, Please to leave your umbrella."

"Faith, Yorick," I returned, "he insisted on my putting so much valuable property into my umbrella, and leaving it all at the foot of the stairs before I entered on the contemplation of many of these pictures – that I tremble to think of the extent to which I have been despoiled. That policeman demanded of me, for the time being, all the best bumps in my head.[3] Form, colour, size, proportion, distance, individuality, the true perception of every object on the face of the earth or the face of the Heavens, he insisted on my leaving at the foot of the stairs, before I could confide in the catalogue. And now I find the moon to be really made of green cheese; the sun to be a yellow wafer or a little round blister; the deep wild sea to be a shallow series of slate-coloured festoons turned upside down; the human face Divine to be a smear; the whole material and immaterial universe to be sticky with treacle and polished up with blacking. Conceive what I must be, through all the rest of my life, if the policeman should make off with my umbrella and never restore it!"

Filled with the terrors of this idea, I retraced my steps to the top of the stairs, and looked over the hand-rail for my precious property. It was still keeping time on the stone pavement like an irregular clock, and the policeman (evidently possessed by no dishonest spirit) was reading a newspaper. Calmed and composed, I resumed my musing way through the many rooms.

Please to leave your umbrella. Of all the Powers that get your umbrella from you, Taste is the most encroaching and insatiate. Please to put into your umbrella, to be deposited in the hall until you come out again, all your powers of comparison, all your experience, all your individual opinions. Please to accept with this ticket for your umbrella the individual opinions of some other personage whose name is Somebody, or Nobody, or Anybody, and to swallow the same without a word of demur. Be so good as to leave your eyes with your umbrellas, gentlemen, and to deliver up your private judgment with your walking-sticks. Apply this ointment, compounded by the learned Dervish, and you shall see no end of camels going with the greatest ease through needles' eyes. Leave your umbrella full of property which is not by any means to be poked at this collection, with the police, and you shall acknowledge, whether you will or no, this hideous porcelain-ware to be beautiful, these wearisomely stiff and unimaginative forms to be graceful, these coarse daubs to be masterpieces. Leave your umbrella and take up your gentility. Taste proclaims to you what is the genteel thing; receive it and be genteel! Think no more of your umbrellas – be they the care of the Police of Scotland Yard! Think no more for yourselves – be you the care of the Police of Taste!

I protest that the very Tax-gatherer does not demand so much of me as the Powers who demand my umbrella. The Tax-gatherer will not allow me to wear hair-powder unmolested; but the Umbrella-gatherer will not allow me to wear my head. The Tax-gatherer takes toll of my spade; but the Umbrella-gatherer will not permit me to call my spade, a spade. Longinus,[4] Aristotle, Doctor Waagen,[5] and the Musical Glasses,[6] Parliamentary Commissions, the Lord-Knows-Who, Marlborough House,[7] and the Brompton Boilers,[8] have declared my spade to be a mop-stick. And I must please to give up my umbrella, and believe in the mop-stick.

Again. The moral distinctions, and the many remembrances, and balances of This and That, which I am required by other authorities to put into my so-often demanded umbrella and to leave in the lobby, are as numerous as the Barnacle family.[9] It was but a session or two ago, that I went to the gallery at the Old Bailey, to hear a trial. Was my umbrella all that I was called upon to leave behind me, previous to taking my seat? Certainly not. I was requested to put so many things into it that it became, though of itself a neat umbrella, more bulgy than Mrs. Gamp's.[10] I found it insisted upon, that I should cram into this unfortunate article all the weighty comparisons I had ever made in my life between the guilt of laying hands upon a pound of scrag of mutton, and upon hundreds of thousands of pounds of sterling money. I found it insisted upon, that I should leave with my umbrella before I went into Court, any suspicions that I had about me (and I happened to have a good many), that distortion and perversion of the truth, plainly for the purpose of so much gain, and for the enhancement of a professional reputation, were to be observed there, outside the dock and beyond the prisoner. I found myself required to take a ticket, conventionally used in that place, in exchange for my natural perception of many painfully ludicrous things that should have become obsolete long ago. Not that I complain of this particular demand at the door; for otherwise how could I have borne the fearful absurdity of the Judge being unable to discharge the last awful duty of his office without putting on a strange little comical hat, only used for the dismissal of a blood-stained soul into eternity? Or how could I have withheld myself from bursting out into a fit of laughter, which would have been contempt of court, when the same exalted functionary and two virtuous Counsel (I never in my life had the pleasure of hearing two gentlemen talk so much virtue) were grimly pleasant on the dressing-up in woollen wigs of certain Negro Singers whose place of entertainment had been innocently the scene of manslaughter. While the exalted functionary himself, and the two virtuous counsel themselves, were at that very moment dressed up in woolley wigs, to the full as false and ridiculous as any theatrical wigs in the world, only they were not of the negro colour!

But, when I went to the Strangers' Gallery of the House of Commons, I had a greater load to leave with my umbrella than Christian[11] had to lay down in the Pilgrim's Progress. The difference between Black and White, which is really a very large one and enough to burst any Umbrella, was the first thing I had to force into mine. And it was well for me that this was insisted on by the Police, or how could I have escaped the Serjeant-at-Arms, when the very same Member who on the last occasion of my going to the very same place I had with my own ears heard announce with the profoundest emotion that he came down to that house expressly to lay his hand upon his heart and declare that Black was White and there was no such thing as Black, now announced with the profoundest emotion that he came down to that house expressly to lay his hand upon his heart and declare that White was Black and there was no such thing as White? If you have such an article about you (said the Umbrella-taker to me in effect) as the distinction between very ill-constructed common places, and sound patriotic facts, you are requested to leave it at the door here. – By all means, said I. – You have there a Noun of Multitude or signifying many, called The Country; please to put that too, in your Umbrella. – Willingly, said I. – Your belief that public opinion is not the lobby of this place and the bores of the clubs, will be much in your way, and everybody else's hereabouts; please to leave that likewise. – You are welcome to it, said I. – But I am bound to admit that, thus denuded, I passed quite a pleasant evening; which I am certain I could not have done, if I had been allowed to take my Umbrella and its cumbrous contents in with me.

Please to leave your Umbrella. I have gone into churches where I have been required to leave my Umbrella in a sham mediæval porch, with hundreds of eventful years of History squeezed in among its ribs. I have gone into public assemblages of great pretensions – even into assemblages gathered together under the most sacred of names – and my Umbrella, filled to the handle with my sense of Christian fairness and moderation, has been taken from me at the door. All through life, according to my personal experience, I must please to leave my Umbrella, or I can't go in.

I had reached this point and was about to apostrophise Yorick once more, when a civil voice requested me, in obliging tones, to "claim my Umbrella." I might have done that, without a ticket, as there was no other on the rack in the hall at Hampton Court Palace, whither I had now worked my way round by another course, without knowing it. However, I gave back my ticket, and got back my Umbrella, and then I and my little reason went dreaming away under its shelter through the fast-falling spring rain, which had a sound in it that day like the rustle of the coming summer.

In Memoriam W. M. Thackeray

First published in *Cornhill Magazine*, February 1864, from which this text is reproduced.

It has been desired by some of the personal friends of the great English writer who established this magazine, that its brief record of his having been stricken from among men should be written by the old comrade and brother in arms who pens these lines, and of whom he often wrote himself, and always with the warmest generosity.

I saw him first, nearly twenty-eight years ago, when he proposed to become the illustrator of my earliest book.[1] I saw him last, shortly before Christmas, at the Athenæum Club, when he told me that he had been in bed three days – that, after these attacks, he was troubled with cold shiverings, "which quite took the power of work out of him" – and that he had it in his mind to try a new remedy which he laughingly described. He was very cheerful, and looked very bright. In the night of that day week, he died.

The long interval between those two periods is marked in my remembrance of him by many occasions when he was supremely humorous, when he was irresistibly extravagant, when he was softened and serious, when he was charming with children. But, by none do I recall him more tenderly than by two or three that start out of the crowd, when he unexpectedly presented himself in my room, announcing how that some passage in a certain book had made him cry yesterday, and how that he had come to dinner, "because he couldn't help it," and must talk such passage over. No one can ever have seen him more genial, natural, cordial, fresh, and honestly impulsive, than I have seen him at those times. No one can be surer than I, of the greatness and the goodness of the heart that then disclosed itself.

We had our differences of opinion. I thought that he too much feigned a want of earnestness, and that he made a pretence of under-valuing his art, which was not good for the art that he held in trust. But, when we fell upon these topics, it was never very gravely, and I have a lively image of him in my mind, twisting both his hands in his hair, and stamping about, laughing, to make an end of the discussion.

When we were associated in remembrance of the late Mr. Douglas Jerrold,[2] he delivered a public lecture in London, in the course of which, he read his very best contribution to PUNCH, describing the grown-up cares of a poor family of young children. No one hearing him could have doubted his natural gentleness, or his thoroughly unaffected manly sympathy with the weak and lowly. He read the paper most pathetically, and with a simplicity of tenderness that certainly moved one of his audience to tears. This was presently after his standing for Oxford,[3] from which place he had dispatched his agent to me, with a droll note (to which he afterwards added a verbal postscript), urging me to "come down and make a speech, and tell them who he was, for he doubted whether more than two of the electors had ever heard of him, and he thought there might be as many as six or eight who had heard of me." He introduced the lecture just mentioned, with a reference to his late electioneering failure, which was full of good sense, good spirits, and good humour.

He had a particular delight in boys, and an excellent way with them. I remember his once asking me with fantastic gravity, when he had been to Eton where my eldest son then was, whether I felt as he did in regard of never seeing a boy without wanting instantly to give him a sovereign? I thought of this when I looked down into his grave, after he was laid there, for I looked down into it over the shoulder of a boy to whom he had been kind.

These are slight remembrances; but it is to little familiar things suggestive of the voice, look, manner, never, never more to be encountered on this earth, that the mind first turns in a bereavement. And greater things that are known of him, in the way of his warm affections, his quiet endurance, his unselfish thoughtfulness for others, and his munificent hand, may not be told.

If, in the reckless vivacity of his youth, his satirical pen had ever gone astray or done amiss, he had caused it to prefer its own petition for forgiveness, long before:

> I've writ the foolish fancy of his brain;
> The aimless jest that, striking, hath caused pain;
> The idle word that he'd wish back again.[4]

In no pages should I take it upon myself at this time to discourse of his books, of his refined knowledge of character, of his subtle acquaintance with the weaknesses of human nature, of his delightful playfulness as an essayist, of his quaint and touching ballads, of his mastery over the English language. Least of all, in these pages, enriched by his brilliant qualities from the first of the series, and beforehand accepted by the Public through the strength of his great name.

But, on the table before me, there lies all that he had written of his latest and last story.[5] That it would be very sad to any one – that it is inexpressibly so to a writer – in its evidences of matured designs never to be accomplished, of intentions begun to be executed and destined never to be completed, of careful preparation for long roads of thought that he was never to traverse, and for shining goals that he was never to reach, will be readily believed. The pain, however, that I have felt in perusing it, has not been deeper than the conviction that he was in the healthiest vigour of his powers when he wrought on this last labour. In respect of earnest feeling, far-seeing purpose, character, incident, and a certain loving picturesqueness blending the whole, I believe it to be much the best of all his works. That he fully meant it to be so, that he had become strongly attached to it, and that he bestowed great pains upon it, I trace in almost every page. It contains one picture which must have cost him extreme distress, and which is a masterpiece. There are two children in it, touched with a hand as loving and tender as ever a father caressed his little child with. There is some young love, as pure and innocent and pretty as the truth. And it is very remarkable that, by reason of the singular construction of the story, more than one main incident usually belonging to the end of such a fiction is anticipated in the beginning, and thus there is an approach to completeness in the fragment, as to the satisfaction of the reader's mind concerning the most interesting persons, which could hardly have been better attained if the writer's breaking-off had been foreseen.

The last line he wrote, and the last proof he corrected, are among these papers through which I have so sorrowfully made my way. The condition of the little pages of manuscript where Death stopped his hand, shows that he had carried them about, and often taken them out of his pocket here and there, for patient revision and interlineation. The last words he corrected in print, were, "And my heart throbbed with an exquisite bliss."[6] G OD grant that on that Christmas Eve when he laid his head back on his pillow and threw up his arms as he had been wont to do when very weary, some consciousness of duty done and Christian hope throughout life humbly cherished, may have caused his own heart so to throb, when he passed away to his Redeemer's rest!

He was found peacefully lying as above described, composed, undisturbed, and to all appearance asleep, on the twenty-fourth of December, 1863. He was only in his fifty-third year; so young a man, that the mother who blessed him in his first sleep, blessed him in his last. Twenty years before, he had written, after being in a white squall:

> And when, its force expended,
> The harmless storm was ended,
> And, as the sunrise splendid
>   Came blushing o'er the sea;
> I thought, as day was breaking,
> My little girls were waking,
> And smiling, and making
>   A prayer at home for me.[7]

Those little girls had grown to be women when the mournful day broke that saw their father lying dead. In those twenty years of companionship with him, they had learned much from him; and one of them has a literary course before her, worthy of her famous name.

On the bright wintry day, the last but one of the old year, he was laid in his grave at Kensal Green, there to mingle the dust to which the mortal part of him had returned, with that of a third child, lost in her infancy, years ago. The heads of a great concourse of his fellow-workers in the Arts, were bowed around his tomb.[8]

EXPLANATORY NOTES

In compiling these notes I am heavily indebted to the work of Madeline House, Graham Storey and Kathleen Tillotson, the editors of the Pilgrim Edition of *The Letters of Charles Dickens* (Oxford: Clarendon Press, 1965–), and have found the annotations to volumes VI, VII and VIII covering the years from 1850–58 particularly useful. Other valuable reference works have been: Arthur Hayward, *The Dickens Encyclopaedia* (London: Routledge, 1924); James S. Stevens, *Quotations and References in Charles Dickens* (Boston: Christopher Publishing, 1929); William Kent, *An Encyclopaedia of London* (London: Dent, 1951); Nicholas Bentley, Michael Slater and Nina Burgis, *The Dickens Index* (Oxford: Oxford University Press, 1988); and Ben Weinreb and Christopher Hibbert (eds), *The London Encyclopaedia* (London: Macmillan, 1993 revised edn). Throughout, I refer to John Forster's *The Life of Charles Dickens*, ed. A. J. Hoppé, 2 vols (London: Dent, 1966; revd 1969) as Forster. For Shakespeare, the Arden (3rd edn) has been used.

A Christmas Tree

1. *Barmecide*: In the story of the Barber's Sixth Brother in the *Arabian Nights Entertainments*, a member of the Barmecide family serves a beggar an imaginary banquet.
2. *Punch's hands*: In the Punch and Judy puppet show.
3. *Jack, who achieved all the recorded exploits*: The adventures described here appear in the fairy tales of 'Jack and the Beanstalk' and 'Jack the Giant-Killer'.
4. *ferocious joke about his teeth*: 'The better to eat you with, my dear' – said by the wolf in the fairy tale just before swallowing Little Red Riding-Hood.
5. *Robin Hood . . . Valentine . . . the Yellow Dwarf . . . and all Mother Bunch's wonders*: The exploits of Robin Hood like the adventures of Valentine (raised at court as a knight) and his brother Orson (carried off by a bear and brought up in the woods) which were first recorded in an early French romance, formed part of young Dickens's imaginative diet. The tale of the wicked Yellow Dwarf, who steals a beautiful princess and kills his rival only to have the princess die of a broken heart, is another of the traditional nursery stories, sometimes collected under the supposed aegis of 'Mother Bunch', which Dickens remembered with delight. Mother Bunch was a noted London ale-wife of the late Elizabethan period, who spend most of her time in the telling of tales. Her name was taken up by the publishers of collections of tall stories.
6. *we all three breathe again*: The allusions here, as in the previous paragraphs, are to stories in the *Arabian Nights Entertainments*, narrated by Scheherazade to postpone her execution by the Sultan: 'trees are for Ali Baba to hide in' and 'cobblers are all

Mustaphas', from 'Ali Baba and the Forty Thieves', usually regarded as part of this collection; 'beefsteaks are to throw down into the Valley of Diamonds', from the second voyage of Sinbad the Sailor; 'the Vizier's son of Bussorah, who turned pastrycook', from the story of Noor-ed-Deen and Shems-ed-Deen; 'cave which only waits for the magician', from 'Aladdin and the Wonderful Lamp'; 'unlucky date', from the story of the Merchant and the Genie; 'fictitious trial of the fraudulent olive merchant', from 'The Story of Ali Cogia, Merchant of Baghdad', traditionally associated with the *Arabian Nights*; 'apple . . . which the tall black slave stole from the child', from the story of the three apples; 'dog . . . who . . . put his paw on the piece of bad money' and 'rice which the awful lady . . . could only peck by grains', from 'The Story of Sidi-Nouman'; and 'fly away . . . as the wooden horse did with the Prince of Persia', from the story of the Magic Horse.

7. *Philip Quarll among the monkeys*: From *The Adventures of Philip Quarll* (1727), describing the exploits of an imitation Robinson Crusoe, by 'Edward Dorrington' (Peter Longueville).

8. *Sandford and Merton with Mr. Barlow*: From *The History of Sandford and Merton* (3 volumes, 1783-9), a famous and influential children's book by Thomas Day, which was written to illustrate the idea that individual goodness may be taught through reason.

9. *devoted dog of Montargis*: Owned by Aubrey de Montdidier, who was slain by Richard de Macaire in 1371. The tale in which which the dog called attention to his master's assassin, fought him in open combat and forced him to confess his crime was popular in chapbooks as well as on the adult and toy theatre stage. It appeared on the London stage in 1814, adapted from *Le Chien de Montargis* by René-Charles Guilbert de Pixérécourt (1773-1844); he was known as the 'Corneille des boulevards'.

10. *Jane Shore*: Mistress of Edward IV, later accused of witchcraft by Richard III and forced to do public penance. She is the subject of Nicholas Rowe's *The Tragedy of Jane Shore* (1714).

11. *how George Barnwell killed the worthiest uncle that ever man had*: Dickens alludes to the action of *The London Merchant: or The History of George Barnwell* (1731) by George Lillo in which Barnwell is encouraged by Millwood, a ruthless whore, to rob his employer and murder his uncle.

12. *"Nothing is, but thinking makes it so"*: Cf. Shakespeare's *Hamlet*, II, ii, 255-7: '. . . there is nothing either good or bad, but thinking makes it so.'

13. *the toy-theatre*: A popular nineteenth-century pastime. The sheets of characters and stage fittings could be purchased at toy shops, and, as Dickens notes, hours of labour went into the 'attendant occupation with paste and glue, and gum, and water colours, in the getting-up of' plays which had been successful in the adult theatres of the day. The actual performance must have offered an excellent opportunity for Dickens to unleash his melodramatic imagination since all parts had to be read by the young producers; while much of the juvenile popularity of Isaac Pocock's *The Miller and his Men* (1813), in which the character of Kelmar appears, was probably due to the explosion with which it ended. A schoolmate of Dickens at Wellington House Academy recalled that 'my brother, assisted by Dickens, got up the *Miller and his Men*, in a very gorgeous form. Master Beverley constructed the mill for us in such

a way that it could tumble to pieces with the assistance of crackers. At one representation the fireworks in the last scene, ending with the destruction of the mill, were
so very real that the police interfered, and knocked violently at the doors. Dickens's
after taste for theatricals might have had its origin in these small affairs.' See Forster
I, p. 42.

14. *Kelmar* : A character in *The Miller and his Men*, see above.

15. *"Forgive them, for they know not what they do"* : Christ's words as reported by
Luke 23: 34.

16. *the Rule of Three* : In mathematics, a rule for finding the fourth term of a proportion
where only three are given. The rule states that the product of the means equals the
product of the extremes.

17. *Terence and Plautus* : Terence (*c.* 190–159 BC) and Plautus (*c.* 254–184 BC),
Roman dramatists famous for their comedies.

18. *the old King* : George III, whose final insanity in 1810 led to the regency (1811–
20) of the Prince of Wales, later George IV.

19. *Legion is the name* : Cf. Mark 5: 9: 'And he asked him, What is thy name? And he
answered, saying, My name is Legion: for we are many.'

20. *This, in remembrance of Me!* : Cf. Luke 22: 19: 'This is my body which is given
for you: this do in remembrance of me.'

Our School

1. *So fades . . . All that this world is proud of* : Slightly misquoted from William
Wordsworth's *The Excursion* (1814), VII, lines 976–8:

> 'So fails, so languishes, grows dim, and dies,'
> The grey-haired Wanderer pensively exclaimed,
> 'All that this world is proud of.'

Lying Awake

1. *"My uncle . . . just falling asleep"* : From 'The Adventure of My Uncle' in Washington
Irving's *Tales of a Traveller* (1824). Dickens wrote from New York on 28 February
1842: 'Washington Irving is a great fellow. We have laughed most heartily together.
He is just the man he ought to be'. See Forster I, p. 201.

2. *"Get out of bed . . . sweet and pleasant"* : From 'The Art of Procuring Pleasant
Dreams' (1786) by Benjamin Franklin (1706–90).

3. *Except Niagara . . . beautiful to see* : Dickens visited Niagara Falls on 26 April 1842,
and sought out the Horseshoe Fall: 'I went down alone, into the very basin. It would
be hard for a man to stand nearer God than he does there. There was a bright rainbow
at my feet; and from that I looked up to – great Heaven! to *what* a fall of bright green
water!' Forster I, p. 248.

4. *great actor . . . playing Macbeth, and . . . apostrophising "the death of each day's life"* :

William Charles Macready (1793—1873), noted tragedian and close friend of Dickens. His last performance was at Drury Lane Theatre on 26 February 1851 in the role of Macbeth. The line quoted here occurs in his frenzied description of sleep as 'The death of each day's life, sore labour's bath, / Balm of hurt minds, great nature's second course, / Chief nourisher in life's feast' (II, ii, 38—40).

5. *MR. BATHE*: The London Tavern, at 123 Bishopsgate Within, adjacent to the offices of Baring Brothers, was a popular haunt for public dinners at this time. Its proprietor was Mr William P. Bathe. Cf. the description of it in 'The London Tavern', *Household Words*, 15 October 1851, by James Hannay and W. H. Wills.

6. *floorcloth* : A material, such as linoleum or oilcloth, used to cover floors.

7. *the Great Saint Bernard*: The mountain pass, 8120 feet above sea level, on the Swiss-Italian border which carries the main road from western Switzerland to the plain of Lombardy. Dickens visited Switzerland in the summer of 1846, and on September 6 he wrote to Forster with an account of his visit to the convent at the top of the pass.

8. *the same happy party*: In a letter to Forster in early September 1846, Dickens listed the members of the climbing party as 'Haldimand, Mr. & Mrs. Cerjat & one daughter; Mr. & Mrs. Watson, two Ladies Taylor, Kate, Georgy & I'. One of those 'now dead' was Richard Watson (1800—52), 'as thoroughly good & true man as ever existed' and whose home, Rockingham Castle in Northamptonshire, provided Dickens with the model for Chesney Wold in *Bleak House*.

9. *the Mannings . . . Horsemonger Lane Jail*: On 13 November 1849, George Manning and his Belgian wife Maria were hanged for murdering their lodger, Patrick O'Connor, whose corpse they buried in quicklime underneath their kitchen floor. The trial caused considerable sensation, not least because of Maria Manning's behaviour in the course of it, when she kept interrupting the judge, and ranted frequently and furiously from the dock; and because of the matter of fact way in which Manning confessed to the murder: 'I never liked him so I finished him off with the ripping chisel.' Approximately thirty thousand people, including Dickens, witnessed the execution; and his attendance led him to write two famous letters to *The Times* (14 and 19 November 1849), both of which denounced public executions. For a full discussion of Dickens's reaction, and his attitude towards capital punishment in general, see Philip Collins, *Dickens and Crime*, 2nd edn (1964), pp. 235ff.

10. *Cremorne reality*: The Cremorne Stadium was originally established in 1832 by Charles Random de Berenger, the self-styled Baron de Beaufainon, 'for the tuition and practice of skilful and manly exercises, such as swimming, rowing, shooting, fencing and boxing'. This soon proved unprofitable, and the gardens were taken over by Renton Nicholson, erstwhile proprietor of the Garrick's Head in Bow Street. In 1846, the grounds, now extending to about twelve acres along the river between Chelsea and Fulham, were reopened and became famed for the shows and amenities they contained, in particular, the balloon ascents. From here, Charles Green made a famous flight accompanied by a lady and a leopard. The main entrance was in the King's Road, where a star illuminated the pay-box; and surrounding the main building, which contained a bandstand and dance floor, were 'a Chinese pagoda, a Swiss chalet, an Indian temple, a large theatre, a marionette theatre, concert room, small circus, restaurant, fernery, menagerie, American bowling saloon, shooting gallery, and gypsy's

tent'. The gardens eventually closed in 1877, and the Lots Road Power Station was built on the site in 1902.

11. *the Morgue in Paris*: See 'Travelling Abroad', note 6.

12. *like that sagacious animal . . . a gone 'Coon*: Frederick Marryat, author, naval captain, and Fellow of the Royal Society related this anecdote about Captain Martin Scott in *A Diary in America* (New York: D. Appleton, 1839), p. 150.

13. *The late brutal assaults*: There had been a wave of street crime in the capital in 1851–2. However, Dickens's critical views of 'the whipping panacea' were by no means fixed. In 1846 he told Forster that he wanted bigamists 'flogged more than once (privately)' before they were deported to Australia; while in 1868, during a similar spate of assaults, he writes of the assailant: 'I would have his back scarified and deep', ('The Ruffian', *All the Year Round*, 10 October 1868).

14. *Pet Prisoning*: Thinking more of the welfare of criminals in prison than of the needs of honest men outside the prison walls, the result, Dickens felt, of the system of solitary confinement currently being tried at the model prison at Pentonville. For a more direct treatment of this theme, see 'Pet Prisoners'; while Philip Collins discusses 'the Pentonville experiment' at length in *Dickens and Crime*, pp. 40–63.

Where We Stopped Growing

1. *SWIFT'S WISE FANCY*: A reference to Part III of Jonathan Swift's *Gulliver's Travels*, when Lemuel Gulliver visits the land of the Luggnaggians, 'where every Child hath at least a Chance for being immortal'. However, this immortality consists of the Struldbrugs, the Immortals, ageing but never dying.

2. *MR. CARLYLE . . . FOR SIX YEARS*: A reference to Part II, ch. 4 of *Sartor Resartus*: 'It were a real increase of human happiness could all young men from the age of nineteen be covered under barrels, or rendered otherwise invisible; and there left to follow their lawful studies and callings, till they emerged, sadder and wiser, at the age of twenty-five.' Dickens became a close friend of Carlyle, and once told Forster, 'I would go at all times farther to see Carlyle than any man alive.' He dedicated *Hard Times* to Carlyle, and the novel incorporates many of his opinions about social ethics.

3. *We have never grown . . . out of Robinson Crusoe*: Defoe's novel long perplexed Dickens. Soon after the completion of this essay, he wrote to Forster: 'You remember my saying to you some time ago how curious I thought it that *Robinson Crusoe* should be the only instance of a universally popular book that could make no one laugh and no one cry. I have been reading it again just now, in the course of my numerous refreshings at those English wells, and I will venture to say that there is not in literature a more surprising instance of an utter want of tenderness and sentiment than the death of Friday.' He continues: 'The second part of *Robinson Crusoe* is perfectly contemptible, in the glaring defect that it exhibits in the man who was 30 years on that desert island with no visible effect made on his character by that experience,' and then concludes: 'I have no doubt he was a precious, dry and disagreeable article himself – I mean De Foe: not Robinson', Forster II, p. 434.

4. *Our growth stopped . . . when nobody had ever heard of a Jin*: Allusions to the Caliph

of Baghdad who figures in many tales of the *Arabian Nights*. Jin are an intermediate order of beings between angels and men, created out of fire, and reputed to have supernatural powers, such as the ability to assume human or animal forms. A genie is one of the jin.

5. *Blue Beard*: A popular tale in an oriental setting of a villainous husband who murders each of his wives, translated from the French of Perrault by Robert Samber (c. 1729). Blue Beard's last bride opens a forbidden closet, discovers the bodies of her predecessors, and very nearly has the same fate, but her brothers rescue her and kill her husband.

6. *Don Quixote*: A satirical romance by Cervantes published in 1605, a second part appearing in 1615.

7. *When Gil Blas had a heart*: Alludes to *The Adventures of Gil Blas of Santillane* (1715-35), a picaresque romance by Alain-René Le Sage, which shows the rise and fall of a young man of humble parentage.

8. *that interesting story in the Sentimental Journey*: See Sterne's *A Sentimental Journey* (1768), II, 'The Fragment. Paris', where 'the poor notary, just as he was passing by the sentry, instinctively clapped his cane to the side of it [his own hat], but in raising it up, the point of his cane catching hold of the loop of the sentinel's hat, hoisted it over the spikes of the balustrade clear into the Seine'.

9. *a tea-tray . . . an exquisite Art*: The picture on the tea-tray may have been taken from the painting by W. R. Bigg, *Black Monday: or the Departure for School*. See Malcolm Andrews, *Dickens and the Grown-Up Child* (Basingstoke: Macmillan, 1994), p. 64.

10. *Colman's Broad Grins*: George Colman the younger (1762-1836), compiled a book of bawdy tales in verse. Forster records that this work 'seized his fancy very much; and he was so impressed by its description of Covent Garden, in the piece called the "Elder Brother", that he stole down to the market by himself to compare it with the book', Forster I, p. 15.

11. *Old Hummums*: A famous London inn situated in Covent Garden. In *Great Expectations*, Pip stays there in a room smelling of 'cold soot and hot dust'.

12. *the two great Theatres*: The Covent Garden Theatre and the Theatre Royal, Drury Lane.

13. *Baron Trenck*: Friedrich, Freiherr von der Trenck, Prussian soldier, whose *Memoirs* (1787) give an account of his sixteen years' imprisonment by Frederick the Great, when he was shackled at the waist, hands, and feet.

14. *Sir Roger de Coverley*: An old-fashioned country dance – one of Dickens's favourites – after whom *The Spectator* named its famous character, 'a gentleman of Worcestershire, of ancient descent, a baronet' (no. 2, by Steele).

Gone Astray

1. *Saint Giles's Church*: A Bloomsbury church designed by Henry Flitcroft (1697-1769) and opened in 1734. The district in which it was situated was notorious for its slums and criminals, and most of the surrounding streets were demolished between 1844 and 1847.

2. *the reigning successor of Bamfylde Moore Carew*: Bamfylde Moore Carew (1693–1770), a fraudster, was the self-styled King of the Gypsies.

3. *the celebrated lion over the gateway*: In 1749, a statue of a lion crest of the Percy family was installed over the entrance of Northumberland House, their London residence at Charing Cross. The house was demolished in 1874.

4. *the Giants in Guildhall*: Guildhall, situated in Gresham Street, was decorated with two effigies, Gog and Magog, 14½ feet high, flanking the council chamber door, which were placed there in 1708 and destroyed in the blitz.

5. *Temple Bar*: Ancient gate of the City of London at the west end of Fleet Street, rebuilt by Wren in 1672. Heads of traitors were impaled on it in the eighteenth century.

6. *St. Dunstan's*: St Dunstan's in the West, Fleet Street, was a medieval church, demolished in 1830. It featured a clock with moving figures – the jacks – that struck the hours and quarters, and was the first in London to have the minutes marked on the dial and a double face. It is mentioned in *Barnaby Rudge*.

7. *the Whittington plan*: Richard Whittington, Lord Mayor of London (d. 1423) and a notable public benefactor. As a young man he sought to leave London, but resting at Holloway, and hearing Bow Bells ringing, as he thought, the words 'Turn again, Whittington', he returned to the city to make his fortune.

8. *Mosaic Arabs*: Arab adherents to the religious system, laws and ceremonies prescribed by the prophet Moses.

9. *Mr. Hudson*: George Hudson (1800–71), British railway magnate, responsible, through his financial speculation, for the railway boom in Britain in the 1840s, but ruined in 1849 when massive frauds were disclosed.

10. *Mr. Fitz-Warren*: The London merchant who employed Dick Whittington.

11. *Smith, Payne, and Smith . . . Rothschild*: Famous city institutions are translated into the adventures of Sinbad, as recounted in the *Arabian Nights*. Smith, Payne, and Smith, originally a Nottingham banking house, established themselves in London (1758) in Lothbury, and by 1806 had settled in Lombard Street. The National Provincial Bank, forerunner of the National Westminster Bank, acquired the company in 1918; Glyn and Halifax were set up by Richard Carr Glyn (1755–1838) and eventually became known as Halifax, Mills, Glyn and Milton of Lombard Street, a firm which had the reputation of having a larger business than any other private banking house in the City; Baring Brothers and Co. Ltd., the longest lived merchant bank in London, was founded in 1762, and continued to trade under that name until its liquidation in 1995; Rothschild was an international banking house set up by Meyer Amschel Rothschild whose London operation (N. M. Rothschild & Sons) was founded in 1804 by Nathan Meyer (1777–1836), one of his five sons.

12. *Austin Friars*: A precinct in the City to the east of Throgmorton Avenue; the name commemorates the priory, dedicated to St Augustine, founded in 1253 by Humphrey de Bohun, which once stood there.

13. *on 'Change*: Royal Exchange, on Threadneedle Street and Cornhill, in the City of London.

14. *Mansion House*: Official residence of the Lord Mayor of London for his year of office, designed by George Dance and completed in 1752.

15. *James Hogg . . . India House*: East India House on Leadenhall Street, built 1610,

rebuilt in 1726 and again in 1799, and demolished in 1862. It was the headquarters of the East India Company, whose chairman in 1852-3 was James Weir Hogg (1790-1876).

16. *Goodman's Fields*: An area of Whitechapel, the site of two eighteenth-century theatres.

An Unsettled Neighbourhood

1. *cannot be called a new neighbourhood*: Camden Town, the area of north-west London to which Dickens's family moved when he was nine – they lived at no. 16 Bayham Street, now demolished – was, in the early years of the century, a semi-rural enclave. However, the coming of the railway changed that. For a fictional version of the construction of the London to Birmingham Railway in the neighbourhood, see *Dombey and Son*, ch. 6.

2. *practising Ramo Samee*: The precise nature of this allusion is untraced. Cf. R. H. Barham, 'The Auto-da-Fé. A Legend of Spain', Canto I, 108-11 in *The Ingoldsby Legends* (1840):

> Which, as Hill used to say, 'I once happen'd to see'
> The great Indian conjuror, Ramo Samee,
> Make, while swallowing what all thought a regular choker,
> *Viz.* a small sword as long and as stiff as a poker.

On 14 January 1856, Dickens identified Mrs Ramo Samee as the writer of a begging letter, and told Wills to give her money: 'Something like a couple of guineas, I should think would be the sum most useful to her. But if there were any hope (I fear there is not), of doing her any real good with more, I should not object to more.' However, *The Times*, 6 March 1856, reported that one Ramo Samee and an accomplice had been arrested for fraudulently offering counterfeit coins; and earlier Samee had been charged with assault.

3. *hardbake*: A type of toffee flavoured with almonds.

4. *Fly the Garter*: A cheating game, also called 'Fast and Loose', 'played with a stick and a belt or string so arranged that a spectator could make the latter fast by placing a stick through its intricate folds, whereas the operator could detach it at once.' Described in J. O. Halliwell, *Dictionary of Archaic and Provincial Words* (1847).

5. *what's-his-name that the Brahmins smoke*: The Brahmans were the highest ranking of the four social castes in Hindu India; Dickens probably has in mind a hookah pipe, occasionally known in India as a narghile.

6. *Bradshaw*: *Bradshaw's Railway Guide*. See 'A Narrative of Extraordinary Suffering', note 6.

7. *the siege of Sebastopol*: Sevastopol, a naval base on the Black Sea, withstood an Allied siege for eleven months (1854-5) during the Crimean War.

8. *parliamentary*: By a special Act of Parliament every railway company had to run at least one train each day for which the fare was a penny a mile, on all major lines. They became known as Parliamentary trains.

9. *the Breaks*: The brakes.

Personal

1. *Three-and-twenty years have passed*: Perhaps Dickens was miscalculating, since the first series of *Sketches by Boz* was published in February 1836, three years after his début in print, the sketch 'A dinner at Poplar Walk', which was printed in *The Monthly Magazine*.

New Year's Day

1. *Mrs. Pipchin*: In *Dombey and Son*, Mrs Pipchin is a boarding-house keeper in Brighton, 'generally spoken of as "a great manager" of children; and the secret of her management was, to give them everything that they didn't like, and nothing that they did – which was found to sweeten their dispositions very much' (ch. 8).

2. *Mrs. Shipton*: Mother Shipton was a witch and prophetess who lived near Knaresborough, Yorkshire, in the early sixteenth century.

3. *Signor Gunter's, della Piazza Berkeley, Londra, Inghilterra*: A tea-shop at 7–8 Berkeley Square, famous for its ices and sorbets.

4. *Abd-el-Kader*: Abd-el-Kader (1807–83), an Arab leader noted for his skilful battles against the French. In 1847 he was forced to surrender and was imprisoned in France until 1852. Dickens here is drawing attention to the promiscuity of the revue. For an account of Dickens's theatregoing in 1856, see Forster II, p. 162.

5. *Sieur Framboisie*: Allusion unidentified.

6. *Pierrot*: A stock character in French pantomime; a greedy thief, lacking moral vision, he is white-faced and dressed in loose white garments.

7. *This spectacle . . . "Not guilty"*: Dickens alludes to *Black-Eyed Susan, or All in the Downs* (1829), a successful melodrama by his friend Douglas Jerrold (1803–57). The play relates the tale of a sailor who, defending his wife's honour, strikes a senior officer and is sentenced to death. He is reprieved at the last minute. Dickens wrote on the play in *The Examiner*, 12 May 1849.

Dullborough Town

1. *Dullborough Town*: Dickens's name for Chatham.

2. *S.E.R.*: The South Eastern Railway.

3. *Seringapatam*: The capital of the Indian State of Mysore at the close of the eighteenth century; the seat of the sultan Tippoo Sahib, killed when the British forces captured the city in 1799.

4. *caudle*: A drink consisting of gruel mixed with wine or ale, sweetened and spiced, and often administered as a tonic.

5. *the model . . . for Aladdin*: In 'Aladdin and the Wonderful Lamp', a tale of the *Arabian Nights*, Aladdin, the son of a poor tailor, acquires a lamp containing a genie who constructs a sumptuous palace for him, and enables him to marry a princess.

6. *struggling for life against the virtuous Richmond*: Dickens is alluding to the opening moments of the last scene of Shakespeare's *Richard III*.

7. *a Panorama*: A picture unrolled or unfolded so as to give the impression of a wide continuous view of a place or an event to a spectator. Panoramas were especially popular at the time, and Dickens wrote about them at length in his article 'Some Account of an Extraordinary Traveller', included in this selection.

8. *"Comin' through the Rye"*: A traditional Scots melody with words by Robert Burns.

9. *Roderick Random*: Eponymous hero of Tobias Smollett's picaresque novel (1748), modelled on Le Sage's *Gil Blas*, a great favourite of Dickens's.

10. *he confounded Strap with Lieutenant Hatchway*: Strap is Random's faithful and generous friend; Lieutenant Hatchway is a character in Smollett's *Peregrine Pickle* (1751), 'a very brave man and a great joker' who has had one leg shot away.

Night Walks

1. *Haymarket*: Extending southward from Coventry Street to Pall Mall, the street was famous in Victorian times as a red-light district.

2. *Yorick's skull*: Yorick is the king's fool, a 'fellow of infinite jest', whose skull is unearthed when Ophelia's grave is dug, *Hamlet*, V, i.

3. *Newgate*: A medieval prison — London's main gaol in the eighteenth century — rebuilt in 1780—83 after its sacking during the Gordon Riots (see *Barnaby Rudge*, chs. 64—5). Dickens wrote an account of the prison in *Sketches by Boz*; and it also appears in *Oliver Twist*, when Fagin waits for his execution in the Condemned Hold; and in *Great Expectations*, Pip is shown inside the 'grim stone building' to view the yard where the gallows are kept, and 'the Debtors' Door, out of which the culprits come to be hanged', see *Dickens and Crime*, pp. 27—41.

4. *Saint Sepulchre*: At the junction of Holborn and Shaw Hill, London.

5. *Aceldama*: Name of the field in Jerusalem bought with the blood money received by Judas Iscariot after he betrayed Christ, Matthew 27: 6—8.

6. *the old King's Bench prison*: A gaol in Southwark, the majority of whose prisoners were debtors. A description of it in 1828 called it 'the most desirable place of incarceration in London'.

7. *Bethlehem Hospital*: Also known as Bedlam, this famous lunatic asylum moved to Lambeth from Moorfields in 1815. It now houses the Imperial War Museum.

8. *St. Martin's church*: The church of St-Martin-in-the-Fields, Trafalgar Square, rebuilt in 1722—6 by James Gibbs.

9. *like the young man in the New Testament*: Cf. Mark 14: 51—2: 'And there followed him [Jesus] a certain young man, having a linen cloth cast about his naked body; and the young man laid hold on him: And he left the linen cloth, and fled from them naked.

Chambers

1. *Ship's Caboose*: A galley.

2. *Bramah erysipelas*: Erysipelas is a contagious skin disease marked by inflammation, fever and formation of large blisters which break and dry into a hard crust; Joseph Bramah (1748–1814) was the English inventor of the door lock and beer pump.

3. *Verulam-buildings*: A range of buildings facing Gray's Inn Road, built between 1803–11, and named after Francis Bacon (1561–1626), 1st Lord Verulam.

4. *Holborn Union*: A workhouse.

5. *Marius among the ruins of Carthage*: An allusion to an incident in the life of Gaius Marius, the Roman general (156–86 BC), who, overcome by his rival Sulla, fled to Africa and landed at Carthage. The Roman Governor attempted to persuade him to leave the country, but he responded with the instruction that he tell the praetor he had seen Gaius Marius, a fugitive, sitting amidst the ruins of Carthage.

6. *flavour of Cockloft*: The smell of a cockloft, a room over a garret where poultry might roost.

7. *Prometheus Bound*: Prometheus stole fire from heaven, and as a punishment Zeus chained him to a rock on Mount Caucasus, where during the daytime a vulture devoured his liver which was restored each night. He was rescued from this torture by Hercules.

8. *Saint Anthony's fire*: Any of several diseased conditions of the skin, but especially erysipelas.

9. *Lyons Inn*: An Inn of Chancery, established in 1420 out of a tavern, its name deriving from the sign of the lion which it bore when a hostelry. It had fallen into decay by 1800 and was sold in 1863. The whole area was demolished in 1899.

10. *Macbeth's Amen*: Cf. 'But wherefore could not I pronounce "Amen"? / I had most need of blessing, and "Amen" / Stuck in my throat" (II, ii, 30–32).

11. *"in furniture stepped in so far"*: Another allusion to *Macbeth*: 'I am in blood / Stepped in so far that, should I wade no more, / Returning were as tedious as go o'er' (III, iv, 136–8).

12. *Clement's*: Established in 1480, and situated on the north side of the Strand close to the western boundary of the Law Courts, part of Clement's Inn was sold in 1868 and the rest in 1884.

13. *New Inn, Staple Inn, Barnard's Inn*: New Inn was established in 1485 out of a tavern named the Inn of Our Lady, and disappeared in the 1890s; Staple Inn, established in 1378, has survived physically and is situated behind a façade of sixteenth-century shops on the southern side of Holborn, and is occupied now by the Institute of Actuaries. In common with other Inns of Chancery, it declined in the later nineteenth century and was sold in 1884. Barnard's Inn, established in 1435, features in ch. 21 of *Great Expectations*, at which point it was in a state of considerable disrepair. In 1892 the premises were purchased by the Mercers' livery company.

Nurse's Stories

1. *belated among wolves, on the borders of France and Spain*: An episode, like those mentioned in the previous paragraph, from Defoe's *Robinson Crusoe*.

2. *the robbers' cave . . . cursing in bed*: chs. 4–10 of the first book of *The Adventures of Gil Blas of Santillane* by Le Sage depict his falling in with outlaws.

3. *Don Quixote's study . . . great draughts of water*: From Part I, chs. 1 and 5 of Cervantes's novel.

4. *the Talisman of Oromanes*: From the first of *The Tales of the Genii* (1764) by James Ridley (1736–65).

5. *the school . . . with a sheet*: The story appears in the first chapter of *The Life of Nelson* (1813) by Robert Southey (1774–1843).

6. *Brobingnag*: Correctly spelled 'Brobdingnag': from Jonathan Swift's *Gulliver's Travels* (1726), where, like Lilliput and Laputa, it is one of the countries visited by Gulliver.

7. *"The Black Cat" . . . for mine*: Deborah Thomas has suggested a similarity to the bloodthirsty young man, hungering for juvenile heart and liver, with which Magwitch threatens Pip in ch. 1 of *Great Expectations* (originally conceived as a short piece in the vein of these *Uncommercial Traveller* sketches which Dickens was writing in 1860). See the letter to Forster of September 1860 in *The Letters of Charles Dickens*, ed. Walter Dexter (London: Nonesuch Press, 1938), vol. III, p. 182.

8. *terrible old Scalds*: Ancient nordic poets.

Some Recollections of Mortality

1. *Cassim Baba*: The brother of Ali Baba.

2. *Blouse-life*: A blouse was a loose blue cotton garment usually belted at the waist, worn by French artisans and peasants; hence, Dickens is thinking of a working-class wedding.

3. *St. Jacques de la Boucherie*: The flamboyant Gothic tower, dating from 1508–22, and since 1798 the only relic of the Church of Saint-Jacques-la-Boucherie, was restored by Ballu in 1858.

4. *costermonger*: A street vendor who sold apples from a cart.

5. *Boulevard de Sébastopol*: Street running north from Châtelet to Boulevard Saint-Denis.

6. *what Melancholy did to the youth in Gray's Elegy*: An allusion to the epitaph which concludes the *Elegy Written in a Country Churchyard* (1751), by Thomas Gray (1716–71):

> Here rests his head upon the lap of earth
> A youth to fortune and to fame unknown.
> Fair Science frowned not on his humble birth,
> And Melancholy marked him for her own.

7. *young Norval*: In John Home's play *Douglas*, young Norval is the son of Lady Randolph by a previous marriage with Douglas. His birth was concealed and he was raised by a shepherd, Old Norval, the 'frugal swain', who found him. Norval is killed by Randolph who discovers too late that his victim is, in fact, the son of Lady Randolph; and she kills herself in despair. The play was a favourite with Kemble and others.

8. *Patagonians*: The indigenous people of Argentina, noted for their great stature. Early explorers represented them as giants.

Birthday Celebrations

1. *a slow torture called an Orrery*: A clockwork model to illustrate relative positions and movements of the planets in the solar system, invented *c.* 1700 by George Graham (1675–1751) and named after Charles Boyle, 4th Earl of Orrery (1676–1731), for whom one was made.

2. *letters more in number than Horace Walpole's*: Horace Walpole, 4th Earl of Orford (1717–97), made a literary reputation from an epistolary one, even though in the nineteenth century this had been clouded by Macaulay's famous attack in the *Edinburgh Review*, denouncing him a gossip-monger. The Yale edition of Walpole's letters, edited by W. S. Lewis *et al.* (1937–81), consists of 42 volumes (not including the index).

3. *P. and O. Steamers*: The Peninsular and Oriental Steamship Company.

4. *My "boyhood's home," Dullborough*: Dickens's name for Chatham. See 'Dullborough Town' in this collection.

5. *Was there sufficient ground . . . Shakespeare ever stole deer?*: An allusion to the biographical question of whether Shakespeare was caught attempting to rustle deer from the Charlecote Estate near Stratford.

A Narrative of Extraordinary Suffering

1. *Ware*: A town in Hertfordshire.

2. *Ravenglass, Bootle, and Sprouston*: Ravenglass is a village in Cumberland; Bootle is an area of Liverpool; Sprouston is a village in the Scottish Borders.

3. *Aynho*: A village in Northamptonshire.

4. *Four Ashes, Spread Eagle, and Penkridge*: Villages in Staffordshire.

5. *Messrs. Moses and Son*: A firm of outfitters located in King Street, Covent Garden, which eventually became known as Moss Bros.

6. *BRADSHAW*: Bradshaw was the colloquial designation of a railway timetable, *Bradshaw's Railway Guide*, a monthly publication detailing all trains running on the 43 railway lines of Great Britain. It was first issued in 1839 by George Bradshaw (1801–53) and ceased publication in 1961. In the previous paragraph, Dickens has recorded the advertisements for accommodation, goods and services typically found at the end of each issue of the *Guide*.

Our Watering-Place

1. *Our Watering-Place*: Broadstairs in Kent, a small village in which Dickens had spent much of his spare time over the years, writing and thinking. Writing to Professor Felton on the 1 September 1843 he described Broadstairs as 'a little fishing-place; intensely quiet; built on a cliff, whereon – in the centre of a tiny semicircular bay – our house stands; the sea rolling and dashing under the windows. Seven miles out are the Goodwin Sands (you've heard of the Goodwin Sands?) whence floating lights perpetually wink after dark, as if they were carrying on intrigues with the servants. Also there is a big lighthouse called the North Foreland on a hill behind the village, a severe parsonic light, which reproves the young and giddy floaters, and stares grimly out upon the sea. Under the cliff are rare good sands (where all the children assemble every morning and throw up impossible fortifications, which the sea throws down again at high water.) Old gentlemen and ancient ladies flirt after their own manner in two reading-rooms and on a great many scattered seats in the open air. Other old gentlemen look all day through telescopes and never see anything. In a bay-window in a one-pair sits, from nine o'clock to one, a gentleman with rather long hair and no neckcloth, who writes and grins as if he thought he were very funny indeed. His name is Boz. At one he disappears, and presently emerges from a bathing-machine, and may be seen – a kind of salmon-coloured porpoise – splashing about in the ocean. After that he may be seen in another bay-window on the ground floor, eating a strong lunch; after that, walking a dozen miles or so, or lying on his back in the sand reading a book. Nobody bothers him unless they know he is disposed to be talked to; and I am told he is very comfortable indeed. He's as brown as a berry and they do say is a small fortune to the innkeeper who sells beer and cold punch. But this is mere rumour.'

2. *Minerva Press*: A printing-house in Leadenhall Street, London, which was famous in the eighteenth century for the publication of popular sentimental novels.

3. *Miss Julia Mills has read . . . these books*: In *David Copperfield* Julia Mills is Dora's friend, 'having been unhappy in misplaced affection, and being understood to have retired from the world on her awful stock of experience, but still to take a calm interest in the unblighted hopes and loves of youth' (ch. 33).

4. *"have been roaming"*: Cf. 'See the Summer Leaves are Coming' by Thomas Bayly (1797–1839): '. . . the plants and on the trees, / And the birds that have been roaming / Under brighter skies than these'.

5. *two dissenting chapels*: Protestant sects refusing to conform to the doctrines or practices of the established Church of England. On the representation of dissent in the Victorian novel, see Valentine Cunningham, *Everywhere Spoken Against* (Oxford: OUP, 1975).

6. *the Fantoccini come*: 'Puppets made to go through certain evolutions by means of concealed strings or wires', *OED*; hence, a marionette show.

7. *Wombwell's Menagerie*: George Wombwell (1778–1850), proprietor of a famous travelling menagerie. On one occasion, after some of his animals died en route to a show, he unfurled a banner proclaiming 'the only dead elephant in the fair'. This still

proved a popular attraction. See Thomas Frost, *The Old Showmen and the Old London Fairs* (1872).

8. *The poet's words*: The final stanzas of Tennyson's 'Break, Break, Break' published in *Poems* (1842).

9. *Do chase . . . comes back*: Cf. *The Tempest*, V, i, 35–6.

A Flight

1. *Deputy Chaff-wax*: An officer responsible for preparing the wax used in sealing documents; he also features in 'A Poor Man's Tale of a Patent', included in this selection. The position was abolished in 1852.

2. *"MEAT-CHELL"*: John Mitchell (1806–74), who had made the St James's Theatre the London location for drama in French at the time of this sketch.

3. *Abd-el-Kader*: See 'New Year's Day', note 4.

4. *Zamiel*: In gnostic sources, the 'God of the Blind', the consort of Lilith and head of the angels of destruction. Known as Samoel in the Cabbala.

5. *Paris in eleven hours!*: This was considered a great feat at the time. Dickens wrote to Forster on 24 June 1850 from the Hotel Windsor on rue de Rivoli: 'The twelve hours journey here is astounding – marvellously done, except in respect of the means of refreshment, which are absolutely none.'

6. *Parliamentary Train*: See 'An Unsettled Neighbourhood', note 8.

7. *Creil*: A town 30 miles north of Paris, in the department of Oise.

8. *statue . . . at Hyde Park Corner*: Matthew Cotes Wyatt's massive bronze statue of the Duke of Wellington on horseback, erected at Hyde Park Corner on Decimus Burton's arch in 1846 (and not removed until more than thirty years after Wellington's death in 1852), was a frequent target of contemporary ridicule. Dickens was generally unsympathetic towards the idea of commemorative statues, and devoted several *Household Words* articles to criticism of the excesses of public statuary. See for instance, 'The "Good" Hippopotamus', 12 October 1850.

Fire and Snow

1. *ghostly dagger of Macbeth*: Cf. 'Is this a dagger which I see before me, / The handle toward my hand?', II, i, 33–4.

2. *blasted heath*: Cf. *Macbeth*, I, iii, 76: 'Upon this blasted heath you stop our way'.

3. *like Christian with his bundle of sins*: Cf. John Bunyan, *Pilgrim's Progress*: 'I dreamed, and behold I saw a man clothed with rags, standing in a certain place, with his face from his own house, a book in his hand, and a great burden on his back.'

4. *time-bills*: Timetables.

Our French Watering-Place

1. *Our French Watering-Place*: Boulogne-sur-Mer where Dickens lived during the summers of 1853, 1854 and 1856, firstly at the Villa des Moulineaux, secondly at the Villa du Camp de Droite and thirdly again at the Moulineaux.

2. *diligence*: A public stage-coach.

3. *"the Bar"*: A breakwater at the mouth of the harbour.

4. *BILKINS*: The name of this authority on taste reappears in 'Why' (*Household Words*, 1 March 1856), where Bilkins is legal counsel for Sharmer, the ruffian pampered in the press.

5. *Juno*: The goddess of women and childbirth and the beautiful wife of Jupiter, queen of the Gods.

6. *lazzaroni*: An Italian term for beggars.

7. *M. Loyal Devasseur*: A faithful portrait of Dickens's landlord, Ferdinand Henri Joseph Alexandre Beaucourt-Mutuel (1805–81), who owned both houses Dickens rented. He grew very fond of this 'liberal fellow', and on 3 November wrote to Wilkie Collins: 'I am glad you like the portrait of Beaucourt so well. It was very pleasant to do, and I hope it may be of some service to him in the letting of his houses.'

8. *castles . . . in Spain*: Dickens is alluding to the French idiom *châteaux en Espagne*, meaning castles in the air.

9. *"arfanarf"*: A mixture of ale and porter.

10. *Ratcliffe Highway*: Infamous district of the East End, replaced by St George's Street.

11. *Féroce*: His real name was Monsieur Sauvage.

12. *Professor Owen*: Sir Richard Owen (1804–92), the first Hunterian professor of comparative anatomy and physiology at the Royal College of Surgeons. He pioneered the reconstruction of the skeletons of prehistoric and extinct animals. In 1856 he became head of the Natural History section of the British Museum. He was a friend of Dickens who brings him into several of his novels.

13. *"Nokemdon"*: A game in which a coconut or similar object was placed on a stick, to be knocked off by players hurling bean bags or balls at this target.

Out of Town

1. *water-patterns*: Water sprinkled on pavements to keep down the dust.

2. *Pavilionstone*: Folkestone.

3. *hollands*: Dutch gin.

4. *petticoat trousers*: An American colloquial name for wide baggy trousers.

5. *Thermoplylæ*: A passage between the Oeta mountains and the marshy shore of Thessaly, Greece, nine miles south-east of Lamia. In 480 BC Leonidas and 300 Spartans fought a rearguard action here to the death to delay the Persian army of Xerxes I during the Persian War.

6. *Susan*: Black-Eyed Susan, see 'New Year's Day', note 7.

7. *its Great Hotel*: The Pavilion Hotel, Folkestone.

8. *the good landlord*: James G. Breach, proprietor of the hotel. Dickens fell ill during his stay, and was grateful for the treatment he received. After completing the piece, he wrote to Wills on 18 September 1855: 'I sent Breach of the Pavilion a Proof of it, and he is in Seventh Heaven of Delight and wants 500 copies of the No. . . . (He was so extraordinarily kind to me when I was ill, that I am glad of the opportunity of being able to make the little present.)'

9. *Mary Bax or, the Murder on the Sand Hills*: Allusion untraced.

10. *Cooke's Circus*: William Cooke, since 1853 manager of Astley's equestrian Amphitheatre, a horse circus which provided Dickens with much material for the depiction of Sleary's circus in *Hard Times*. See the letter to Forster, 18 October 1856, in which he describes the visit of Cooke to Gad's Hill.

Railway Dreaming

1. *Café de la Lune*: The Café de Paris.

2. *in weather that would have satisfied Herod*: In inclement conditions.

3. *the virtuous farmer in . . . comedy*: Possibly an allusion to Dickens's play *The Village Coquettes* (1836), in which John Benson, an old farmer, is threatened with eviction from his farm by Squire Norton.

4. *Holbein . . . linen-draper*: A procession or dance in which the living and the dead take part. The most well known of all representations of the Dance is the series of forty woodcuts designed by Hans Holbein the younger (1497–1543), published in 1538.

5. *Paillasse*: A generic term for clown, buffoon.

6. *Circumlocution*: The name Dickens coined in *Bleak House* for the Civil Service.

Out of the Season

1. *a watering-place out of the Season*: Dover.

2. *a chapter of unheard-of excellence*: In spring 1856, Dickens was in the early stages of *Little Dorrit*, but his residence in Dover does not seem to have furthered the novel. He wrote to his wife on 5 May 1856: 'I did nothing at Dover (except for Household Words) and have not begun little Dorrit no. 8 yet. But I took twenty mile walks in the fresh air, and perhaps in the long run did better than if I had been at work.'

3. *Moore's Almanack or the sage Raphael*: Francis Moore (Old Moore) (1657–1714) was a physician and astrologer, who in 1700 published the first number of his *Vox Stellarum, an Almanac for 1701 with astrological observations*. His *Almanac* was very popular in the nineteenth century, and remains available to this day. Raphael was an archangel who in the Book of Tobit accompanies, instructs, and rescues the hero on his journey. He also appears in *Paradise Lost*.

4. *a seaside town without a cliff*: Deal, eight miles north-east of Dover.

5. *thick pint crockery mugs . . . frayed-out roots*: This is a good description of Mocha

ware named after the stone with dentritic markings originally from Mocha in Arabia. Utilitarian earthenware was decorated with coloured bands between which the potter applied a mixture of 'tea' (tobacco-juice, manganese and urine) which fanned out into the typical root-like markings. Also known as 'tobacco-spit ware'.

6. *the celebrated Black Mesmerist*: Unidentified.

7. *Madame Roland*: Marie Jeanne Phlipon, Mme Roland de la Platière (1754-93), was a French revolutionist, who inspired Girondist policy through her *salon*. She despised Danton and Robespierre, and the enmity of these and other Montagnards, members of the extreme revolutionary party in the Convention Nationale, led to her execution. She wrote her unfinished *Memoires*, which Dickens reads here, and from prison just before her death, *Appel à l'impartiale postérité* (1795).

8. *Dr. Faustus . . . blade-bones*: Allusion to Christopher Marlowe's play (1604, 1616) which concludes with the hero dragged down to hell by demons.

9. *. . . infinite delights to me*: As ever, Dickens seeks to resurrect his own childhood reading.

10. *the Downs*: A grass-covered range of chalk hills in southern England, they are generally divided into the South Downs (Sussex) and the North Downs (Surrey and Kent).

11. *the Whole Duty of Man*: The title of the most famous chapter of Mme Roland's *Memoires*, see note 7 above.

12. *Mr. Baines of Leeds*: Matthew Talbot Baines (1799-1860), MP for Leeds since 1852, Chancellor of the Duchy of Lancaster since 1855, was renowned for his puritanical views.

13. *May they find themselves in the Season somewhere!*: Dickens wrote to Georgina Hogarth on 5 May 1856: 'I went to the Dover Theatre for Friday Night, which was a miserable spectacle. The pit is boarded over, and it is a drinking and smoking place. It was "for the Benefit of Mrs. A. Green" and the town had been very extensively placarded with "Don't forget Friday". I made out four-and ninepence (I am serious) in the house, when I went in. We may have warmed up, in the course of the evening, to twelve shillings. A Jew played the Grand Piano, Mrs. A. Green sang no end of songs (with not a bad voice, poor creature), Mr. Green sang comic songs fearfully, and danced clog hornpipes capitally, and a miserable woman, shivering in a shawl and a bonnet, sat in the side-boxes all evening, nursing Master A. Green, aged seven months. It was a most forlorn business, and I should have contributed a sovereign to the treasury if I had known how.'

Refreshments for Travellers

1. *Walworth*: An area of the London borough of Southwark, bounded on the north by the New Kent Road, on the west by Kennington Park Road, on the south by Camberwell, and the east by the Old Kent Road.

2. *SIR RICHARD MAYNE* (1796-1868), Commissioner of the London Metropolitan Police.

3. *conversazione*: A social gathering intended for the discussion of travels, culture and so on.

4. *like Dr. Johnson, Sir, you like to dine* : Boswell says about Samuel Johnson, 'I never knew any man who relished good eating more than he did' (Boswell's *Life of Johnson*, ed. George Birkbeck Hill, rev. L. F. Powell (Oxford: Clarendon Press, 1934), vol. I, p. 468).

5. *spermaceti ointment* : Spermaceti was a fatty substance found in the head of the sperm whale, and used in a refined state in certain medical preparations and in candles.

6. *D'Oyleys* : Small round ornamental paper mats placed under cakes etc., and named after Doyley, a London haberdasher.

Travelling Abroad

1. *Shooter's Hill* : The main Dover Road passes over the hill, 432 feet at its summit; in the eighteenth century it was notorious as a haunt of highway robbers.

2. *a very queer small boy* : Dickens as a child. Gad's Hill became Dickens's home in 1856, and according to Forster, 'amid the recollections connected with his childhood it held always a prominent place, for upon first seeing it as he came from Chatham with his father, and looking up at it with much admiration, he had been promised that he might himself live in it or in some such house when he came to be a man, if he would only work hard enough', I, p. 5.

3. *where Falstaff . . . ran away* : Cf. Shakespeare's *1 Henry IV*, II, ii.

4. *"Blow, blow, thou winter wind"* : From Shakespeare's *As You Like It*, II, vii, 174.

5. *Sterne's Maria* : The half-witted French girl of vol. IX of *The Life and Opinions of Tristram Shandy* (1760–67) who reappears in *A Sentimental Journey through France and Italy* (1768).

6. *I am dragged . . . into the Morgue* : See, for instance, 'Some Recollections of Mortality' and 'Railway Dreaming'; and the discussion of these works in the Introduction.

7. *The British Boaxe* : Boxing.

8. *shako* : A cylindrical military hat with a peak and a plume or pompon.

9. *nursery rhyme about Banbury Cross* : From the nursery rhyme which begins 'Ride a cock-horse to Banbury Cross'. In modern versions, the lady is usually described as 'fine', but, in some earlier versions, she was termed 'old'.

10. *a new Gesler in a Canton of Tells* : Austrian bailiff of the canton of Uri, killed, according to Swiss legend, by William Tell.

11. *a glorified Cheap-Jack* : Cheap Jacks sang and performed confidence tricks in order to attract customers to buy their wares.

12. *Don Quixote on the back of the wooden horse* : From Part II, ch. 41 of *Don Quixote*.

Shy Neighbours

1. *Mr. Thomas Sayers . . . and Mr. John Heenan* : The bareknuckle fighters, Sayers (1826–65) and Heenan (1835–73), fought a famous bout in 1860 which was considered a draw.

2. *in the manner of Izaak Walton* : An allusion to the descriptions in Walton's *The*

Compleat Angler (1653, continued by Charles Cotton 1676), a handbook of the art of fishing.

3. *St. Giles's* : Dickens is alluding to the rookeries (i.e. slums) of St Giles, by New Oxford Street, whose inhabitants were mainly Irish immigrants.

4. *Spitalfields* : An area east of the City. Many of the area's worst slums were cleared when Commercial Street, the main artery through the East End of London, was constructed in 1848. See 'Spitalfields', in this selection.

5. *Jacob's Island* : An infamous rookery in Bermondsey, situated between Jacob Street and London Bridge Street, the place of Bill Sikes's demise in *Oliver Twist*.

6. *the Green Yard* : A municipal pound for holding stray animals and lost vehicles.

7. *dogs . . . in Punch's shows* : A dog called Toby was a traditional figure in the Punch and Judy show.

8. *Somerstown* : Somers Town lies between St Pancras and Euston stations. In the early nineteenth century it accommodated large numbers of Spanish refugees from the Peninsular war. In 1824, Dickens lived in the area before it became dominated by the two great railway stations.

9. *Burlington House Gardens . . . the Arcade . . . the Albany* : Burlington House was one of a number of mansions built on the north side of Piccadilly in the 1660s, remodelled in the Palladian style in the eighteenth century. In the 1850s, the Government bought the house and it subsequently became the home of the Royal Academy. Burlington Arcade, famous for its shops, was designed in 1819 for Lord George Cavendish to prevent vagabonds throwing rubbish into the gardens. The Albany on Piccadilly was built in 1774, converted into residential chambers originally for bachelors only and still fashionable.

10. *Notting-hill* : An area of West London sometimes called North Kensington, known for extreme contrasts, with fine houses and noxious rookeries coexisting in close proximity.

11. *surplus population* : In *An Essay on the Principle of Population* (1798, 1803) Thomas Malthus (1766–1834) predicted that population, if allowed to grow unchecked, would increase more quickly than the food supply. Dickens disliked the theory, and in *A Christmas Carol*, when Scrooge is told of the plight of the starving poor, he replies, 'if they would rather die . . . they had better do it and decrease the surplus population' (ch. 1).

12. *the Obelisk in Saint George's Fields* : St George's Fields was a large open space between Southwark and Lambeth, taking its name from the nearby church of St George the Martyr. The area was used for large gatherings: during the day the fields would be used for the drilling of soldiers or for executions, and on Sundays they became the resort of Londoners. The obelisk, a convenient meeting place, was erected in 1771, and later removed to the ground of Bethlehem hospital.

13. *Mrs. Southcott* : In 1792, Joanna Southcott (1750–1814), a farmer's daughter and domestic servant, began writing doggerel prophecies and claiming supernatural powers. She attracted a large following; she died of brain disease.

14. *Bethnal-green* : At the time, Bethnal Green was the poorest district of the capital.

15. *Phœbus* : In Greek mythology, the sun or sun-god, from *phao*, 'to shine'.

Arcadian London

1. *a Volunteer*: According to Gwen Major the subsequent details seem drawn from the Middlesex Volunteer Rifle Corps. See her 'Arcadian London' in *The Dickensian*, 40 (1949), p. 209.

2. *Knickerbockers*: Loose-fitting trousers gathered in just below the knees, named after Diedrich Knickerbocker, the imaginary author of Washington Irving's burlesque, *A History of New York* (1809).

3. *chasing the ebbing Neptune on the ribbed sea-sand*: Cf. Prospero's valediction to his magic in Shakespeare's *The Tempest*, V, i, 33–5:

> Ye elves of hills, brooks, standing lakes, and groves,
> And ye that on the sands with printless foot
> Do chase the ebbing Neptune . . .

4. *the Every-Day Book*: Written by William Hone, bookseller and polemicist, it contained descriptions of 'the popular amusements, sports, ceremonies, manners, customs, and events, incident to the three hundred and sixty-five days, in past and present times'. First published weekly from January 1825 to December 1826; it was dedicated to Lamb and highly praised by Southey and Scott.

5. *the taking of Delhi*: Recaptured by the British from Indian mutineers in September 1857.

6. *deserted Westminster . . . Two Houses shut up*: Dickens is describing the Palace of Westminster. Westminster Hall, adjoining the north side of the House of Commons, accommodated the Royal Courts of Justice until 1882; the Two Houses were the rebuilt House of Lords, opened in 1847, and the new House of Commons, first used three years later.

7. *New Zealander of the grand English History*: An allusion to Macaulay's prediction that one day 'some traveller from New Zealand shall, in the midst of a vast solitude, take his stand on a broken arch of London Bridge to sketch the ruins of St Paul's'. The prediction occurs not in Macaulay's *History of England* but in his essay 'Von Ranke', *Edinburgh Review*, October 1840.

8. *to-morrow, and to-morrow, and to-morrow*: Dickens alludes to *Macbeth*, V, v, 19.

9. *Agapemone*: Greek for 'place of love', and the name of a religious community established in 1849 near Bridgwater, Somerset, by Henry James Prince (1811–99).

10. *Lord Shaftesbury . . . ragged school*: Anthony Ashley Cooper, 7th Earl of Shaftesbury (1801–85), an English philanthropist active in organizing so-called 'ragged schools', the colloquial term given to primitive schools established by private individuals and organizations to teach slum children.

The Calais Night Mail

1. *dogs of Dover bark . . . Richard the Third*: See Richard's description of himself in the opening scene of Shakespeare's *Richard III* (I, i, 20–23):

Deformed, unfinished, sent before my time
Into this breathing world, scarce half made up,
And that so lamely and unfashionable
That dogs bark at me as I halt by them.

2. *"Rich and rare were the gems she wore"*: This is the opening line of one of the *Irish Melodies* by Thomas Moore (1779–1852), a collection of songs published in ten parts between 1808–34. Dickens much admired Moore's work, and here he weaves several other lines into the description of his surroundings.

Rich and rare were the gems she wore,
And a bright gold ring on her wand she bore:
But Oh her beauty was far beyond
Her sparkling gems, or snow-white wand.

'Lady! dost thou not fear to stray,
So lone and lovely through this bleak way?
Are Erin's sons so good or so cold,
As not to be tempted by woman or gold?'

'Sir Knight I feel not the least alarm,
No son of Erin will offer me harm: –
For though they love women and golden store,
Sir Knight they love honour and virtue more!'

On she went, and her maiden smile
In safety lighted her round the Green Isle;
And blest for ever is she who relied
Upon Erin's honour and Erin's pride.

3. *the Mississippi*: Dickens and his wife arrived in America in January 1842 and remained there for six months. His account of the Mississippi appears in *American Notes*, where he describes it as 'an enormous ditch . . . running liquid mud' (ch. 12).

4. *Franconi's Circus*: The Cirque Olympique, a famous show founded in Paris in 1807 by the Franconi family.

5. *a bull's eye bright*: A bull's-eye lantern.

6. *those Calais burghers . . . ropes round their necks*: One of the conditions on which Calais was surrendered to Edward III in 1347.

7. *Calais will be found written on my heart*: Calais was retaken by the French in 1558 during the reign of Queen Mary who is reputed to have said in her final illness, as Dickens quotes in *A Child's History of England*, 'When I am dead and my body is opened . . . ye shall find Calais written on my heart.'

8. *"an ancient and fish-like smell"*: Cf. Shakespeare, *The Tempest*, II, ii, 26–7.

9. *VAUBAN*: Sébastien le Prestre de Vauban (1633–1707), a great French military engineer who directed fifty-three sieges, and fortified the frontiers of the nation.

10. *such corporals . . . many a blue-eyed Bebelle*: Described in the story contained

in 'His Boots', in the extra Christmas number of *All the Year Round* for 1863.

11. *Richardson's*: John Richardson (1761–1837), the Penny Showman, offered many cheap and popular shows. There is an account of a Richardson's Show in 'Greenwich Fair', one of the *Sketches by Boz*.

Chatham Dockyard

1. *the Nore Light*: The Nore is a large sandbank in the centre of the Thames estuary, marking the mouth of the river. It is marked by a lightship.

2. *"the dumb-ague"*: 'An irregular form of malarial fever which lacks the usual chill', *OED*.

3. *the Achilles*: HMS *Achilles* was commissioned in 1863, and remained in service until the early twentieth century.

4. *amphitheatre (say, that at Verona)*: The Arena – which is still in use – dates from the first century A D, and was the third largest of all Roman amphitheatres.

5. *Doctor Johnson ... near-sighted*: Boswell records, 'I supposed him to be only near-sighted; and indeed I must observe, that in no other respect could I discern any defect in his vision; on the contrary, the force of his attention and perceptive quickness made him see and distinguish all manner of objects, whether of nature or of art, with a nicety that is rarely to be found' (Boswell's *Life of Johnson*, ed. George Birkbeck Hill, rev. L. F. Powell (Oxford: Clarendon Press, 1934), vol. I).

6. *Pope Joan board*: A round painted board with fish shaped counters used in the card game, Pope Joan, in which any number of players can participate.

7. *Charon*: The boatman who ferried the souls of the dead over the rivers Styx and Acheron to the infernal regions.

8. *the old Medway ... starved in the streets*: The 'merry Stuart' was Charles II, during whose reign, in 1667, the Dutch fleet sailed up the Medway and destroyed a large part of the English fleet in dock.

9. *the shadow of Russian Peter*: Peter the Great of Russia (1672–1725) travelled incognito for sixteen months in Europe amassing western technology. He worked as a shipwright (1696–7) in the dockyards of Deptford, and returned to Russia with thousands of craftsmen and military personnel.

10. *braggart Pistol*: Ancient Pistol, a bombastic soldier who appears in *2 Henry IV*, *Henry V* and *The Merry Wives of Windsor*.

A Walk in a Workhouse

1. *a large metropolitan Workhouse*: Dickens wrote to Jacob Bell on 12 May 1850 to explain that 'Without identifying the Workhouse, I have written a fanciful kind of description of our walk'. Although the workhouse is unnamed, the editors of the Pilgrim Dickens's letters suggest it is 'possibly the Wandsworth and Clapham Union' which housed between 1500 and 2000 paupers.

2. *a woman such as HOGARTH has often drawn*: William Hogarth (1697–1764).

Dickens may be alluding to the image of the inebriated woman dropping her baby in *Gin Lane*. Forster recorded Dickens's views on this engraving in *Life*: 'I think it a remarkable trait of Hogarth's picture, that, while it exhibits drunkenness in the most appalling forms, it also forces on our attention a most neglected wretched neighbourhood, and an unwholesome, indecent abject condition of life that might be put as a frontispiece to our sanitary report of a hundred years' later date' (II, p. 42). The woman made a great impression on Dickens, and he asked Bell how he might assist her.

3. *sodgers*: Soldiers.

4. *enormity committed at Tooting*: See 'Pet Prisoners', note 6.

5. *Middlesex House of Correction*: Coldbath Fields Prison at Mount Pleasant, constructed in 1794 and demolished in 1889. Here, criminals sentenced to short terms of imprisonment were accommodated.

6. *like dispirited wolves or hyænas*: Dickens was especially struck by this image, and wrote to Wills on 10 March 1853: 'look to my walk in a workhouse (in H.W.) and to glance at the youths I saw in one place, positively kept like wolves'.

Detective Police

1. *the old Bow Street Police*: The Metropolitan Police Act of 1829 created a single uniformed force of over 1000 men for the London area; however, the Bow Street Runners were excluded from this new body and remained under the control of their own magistrates' office until 1839, when they were disbanded. Three years later, in 1842, after two sensational murders, a Detective force was formed consisting of two inspectors and six sergeants.

2. *penny-a-liners*: Freelance contributors to newspapers who were paid a penny per line.

3. *Theatre opposite*: The Lyceum, situated on Wellington Street, Covent Garden, and, in its heyday from 1847–55, managed by Mme Vestris and C. J. Mathews.

4. *Inspector Wield*: Charles Frederick Field (1805–74), who had begun his career in the Bow Street Runners, but, by 1846, had risen to become Chief Inspector of the Metropolitan Detective Department at Scotland Yard. He retired in 1852, but continued to work as a private detective. Dickens made use of Field's mannerisms in his depiction of Bucket in *Bleak House*.

5. *Normal Establishment at Glasgow*: A government controlled teacher-training college, founded in 1826, and regarded as exemplary in its day.

6. *The sergeants are presented*: William Long has identified all the members of the Detective Force mentioned here: see his article 'The "Singler Stories" of Inspector Field', *The Dickensian* (1987).

7. *Wilkie ... the Reading of the Will*: David Wilkie (1785–1841), Scottish painter, appointed Painter-in-Ordinary to George IV in 1830, and best known for his narrative pictures. *The Reading of the Will* is currently exhibited in the Pinakothek in Munich.

8. *the swell mob*: Thieves who dressed expensively and fashionably, and who could therefore gain entrance to situations that might prove profitable.

9. *"gonophing"*: A slang term for pickpocketing. According to the *OED*, the first recorded use of the word is ch. 19 of *Bleak House*, first published August 1852; here almost two years before, Dickens is reporting its existence.

10. *the murderess last hanged in London*: Maria Manning, who, it was suspected, had boarded a ship bound for the United States; see 'Lying Awake', note 9.

11. *Fikey*: William Edward Eike, a clerk in the treasurer's office of the London and South Western Railway Company, had forged a debenture bond worth £2000, which he then cashed using a false name, John Windsor. With the proceeds, he set up a factory in Battersea.

12. *Newgate . . . Carnaby*: Newgate Market was a meat market, superseded by Smithfield; Newport Market, also specializing in meat, was established in the seventeenth century on the area which is now the Charing Cross Road, but by the time Dickens was writing it had become one of the most notorious slums in London; Clare Market, specializing in meat and fish, took place in what is now the Aldwych area of the West End; and Carnaby Market was founded in the 1690s adjacent to the then newly built Carnaby Street.

13. *cove*: Thieves' slang for a customer or fellow, cf. 'That old cove at the book-stall', *Oliver Twist*, ch. 10.

14. *the Tombs*: A notorious New York prison constructed in the 1830s, and modelled on ancient Egyptian mausoleums.

15. *LEVERRIER or ADAMS . . . new planet*: Urbain Jean Joseph Leverrier (1811–77) was a noted French physicist who, in 1846, predicted the existence of Neptune after observing irregularities in the orbit of Uranus. The previous year, the Englishman John Couch Adams (1819–92) had made a similar prediction. The planet was finally 'discovered' by Johann Gottfried Galle, a German astronomer, in 1846.

A Paper-Mill

1. *Wat Tyler*: Wat Tyler (d. 1381), blacksmith and leader (with Jack Straw) of the Peasants' Revolt of 1381. He was reputed to have murdered a tax collector who insulted his daughter. Tyler was killed by William Walworth, then Lord Mayor of London, while arguing with Richard II at Smithfield.

2. *the pious Orange-Lodges*: In 1795, in Belfast, two members, Cope by name, of the 'Orange Lodge' of Masons (named after William of Orange) helped organize an ultra Protestant party, the members of which were known as Orangemen.

3. *put his trust . . . kept his paper damp*: When his troops were about to cross a river, Cromwell told them: 'Put your trust in God; but mind to keep your powder dry!'

4. *books in the running brooks*: Cf. 'Finds tongues in trees, books in the running brooks, / Sermons in stones, and good in every thing', *As You Like It*, II, i, 16.

5. *Spielman*: Probably John Spielmann, a German jeweller and goldsmith, who worked in London from 1583–97.

6. *the Mill of the child's story*: A version of the legend of the Fountain of Youth, which is alluded to in *Edwin Drood* (ch. 22). In her book, *The Industrial Muse* (London: Croom Helm, 1974), Martha Vicinus quotes the following rhyme:

The spinning jennies whirl along,
Performing strange things, I've been told sir
For twisting fresh and making young
All maids who own they're grown too old, sir.

7. *like the sailor's wife in MACBETH*: Cf. 'A sailor's wife had chestnuts in her lap, / And munched, and munched and munched', I, iii, 4.

8. *Mr. Emden . . . groats!*: Cf. 'Emblem groats: crushed barley or oats', *OED*.

9. *Witney hills*: Witney is a market town fifteen miles west of Oxford, famous for its woollen blankets which were first produced intensively in the seventeenth century.

10. *a mighty Duty, set forth in no Schedule of Excise*: Dickens is playing on the word 'duty' and attacking the tax on paper (which was repealed in 1861).

Three 'Detective' Anecdotes

1. *Eliza Grimwood*: Eliza Grimwood, a prostitute in her late twenties, was found on the morning of 26 May 1838 with her throat cut in her bedroom at 12 Wellington Terrace, a side street off Waterloo Way. Suspicion fell on her cousin, William Hubbard, with whom she shared the house, but the case against him was never proven and the crime remains unsolved.

2. *Lyceum Theatre*: See 'Detective Police', note 3.

3. *a drain*: A slang term for drink, first recorded by the *OED* in 1836 from Dickens's 'Ginshops', included in *Sketches by Boz*: 'Two old men who came in "just to have a drain".'

4. *a free-and-easy*: A convivial gathering where drinking takes place.

5. *Jenny Lind*: (1820–87), Swedish singer, known as the Nightingale.

6. *prop*: Thieves' slang for scarf-pin.

7. *braggadocia*: Empty boasting, arrogant pretension.

8. *slow justices*: After the appearance of the article, Field complained that *Household Words* had misquoted him. Dickens informed Wills on 14 September 1850: 'You may tell Mr. Field that the only word in that passage which he did not use is "slow" as applied to "Justices". I put that in, to express what his manner expressed. But, that if he means to say he didn't mention about "while they were looking over the acts of Parliament" he means to say the thing which is not . . . what Mr. Field did say shall not be unsaid – can't be.'

Railway Strikes

1. *the port . . . the world*: Liverpool.

2. *MR. GLYN'S*: George Carr Glyn (1797–1873), banker, MP for Kendal (1847–68), and chairman of London and North West Railway Company, whose workers had been on strike between 22 December 1850 and 1 January 1851.

3. *Railway accidents . . . loss of life*: Dickens was himself involved in a railway accident

in 1865, an event which caused great perturbation to him. See Introduction, pp. xxiv–xxv.

Bill-Sticking

1. *Belshazzar's palace*: Belshazzar, the son of Nebuchadnezzar and the last king of Babylon, whose doom was foretold by the writing on the wall, as interpreted by Daniel in Daniel 5: 5–6, 25–8. Hence, the panels of the omnibus are covered in writing (that same one line) which, prophetically interpreted, would announce the demise of Dickens's notional 'enemy'.

2. *Knowing all the posters . . . be happy*: The whole of this paragraph refers to prominent advertisers of the day. M. Jullien was Louis Jullien (1812–60), an ostentatious musician and conductor, who died in an asylum; Madame Marie Tussaud (1760–1850) was founder of the waxwork exhibition which still bears her name today; Professor Holloway was Thomas Holloway (1800–83), a dispenser of quack medicines; Cabburn produced a popular hair-oil; Moses and Son was a firm of tailors, which eventually became known as Moss Bros; John Joseph Mechi, Leadenhall Street, was a cutler and purveyor of 'fancy-goods'; H. J. and D. Nicoll were Merchant Clothiers. 'Revalenta Arabica', made by Du Barry & Co., was a potion consisting of barley, lentils and gum arabic designed to relieve constipation; while 'Number One, St Paul's Churchyard' was the address used in advertisements by the tea merchants, Dakin & Co.

3. *a public-house*: The Blue Boar Inn.

4. *I am the inventor of these wans*: The advertising vans, for whose existence he claims responsibility, obstructed the traffic to such an extent that they were the object of banning orders issued by the Metropolitan Police.

5. *Assessed*: Duties payable on, among other things, inhabited houses, male servants, carriages, horses, mules, dogs, horse-dealing, hair-powder, armorial bearings and game.

6. *winders*: The King is alluding to the hated Window Tax, which would not be repealed until 1851, see 'Red Tape', note 3.

7. *taking tea . . . according to the song*: Allusion to the contemporary popular song 'Come and take Tea in the Arbour'.

8. *a surprising fancy of dear THOMAS HOOD'S*: Thomas Hood (1799–1845), a writer and friend of Dickens's, best known for 'The Bridge of Sighs' and 'The Song of the Shirt'; the precise nature of the allusion is untraced.

9. *the murdered Eliza Grimwood*: For an outline of this notorious case, see 'Three "Detective" Anecdotes', note 1.

10. *State Lottery*: This was established in 1802 and abolished in 1826.

11. *the New Police Act*: The Police Act of 1839.

12. *the Seven Dials*: A slum area of St Giles, between Bloomsbury and Covent Garden, so named because it was a point of convergence of seven streets.

13. *(Vestris, understood)*: Eliza Vestris (1797–1856) was an actress, and, between 1831–9 was manager of the Olympic Theatre on Wych Street, the Strand; and later of the Lyceum.

Spitalfields

1. *Spitalfields*: An area east of the City (so named from its being the property of the Priory and hospital of St Mary Spittle), founded in 1197; resettled in the seventeenth century by French Huguenot refugees who quickly established a silk weaving industry there. At the time Dickens was writing, such weaving techniques were outdated and uneconomic, and the industry was moribund.

2. *Lancashire . . . Suffolk*: These were modern, industrialized weaving centres.

3. *the "ragged school"*: See 'Arcadian London' and 'A Sleep to Startle Us'.

4. *the Dramatic Authors' Society*: Founded in 1833 by T. J. Serle (1798—1889) and Douglas Jerrold (1803—57) in order to encourage the writing of 'Legitimate Drama' as opposed to musicals, burlesques and the like. Dickens was an enthusiastic supporter of its ideals, and here he is thinking of French melodrama, popular at the time in translation.

5. *the School of Design*: The Government School of Design in Somerset House, established in 1837. The painter, William Dyce, was Director from 1838—43. In 1842, a branch school was set up in Spitalfields, and in 1857, the institution was moved to the South Kensington Museum.

6. *A nearer one / Yet and a dearer one*: Paraphrased from 'The Bridge of Sighs' (1844) by Thomas Hood: 'Had she a sister? / Had she a brother? / Or was there a dearer one / Still, and a nearer one / Yet, than all other?'

On Duty With Inspector Field

1. *Saint Giles's clock*: The clock of the church of St Giles in the Fields (1734), St Giles's High Street.

2. *"Gonoph"*: See 'Detective Police', note 9.

3. *flaming eye . . . waist*: A bull's eye, or standard issue police lantern.

4. *New Oxford Streets*: New Oxford Street was completed in 1847 as an extension of Oxford Street, and cut through a notorious slum area to permit traffic to reach Holborn without passing through St Giles.

5. *vestrymen*: Members of a parochial parish council.

6. *the Old Mint in the Borough*: The site of a mint established by Henry VIII at Suffolk Place, demolished in 1557. The area around the old mint was a recognized haven for debtors and recidivists into the nineteenth century.

7. *the eminent Jack Sheppard*: John 'Jack' Sheppard (1702—24), a notorious thief, highwayman, and prison escapee eventually executed at Tyburn.

8. *Saint George of Southwark*: A twelfth-century church, rebuilt in 1734, in which Little Dorrit was baptized and married.

9. *the Minories*: Named after an abbey of nuns of the order of St Clare called the Minories, this area of the City had originally been associated with gunsmiths but by the mid-nineteenth century had become a place of general trade.

10. *Wentworth Street*: Lying between Middlesex Street and Brick Lane, east of the City's precincts.

11. *almost at odds with morning, which is which*: The line is from *Macbeth*, III, iv, 126, and is spoken by Lady Macbeth.

A Curious Dance Round A Curious Tree

1. *Windmill Hill, "Fensbury"*: Takes its name from a windmill which stood at the top of the hill in Finsbury from at least the fourteenth until the early eighteenth century.

2. *Sir Thomas Ladbroke ... Thornton*: Dickens may have in mind Robert Ladbroke, Lord Mayor of London in 1747; Bonnel Thornton (1724–68) was a scholar and wit, editor of the *St James Chronicles*, and translator of Plautus.

3. *monomania*: Cf. *David Copperfield* ch. 16: 'I call it quite my monomania, it is such a subject of mine'.

4. *With the benevolence ... the Good Doctor ... cotton*: The allusions in this paragraph are to the practices advocated in *Observations on Madness and Melancholy, including Practical Remarks on those Diseases* (1809) by John Haslam (1764–1844). In 1815, a Parliamentary inquiry revealed inhumane practices at Bethlehem Hospital, and Haslam was dismissed from that institution.

5. *"Saint Luke's"*: St Luke's Hospital for the Insane in Old Street, founded in 1751. The hospital moved in 1916.

6. *an inconvenience ... inestimable Corporation*: Dickens is alluding to practices at Smithfield cattle market, where beasts were still being driven through crowded streets and then slaughtered in the market. He was frequently exercised at this, and depicted it in *Oliver Twist* and, among other articles, in 'A Monument of French Folly' and 'Lively Turtle', both included in this selection. The woman in question, so severely traumatized by her encounter with the ox was, it seems, later released uncured.

7. *not inexpressive of "Boxing" ... reposing on the straw within*: Dickens's and Wills's visit occurred on Boxing Day, and some of the drivers seem to have spent their tips on drink.

8. *Ladies' Chain*: A part of the second figure in a quadrille.

9. *shining everywhere, his wife*: Charlotte Eliza Walker was the matron; her husband, Thomas Collier Walker, was the master.

10. *American aloe*: The century plant, *Agave americana*, maturing and flowering only once in many years, then dying.

11. *Wherever in your sightless substances, / You wait*: The allusion is to *Macbeth*, I, v, 50–51.

A Sleep To Startle Us

1. *At the top of Farringdon Street ... in a state of transition*: The thoroughfare Dickens describes is the Farringdon Road, which during 1845–6 had been built through some of the capital's most notorious slums. It followed the course of the Fleet River through

the Saffron Hill rookeries, destroying, among others, the notorious area around Field Lane.

2. *the first Ragged School*: The Field Lane Ragged School had recently moved from West Street, Saffron Hill, to larger premises in Farringdon Street. Dickens wrote to Mary Carpenter on 20 May 1852: 'The most remarkable collection of Ragged School attendants in London is to be found (I think) at about ½ past 7 o'Clock in the evening at the Field Lane Ragged School and Dormitory at the Northern end of Farringdon Street.' See also 'Arcadian London', note 10.

3. *young pupil teacher*: Cf. *Our Mutual Friend*, II ch. 1: 'In some visits to the Jumble his [Headstone's] attention had been attracted to this boy Hexam. An undeniable boy for a pupil-teacher . . . to do credit to the master who should bring him on.'

4. MR. *CHADWICK*: Edwin Chadwick (1801–90), a social reformer and author of *Report on the Sanitary Condition of the Labouring Population of Great Britain* (1842).

5. DOCTOR *ARNOTT*: Neil Arnott (1788–1874), a physician who specialized in diseases resulting from bad sanitation, argued for the importance of clean clothing and good ventilation as preventive measures.

6. *as if he were going into his grave*: It has been suggested that this description of the dying orphan boy influences the depiction of Jo in *Bleak House*, on which Dickens was working at the time of his visit to the school. See K. Tillotson, '*Bleak House*: Another Look at Jo', in Colin Gibson, ed., *Art and Society in the Victorian Novel: Essays on Dickens and his Contemporaries* (Basingstoke: Macmillan, 1989).

7. *Dearly beloved . . . low down!*: The Gorham controversy was an ecclesiastical law-suit which arose out of the refusal of the Bishop of Exeter (a High Churchman) to institute the Revd Cornelius Gorham into the living of Brampford Speke on account of his allegedly unorthodox views on infant baptisms; Edward Pusey (1800–82) and John Henry Newman (1801–90) were among the leaders of the Tractarian Movement.

A Plated Article

1. *one of the chiefest towns of Staffordshire*: Stafford, where Dickens spent the night on 2 April 1852.

2. *the Dodo, in the dull High Street*: The Swan Inn situated in Green Gate Street.

3. *Miss Linwood, erst of Leicester Square*: May Linwood (1755–1845), a needlework artist who exhibited her textile copies of the old masters in a gallery in Leicester Square.

4. *Bradshaw, and "that way madness lies"*: *Bradshaw*, the monthly railway timetable, had a reputation for its complexity (see 'A Narrative of Extraordinary Suffering'); 'that way madness lies' quoted from *King Lear*, III, iv, 21.

5. *COPELAND*: The partner of Josiah Spode, who in 1799 first produced the fine bone china which bears his name. At the time of Dickens's visit, William Copeland (1797–1868) was head of the firm.

6. *Macadamised*: The technique by which a road is constructed from layers of small broken stones, bound together by tar and compressed by rollers in order to constitute

an even and durable surface. The process was named after its inventor, John Loudon McAdam (1756–1836), a Scottish civil engineer.

7. *new material called Parian*: Cream-coloured porcelain introduced by Copeland around 1846, used for modelled decoration and small marble-like statues, after the famous marble of the Greek island of Paros.

8. *Miss Biffin*: Sarah Biffin (1784–1850) was born without legs or arms, and never grew more than 3 feet tall. Despite her disability, she became famous for her miniatures, which she executed by manipulating paintbrushes with her mouth.

9. *pre-Adamite*: Existing before Adam; but Dickens is also aluding to the existence of Adamite, a yellow, green or colourless zinc arsenate invented in the early nineteenth century by the French mineralogist, G. J. Adam (1795–1881).

10. *Giant Blunderbore*: A nursery story giant, brother of Cormoran, who tried to kill Jack the Giant Killer.

11. *Cerulean Empire*: i.e. China; but perhaps Dickens also means Cerulein, an intensely blue oily compound obtained from indigo.

12. *When Mr. and Mrs. Sprat*: From the nursery rhyme, 'Jack Sprat would eat no fat, / His wife would eat no lean'.

13. *the landscape after Turner*: Joseph Mallord William Turner (1775–1851), landscape painter, famous for his rendering of light effects.

Down With The Tide

1. *pea-coat*: A short double-breasted navy blue or black overcoat worn especially by seamen.

2. *drawing his pension at Somerset House*: At the time, the Navy had the west wing and part of the river wing of Somerset House in the Strand, a large government building which was designed by William Chambers in 1775.

3. *"if he be . . . so generously minded"*: An allusion to Ben Jonson's *Every Man in His Humour* (1598) where the boastful and cowardly soldier Bobadil says, 'You shall kill him, beyond question: if you be so generously minded' (IV, vii). Several times in the 1840s, in productions of the play by his Amateur Company, Dickens took the part of Bobadil.

4. *Kean's Prize Wherry*: An annual contest run during the 1820s on the river at Battersea between twin-oared rowing boats for the prize of a wherry donated by Edmund Kean.

5. *Pool*: The Pool of London is that stretch of the Thames immediately below London Bridge.

H. W.

1. *We have already described the manufacture of paper*: See 'A Paper-Mill'.

2. *His name is Legion*: Mark 5: 9. See 'A Christmas Tree', note 19.

3. *"tragedy, comedy . . . poem unlimited"*: Cf. *Hamlet*, II, ii, 416.

4. *the tears of school-boys*: 'A reference to the arithmetic problem concerning the man who agrees to have his horse shod at the cost of a penny for the first nail, two for the second and so on – thereby binding himself to pay a very large amount' (Stone's note).

5. *regular fellow labourers . . . our existence*: Regular contributors who had originally emerged by sending unsolicited manuscripts to *Household Words*, such as George Augustus Sala and Adelaide Anne Procter.

6. *Guttenberg, or Faust, or Peter Schæffer*: Johannes Gutenberg (*c.*1400–*c.*1468?) invented the printing-press using movable metal type. A loan from Johannes Fust (*c.* 1400–66) enabled him to build the press in Mainz, but by 1458 Gutenberg was bankrupt and so the business was continued by Fust and his son-in-law, Peter Schöffer (*c.* 1425–1502).

7. *the miller and his men*: Allusion to Isaac Pocock's *The Miller and his Men* (1813), a play which had made a great impression on Dickens as a child. See 'A Christmas Tree', note 13. According to Professor Stone, two of Dickens's favourite catch phrases from the play were 'More sacks to the mill!' and 'When the wind blows, then the mill goes', both of which are alluded to in the last few lines of the article.

8. *sixteen, Wellington Street North, Strand, London*: Address of the offices of *Household Words*.

A Nightly Scene In London

1. *the Conductor of this journal*: Every title-page of *Household Words* declared that it was 'A Weekly Journal Conducted by Charles Dickens'.

2. *a friend well-known to the public*: John Forster, whose account of the experience is worth quoting in full:

He had sallied out for one of his night walks, full of thoughts of his story [*Little Dorrit*], one wintry rainy evening (8 November), and 'pulled himself up,' outside the door of Whitechapel Workhouse, at a strange sight which arrested him there. Against the dreary enclosure of the house were leaning, in the midst of the downpouring rain and storm, what seemed to be seven heaps of rags: 'dumb, wet, silent horrors' he described them, 'sphinxes set up against that dead wall, and no one likely to be at the pains of solving them until the General Overthrow.' He sent in his card to the Master. Against him there was no ground of complaint; he gave prompt personal attention; but the casual ward was full and there was no help. The rag-heaps were all girls, and Dickens gave each a shilling. One girl, 'twenty or so,' had been without food a day and night. 'Look at me,' she said, as she clutched the shilling, and without thanks shuffled off. So with the rest. There was not a single 'thank you.' A crowd meanwhile, only less poor than these objects of misery, had gathered round the scene; but though they saw the seven shillings given away they asked for no relief to themselves, they recognised in their sad wild way the other greater wretchedness, and made room in silence for Dickens to walk on (Forster II, p. 131).

3. *the Casual Ward*: An area of the workhouse reserved for those who needed occasional relief, and were not permanent members of the institution.

Wapping Workhouse

1. *India House ... Charles Lamb*: East India House on Leadenhall Street, constructed in 1610, rebuilt in 1726 and enlarged in 1799. Tippoo Sahib was a virulent Anglophobe killed during the capture of Seringapatam in 1799, whose 'Man-Tiger Organ', a mechanism which represented the sight and sound of a tiger overwhelming a red-coated Englishman, was housed in the museum on the premises. Charles Lamb (1775–1834) worked in East India House for thirty-three years, retiring in 1825. 'My printed works were my recreations,' he claimed, 'my true works may be found on the shelves in Leadenhall Street filling some hundred volumes.'

2. *little wooden mid-shipman*: At 157 Leadenhall Street stood the Little Wooden Midshipman, which in *Dombey and Son* indicated the shop of the nautical instrument-maker, Solomon Gills.

3. *Aldgate Pump*: A communal water pump, moved several feet to the west of its original site during the widening of Leadenhall Street in the 1860s.

4. *Saracen's Head*: An ancient hostelry on Snow Hill, demolished in 1868, whose sign was famous for the ferocity of the Saracen's visage. Nicholas Nickleby meets Wackford Squeers in this tavern.

5. *Black or Blue Boar, or Bull*: The Blue Boar was situated in Leadenhall Market; the Bull Inn, demolished in 1866, was a coaching house used by travellers from the eastern counties.

6. *the young woman who told her sea-going lover ... taken in*: Cf. the following lines from 'Faithless Sally Brown: an Old Ballad' by Dickens's friend Thomas Hood:

> 'O Sally Brown, O Sally Brown,
>   How could you serve me so?
> I've met with many a breeze before,
>   But never such a blow.'

> Then reading on his 'bacco-box,
>   He heaved a bitter sigh,
> And then began to eye his pipe,
>   And then to pipe his eye.

> And then he tried to sing 'All's Well,'
>   But could not though he tried;
> His head was turn'd, and so he chew'd
>   His pigtail till he died.

7. *St. George's*: In the 1850s, the church of St George in the East, on Cannon Street Road, became a centre of religious controversy. The rector and curate introduced what were considered as Roman Catholic practices, and, in retaliation, the Bishop of London appointed a Low Church preacher. At this schism, demonstrations ensued: men entered church with hats, smoking pipes and unleashing barking dogs; rubbish

was often strewn over the altar. Because of this uproar, the church was closed down in 1859.

8. *Mrs. Gamp's*: Sarah Gamp is an untidy nurse in *Martin Chuzzlewit*. A 'fat old woman . . . with a husky voice and a moist eye' (ch. 19), she was the subject of one of Dickens most popular monologues. See also 'Please to Leave your Umbrella', note 10.

9. *The Refractories were picking oakum*: 'Refractories' were the rebellious and difficult inmates of the workhouse; oakum was the loose fibre obtained by unravelling old rope, a common employment in such institutions.

10. *Boston . . . Massachusetts*: On his visit to Boston in 1842, Dickens had been most impressed by the provision for the poor, and the humane conditions of the House of Industry in which the authorities accommodated the destitute. See *American Notes*, ch. 3.

11. *When Britain . . . besung*: An allusion to James Thomson's 'Rule Britannia', from *Alfred* (1740), II, v: 'When Britain first, at Heaven's command, / Arose from out the azure main, / This was the charter of the land / And guardian angels sung this strain: / "Rule, Britannia, rule the waves; / Britons never will be slaves".'

12. *Poor Rates*: A rate or local tax introduced in the late sixteenth century, and levied for the relief or support of the poor.

13. *countersign*: A private signal – usually a handshake or an arm gesture – used by Freemasons.

A Small Star In The East

1. *"Dance of Death"*: See 'Railway Dreaming', note 4.

2. *Ratcliff*: An area of dockland between Wapping and the Isle of Dogs in the East End of London. During the nineteenth century it became home to many poor Irishmen who worked as dockers.

3. *the lead-mills*: For a description of the lead-mills, see 'On an Amateur Beat'.

4. *She did slop-work*: Slop-work is the making of cheap ready-made clothing, often provided for sailors.

5. *Bosjesman*: An Afrikaans word referring to a 'bushman', a member of the aboriginal race of southern Africa.

6. *Adelphi Theatre . . . Victorine*: The Adelphi on the Strand, so named in 1819, was famous for its melodramas; Fanny Elizabeth Fitzwilliam (1801–54) first played at the theatre in 1825, and continued an association with it for the next two decades; *Victorine* was a play by J. R. Planché (1796–1880).

7. *A gentleman and lady*: Nathaniel Heckworth and his wife, Sarah, had set up the hospital in 1868, the year the article was written.

8. *An affecting play . . . "The Children's Doctor"*: During his stay in Paris in spring 1856, Dickens had seen *Le Médecin des Enfants* (1855) by Anicet Bourgeois and Adolphe-Philippe Dennery, and he wrote to Forster on 17 April 1856: 'That piece you spoke of (the *Médecin des Enfants*) is one of the very best melodramas I have ever read. Situations admirable . . . it is an instance to me of the powerful emotions from which art is shut out in England by the conventionalities.'

On An Amateur Beat

1. *the new Chief Commissioner*: Colonel Edmund Henderson was appointed Chief Commissioner of the Metropolitan Police in 1868, after the death of Richard Mayne, who had been in control of the force since 1829.

2. *Houndsditch Church*: Houndsditch, an area near Bishopsgate, whose name may derive from the City Kennels which were in the moat that bounded the City wall, and in which were kept the hounds for the City hunts. In the 1860s, the area was, according to Henry Mayhew, 'inhabited by Jewish shopkeepers, warehousemen, manufacturers and inferior jewellers'.

3. *kennel . . . Canon-gate . . . Holyrood . . . catchpoles on the free side*: Canongate was the principal thoroughfare in the old town of Edinburgh, and Holyrood the ancient Royal Palace of Scotland, founded in 1128; a catchpole was a sheriff's officer. Dickens is alluding to Sir Walter Scott's *Chronicles of the Canongate* (1827–8), as told by Mr Chrystal Croftangry, who, in giving an 'Account of Himself' in the opening chapter, describes how the precincts of the palace beyond the ditch offered an asylum for civil debtors: 'Day after day I walked by the side of the kennel which divides the sanctuary from the unprivileged part of the Canongate . . . For my part all Elysium seemed opening on the other side of the kennel.'

4. *that sweet little child is now at rest for ever*: Here and in the paragraphs that follow, Dickens is recalling his earlier article, 'A Small Star in the East'.

Pet Prisoners

1. *The system of separate confinement*: Solitary confinement, by which all prisoners were prevented from meeting or mixing with one another. For a full account of the penological background to the 'Pentonville Experiment' see Philip Collins, *Dickens and Crime*, ch. 6.

2. *St. Stephen*: The first Christian martyr; his stoning to death is recounted in Acts 7.

3. *Lord Grey*: Sir George Grey (1799–1882), Home Secretary in 1850.

4. *Captain Macconnochie*: Alexander Maconochie (1787–1860), a penal reformer who advocated that convicts should work together in groups which should share a common responsibility for rewards and punishments.

5. *Archbishop Whateley*: Richard Whately (1787–1863), Archbishop of Dublin, had proposed the abolition of all punishments for criminal offences except those sentences which existed only to deter.

6. *DROUET*: Bartholomew Drouet ran the Juvenile Pauper Asylum at Tooting, in whose insanitary and overcrowded conditions over 100 children died during the cholera outbreak of 1848–9. Drouet was eventually charged with, but acquitted of, manslaughter. Dickens wrote several articles on this 'baby-farming' scandal, most famously those in *The Examiner* on 20, 27 January and 21 April 1849.

7. *Mr. Manning . . . ripping chisel*: See 'Lying Awake', note 9.

8. *Associated Silent System*: In this system, which had been implemented at the

Middlesex House of Correction at Coldbath Fields since 1829, prisoners mixed together, but were prohibited from communicating with each other, any breaking of the silence being harshly punished. As it necessitated round-the-clock surveillance of the inmates, it was therefore expensive.

9. *Reverend Mr. Field . . . favourite principles*: Revd J. Field, author of *Prison Discipline: the Advantages of the Separate System* (1846); 2nd edn, 2 vols (1848). In the long footnote at this point in his paper, Dickens defends himself against Field's misrepresentations of his own views about the system set out in *American Notes*.

10. *Miss Martineau*: Harriet Martineau (1802-76) was a writer and social reformer who visited and wrote about the United States in the 1830s. The passage in question is excerpted from her *Retrospect of Western Travel* (1838).

11. *Dr. Dodd*: William Dodd (1729-77), a forger and clergyman. He forged a bond for over £4000 in the name of a former pupil, the 5th Lord Chesterfield, and, despite many appeals, was executed. On death row, he wrote 'Thoughts in Prison' (1777), to which Dickens here alludes.

12. *Mr. Croker . . . must be off*: In Act IV of Oliver Goldsmith's *The Good Natur'd Man* (1768), Mr Croaker, a gloomy middle-aged guardian, says, 'My hat must be on my head, or my hat must be off.'

A Poor Man's Tale of a Patent

1. *I am not a Chartist*: A Chartist was an adherent of Chartism, a working-class movement set on achieving the political reforms contained in the 'People's Charter' (1838). It demanded manhood suffrage, vote by ballot, payment of MPs, equal electoral districts, the abolition of property qualifications for MPs and annual Parliaments. The movement ended in 1848, partially successful in its aims.

2. *the Clerk of the Hanaper*: Hanaper was the department of Chancery into which fees were paid for the enrolment of charters and patents. It was, in fact, abolished in 1832.

3. *Deputy Chaff-wax*: The officer whose ceremonial duty was to prepare the wax for the imprint of the Lord Chancellor's seal. The post was abolished in 1852.

Lively Turtle

1.. *the Clarendon*: At 169 New Bond Street; at the time one of the most luxurious hotels in London.

2. *the Common Council*: A body of aldermen who managed the affairs of the City of London. Noted for their conservatism, they were opposed to sanitary reform, and wanted the Smithfield meat market to remain in the City.

3. *Groggles*: According to the editors of the Pilgrim *Letters of Charles Dickens*, Groggles was probably Henry Lowman Taylor (1803-83), an ironmonger of Cheapside and spokesman for the Court of Common Council. Dickens wrote to Wills, 12 July 1850: 'I observe a Report in The Times this morning of a most intolerably asinine speech about Smithfield, made in the Common Council by one Taylor . . . If you will look

to the other papers and send me the best Report, or a collation of the greatest absurdities enunciated by this wiseacre, I will try to make something of it.'

4. *Birch's*: Allusion unidentified.

5. *the house of Mr. Groggles's recommendation*: Dickens may have had in mind The Ship and Turtle, a tavern at 129 and 130 Leadenhall Street.

Red Tape

1. *rout-supper*: A large and fashionable evening party or social gathering, much in vogue in the nineteenth century.

2. *girdle . . . round the earth . . . quicker time than Ariel*: Dickens is confusing the actions of Puck in *Midsummer Night's Dream*, II, i, 175, 'I'll put a girdle round about the earth/In forty minutes', with those of Ariel, the winged spirit in Shakespeare's *The Tempest*.

3. *Window Tax*: First levied in 1695. In the 1830s, all dwellings except those liable to Poor or Church Rates, were assessed at 2s a year, an extra sum being payable according to the number of windows. The tax was repealed in 1851.

4. *the Chancellor of the Exchequer*: Henry Goulburn (1784–1856) served as Chancellor in the Peel Government (1841–6).

5. *Doctor Southwood Smith*: Thomas Southwood Smith (1788–1861), a sanitary reformer instrumental on a number of committees, including the Metropolitan Association for Improving the Dwellings of the Industrial Classes, whose ministrations lie behind this article. He was a close friend of Dickens's.

6. *Lord Althorp*: John Charles Spencer, Viscount Althorp and 3rd Earl Spencer (1782–1845), Leader of the Commons and Chancellor of the Exchequer (1830–34).

7. *Westminster Review*: A radical journal founded in 1824 by Jeremy Bentham. George Eliot became its assistant editor in 1851 under John Chapman.

8. *Doctor Gardner's*: Dr John Gardner (1804–80), medical practitioner and pharmaceutical chemist, author of *Household Medicine*.

9. *"blush to find it fame"*: Cf. Alexander Pope, 'Epilogue to the Satires' (1738), Dialogue I, 135–6:

> Let humble ALLEN, with an awkward Shame,
> Do good by stealth, and blush to find it Fame.

A Monument of French Folly

1. *Belcher handkerchiefs*: Dark-blue, white-spotted handkerchiefs, named after Jim Belcher (1781–1811), a boxer.

2. *PROFESSOR OWEN*: See 'Our French Watering-Place', note 12.

3. *Mrs. Quickly . . . green wound*: Dickens is either punning on or misremembering the lines in *2 Henry IV*: 'she had a good dish of prawns, whereby thou didst desire to eat some, whereby I told thee they were ill for a green wound' (II, i, 100).

4. *BRUCE found to prevail in ABYSSINIA*: James Bruce (1730–94), a celebrated explorer of Africa, who travelled in Abyssinia (1771–3), and later related in his *Travels to Discover the Source of the Nile* (1790) how the corpses of criminals in that country went unburied, and instead were eaten by wild beasts.

5. *charter . . . granted to you by King Charles the First*: In 1638, the City of London Corporation formally established a cattle market on the site under Royal Charter; but soon the City spread to surround the market on all sides. In 1852, after much pressure, the market was eventually transferred to Copenhagen Fields, Islington.

6. *Poissy*: Situated west of Paris; Dickens made a visit there on 12 February 1851, a trip which, as he told Kate Dickens, 'involved the necessity of getting up at 5'.

7. *sublimated Frenchman*: Napoleon.

8. *Franconi's*: See 'The Calais Night Mail', note 4.

Trading in Death

1. *The late Duke of Sussex*: Augustus Frederick (1773–1843), 6th son of George III; a progressive politician and President of the Royal Academy.

2. *the cemetery of Kensal Green*: All Souls, Kensal Green, was the first of the great commercial cemeteries in London, and, laid out according to a Greek Revival plan, with Doric arches and colonnades, it was consecrated in 1833.

3. *Sir Robert Peel*: (1788–1850), Conservative statesman and Prime Minister (1834–5 and 1841–6). As Home Secretary he reorganized the London Police; as PM he reintroduced Income Tax, and in 1846, largely as a result of the Irish famine, repealed the Corn laws. He died of injuries received after falling from his horse.

4. *The late Queen Dowager*: Queen Adelaide of Saxe-Coburg-Meiningen, widow of William IV, who died on 2 December 1849 and was buried beside her husband.

5. *the late Duke of Wellington*: Arthur Wellesley, 1st Duke of Wellington (1769–1852), British soldier, statesman and Prime Minister (1828–30).

6. *BLUCHER*: Gebhard Leberecht von Blücher (1742–1819), commanded the Prussian army at Waterloo (1815) where his timely arrival helped ensure Napoleon's final defeat.

7. *Alexandre Manzoni*: Alessandro Manzoni (1785–1873), Italian poet and novelist.

8. *vain shadow . . . in vain*: Cf. 'For man walketh in a vain shadow, and disquieteth himself in vain: he heapeth up riches, and cannot tell who shall gather them', *Book of Common Prayer*, Psalm 39.

9. *Mr. Hume*: Joseph Hume (1777–1855) was a radical parliamentarian who challenged and brought to direct vote in the Commons many items of public expenditure.

10. *tawdry Car*: A giant funeral carriage, weighing eighteen tons, drawn by twelve horses and adorned with trophies and heraldry. Dickens wrote to Miss Burdett Coutts, 19 November 1852: 'I suppose for forms of ugliness, horrible combinations of color, hideous motion and general failure, there never was such work achieved as the Car.'

Proposals for Amusing Posterity

1. *"– to this extent, no more"*: Cf. *Othello*: 'The very head and front of my offending / Hath this extent, no more' (I, iii, 80–81).

2. *Puisne Judges*: A junior judge in the superior courts of common law; i.e. one inferior to the Lord Chancellor, the Lord Chief Justice, the Lord Chancellor etc.

3. *Jenner or Vaccination Dukedom ... garter*: Dickens is crossing Edward Jenner (1749–1823), the English physician who discovered that inoculation with cowpox vaccine created immunity to smallpox, with his namesake, the 'noble and scientific Duke', Sir William Jenner, 1st Baronet (1815–98), the Royal Physician, best known for his work distinguishing typhoid and typhus. *Watt or Steam-Engine peerage*: James Watt (1736–1819), Scottish engineer who made fundamental improvements to the Newcomen steam engine, leading to the widespread adoption of steam power in mines, factories, etc. *Iron-Road Earldom*: George Stephenson (1781–1848), with his son Robert Stephenson (1803–59), engineered many of the earliest railways, in Britain and abroad. *Tubular Bridge Baronetcy*: Robert Stephenson pioneered tubular construction in the bridge he built across the Menai Strait. *Faraday Order of Merit*: Michael Faraday (1791–1867), an English physical scientist, discovered electromagnetic induction and many important electrical and magnetic phenomena. *Electric Telegraph Garter*: The electric telegraph was developed in 1836–7 by William Cooke (1806–79) and Charles Wheatstone (1802–75).

On Strike

1. *Mr. McCulloch's dictionary*: John Ramsay McCulloch (1789–1864), statistician and political theorist, whose most influential work, *The Principles of Political Economy: with a Sketch of the Rise and Progress of the Science* (1849), is alluded to here. Dickens once called him 'that Great Mogul of impostors', Forster II, p. 387.

2. *combine*: Form a union.

3. *Preston masters*: Following strikes at some Preston mills the Masters' Association, a confederation of local industrialists, announced a general lock-out to begin on 15 October 1853.

4. *Drum-head*: So that appropriate action could be taken even in the heat of battle, courts martial were often held round an upturned drum, which thus became a symbol of rough and ready justice.

5. *Gorton*: A town south-east of Manchester.

6. *this quotation from MR. CARLYLE*: From the conclusion of Thomas Carlyle's 'The Hero as Man of Letters', the fifth lecture of *On Heroes, Hero-Worship and the Heroic in History* (1841). The comment is made in relation to Robert Burns.

7. *winder*: A mill-worker whose job was to put silk, cotton or thread on the bobbins.

8. *the Speaker himself*: Charles Shaw Lefevre (1797–1888) was speaker of the House of Commons between 1839 and 1857.

9. *Ernest Jones*: (1819—69), a Chartist writer and agitator, editor of *The People's Paper* who was imprisoned for two years (1848—50) for sedition.

10. *Throstletown*: Warrington.

11. *Gruffshaw*: Mortimer Grimshaw, one of the leaders of the striking weavers.

12. *"Chadwick's Orchard"*: Cf. the entry in Charles Hardwick, *History of the Borough of Preston and its Environs, in the county of Lancaster* (1857), p. 436: 'The orchard, so well-known as an arena for public meetings, is merely a large part of valuable building land, in the centre of the town . . . It was formerly a fruit garden, in the occupation of Mr. Chadwick; hence its name.'

13. *morning-party in the Adelphi*: The Adelphi was an imposing and exclusive riverside development of twenty-four terraced houses designed and built by the Adam brothers during the 1770s. The properties were renowned for the sumptuousness of their interior decoration.

To Working Men

1. *awful pestilence*: After an absence of five years, Asiatic cholera had broken out again in London during August and September 1854, claiming 10,700 lives. At one point infection was so serious that a cordon sanitaire had to be established around the worst affected areas of Southwark and Vauxhall.

2. *this Journal*: *Household Words*, which regularly published articles campaigning for better public sanitation.

3. *last great outbreak . . . five years ago*: In the epidemic of 1848—9, out of roughly 30,000 cases some 14,000 people died.

4. *Lord Seymour*: Edward Adolphus St Mawr Seymour (1805—85), MP for Totnes and First Commissioner of Works (1851—2). According to Hansard, the speech took place on 1 August 1854 in a debate on public health.

5. *the College of Maynooth*: Established in 1795, St Patrick's College, Maynooth, was the largest Roman Catholic Seminary in the British Isles. Its public funding was a point of controversy for Prime Minister Peel in 1845.

Insularities

1. *Old Boguey*: The Devil; hence, an object of terror or dread.

2. *the Royal Exchange*: City Stock Market in Cornhill, rebuilt after a fire in 1844.

3. *wide-awakes*: Soft felt hats with broad brim and low crown.

4. *Smith Payne and Smith, or Ransom and Co.*: Smith, Payne, and Smith, originally a Nottingham banking house, established themselves in London in 1758 in Lothbury, and by 1806 had settled in Lombard Street; Ransom, Bouverie & Co., founded in 1786, were based in Pall Mall.

5. *Zouave*: A member of a French light infantry corps re-formed in 1854, but originally raised in 1831 in Algeria from the Kabyle tribe of Zouaoua. The soldiers were renowned for their exotic uniforms.

6. *Griggs and Bodger*: A representative banking house. These names appear elsewhere in Dickens: in *The Pickwick Papers*, the Griggses are the great social rivals of the Nupkins; and in 'Chambers', included in this selection, Bickle, Bush, and Bodger is a firm of barristers.

7. *the Gazette*: The *London Gazette*, founded in 1665, and the official journal of the British Government, in which formal announcements were and are still made.

8. *Fine Arts department of the French Exhibition*: The 1855 Paris Exhibition; the closing ceremony took place on 15 November.

9. *Clapham . . . Richmond Hill*: At the time, both Clapham and Richmond Hill, Surrey, were home to many wealthy businessmen.

10. *Madame Grundy*: A character referred to but never encountered in Thomas Morton's *Speed the Plough* (1798). She symbolized the exaggerated social concern with respectability and etiquette that Dickens is considering in this paper.

11. *Mr. Macaulay . . . "Loch Lomond"*: Thomas Macaulay (1800–59), author of *The History of England from the Accession of James II*, the third volume of which had just appeared in December 1855. Discussing Oliver Goldsmith's *History of England*, Macaulay observed: 'It is difficult to believe that the author of the Traveller and of the Deserted Village was naturally inferior in taste and sensibility to the thousands of clerks and milliners who are now thrown into raptures by the sight of Loch Katrine and Loch Lomond.'

12. *Early Closing Movement*: A movement for the reduction of the daily hours of labour in wholesale and retail trades. *The Times* first reports it in 1846.

13. *Prince Consort . . . Mr. Gibbs*: HRH Prince Albert (1819–61) was Prince Consort to Queen Victoria; Frederick Waymouth Gibbs was Prince Edward's tutor from June 1851 until late 1858.

14. *Lord Aberdeen . . . Lord Aldborough*: George Hamilton Gordon, the 4th Earl of Aberdeen (1784–1860), was a great statesman and politician who led a coalition Government of Whigs and Peelites (1852–5); Edward Stratford, 2nd Earl of Aldborough (d. 1801) was an Irish politician.

15. *our Premier*: Lord Palmerston (1784–1865).

16. *our Ambassador in the French capital*: Henry Richard Charles Wellesley, 1st Earl Cowley (1804–84), Ambassador in Paris 1852–67.

17. *Orson*: In an old French Romance, subsequently transformed into a children's tale, Orson is carried off by a bear, and subsequently becomes a wild-man of the forest.

18. *King of Brentford . . . Tooley Street*: A comic equestrian act which recounted the journey to Brentford of Billy Button, a tailor. Little more than a display of daredevil riding, the entertainment was first devised by Philip Astley in 1768, and was revived frequently thereafter until 1853 when it became a Christmas pantomime. In *Hard Times*, Sleary's horse troupe presents the 'highly novel and laughable hippo-comedietta of the Tailor's Journey to Brentford' in which Signor Jupe appeared in his favourite character of Mr William Button, of Tooley Street (I ch. 3). See Paul Schlicke, *Dickens and Popular Entertainment* (London: Allen & Unwin, 1985), ch. 5.

The Demeanour of Murderers

1. *The recent trial*: Dr William Palmer (1824-56), the 'Rugeley Poisoner', was convicted on 27 May 1856 at the Old Bailey of the murder by strychnine of his friend, John Parsons; he had also poisoned his wife and brother. He was hanged on 14 June. Dickens described this article as 'a quiet protest against the newspaper description of Mr. Palmer in court: shewing why they are harmful to the public at large, and why they are even in themselves, altogether blind and wrong. I think it rather a curious and serviceable essay' (letter to Miss Burdett Coutts, 1 June 1856).

2. *RUSH*: James Rush, a tenant farmer, was executed in 1849 for the murder of his landlord, Isaac Jermy, and the landlord's son, also named Isaac.

3. *THURTELL*: John Thurtell (1794-1824), famous murderer. Massively in debt, he killed William Weare in 1823, was tried and hanged.

4. *Edmund Kean*: Kean (1789-1833), the most famous tragic actor of his day, who died an alcoholic.

5. *Mr. Manning*: See 'Lying Awake', note 9.

6. *the Evening Hymn for a Young Child*: Dickens probably has in mind the Evening Hymn, 'Glory to Thee, my God, this night,' by Thomas Ken (1637-1711), the third verse of which is:

> Teach me to live, that I may dread
> The grave as little as my bed;
> Teach me to die, that so I may
> Rise glorious at the awful day.

Nobody, Somebody and Everybody

1. *the late war*: The Crimean War, in which Britain was involved from 1854-6.

2. *Balaklava harbor . . . cavalry charge*: A military engagement, in which the Russians attempted to capture the Black Sea supply port of the British, French and Turkish forces. The famous charge took place on 25 October 1854, after an order from Lord Raglan was misunderstood: Lord Lucan instructed Lord Cardigan's Light Cavalry to charge the Russian army, not knowing that they would face heavy artillery. This 'hideous blunder', as *The Times*' correspondent called it, resulted in the deaths of 113 men out of the 673 who took part.

3. *Kars*: A city in north-eastern Turkey, which fell to the Russians in 1855.

4. *a deposed iron king*: Possibly George Hudson (1800-71), a railway tycoon who was exposed as corrupt in the late 1840s. Dickens wrote on 10 May 1847: 'I disavow any allegiance to the Railway king – believing His Majesty to be the Giant humbug of this time.' See 'Gone Astray', note 9.

5. *Newgate*: London's main gaol, rebuilt in 1770, and demolished in 1902. See *Sketches by Boz*.

6. *look at that carcase . . . London town!*: Dickens is alluding to the suicide of John

Sadleir (1814–56), an Irish MP, junior Lord of the Treasury (1853–4) and fraudster, who poisoned himself on Hampstead Heath, after the collapse of the Tipperary Bank, to whose creditors he owed £200,000. A silver milkpot containing traces of cyanide was found beside the corpse.

7. *daguerreotyped*: An early photographic process, devised by Louis Daguerre (1789–1851), in which polished silver plates were covered with a thin film of silver iodide exposed to iodine vapour, to create a positive image.

8. *My heart . . . is sore for Somebody*: Cf. the final verse of 'The Dirge of Athunree' by Aubrey de Vere (1814–1902): 'Athunree! Athunree! All my heart is sore for thee'.

The Murdered Person

1. *In an early number of this journal*: Dickens is referring to 'Pet Prisoners', first published six years earlier, and included in this selection.

2. *MR. DOVE*: John Dove poisoned his wife Harriet in Leeds on 8 March 1856; he was tried and convicted later that year, and hanged at York on 10 August 1856.

3. *wings of a Dove*: Cf. 'Oh that I had wings like a dove', Psalm 55: 6.

4. *Home Secretary . . . Professor Holloway*: Sir George Grey (1799–1882) was Home Secretary at the time; Thomas Holloway (1800–83) was a dispenser of patent medicines.

5. *Morrison's pills*: A primitive purgative.

6. *Saint John Ketch*: A generic term for an executioner. Jack Ketch (d.1686) became synonymous with clumsiness after his botched execution of the Duke of Monmouth in 1685. The axe was blunt, and after the first blow failed to despatch Monmouth, the Duke rebuked Ketch. After two further attempts with the axe on the condemned man's neck, the executioner had to resort to a knife to finish the job.

7. *Two noble lords . . . They demand enquiry*: Dickens is alluding to the Crimean Board of Enquiry, a Board of Officers set up to investigate the severely critical account, given by Colonel Alexander Tulloch and Sir John McNeill in their 1855 report, of the conduct of the Commissariat and the general deployment of troops in the Crimea. The Board sat in spring 1856, and reported to Parliament. See 'Nobody, Somebody, and Everybody'.

8. *the Editor of the Times*: John Thaddeus Delane (1817–79), editor 1841–77.

9. *Mr. Calcraft*: William Calcraft (1800–1879), hangman from 1829 until 1874.

10. *the fallen governor of Barataria*: An allusion to Cervantes's *Don Quixote*. Barataria was the island city over which Sancho Panza was made Governor: 'one there was, who, getting a-top [the prostrate Sancho], stood there for a good while, and from thence . . . commanded the troops' (II ch. 53).

11. *Mr. Palmer*: Dr William Palmer, see 'The Demeanour of Murderers', note 1. For an account of Palmer's behaviour at his trial see that article.

12. *SIR CHARLES BARRY'S palace*: The Houses of Parliament. After the old chambers were destroyed by fire on 16 October 1834, Sir Charles Barry (1795–1860) was appointed architect of the new Palace of Westminster, and was assisted by Pugin. Work began in 1840; the new House of Lords was first used on 13 April 1847 and the House of Commons on 30 May 1850.

The Best Authority

1. *Croxford's*: A recollection of Crockford's, a private club and gambling house established in 1828 at 50 St James's Street, whose membership was made up of 'the chief aristocracy of England'. After the death of the founder, William Crockford, in 1844, the premises were sold and occupied in turn by the Naval, Military and Civil Service Club, and then The Wellington, a restaurant.

2. *the Boy Jones*: Edmund Jones, a seventeen-year-old apothecary's assistant, broke into Buckingham Palace on three separate occasions between December 1840 and March 1841. After being arrested on 16 March 1841, while eating cold mutton from the palace larder, he was deemed unfit to stand trial and sent to an asylum.

3. *ninth time . . . Doctor Locock*: Sir Charles Locock (1799–1875), the Royal Obstetrician, who attended at the birth of all Victoria's children. Her ninth and last child was Princess Beatrice (1857–1944), born 14 April.

4. *the late Mr. Palmer*: See 'The Demeanour of Murderers', note 1.

5. *the Conductor*: See 'A Nightly Scene in London', note 1.

6. *Mr. Russell*: William Howard Russell (1820–1907), *The Times'* war correspondent whose reports about the mismanagement of the Crimean Commissariat and Medical Departments led to the resignation of the Aberdeen Ministry in January 1855.

7. *the Redan*: A fortification with two parapets forming a salient angle against an expected offensive. At the siege of Sevastopol, Redans 2 and 3 were celebrated for their fortitude in withstanding attacks.

8. *the Malakhoff*: The fortress of Malakhov at Sevastopol, captured by the French, 8 September 1855.

9. *Gesler-like*: See 'Travelling Abroad', note 10.

10. *retired, like Iago, and word spake never more*: Cf. Iago's last words in *Othello*: 'From this time forth I never will speak word' (V, ii, 310).

11. *acting Midas to everybody else's Reed*: Midas was a legendary King of Phrygia who having offended Apollo by judging Pan to be a better musician than the god, developed the ears of an ass; he hid them from all but his barber who, burdened by the secret, whispered the truth into a hole in the ground from which reeds grew and rustled.

12. *O' Boodleom*: Perhaps an Irish member of Lord Boodle's cabinet? Cf. *Bleak House*, ch. 40.

The Amusements of the People

1. *The Polytechnic Institution in Regent Street*: The Polytechnic at 309 Regent Street received its Royal Charter as the Royal Polytechnic Institution in 1839.

2. *a Maid and a Magpie*: A number of plays about thieving magpies were performed in London theatres during the first half of the century. The first was S. J. Arnold, *The Maid and the Magpie, or Which is the Thief* (1815); and the most recent was C. Stansfield Jones, *The Maid and the Magpie* (1848). All were adaptations of the massively successful

melodrama, *La Pie Voleuse; ou la Servante du Palaiseau* (1815) by Jean-Marie-Théodore Baudouin d'Aubigny and Louis-Charles Caigniez.

3. *Forest of Bondy* : The subtitle of *The Dog of Montargis*, see 'A Christmas Tree', note 9.

4. *JOE WHELKS, of the New Cut, Lambeth* : The area around New Cut was infamous for the thieves and prostitutes who used to frequent its weekend market.

5. *Victoria Theatre* : The Royal Victoria Theatre in the Waterloo Road, whose lessee at the time was R. W. Osbaldiston.

6. *Mirror up to Nature* : Cf. 'to hold, as it were, the mirror up to nature', *Hamlet*, III, ii, 25.

7. *like the dyer's hand* : Cf. Shakespeare's *Sonnet* 111: 'my nature is subdued / To what it works in, like the dyer's hand'.

8. *an attractive Melo-Drama* : Dickens wrote to Daniel Maclise on (?29) January 1850, 'I am alone . . . and want to go to the Victoria tonight, with a view to some articles I am writing, to see a Melo-Drama.' The play he saw was *May Morning; or the Mendicant Heir*, first produced on 26 January 1850, author unknown.

9. *Doctors' Commons* : A college of lawyers founded in the thirteenth century for the study and practice of civil and canon law, and which acquired in the sixteenth century a site near St Paul's for the residences of the judges and advocates, and buildings for holding the courts. There were five courts: the Court of Arches; the Prerogative Court; the Court of Faculties and Dispensations; the Consistory Court of the Bishop of London; and the High Court of the Admiralty. The Commons was on the wane by the 1850s partly through the reforms introduced by the Probate Act of 1857, and the buildings were finally demolished in 1867. Between 1829 and 1831, during his tenure as a shorthand writer for the proctors in the Consistory Court, Dickens shared an office at 5 Bell Yard, Paul's Chain, leading into the Commons.

10. *the saloon in question* : The Royal Britannia Saloon, Hoxton, opened in 1841 by Samuel Lane.

11. *the Eagle, in the City Road* : Once a tea shop, in 1825 it became a music-hall, and later in the nineteenth century, the Grecian Theatre. The Eagle gives rise to the popular song: 'Up and down the City Road, / In and out the Eagle / That's the way the money goes, / Pop goes the weasel'. ('Weasel' was slang for a tailor's iron; 'pop' meant pawn.)

12. *All the queen's horses* : This alludes to the nursery rhyme 'Humpty Dumpty' where after his fall from high, 'all the king's horses and all the king's men / Couldn't put Humpty together again'.

13. *Bosjesmen* : See 'A Small Star in the East', note 5.

14. *In the remote interior . . . creature's death?* : For Dickens's account of his encounter with the 'Bush-people', see 'The Noble Savage' included in this selection.

15. *Dramatic Licenser . . . educational trust* : The office of the Lord Chamberlain had been strengthened in 1843 by the Theatre Regulations Act, and had jurisdiction over all dramatic works intended for performance throughout Britain. However, Dickens wanted the office to be more critical than censorial.

16. *Mr. Chorley's play* : Henry Fothergill Chorley (1808–72), music critic of *The*

Athenaeum since 1833, whose play *Old Love and New Fortune* opened at the Surrey Theatre on 18 February 1850, but closed the following day as it had not yet been licensed with the Lord Chamberlain's office.

17. *a mutilated theme of the late THOMAS INGOLDSBY*: On his visit to the Royal Britannia, Dickens saw *Lady Hatton; or, the Suicide's Tree*, adapted by the house dramatist, Dibdin Pitt, from 'The House-Warming! A legend of Bleeding-Heart Yard', one of the *Ingoldsby Legends*, 3rd Series (1847) by R. H. Barham (1788–1845).

18. *Tartarus*: One of the regions of Hades where the most guilty among mankind were punished.

19. *"Prometheus . . . liver"*: A son of a Titan, he stole fire for the benefit of mankind, and in punishment, was chained to a rock on Mt Caucasus where during the daytime a vulture fed on his liver, which was regenerated each night.

20. *"hurries"*: Tremolo passages played on violins or other instruments to accompany exciting scenes. Cf. 'Greenwich Fair' in *Sketches by Boz*: 'The wrongful heir comes in to two bars of quick music (technically called a "hurry")'.

Some Account of an Extraordinary Traveller

1. *Choctawas*: The Choctaw were a tribe of North American Indians, orginally inhabiting Alabama.

2. *Mandans*: The Mandan were a Sioux Indian people, originating in North Dakota.

3. *Captain Cook . . . at Owyhee*: James Cook (1728–79), naval explorer, killed on Hawaii by natives.

4. *the tubular bridge across the Menai Straits*: The Menai Strait is a channel which separates the Isle of Anglesey from the mainland of Wales, and across which Robert Stephenson built the wrought-iron tubular Britannia bridge.

5. *the second cataract*: Cataract was a term for a Nile waterfall.

6. *in the days of Herodotus*: A Greek historian (480–425 BC), known as the father of history, he wrote about the conflict between Europe and Asia, and, recounting the expedition of Cambyses into the Nile, detailed Egyptian history.

7. *the Simoon*: A hot dry wind which blows across North African and Arabian deserts in late spring and early summer.

8. *Bruce*: James Bruce (1730–94), African explorer, who in 1770 traced the course of the Blue Nile from Khartoum to its source in the Ethiopian mountains.

9. *Mamelukes, and Mooslmen*: Mamelukes were an army, originally made up of Caucasian slaves of the Sultan of Egypt, who seized the government of Egypt in 1254, and made one of their number Sultan. The Mameluke sultans were in power until 1517. Mussulman is an archaic term for muslim.

10. *expedition under Sir James Ross . . . entered Port Leopold Harbor*: Sir James Clark Ross (1800–62), an Arctic and Antarctic navigator. The voyage mentioned here, the first expedition for the relief of Sir John Franklin (1786–?1847), was Ross's last. No trace of Franklin was ever found, but Ross, frozen in during the winter at Port Leopold, was subject of a panorama by Robert Burford at Leicester Square in February 1850.

11. *Polka-jacket*: A woman's tight-fitting jacket, usually woollen.

12. *When I was a boy . . . not been attempted*: Panoramas were invented when Robert Barker developed a system of bending lines of perspective in a scenic painting on a cylindrical surface so that they would appear true when viewed from the centre of the cylinder. He opened his famous panorama on Leicester Square in 1793. The first diorama was patented by John Arrowsmith in February 1824, and differed from the panorama in that it was a flat picture with an illusion of depth, and capable of dramatic changes in lighting.

13. *Mr. Banvard . . . Mr. Burford*: Names of panorama artists and impresarios. John Banvard was a New York-born painter whose panorama of western America was successfully shown in late 1848, and reviewed by Dickens in *The Examiner* on 16 December 1848. In 1850, S. C. Brees exhibited his 'Colonial Panorama' of New Zealand at the Linwood Gallery, Leicester Square. From July 1849, the team of Henry Warren, Joseph Fahey and Joseph Bonomi exhibited their massive panorama of the Nile (painted on to a transparency) at the Egyptian Hall, Piccadilly. In preparation for the article, Dickens invited Maclise with him to see it on 22 February 1850. Thomas Grieve was involved in the consortium of artists responsible for *The Overland Mail to India*, which opened in early 1850 at the Gallery of Illustration, 14 Regent Street. For Robert Burford, see note 10 above.

Old Lamps For New Ones

1. *Maclise*: Daniel Maclise (1806–70), highly-regarded portrait painter and close friend of Dickens.

2. *The pre-Raphael Brotherhood*: The mysterious initials 'P R B' first appeared following Rossetti's signature of his *Girlhood of Mary Virgin* exhibited in 1849. They were the outcome of talks between Holman Hunt and Millais although the choice of 'Pre-Raphaelite' was largely fortuitous.

3. *You behold the interior of a carpenter's shop*: The central section of the essay is an extended description of J. E. Millais's painting of *Christ in the House of His Parents* (1849–50), whose symbolism Dickens perhaps felt was associated with High Church beliefs and practices. Dickens was not the only writer to be disconcerted by this plebeian representation of the Holy Family. *The Times*' reviewer said, 'the picture is plainly revolting'; and the *Literary Gazette* attacked it as a 'nameless atrocity . . . in which there is neither taste, drawing, expression, or genius'.

4. *Saint Giles's*: See 'Shy Neighbourhoods', note 3.

5. *Hogarth's idea of a man . . . in the foreground*: The allusion is to the print, *Satire on False Perspective*, designed by Hogarth but engraved by Sullivan, and first published in 1754. For Dickens's views on Hogarth see 'A Walk in a Workhouse', note 2.

6. *Bluchers*: Strong leather half-boots.

7. *Pre-Harvey Brotherhood*: William Harvey (1578–1657) was an English physician who discovered and demonstrated the circulation of the blood (1628).

8. *Pre-Gower*: John Gower (1330?–1408), poet and acquaintance of Chaucer, best known for his *Confessio Amantis*.

9. *Pre-Laurentius*: Alludes to the Laurentian Library in Florence which originated in the collections of manuscripts amassed by Cosimo and Lorenzo de' Medici in the fifteenth century.

10. *Mr. Pugin*: A. W. N. Pugin (1812–52), English architect (one of the leaders of the Gothic revival), was best known for his Catholic churches and his role, in association with Barry, in designing the Houses of Parliament (1836–43), to which Dickens is alluding.

11. *Pre-Henry-the-Seventh Brotherhood*: Dickens here probably has in mind Disraeli's Young England movement, which was aiming to create a new Toryism based on the aristocracy, the Queen and the Church, but which also protected the working classes.

The Ghost of Art

1. *Temple*: The Inner Temple and the Middle Temple of the Inns of Court.
2. *little man in the nursery-story*: Cf. the eighteenth-century nursery rhyme:

> When I was a little boy I lived by myself,
> And all the bread and cheese I got I laid upon a shelf;
> The rats and the mice they made such a strife,
> I had to go to London town and buy me a wife.

3. *Honourable Society*: Either the Inner or Middle Temple.
4. *the new discovery called Gas*: Dickens is perhaps being a little ironic. In 1812, after a series of failed attempts, the Gas-Light and Coke Co. became the first gas company to supply light to the City of London, Westminster and Southwark. However, only after the 1830s, during which time competition between gas supply companies was intense, did the consumption markedly increase. In the course of the 1840s, the Houses of Parliament and Buckingham Palace went over to gas lighting, as did many theatres and galleries.
5. *Royal Academy . . . Church of England*: The Royal Academy, established under the patronage of George III in 1768, for the annual exhibition of works of contemporary artists and for the establishment of an art school, was commonly known as 'The Forty', from the number of Academicians at any one time. The Thirty-Nine Articles are the statements to which those who take holy orders in the Church of England subscribe; they received parliamentary assent in 1571.
6. *Vicar of Wakefield . . . Great Plague of London*: Popular subjects for exhibits at the Summer Exhibition.
7. *Whether he was the Vicar . . . Primrose blood*: Characters in Goldsmith's novel *The Vicar of Wakefield* (1766); the Vicar's name was Dr Primrose. In his fine account of eighteenth- and nineteenth-century British art, *Paintings from Books*, Robert Altick observed that in the 1840s, such was the popularity of Goldsmith's novel, that over thirty pictures were exhibited which featured scenes and personages from it.
8. *Sir Roger de Coverley*: A famous character in *The Spectator*, 'a gentleman of Worcestershire, of ancient descent, a baronet' (no. 2, by Steele).
9. *warses . . . table-kivers*: Vases and table-covers.

10. *Pratt's shop . . . Davenportseses*: Pratt's in Bond Street was a well-known theatrical costumier; Storr & Mortimer, Garrard & Co. and Davenports were all jewellers and silversmiths of the West End.

11. *The German taste*: The Romantic style of *Sturm und Drang*, storm and stress, originating in the late eighteenth century, and directly imitated in British art of the 1840s.

Epsom

1. *Derby Day*: Founded by the 12th Earl of Derby in 1780, the Derby Stakes in 1851 were run on Wednesday 21 May.

2. *the Palace of Glass in Hyde Park*: The Great Exhibition opened on 1 May 1851, and took place in Joseph Paxton's Crystal Palace, based on the conservatory at Chatsworth where he was in charge of the gardens.

3. *the animal described in the Book of Job*: Cf. Job 39: 20–22: 'the glory of his nostrils is terrible. He paweth in the valley, and rejoiceth in his strength: he goeth on to meet the armed men. He mocketh at fear, and is not affrighted; neither turneth he back from the sword. The quiver rattleth against him, the glittering spear and the shield. He swalloweth the ground with fierceness and rage'.

4. *St. James's*: An exclusive area of central London around St James's Square.

5. *thimble-rigger*: A cheat who ostensibly concealed a pea under one of three thimbles, and challenged bystanders to bet on its location. Dickens describes the trick later in the article.

6. *tilted vans*: A tarpaulin-covered wagon.

7. *heather . . . field of gold*: As Dickens was writing in early summer, it is more likely that he is describing gorse rather than heather.

8. *jobbing . . . [importunate?]*: Comparing the *Household Words* text with that published in Wills's *Old Leaves*, Professor Stone suggests the emendations in this paragraph.

9. *Juggernaut-car*: A massive wheeled car which transported the Hindu idol in procession.

10. *Fortnum and Mason's*: A high-class grocer on 181 Piccadilly opened in the 1770s by Charles Fortnum, a retired footman in the household of George III and his friend, John Mason. The famous hamper was a relatively new venture, and had been developed for the Great Exhibition earlier in the month.

11. *"do his duty"*: Prior to the Battle of Trafalgar (1805), Admiral Nelson (1758–1805) ordered signal flags to be displayed which read 'England expects every man will do his duty'.

12. *Devonshire Lad . . . the Bantam*: Names of pugilists.

13. *Ethiopians*: Musicians in black-face.

14. *bones*: Small pieces of bone rattled together between the fingers of each hand as an accompaniment to the banjo.

15. *ring the Bull*: An alternative for Hoopla, in which one attempts to toss a ring on to a hook fixed to a target.

16. *knock-em-downs*: A coconut shy.

17. *splinter-bars*: Cross bars in a carriage, coach or other vehicle, to which the leather traces are attached.

18. *leads*: Leaded parts of a roof.

19. *Clapham*: A genteel suburb, where many such Establishments for Young Ladies could be found.

Betting-Shops

1. *Pleased to the last . . . surely Done!*: Cf. Alexander Pope, *An Essay on Man*, Epistle I, 83–4: 'Pleas'd to the last, he [the lamb] crops the flow'ry food, / And licks the hand just rais'd to shed his blood.'

2. *our neighbourhood*: The *Household Words* office was situated on Wellington Street North, off the Strand.

3. *like that of the apothecary in Romeo and Juliet*: Dickens has in mind Romeo's remembrance in Act V, i, 35–47:

> I do remember an apothecary,
> And hereabouts he dwells, which late I noted
> In tattered weeds, with overwhelming brows,
> Culling of simples. Meagre were his looks.
> Sharp misery had worn him to the bones,
> And in his needy shop a tortoise hung,
> An alligator stuffed, and other skins
> Of ill-shaped fishes; and about his shelves
> A beggarly account of empty boxes,
> Green earthen pots, bladders, and musty seeds,
> Remnants of packthread, and old cakes of roses
> Were thinly scattered to make up a show.

The Spirit Business

1. *The Spiritual Telegraph*: A paper which commenced publication in Boston in July 1850. Though a believer in (and practitioner of) mesmerism, Dickens frequently ridiculed the excesses of the Spiritualist movement. See 'Well-Authenticated Rappings', in this selection; 'Stores for the First of April', *Household Words*, 7 March 1857; 'Rather a Strong Dose', *All the Year Round*, 21 March 1863; and 'The Martyr Medium', *All the Year Round*, 4 April 1863.

2. *The Shekinah*: A monthly journal begun by S. B. Brittan in 1850.

3. *Thomas Paine*: (1737–1809), Anglo-American political writer and free-thinker.

4. *fonography*: A system of phonetic shorthand invented by Isaac Pitman in 1837.

5. *Mrs. Fish and the Misses Fox*: Leah Fish (b.1814) and her younger sisters Margaret (1835–95) and Katie Fox (1837–95) of New York State were the first mediums; their public seances, which began in 1848, soon became world-famous.

6. *Melodeon*: American term for music-hall.

7. *Andrew Jackson Davis ... Mr. Sunderland*: Davis (1826–1910), clairvoyant and trance medium, dubbed the 'Poughkeepsie Seer', whose book *The Principles of Nature, Her Divine Revelations, and a Voice to Mankind* (1847) provided a theoretical framework for the Spiritualist Movement; the Reverend LeRoy Sunderland (1804–85) was an American preacher and author of, among other works, *The Spirit World* (1850–51).

8. *Mr. Robert Owen*: (1771–1858) social reformer, politician and eventually spiritualist.

9. *Dr. Conolly*: John Conolly (1794–1866), physician and director of Hanwell asylum (1839–44) where he abandoned the routine strait-jacketing of patients, and introduced the principle of 'non-restraint'.

The Noble Savage

1. *There was Mr. Catlin ... with his Ojibbeway Indians*: George Catlin, an ethnologist who attempted to bring the plight of the American Indian to the attention of the world by mounting touring exhibitions which demonstrated the customs and activities of an authentic group of Ojibbeway Indians. In 1841 he published *Letters and Notes on the Manners, Customs and Condition of the North American Indians*.

2. *BUFFON*: Georges-Louis Leclerc, Comte de Buffon (1707–88), a naturalist famed for his work on the monumental *Histoire naturelle, générale et particulière*, 36 vols. of which he had completed at his death.

3. *refer to his "faithful dog" ... brought down ... by POPE*: Dickens is alluding to a passage in Alexander Pope's *Essay on Man*, Epistle I, 99ff:

> Lo! the poor Indian, whose untutor'd mind
> Sees God in clouds, or hears him in the wind;
> His soul proud Science never taught to stray
> Far as the solar walk, or milky way;
> Yet simple Nature to his hope has giv'n,
> Behind the cloud-topt hill, an humbler heav'n;
> Some safer world in depth of woods embrac'd,
> Some happier island in the watry waste,
> Where slaves once more their native land behold,
> No fiends torment, no Christians thirst for gold!
> To Be, contents his natural desire,
> He asks no Angel's wing, no Seraph's fire;
> But thinks, admitted to that equal sky,
> His faithful dog shall bear him company.

4. *the Bushmen*: In 1847, a group of Bushmen were exhibited at the Egyptian Hall in Piccadilly, on a raised stage against a painted background of African scenery. Normally they posed, but occasionally went through a series of acts, punctuated by frightening yells.

5. *There is at present ... London*: In 1853, at the St George's Gallery, eleven men, a

woman and a child from Port Natal portrayed 'the whole drama of Caffre life' against a series of scenes painted by Charles Marshall. According to R. D. Altick:

They ate meals with enormous spoons, held a conference with a 'witch-finder . . . to discover the culprit whose magic has brought sickness to the tribe,' and enacted a wedding, a hunt, and a military expedition, 'all with characteristic dances', the whole ending with a programmed general mêlée between rival tribes (*The Shows of London* (Cambridge, Mass.: Harvard University Press, 1978), p. 282).

Frauds on the Fairies

1. *Mr. George Cruikshank*: Cruikshank (1792—1878) was an illustrator and caricaturist, who had collaborated with Dickens on *Sketches by Boz* and *Oliver Twist*, and who, in 1853, published a version of the children's story 'Hop o' My Thumb' specially designed to promote teetotalism.

2. *Goody Two Shoes . . . bruise your oats yet*: E. Moses and Son, a firm of tailors, who became known as Moss Bros; Holloway's Pills were patent tonic medicines; Mary Wedlake was a firm of agricultural toolmakers, whose oat-bruising machine was marketed widely.

3. *Montgolfian persuasion*: The Montgolfier brothers, Joseph (1740—1810) and Étienne (1745—99), were inventors of the air balloon which had its first manned flight in 1783. Dickens is implying hot air, and high-mindedness on the part of the groom.

4. *Mrs. Colonel Bloomer*: An allusion to Mrs Amelia Bloomer, a pioneer of women's rights, whose name was also given to the type of baggy trousers often worn by followers of the movement.

5. *Vicar of Wakefield . . . being always wise*: An allusion to Goldsmith's *Vicar of Wakefield*, ch. 10: 'But we could have borne all this, had not a fortune-telling gypsy come to raise us into perfect sublimity. The tawny sybil no sooner appeared, than my girls came running to me for a shilling a piece to cross her hand with silver. To say the truth, I was tired of being always wise, and could not help gratifying their request, because I loved to see them happy.'

6. *The world is too much with us, early and late*: Dickens is alluding to Wordsworth's sonnet, 'The world is too much with us':

> The world is too much with us; late and soon,
> Getting and spending, we lay waste our powers:
> Little we see in Nature that is ours;
> We have given our hearts away, a sordid boon!
> This Sea that bares her bosom to the moon;
> The winds that will be howling at all hours,
> And are up-gathered now like sleeping flowers;
> For this, for everything, we are out of tune;
> It moves us not. — Great God! I'd rather be

A Pagan suckled in a creed outworn;
So might I, standing on this pleasant lea,
Have glimpses that would make me less forlorn;
Have sight of Proteus rising from the sea;
Or hear old Triton blow his wreathèd horn.

Gaslight Fairies

1. *Mr. Beverley*: A character in *The Man of Business* (1774) by George Colman, the elder (1732–94).

2. *Somers' Town*: See 'Shy Neighbourhoods', note 8.

3. *obelisk in St. George's Fields*: See 'Shy Neighbourhoods', note 12.

4. *as Sterne took his Captive*: Allusion to Sterne's *Sentimental Journey*: 'I took a single captive, and having first shut him up in his dungeon, I then look'd through the twilight of his grated door to take his picture', II, 'The Captive. Paris'.

5. *John Kemble Fairy*: John Kemble (1757–1823), a celebrated English actor.

6. *Rolla*: A character in Sheridan's tragedy *Pizarro* (1799), the commander of the army of Ataliba. The play, adapted from a German drama by Kotzebue, depicts the Spanish colonization of Peru in the early sixteenth century.

Well-Authenticated Rappings

1. *blue pill . . . black draught*: Blue pill was a preparation containing mercury designed to counteract biliousness; black draught was a purgative compound made of liquorice, senna and magnesium sulphate.

2. *Cape. Gamboge*: Cape denotes South African wine; gamboge is a gum resin obtained from south-eastern Asian trees, used as a yellow pigment and a cathartic.

Please to Leave Your Umbrella

1. *Hampton Court*: Queen Victoria had declared the Palace open to the public, 'free and without restriction', on certain days of the week, and in 1851 the administration passed from the Crown to the Government.

2. *in the manner of the Sentimental Journeyer*: An allusion to Parson Yorick, the charming and gallant narrator of Sterne's *Sentimental Journey* who has the habit of holding conversations with himself.

3. *the best bumps in my head*: Dickens is alluding to the science of phrenology, which suggested that the shape of the cranium could offer a guide to the mental faculties.

4. *Longinus*: *Longinus on the Sublime*, a Greek work of unknown date and authorship, examines what constitutes sublimity in literature.

5. *Doctor Waagen*: Gustav Friedrick Waagen (1794–1868), author of an influential guide to works of art in English and Paris museums, *Kunstwerke und Kunstler in England und Paris* (1837).

6. *Musical Glasses*: A set of drinking glasses tuned to the scale and played by rubbing their rims with moistened fingers; also known as a glass harmonica.

7. *Marlborough House*: Designed by Wren in 1710 and used at the time to house the Vernon and Turner collections of paintings and the Department of Practical Art.

8. *Brompton Boilers*: A massive prefabricated structure of sheet iron, cast iron and glass, built by Sir William Cubitt, to house the Museum of Science and Art (opened 1857). At the suggestion of Prince Albert it was painted in green and white stripes to make it less austere. Finally it was dismantled and replaced by the V & A.

9. *the Barnacle family*: In *Little Dorrit*, the Barnacles, an extended establishment family, provide types of government officials in the 'Circumlocution Office'.

10. *Mrs. Gamp's*: For Sarah Gamp, see 'Wapping Workhouse', note 8. Her 'umbrella with the circular patch was particularly hard to be got rid of, and several times thrust out its battered brass nozzle from improper crevices and chinks, to the great terror of other passengers'. *OED* gives: 'An umbrella, especially one tied up in a loose, bulgy fashion, 1864 (after Mrs Sarah Gamp)'.

11. *I had a greater load . . . than Christian*: In the opening lines of John Bunyan's *The Pilgrim's Progress*, Christian is described as 'a man cloathed with rags, standing in a certain place, with his face from his own house, a book in his hand, and a great burden upon his Back'.

In Memoriam W. M. Thackeray

1. *illustrator of my earliest book*: In 1837, Thackeray had tried to persuade Dickens to employ him as illustrator for *The Pickwick Papers*, and Forster gives an account of the rejection:

An incident which I heard related by Mr. Thackeray at one of the Royal Academy dinners belongs to this time. 'I can remember when Mr. Dickens was a very young man, and had commenced delighting the world with some charming humorous works in covers which were coloured light green and came out once a month, that this young man wanted an artist to illustrate his writings; and I recollect walking up to his chambers in Furnival's Inn, with two or three drawings in my hand which strange to say, he did not find suitable' (I, p. 61).

2. *Douglas Jerrold*: Thackeray was a pall-bearer at the funeral of Jerrold (1857). Later in the same year he read his old lecture on 'Charity and Humour' (or 'Weekend Preachers') at the memorial service.

3. *his standing for Oxford*: Thackeray stood as a Liberal for the Parliamentary constituency of Oxford in July 1857, but lost to Edward Cardwell by 65 votes.

4. *I've writ . . . wish back again*: Excerpted from Thackeray's poem 'The Pen and Album' (1853), lines 22–5.

5. *his latest and last story*: At the time of his sudden death on Christmas Eve, 1863,

Thackeray had only recently begun *Denis Duval*, a novel set in Rye among a colony of French refugees.

6. *"And my heart throbbed with an exquisite bliss"* : The last line of ch. 7 of *Denis Duval*.

7. *And when . . . A prayer at home for me* : The closing lines of Thackeray's poem, 'The White Squall' (1846).

8. *The heads . . . were bowed around his tomb* : An anonymous contributor to *Harper's Monthly Magazine* of September 1870 recalled that, at the side of Thackeray's grave, Dickens 'had a look of bereavement in his face which was indescribable. When all others had turned aside from the grave he still stood there, as if rooted to the spot, watching with almost haggard eyes every spadeful of dust that was thrown upon it. Walking away with some friends, he began to talk, but presently in some sentence, his voice quivered a little, and shaking hands all round rapidly he went off alone.'

pages 239-245 - A walk in a workhouse.
pages 111-119 - Birthday Celebrations.
pages 73-80 - Night Walks

READ MORE IN PENGUIN

In every corner of the world, on every subject under the sun, Penguin represents quality and variety – the very best in publishing today.

For complete information about books available from Penguin – including Puffins, Penguin Classics and Arkana – and how to order them, write to us at the appropriate address below. Please note that for copyright reasons the selection of books varies from country to country.

In the United Kingdom: Please write to *Dept. EP, Penguin Books Ltd, Bath Road, Harmondsworth, West Drayton, Middlesex UB7 0DA*

In the United States: Please write to *Consumer Sales, Penguin USA, P.O. Box 999, Dept. 17109, Bergenfield, New Jersey 07621-0120*. VISA and MasterCard holders call 1-800-253-6476 to order Penguin titles

In Canada: Please write to *Penguin Books Canada Ltd, 10 Alcorn Avenue, Suite 300, Toronto, Ontario M4V 3B2*

In Australia: Please write to *Penguin Books Australia Ltd, P.O. Box 257, Ringwood, Victoria 3134*

In New Zealand: Please write to *Penguin Books (NZ) Ltd, Private Bag 102902, North Shore Mail Centre, Auckland 10*

In India: Please write to *Penguin Books India Pvt Ltd, 706 Eros Apartments, 56 Nehru Place, New Delhi 110 019*

In the Netherlands: Please write to *Penguin Books Netherlands bv, Postbus 3507, NL-1001 AH Amsterdam*

In Germany: Please write to *Penguin Books Deutschland GmbH, Metzlerstrasse 26, 60594 Frankfurt am Main*

In Spain: Please write to *Penguin Books S. A., Bravo Murillo 19, 1° B, 28015 Madrid*

In Italy: Please write to *Penguin Italia s.r.l., Via Felice Casati 20, I–20124 Milano*

In France: Please write to *Penguin France S. A., 17 rue Lejeune, F–31000 Toulouse*

In Japan: Please write to *Penguin Books Japan, Ishikiribashi Building, 2–5–4, Suido, Bunkyo-ku, Tokyo 112*

In South Africa: Please write to *Longman Penguin Southern Africa (Pty) Ltd, Private Bag X08, Bertsham 2013*

READ MORE IN PENGUIN

CHARLES DICKENS

'A popular and fecund, but yet profound, serious and wonderfully resourceful practising novelist' – Q. D. Leavis

'He was successful beyond any English novelist, probably beyond any novelist that has ever lived, in exactly hitting off the precise tone of thought and feeling' – Leslie Stephen

'All the political futility which has forced men of the calibre of Mussolini, Kemal and Hitler to assume dictatorship might have been saved if people had only believed what Dickens told them in *Little Dorrit*' – Bernard Shaw

'Heaven for the just: for the wicked, Hell. Herein Dickens is true to the opinion of his countrymen and of his time' – André Gide

'Language and morality add dimensions to his cartoons and turn them into literature' – Anthony Burgess

Barnaby Rudge
The Christmas Books
Dombey and Son
Hard Times
Martin Chuzzlewit
Nicholas Nickleby
Oliver Twist
The Pickwick Papers
American Notes for General
   Circulation
Sketches by Boz

Bleak House
David Copperfield
Great Expectations
Little Dorrit
The Mystery of Edwin
   Drood
The Old Curiosity Shop
Our Mutual Friend
A Tale of Two Cities
Selected Short Fiction